1620–1800

BAROQUE

Style in the Age of Magnificence

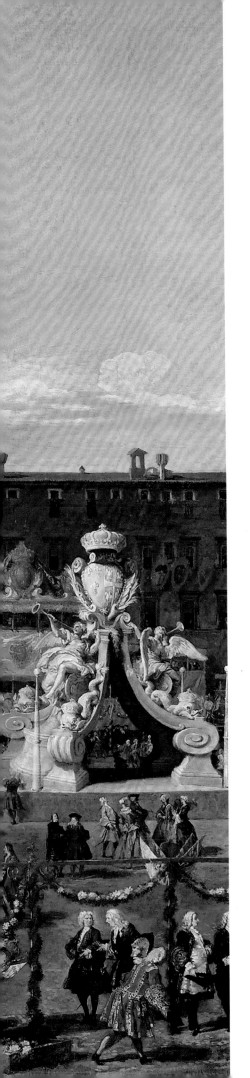

BAROQUE

1620–1800

Style in the Age of Magnificence

EDITED BY **MICHAEL SNODIN AND NIGEL LLEWELLYN**
ASSISTED BY **JOANNA NORMAN**

V&A Publishing

First published by V&A Publishing, 2009
V&A Publishing
Victoria and Albert Museum
South Kensington
London SW7 2RL

Distributed in North America by Harry N. Abrams, Inc., New York

Hardback edition
ISBN 978 1 85177 558 3
Library of Congress Control Number 2008939262

10 9 8 7 6 5 4 3 2 1
2013 2012 2011 2010 2009

Paperback edition
ISBN 978 1 85177 591 0

10 9 8 7 6 5 4 3 2 1
2013 2012 2011 2010 2009

A catalogue record for this book is available from the British Library.

Designer: Janet James
Copy-editor: Elisabeth Ingles
Indexer: Vicki Robinson
Maps: David Hoxley at Technical Art Services
Additional Picture Research: Caitlin Arner, Clare Coleridge and Silvia Bence-Jones
New V&A photography by Christine Smith and Richard Davis, V&A Photographic Studio

Front illustration: Kaleidoscoped image of Ceremonial mace made for a cardinal,
Giovanni Giardini (pl.4.7)

Back illustration: Extended fan leaf depicting Mme de Montespan in the *Trianon de
Porcelaine* (pl.5.73)

Half-title: *Ewer with The Triumph of Neptune*, Massimiliano Soldani Benzi (pl.2.31)

Frontispiece: *Preparations for the festivities to celebrate the birth of the Dauphin in Piazza
Navona in 1729* (detail), Giovanni Paolo Panini (pl.3.29)

Printed in Great Britain by Butler Tanner & Dennis Ltd, Frome, Somerset

V&A Publishing
Victoria and Albert Museum
South Kensington
London SW7 2RL
www.vam.ac.uk

Contents

List of Lenders

Brazil
Museu de Arte Sacra de São Paulo-Organização Social de Cultura/Secretaria de Estado da Cultura/Governo do Estado de São Paulo

Czech Republic
The Castle of Ceský Krumlov, The National Institute for the Protection and Conservation of Monuments and Sites

Denmark
The Royal Danish Collections, Rosenborg Castle, Copenhagen

France
Musée Carnavalet, Paris
Musée du Louvre, Paris
Musée national des châteaux de Versailles et de Trianon, Versailles

Germany
Grünes Gewölbe, Staatliche Kunstsammlungen Dresden
Kunstgewerbemuseum, Staatliche Kunstsammlungen Dresden
Kupferstich-Kabinett, Staatliche Kunstsammlungen Dresden
Rüstkammer, Staatliche Kunstsammlungen Dresden
Hamburger Kunsthalle, Hamburg
Bayerische Verwaltung der staatlichen Schlösser, Gärten und Seen, Munich
Bayerisches Nationalmuseum, Munich
Stiftung Preussische Schlösser und Gärten Berlin-Brandenburg, Potsdam
Staatliches Museum, Schwerin

Indonesia
Museum Sejarah Jakarta

Ireland
National Gallery of Ireland, Dublin

Italy
Archivio Storico della Fondazione Teatro Comunale di Bologna
Palazzo Reale Caserta
Fabbrica di San Pietro in Vaticano
Galleria degli Uffizi, Florence
Museo Degli Argenti, Palazzo Pitti, Florence
Provincia d'Italia della Compagnia di Gesù, Rome
Galleria Nazionale d'Arte Antica di Roma, Palazzo Barberini, Rome
Museo di Roma, Rome
Museo Nazionale di Palazzo Venezia, Rome
Private Collection, Rome

Mexico
Fundación Televisa AC., Santa Fé

Norway
Norsk Folkemuseum, Oslo
Ringsaker Church, Norway

Portugal
Museu Nacional de Arte Antiga, Lisbon
Santa Casa da Misericórdia de Lisboa/Museu de São Roque, Lisbon

Spain
Colección del Marqués de los Balbases, Madrid
Museo de América, Madrid
Museo Nacional del Prado, Madrid
Museo Nacional Colegio de San Gregorio. Valladolid

Sweden
Skoklosters Slott, Stockholm
Livrustkammaren, Stockholm
Nationalmuseum, Stockholm
The Royal Collections of Sweden, Stockholm
The Office of the Marshal of the Realm of Sweden
Västerås Cathedral, Church of Sweden, Västerås

Switzerland
Historisches Museum Basel, Basel

United Kingdom
Duke of Northumberland, Alnwick Castle, Alnwick
The Trustees of the Chatsworth Settlement, Chatsworth
Marquess of Salisbury, Hatfield House, Hatfield
Charles Stopford Sackville
Collection of The Trustees of the 9th Duke of Buccleuch's Chattels Fund
Leeds Museums and Galleries (Temple Newsam House)
Collection Dr Gert-Rudolf Flick
RIBA Library Drawings and Archives Collections, London
The British Museum, London
The Samuel Courtauld Trust, The Courtauld Gallery, London
The National Gallery, London
Knole, The Sackville Collection (The National Trust)
The Vyne, The Chute Collection (The National Trust)
Ham House, The Dysart Collection (The National Trust)
Viscount De L'Isle MBE DL, from his private collection at Penshurst Place, Kent
Viscount Coke and Trustees of Holkham Estate, Wells-next-the-Sea
The Royal Collection
English Heritage, London

United States of America
The Detroit Institute of Arts, Detroit
The Metropolitan Museum of Arts, New York

Director's Foreword

From several standpoints, *Baroque 1620–1800: Style in the Age of Magnificence* belongs in the series of major exhibitions that have been presented at the V&A since the 1970s. Firstly, its subject belongs in the familiar sequence of style-period labels used to trace change through art-historical time. On these grounds the show belongs within a tradition that includes *Rococo: Art and Design in Hogarth's England*, held at the museum in 1984. But *Baroque*, though, deals with the art and design not only of this country but of all four known continents. Its scope reminds us of the global remit of the V&A's collections and the challenge that the museum sets itself to explore the cultural transmission of art and design wherever it occurs. Finally, this show rejects the orthodox principle that the art of painting should be privileged in historical accounts of visual culture. Of course, the fine arts play a decisive key part in the development of the Baroque style, but, as visitors will find, equal roles importance must be given attached to the applied and decorative arts.

As do so many twenty-first century artists, the exponents of the Baroque were restless innovators, constantly exploring the potentials of new materials and crossing boundaries, both geographical and conceptual. We have matched these principles in assembling our curatorial team to bring together curators, and academics and specialists in the histories of religion, music and popular culture as well as art, architecture and design. Some of these skills were made available through the V&A's partnerships and it is a pleasure to acknowledge the long long-standing faculty-curator exchange programme that the V&A has with the University of Sussex and the Arts and Humanities Research Council's support, that which brought research students into the project thanks to the Collaborative Doctoral Awards Scheme and music into the exhibition via the Knowledge Transfer Grant, in collaboration with the Royal College of Music. The V&A also acknowledges Tate's willingness to allow the co-curator to complete his work on the project over the last two years and we are delighted that *Baroque* overlaps with Tate Britain's *Van Dyck and Britain* exhibition, which will form a thrilling counterpart to our own show. These shows will together bring a spotlight to fall on to seventeenth-century culture and London's public will be able to enjoy them as part of *Baroque '09*, a year of events celebrating Baroque music and culture.

The concept of the Baroque was first expounded by the later nineteenth-century German-speaking scholars who were the founders of academic Art History. They were designing a conceptual framework that would allow them to articulate that great sweep of art history between the Renaissance and the Neo-classical revivals of their own day. In London in those same years, the V&A was starting to assemble the great collection that we still care for and – sometimes against the prevailing currents of taste – V&A curators were taking decisions about acquisitions and displays that show that they too were impressed by the technical and aesthetic sophistication that is so characteristic of the Baroque style. We hope that visitors will find in this exhibition new understandings about issues and objects which that have always been at the very foundations of the museum's work.

MARK JONES
Director of the Victoria and Albert Museum

Acknowledgements

Major exhibitions and their publications demand a huge amount of collaborative effort, both inside and outside the organizing institution. This exhibition has been no exception. First, we are grateful to the V&A Director's Circle for their most valuable support of the exhibition. The V&A would like formally to thank the institutional and private lenders who have so generously made available the precious objects in their care. The Arts and Humanities Research Council (AHRC) has provided important support in the form of two doctoral bursaries, and the V&A would like formally to acknowledge their enlightened support for inter-institutional research, represented by their Collaborative Doctoral Award bursary scheme.

This exhibition project has been developed by a curatorial team led by Michael Snodin (V&A) and Nigel Llewellyn (formerly University of Sussex, now at Tate), who also acted as editors of this volume. As co-curators, we would like to acknowledge the essential contribution of Joanna Norman, who has acted as Assistant Curator and has played a central co-ordinating and managing role on almost every aspect of the project, including much of the detailed editing of this book. We would also like to thank, for their vital work on the team, Antonia Brodie, who ably edited the catalogue section, Loraine Long and Clare Coleridge and the AHRC doctoral students, Jane Eade, Elaine Tierney and initially Caroline Maddox, who valuably augmented the interdisciplinary range of the curatorial team. Volunteers attached to the team have made a valuable contribution: Caitlin Arner, Silvia Bence-Jones, Maddalena di Sanfilippo, Katherine Parkins, Katrina Ramsey, Elizabeth Simpson, Leonor Veiga and Ned Younger.

A project of this size and ambition depends on the support and expertise of many departments and colleagues within the museum. The curatorial team would like to acknowledge the support and personal interest of the Director and other senior colleagues, especially Linda Lloyd Jones (Head of Exhibitions & Loans) and the expert involvement of the managers and staff of the museum's Research Department: Carolyn Sargentson, Christopher Breward, Liz Miller, Glenn Adamson, Philippa Glanville, Angela McShane, Alex Klar, Katrina Royall, Julia Sachs, Vanessa Sammut, Jana Scholze and Lindsay Flood. We have made innumerable calls on the expertise and time of many curators, in particular Guy Baxter, Janet Birkett, Susanna Brown, Clare Browne, Marian Campbell, Katie Coombes, Rosemary Crill, Judith Crouch, Ann Eatwell, Richard Edgcumbe, Mark Evans, Patricia Fergusson, James Fowler, Alun Graves, Ruth Hibbard, Louise Hofman, Norbert Jopek,

Kirstin Kennedy, Sophie Leighton, Reino Liefkes, Geoffrey Marsh, Christopher Maxwell, Beth McKillop, Daniel Milford-Cottam, Lesley Miller, Susan North, Angus Patterson, Helen Persson, Stephanie Seavers, Suzanne Smith, Tim Stanley, Abraham Thomas, Mor Thunder, Marjorie Trusted, Rowan Watson, Christopher Wilk, Paul Williamson, Sarah Woodcock, James Yorke, Hilary Young, Heike Zech and Hongxing Zhang. We would like to extend our especial thanks to Sarah Medlam, Tessa Murdoch and Lucy Wood, who joined the team on its trips at home and abroad.

Central to the practical realization of the exhibition was the contribution of Rocío del Casar, in her role as Exhibition Co-ordinator. In the Exhibitions & Loans section we would like to thank Rebecca Lim, Poppy Hollman, Anu Ojala, Alex Westbrook, Penny Wilson and Alison Pearce. In Conservation, the exhibition project was led by Nicola Costaras, assisted by Roisin Morris. In the photographic studio we would like to thank Ken Jackson, Christine Smith and Richard Davis, and in Technical Services and Collections Services, Richard Ashbridge, Andrew Monks, Matthew Rose, Robert Lambeth and Matthew Clarke. The gallery texts were edited by Lucy Trench and Learning and Interpretation was in the hands of Jo Banham. In Public Affairs we would like to thank Debra Isaac, Sarah Armond, Meera Hindocha, Naomi Saffery, Dorothee Dines and, from the Web Team, Cassie Williams. Project management was in the capable hands of Mike Cook and Adrian Milner of Cultural Innovations.

Land Design Studio have risen wonderfully to the challenge of designing the exhibition: Peter Higgins, supported by Fernando Lai Couto, Simon Milthorp and Jona Piehl and, for the films, Simona Piantieri and Victoria Evans. The project to introduce music in and around the exhibition was led by Giulia Nuti, Aaron Williamon and Ashley Solomon of the Royal College of Music, generously funded by an AHRC Knowledge Transfer Grant, and Felix Warnock and Nick Morrison of The English Concert. We would like to thank Sir Nicholas Kenyon and Christopher Purvis for their unstinting support of the exhibition in the context of the Baroque '09 Festival.

The writing of this book represents another substantial collaborative effort and the editors would like to extend their gratitude to the authors of chapters, feature spreads and catalogue entries, both V&A staff and others. The production and publication of the book was expertly guided first by Mary Butler, then by Mark Eastment, Anjali Bulley, Laura Potter and our long-suffering copy-editor Elisabeth Ingles. It was beautifully designed by Janet James.

An exhibition and publication of this international scope and scale could not happen without the generous contributions, practical and intellectual, of scholars and curators across the world. They have included, in Australia: Luke Morgan; in Austria: Christian Benedik, Markus Christian, Monika Kurzel-Runtscheiner, Hellmut Lorenz, Monika Platzer and Karl Schütz; in Canada: Evonne Levy; in the Czech Republic: Kateřina Cichrová, Helena Koenigsmarkova, Martin Opatrny, Andrea Rusova, Evermod Gejza Sidlovsky and Pavel Slavko; in Denmark: Mogens Benckard, Erik Lennesgreve Danneskiold, Jørgen Hein, Søren Bo Jensen and Henrik Wedell Wedellsborg; in France: Pierre Arizzoli-Clémentel, Marc Bascou, Geneviève Bresc-Bautier, Peter Fuhring, Stéphane Loire, Henri Loyrette, Philippe Malgouyres, Nicolas Milovanovic, Alexandre Pradère, Bertrand Rondot and Xavier Salmon; in Germany: Tania Baensch, Susanne de Ponte, Dorothee Feldmann, Fritz Fischer, Burckhardt Göres, Regina Hanemann, Gisela Haase, Werner Helmberger, Hans-Ulrich Kessler, Sigrid Sangl, Rudolf Scharmann, Astrid Scherp, Claudia Schnitzer, Graf von Schönborn-Wiesenthied, Holger Schuckelt, Lorenz Seelig, Martina Sitt, Achim Stiegel, Dirk Syndram, André van der Goes, Moritz Voelk, Jutta Charlotte von Bloh, Rudolf Wackernagel and Ulrike Weinhold; in Ireland: Sergio Benedetti; in Italy: Maria Giulia Barberini, Ilaria Bartocci, Lucia Bellofatto, Maria Rosaria Boccuni, Fausto Calderai, Chiara Calvelli, Maria Cristina Carlo-Stella, Enrico Colle, His Eminence Cardinal Angelo Comastri, Francesca de Luca, Annamaria Giusti, Alvar González Palacios, Paolo Jorio, Elizabeth Kieven, Isabella Leone, Padre Daniele Libanori SJ, Anna Lo Bianco, Giorgio Marini, Miria Nardi, Angela Negro, Serena Padovani, Sara Piagno, Patrizia Piergiovanni, Emiliana Ricci, Father Ferrucio Romanin SJ, Hermann Schlimme, Maria Selene Sconci, Nicola Spinosa, Padre Massimo Taggi SJ, Magda Tassinari, Mario Tavella, Maria Elisa Tittoni and Simonetta Tozzi; in Mexico: Clara Bargellini; in The Netherlands: Reinier Baarsen, Paul Beghein, Eloy Koldeweij, Jet Pijzel-Dommisse and Mariet Willinge; in Norway: Ulf Grønvold, Inger Jensen, Geir Riisse and Marie Fongaard Seim; in Portugal: Maria João Vilhena Carvalho, Paulo Costa, Leonor D'Orey, Alexandra Markl, António Meira, Teresa Morna, Luísa Penalva, Conceição Sousa, Nuno Vassallo e Silva, Teresa Leonor Vale and Teresa Vilaça; in Spain: Letizia Arbeteta Mira, Alberto Bartolomé Arraiza, Paz Cabello, Ana Cabrera, Mira Concepción, Juan José Luna, García Sáiz, Letizia Sánchez, Jesús Urrea and Adrián Zunzunegui; in Sweden: Countess Caroline Bielke, Ulf Cederlöf, Torsten Gunnarsson, Margareta Isberg, Helena Kaberg, Eva-Lena Karlsson, Johan Knutsson, Bengt Kylsberg, Lars Ljungström, Birgitta Martinius, Wolfgang Nittnaus, Magnus Olausson, Martin Olin, Inger Olovsson, Lena Rangström, Cilla Robach, John Rothlind, Monica Sargren, David von Schinkel, Elisabet Stawenow-Hidemark, Elisabeth Westin Berg, Anna Womack; in Switzerland: Eduard Belser; in the United Kingdom: Bruce Bailey, Clare Baxter, Victoria Bradley, Stephanie Buck, Caroline Campbell, Beatriz Chadour, Yannick Chastang, Martin Clayton, Michael Daley, The Rev. Sally Davenport, Aileen Dawson, Lord and Lady De L'Isle, Carmen Fracchia, Valerie Fraser, Anthony Geraghty, Antony Griffiths, Robin Harcourt-Williams, Joanne Harwood, Helen Hills, Charles Hind, Amin Jaffer, Father Julian Large, Sophie Lee, Peter le Rossignol, Charles Lister, Judi Loach, Adrian Locke, James Lomax, Father Rupert McBain, Jean Michel Massing, David Mitchell, Jennifer Montagu, Irena Murray, Charles Noble, Hannah Obee, Rodney Palmer, Cathy Power, Jane Roberts, Christopher Rowell, Judy Rudoe, Emma Slocombe, Anna-Brita Snodin, Mario Tavella, Dora Thornton and Lucy Worsley; in the USA: Julia Marciari Alexander, Graham Beal, Andrew Bolton, Thomas P. Campbell, Mark Castro, Alan Darr, Eric Garberson, Alden Gordon, Herbert Heyde, Thomas DaCosta Kaufmann, Florian Knothe, Mallica Kumbera Landrus, Kenneth J. Moore and Joseph Rishel.

Nigel Llewellyn would personally like to thank a number of colleagues for the support they have offered over the duration of this project. The invitation to become involved came from Dr Carolyn Sargentson, former Head of Research at the V&A. In the earlier phases of this project, encouragement came from all his departmental colleagues at the University of Sussex, especially Professors Maurice Howard and Liz James, and his Dean, Dr Stephen Burman. Since January 2007 and with a move to a new post in a new institution, his senior colleagues at Tate have given him every encouragement to see the project through, especially Sir Nicholas Serota, Caroline Collier and Stephen Deuchar. His greatest debt is owed to his family, to Clare and to Jasper, who remained supportive throughout and heard more about the Baroque than they bargained for. For his part, Michael Snodin would like to thank his family, Patricia and Oliver, for their understanding and support during a project that became bigger than he had ever imagined.

MICHAEL SNODIN
NIGEL LLEWELLYN

Map of Europe after the Peace of Westphalia, 1648

The dotted line marks the boundaries of the Holy Roman Empire

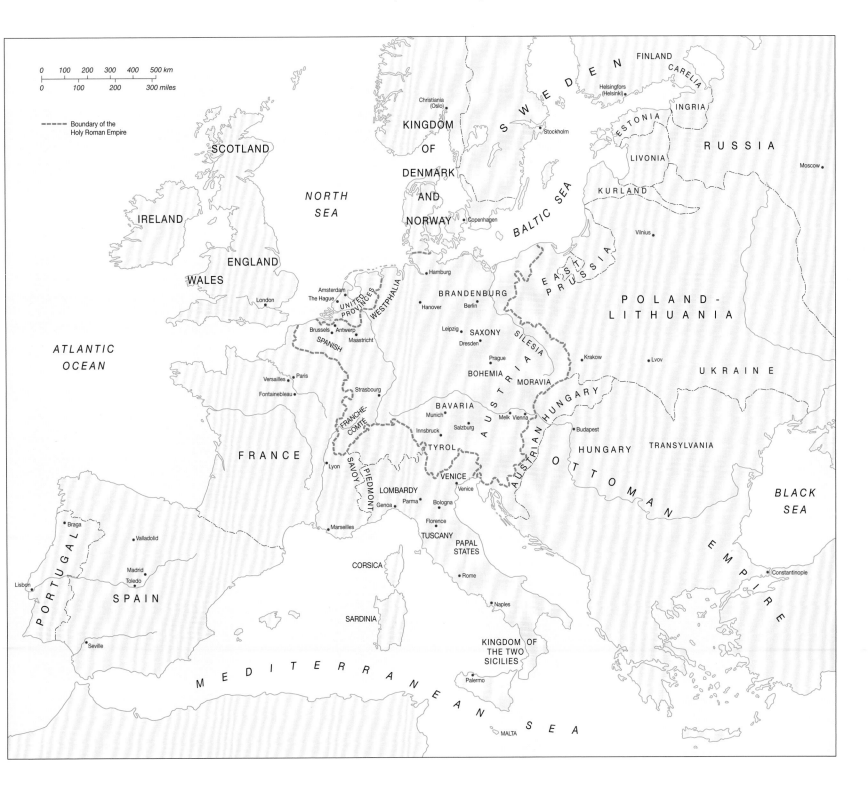

- - - - - Boundary of the
Holy Roman Empire

0   100   200   300   400   500 km
0   100   200   300 miles

SCOTLAND

IRELAND

ENGLAND

WALES

London

NORTH
SEA

ATLANTIC
OCEAN

FRANCE

Versailles • Paris
Fontainebleau •

Lyon •

SAVOY

PIEDMONT

Marseilles •

Genoa •   LOMBARDY
Parma •

FRANCHE-
COMTE

Strasbourg •

Innsbruck •   Salzburg •

TYROL

VENICE
Venice •

Bologna •
Florence •

TUSCANY

CORSICA

PAPAL
STATES

• Rome

SARDINIA

PORTUGAL

Lisbon •

Braga •

Valladolid •

Madrid •
Toledo •

SPAIN

Seville •

M E D I T E R R A N E A N   S E A

MALTA •

KINGDOM OF
THE TWO
SICILIES

Palermo •

• Naples

KINGDOM

OF

DENMARK

AND

NORWAY

Christiania
(Oslo) •

• Copenhagen

S W E D E N

BALTIC SEA

• Stockholm

FINLAND

CARELIA

Helsingfors
(Helsinki) •

INGRIA

ESTONIA

LIVONIA

KURLAND

RUSSIA

• Moscow

Vilnius •

E A S T   P R U S S I A

POLAND-
LITHUANIA

• Hamburg

Amsterdam •
The Hague •

UNITED
PROVINCES

WESTPHALIA

Brussels • Antwerp •
SPANISH   Maastricht •

BRANDENBURG

Hanover •   Berlin •

Leipzig •   SAXONY
Dresden •

• Prague

BOHEMIA

SILESIA

MORAVIA

Krakow •   Lvov •

UKRAINE

A U S T R I A

BAVARIA

Munich •

Melk •   Vienna •

AUSTRIAN   HUNGARY

• Budapest

HUNGARY

TRANSYLVANIA

O T T O M A N   E M P I R E

BLACK
SEA

• Constantinople

Map of the world, showing Spanish, Portuguese and Dutch trade routes

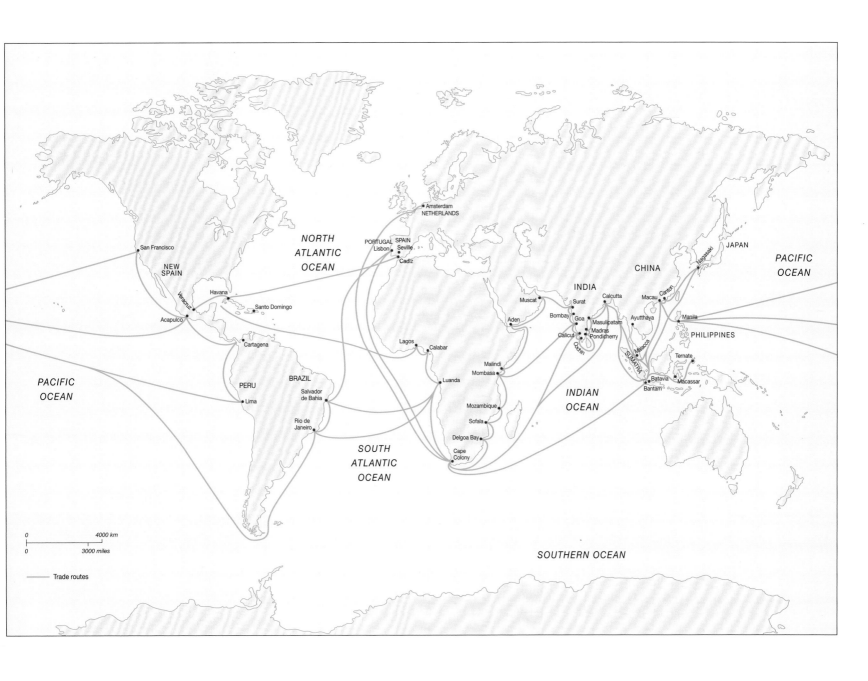

NORTH
ATLANTIC
OCEAN

Amsterdam
NETHERLANDS

PORTUGAL SPAIN
Lisbon Seville

Cadiz

JAPAN

Nagasaki

PACIFIC
OCEAN

CHINA

Macau Canton

INDIA

Calcutta

Muscat Surat

Bombay Goa

Masulipatam

Madras

Calicut Pondicherry

Cochin

Ayutthaya

Manila

PHILIPPINES

San Francisco

NEW
SPAIN

Veracruz

Havana

Santo Domingo

Acapulco

Cartagena

PERU

Lima

BRAZIL

Salvador
de Bahia

Rio de
Janeiro

PACIFIC
OCEAN

Aden

Lagos

Calabar

Luanda

Malindi

Mombasa

Mozambique

Sofala

Delgoa Bay

Cape
Colony

SUMATRA

Malacca

Batavia

Bantam

Ternate

Macassar

INDIAN
OCEAN

SOUTH
ATLANTIC
OCEAN

0   4000 km

0   3000 miles

—— Trade routes

SOUTHERN OCEAN

13

CHAPTER 1

THE WORLD OF THE BAROQUE ARTIST

Nigel Llewellyn

Fanzago's Flight

On 7 July 1647, the common people of Naples, weakened by plague and angry about new taxes imposed on their staple foodstuff – fruit – but strengthened by a charismatic leader named Tommaso Masaniello, rose up and took over the city. Masaniello died a few days into the revolt but the authorities did not regain control until April 1648. In consequence, the professional world of the Baroque artist Cosimo Fanzago (1591–1678) collapsed. Fanzago – intimately associated with the court – received threats of capital punishment and promptly fled to Rome; many years of careful career-building and artistic endeavour were undone in a few short hours. A famous picture painted by Michelangelo Cerquozzi (1602–60) and owned by the patrician Roman connoisseur Virgilio Spada in that same year shows the Piazza del Mercato in Naples with Masaniello centre-stage and riding a white horse (pl.1.1).[1] Quite why a member of the Roman aristocracy would have valued a painting showing such a gross reversal of the natural order is unclear – perhaps it was to remind his fellow nobles of the potential fragility of their

1.1 *The Revolt of Masaniello*, Michelangelo Cerquozzi and Viviano Codazzi, oil on canvas. Rome, 1648 (Galleria Spada)

dominance. Certainly, across Europe as a whole the political landscape was monarchical, not republican, although a medal was struck in Holland showing Lord Protector Cromwell on one side and Masaniello, as people's leader (*capopopolo*), on the other.

Typical of street revolutionaries the world over, the discontented Neapolitan masses have not left us their views on contemporary art, but some of Fanzago's works escaped destruction. Though resulting from élite patronage, the votive column (or *guglia*) that he had designed in 1636–7 was of compelling local interest to Neapolitans, since it was built in response to a communal vow to construct a splendid memorial should S. Gennaro, their patron saint, intervene on behalf of the city in the midst of a Vesuvian eruption (pl.1.2). By 1660, communal order had been restored; Fanzago was back at his post and sufficiently confident to include a self-portrait low relief on the basement of the completed column.

Fanzago, a native of northern Lombardy, had arrived in Naples in 1608 as a very young man and had taken many years to establish himself in Naples, which was not a welcoming environment for foreign artists. After all, his native language and culture were as alien to Naples as if he were from German- or French-speaking Europe. In fact, Naples in the mid-1600s was not only one of the largest cities in Europe, it was the capital of a southern Italian satellite state of the Spanish crown, in its possession until 1707 (when it passed to the Habsburgs until 1734). Naples was not only Spanish, it was also so populated with religious orders that contemporary European intellectuals regarded it as a latter-day Oxyrhynchus (now Behnesa), a semi-mythical city of ancient Egypt reputedly the dwelling place of 40,000 monks and nuns.

After about 20 years in this alien environment, Fanzago secured a major royal commission to build a Carthusian monastery (a *certosa*) dedicated to St Martin, on a dramatic hill-top site immediately beneath the Castel S. Elmo, a fortress designed to survey and control the volatile inhabitants (pl.1.3). Work on the Certosa continued during the 1650s when Fanzago was in exile in Rome, although the work of other artists was also disrupted. Viviano Codazzi (*c*.1604–70), also from Bergamo, had been intending to paint a series of frescoes showing the travails of the Carthusian order in Reformation

England but left them unfinished when he fled: subsequently there were long, unresolved disputes with the monks over payment. On his way south to Naples from Lombardy, Codazzi had worked in Rome in close association with Cerquozzi and a circle of northern painters, known as the *Bamboccianti* ('triflers'), specialists in painted narrative set in ruins. It was typical of the world in which the Baroque artists worked that this loose confederation recognized both international and local interests.

EUROPE EAST AND WEST: CENTRES OF DIPLOMATIC POWER c.1700

Nigel Llewellyn

Towards the year 1700, the political balances that had been maintained across Europe since 1648 were becoming increasingly unstable. The unprecedented longevity of Louis XIV, along with the vitality, competence and aggression of France's economy, diplomats and generals, were one constant source of pressure. From the opposite side of Europe arose the ambition of the Ottoman Sultan, Mehmet IV, aided by his Grand Vizir, Kara Mustafa, who in 1683 attacked the Holy Roman Empire to set siege to Vienna. The invasion of the Holy Roman Empire by a huge army of Turks, supplemented by bands of Tartar horsemen and their Magyar allies, generated a pan-European crisis of the first order. In response, a victorious alliance including Poland, Bavaria and other central European states – the French remained aloof – was formed across much of Christendom that together finally reversed generations of Christian defeats at the hands of the Ottomans.

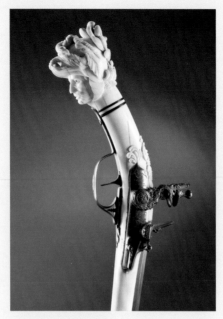

1.4 Flintlock pistol with the head of a classical warrior, Jean Louroux. Maastricht, The Netherlands, c.1661–87 (cat.38)

1.5 Flintlock pistol with the head of a Polish hussar, Michel de la Pierre. Maastricht, The Netherlands, c.1650–65 (cat.38)

1.7 Upper Belvedere, designed by Johann Lukas von Hildebrandt. Vienna, 1720–23, engraved by Salomon Kleiner 1737 (Private Collection)

1.8 (*right*) Prince Eugene of Savoy, artist unknown. Italy, 1710 (Musée des Beaux-Arts, Cambrai)

1.6 (*opposite*) Battle of Blenheim Tapestry, woven by Judocus De Vos after Lambert de Hondt. Brussels, 1710 (Blenheim Palace)

Furthermore, the papacy encouraged a new crusade and, supported by the Venetian Republic, the Christians secured an east European realignment that was maintained more or less intact until the outbreak of World War I. There were cultural as well as martial consequences to the Turkish presence on Europe's south-eastern flank (pls.1.4, 1.5).

Within twenty years another great issue arose, the monarchical succession in Spain; for among absolutist rulers, succession remained a topic of overriding importance. The new crisis followed the death in Madrid in 1700 of King Charles II, who left no children and no agreed heir. Spain's possessions were vast, and included not only half the nations that made up Italy and the politically sensitive and strategically important southern Netherlands (present-day Belgium), but also a world empire that embraced Mexico (indeed, most of central America), much of South America, the rich trading islands of the Philippines, the Canary Islands and some of the West Indies. Governments across Europe – especially the thriving trading nations of Britain and the Netherlands, as well as Spain's Habsburg cousins in Austria – grew increasingly concerned that this vast territory might fall to the French.

A will of Charles's did indicate that his successor was to be the grandson of the king of France, and since Louis seemed determined to recognize this inheritance, war was unavoidable. During the hostilities, reputations and fortunes were made that had a direct bearing on the patronage of Baroque art and architecture. In particular, the two field commanders who successfully fought the French, the Duke of Marlborough, who led the British, Dutch and German alliance, and Prince Eugene of Savoy, commander of the imperial armies, are intimately associated with the Baroque style. The architecture and decorated interior of the extraordinary palace at Blenheim, designed by Sir John Vanbrugh for Marlborough in the heart of the Oxfordshire countryside and paid for by a grateful nation, is named after the decisive battle in August 1704 (pl.1.6) and is one of the most ambitious Baroque monuments in England (see pl.1.9). When he was not riding against the Turks, Prince Eugene was patronizing the architect Hildebrandt, for example, at Eugene's Upper Belvedere palace, the epitome of progressive but cosmopolitan High Baroque design (pl.1.7).

Argomenti

Many Baroque opera libretti carried printed *argomenti*, typical Baroque devices, both explaining the piece and displaying the author's erudition.[2] Our *argomenti* on the Baroque start with the observation that the term itself post-dates the art to which it applied but is a label which can be usefully affixed to an identifiable style, one that occurs across all the visual arts (fine and applied), over a period of about seven or eight generations and right across the known world. Precise questions of definition and thematic currency are explored more fully in Chapter Two. We do not aim to give a general account of the Age of the Baroque but to consider the style itself. More than one hundred years after they published their definitions and theories, the ideas of the innovative German art-theorists who explored the Baroque in about 1900 – especially Wölfflin and Riegl – are still relevant.[3] Basing his theories on the history of applied art ornament, Riegl argued that art styles should be understood not as events but as processes, transformations of natural pattern resulting from purely artistic forces. The developing Baroque patterns of ornament resulted from the search for richer and more integrated forms.

What is intriguing about the Baroque is that even in its heyday it was never the exclusive style. Other styles ran alongside and overlapped with it: Mannerist ornament, various other dialects of classicism and a range of realist and naturalist tendencies were all fashionable at the same time. Stressing the continuity of what they see as a national classical tradition, French scholars continue to argue that 'French Baroque' amounts to a contradiction in terms. Many who have described a Baroque phase in British architecture have been sharply rebuked, especially over claimed linkages with a sympathy for Roman Catholicism. In Spain the Baroque is associated with severe order, while in neighbouring Portugal art historians have identified a 'plain' style to stand in opposition to Baroque. Many of our artists had the Baroque style in their repertoire and selected it for use, depending on the nature of the commission. When Luca Giordano (1634–1705), a much-travelled Neapolitan, painted in Florence in the 1680s he used the Baroque style for religious works but not for secular subjects. But in other cultures Baroque was the standard and dominant stylistic mode; it appeared in all media, it was highly adaptable, and it was mobile and prone to migration across cultural boundaries. Most of all, it was a style that challenged both the creative skills of the artists and the viewing skills of its audiences; in fact, it has challenged viewers ever since. Despite Riegl's claims about the style's independent formation, the Baroque has long been associated with magnificent performances – both religious and secular – by social élites, an idea that will be examined in Chapter Three. Typical of art history's tendency to use style-period labels that assume hegemonic European-centred contexts and conditions, accounts of the Baroque style have also tended to be Eurocentric. However, as we shall see, the Baroque had a global impact (see Potosí, p.28, and Goa, the 'Rome of the Orient', p.42).

In the hands of many historians, the Baroque has connoted pre-Enlightenment intellectual systems and an assumed sympathy for political absolutism. In fact, as Downes points out, the artists who adopted the Baroque regarded themselves as progressive and fashionable, although into the eighteenth century a rigid adherence to the style did express an increasingly conservative outlook.[4] For those seeking an anchor in cultural history the challenge lies in the fact that the Baroque is demonstrably not uniquely the style of the Counter-Reformation, nor uniquely that of the Jesuit Order and certainly not the approach to art-making encouraged by the Council of Trent.

The Baroque means many different things even across the visual cultures of western Europe, depending on the date and character of the work of art under consideration. There is no convincing Baroque *Zeitgeist*, in the fullest sense, argued by the great cultural historian Jakob Burckhardt, nor does Wölfflin's model of the Baroque – as a reaction against the Renaissance – always apply. We present the Baroque as a complex stage in the development of the post-Renaissance classical language of design and we explore it through themes such as assemblage and synthesis, the visual exploration of physical space, the illusion of movement and naturalistic ornament. Common to nearly all the works of art discussed is that they result from the transmission of people, ideas, motifs or materials.

This chapter sets the scene by exploring the circumstances and contexts within which Baroque artists worked, seeking to describe the Baroque-period 'eye', or rather 'eyes', for in relation to questions of patronage, making, distribution, display, viewing and response, Baroque art was many-layered and various. The boundaries that were crossed were intellectual, social, cultural and geographical.

1.9 North front of Blenheim Palace, designed by
Sir John Vanbrugh and Nicholas Hawksmoor, hand-coloured
engraving by Paul Foudrinier. 1745 (Blenheim Palace)

The World of Action – Early Modern Society

The early modern society that produced the Baroque was, above all else, hierarchical and patriarchal. Social mobility tended to be dependent on patronage and the élite were deeply preoccupied with questions of precedence. In Papal Rome, perhaps the greatest centre for the patronage and production of the Baroque, artists moved in and out of favour as new popes were elected and as new papal nephews (*nepoti*) took the reins of nepotism. Given the advanced age of those elected popes, such change-overs were frequent.[5] The noble status of an artist's patron was key to a successful career. In Protestant England, the acclaimed dramatist John Vanbrugh (1664–1726) was taken up by the Earl of Carlisle, a fellow Kit-Cat Club member. Carlisle, who was First Lord of the Treasury, having persuaded Vanbrugh to design Castle Howard, appointed him Comptroller of the Board of Works and Clarenceux King-of-Arms, the second highest rank in the College of Arms (the

heralds' professional body). Vanbrugh had no architectural training and such contempt for heraldry that he sold that office for £2,500. But he did stick with architecture long enough to design and oversee the building of Blenheim Palace (from 1705), a memorial to the Duke of Marlborough's military victories in the War of the Spanish Succession and often described as an 'English Versailles', although in fact resembling it little (pl.1.9).

Landed estates and great houses like Blenheim were the basis of noble status in England; in other Continental countries, it was often blood lineage that determined such matters. The incredible expense of Blenheim was carried by the crown, and we can find evidence of state support behind many of the most significant Baroque building projects. France set the tone: Louis XIV set out city squares, constructed hospitals; his architectural vision was emulated across Europe and beyond. For example, after the Great Fire of London Charles II set down great plans

for the City, the hospital at Chelsea and the monumental complex at Greenwich.[6] Gascar's portrait of Charles II's brother and heir, James, Duke of York, shows him as Lord High Admiral against a naval backdrop (pl.1.11).[7]

Throughout most of the Baroque world, public and private behaviour were subject to ecclesiastical influence and control (pl.1.10). Monarchs wielded temporal power but that power was ordained by God and significant areas of Baroque Europe were governed by theocracy – such as the Papal States in central Italy and the electorates of the central European prince-bishops. Invariably, the patterns of everyday life were deeply dependent on religious practice. Holy observances such as fasting had set rules and cases of ambiguity or applications for exemption, even from the élite, had to be referred to the priesthood.

1.10 (*opposite*) Cabinet on a console table, with a nocturnal clock and virginal, Giacomo Herman and Johannes Meisser (cabinet), Giovanni Battista Maberiani (virginal), Giovanni Wendelino Hessler (clock), Rome, 1669–75 (cabinet), 1676 (virginal), 1700–25 (console table). The cabinet is decorated with papal symbols and painted scenes of the principal churches and monuments of Rome. (cat.24)

1.11 *James, Duke of York as Lord High Admiral*, Henri Gascar, oil on canvas. England, 1672–3 (National Maritime Museum, Greenwich)

Le Frostin que Clement IX. fit a La Reyne de Suede, a monte cauallo l'an 1667.

1.12 *Queen Christina of Sweden dining with Pope Clement IX*, Pierre Paul Sevin, gouache. Probably Sweden, 1668 (National Library of Sweden – Royal Library, Stockholm)

1.13 Funerary catafalque of King Philip IV of Spain in Mexico City Cathedral, engraving. Mexico, 1666 (Biblioteca Nacional de España)

At higher social ranks, precedence was supremely important: who was to be addressed first? Who should walk on which side, given that the place of honour – but of lower rank – was to the right? After her abdication as queen of Sweden, Christina was still accorded princely status by the Vatican and permitted to dine with the pope, a ceremonial occasion.[8] A contemporary drawing shows the pontiff seated higher than the queen (pl.1.12). In France, precedence and rank were determined by the point of origin of a noble line: in the first rank were those with *noblesse de race* who benefited from hereditary nobility; at the bottom those whose *noblesse de dignité* was conveyed by office-holding. The individual's rank determined every issue about behaviour and identity – what they wore, the numbers of servants that might attend them, where they stood, when and what they said, the language used and how they were portrayed in art. Alertness to these distinctions was a key determinant of the Baroque eye.

The rules of precedence also blurred the universal acceptance of religious truth. Privilege was central to this system and touched on every social exchange, but was a social as well as a spiritual reality. Reflecting on the existence and nature of hell, one Protestant minister wrote: 'I don't believe any more than you do that hell is eternal; but it's a good thing for your maid, your tailor and even your lawyer to believe it.'[9] Precedence concerned the dead and the living. The death of a single individual such as the king of Spain generated multiple

1.14 *Celebrations in St Peter's, Rome, for the Jubilee year of 1700*, Johann Ulrich Kraus. Augsburg, 1700 (cat.80)

ceremonies across the known world (pl.1.13).[10] Elaborate funerals would be held in Mexico and other colonies, in the Spanish church at Rome and, of course, across the home country itself, designed to help achieve an orderly transition of power. The absence of a corpse at nearly all these ceremonies was overcome by means of art, with splendid catafalques and dressed effigies representing the natural body of the dead monarch and accorded every necessary sign of obeisance. Such ephemeral or temporary projects were the stock-in-trade of Baroque artists often associated with the various kinds of public performance that will be discussed in Chapter Three (pl.1.14).

At Mdina, the ancient spiritual capital of Malta, a movable and emotionally moving 'Altar of Repose' (1751–2) was erected every year in the cathedral during Holy Week, designed by Troisi and constructed and painted by Zara.[11]

From God himself to the very destitute, Baroque artists' awareness of precisely how to represent all the ranks of degree was a prerequisite for their career success. In the secular ranks, beneath the anointed prince came the nobility, the knights, the religious, the professionals (academics and lawyers), the trades and manufactures and finally the lower orders who were marked, indeed stigmatized, by their manual practice. For any visual artist, trained in a workshop tradition and earning a living by skilful manipulation of the hand to create art that deceived the eye, to be appointed into one of the innumerable orders of knighthood represented a radical revision to the ranks of degree.[12]

Despite the domination of inherited status, the massive growth in the world economy created fortunes that were made and lost with great rapidity, even by some élites. Meritocracies were slow to develop even in areas where professional experience and skill were clearly of benefit. Nobles appointed untrained architects, just as rulers appointing generals tended to look for high social rank rather than strategic skill or experience. Only in the 1670s did the French army take a first step towards subordinating social rank and blood ties to military rank and length of service. But one hundred years later, entrance to the *Ecole Militaire* still depended on a four-generation nobility test. In contrast, military professionals were mainly of humble birth – the engineers, sappers, cannoneers, etc.

Status remained for the most part an inalienable right conferred by lineage and not subordinate to man-made hierarchies. In fact, throughout the seventeenth century, when the Baroque was at its height, meritocratic tendencies tended to be ever further rebutted. Birthright counted even higher in about 1730 than it had around 1670. Only in some seventeenth-century Protestant states can we identify educated rather than social élites, seeking to establish the religious status of an elect, autonomous and unified nation.

This dominant culture of aristocratic favour had a direct bearing on Baroque art practice. Aristocrats were expected to engage in conspicuous consumption, whatever their actual wealth (pl.1.15). The display of luxury was itself a sign of nobility, which was why costume-wearing was subject to sumptuary law. A modest display by a member of the élite was potentially a subversive act. Princes, keen to preserve their mystique, tended to be cautious about public performance of, for example, music, fearful that it might confuse social distinction. With some very carefully organized and choreographed exceptions – the danced masques of Charles I or of Louis XIV – seventeenth-century Baroque princes were generally reluctant performers.

Among the military, expensive displays, ceremonies and present-giving marked key stages in warfare and reinforced the aristocratic and cosmopolitan officer code that operated across competing dynastic and military boundaries and acknowledged commonly held aristocratic values.[13] Voltaire called warfare the caprices of the few and, in general, princes tended to ignore theological arguments favouring peace. Baroque art was deeply

concerned with marking, celebrating and glorifying warfare in the form of countless portraits, increasing numbers of history paintings and churches dedicated to victory. Notre-Dame des Victoires, Paris, was started in 1629 and S. Maria della Vittoria, Rome (see The Cornaro Chapel, p.96), celebrates the 1620 massacre of Protestants outside Prague by troops hired by the Catholic Holy Roman Emperor. Warfare was conspicuous expenditure on a monstrous scale and most government income (raised through taxation or borrowing) was spent on fighting. The ancient systems of raising troops through feudal ties and the acknowledgement of the rules of military chivalry were largely ended during the period when the Baroque was fashionable. By 1700, such traditions no longer fitted comfortably with the demands of modern warfare.[14] The continuing traditions of Baroque equestrian portraiture were less and less to do with recording contemporary events and more and more about creating idealized visions (see The Portrayal of Absolutism, p.30).

Power and authority were usually transmitted via the male bloodline, and actual or potential failure in the hereditary succession tended to destabilize the Baroque state. Almost every year of the High Baroque period, 1618–80, saw armed conflict between rival states somewhere in Europe. Contested symbolic actions and behaviour were the most likely causes of wars: disputes around succession, a prince's urge to heighten his personal prestige, squabbles over territory or birthright or social precedence. A few wars were fought over territory. Religious difference was often a secondary motive, but only rarely were wars fought over the controls on trade and economic resources or to settle economic rivalries. The Anglo–Dutch naval war of 1652–4 was an exception.

All this fighting created a deep-rooted hatred of soldiers. Civilian communities in the theatres of war – much of Baroque Europe – suffered enormously from loss of life through battle and disease, from the destruction of agricultural life and of the peasant economy, and from the lowering of the conception rate, which further endangered economic sustainability. The only beneficiaries of warfare were some manufacturers in towns and the money-lenders.

Ordinary people had no conception of the states that waged war with one another; in fact, in modern terms the scale and reach of the Baroque state were unrecognizably tiny. The great and growing standing armies fought out of loyalty to prince or lord, not to states. Armies were often made up of foreigners, serving in regiments raised by their colonels. These were heterodox organizations within which religious, linguistic and national differences counted for little, although their

1.15 Ruby glass beaker, mark of Tobias Baur (mounts). Probably Nuremberg (glass) 1660–1700 and Augsburg (mounts) 1675–1700. Ruby glass was extremely expensive, as it was made using real gold, and so was highly desired by collectors. (cat.39)

Potosí: The Silver Mountain

Marjorie Trusted

Potosí, known as the Villa Imperial de Potosí during the period of Spanish colonial rule, is in present-day Bolivia; from the time of the Spanish conquest until 1776 it was in the Viceroyalty of Peru. Its importance lay in its extensive silver mines, which were revealed in 1545; the discovery of mercury some 700 miles to the north, at Huancavelica, in 1566 led to more intense mining activity, since mercury was crucial for refining silver ore. The legendary story of the finding of the silver by a native Indian shortly after the Spanish conquest established the myth that it had been preserved for the Spaniards by divine providence. From being not much more than a mining site Potosí became a flourishing city, with tens of thousands of inhabitants, from the mid-sixteenth century onwards. Black slaves were imported from Africa to work the mines, and an artificial river was created across the town, dividing the dwellings of the indigenous Indians from those of the Spaniards, the black slaves, *criollos* (Spaniards born in the New World) and *mestizos* (those of mixed race). Coins were minted from 1572 to 1767 at the Casa Real de la Moneda (the royal mint), founded by the Viceroy of Peru, Don Francisco de Toledo (1515–84; viceroy 1569–81). In 1613 a Mercedarian friar noted that residents were 'interested only in getting silver and more silver'. Much of the metal was exported to Spain, where it was used for goldsmiths' work, including great monstrances and other ecclesiastical silver vessels (pl.1.16).

The city was dominated by the Cerro Rico (the rich hill), beneath which lay the silver mines. Previously this had been a sacred site for the Incas, who had identified it with Pachamama, or Mother Earth. In the late sixteenth century the Spanish decided to convert this spiritual location into a Christian place, and three chapels were built on the hill. A number of paintings executed probably in the seventeenth or eighteenth century show the Cerro Rico as the Virgin (pl.1.19) . In these extraordinary images her head and hands are shown, but the rest of her body is contained in the hill. She resembles dressed Baroque images, whose heads and hands are carved but whose bodies are merely wood frameworks enveloped in robes. The sanctity of the hill is underlined

1.16 Monstrance, maker unknown, silver-gilt and quartz crystal. Spain, *c*.1630 (V&A:M.252-1956)

1.17 *The Entry of Viceroy Archbishop Morcillo into Potosí*, Melchor Pérez Holguín, oil on canvas, Bolivia, 1718 (Museo de América, Madrid)

1.18 *Artesonado* woodwork ceiling, Church of S. Francisco. Sucre, Bolivia, *c.*1618

1.19 The Virgin of the rich mountain of Potosí, the Cerro Rico, artist unknown, Potosí. Bolivia, *c.*1740 (Museo de la Casa Nacional de la Moneda, Potosí)

not only through the figure of the Virgin herself, but through the presence of the Holy Trinity crowning her, flanked by angels. Below, the Emperor Charles V and Pope Paul III (both in power in 1545, when the silver was discovered) kneel before the sacred scene. The combining of an indigenous deity, Pachamama, with a representation of the Virgin, fusing the native pagan religion with Christian beliefs, and with the yield of the land through its mineral resources, was characteristic of Spanish colonial images. Often these were made by *mestizo* artists, whose native beliefs underlay the Christian dogma they had been taught, and who therefore sometimes fused the two in their imagery. The Baroque church architecture of Potosí similarly reveals a synthesis of the European and Indian traditions: classical motifs, such as columns and capitals, and Muslim architectural forms, such as the *artesonado* woodwork ceilings, are combined with fleshy foliate decorative details, derived from the Indian culture and environment (pl.1.18).

THE PORTRAYAL OF ABSOLUTISM

Nigel Llewellyn

In the preamble to the so-called 'Authorized Version' of the Bible (1611), King James I is described as a 'blessing' sent by 'Almighty God … to rule and reign over … England…'. In the Baroque age, anointed monarchs were regarded as empowered directly by the hand of God and not accountable to human authority. This relationship with the deity signals the monarch's 'Divine Right' to rule and is the foundation of absolutism, the political and cultural system at the core of the Baroque state, epitomized by France under Louis XIV.

In the 1680s, Louis's son was tutored by Bishop Bossuet (1627–1704), who wrote about the four qualities essential to royal authority, regarded by him as 'sacred … paternal … absolute … [and] subject to reason'. Bossuet explained that '[a]ll power comes from God …

Princes act … as ministers of God, and [are] his lieutenants on earth … the royal throne is not the throne of a man but the throne of God himself … the person of kings is sacred … to make an attempt on their lives is sacrilege. … The prince is accountable to no one for what he orders. … Majesty is the image of the grandeur of God in the prince …'. This was the kind of imagery projected in apotheoses and portraits of absolutist rulers across Europe and their world empires (pl.1.20). They sought to project an air of lofty superiority, showing individuals not entirely of the real world, who were dread

1.21 *Louis XIV*, after Hyacinthe Rigaud. Paris, after 1701 (cat.18)

1.20 (*left*) *The Apotheosis of James I*, detail of the ceiling painting of the Banqueting House, London, Peter Paul Rubens. *c.*1630

1.23 (*right*) *Louis XIV Crowned by Fame at the Siege of Maastricht*, Pierre Mignard, oil on canvas. Paris, 1673 (Galleria Sabauda, Turin)

1.22 Bozzetto for the equestrian statue of Louis XIV, Gianlorenzo Bernini, terracotta. Rome, 1669–70 (Galleria Borghese, Rome)

judges on matters of life and death and who projected a near-timeless dignity, magnificence and grandeur.

These were not necessarily the elements of exciting and innovative portrait practice, but, as with other cultural patterns, the court of the Sun King generated some of the most influential and effective examples. In a famous portrayal of Louis (pl.1.21), Rigaud balances the ideological necessities with some fashionable references in the full wig and the elegant pair of stockinged legs. The body of Louis, by now an old man, is almost entirely masked by his formal robes, which prominently display the royal *fleur-de-lis*, yet his frame seems hardly capable of supporting the enormous sword at his side.

He stands on a throne-room platform in an unreal environment of swirling drapery amidst the traces of gigantic architecture. The natural body of the man is barely discernible: it is the political person of the monarch that is portrayed.

The theme of divine intervention – in the person of a winged Victory – is explicit in a portrait by Mignard (not a Baroque painter) of 1673 (pl.1.23) showing Louis wearing timeless Roman armour and effortlessly managing his massive steed with one hand. Such equestrian imagery was especially appropriate in the public spaces of city squares and palace courtyards (pl.1.22). Hardouin Mansart's Place Vendôme, built in Paris (after 1698), included at its centre Girardon's statue of the king, such effective propaganda that it was an early casualty of the 1789 Revolution. Bernini's adaptation of the rearing horse motif set the model for the conquering absolute ruler.

commanders might be seeking to impose ideological or spiritual uniformity on the countries they defeated.

Nationalism features but rarely in this world. Some artists adopted styles which appeared to connote national identities, for example, the French who were encouraged to adopt a distinct national style in music, despite the fact that, at the French court, taste was international. Where we might expect to find state responsibilities, we find private enterprise. For example, navies made extensive use of privateer captains, who were rewarded with money and with lavish gifts such as elaborately worked precious metal chains and weapons, often designed in the Baroque style. Even the most significant enterprises were administered only very lightly; religious life was often the exception to this rule. Taxes were irregularly collected and education was incidental, rather than general. Although armies were usually a rabble, the imposition of the Baroque aesthetic could sometimes turn them into works of art. Some princes recruited soldiers of equal height to the ranks, others demanded bodily elegance from their officers and Martinet, Inspector-General of French infantry from 1667, was famously enthusiastic about uniformity. Only in the 1660s, under Colbert, was the French army administered at all seriously and its effectiveness was soon celebrated by Le Brun's designs for the *Galerie des Glaces* (Hall of Mirrors) at Versailles (see The Gallery p.310). In contrast, Prince Eugene of Savoy, the commander of the Habsburg armies in about 1700, struggled to impose any kind of effective order on his forces, a telling defect in the battles waged against the Turks and during the War of the Polish Succession. The French modernization included the building of a naval training school in the 1660s, designed, of course, in the Baroque style.

Sieges were perhaps the exemplary mode of Baroque warfare (pl.1.24), since they offered ample opportunity for ritual practice such as ceremonial exchanges between the adversaries, they encouraged the development of new technology and they secured booty for the victor. They also challenged the intellectual faculties of the generals, who sought to control the rival forces with unseen hands. Improved fortifications were a legacy of Renaissance architectural theory, but around those walls and bastions there took place actions that were exemplary of Baroque representation.

Central to the Baroque was a paradox: an apparently unchanging world of clear social distinctions and unassailable princely authority that was frequently opposed by disruptive and violent disputes about the precise location of that authority. Many of the states that were significant exponents of the Baroque style endured factional rebellion, especially in the

mid-seventeenth century when England was engaged in civil war, the hardly united British nations fought one another, France suffered uprisings known as the *Fronde*, Spain experienced provincial revolt and lost its dominance in Portugal, and across the globe many of these European nations fought bloody colonial wars.

The leading dynasties engaged one with the other with a view to preserving and raising their prince's status but without disturbing the equilibrium between power centres. Clipping the wings of France became a Europe-wide preoccupation during the later 1600s. Louis XIV's public policy was to fulfil his dynastic responsibilities and establish France's 'Glory', a performance that sometimes conflicted with the needs of his body and soul. His marriage to Maria Theresa met certain dynastic aims, his mistresses – Louise de la Vallière, Françoise-Athénaïs de Montespan and Marie-Angélique de Fontanges – satisfied his body and Madame de Maintenon appears to have taken care of his soul.[15] Through the later Baroque period (*c.*1650–1740) the power of France steadily grew, marked by Louis's propagandists, including his painters, as dating from the early 1660s when he took personal charge of his government. His major strategic aim – supported by military action – was to protect the core territory of France. In response, grand alliances formed against her. The War of the Spanish Succession was Louis's final great conflict, fought against two great allied commanders, both of them considerable patrons of the Baroque style, the Duke of Marlborough and Prince Eugene of Savoy.

The papacy, elected and always in Italian hands, was a political exception within Europe but by now no longer with the power to direct the policies even of the 'Most Catholic' princes. The Habsburg Empire, despite dominating central and eastern Europe, was much threatened by the Swedes in the mid-1600s (pl.1.25).[16] Less relevant to the development of the Baroque style was the unexpected and unprecedented growth of Russia, which became a European power under Peter I in the early eighteenth century, replacing Sweden in the dominance of the Baltic region and certain parts of the north German lands. Thirdly, in the south-east corner of the European Baroque region, the Turks were effectively put out of commission by the forces of the Holy Roman Empire in the years around 1700, although the retaking of parts of Turkish Serbia in the late 1730s reflected the inherent weakness of the Habsburg government.

The German-speaking lands were increasingly weak politically and economically and poorly placed to patronize the visual arts. It took several generations to recover from the effects of the Thirty Years War (1618–48) following the rebellion by Bohemian nobles seeking political independence and religious emancipation from the Habsburg state. By the end of the Baroque era, the great European powers were France, Russia and Austria, and the power of Britain was steadily growing. Several former great powers were in decline – Venice, Spain, the Dutch Republic, the Ottoman Empire and the Nordic states of Sweden and Denmark – and most of present-day Italy and Germany was marking time.

1.24 *Siege of Namur*, Jean-Baptiste Martin, oil on canvas. France, 1692 (Musée national des châteaux de Versailles et de Trianon)

1.25 Binding of the *Codex Argenteus*, the 'Silver Bible'. The bible, written in silver and gold on purple vellum, and made in Ravenna *c.*520, fell into the hands of the Swedes during their occupation of Prague in 1648; the silver binding was later made at the orders of the Swedish Count Magnus Gabriel De La Gardie, to designs by David Klöcker Ehrenstrahl. (Uppsala University Library)

The Material World

The transmission of the Baroque style across the globe followed the routes taken by the great Renaissance discoveries as colonization was stimulated by dynastic ambition, trade and missionary fervour. From the European standpoint, the world was inexorably changing its shape. The new materials and commodities that became available were generally welcomed and are celebrated in some works of art (pl.1.26); but there was some disquiet too. Charles II, who knew a great deal about physical pleasure, regarded the newly available liquid stimulants as too dangerous for common distribution and strove to suppress the London coffee-houses that had started to open in the 1650s, fearing that coffee might foment discussion, which might in turn encourage dissent.[17]

Across Europe, the focus of economic activity shifted westwards, a trend especially marked in the Mediterranean as markets moved from the Near East to the Atlantic seaboard. Although economic foundations were shifting, at a local level élite privileges tended to be maintained. For example, Genoese trade – mediating between Spain and its possessions in Lombardy – remained in the hands of the aristocrats. These families were also the grandest art patrons in the city. The materials that the Baroque artists used reflect the steady globalizing of commodities: the panels provided for Dyrham Park in Gloucestershire by Alexander Hunter in about 1700 used Virginian cedar and walnut (presumably the European *Juglans regia* imported into America). These were supplemented by decorated leather from Holland. As in Iberia, the Dutch enjoyed grand, ornamented ebony chairs made in India. Soon after 1600, mirrors were developed in India, initially for Muslim consumption,[18] but the Europeans were soon attracted to the new decorative form and also sought local alternatives, for example, in South America where mica was mined in East Bolivia. In fact, across South America, the European colonists discovered that the indigenous makers were brilliant copyists: almost no form or pattern defeated them. By the time the Baroque style became current, North and South America were connected to Europe, Asia and Africa by a comprehensive network of trading routes. Cultural exchanges were dynamic, affecting diverse art forms in all continents (pl.1.27).[19]

1.26 Extended fan leaf depicting an imagined interior of a shop selling export wares, artist unknown. Possibly The Netherlands, 1680–1700. This fantasy of exotic luxury goods includes Japanese lacquer furniture, Chinese porcelain, ivory devotional sculptures, Indian chintzes and Turkish or Persian paintings. (cat.42)

Trade rather than manufacture was the major generator of European wealth and in the 1740s and '50s, as the popularity of the Baroque style started to wane, Britain waged a series of wars against her Continental rivals, turning her into the most successful imperial and trading power in the world. By contrast, the collapse of the Spanish economy late in the seventeenth century triggered a general loss of Spain's military power and eventually of most of her vast colonies. Although there is no general thesis to describe the relationship between economic performance and the adoption of the Baroque, contemporary theory imagined a stable, God-made universe comprising a fixed ration of wealth or trade. Competitors struggled to secure a greater percentage or to protect their interests: the economy was not regarded as capable of growth overall. Changes in the distribution of the wealth that God had provided became possible when that which was previously hidden was miraculously revealed to his faithful servants, such as the kings of Portugal, whose Brazilian territories yielded up vast supplies of gold, diamonds and emeralds, swiftly turned into works of Baroque decorative art in unprecedented volume and dedicated in gratitude to God (pl.1.28).[20] Warfare encouraged some mass-production, which had an impact on the development of Baroque design, and since warfare was becoming more concerned with trade and colonization, navies started to outweigh land armies in importance. The Dutch became the leading economic power of the seventeenth century and when times were good, were enthusiastic patrons of painting, though rarely in the Baroque style.

1.27 'Bucchero' vase, maker unknown. Mexico (vase) and Florence (mounts), 1600–1700 (vase), *c.*1700 (mounts) (cat.41)

1.28 Breast jewel, maker unknown. Portugal, 1700–25 (cat.33)

1.29 *St John Nepomuk hearing the confession of the Queen of Bohemia*, Donato Creti, oil on canvas. Bologna, Italy, 1730–33 (Galleria Sabauda, Turin)

The World of Ideas – Religion

Alongside warfare and dynastic ambition, a great deal of Baroque art was directed at religious subject-matter and produced for ecclesiastical sites and patrons. However, this was an age not only of deep religiosity but also of reform, controversy and dispute. Disagreements between Protestants and Roman Catholics centred on questions of authority, the boundary between the religious and secular and on theological and cultural issues – for example, the celibacy and role of the priesthood. Protestant Christians used the term pastor, while Catholics reaffirmed the function of priests as intermediaries, a strengthening of traditional policy that had directly affected the

character of the Baroque-period eye. An aspect of devotional practice such as the individual sinner's penitence confessed to a priest became exemplary of Catholic orthodoxy, its status created and secured in part by Baroque art. In the early 1730s, the Bolognese painter Donato Creti painted a scene from the life of St John Nepomuk (*c*.1345–93), whose image is prominent in Baroque central Europe (pl.1.29). Nepomuk had been martyred for his refusal to reveal the secrets of the confessional and Creti shows him hearing the confession of the queen of Bohemia, which was to lead to his martyrdom.[21] In the same years, in neighbouring Bavaria, Cosmas Damian (1686–1739) and his brother Egid Quirin Asam (1692–1750)

1.30 (*opposite*) Confessional in the church
of St John Nepomuk (Asamkirche), Munich,
Egid Quirin Asam and Cosmas Damian
Asam. 1733–46

1.31 Interior of St Peter's Basilica,
Rome, Giovanni Paolo Panini
and studio. Rome, before 1742
(cat.79)

built and decorated their local church in Munich – dedicated to
Nepomuk – and included confessionals, each designed with an
elaborate architectural frame, richly carved woodwork and inset
stucco figure sculpture (pl.1.30).

These religious controversies affected cultural production in
complex ways and tested the diplomatic sensitivities of artists,
patrons and audience. The English composer Henry Purcell
(1659–95) wrote Protestant (Anglican) music for Charles II's
court but also some settings of sacred Latin texts, perhaps
intended for the Catholic chapel of the queen, Catherine of
Braganza. Risking confusion with pre-Reformation practice,
Purcell also wrote 'odes' in the form of light banquet pieces for
the name day of St Cecilia, the patron saint of music. These
were, in fact, secular in tone: 'Welcome to all the pleasures/Of
every sense the grateful appetite'.[22] Archbishop Thun of

Salzburg – one of the architect Johann Bernhard Fischer von
Erlach's most important patrons – was a Catholic grandee but
closely involved in the entrepreneurial activities of the Dutch
East India Company, so central to the financial well-being of
the Protestant Netherlands. Thun invested his trading profits in
church bells, religious foundations, hospitals and charitable
institutions.

The Catholics' claim to universal power was based on
historical precedent: the popes claimed a direct lineage from
Christ via his token, the keys, given to Peter, his apostle,
therefore Christ's vicar on earth and the first pope. This
message of institutional authority was spoken forcefully and
eloquently in the design and decoration of the Vatican Basilica
of St Peter (pl.1.31), and countless square metres of Baroque
painting were committed to reinforcing this position. A huge

painted view of the council taking place within Benedict XIII's diocesan church of S. Giovanni in Laterano in spring 1725 by Pier Leone Ghezzi (1674–1755) shows the east end of the church set up for the bishops' deliberations with an audience accommodated on pews stretching right across the church. Rich embroidery hangs from the clerestory and dogs, soldiers and civilians witness the scene (pl.1.32).[23]

The visual arts were themselves a field of theological dispute. Catholic reformers argued strongly and traditionally that religious images were legitimate on functional grounds: they could teach and move the emotions of beholders in beneficial ways. Such images had, however, to be error-free because the power of the visual sense could easily be abused by the wrong kinds of images in the wrong settings. Potentially idolatrous images, set before the eyes of the weak or unwary, could lead to sinfulness, could arouse harmful emotions and stimulate inappropriate sensory responses, distracting the worshipper's attention from the true path.[24]

As we shall see in Chapter Four, religious experience overlapped directly with optical science and psychology in the Baroque fascination with illusory visions. There were passionate discussions from every intellectual standpoint about what exactly could be perceived by the organ of sight as distinct from what might be perceived internally through the imagination or the intellect. In seventeenth-century terms, an experience need not be perceived optically to be experienced as genuine and the Baroque style has often been understood as associated with a new bodily intimacy between object and viewer, appealing directly to the sense of sight and engaging with the space occupied by the body.

New challenges to the Roman Catholic Church generated new kinds of devotion supported by innovations in imagery. In the face of Protestant scepticism, the Vatican formula confirming the interrelations of the Holy Trinity was personified in art. New devotional practices were introduced in which the laity could share, for example, the daily devotion centred on the Rosary, which was especially promoted by the Dominican order.[25]

There were also the lives, works and miracles of the radical cohort of counter-reformatory saints, many associated with the new colonies in the Americas. The image of 'Our Lady of Guadalupe' has its origins in a miraculous apparition experienced by a newly converted Mexican peasant named Juan Diego in 1531 (see Religious Processions, p.254). Finding a barren, rocky hillside miraculously carpeted in flowers, he gathered them in his cape, and on delivering them to his sceptical bishop found the fabric impregnated with the image of the heavenly lady as she had appeared on the hillside.[26]

With the exception of the Erastians, who believed that the Church depended on the state, Catholics and Protestants accepted that the Church had a legitimate interest in social policy and in the political functions of the state. The Roman Church presented itself as Catholic (or universal), although many princes sought to establish political independence from the Vatican while accepting the theological authority of the pope. The administrative provinces of the Roman Church were governed by archbishops superintending diocesan bishops. These prelates were at the top of a vast hierarchy of Holy Orders including ordained priests, deacons and sub-deacons being prepared for ordination. Below them, the 'minor orders' included door-keepers (ostarii), exorcists, lectors and acolytes. The religious orders (monastic, mendicant and military) were the organizing bodies for nuns and monks, including friars and regular canons and canonesses.

Of all the monastic orders, the recently established Jesuits were especially influential on two levels: first, they were effective ministers, the emphasis of their teaching being placed on devotions that resulted in important new iconographic categories such as the Forty Hours Devotion or Quarant'ore, and the achievement of a good death. Secondly, they founded powerful institutions – new churches, priestly colleges and lay confraternities – that were influential on teaching, patronage, the attitudes of the lay public and other conditions important in the Baroque period. The popularity of the Jesuit saints was a stimulus to the production of Baroque art. In 1622, just as the style was reaching a defined visibility, the founders of the Jesuit order, Ignatius of Loyola and Francis Xavier, were canonized and as a result their images circulated across the globe. In 1726, another Jesuit saint, Aloysius Gonzaga, was canonized, bringing the order additional exposure (see The Bizarre, p.80, pl.2.9).[27] Such religious changes and tensions encouraged new artistic forms across the religious divide and in all media: for example, in music, the highly meditative cantata developed in the German-speaking lands in the last quarter of the seventeenth century and made famous by J.S. Bach.

The visualizing of religious experience was a compelling issue during the Baroque age and was passionately debated by theologians and philosophers. Visual images were assumed to be effective surrogates for whatever they represented – in most religious contexts, for example, at royal funerals, but also in secular contexts. A portrait of the museologist Elias Ashmole, mounted in a highly ornamental 'Gibbons' frame, stood in for him at the opening of the museum he founded at Oxford.[28]

1.32 *Lateran Council in the Church of S. Giovanni in Laterano,* Rome, Pier Leone Ghezzi, oil on canvas. Rome, 1725 (North Carolina Museum of Art, Raleigh)

GOA: THE 'ROME OF THE ORIENT'

Mallica Kumbera Landrus

When the Portuguese first arrived in India in 1498, they had mercantile aspirations. Indeed, the French monarch called the Portuguese king, Manuel (1495–1521), *le roi épicier*. Dom Manuel himself said, 'For our ancestors the main basis of this enterprise was always the service of God our Lord and our own profit.' The Portuguese objectives were thus not one but a combination of souls and spices, and encompassed the desire of the king to be crowned emperor of the East. Hence, after Alfonso de Albuquerque conquered the port city of Old Goa in 1510, Goa was embellished with churches as the capital of the Catholic Portuguese eastern empire. Indeed, early travellers compared the city of Goa to both Lisbon and Rome, and called it the 'Rome of the Orient'.

Architecture in Portuguese Goa played a highly political role, defined in large part by the close relationship between religion and politics. Hundreds of Catholic churches and chapels were conceived as visual symbols of Portuguese power and dominance in the region, representing the power of the Portuguese administration, the occupation of Goa, and the rule of a colonial master. The effects of these monumental churches on the indigenous population were thus calculated and carried a message of hegemony. The European styles of the churches confirmed Goa's ties with Catholic Portugal and Rome. Few examples survive from the sixteenth century; the seventeenth and eighteenth centuries are best represented in Goa today (pl.1.33).

1.34 Pulpit, Church of the Bom Jesus. Old Goa, 1681–95

1.33 Interior of the Church of the Holy Spirit. Old Goa, 1661–8

1.36 Façade of the Church of the Bom Jesus. Old Goa, 1695

1.35 *The Child Jesus as the Good Shepherd*, maker unknown. Indo-Portuguese, probably Goa, 1675–1750 (cat.6)

The Baroque styles that proliferated in this period constitute the majority of what remains in the form of ecclesiastical structures. The interiors were richly decorated with carved walls, as well as ornately polychromed and gilt altars and pulpits (pl.1.34). The popularity of the box-like simple interior adopted in most Goan churches was economical, but, importantly, provided an unobstructed view of the chancel and aided the process of mass conversion. Baroque influences in Portuguese Goa show ties not just to Portugal, but also to Rome and the Roman Catholic traditions brought to Goa by the various religious orders (pl.1.35).

Built within large open areas or on hills, the churches command attention. They are easily visible and appear to be superior, distinct and distant from all other structures. The Portuguese built in their new colony what they knew back home. If these churches were not exact clones of their Baroque antecedents, this was simply the result of local building conditions and a lack of the right materials.

In Goa the churches achieved a sense of awe, impressing the indigenous population and European travellers. They expressed triumphant power and control, exemplified through their dramatic and exuberant presence in an otherwise diverse cultural landscape. The Catholic Portuguese transformed the face of Goa with grand religious architecture that held symbolic significance for them. That these were European buildings in India is what sets the churches in Goa apart from all other religious structures.

Encouraged perhaps by high levels of bigotry, engendered by radical distinctions habitually drawn between minor shades of religious difference, the interweaving of religious practice with secular culture was total. The Knights of Malta, builders of Valletta, one of the great Baroque cities of Europe, monks but also soldiers and temporal lords, exemplify the blurring of lines between the religious and the secular, the militaristic and the artistic (pl.4.26). Religious controversy was as likely to be couched in terms derived from differences in ethnicity or social class as in theology. Many Protestants who visited unreformed Baroque Europe were put off papist images not because they feared their magic powers but because they saw that they encouraged the masses to become 'an irregular mob of penitents ... bawling and bellowing' and to misbehave in public.[29]

The organization of spirituality and of religious practice in Catholic Europe in the age of the Baroque was substantially determined by a set of principles agreed in the later sixteenth century, in the immediate aftermath of the Protestant revolt. This was a set of decrees hammered out after years of discussion – the Council of Trent (1545–63) – in the small north Italian Alpine town of Trento and which comprised the so-called post-Tridentine settlement.

One set of decrees related to the daily lives of the monastic religious – monks and nuns. Important assumptions about gender difference in the context of religious experience are revealed by the Tridentine emphasis on the shutting away of nuns from the world, in enclosed communities, as chaste brides of Christ, necessarily kept from pollution because their own feeble wills would not otherwise have preserved them from Satan's works. This arrangement was also attractive on overtly secular grounds, especially amongst the social élite, for whom the marriage of a daughter required a costly dowry or a risk of losing status. In certain Baroque centres as many as 40% of daughters were sent to convents, where many of them engaged in intellectual and cultural pursuits at the highest level.[30]

The God-fearing looked for signs of God's handiwork in every event and natural phenomenon. The Portuguese took a beautiful climbing plant (*Passiflora caerulea*) found in the Amazon basin as evidence of God's presence and called it the passion flower on the grounds that its flowers contained emblems of the Redemption. The leaves were shaped like the spear that pierced Christ's side; the corona threads like the scourge that beat him; the five stamens like the Crown of Thorns, and the three clavate stigmas above the flower resembled the nails that secured him to the Cross. The flower had only ten petals and sepals to represent the apostles because Judas and Peter had indulged in betrayal in Passion Week.

Cosmologies

The Baroque age saw a reappraisal of the concept of nature, which, in philosophical and theological terms, had been regarded as imperfect, non-essential and inferior to the ideal. Natural things were of lower status (more feminine) and they appealed to the senses rather than to the higher, intellectual faculties. In the late Baroque period some of these assumptions were challenged and the natural condition seen as ideal, innocent and meditative rather than simply as primitive. The creative, natural retreat also became fashionable again.[31] The natural theme in the visual arts was contested. The painter's capacity to replicate nature was an embarrassment to academic theorists but was an important thread in artistic production, and powerfully expressed in works in various styles and genres across the Baroque world, for example, in *paso* figures carried through Spanish streets during Holy Week. These were life-like in scale and coloration, with glass eyes and tears, and they sometimes wore wigs made from real hair. Their limbs were movable and their heads interchangeable to accommodate the demands of the narrative: they represented the antithesis of academic good taste.

Baroque artists and their audiences were moving through a social and physical universe that was growing larger before their eyes and minds. Geographers were accommodating new lands, new continents and also new understandings of the heavens. As today, the expressions 'sunrise' and 'sunset' were used, but most people of the Baroque era believed them to be literal. When Bellori published his famous essay on the principles of artistic idealization in 1670, he expounded a view of the material universe that had been definitively challenged several generations earlier by Galileo's confirmation of Copernicus's heliocentric theory.[32] To quote Koyré on the Galilean telescope: '... mountains on the moon, new "planets" in the sky, new fixed stars in tremendous numbers, things that no human eye had ever seen, and no human mind conceived before ... [the invention] enabled Galileo to transcend the limitation imposed by nature – or by God – on human senses and human knowledge'.[33] Famously, Galileo's championing of new technology in the form of the telescope did not carry the day: orthodox theologians, conservative scholars and rival philosophers all objected to trusting information gathered from such a source.

Astronomers did not simply contest rival definitions of scientific truth; they challenged the authority of ancient sources and potentially undermined political and ecclesiastical authority. A painting by Niccolò Tornioli, acquired for Palazzo Spada, Rome, in 1645, shows ancient and modern astronomers

disputing the opposing merits of the Ptolemaic and Copernican
viewpoints, representative sources for the ancient and modern
systems (pl.1.37).[34] In the centre, Copernicus points out the
lunar phases as evidence of his heliocentric theory. This seems
serious enough, but in another picture in the same collection,
'Astronomy' could be personified as a comely young woman,
holding a pair of compasses and engaging the eye of the
beholder in a way suggestive of bodily rather than intellectual
pleasures (pl.1.38).[35] This latter image adapts one of the
important iconographic categories in the Italian Baroque, the
portrayal of the wise woman – fortune-tellers, sibyls, and so on.

1.38 (*opposite*) *Personification of Astronomy*, Giovanni Battista Magni, called Il Modenino, oil on canvas. Rome, *c.*1644 (Galleria Spada)

1.39 *Jupiter*, Donato Creti, oil on canvas. Bologna, Italy, 1711 (Pinacoteca Vaticana)

The period of Baroque's popularity is bracketed by the slow acceptance of the theoretical implications of Galileo's discoveries and Sir Isaac Newton's demonstration of the existence of gravity, '... an absolute space, which being unperceivable to sense, remains in itself similar and immovable...'.[36] For Bishop Berkeley, an unperceivable reality was a contradiction in terms. The image that appeared through the telescopic lens to be four times larger than the image discerned by the natural eye, and four times smaller when reversed, was evidence that the existence of the body was simply a sensory manifestation of an idea.[37] The scholar-philosopher Gottfried Wilhelm Leibnitz (1646–1716) understood Newtonian gravity differently and his reaction is a powerful revelation of Baroque aesthetics: he complains that the idea – not being based on the evidence of sensory perception – brought an unwelcome 'occult quality into

philosophy'.[38] Stung by this criticism, Newton added to a later edition a clear statement about the religious conceptions that he claimed supported his method and his discoveries: 'This most beautiful system of the sun, planets, and comets, could only proceed from the counsel and dominion of an intelligent and powerful Being.'[39]

The depiction of mundane and heavenly space reflects these concerns with the natural structure of the universe. Donato Creti was commissioned in 1711 to paint eight pictures for the pope, hoping that he would sanction the purchase of a telescope for the institute at Bologna, and these evidence this sense of a 'beautiful system' irrespective of Protestant and Catholic factionalism.[40] Creti's pictures show the heavenly bodies, each massively exaggerated in size, hanging in the sky and the object of learned attention from small groups of scientists. *Jupiter* shows a short string of moons alongside the mother planet (pl.1.39).

1.41 (*opposite*) The Triumph of the Name of Jesus, ceiling fresco of the nave of the church of the Gesù, Rome, Giovanni Battista Gaulli, called Baciccio. 1678–9

1.40 *A Witch Frightening a Young Man*, Lionello Spada, pen and ink. Bologna, Italy, 1620 (The Royal Collection)

Bologna – a city within the papal territory – was scholarly and the acknowledged centre for the artistic technique of *quadratura*. This, derived from Renaissance linear perspective, relied on the artist's competence in geometry and enabled decorative painters comprehensively to confuse onlookers about where the real architecture of vaults and walls ended and where fictive, painted architecture began. It was an artistic practice that brought together the representational and performative worlds of theatre and religion (pl.1.41).

The systems of thought that operated around 1700, and the academic boundaries that supported those systems, need careful definition. The word 'philosophy' was taken to indicate scepticism, what we might term 'free thinking' or 'rationalism'. The contemporary term to describe the understanding of thought and knowledge was termed 'metaphysics'. Far from signifying outlandish superstition, alchemy was commonly accepted as a legitimate form of useful knowledge and astrology was for the most part treated as an acceptable

superstition but a form of knowledge (or science) nevertheless. Faced by dark forces, the visual arts could function palliatively. A drawing by Lionello Spada shows an artist, assailed by nightmares, who tries to free himself from them by drawing a young man in torment, begging the recipient to seek an elixir to remove the spell (pl.1.40).[41]

Significant echoes of scepticism occur first in René Descartes's *Discourse on Method* (1637), which was published in the French vernacular rather than in standard academic Latin. Descartes had fought on the Catholic side in the Thirty Years War, then found fame as a philosopher and died in 1650 in frozen attendance on Queen Christina of Sweden. The *Discourse* explores the theory of knowledge – how we know the things we think we know – and sets out principles that were to underpin the academic theory of art developed across Baroque Europe over subsequent generations. Descartes regarded the human senses as inadequate tools for the collection of secure scientific data and argued that the information gained by the

senses required processing by the intellect. Adapting this principle, academic art theory taught that the higher genres of the figurative arts – the visual arts that would improve and instruct, for example, pictures in churches or paintings that teach instructive lessons about ethics or history – should be based not simply on manual skill and the capacity of the hand to deceive the eye but on an intellectual process that improved on nature. The artist's intellect was needed to process what the sense of sight supplied. The classic formulation of these ideas was developed by Charles Le Brun (1619–90), royal painter to Louis XIV, who used the Cartesian theory of knowledge as the basis of the syllabus at the Royal Academy of Painting and Sculpture. The origins of Neoclassicism lay in the Baroque.

In eastern Europe, rival philosophical systems were being developed that may also have had a direct bearing on the arts of design. The architecture of Fischer von Erlach (1656–1723) is a characteristic late Baroque attempt to synthesize various stylistic interests by reconciling elements that might be regarded as incompatible, such as ancient and historical references in a contemporary building. His European training had included a long stay in Rome (c.1671–87), where his contacts included Philipp Schor (son of Giovanni Paolo Schor, known as 'Il Tedesco', the decorator of the Palazzo Colonna), the workshop of Bernini, the art theorist Bellori, Queen Christina and the polymath Athanasius Kirchner. Establishing his career in imperial Vienna, Fischer was drawn into the circle of Leibnitz, who visited the city in 1712–14 to expound a new philosophical system to Prince Eugene of Savoy, the leading figure at court. Leibnitz's fundamental principle was based on the ancient idea that God was the architect of the world, which

was his 'perfect' building. Leibnitz assumed that the natural universe reflected a theocentric 'order' with basic building blocks or constituent substances known as 'monads', emanating from God and moving in harmonious correspondence with one another. Visual harmony was a goal of Fischer's architectural designs (even to the point of sacrificing physical comfort), just as the harmonic ideal was the key principle in Leibnitz's metaphysics. The parallel interests of the architect and the metaphysician do remind us that the Baroque eye is directed at ideas and the intellect as well as searching for stimulants for the sense of sight. As we shall see in Chapter Four, the Leibnitzian monad can be traced in Fischer's most important building, the Karlskirche in Vienna, the key lying in its harmony and the supreme integration of all its arts, architectural and decorative (pl.1.42).

Subjects hotly debated in Baroque theology tended to be non-scriptural, a feature compensated for by a vast, complex set of competing definitions and arguments offered by every branch of Baroque science and philosophy. The debate about the Trinity had, in Voltaire's words, 'exercised curiosity, sophistic subtlety, acrimony, intrigue, fury to dominate, rage to persecute, blind and bloody fanaticism, barbarous credulity and ... more horrors than the ambitions of princes'.[42] So baffling were the results that Voltaire was to remark many years later: 'Oh Man. This God has given you understanding in order to behave well, and not to penetrate the essence of the things he has created.'[43] The nature of the Soul was disputed but the Body was regarded mechanically: blood inflamed by the warmer southern climes was more inclined to sensual pleasures than the cooler blood of the North.

1.42 Karlskirche, Vienna, Johann Bernhard Fischer von Erlach and Joseph Emanuel Fischer von Erlach. Begun 1715

THE PEACE OF WESTPHALIA

Nigel Llewellyn

In May 1648, at the small north German town of Münster, in Westphalia, a treaty was signed that brought peace to much of Europe by ending the Thirty Years War. The lengthy diplomatic processes had been witnessed by the Dutch painter Gerard ter Borch (1617–81), who commemorated the final events in a small oil painting recording the faces of the dozens of male envoys and politicians who took part; the artist himself is included on the left (pl.1.43). In its balance and organization, the picture registers the political realities of the day, with the two opposing camps of the United Provinces of the Netherlands and their erstwhile colonial masters, Spain, distributed in equal balance on each side.

Ter Borch was a typical international artist of the mid-seventeenth century. Working in the Netherlands, England, France, Italy and Spain, he was commissioned by both Protestant and Roman Catholic patrons. Although his painting does not represent exactly what happened, some key signs of cultural difference are included. The Dutch delegates extend their fingers in Protestant gestures of oath-taking, while the Catholic Spanish plenipotentiaries set theirs on the Bible and crucifix.

The discussions at Münster had focused on new patterns of political control over constitutions, territory and religious practice across much of mainland Europe. After much argument, the Holy Roman Emperor agreed to recognize the confessional realities of post-Reformation Europe and his envoys conceded that Protestants of both Lutheran and Calvinist faiths could be party to the final settlement. Unsurprisingly, Pope Innocent X (pl.1.44) sent an open letter of complaint.

1.43 *The Swearing of the Oath of Ratification of the Treaty of Münster*, Gerard ter Borch, oil on canvas. The Netherlands, 1648 (The National Gallery, London)

1.44 *Pope Innocent X*, Domenico Guidi, after Alessandro Algardi. Rome, *c*.1690 (cat.78)

1.45 *William III on Horseback*, Godfrey Kneller, oil on canvas. England, 1701 (The Royal Collection)

interests. Thirdly, there was peace between the Austrian-Habsburg Holy Roman Emperor (Ferdinand III, r.1637–57) and the allied forces of France and Sweden (the latter under Queen Christina, r.1632–54). In the early 1600s the Swedes had become dominant in northern Europe, occupying Prague for a while and even threatening Vienna, and at Münster they gained important coastal trading outlets. The Swedes were to continue their warlike policies over the next decades and to dominate their Danish rivals and neighbours (pl.1.46). France, in 1648 yet to capitalize on the reforms of Louis XIV (r.1643–1715), merely consolidated its eastern border.

Contrasting with the ordered composition of Ter Borch's picture, the Peace itself registered how, in the mid-century, ancient structures of belief, understanding and social organization were being subjected to massive pressure for change. Despite the long negotiations, the effect of the settlement was neither universal nor immediate. Fighting continued, but the cultural chaos that had been so antipathetic to the arts for so long was reduced. As one contemporary German painter noted at the time, 'Dame Painting, who had been sleeping, woke again.'

At least three processes were linked at Westphalia: the first ended an eighty-year war of independence fought against Spain (Philip IV, r.1621–65) by the Dutch republic, led now by William II, Prince of Orange (r.1647–50, whose son William III, r.1650–1702, also took the throne jointly in Britain after 1688 [pl.1.45]). Secondly, there ended thirty years of fighting in Germany and Bohemia which had been mostly about tensions between imperial and local

1.46 *Christian IV of Denmark*, François Dieussart, bronze. Copenhagen, 1643 (The Royal Danish Collections, Rosenborg Castle, Copenhagen)

The World of Signs

The belief that the universe was God's perfect creation inclined the curious to seek comprehensive solutions and universal systems. The painter John Smibert (1688–1751) was seduced by Bishop Berkeley's vision of a universal college of the arts and sciences for the instruction of heathen children, to be established in the paradise of Bermuda.[44] Theologians had not yet learned the polemical practice, forced upon them in the later eighteenth century by attacks from Enlightened sceptics, of engaging in selective symbology. The prevailing assumption was that Scripture was literally true; these were sacred and inspired texts that were assumed to mean exactly what they said: to select or ignore would be blasphemous. In 1724 Richard Cumberland, an Anglican bishop, published a famous, learned tract taking the Bible as a secure guide to ancient genealogies, which he painstakingly reconstructed.[45] Theological gloss and exegesis had a direct bearing on Baroque iconography: for example, the ranks of angels first identified by Jewish scholars then formalized by papal bull, with seraphim and cherubim below and an élite corps of archangels. In the mid-1680s, the Prior of El Escorial confirmed to his royal patron Charles II of Spain that Luca Giordano had had two learned theologians working alongside him to instruct him in the 'mysteries', an important safeguard because Giordano painted so quickly that errors were prone to creep in (pl.1.48).

Allegory, the continued metaphor whereby a subject or character is treated under the guise of another, was an important system of sign-usage for the visual arts, especially in the secular sphere. When it came to planning allegorical histories in the Baroque manner, artists gave priority to effect, for example, that of heroic grandeur, rather than historical truth.[46] Such corrections were legitimate, according to the early eighteenth-century theorist Jonathan Richardson: 'A painter is allowed sometimes to depart even from Natural and Historical truth.'[47] In planning a painting about the historic landing of George I on British territory in 1714, Sir James Thornhill (1675–1734) foresaw that there would be 'Objections [to] the plain representation of the king's landing as it was in fact and in the modern way and dress' (pl.1.47). The time was changed from dead of night to evening; nobles disgraced since the event were removed from the welcome party; the king's costume was made graceful and timeless; finally, a large cast of mythological and allegorical personifications was introduced to clarify the artist's pedagogic and moralizing intentions. Such alterations were done with careful judgement; the key to creating an exemplary and powerful impact was to avoid excessive variety,

1.47 *Landing of George I at Greenwich*: design for decoration of Greenwich Hospital, Sir James Thornhill, pen and brown ink, with brown-grey wash, over graphite. London, 1718–25 (The British Museum)

1.48 (*opposite*) St Lawrence in Glory, Ceiling Fresco of the Imperial Staircase, El Escorial, Madrid, Luca Giordano. 1690s

since it might offer unnecessary distraction to the eye.[48] The interpretation of systems of allegorical signs required extensive education in the necessary conventions and, since access to education was restricted, such systems were class-specific. In some Baroque cultures, the noble classes were those qualified by blood, marriage or promotion to bear heraldic arms, which were key social indicators and occur frequently on Baroque works of art. Clothing was of course another key indicator of class, ethnicity and livelihood, although armies did not have standard uniforms in the early seventeenth century. In the Baroque period, military conduct came gradually to be seen as an exemplary code of social conduct and its trappings became standard signs of this code. Louis XIV had himself represented in military uniform but he never in fact wore it. Nor did he allow his nobles to appear at court wearing it, whereas many monarchs habitually dressed themselves as commanders-in-chief, a mode of dress that survives to this day.

By the 1650s, armies were employing symbolic colours to associate themselves with dynasties rather than with nations: red for Spain, white for France, black referring to the double-headed Habsburg imperial eagle. The prime example was orange, referring to the ruling dynasty of Orange and to the Dutch Republic. The taste for ceremony, display and conspicuous consumption among the higher ranks of the military contrasted with the brutality of the fighting between the common soldiery. There were pricey flags too large actually to unfurl in battle, and in 1676 the gilding and decorating of a Mediterranean fleet galleon cost the French crown three times more than did the actual building of it.[49]

Science and Language

Given the opportunity, Baroque artists would have witnessed a transition in medical knowledge, from age-old Galenic principles to startling modernity. As with other fields of knowledge, the distinction between science and religion was not drawn and in most quarters the theories of the humours and their balance continued to be central to an understanding of the physiognomic workings of the human form and the treatment of illness. The genders had what were regarded as their natural humoral states – Hot/Dry, Wet/Cold and Male/Female. The visual arts were a field of activity appropriate for the pursuit of knowledge and the exercising of curiosity about the natural world. Precious things were collected from all quarters of the globe, and alongside wondrous rarities the naturalist might well display coloured dyes and materials of art such as lapis lazuli, charcoal black and cochineal red.[50] Visiting Paris in the 1640s, John Evelyn saw objects 'of Purselan, of Currall [porcelain and coral], … one carved in a large Crucifix … bookes of Prints … all sorts of Insects … so plac'd that they present you with a most surprizing & delightful tapissry' (pl.1.49).[51]

1.49 Amber tankard, maker unknown. Probably Königsberg (now Kaliningrad), 1659 (cat.35)

1.50 *Self-portrait with the Marchese Pallavicini*, Carlo Maratta, oil on canvas. Probably Rome, 1705 (The National Trust, Stourhead). The allegory presents the Marchese as an enlightened patron of the arts, being welcomed by Apollo and the Muses, with the artist himself seated among them. The Temple of the Muses is shown above to the right, up a steep and difficult path.

The so-called new science did have an impact on the visual arts in relation to the understanding of sight and the dawning realization of the infinity of the universe. What did Baroque artists engaged in, say, a depiction on a church vault of the heavens opening to receive a martyred saint, or to reveal the deity, actually think they were painting in terms not just of subject but of materiality? To claim that God's universe is infinite was a means of honouring God's creation; however, it could also be taken to challenge assumptions about the central place of humankind in that universe, which might in turn challenge other scriptural teaching. Some preferred to consider the heavens as 'indeterminate' rather than 'infinite', although neither term offered much encouragement to figurative artists employed to use conventional languages of visual signs to illustrate agreed iconographies. If an artist cannot conceive of the motif, it cannot be painted, a task made more difficult by the new theories arguing that the universe was not static and ordered but unstable and indeterminate; that the place of the earth in the scheme of things is at the very least uncertain and often contestable and that the earth is not dark and flawed in contrast with the perfect lightness of the sun.

When Leibnitz engaged in his published dispute on the existence of gravity, he wrote in French and his adversary, Newton, replied in English. When the elected king of Poland, John Sobieski, met Emperor Leopold in the immediate aftermath of the relief of the siege of Vienna in 1683, complex questions of precedence and authority were foremost in the two men's minds: they faced one another to avoid either being given precedence to the right and their heads were uncovered for precisely the same period of time; however, there was no recorded disagreement on their common language, Latin. The ability to conduct oneself in the common European language of scholarship was the key indicator of educational attainment among Baroque patrons, who came from a class where rhetorical and grammatical competence was the norm. These skills were learned from Cicero and required the acquisition of verbal dexterity in planning, explaining, persuading, deploying authoritative sources and interpreting complex allegories (pl.1.50). Latin phrases and constructions echo behind the Baroque eye.

The World of the Baroque Artist

With a few notable exceptions such as Rubens, Baroque artists were not expert Latinists and the arguments that took place about the basis of artistic education were not about the acquisition of ancient verbal languages. In 1733, Antonio Balestra, a figure of some authority in north-east Italy, commented: 'All the present evil derives from the pernicious habit, generally accepted, of working from the imagination without having first learned how to draw after good models and compose in accordance with good maxims. No longer does one see young artists studying the antique.'[52]

The disinclination of some artists to study the surviving works of the Greeks and the Romans was not a sign that they were at odds with the priorities of their patrons. For the most part, Baroque artists did not conform to the post-Romantic art-historical stereotype of the artist as eccentric genius or social non-conformist. Mostly, their aspirations were towards the elegant courtier, an image that had been envisioned by Alberti in the early Renaissance and one fulfilled by several

prominent exponents of the Baroque – Bernini, Rubens, Velasquez, Maratta and Solimena. Portraits and self-portraits of Baroque artists set out the kind of self-fashioned images that they sought to cultivate. Charles Le Brun appears as a scholar, surrounded by images and texts alluding to his liberal education and intellectual approach to picture-making (pl.1.51).

Within the figurative arts, the categories or genres of subject-matter – history, landscape, still life, and so on – were each regarded as having a distinctive professional character and were seen as a hierarchy, with history at the top. For this reason, artists were known by the genres with which they were most associated, the higher the better, and many sought to raise their professional profiles by associating with a higher genre. Even when their subjects were not taken from history, artists could make historical references and thus improve the reputation of their work.

In terms of perceived historical significance and career achievement, the leading exponents of the Baroque style were nearly all men. Sofonisba Anguissola (c.1532–1625) and Artemisia Gentileschi (1593–c.1654) ended their careers before the style developed and Rosalba Carriera (1675–1757) was enormously successful but was not a Baroque artist. Her practice was in crayon or pastel portraiture, which did not require her to risk her social reputation by exposing herself either to the nude anatomical model in the drawing school or to the intellectual demands of idealization. Experience in both life-drawing and the ideal were prerequisites for history painters. Furthermore, the portraiture business, even on an international stage, could be regulated and domesticated: during Carriera's celebrated stay in Paris in the early 1720s, she was accompanied by her brother-in-law Pellegrini, also a painter.

Van Dyck made a note on a sketched portrait of Anguissola, done in 1624 when she was in her 90s, which illustrates the Baroque artists' theoretical and practical fascination with representation, their veneration for tradition and that self-reverential quality typifying so much early modern art discourse (pl.1.52). Van Dyck records that Anguissola's brain was 'most alert ... though ... she has lost her sight, she would all the same delight in putting pictures in front of her. ... As I was making her portrait, she gave me many hints, such as not to

1.51 *Charles Le Brun*, Nicolas de Largillière, oil on canvas. Paris, before 1686 (Musée du Louvre)

1.52 (*opposite*) *Sofonisba Anguissola*, from the Italian Sketchbook, Anthony van Dyck, pen and brown ink. Italy, 1624 (The British Museum)

Ritratto della Sig.ra Sofonisba pittrice fatto dal vivo in Palermo
l'anno 1624 li 12 di Iulio. l'età di essa 96 havendo ancora la memoria
et il cervello prontissimo, cortesissima. Et se bene per la vecchiaia li
mancava la vista, hebbe con tutto ciò gusto di mettere gli quadri avanti
ad essa, et con gran stenta   mettendo il naso sopra il quadro, veniva
a discernere qualche poco   Et piglò gran piacere ancora
in quel modo, facendo   il ritratto de essa, me diede
diversi advertimenti   non dovendo pigliar il lume
troppo alto, acciò   che l'ombre nelle
ruge della vecchiaia   non diventassino troppo
grande, et molti   altri buoni discorsi
come ancora con te   parte della vita di essa
per la quale si conobbe essere pittora di natura maravigliosa
et la pena maggiore che hebbe fu per mancamento de vista il
non poter più dipingere. la mano era ferma senza
tremare alcuna.

take the light from too high ... I came to know that she was a painter from nature.' Of course, any male Baroque artist, however sensitive, would expect a woman artist to be close to nature and less capable intellectually of undertaking the abstract reasoning necessary for the idealizing enterprise.

The capacity to engage intellectual faculties as well as manual skills was an aspect of a liberal education and outlook and was identified with the social ranks above the professional class, but such recognition was hard for Baroque artists to gain. As late as the 1720s, the English theorist Richardson noted that 'the Word *Painter* does not generally carry with it an Idea equal to that we have of other professions'. The artists strove constantly to show that they relied not only on manual gifts and that theirs was a practice suitable for gentlemen. The French scholar Roland Fréart de Chambray took a resolute, radical and modernist stance against his 'ancient' adversaries, arguing that the intellectual achievements of painters had gained them ascendancy over their ancient forebears: 'The days of *Apelles* are now past, and our Modern *Painters* are quite another strain from those Old Masters, who never came to be *Considerable* in their *Profession*, but by the study of *Geometrie* and *Perspective*, the *Anatomy* of *Bodies*, the assiduous Observation of those *Characters* which express'd the *Passions* and *Emotions* of the Soul; by the Lecture of the *Poets* and good *Historians*; and, in fine, by a continual *re-search* of whatever might best contribute to their Instruction.' These kinds of patterns are discernible among other kinds of artists too: composers of music were regarded as artisans, at a lower intellectual level than librettists, practitioners of the word. Few early modern artists would have had a high enough level of creative self-esteem to have emulated Bernini, who felt that it was beneath his dignity to deal with the practical details of design.

Career categories among Baroque artists generally remained fluid; for example, architecture was not yet recognized as a profession and building designers came from a variety of educative backgrounds. Some were sophisticated stonemasons, others fully rounded scholars. Balthasar Neumann (1687–1753) applied his mathematical skills in a number of fields – cannon-founding, logistics, geometry, surveying, and civil and military engineering – before he turned his hand to architecture *per se*. His staircase ceiling at Würzburg, painted by Giambattista Tiepolo (1696–1770), encouraged what is perhaps the greatest example of late Baroque visual complexity (pl.1.53).

1.53 Imperial staircase of the Residenz at Würzburg, Germany, designed by Balthasar Neumann, 1737, with the ceiling fresco by Giambattista Tiepolo. 1752–3

1.54 High Altar of Sint Jacobskerk, Antwerp, Belgium, with *The Assumption of St James*, Willem Kerricx and Artus II Quellin. 1685

Artists Crossing Boundaries

Increasing numbers of artists became art collectors in the Baroque period. Sir Peter Lely (1618–80) started buying works on paper in the late 1640s and continued through the politically difficult 1650s, claiming that 'for Drawings and Prints his [collection] was the best'. Lely's motives were artistic, financial, social and pedagogic. He hoped that his investment would enhance his prestige, give him access to models and help compensate him for not visiting Italy during his apprenticeship. By Lely's day, it was commonplace for northern artists to undertake challenging Italian journeys, which were made in response to the developing international market for their skills and the increasing sophistication of their clients. Only a small minority of established practitioners of the Baroque style restricted their practice to their home towns, and most found it necessary or advantageous to travel abroad to seek commissions or to train. Nearly all artists had to be able to cover a range of subject-matter and many had to offer the public work in more than one medium.

These broad trends obscure other revealing patterns. By and large, the Netherlanders travelled abroad more than their Italian counterparts, partly a response to the healthy state of the Italian market – markedly less healthy as the seventeenth century progressed – and partly as a consequence of the religious tensions across Europe. Some courtier artists undertook foreign journeys in the diplomatic interests of their masters. Carriera, whose Paris sojourn we have already noted, was one of a number of contemporary peripatetic and internationally experienced Italian artists, many of them Venetian: Amigoni, Canaletto, Franceschini, Giordano, Pellegrini, Ricci. These artists travelled to find new markets elsewhere in Europe as the Italian economy came under increased pressure. Inevitably, fate played a hand in deciding the outcome of such travels. John Smibert moved from Edinburgh to Rome to London during his training. Then a voyage to Bermuda was re-routed, and Smibert was stranded in New England with a collection of graphic art that proved seminal in establishing the painting profession in the American North-East.

Despite the development of new genres and markets and this increasing tendency to travel, artists and their pupils still tended to evolve dynastically. The Quellin clan was extensive and typical. Erasmus I Quellin (1548–1639) operated in Antwerp. His older son, Erasmus II (1607–78), was a painter and Rubens's assistant, his younger son Artus I (1609–68) moved to Rome and was a sculptor. So was his nephew, Artus II (1625–1700, pl.1.54), who lived in Antwerp and Brussels and trained Gabriel Grupello (1644–1730), a successful and prolific

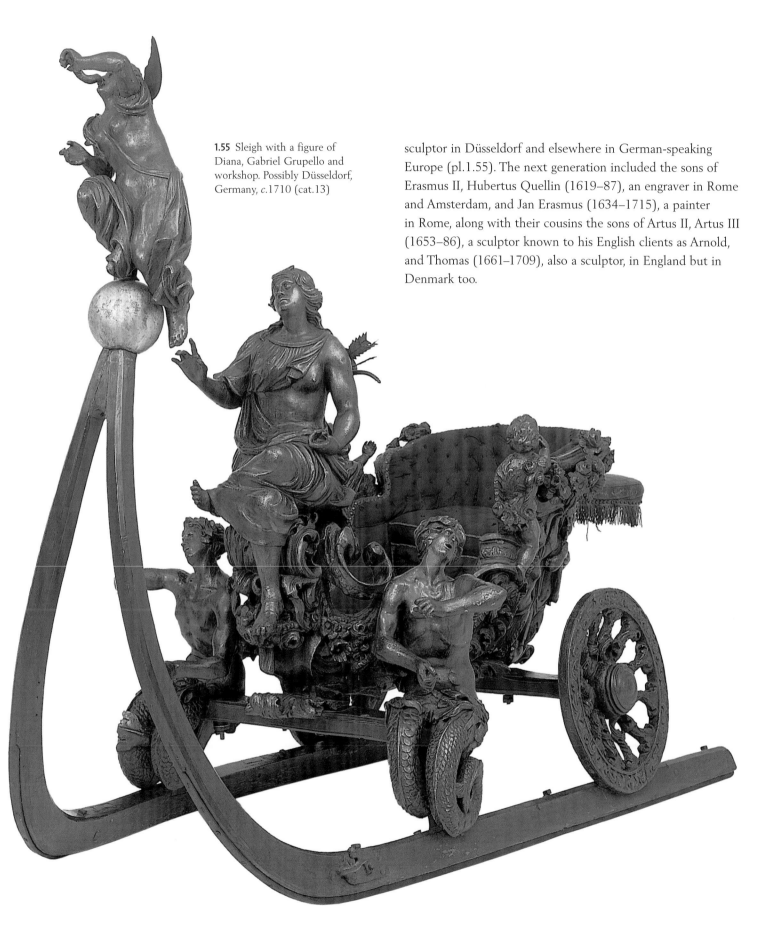

1.55 Sleigh with a figure of Diana, Gabriel Grupello and workshop. Possibly Düsseldorf, Germany, c.1710 (cat.13)

sculptor in Düsseldorf and elsewhere in German-speaking Europe (pl.1.55). The next generation included the sons of Erasmus II, Hubertus Quellin (1619–87), an engraver in Rome and Amsterdam, and Jan Erasmus (1634–1715), a painter in Rome, along with their cousins the sons of Artus II, Artus III (1653–86), a sculptor known to his English clients as Arnold, and Thomas (1661–1709), also a sculptor, in England but in Denmark too.

Often working away from their home ground, the artists acquired nicknames that throw light on the social world they inhabited. Some of these names related to appearance, a way of distinguishing an individual foreigner: Gian-Francesco Barbieri (1591–1666), from near Bologna but working in Rome, was called *Guercino*, because he had a squint; little Domenico Zampieri (1581–1641), also from Bologna, was *Domenichino*; being small and dark, Giovanni Benedetto Castiglione from Genoa (*c*.1609–64) was known as *Grechetto*, the little Greek; Giuseppe Maria Crespi (1665–1747), not from Spain but from Bologna, was known as the little Spaniard; *Spagnoletto* was the name that the Neapolitans also gave Jusepe de Ribera (1591–1652), who really was a small Spaniard. Other names related to origin and remind us that the continent of Europe comprised towns, cities and regions rather than nation-states. Pietro Berrettini (1596–1669) was called Pietro from *(da) Cortona*; Michelangelo Merisi (1571–1610) was always known as *Caravaggio*, after his birthplace near Milan; Mattia Prete (1613–99) was from Calabria, hence his nickname, the *Cavaliere calabrese*, the Calabrian knight.

Another category of names relates to personal or professional habits: Bernardo Strozzi (1581–1644) was a strict Franciscan (Capuchin) friar from Genoa, hence *Il Cappuccino* or *Il Prete Genovese*, the Genoese priest; Luca Giordano (1634–1705), who worked fast, was known as *Luca fa presto*; Gerrit van Honthorst (1592–1656) was a specialist in night scenes and was called Gherardo *della Notte*; the career of Gaspard Dughet (1615–75) was doubtless helped by his being known as Gaspard 'Poussin' after his famous brother-in-law Nicolas Poussin (1594–1665).

Often these informal means of identification were only loosely accurate in terms of ethnicity and geography. The Austrian sculptor Balthasar Permoser (1651–1732) worked in Italy from the mid-1670s to the end of the 1680s and was known there as Baldassare *Fiammingo*, the Fleming, or by a diminutive, *Balmosel* or sometimes *Delmosel*.

Like nearly everyone else, most Baroque artists were devout Christians, some of them displaying their piety in remarkable ways. Michiel Sweerts (1618–64) worked in Rome from around 1646 to 1654 and then opened a drawing academy in Brussels. Some time after 1661, he joined an order of missionaries, started to observe an extraordinarily strict daily round of devotions and gave away his material possessions to the poor. He then gave up his professional practice and travelled across the Near East to join the Portuguese Jesuits, dying soon afterwards in the Indian missionary centre of Goa.[53]

Although there are dangers in over-generalizing as regards the social identity of the Baroque artist, it is clear that the senior practitioners were located firmly in the professional class. Above that, an élite group even became courtiers and were ennobled (Arpino, Bandinelli, Bernini, Coustou, Kneller, Le Brun, Medina, Rubens, Titian, Van Dyck, Velasquez, Werff). The less successful remained as skilled artisans. In parallel with the increasing fashionability of the Baroque style, outward-looking and status-conscious princes recognized that it was advantageous to be associated with great artists – very few of whom came from high-status families – and to be seen to reward their extraordinary skills and achievements: Rubens, Van Dyck, Bernini and Velasquez were all rewarded with titles, lands and expensive gifts.

The Baroque style was executed within a tempered meritocratic system that developed to embrace the visual artist. In an extraordinary and complex way, Velasquez's *Las Meninas* illustrates how the élite market worked. It shows the painter at work in the setting of the court on a picture that challenges age-old conventions by which the size of a painted figure was governed by the social importance of the person represented: here we see the artist giving himself the same space on the canvas as his royal master. The way the picture interprets space and portrays narrative action is intentionally mystifying but measured – as befits a courtier's gift to his prince. The picture shows the artist himself, some of his sitters in the form of the young princess and her retinue, the back of his canvas, other courtiers and, reflected in a mirror, the painted representations of the king and queen, who are, like so much royal imagery in early modern Europe, both absent and present. The demonstrable value of the painted portrait, quoted here by Velasquez in his own picture, is evidence in itself of his value to the monarch as the creator of powerful imagery.

Other kinds of picture-making were less esoteric. The cosmopolitan John Medina (1659–1710) was born in Brussels to Spanish parents and made his career in Scotland painting half-length portraits of the nobility. He worked first in England, but the international context of his trade forced him to adopt an efficient system of production. When he arrived in Scotland in the winter of 1693–4 he was accompanied by a rather sinister selection of paintings (done by sub-contracted painters, incidentally) which simply wanted the heads and faces of the actual sitters. There were headless armoured knights, headless sets of children's breeches and headless draped bosoms.[54]

Some artists worked in isolation, ploughing single creative furrows, often with great personal success, and the market was increasingly able to get such work into the hands of patrons and collectors, especially smaller, movable works rather than

1.56 *Still life with musical instruments and a globe,*
Evaristo Baschenis, oil on canvas. Probably Bergamo, Italy,
*c.*1667–77 (Galleria dell'Accademia, Venice)

large-scale decorative works, which usually required the actual presence on site of the artist or at the very least a trusted henchman. Evaristo Baschenis (1617–77) was a markedly original artist who worked at Bergamo in northern Italy (pl.1.56). By the end of his life his extraordinary painted assemblages of sets of musical instruments hung in prominent collections across Italy. Although still life was one of the lower genres, collectors were fascinated by his work, which was highly intelligent in its aims, despite the apparent absence of

figurative content or verbal narrative; it frequently related to the performance of music – instruments and fragments of notation held by a plaster-cast hand. Baschenis was an ordained priest and the rules of his clerical life made it difficult for him to pursue an active career as an artist. The references in his works are secular, not religious, although music was often interpreted symbolically; the inevitability that a musical note, however beautiful, would die on the air was taken to represent allegorically the ephemeral nature of worldly existence.

THE MEDALLIC HISTORY OF LOUIS XIV

Mark Jones

The publishing event of 1702 was the appearance, in a specially designed typeface *Romain du Roi*, of a great history of the reign of Louis XIV told through 302 medals. This significant undertaking had been pursued by the king and his ministers with renewed vigour since the moment in 1694 when defeat and financial crisis had forced the interruption of other, more expensive programmes of celebration and commemoration. The frontispiece has an image of defeated Time acting as lectern for Clio, muse of history, his hourglass rendered useless by the medals around it; this last feature reminds us that the commemorative power of medals was still highly valued at the beginning of the eighteenth century.

Early in the reign, Colbert had systematically examined ways in which the greatness to come could best be recorded, communicated and commemorated. In 1662 he set the great medallist Jean Warin, shown here instructing Louis in the art of understanding the historical and moral significance of ancient coins, to work on a medallic history of events as they unfolded. The following year he appointed a 'Little Academy' (later known as the Academy of Inscriptions and Belles-lettres) to advise on and carry out various commemorative schemes, including the production of tapestries and medals. The secretary was Charles Perrault, and the members were to include Jean Racine, Jean Chapelain and Nicolas Boileau-Despréaux.

Selecting and representing the subject-matter proved problematic. How to decide what merited inclusion? How to avoid any suggestion of defeat while recording the capture of the same town on a number of different occasions? How to avoid undue offence to fellow rulers and potential or current allies? It was difficult to encompass the grandeur of ambassadorial receptions at Versailles within a circle 41mm in diameter. The best available draughtsmen – Sebastien Le Clerc and later Antoine Coypel – provided drawings for the most skilful engravers in Europe, led after Warin's death by Jean Mauger. The grandeur of the king was subtly emphasized by ensuring that apparently correct perspective allowed the royal figure to be larger than anyone else's, a trick also widely used in other media. As the world changed, injudiciously chosen subjects were personally eliminated by the king and his ministers and the

1.57 Frontispiece to The Medallic History of Louis XIV (*Medailles sur les principaux evements du regne de Louis le Grand, avec des expoi quations historiques*) engraved by Simonneau the Elder after Antoine Coypel. Paris, 1702 (V&A:75.M.29)

1.58 *Jean Warin instructing the young Louis XIV in the appreciation of medals,* François Lemaire, oil on canvas. Paris (Musée de la Monnaie)

gold pieces presented as diplomatic gifts were carefully selected from the history as a whole, in order to emphasize the more pacific accomplishments of the reign.

A major preoccupation, as we learn from the academy's preface (quickly suppressed by Louis XIV because it distracted attention from himself), was the manner in which events should be portrayed. Early in the reign the 'modern' style drew on newly invented devices such as Louis Douvrier's famous *nec pluribus impar*, originally conceived for a medal and widely used as symbol of both king and reign, and on realistic representations of events. Later in the century the 'quarrel' between Ancients and Moderns found a forum in the Little

1.59 Reception by Louis XIV of the Siamese Ambassadors at Versailles, Jean Warin, copper. Paris, 1686 (The British Museum)

1.60 Louis XIV's device *Nec Pluribus Impar*, Jean Warin, gold. Paris, 1672 (The British Museum)

1.61 Louis XIV directing the French army's crossing of the Rhine, Jean Warin, copper. Paris, 1672 (The British Museum)

Academy. Yet, though the former were victorious after the ejection of the 'modernist' Charles Perrault, and they stuck wherever possible to classical precedent in the representation of events, the selection of inscriptions and the use of Latin, the enterprise as a whole is thoroughly modern in impact. Louis himself, dressed in Roman armour but with a contemporary *pérruque*, is represented as more than equal to any of the Roman emperors on whose example his history is modelled. Here, the medallic history asserts, is an emperor whose radiance warms the whole globe and whose exploits and achievements are worth recording and preserving forever, not just in a few dozen images on large bronze coins as his Roman predecessors' were, but on hundreds of modern medals struck on the latest machinery in the finest mechanical mint in Europe.

The Market for Art

Only rarely did early modern artists produce work for their own private purposes; by and large Baroque art was either bespoke or produced for sale in specified markets. A rare exception to this rule was Bernini's extraordinary female figure intended to form part of the marble group *Time Discovering Truth*, made when the sculptor was being subjected to personal and political attacks by his enemies in the papal curia in the late 1640s. Very few artists could afford such freedom of action, especially where an expensive material like marble was concerned.

An élite group of court artists worked for their masters in return for pensions, salaries and other rewards. In his prime, Bernini's remuneration for the post of architect to St Peter's was some 36 times higher than the level of salary enjoyed by Frescobaldi, the celebrated chapel organist there, though the privileges of courtier artists were subject to every whim and fancy. In Florence, the grand duke's collection of self-portraits was on permanent exhibition, and for an artist to be asked to contribute to the series was regarded as a signal honour and rewarded not with money but with a rare gift. Carlo Maratta (1625–1713) was given a hard-stone casket and Charles Le Brun had a hamper of cloth, wine and foodstuffs. Successful artists tended to have regular clients or client groups and worked to commission; less successful artists produced standard lines for retailing. Many practitioners of the Baroque style ran complex workshop operations, exploiting economies of scale and dividing skilled from unskilled labour; they sought to maximize the number of works that could be produced collectively while still carrying the brand label.

The lack of secure data makes it impossible to gauge with any accuracy the total numbers of works produced for the market. Few artists have been more closely studied than Rembrandt, however; expert estimates of his output over a 40-year career range from about 1,000 works (or about one painting per month) to less than half of that figure. The high levels of demand for paintings in the Netherlands in the early 1640s must have produced hundreds of thousands, if not millions, of works, although some 90% have probably been lost. Despite the fact that the art market was growing, the demand for new pictures was vulnerable to calamitous disruption. Political events encouraged mass migrations of artists from one country to another, for example in 1685, when Louis XIV revoked the Edict of Nantes and thousands of French Protestants, including numerous visual artists, sought refuge in sympathetic states such as England.

Major shifts in the economy had their effect on the visual arts, with periods of growth encouraging the numbers of artists to grow as the reputed profitability of the profession grew. Jan de Vries has marked a massive increase in artists' numbers in the Netherlands late in the 1500s, although they fell away again after about 1640. In such periods of high growth, the sale potential of a painting on the open market could be improved if its meaning was generalized rather than specific. In these particular circumstances ambiguity of meaning helped sales, since a work that might mean several different things might appeal to a wider range of customers. Art was often, if not invariably, produced in response to a combination of demand and a sufficient economic surplus; for example, painted interior decorations required dwellings to be built, enlarged or converted in accordance with a change in fashion or a patron's taste. Such investments in the luxury trade were costly and vulnerable to the vagaries of personal health, politics and the economy. Paintings and sculpture were produced in a broad market context, many centres having established reputations for the manufacture of a range of luxury goods and services. The Netherlands in the mid-seventeenth century was a world leader in commerce, trade and banking, and made and sold the best lenses and maps. The marked rise in consumption in the British economy throughout the early eighteenth century helps to explain the increase in art institutions and the rise in the status of artists.

Exhibitions were at this period a modest means of marketing an artist's work, since they gave only limited public access to art and were highly regulated by invitation, admission fees or by the necessity of purchasing a catalogue. However, these controls did nurture the increasing sense of politeness that surrounded the consumption of art and in the longer run acted in the artists' favour. In Italy, exhibitions were events controlled by the various states and closely linked to other formal institutions such as guilds, religious festivals or academies. The first public exhibition in Florence took place in 1680, although a second followed only in 1706 (on 18 October, the name day of the patron saint of artists, St Luke). Only rarely were artists willing or able to resist the constraints represented by these official structures. Salvator Rosa (1615–73) expressed his unhappiness with the standard system whereby an artist worked to a patron's behest and created exhibitions of his work as the best way of attracting sales (pl.1.62). The eighteenth-century Salon exhibitions in Paris, open only to royal academicians, gave that élite group of painters enormous commercial advantage, although the exhibition spaces were sites of struggle between individual artists, the system of

1.62 *Self-portrait*, Salvator Rosa,
oil on canvas, Florence. *c.*1645
(The National Gallery, London)

ANN DVTCHESS O.
YORK

patronage and the institution of the Academy itself.

Artists emigrated across national boundaries to establish themselves in relatively restricted markets. The Dutchman Peter Lely moved to Britain during the early 1640s; competent in a range of genres, he found fame and fortune as a portraitist at the Restoration court, accommodating its culture with great success (pl.1.63). The kind of narrow niche marketing so successfuly practised by Lely required a close identification between the artist and the concerns of his identified patron group.

The market for art in the seventeenth century was increasingly characterized by strong differentiation between products and niche operation by the producers. Individual painters and families of painters were specialists in particular subjects. In some areas of Europe this pattern was less marked as a consequence of smaller numbers of individuals taking part in the trade. In relation to the painting of ruins, there was Giovanni Ghisolfi (1623–83), a Milanese specialist, and Codazzi, whom we have already met in riot-torn Naples in the later 1640s. Seventeenth-century Dutch landscape painting had especially complex national and local markets, with Utrecht acting as a gateway to Italy and fostering a taste for the Italianate. Meanwhile, Amsterdam was the specialist location for art in the national style. From about 1590 to about 1620 there was a huge growth in the Dutch painting market, with ever-increasing numbers of artists, more and more specialized and working for growing numbers of patrons. Then the economy saw a downturn, trade went into recession, and the financial surpluses were simply not sufficient to justify such huge expenditure on art. The spread of the Baroque would have followed a different pattern had the economic history of the Netherlands been different.

1.63 (*opposite*) *Anne Hyde, Duchess of York*, Peter Lely, oil on canvas. England, 1661–2 (Scottish National Portrait Gallery)

International Markets and Collectors

At the higher social levels, the patronage of art and architecture was an international business in the sense that patrons were accustomed to look across international borders to satisfy their tastes. When the prince-bishop, Lord of Würzburg, in south central Germany decided to rebuild the family palace in the second decade of the 1700s, a team of architects from various German states, from France and from Italy was consulted. The interior was finally decorated by a range of artists, some of them Italian, most famously by members of the Venetian workshop of Giambattista Tiepolo, who at the end of his life was to live and work in Spain. One could retrace countless patterns of this kind. Claude exported works from Rome to patrons in France, Bohemia, Scandinavia and Spain. In search of commissions, Pellegrino undertook extraordinary journeys across Europe; in the space of a few months in the mid-1720s much of central Europe was on his itinerary – Würzburg, Prague, Dresden and Vienna.

Such travels presented significant challenges, since social and diplomatic manners varied markedly across the Continent and it was no easy matter for an artist or a patron to engage with foreign markets and cultures. Immigrants found it hard accurately to read social signals and to avoid giving offence. To oil the wheels of commerce there developed a class of agents, such as the numerous individuals documented as working in Rome. Having retreated from Rome in 1623 after the death of his patron Pope Gregory XV, Guercino returned home to the Emilian town of Cento to conduct an international business in altarpieces and smaller works sent out to discriminating collectors; he refused invitations to take up court positions in France and England, where the reputation for heresy especially alarmed him. Francisco de Zurbarán (1598–1664) made efforts in the 1640s to offset his loss of popularity in the domestic markets in Madrid and Seville and started to produce works for Spain's colonies on a speculative basis. Zurbarán's colleague Juan Martínez Montañés (1568–1649) supplied wooden sculpture to the New World on the same basis. Giuseppe Maria Crespi stayed in Bologna and turned down court positions at Rome, Vienna and Savoy, but conducted a mail-order business with the support of a local entrepreneur who sent the painter on study trips to Modena, Parma, Pesaro, Urbino and Venice.

Collectors represented an increasingly important force in the market. Living artists had to contend with a lively taste for antiquities and old masters in collections. Before the establishment of museums, these collections of works were studied and emulated by other collectors. Some great families of patrons have left rich archives of records that allow us fully to reconstruct the detailed mechanisms of their investment in the visual arts. One of the richest of all archives is that of the Barberini family, who were Florentines prominent in early seventeenth-century Rome and who owed their final triumph to the election of Maffeo Barberini as Pope Urban VIII in 1623. The monies at the disposal of a papal family like the Barberini were enormous and included income from taxation and the sales of various officerships and benefices. The Barberini regarded the visual arts – as they did other scholarly and cultural interests – as an acceptable form of consumption supported by a private fortune and papal funds. In the earlier part of Urban's reign, the family palace was enlarged and decorated with ambitious allegorical frescoes by Andrea Sacchi (1629–31) and Pietro da Cortona (1633–9), the iconographic programme of the latter's 'Divine Providence' picking up the themes explored less permanently in the coronation ceremonies that had marked Urban's election some seven years earlier.

An extraordinary monument in the retrochoir at Salisbury Cathedral symbolizes the international quality of the Baroque style (pl.1.64). It adapts Baroque inventions: the Salomonic column shafts are used here in a composition that closely resembles Bernini's Vatican Baldacchino. The decoration of the Gorges monument employs scrollwork, heraldic devices, cherubim, acanthus and other foliate forms together with allegorical signs that are both pagan and Christian. The inscriptions and captions tell the familiar story of bereavement, widowhood and of a career cut short. However unique it is in its particular combination, much of the formal language of the Gorges tomb is international and can be found in countless places across the Baroque world. It illustrates the rich exchanges that took place between the high arts of Baroque design and popular cultural imagery.

1.64 Monument to Thomas Gorges, Salisbury Cathedral. 1635

CHAPTER 2

THE BAROQUE STYLE

Michael Snodin

In Search of a Style

Style names are often adopted as signals of disapproval, and Baroque was no exception. Its distortions and extravagances, seen through the eyes of those working to revive classical forms in the middle of the eighteenth century, prompted the transfer of the Portuguese name for a misshapen pearl (*pérola barroca*) (pl.2.1) and an Italian word for a far-fetched or fanciful argument to a whole approach to art and design.[1] Baroque was seen as having knowingly distorted the sacred norms of classical design based on the rules of the ancient Greeks and Romans that had been carefully systematized in the Renaissance. The word is of course still used in much the same sense today to describe anything elaborately or grotesquely ornate, whimsical or bizarre. It has also been applied to other areas, including the name of an 'age', a period in music, and even sets of ideas in philosophy and religion. That such various extensions of meaning should have occurred is not perhaps surprising, for the art and design ideas that are most often associated with the Baroque are closely linked to the seventeenth-century rise of political absolutism and the simultaneous revival of the Roman Catholic Church.

It was not until the late nineteenth century, with the historian Heinrich Wölfflin's comparative analysis of the Baroque with the Renaissance, that the Baroque, which he defined as a style of grandeur, richness and vitality, came to be seen in a more positive light. Since then, much academic ink has been spilled on the question of what exactly can be called Baroque, as scholars have worked to tease out the complex strands of art and design in the seventeenth and eighteenth centuries.[2] It is, however, generally agreed that Baroque was but one dialect, although the dominant one, within the language of the revival of the ancient art and architecture that began with the Renaissance. Some scholars have focused on the great artistic and architectural triumvirate of Gianlorenzo Bernini, Francesco Borromini and Pietro da Cortona, working mainly in Rome for successive popes in the middle years of the seventeenth century. Others have included slightly later developments in France under Louis XIV, which were more classical in character, but nevertheless indebted to recent developments in Italy. But it is clear that, from the late seventeenth century onwards, the visual language of both Roman and French forms of the Baroque came to be adopted in varying degrees across Europe, from Portugal to Russia, as well as the territories of the European powers in the rest of the world.

2.1 Figure of a camel made from Baroque pearls, maker unknown. Probably Frankfurt am Main, before 1706 (cat.1)

2.2 *Carousel for Queen Christina of Sweden held in the courtyard of Palazzo Barberini, Rome, 1656, Filippo Lauri and Filippo Gagliardi. Rome, 1656–9 (cat.2)*

The Baroque, however, was not just a matter of particular motifs and approaches to design. At a deeper level, the Baroque style that emerged against the background of the great secular and sacred powers was at root about performance. It was made to persuade as well as impress, to be both rich and meaningful. This approach to design was evident across the whole span of visual culture, from painting and sculpture to architecture, gardens, the applied arts, theatre and public events and even the decoration of coaches and ships. It can be seen in the paintings of Rubens and the sculpture of Bernini, the ceiling paintings of Pietro da Cortona in Italy and Thornhill in England, and the palaces and gardens of Versailles and Vienna. The effects of the Baroque approach were felt over a long period, coming to life in one place as they faded out in another: Borromini's architectural ideas of the 1640s were taken up by the sculptor and architect Aleijadinho in Brazil 150 years later, while the dazzling reputation of Louis XIV's great silver furniture, which had been melted down in the 1680s, was strong enough to prompt a rash of imitations in the courts of Germany and Austria in the following century.

A Baroque Party

On a dark night on 28 February 1656, the powerful Roman family of the Barberini presented a great performance (pl.2.2). Beside their handsome palazzo on the edge of the city, they had built a special arena seating 3,000 people. The party was for Christina, who four years earlier had relinquished the crown of Sweden. From her box overlooking the arena, she was serenaded by a parade of players dressed as ancient gods, led by Apollo, and watched a mock battle between fabulously costumed knights and Amazons. The Amazons, victorious as befitted the queen, concluded the show by defeating a fire-breathing dragon. But this lavish spectacle, which might now seem appropriate only for a circus or carnival, had a profoundly serious purpose. Such great performances were not just about colour and invention, excitement and entertainment; they were also about political power. For Christina, from Protestant Sweden, had become one of the Roman Church's most spectacular catches when she had converted to Catholicism the

year before. Following her triumphal entry into Rome in December 1655, Rome's great families vied with each other to impress her, most especially the Barberini and the Chigi, who were in competition for election to the papacy, the greatest prize of all. It was not only a matter of conspicuous expenditure, but also, for those who could understand it, the use of symbolic language to drive home political points.

The Barberini party's concentrated and carefully composed combination of pomp, power and persuasion was typical of Baroque visual culture. The Baroque was a rhetorical style that aimed to engage the senses, as much through the emotions as through the intellect. To do so it employed a certain set of visual motifs and approaches to design. These included the idea of fusing the arts of painting, sculpture and architecture into a single work and the extensive use of the human figure as a carrier both of meanings and of emotions. Baroque art and design manipulated the beholder into a particular viewpoint, using devices that bridged the barrier between the world of the image or object and that of the viewer. But it is important to remember that, for all its elaboration, the Baroque was not a frivolous style. Its works were usually profoundly serious in their purpose, and its leading practitioners were often multi-talented individuals, as John Evelyn wrote of Bernini:

> A little before my Coming too the City, Cavaliero Bernini, Sculptor, Architect, Painter and Poet … gave a Publique Opera (for so they call Shews of that kind) where in he painted the Seanes, cut the Statues, invented the Engines, composed the Musique, writ the Comedy and built the Theater all himself.[3]

Such Baroque conceptions can be huge and overwhelming, encompassing whole cities and landscapes, or quite small, but whatever their scale they share a sense of the monumental. They also share a sense of movement and drama that is in sharp contrast to the studied control and proportion that art historians have associated with the Renaissance. The strongly sculptural façades of Baroque buildings can curve in and out, and often have their ground plans based on a series of ovals. The poses and draperies of human figures are contorted into dramatic sweeps, and the forms of furniture and metalwork are modelled into deep contrasts of light and shade. Baroque breaks the rules.

2.3 The Porta Pia, Rome, from *Regola delli cinque ordini d'architettura* by Giacomo Barozzi da Vignola, engraving. Italy, 1635 (V&A:62.C.53)

Breaking the Rules

The idea of rule-breaking was not of course new. The Baroque's immediate precursor, the style now known as Mannerism, in use across Europe for much of the sixteenth century, was also based on a breaking of the classical rules. In architecture, these rules, drawn from ancient Greece and Rome and codified in the Renaissance into a logical grammar, set out a system of orders, based on the principle of the column, capital, and beam or entablature. Each of the orders had particular types of ornament and was proportioned and spaced in a particular way. The orders' varying proportions and increasing complexity of ornament were reflected in the way they were used. This is most clearly seen in the Colosseum in Rome, in which the ground floor is in the Doric order, the second in the Ionic, the third in the Corinthian and the fourth in the Composite order. Accompanying the orders were sets of conventions controlling how they were to be combined with other elements, such as doors and windows, arches and pediments.

Both Baroque and Mannerism were greatly indebted to the work of Michelangelo, who invented a new type of rule-breaking design as well as a whole set of new ornamental motifs. Michelangelo's approach to design produced an architecture of feeling that was intensely sculptural in character. A particularly famous example was his scheme for the Porta Pia in Rome, whose influence was spread by an engraving of it in Giacomo Vignola's book of architecture from 1562 (pl.2.3).

Designed in 1561, it is a fantasy on the theme of classical architecture 'crammed with alternative ideas, suddenly frozen solid'.[4] It mixes up two of the classical orders (the Greek and Tuscan Doric) and manages, against all the rules, to combine a triangular pediment with an 'open' scrolled one. Even without knowing the rules, we can sense that there is something amiss. The distortions of scale and clash of elements are distinctly uncomfortable, even slightly nightmarish. These qualities were seized upon by Mannerist designers, who invented many imaginative variants of classical motifs, piling them up in a pursuit of novelty and complexity for its own sake, often with bizarre results.

Baroque, too, had many such bizarre elements. In fact this was the word that was used from the mid-sixteenth century onwards to describe art and design that opposed the norm (see The Bizarre, p.80). While some effects described as bizarre were part of a broad tendency towards the fantastical that had grown since the mid-sixteenth century, others were imaginative departures from the classical of the type triggered by Michelangelo. Indeed, the Porta Pia itself was singled out for censure in Teofilo Gallaccini's *Treatise on the Errors of Architects*, written in about 1625, but not published until 1767, and enlarged by Antonio Visentini in 1771. While Gallaccini was writing when the Baroque was first emerging, Visentini wrote at a moment when it was well past its full flowering in much of Europe, and he was thus able to fill his additional volume with innumerable examples of architectural errors in Rome, Venice and Florence. As a Venetian schooled in the texts of the ancient Roman architect Vitruvius and the buildings of the local hero, Andrea Palladio, Visentini took the designers of almost all the Baroque decorative and compositional devices to task for their transgression of the logical load-bearing language of classicism, as well as for employing what he saw as an excess of inappropriate ornament that broke the Vitruvian tenet of architectural decorum. Among the condemned forms was the Salomonic or twisted column, so named because of the famous ancient Roman examples kept in St Peter's, which were believed to have come from the temple of Solomon in Jerusalem. When, in 1629, Bernini created the great symbolic bronze canopy of the Baldacchino over the tomb of St Peter, he used the same forms hugely enlarged in a design of the highest theatricality, elements of which were to be echoed in Baroque designs for the next 150 years (pl.2.4).

2.4 Design for a capital and part of a column for the baldacchino in St Peter's Basilica, Rome, Francesco Borromini. Rome, *c.*1625 (cat.21)

THE BIZARRE

Rodney Palmer

Unlike 'Baroque', a later invention, the word 'bizarre' was used at the time for a number of the characteristics we now associate with the Baroque. *Bizzarria* (the bizarre) played a subversive role in Italian art from the mid-1500s to the 1700s, describing works that irreverently opposed the rules.

The 'bizarre' of the Baroque period is exemplified by Giovambattista Braccelli's *Bizzarie of Various Figures* (pl.2.5), a series of engravings of fantastic ideas for theatrical costumes dedicated to Piero de' Medici, published in 1624. In painting, the work of Caravaggio and Salvator Rosa struck their contemporaries as 'bizarre'. Caravaggio's *Seven Works of Mercy* was called 'thoroughly bizarre', because it broke the rules of religious decorum. Salvator Rosa's art challenged the unwritten rules of the patron-artist relationship. In his biography of Rosa Filippo Baldinucci called the artist's *Allegory of Fortune*, in which fortune showers her riches on dumb animals, 'bizzarissimo'.

2.5 (*above*) Plate 43 from *Bizzarie of Various Figures*, Giovambattista Braccelli, engraving. Livorno, 1624 (Bibliothèque Nationale de France)

2.6 (*far left*) Altar of St Ignatius, church of the Gesù, Rome, Andrea Pozzo. 1695–9

2.7 Figure 75 from Volume II of *Perspectivae Pictorum et Architectorum*, Andrea Pozzo, engraving. Rome, 1693–1700 (V&A:99.D.20)

2.8 (*below*) Figure 45: 'Bizara cima di Altare proposte dal P. Pozzi dissonante nelle sue parti', *Trattato degli errori degli architetti*, Teofilo Gallaccini, ed. Antonio Visentini, engraving. Venice 1771 (V&A:34.G.57)

2.9 Altar of St Aloysius Gonzaga, church of S. Ignazio, Rome, Andrea Pozzo and Pierre Legros II. 1697–9

To his contemporaries, the work of Francesco Borromini epitomized 'bizarre' architecture. In his so-called *Opus Architectonicum* (*My Work in Architecture*), Borromini himself described how he used a *bizzarria* and inserted leaves at the bases of the columns in the vestibule at the foot of the main staircase of the Oratory, to compensate for their shortness. This motif became emblematic of his inventiveness. Borromini's pursuit of the 'bizarre' was taken up by the Jesuit painter and architect Andrea Pozzo, in his two-volume *Perspective for Painters and Architects* (pl.2.6). Pozzo's more fantastic design ideas were gathered in the second volume (1700), in which he 'pleased himself'

and showed off the *bizzarria* in his rejected plan for the St Aloysius Gonzaga altar at S. Ignazio in Rome, in which he proposed to raise the urn containing Gonzaga's ashes to the top of the altar. In another design, in order to 'vary' or differ from other altars, he replaced the norm of Vitruvian 'standing' columns by the 'novelty and *bizzarria*' of crooked 'sitting columns' (pl.2.7).

In the middle of the eighteenth century the old concept of the 'bizarre' and the newly minted 'Baroque' were conflated, as erroneous and even vicious, by orthodox neo-classicists. Antonio Visentini, editor of a *Treatise on the Errors of Architects*, denigrated one of Pozzo's Baroque altar tops as 'bizarre' (pl.2.8).

But in spite of its use of the bizarre, the Baroque approach to design was very different from that of Mannerism. In Mannerist design and architecture, restless ornament is the most distinctive feature, at the expense of any strongly marked architectural design. Baroque designers and architects, on the other hand, respected the fundamental language of classicism, while turning it into a consciously expressive form. This can clearly be seen in the church façades of the Roman pioneers, in which the orders, although observing the ancient hierarchies, are manipulated in a game of scale, to drive the eye powerfully towards points of focus, in ways that convey both meaning and emotion. This rhetorical approach first became evident in Carlo Maderno's S. Susanna, completed in 1603, in which the columns are so disposed as to emphasize the centre. Some 30 years later, in Pietro da Cortona's SS Luca e Martina, we can see the classical language developing a new dynamism: the crucial point is that the façade is gently curved in the centre. Some twenty years later elements of this façade were used in the same architect's S. Maria della Pace, but incorporated into a bold composition of concave and convex curves that seem to model the space they occupy.

The most dramatic inventions of all came from Francesco

2.11 Elevation and plan of the façade of the Oratory and House of the Order of St Philip Neri, Rome, Francesco Borromini. Rome, 1638 (cat.20)

Borromini. His double-curved façade of S. Carlo alle Quattro Fontane is made up of individual elements of a strong character working closely together in pursuit of a single theme that can immediately be grasped in purely visual terms (pl.2.10). In another building by Borromini we know what its theme was, for he described the façade of the Oratory as being like a man with his arms outstretched to welcome the faithful. The convex lower section in the centre represented the chest and the concave wings the arms (pl.2.11).[5] A similar approach was taken by Bernini, who believed that art was not only concerned with beauty of form but beauty of conception, or

'bellezza di concetto'. According to his biographer, he based his way of working on that of the ancient orators: 'First the general conception, then the planning of the parts, finally adding softness and grace to achieve perfection. Here he followed the example of the orator, who first defines, then deploys, and then beautifies and adorns'.[6]

2.13 (*opposite*) Interior of the church of Vierzehnheiligen, South Germany, Balthasar Neumann. 1743–72

The swinging columned façade of Borromini's S. Carlo introduces its interior. The ground plan, as with much Baroque design, is based on a dynamic geometry. Formed as an extended oval, it is geometrically composed using a series of triangles and circles (pl.2.12). The oval dome topped by a lantern floods the church with light.

Compact centralized plans of this type became common in Baroque churches. They were in part prompted by a change in Church practice, following the Council of Trent, which emphasized the need to allow silent contemplation of the Holy Sacrament in a tabernacle on the main altar. The same principles govern the design of perhaps the greatest of the pilgrimage churches of Southern Germany, Vierzehnheiligen ('Fourteen Saints') near Bamberg, designed by Balthasar Neumann from 1743 (pl.2.13). Its plan is based on a series of ovals that combine a traditional (and symbolic) cross-shaped format with a centralized emphasis over the sacred spot, the site of a miraculous vision. Both interiors are lined with an unbroken series of monumental columns in the Corinthian order that clearly articulate the space. At Vierzehnheiligen, however, the walls are pierced to produce a space of great complexity and movement, an active composition of curves and vaulting. While the columns of Borromini's Corinthian order conform to conventions, Neumann's break the rules with playful scrolls and curves in a manner characteristic of the last stages of the Baroque in Germany. The signal for such rule-breaking had, as we have seen, been given in Italy from the 1630s with the adoption and development of Michelangelo's ideas. Such features as the open and broken pediments were developed into ever more daring space-defying forms on façades, roofs and altarpieces as well as a dizzying variety of interesting ways in which to show off doors and window openings.

2.12 Ground plan of the church of S. Carlo alle Quattro Fontane, Rome, Francesco Borromini. 1638–41

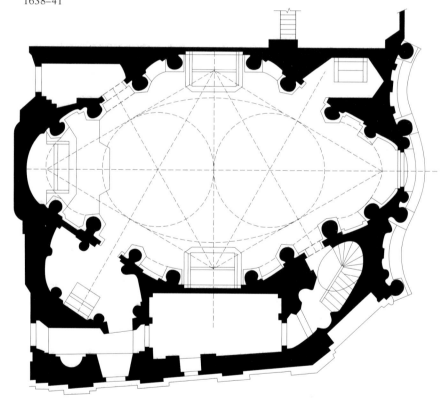

Ancients and Moderns

In France a new and richly classical style was also developing in the 1630s, notably in architecture and interior decoration. Eighty years earlier, France had been the only country outside Italy to develop a coherent Renaissance style of its own, and it never adopted the extreme forms of Mannerism current in the rest of northern Europe. From the early seventeenth century French artists and architects had very close links with Italy. In Rome, the painter Nicolas Poussin developed a style founded on Raphael and classical antiquity, and was persuaded in 1640 to return to France to work for King Louis XIII and Cardinal Richelieu.

At the same time French architects were being sent to Italy to study and measure the ancient remains and compare them with the rules as set out by Vitruvius. Roland Fréart de Chambray, who had been sent there by Richelieu, published his findings in 1652, with the expressed aim of returning the art of architecture to its original ancient splendour. In 1664 this work was translated by John Evelyn as *The Parallel of the Ancient architecture with the modern*. This was the first attempt to sort out a set of rules based on the great variety of real examples of ancient and modern architecture as well as the writings of Vitruvius. The impulse culminated in Charles Perrault's treatise on the five orders of architecture published in 1676, in which each perfected order was set out according to an easily memorable modular scale. This was also the period which saw the establishment in Paris of the Royal Academy of Painting and Sculpture (1648) and of Architecture (1671), as well as the French Academy in Rome (1666). It was against this background that an officially sponsored, classically based French design style was developed, but not without dispute. The two sides polarized as the Ancients and Moderns, first of all in the field of literature (those who supported the classical authors as opposed to modern writers) and then in the visual arts. For all their work on achieving the perfect set of orders, French architects also had a long record of creating imaginative modern variations, beginning, in 1567, with a patriotic 'French' order used on the front of the Louvre.

It is significant that one of the first major examples of the new French classical style was not a church but a great country house. The château of Vaux-le-Vicomte was built between 1657 and 1661 by Louis Le Vau for Nicolas Fouquet, the king's superintendent of finances (pl.2.14). Its plan adopted the formula of a ceremonial centre with pavilion wings (with separate apartments for Fouquet and for the king) that originated in France in the previous century and was, after its adoption at Versailles, to become standard in Baroque palaces

2.14 Château of Vaux-le-Vicomte, France, Louis Le Vau. 1612–70

across Europe. The strong, domed silhouette, although in part descended from earlier French houses, has a Baroque sense of mass and drama. The house was set in gardens laid out in geometrical parterres by André Le Nôtre. The richly decorated interior is even more Baroque. It combines plaster, painting and gilding in a manner directly inspired by near-contemporary examples in Italy, such as Pietro da Cortona's decorations of the early 1640s in the Palazzo Pitti in Florence (pl.2.35). This scheme, which established a new type of French aristocratic decoration, was the creation, under the leadership of Le Vau, of the painter Charles Le Brun. The completion of the château was celebrated in 1661 with a famous party given for Louis XIV and the royal family, which included the performance of an opera-ballet by Jean-Baptiste Lully (with scenery by Le Brun) and finished with fireworks. The party had unexpected consequences, for three weeks later Fouquet was imprisoned for embezzlement and eventually most of his creative team (including Lully and Le Brun) was taken over by Jean-Baptiste Colbert, the king's superintendent of buildings, to work on the royal palaces and other royal projects.

As part of the project to complete the Louvre, at that date the king's chief residence, Colbert sent Le Vau's design for the east front to Italy to be criticized, but then asked Bernini and Pietro da Cortona for their own ideas. Bernini's first design was dramatically curved, with its great oval salon at the centre and giant columns fronting a series of arched openings in the Venetian style, which he imagined the French might like (pl.2.15). In the end all his schemes were rejected, although his and Pietro da Cortona's ideas, suitably toned down, were to provide the basic models for the French approach to palace

2.16 East front of the Louvre, Paris, Claude Perrault, Louis Le Vau and Charles Le Brun. 1667–74

design and its many progeny outside France. The Louvre east front as eventually executed, designed by the Fouquet team and Claude Perrault, combined a line of paired columns balanced with the calm central pediment and end pavilions, turning it into a composition of majestic dignity and drama (pl.2.16).

It was on the vast works at Versailles that the Fouquet team really came into its own, with the addition of Jules Hardouin-Mansart as its architect. Just as Roman church interiors were designed to be seen as a whole, so those at Versailles and other palaces were provided with their own specially created furniture and fittings, usually designed by Le Brun, manufactured in the royal workshops and using the same classical vocabulary of ornament.

Engaging the Senses

Baroque art and design made a direct appeal to the senses, and through them to the emotions and intellect. It did so in three main ways: by manipulating the viewer into looking at a work in a particular way, by synthesizing different art forms into a complete whole with a single message or meaning, and by using the human figure to communicate emotion and meaning. The geometry that played such a vital role in Baroque architecture and planning was used consciously to make the viewer see and experience things in particular ways. We only have to look at the great space in front of St Peter's, the plan of the town and gardens of Versailles and Pietro da Cortona's painted ceiling in Palazzo Barberini (pl.5.21) to see how the use of perspectival geometry draws us into the visual world the architects are seeking to create. The entrance to St Peter's, one of the greatest achievements of Baroque architecture and town planning, was the conclusion of a process of rebuilding that had begun in 1506 and had included the creation of Michelangelo's dome. Pope Alexander VII asked Bernini to design an approach that would symbolize the Church's embrace as well as providing a space for public events before its greatest building. By narrowing and then opening up the space in front of it, Bernini makes the façade seem wider than it really is as well as further away (pl.2.17). The great welcoming arms of the enormous porticoes, with their dizzying rows of huge columns, seem to urge us forward to enter the church with, at its far end, the great Baldacchino and throne of St Peter raised in Glory. As so often with Baroque architecture and design, the space is best experienced while moving through it. You are not only at the theatre, but actually invited on stage.

While the plan of the scheme for St Peter's can be understood on the ground, other Baroque planning schemes were so large that they could be fully appreciated only through a plan, model, or bird's-eye view. The symmetrical fanning avenues at Versailles, centred on the great palace, determined the plan of the town as well as the garden (see pl.5.4), creating both a physical and a symbolic expression of the king's power and his control over man and nature. Fanning avenues, in part inspired by the scenic devices of the Renaissance theatre,[7] had first appeared in the late sixteenth-century papal replanning of Rome, which linked the great pilgrimage basilicas. As at Versailles, such Baroque planning came to be applied to gardens, town plans and whole landscapes all over Europe, among them Sir Christopher Wren's ideal scheme for the rebuilding of London after the fire of 1666.

2.17 *View of St Peter's Square, Rome,* Gaspar Van Wittel, also called Gaspare Vanvitelli. Rome, 1715 (cat.77)

2.18 View of the Scala Regia in the Vatican. Rome, Gianlorenzo Bernini. 1663–6

Theatrical perspective devices were also used in interior contexts. For the Scala Regia, the great staircase to the main hall of the papal palace, Bernini created a rising tunnel vault in which the side columns get progressively shorter as the stair rises, increasing its apparent length (pl.2.18). Unlike the mathematically conceived effects of the Renaissance theatre, Bernini's design interrupted the stair to make it appear more monumental, and dramatized it with cross-lit landings. While Bernini was working within the constraints of an existing building, the designers of staircases in German and Italian palaces, with no such limitations, were able to develop the same devices in creating some of the most exciting and dynamic spaces in Baroque architecture. One of the last and greatest examples was the huge staircase in the core of the king of the Two Sicilies's palace at Caserta, which rises majestically then doubles back to reach a domed hall at the top. The dramatic perspective effects in the upper hall are carried out using a form of scenic perspective system called *scena per angolo*, first exploited by Ferdinando Galli Bibiena for use in the theatre (p.160). It abandoned the old Renaissance axial perspective for a technique in which walls disappear at angles, creating an illuson of almost limitless space (see pl.5.52).

Great entrance stairs were the most impressive spaces in the palaces of the German electors and prince-bishops. The spatial games of the rising flights of stairs, often lit from three sides and surrounded by open arcades, were matched by the unbroken expanse of the painted ceiling, which often appeared to open the room to the sky. At Pommersfelden, built for the prince-bishop of Mainz, Lothar Franz von Schönborn, the ceiling shows the gods surrounding Apollo, with the four continents at the edges (see pl.5.53). The same subject was used for the huge staircase ceiling of the palace of the prince-bishop at Würzburg, painted by Giambattista Tiepolo. As at Caserta, the stair rises up the centre and then doubles back, allowing the painting to reveal itself in a significant sequence, first showing America, then Apollo, next Asia and Africa and finally, at the turn of the stair, Europe, with the prince-bishop's portrait borne up by figures of Fame and Glory (see pl.1.53).

Reaching to Heaven

Ceilings and domes painted with illusionistic architecture, figures and openings to the sky first appeared in Italy in the late fifteenth century. The later sixteenth and early seventeenth centuries were marked by great developments in the art of ceiling painting, not only in terms of the perspective techniques needed to show architecture and figures '*da sotto in su*' (foreshortened as if seen from below to above), but also by creating the illusion that the whole ceiling has been opened up to the sky. The result was an art form that lent itself as well to showing the glories of heaven as to underscoring the power of rulers. Both ideas were combined in Pietro da Cortona's ceiling for the *salone* of Palazzo Barberini, which showed, in the words of a contemporary author, 'The Triumph of Divine Providence and the fulfilment of her ends under the Papacy of Urban VIII' (see pl.5.21). It was the first great demonstration of the complex intermingling of illusionistic painted figures, sculpture and architecture that was to become characteristic of Baroque ceiling and mural decoration. The dynamic perspective of the painted architecture and the diminishing size of the figures transform the depressed vault of the real ceiling into a convincing rising dome.

The development of the illusionistic architectural elements in Baroque ceiling painting, called *quadratura*, culminated in the work of Andrea Pozzo, a Jesuit scenic designer, architect and artist. His technique allowed the centralized perspective of the ceiling painting to continue the real architecture of the space, creating a completely convincing opening to the sky. Generating such illusions required extremely careful preparation, as can be seen in the elaborate drawing for the *quadratura* elements of his most famous ceiling, at the church of S. Ignazio in Rome, before the addition of figures and clouds (pl.2.19).

While Pozzo relied on centralized perspective tricks to eliminate the transition between the real and the imaginary, other artists used a range of different techniques. For the *Triumph of the Name of Jesus* on the ceiling of the Jesuits' chief Roman church, the Gesù, Giovanni Battista Gaulli combined painting, sculpture and the building's own architecture to create an overwhelming illusion of the heavenly host adoring the Holy Name in layers of cloud. The damned, painted (complete with shadows) on the stucco laid over the ornamented plaster vault, seem to fall towards us into the real space of the church. Just as St Peter's turns the viewer from a spectator into an actor, so these painted and modelled ceilings draw the spectator in by suggesting that the heavenly scene is happening here and now (see pl.1.41).

2.19 Design for the fictive architecture of the vault of the church of S. Ignazio, Andrea Pozzo, pen, grey and brown ink and grey wash, Rome. 1685–90 (National Gallery of Art, Washington)

The Total Work of Art

The Gesù vault's combination of architecture, sculpture and painting to form a single work of art was characteristic of the Baroque. These three art forms had of course been used together for centuries, but they had always been kept within their own distinct areas. Baroque artists not only encouraged the blurring of the old boundaries but also combined the disparate forms to deliver a single unmistakable message. The richly decorated and furnished interiors of Baroque palaces achieved an unprecedented visual unity through the use of a single controlling designer. The most striking examples, however, were made for the Church, prompted by the need to bring back the faithful as well as to convert others. The most famous and influential expression of this new design approach was one of Bernini's masterpieces, the Cornaro family chapel dedicated to St Teresa in the Roman church of S. Maria della Vittoria (see The Cornaro Chapel, p.96). The ensemble achieves the intimate union of form and content. The immediate impression of the small chapel is less that of a picture than of a scene in the theatre, in which the worshipper is invited to share in the ecstasy of the central white marble figure of the saint.

The design approach pioneered at the Cornaro Chapel was further developed in the enormous marble, bronze and glass setting for the reliquary that contains the *Cathedra Petri*, the traditional wooden throne of St Peter (see pl.4.41). Bronze statues of the doctors of the Greek and Latin Churches bear up, apparently without effort, the throne-shaped reliquary towards the painted window through which the Holy Dove descends, surrounded by innumerable angels and cherubim. Intended to be seen through the Baldacchino as the visual culmination of the great church, the *Cathedra Petri* was not only a focus for worship. Placed in the position normally occupied by the bishop's throne, it was designed to be a powerful expression of the ancient power of the Church and the papacy.

Bernini's design ideas were quickly imitated in other Roman churches and subsequently found their way across the Catholic and even into the Protestant world. Andrea Pozzo's altar to St Ignatius Loyola in the Gesù, based on the scheme of the Cornaro Chapel, adds another theatrical device in the form of a painting of the apotheosis of the saint, which during solemn feast days drops away to reveal a precious silver statue of him. Thanks to Pozzo's book of 1693–1700 on the theory of perspective painting, the design became the standard model for altars across the world, spawning examples in central and eastern Europe and Portuguese Goa (see The Bizarre, pl.2.9). Pozzo himself devised a more complex variant in the later altar to St Aloysius Gonzaga in the church of S. Ignazio, which instead of a painting substitutes a fixed carved relief and the straight columns with Salomonic variants. In Spain, much later, altars of this type reached an unequalled level of fantasy, culminating in the famous Trasparente in the cathedral of Toledo, which deploys all Bernini's theatrical devices and use of mixed marble and other materials, although its ornamental vocabulary actually combines borrowings from northern European Mannerism with late Baroque ornamental ideas from Italy.

The term *Gesamtkunstwerk*, often used to describe this Baroque phenomenon of the total work of art, was first applied by art historians to those Baroque churches of central and eastern Europe in which, in a manner ultimately indebted to Bernini, a rich and complex interaction between architecture, painting, sculpture and ornament is unified through the dramatic use of light. While some interiors, such as that of the Asam brothers' jewel-like church of St John Nepomuk in Munich, are the product of a single effort (see The Cult of Saints, p.230), others, such as the court chapel in the Residenz at Würzburg, are in fact the product of a range of painters, sculptors and craftsmen working together in the same style over an extended period. The interiors of the churches of Portugal and Brazil use different means to achieve the same ends. Entirely decorated in a rich layer of carved ornament covered in Brazilian gold leaf, they are designed to focus the congregation's attention on the main altar, which is backed by a tall stepped *trono* for the display of the consecrated host, contained in a small room-like space (see pl.4.1).

THE CORNARO CHAPEL

Evonne Levy

On a cloudy day the Cornaro Chapel, in the Roman church of S. Maria della Vittoria, is dimly lit, though dazzlingly patterned (pl.2.21). Facing the altar, which is surrounded by rare and intensely patterned coloured marbles framed by black marble pilasters, the spectator feels submerged in the substratum, at bedrock, like the two cadavers shown on the floor emerging from their sepulchres (pl.2.20). When the clouds part, light suddenly streams into the chapel from a hidden window, illuminating the white Carrara marble group of the smiling angel and St Teresa floating in ecstasy on a cloud (pl.2.22), bathing everything around in a golden glow. The alabaster panels beside the altar suddenly become transparent, living up to their reputation as representations of clouds. Framed like pictures, they seem to show the landscape of Paradise, suggesting that one of the tasks of the artist, Gianlorenzo Bernini, is to convince us that we have entered heaven.

Enacted on the altar are St Teresa's closely related experiences of a vision of an angel plunging its flaming arrow into her and the sweet taste of ecstasy that ensued. In this weightless state, supine, with her senses closed to the world, her limbs fall limp, her mouth opens. The heavy folds of her drapery, alive in

their complexity around her enflamed entrails, make visible the movements of a soul on fire with love of God. The face of the angel, Teresa wrote, 'was so aflame that he appeared to be one of the highest rank of angels who seem to be on fire', and fire is a leitmotif of the chapel, from the gilded heart ablaze on the chapel gate to the flame-like drapery of both angel and saint, to the light made permanent in gilt bronze rays framing the marble group.

2.21 *View of the Cornaro Chapel in S. Maria della Vittoria,* attributed to Guidobaldo Abbatini. Rome, *c.*1651 (cat.81)

2.20 (*left*) Praying skeleton, floor relief from the Cornaro Chapel, Gianlorenzo Bernini, marble intarsia. Rome, 1647–51

The sunlight illuminates an already luminous fresco of the Holy Spirit celebrated by music-making angels (pl.2.23). The fresco partially obscures the relief scenes from Teresa's life on the upper reaches of the vault, making the clouds seem real. Cloud-shaped shadows painted in dark varnish support the illusion that a patch of heaven has dropped to earth. The changes in natural lighting create the sensation of an event in progress.

Bernini engages the viewer's senses in a 'narrative enactment'. The unfolding action, superseding the narratives taking place on the altar and in the vault, appears to be caused by a divine force. In a chapel executed in different media and materials, Bernini creates what seems like a temporally unified event, and, in the words of his biographer Filippo Baldinucci, a 'beautiful whole' (*bel composto*).

The chapel served two purposes: it commemorated the newly canonized Spanish mystic St Teresa of Ávila and it provided a memorial to the Venetian Cardinal Federico Cornaro, who paid Bernini an extraordinary sum to honour his family and to support his own aspirations to the papacy. One doge and seven cardinals from the Cornaro family, all but one long dead, sit in *coretti* on the side walls of the chapel as if attending Mass (pl.2.24). A family that existed through time has been catapulted over time into our time. Their responsiveness to the events that surround them convinces us that the divine is acting around us and upon us now, in this very space.

2.22 (*top*) *The Ecstasy of St Teresa*, sculpture from the Cornaro Chapel, Gianlorenzo Bernini, marble. Rome, 1647–51

2.23 (*above*) *The Holy Spirit and Musical Angels*, fresco from the vault of the Cornaro Chapel, Guidobaldo Abbatini. Rome, 1647–51

2.24 (*top right*) Federico and other members of the Cornaro Family, relief from the west (right) wall of the Cornaro Chapel, Gianlorenzo Bernini, marble. Rome, 1647–51

The Human Figure

The swooning figure of St Teresa in the Cornaro Chapel and the multitudes of cherubs, saints and angels on the ceiling of the Gesù are a reminder of the vital part played by the human figure in Baroque art and design. Allegorical, sacred and mythological figures had of course long played a dominant role in art, but it was in the Baroque period that they seemed to take over the whole work of art, turning it into a drama in which the actors energetically strove not only to convey a particular message, but to do so by engaging the viewer with overt expressions of emotion. The ways in which this was achieved were very largely developed in Rome in the circle of Bernini and his contemporaries. Bernini, in particular, found the means of endowing the whole figure with emotion, in pose, gesture and drapery as well as facial expression. Above all, he gave his figures a sense of realistic immediacy, as if they had been stopped in mid-action, made all the more actual by the treatment of detail and texture. This is most clearly seen in his figure of St Teresa, captured at the moment the smiling seraph pierces her heart with the flaming arrow of love, symbolizing her mystical union with Christ.

Bernini was also responsible for inventing two forms of secular figure sculpture that came to be characteristic of the Baroque. The first was the heroic bust, with the head held proudly above a mass of billowing drapery. A secular echo of the devices developed for sacred subjects, this also solved the age-old problem of how to finish off the bottom of a bust in a convincing manner. Bernini used it first for Francesco d'Este, but more significantly and magnificently for Louis XIV (pl.2.26). Other rulers quickly demanded a similar treatment for their own portraits (pl.2.25). Bernini's second invention, the rearing equestrian statue, was equally attractive to absolute rulers. He first used it for his sculpture on the Vatican Scala Regia showing the Roman emperor Constantine, set in front of a great curtain, seeing a vision of the sign of the cross in the sky before his victory at the Milvian Bridge, with the message 'In this sign, you will conquer'. Just as the Constantine statue underlined the pope's power, so Bernini's adaptation of the theme for Louis XIV (see The Portrayal of Absolutism pl.1.22) set the model for the conquering absolute ruler, although this statue was ultimately to be translated into a sculpture of the Roman Marcus Curtius.

2.25 *Charles II*, Honoré Pelle. Probably Genoa, Italy, 1684 (cat.19)

2.26 (*opposite*) *Louis XIV*, Gianlorenzo Bernini, marble. Paris, 1665 (Musée national des châteaux de Versailles et de Trianon)

2.27 *The Descent from the Cross*, Peter Paul Rubens. Antwerp, 1611 (cat.15)

2.28 *William and Mary presenting the cap of liberty to Europe*, ceiling design for the Royal Hospital for Seamen, Greenwich, Sir James Thornhill, oil on canvas. London, 1710 (V&A:812-1877)

While such treatments were new in sculpture, they were not new to painting, which had been developing an increasingly dramatized mode of representation since the early years of the seventeenth century, both in the chiaroscuro treatments of Caravaggio and the more classical treatments of the Bolognese mural and ceiling painter Annibale Carracci, as well as in the work of Peter Paul Rubens, the greatest artist of the northern European Baroque. Rubens developed a strongly dramatic style based on the close study of earlier art, including the colouring and handling of Titian, the dramatic lighting of Caravaggio and the figure treatments of ancient classical sculpture. The result was a series of religious and secular works of unprecedented emotional power (pl.2.27).

In France, the king's painter, Charles Le Brun, who was also director of the Royal Academy of Painting and Sculpture, devised a set of formulae for showing the human moods, known as the passions, in facial expression (see pl.4.47). By the end of the seventeenth century such emotionally based treatments had found their way into sculpture and painting across Europe. Figures secular and sacred filled the churches, more vigorously modelled and more densely deployed than they ever were in Italy. The carefully devised representations of martyrdoms and ecstatic visions used in churches had their secular equivalents, prompted by the example of Pietro da Cortona. On the ceiling of the great dining hall of the Royal Hospital for Seamen at Greenwich, the cloud-enthroned King William III and Queen Mary expel their enemies out of the oval frame, in exactly the same way as the damned in the ceiling of the Gesù (pl.2.28). In palaces, the painted and sculpted decorations followed a careful programme glorifying the ruler, in which the actors often took on the attributes of the classical gods. The best-known example was of course Louis XIV

himself, who promoted a link with the classical sun god Apollo by using the god's image or his own image coupled with a sun mask emblem. While some rulers imitated Louis XIV in their connection to Apollo, others, such as William of Orange, later King William III of England, chose Hercules. In King William's new palace at Het Loo, Hercules appears not only in the ceilings but also as the supports of the pier table in his state bedchamber, as part of a carefully devised iconographical programme.

The Hercules figures supporting the Het Loo table were examples of a growing trend in the applied arts of the Baroque of employing figures which combined a symbolic meaning with a practical function. As with Baroque architecture, there were antique precedents. The renewed and increasingly serious study of antique statues by Rubens and others from the early

seventeenth century onwards encouraged the creation of objects illustrating antique themes. Some of the earliest examples did indeed come from Rubens and his circle, including a silver ewer and basin made for King Charles I (pl.2.29), and Rubens's own salt-cellar, carved by Georg Petel with an exquisite, vigorous and complex Triumph of Venus, both based on the compositions found on Roman sarcophagi.[8] Petel also devised a version of Rubens's *Drunkenness of Silenus*, which became a popular subject for ivory and silver tankards. (pl.2.30). Figures could also dictate almost the whole form of an object, as in

2.29 Design for a silver basin with the Birth of Venus, Peter Paul Rubens. Antwerp, Belgium, *c*.1632–3 (cat.14)

2.30 Tankard with the *Drunkenness of Silenus*, Johann Baptist I Weinold, after a design by Rubens. Augsburg, Germany, *c*.1645–50 (cat.16)

2.31 Ewer with The Triumph of
Neptune, Massimiliano Soldani
Benzi. Florence, *c*.1721 (cat.17)

Massimiliano Soldani Benzi's vase illustrating *The Triumph of
Neptune* (pl.2.31).

Based similarly on an antique marine theme was one of the
high points of the composer Michele Todini's *Galleria Armonica
e Matematica* in Rome, created to promote his manufacture
of musical instruments (pl.2.32). In a characteristically Baroque
synthesis of sculpture, painting and music, the 'machine of
Polyphemus and Galatea' combined a harpsichord with two
figures, originally backed by seascapes painted by Gaspard
Dughet. The Cyclops Polyphemus plays a bagpipe, the sound
of which was produced by a small organ. The sea nymph
Galatea, the object of his infatuation, probably once played
a lute, perhaps imitated by the harpsichord. On the side of the
harpsichord Galatea is borne along in triumph, while a
triumphant procession of tritons and nereids supports the
instrument. The type of composition and the figure treatment
in this typical example of the Roman Baroque were pioneered

2.32 Harpsichord with Polyphemus and Galatea,
Michele Todini and Jacob Reiff (carving). Rome, *c*.1675
(The Metropolitan Museum of Art, 84.4.2929)

by Bernini and Pietro da Cortona. While Bernini himself designed examples of applied arts for only the most exalted clients, such as Queen Christina, his ideas were taken up by his collaborator, Giovanni Paolo Schor, whose designs for a wide range of applied arts also showed the influence of his master, Pietro da Cortona. An extraordinary state bed, designed by Schor to celebrate the birth of Maria Mancini Colonna's first son, was in the form of an enormous shell pulled in triumph by hippocamps (see pl.5.70).

Perhaps the biggest assemblages of such symbolic figural compositions were to be found in the many works, from coaches to table decorations, created for the official entries of foreign ambassadors, especially into Rome. Among the grandest were the five carriages made in Rome for the Portuguese ambassadorial procession to Pope Clement XI in 1716, carved with allegorical figure sculpture. Of the three surviving coaches, one is devoted to the oceans and their exploration, a second has at the front an allegory of heroism and immortality and at the back an allegory of the city of Lisbon and of the royal house breaking Muslim power in Asia and Africa (pl.2.33), while the ambassador's coach glorifies King John V of Portugal and his country's role in navigation and conquest. The triumphal entry of Viscount Castlemaine, in 1687, ambassador for the Catholic James II of England, was, like that of Queen Christina, an event of great political significance. The ambassador's two-month journey from London to Rome via Paris and Avignon was marked with festivities en route. Once in Rome, a band of artists worked for nine months to create the elements required for the official entry, including the coaches, allegorical figure sculptures one metre high in sugar for the banqueting table (see Dining at Court, p.288) and painted allegorical decorations for the outside of his palazzo. All were carefully recorded and published in an illustrated account the following year by the royal portrait painter John Michael Wright.[9] A comparable visual vocabulary was used for the carved decoration of warships, in particular their sterns, which used symbolic figures and architectural forms to convey messages of national power.

2.32 Rear view of the 'Lisbon' Ambassadorial Coach from the Embassy of John V of Portugal to Pope Clement XI, maker unknown. Rome, 1716 (Museu Nacional dos Coches, Lisbon)

Baroque Ornament

Just as Baroque art and design gave prominence to the human figure, so Baroque ornament was heavily indebted to the vegetable and animal world: leaves and flowers especially, but also motifs derived from human and animal figures. The style sprang from Renaissance and Mannerist ornament as well as ancient Roman decoration. An important founding element was a form of late Mannerist ornament now called auricular, named after the fleshy parts of the ear, which it somewhat resembles. The auricular style, which fully emerged in the earliest years of the seventeenth century, sprang from an interest in fleshy forms, shells and scaly shapes, which began in the Low Countries in the 1550s, inspired by a fashion for dripping grottoes inhabited by scaly creatures. Essentially ambiguous, suggestive and bizarre, it was a zoomorphic style derived from marine, animal and human forms, and was not a little inspired by the new interest in human anatomy and dissection.

The style was pioneered by goldsmiths and artists in Haarlem and Prague, most notably the members of the Van Vianen family, whose work in Prague for the Emperor Rudolf II, and in London for kings Charles I and II, as well as a set of prints of their work published in 1650, helped to spread it. Among the Van Vianens' earliest and greatest achievements was the extraordinary ewer made in 1614 by Adam van Vianen in memory of his brother Paul. More a work of art than a practical object, its female-figure handle and monkey-like foot have been smoothed off into a new melting 'substance' that takes over the ewer's whole shape in a manner prefiguring the Baroque (pl.2.34). The soft natural forms of the auricular were particularly popular in Holland, but elements of it found their way across Europe, most especially into Germany and the Scandinavian and Baltic countries within the German cultural orbit. By about 1660 auricular forms had become incorporated into the standard naturalistic repertoire of Baroque ornament, most especially as a framing device for pictures and for the borders of shields or cartouches. The ambivalent nature of the auricular style and its references to dissection seem to have made it particularly suitable for inclusion in memento mori paintings and memorial tablets (see pl.4.28).

The strongly modelled forms of the auricular style were part of a late Mannerist trend towards ever broader and more sculptural forms, which began in Italy and formed the seed-bed of later Baroque ornamental developments. The Italian examples were soon taken north. Between 1610 and 1615, Rubens added to his house in Antwerp an encrustation of ornament partly based on what he had seen on the palaces of Genoa, engraved illustrations of which he published in 1622.

2.34 The 'Dolphin' Ewer, mark of Adam van Vianen, silver-gilt. Utrecht, 1614 (Rijksmuseum)

The new Italian style of interior decoration had arrived in France by 1615. The French appetite for particular types of Italian design is shown by the plates in a compendium of ancient and modern Italian decorative motifs, published in 1645 by Adam Philippon, who had been sent to Rome by Cardinal Richelieu in 1640. Among the ancient Roman and the Renaissance material are motifs in a style close to the auricular. But by that point up-to-date ornament in Italy had taken a new turn, initiated by Pietro da Cortona. In a decisive shift from the distortions of Mannerism, Cortona employed a massive and dense overlayering of correctly classical swags, scrolls and masks, combining them with figures and cartouches (pl.2.35).

2.35 Sala di Giove, Palazzo Pitti, Florence, with the ceiling painted by Pietro da Cortona and Ciro Ferri. 1643

2.36 Altar card, Johann Adolf Gaap and Charles Germain. Rome, 1699 (cat.99)

In France, as we have seen, it was Cortona's classicizing design approach that became, in the 1660s, the official court style, applied to interiors, furniture and furnishings. In Italy, by the 1660s, largely through the efforts of Cortona's pupil Giovanni Paolo Schor, a style had emerged that combined Cortona's ideas with those of Bernini, and this found its way into a wide range of interior decoration and the applied arts. It combined richly modelled curved forms with cartouches, figures, and scrolling leaf ornament based on the acanthus plant. In a typical example from the late 1660s, the curves form the frame of an extravagant cartouche, one of the most characteristic motifs of Baroque ornament (pl.2.36). By the early years of the eighteenth century the shaped scrolls had developed a character between vegetation and architectural mouldings and could sometimes take over the whole object (pl.2.37). By the 1730s the forms had separated into a series of broken angular mouldings. This style, known as Barochetto, or little Baroque, had a light-hearted character that made it the Italian equivalent of the French Rococo. Perhaps its most characteristic expression was in the work of travelling north Italian and Swiss mural painters working chiefly across central and eastern Europe.

2.37 Console table, maker unknown. Rome, c.1700 (cat.143)

The Acanthus

The scrolling leaves supporting Italian tables of the late seventeenth century were part of a passion for acanthus ornament that gripped much of Europe from about 1650 to about 1720. The acanthus motif had been in unbroken use since it first appeared in ancient Greece. An imaginary plant only loosely linked to the real plant of the same name, the acanthus was endlessly adaptable to both decorative and functional purposes. In its ancient Greek and Roman form it was used as a running frieze, or as part of a centralized composition rising from the ground or a vase, and was often combined with flowers and human, animal and fantastic figures. In the early sixteenth century Raphael and his pupils rationalized the forms of ancient acanthus in their painted decorations. A hundred years later these forms were revived, first of all in Italy, coinciding with a return to antique sources.

The way in which the ornament spread beyond Italy is hinted at by the publishing history of Polifilio Giancarli's ideas for acanthus friezes,

of a fleshy and rather Baroque character and with a full complement of birds, beasts, putti and mythical figures. First published in Venice, they were subsequently copied in Rome (1628), Amsterdam (1636), Paris (1646) and London (1672) (pls 2.38–41). Acanthus was the ornamental mainstay of the French official classical style, and thus of its later derivatives

elsewhere. At Vaux-le-Vicomte in the 1650s, Le Brun's painted wall panels of vases, acanthus and flower garlands were adapted from Raphael. The large scrolling acanthus on the so-called Anne of Austria casket is derived from the ancient Ara Pacis or Altar of Augustan Peace in Rome (which still survives but was then known through sixteenth-century prints),[10] but is combined with much smaller leaves and flowers, giving it a richly dense character very different from the Roman original (pl.2.43). In the same way, the scrolling acanthus designs of Jean le Pautre of the 1660s, with their wind-blown leaves and figures in violent action, far exceed their antique models in vigour and complexity. Acanthus was most keenly taken up in central Europe, reflecting a continuing tradition of vigorous leaf-work that had begun in the late Gothic period. Locally made acanthus candle-stands furnished the new Baroque palaces in Berlin in the 1680s, while in church altarpieces from Bavaria to Norway the architectural structure almost disappeared under a mass of leaf-work. It was this form of acanthus that became the basis of a vernacular decorative style still current in many parts of Europe.[11]

Baroque Flowers

Baroque floral ornament, although often found associated with the acanthus, had a largely independent origin. Like the acanthus, flowers have been used for ornament since ancient times. Running scrolls and hanging garlands incorporating flowers had been taken over from ancient Roman sources by artists of the Renaissance, but the blooms were often very generalized in form. A leading characteristic of flowers in Baroque ornament was the prominent naturalistic depiction of particular species. This was a reflection of the growing scientific and general interest in botany signalled by the increasing popularity, from the late sixteenth century, of flowers in gardens, the high prices paid for exotic rarities such as tulips and the emergence of the floral still-life. The first specialist flower painters emerged in Antwerp in the late sixteenth century. They were matched by printmakers, who not only copied the paintings (pl.2.42) but also produced sets of engraved prints that included flowers among other natural history subjects which were then used by artists in other media.[12] Perhaps most significant for the future of Baroque floral decoration was the work of Jan Breughel the Elder, whose garlands of flowers and fruit, which were often combined with Rubens's figure painting, anticipated the forms of later ornament. While such depictions were decorative they could also be freighted with meaning, for particular species carried sacred or secular messages (see pl.4.51) related to the figurative subject of the painting.

2.42 Tile panel, after an engraving by Theodor de Bry after Jacob Kempener, tin-glazed earthenware, painted. Lisbon, 1650–75 (Museu Nacional do Azulejo)

2.43 (*above*) 'Casket of Anne of Austria', maker unknown, gold over wood covered in blue silk. Paris, *c*.1660 (Musée du Louvre)

2.45 Benefactor's panel for Isaac Barrow
from the Wren Library, Trinity College,
Cambridge, England, Grinling Gibbons,
carved wood. England, 1691–5
(Trinity College, Cambridge)

The introduction of floral ornament is well tracked in
ornament prints and the finished products made by French
jewellers and enamellers. The first hint is to be found in the
flower-like elements in a type of ornament now called pea-pod,
which appeared in jewellery prints in the 1620s. In the 1630s
the prints included naturalistic flowers among the pea-pods.
By the 1640s, French enamelled cases for watches and
miniatures were being painted with scattered flowers or floral
garlands which also found their way on to furniture (pl.2.44).
In other fields, richly naturalistic flower bouquets and garlands

2.44 Cabinet on a stand,
attributed to Pierre Gole. Paris,
1660–71 (cat.174)

adorned French tapestry borders of the 1630s designed by the
decorative painter Jean Cotelle.[13] A little later, painted floral
still-lifes became a common component, often incorporated into
the decoration of French rooms. Their appeal lay in the startling
illusion of reality, as Samuel Pepys wrote in 1669 of a painting
by Simon Verelst: 'a little flowerpot of his drawing, the drops of
dew hanging on the leaves so that I was forced again and again
to put my finger to it to feel whether my eyes were deceived or
no … a better picture I never saw in my whole life'.[14] The
bouquet and garland compositions of the still-life painters were
copied in marquetry on cabinets, painted on to ceramics and
turned back into three dimensions by plasterers and carvers,
most famously by Grinling Gibbons, who developed a form of
naturalistic carving that had originated in the Netherlands
(pl.2.45). The most widespread form of Baroque floral
ornament, however, was the running scroll, often combined
with acanthus, together with the large bloom on a single stem.

2.46 Dish, silver-gilt. Copenhagen, *c.*1680 (V&A:M.49-1963)

Towards the end of the seventeenth century this became the characteristic border ornament on silver, most especially on the embossed dishes made for display on dining buffets, where the aim was to make a maximum impression, without, it was hoped, using too much silver (pl.2.46). Flowering scrolls and single blooms also formed the basis of the great seventeenth-century development in repeat patterns in woven textiles, stamped leathers or wallpapers, either in the form of single sprigs or as part of a complex pattern (see pl.5.24).

Ornament and the Grotesque

The botanical and animal forms used in Baroque ornament very often came together in the context of the grotesque (called in France the arabesque): a type of ancient Roman wall decoration based on a structural framework often inhabited by a strange collection of human figures, animals and fantastic creatures. It was named after the grotto-like buried rooms of Roman palaces in which it was discovered in the Renaissance. Both classical and imaginative, it created a design revolution after being established as an ornamental system by Raphael in 1517, in the decorations of the Vatican. Raphael's type of grotesque wall decoration became part of the French classical style in the 1640s; it was, for instance, used at Vaux-le-Vicomte some ten years later. In the late 1670s, Jean Berain, Louis XIV's official designer, developed a new type of grotesque composition using bands of inanimate strapwork from which leaves sprouted. This form of strapwork was based on a type of Mannerist grotesque indebted to Islamic interlace ornament, but Berain's handling of the strapwork was wonderfully adaptable and came to be used on surfaces large and small, from watch cases to garden parterres, as well as being capable of forming the whole shape of an object (pl.2.47). In France, Berain's compositions were part of a trend towards a lighter and more whimsical approach

2.47 Design for a grotesque, Jean Berain, engraving. France, c.1685–93 (V&A:29876.2)

to design that eventually, in the 1720s, produced the Rococo style. Outside France, however, Berain's strapwork enjoyed a long life, especially in central Europe where *Laub- und Bandelwerk* (leaf- and strapwork) replaced the acanthus as the leading form of ornament and was combined with the architectural elements of contemporary Italian ornament to create a distinctive late Baroque style in the German and Austrian courts (see pl.5.86).

Baroque as a World Style

The seventeenth century was characterized by the crossing of boundaries: natural ones through voyages, political ones through conquests, intellectual ones through ideas and material ones through the movement of goods and commodities. All these factors helped to make the Baroque the first style to appear in both world hemispheres and all the continents except for Australasia. Its spread outside Europe was a product of the development of territories by the European powers in South and Central America and along the sea routes to East Asia via the Cape of Good Hope and across the Pacific. The export from Europe of goods in the Baroque style extended from furniture, textiles and other movables to elements of building, such as the statuary, cut stonework and wall tiles sent from Portugal for incorporation into churches in Brazil and Angola. But the traffic of goods and of ideas in design went both ways. Objects made in the Baroque style for local European consumption, such as the ebony chairs produced in South Asia on the Coromandel coast, were also on occasion sent back home, where they seem to have helped to introduce the fashion for caned seats. At the same time, Europeans in South Asia set up the production of goods, notably printed chintzes, specifically for export to Europe, which joined the porcelain and other goods made in China shipped to satisfy the demand for brightly coloured 'India' goods in Baroque furnishing. Goods also circulated between territories, carried by company servants as they changed posts or sent to supply a need. Church altarpieces for Portuguese Angola were made in Portuguese Goa.[15] Sacred figures made by Chinese craftsmen in Spanish Manila were exported to Mexico, while the European-style ebony furniture used by the Dutch East India Company in Java, if not made locally by enslaved South Asian craftsmen, was brought in from the Coromandel coast.

The origins of such goods were very often reflected in their mixture of local and European themes. The export chintzes of South Asia, often based on drawings sent out from Europe, were carefully aimed at the European market by combining local Persian-derived elements, Chinese motifs and Baroque flowers, and even the grotesque designs of Jean Berain. Coromandel coast furniture and Goan church pulpits combined Baroque forms and vegetal motifs with figures taken from Hindu mythology (see Goa: the 'Rome of the Orient', p.42). Such mixtures could involve both design and function. The great council room screen in the governor-general's fort in Batavia (Jakarta) was carved by Chinese craftsmen very largely in the Baroque vegetal style, and was placed before the main entrance (pl.2.48). The central figure of Perseus, carrying the

2.48 Screen for the Council Room of Batavia Fort, made by Chinese craftsmen. Batavia (Jakarta), Indonesia, 1700–20 (cat.11)

shield of Medusa, suggests that the screen was intended to repel evil spirits, as such a screen would do in a traditional Chinese house. This intimidating object, adorned with the royal crown and the arms of the Dutch East India Company's towns in Holland, must have transmitted a combination of several messages to its Indonesian audience.

Such patterns of export and local adaptation were not of course unique to the Baroque style outside Europe. The various design elements in the characteristically Baroque cane-seated 'English chair' were modified to conform to local tastes as the type moved across Europe (see The International 'English Chair', p.118). While it is unclear why this particular chair type became so popular, it seems that the fashion may have spread through a vigorous export market in the chairs themselves. Other transfers of ideas occurred through the movement of paper and people, in the form of prints and drawings and of artists, craftsmen, designers and architects. Printed images had been used for the transfer of design ideas since the invention of engraving in Germany in the 1430s and had played a key role in the spread of Renaissance ornamental motifs from Italy to the rest of Europe in the early sixteenth century. By the end of that century print production had become big business, mainly based in Antwerp, whose wholesale publishers had offices in most of the major cities of Europe. By the mid-seventeenth century the centre of production had shifted to Paris, and then, in terms of the number of ornament prints produced, Augsburg took the lead in the early eighteenth century. The international nature of this trade is exemplified by the manner in which publishers worked to target particular markets, such as the Augsburg ornament prints in the Baroque and Rococo styles made for the Spanish and Portuguese markets, and by extension those of Central and South America.[16]

The design ideas carried by prints were, perhaps surprisingly, only rarely copied in their entirety. Among the examples are the monumental chimneypieces in the Swedish castle of Skokloster, copied exactly from a set of prints of fashionable French examples of the 1620s, which still survive in the castle.[17] One of the Skokloster summer firescreens is adapted from a print by Jean Le Pautre, whose huge production of seductively atmospheric etchings of interiors, palaces and gardens in the

official French court style had an enormous influence, chiefly in northern Europe. Much more usual was a form of imaginative adaptation of the type seen in the engraved and chased decoration on a salver of the 1690s (pl.2.49). Its outer border is adapted from a design by Stefano della Bella, whose ornament prints of the 1630s to 1650s had an effect out of all proportion to their small number (pl.2.50). The figures over the curling Baroque cartouche in the centre are derived from the title page of a set of prints of putti and masks after the sixteenth-century artist Paolo Farinati (pl.2.51). The emergence in the seventeenth century of books illustrated with copper engravings, such as Andrea Pozzo's *Perspective for Painters and Architects*, was also very significant. On its first publication in 1693 the usefulness of the *Perspective* was immediately recognized by a Leipzig reviewer, who praised its ability 'to accomplish and by the fastest method and as succinctly as possible optical delineations of every kind'.[18] At the end of 25 years it had been translated into at least seven European languages. The effect of its clear and dramatic plates was to spread the composition of the Roman Baroque altar to the whole of the Catholic world and beyond.

The second way in which Baroque design ideas travelled was of course through the movement of people. Artists, architects and craftsmen had, of course, been carrying their skills and design ideas out of their home areas for centuries. Crucial to this process had been the process of craft training under the guild system, which determined that apprentices should hone their skills through a lengthy period working away from the guild. Since the sixteenth century, Italy had not only been the source of the most fashionable design ideas but also of the architects and craftsmen who could turn them into reality. In the seventeenth century a close-knit network of families based in the area around Lake Como and the Graubünden region of Switzerland, bordering Italy, produced an astonishing number of travelling builders, fresco painters and plasterworkers, who helped to bring the Italian Baroque to central Europe and Scandinavia. But they were not without their local rivals, such as the very large school of plasterers and painters that emerged from Wessobrunn in Bavaria, who teamed up with the builders of the Bavarian Vorarlberg to produce much of the Baroque church architecture of southern Germany, and took their skills further afield, to Poland and Russia.

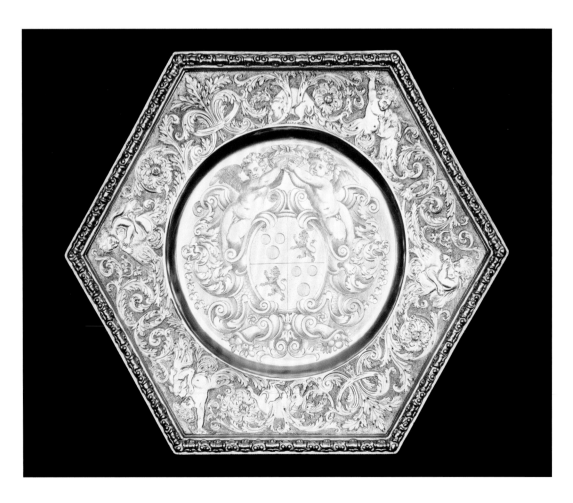

2.49 Salver, mark of Benjamin Pyne, silver-gilt. London, 1698–9 (V&A:M.77A-1947)

2.50 Frieze from *Ornamenti di fregi et fogliami*, Stefano della Bella, etching. Italy, after 1647 (V&A:28190.9)

2.51 Title-page to *Diverses Figures à l'eau forte de petits Amours*, Abraham Bosse after Paolo Farinati. Paris, 1644 (V&A:93.D.184)

THE INTERNATIONAL 'ENGLISH CHAIR'

Lucy Wood

2.52 A 'crown' chair, stamped with the initials of the joiner, 'MR', walnut. London, c.1685–95 (V&A:W.12-1949)

The London trade in caned chairs began in the mid-1660s, probably stimulated by the Great Fire of 1666, and by 1690 some 70,000 chairs were made per year. About 24,000 were allegedly exported annually to India and South-East Asia, where the heat made cane much more practical than upholstery (and where the technique of caning had in fact originated). All of these have seemingly been destroyed (probably ravaged by termites), but the trade is attested by some derivative Indian chairs, made in more durable tropical woods.

Others were exported within Europe, especially to Holland, Germany and Scandinavia, and after 1700 to North America. In the principal importing cities imitations were soon manufactured, and the type came to be known universally as an 'English chair'. In Germany the Margrave of Brandenburg-Schwedt ordered from Berlin, in 1696, a dozen 'English chairs with Spanish cane', which doubtless came from London; but a set of 'caned English chairs' supplied in 1732–3 to Queen Sophie Dorothee were probably manufactured in Berlin. In Sweden, London-made chairs were being imported as early as the 1670s, and still in the mid-1720s; by that time apprentice chair-makers in Stockholm were required to make chairs with caned seats, 'like English chairs'. Even in France, cane-seated furniture of the 1690s, though very different in style from any English pieces, was described as *d'anglaise*.

The English patterns themselves developed over the period of this international fashion. One of the earliest forms to be exported was decorated with one or more crowns on the back-frame and another on the front stretcher (pl.2.52); a slightly later type had crowns

2.53 A 'boyes and crowns' armchair, walnut. Probably The Netherlands, c.1690 (Rijksmuseum, Amsterdam).

2.54 Armchair, teak. Indonesia, c.1700–25 (Rijksmuseum)

2.55 Armchair, walnut. London, c.1685–1700. (cat.8)

supported by naked putti, known as 'boyes and crownes' (pl.2.53). Derivatives are known in Sweden, Norway, Holland and – through Dutch mediation – Indonesia (pl.2.54).

From around 1700 English caned chairs became much taller, and were typically carved with pierced scrolls and foliage (and rarely with crowns). Soon the back uprights were treated as columns rather than spirals, and surmounted by an elaborate top rail (which previously would have been set between them). This model too was widely adopted in northern Europe, notably in The Netherlands (pl.2.55). Sweden and Denmark favoured a hybrid model, retaining the crown or 'boyes and crownes' motif (pl.2.56).

The final development in London, from c.1715, was to merge the back uprights and caned panel into one – a full-width caned, moulded back-frame (pl.2.57). This type, too, was widely favoured in Europe, and a midway form was adopted in America.

The 'English chair' inspired imitations in manufacturing centres where caning itself was not practised: a variant of the 'simple' crown chair, with a solid wood seat and slatted back, was made in Scotland. And a distinctive Portuguese type, with stamped leather back and seat, is clearly – if perhaps unconsciously – inspired by the final development of the form (pl.2.58). So the influence of the 'English chair' was seemingly even more pervasive than the international recognition of this term implies.

2.56 Chair, Johan Henrik Spåre, ebonized wood, Breslau (now Wrocław, Poland), 1710–16 (Helsinki City Museum). Spåre, originally from Finland, escaped from Russian captivity during the Great Northern War to Breslau. The carving of the top rail of this chair matches a distinctive Swedish model.

2.57 *One of a pair of chairs possibly made for Thomas, 1st Viscount Windsor. London, c.1705–15 (cat.9)*

2.58 Chair with stamped-leather covers. Portugal (probably Lisbon), c.1720–40 (cat.10)

The next stage in the process of a style being spread through the movement of craftsmen is well shown by the progress of acanthus ornamentation in Norway. It was initiated by the work of a wood-carver recorded simply as a 'hollender' (perhaps a German) who in 1699 made the reredos and pulpit of St Saviour's church in the central enclave of Christiania (now Oslo). The spread of acanthus ornament beyond the town was made possible by the travels of urban carvers working in country churches. The best of these, Lars Borg, created at Ringsaker in 1704 the finest of all the Norwegian font-houses and a pulpit based on the one in Oslo (see pls 4.24, 4.25). It was the acanthus ornament employed by these urban craftsmen, combined with the freer forms of the Rococo, which led, towards the end of the eighteenth century, to the vigorous acanthus-leaf-based folk style now seen as typically Norwegian.

As often with the movement of people, politics also had a major role to play. In 1686 Louis XIV, in response to an embassy to France, sent to Siam Jesuit scholars with an array of scientific instruments and six specialist craftsmen, with the aims of opening up trade and evangelizing.[19] The same king's revocation in 1685 of the Edict of Nantes, which for many years had allowed Protestant Huguenots freedom of worship, prompted a mass exodus of technical skill and design talent from the main centre of European fashion. Among the refugees was Daniel Marot, whose father was the court designer Jean Marot. As a designer to Louis XIV's rival, Prince William of Orange (later King William III of England), Daniel Marot developed a variant of the French style that passed to England and her colonies, as well as to Germany via royal marriages (see The State Bedchamber, pl.5.48). William's desire to copy French styles was characteristic of many European rulers, whether they were enemies of France or not, although political alliances could have an influence. While the Danish court did absorb some French ideas, its strongest artistic links were with Germany, reflecting its political allegiance to the Holy Roman Emperor. The love of things French in Sweden, Denmark's traditional enemy, was linked to her allegiance to Louis XIV. The manner in which such courts adopted the Baroque style varied according to local circumstances, but almost always it involved the employment of foreign artists or designers and the conscious gathering of information from outside sources.

In England, the Restoration in 1660 of Charles II after his continental exile had prompted the fashionable updating of the royal residences in a style that combined both French and Dutch elements. At Windsor Castle, the Upper Ward was turned into a Baroque palace from 1675 by a team consisting of the architect Hugh May, who had been with the king in exile,

the woodcarver Grinling Gibbons, who had been trained in Holland, and the painter Antonio Verrio, who introduced into England mural and ceiling painting in the Franco-Italian manner. For courts such as those of Portugal and Sweden, further from the centres of aesthetic authority, the process of design was more difficult and complex. In Portugal, the absolutist King John V, rich through Brazilian gold and diamonds, looked directly to France for guidance in secular decoration and ceremonial. In 1728 he recruited the goldsmith Juste-Aurèle Meissonnier, Louis XV's designer of festival and ceremonial decorations, as an adviser on artistic matters, designing for the Portuguese king a silver throne in the manner of that made for Louis XIV, which had been melted down many years before.[20]

In ecclesiastical matters, including design, manufacture and ritual, John V's court turned to Rome. Between 1740 and 1744, a team of artists, designers and makers were recruited by the ambassador at the Vatican, Manuel Pereira de Sampaio, and seemingly managed by the architects Luigi Vanvitelli and Nicola Salvi, while in Portugal the works came under the charge of João Frederico Ludowice (or Ludwig), a goldsmith and architect born in Swabia and trained in Munich and in Rome, where he worked on the S. Ignazio altarpiece in the Gesù. For the basilica in the Lisbon patriarchal palace, chapel fittings, furnishings and silver were designed and made in Rome and Florence, including full-size replicas in wood of the monstrances used on the altars of St Peter's. The artists were carefully directed to look for inspiration at particular items in Rome.[21]

About 60 years earlier, an absolutist monarchy at the other end of Europe had had the same need to develop Baroque forms of design. Sweden had emerged in the 1650s as a great power, with territories around the Baltic and a scattering of colonial settlements. Her adoption of absolutist rule in the 1670s coincided with the start of the career of Nicodemus Tessin the Younger, who became the royal architect and eventually, like Colbert in France, superintendent of public works, and thus the controller of all court design. Aware that in Sweden he had 'the most obdurate of climates to contend with, together with the ignorance of the craftsmen', he made a series of trips abroad between 1673 and 1688, in particular to France and Italy. His first purpose was to collect information on architecture and 'all those concerns on which architecture is dependent or to which it is related, viz. sculpture, painting, landscape, gardening, hydraulics, mechanics and festivities for both glad and solemn occasions'.[22] The resulting huge collection of drawings, books and prints, organized by subject for easy reference, was augmented, after his return, by specially commissioned record drawings of the latest trends, which included Roman sculpture and sheets showing the latest types of French silver tableware and fashions in table arrangements. His second purpose was to make contacts that would produce foreign craftsmen and artists willing to work in Sweden, as well as commissioning objects from foreign designers.

In Rome in the 1670s, Tessin attended the studio of the architect Carlo Fontana, a training ground in the Baroque for a number of foreign architects, including the Austrian Fischer von Erlach and the Scot James Gibbs. Tessin's careful academic drawings of such modern buildings as the churches of S. Ignazio and S. Carlo Borromeo were shown to Bernini for examination (pl.2.59). But he also made designs or 'inventions' on appropriate subjects, including dramatic schemes for thrones and state bedchambers in the Bernini manner. In France in the 1670s, he made a special study of gardens, including those at Versailles, and detailed notes on furniture and furnishings in 1687. Le Nôtre took him round the Versailles gardens, while Le Brun received him at home. Tessin's studies led him to create a synthetic Baroque style that combined elements from Italy, most especially for exteriors, with ideas from France (especially from the 1690s), largely employed in secular interiors, state events and gardens. A clue to his choice of architectural and artistic heroes is provided by those depicted on the ceiling of the main hall of his private palace in Stockholm: the architects Bramante and Bernini, the sculptors Michelangelo and Algardi, the painters Raphael and Annibale Carracci and the engineers Domenico Fontana and Agostino Ramelli. The gilt-wood royal thrones in the 'great church' in Stockholm, carved by Burchardt Precht in 1684 after designs by Tessin, are a close reflection of his Roman 'inventions' inspired by Bernini. His high altar for Uppsala Cathedral, carried out by Precht in the 1720s, is one of the numerous progeny across the world of Andrea Pozzo's S. Ignazio altar in the Gesù.[23] Pozzo's figures of the New Testament and Faith casting their enemies into the abyss have, however, been shifted from their anti-Protestant message to Tessin's anti-Catholic one, without altering the iconography. A design for a luxurious bed, while being inspired by examples at Versailles, includes elements taken directly from Italian drawings in his own collection (see pl.5.71).

For his biggest project, the building of the Stockholm royal palace, completely reconceived after a fire in 1697, Tessin had brought over from France a group of artists and craftsmen who had trained under Berain, Le Brun and the sculptor François Girardon. The design of the imposing exterior synthesized ideas from several Italian palaces and villas, including Michelangelo's Palazzo Farnese and Bernini's Palazzo Chigi, as well as the same

2.59 View of the dome of the church of S. Carlo al Corso, Rome, Nicodemus Tessin the Younger, pen and brown ink with blue and grey wash. Rome, 1673 (cat.23)

architect's design for the Louvre (see pl.5.6). For the planning and decoration of the interior Tessin turned to French royal examples, above all Versailles. In the centre of the courtyard was to stand an equestrian statue, largely based on Girardon's famous statue of Louis XIV in the place Vendôme, of Charles XI by Bernard Fouquet, one of the artists brought to Stockholm. A drawing of the final idea was sent to Paris to be shown to the leading artists as well as to Louis XIV himself. The responses were reported by Daniel Cronström, Sweden's permanent envoy in France; the plinth, designed by Tessin, was found not to be to French taste, but Fouquet's work got full

2.60 Casket, grand-ducal
workshops after Giovanni Battista
Foggini, Florence, c.1720.
The stand is attributed to William
Vile, London, 1752 (cat.34)

approval. Tessin also turned to French artists and craftsmen for
the production of movable items. These included the state
coach from a design ordered from Jean Berain after the older
coaches had been destroyed by a fire in 1696. The wooden
framework was made in France, but the coach was finished by
the French artists in Stockholm. For the silver in the royal
chapel, including the candelabra and the great font, Tessin used
Jean-François Cousinet, who worked in Sweden using, in the
case of the font, a model made by Bernard Fouquet (pls 2.61
and 2.62). A suite of tapestries showing victories was designed
and woven in France, although the battle subjects were taken
from Swedish paintings.

Court Workshops

Artists and craftsmen had of course been attached to courts
since the Middle Ages, working outside the restrictive, media-
based regulations of the guild system, to produce works of art
and luxury objects. The ability of such artists to operate across
the whole field of the fine and applied arts, from paintings to
textile design, helped to lay the foundations for the
seventeenth-century phenomenon of the court-sponsored
manufactory that worked across a broad range of media, most
significantly the much admired and imitated French royal
manufactory of the Gobelins, founded in 1662 (see The
Gobelins Workshops, p.124). The Gobelins was an innovator
not in its range of luxury products, for in that it had been
anticipated by the example of Prague workshops of the
Emperor Rudolf II some 60 years earlier, and by the Medici
workshops founded in 1588, but because its products came
under the design control of a single individual, the artist
Charles Le Brun, with a resulting unity of style.

Manufactories like the Gobelins served several purposes
beyond their main function of supplying luxury products and
furnishings to the court. Not only did they strive to make
things of the highest quality and in the latest fashion, they also
tried to develop a range of difficult and sought-after technical
processes. Carrying out such work, as Tessin knew, often
depended on expertise from abroad. The Flemish domination of
the production of tapestry, the most expensive and prestigious
of all luxury products, was challenged by several court
initiatives using immigrant skill, including the English royal
works at Mortlake, the Gobelins and the Berlin royal works
early in the eighteenth century. Mirror glass, which became
increasingly fashionable from the 1660s, was a Venetian
monopoly until challenged from 1665 by the *Manufacture
royale de glaces de miroirs*, in turn imitated by the factories set
up by the German princely courts. The working of hardstones,
which since 1588 had been centred on the grand-ducal
workshops in Florence, was begun at the Gobelins with the
assistance of Italians, including Domenico Cucci (see The
Gobelins Workshops, pl.2.63). The long European search for
the secret of true porcelain was finally ended in 1709 by
Johann Friedrich Böttger, working for Augustus the Strong, king
of Poland and elector of Saxony. The products of the Meissen
porcelain factory, established a year later, played a major role in
the presentational aspects of the Saxon court, not only in the
extraordinary porcelain-decorated interiors of the Japanisches
Palais but also as gifts to important visitors. In the same way, for
a long period the sought-after hardstones from the Florentine
court workshops could only be obtained as state gifts (pl.2.60).[24]

2.61 Royal font, mark of
Jean-François Cousinet, silver.
Stockholm, 1696 (The Royal
Collections, Stockholm)

2.62 Candelabrum made for
the Royal Chapel, Stockholm,
mark of Jean-François Cousinet.
Stockholm, 1695 (cat.5)

THE GOBELINS WORKSHOPS

Florian Knothe and Carolyn Sargentson

During the 1660s, Louis XIV (1638–1715) established a series of royal *manufactures* as a means of encouraging and controlling French artistic production. These large-scale enterprises furnished the French and foreign courts, and produced some of the most extraordinary and innovative designs of Louis's reign. The king's principal agent in this programme was Jean-Baptiste Colbert (1619–83), minister of finance, who, between 1681 and 1683, created a distinctive French version of European mercantilism (now called Colbertism). With the intention of reducing imports and placing Paris at the centre of Europe's luxury production, Colbert's domestic economic campaign included the fostering of both the new royal *manufactures* and the existing, highly skilled workshops of seventeenth-century Paris. In terms of propaganda, design was a crucial tool. Not only were the products of royal patronage to be among the most impressive, and expensive, in Europe: they were rich in iconographical decoration celebrating the life and power of the French king.

Colbert housed the new Gobelins *manufacture* in the existing textile workshops of the Hôtel des Gobelins, to which site were relocated four existing tapestry ateliers from Paris and Maincy. In 1663 the artistic and business leadership of this new *manufacture* was placed in the hands of Charles Le Brun, former head of the Maincy workshops and First Painter to the king from 1662. The workshops expanded as weavers, dyers, painters, sculptors, cabinetmakers, lapidaries, silversmiths, gilders, engravers and embroiderers arrived to take up new positions. In total there were about 300 male employees, and, as indicated by rare individual accounts, a number of female household members also joined the workforce. Protected by royal letters patent of 1667, these craftsmen worked to Le Brun's designs, creating some of the most ambitious projects of seventeenth-century Europe.

The Gobelins is best known for its series of sumptuous high-warp tapestries, many of which glorified the king's moral virtues and political power, either through allegory, as in the *Elements* and *Seasons*, or by allusion, as in the *History of*

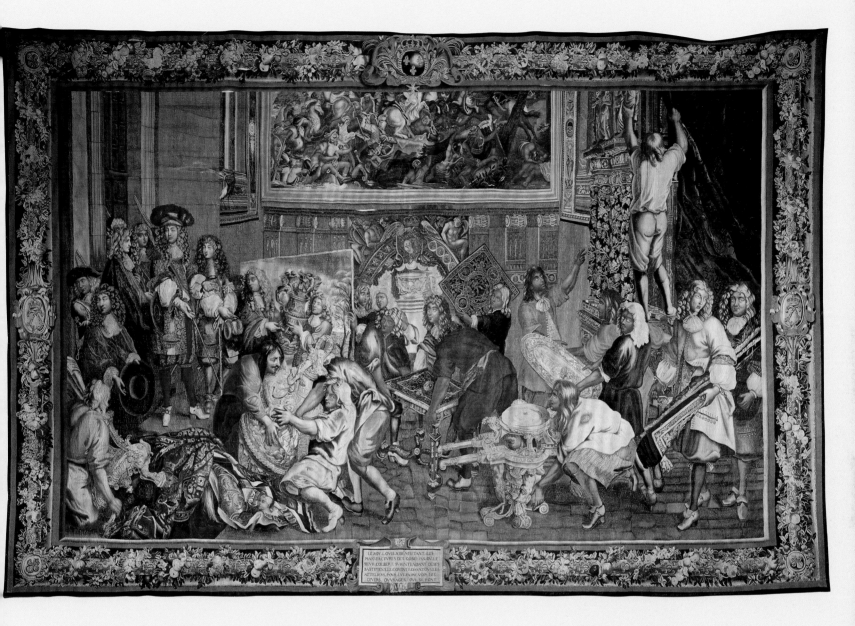

2.64 *Visit of King Louis XIV to the Gobelins* (15 October, 1667), from the series *The History of the King*, tapestry, after a design by Charles Le Brun, woven at the Manufacture Royale des Gobelins. Paris, 1665–80. The figure on the right, gesturing towards the cabinet, is thought to be Domenico Cucci. (Musée national des châteaux de Versailles et de Trianon)

2.63 *(opposite)* Cabinet, Domenico Cucci. Paris, 1679–83 (cat.3)

Alexander. Other weavings, including those of *The History of the King* (pl.2.64) and the *Royal Residences*, illustrated more overtly Louis XIV's diplomatic and military victories, royal wealth and leisure. The workshops produced innovative designs in all kinds of materials, notably the furniture cast from silver or mounted with panels of semi-precious stones, which challenged the status of renowned foreign workshops such as the Florentine *Opificio delle Pietre Dure*, and testified politically to the strength of the Bourbon empire. The direct influence of the Gobelins designs was extended as some were engraved and made available as prints. These had an impact both on European taste and on Parisian production, as the city's artisans took

up the engraved designs, or parts of them, and deployed them in all kinds of media.

Without doubt, the *manufacture*'s greatest achievements date to its first 20 years. Following Colbert's death and the shift from Le Brun's to Pierre Mignard's direction, it became less inventive. Furthermore, the War of the League of Augsburg (1688–97) committed the French crown to enormous financial outlay, drastically reducing funding for the arts. The solid silver furniture was melted down some seven years after it had been made, and entire workshops were closed. The tapestry workshops were to survive, reorganized in 1699 by Robert de Cotte, and they alone were to maintain a major influence during the eighteenth century.

Perhaps the biggest of all state gifts was that of the Amber Room, designed by the Prussian court sculptor Andreas Schlüter, made by craftsmen from Denmark and Danzig (now Gdansk) and installed in Schloss Charlottenburg in Berlin. In 1716 it was given by Frederick Wilhelm I of Prussia to Peter the Great of Russia, an act that helped to seal their political alliance against Sweden.

But the promotion of court manufacture had a still deeper purpose, born of the close identification of the absolute monarch with the nation. The Gobelins and the other newly established French royal manufactories were part of a broader policy, introduced by Colbert as minister of finance, to foster French manufactures, both for home consumption and for export. Part of the same project was the promotion of both the king and the nation through state-sponsored prints.[25] In the same way, Tessin recognized the power of design in promoting both the national interest and royal prestige.

2.65 Trochus shell cup, maker unknown, shell mounted in silver, partially gilded. Possibly Nuremberg, c.1680–99 (V&A:276-1878)

2.66 (*opposite*) *A Cabinet of Curiosities*, Georg Hinz, also called Johann Georg Hainz. Hamburg, Germany, 1666 (cat.27)

Marvellous Materials

As the activities of the court manufactories suggest, a fascination with physical materials, both real and imitation, played a central role in the complex visual language of the Baroque. The waving plumes and pasteboard armour of Queen Christina's evening reception were matched by an interest in real materials, their nature and their meaning, characteristic of a period that saw both the birth of modern science and the geographical opening up of the world beyond Europe. In external architecture, the ideal stone could be imitated in plaster, but a strong awareness of materials could also produce such buildings as the Palazzo Carignano in Turin, with its huge sculptural façade of moulded brick. In interior architecture, the counterpoint to the heavenly illusion in paint and plaster up above was a real world of bronze and expensive patterned marble below, reassuring even if only skin-deep. The concentration of coloured marbles, bronze, lapis lazuli, gilding and paint in Bernini's Cornaro Chapel turned it into a precious and richly coloured setting for the white marble figures of the central drama. It is like a jewel box, but was also modelled on an imaginative reconstruction of the lost marble-lined secular interiors of imperial Rome. This was true of the concentration of bronze, paint, marble and gilding in state rooms at the palace of Versailles and even, by extension, of the conspicuous painted imitations of marble in the Baroque interiors of Scandinavia. In Portugal and Brazil these materials were replaced by equally assertive gilt-wood carving and painted tiles. As always, the viewer is aware of the material as well as the total effect.

By the early seventeenth century, rare and precious materials, both natural and man-made, had long played a major role in princely collections. The princely *Kunst- und Wunderkammer* (or room for artificial and curious objects) that evolved in the sixteenth century contained natural history specimens and curiosities as well as scientific materials and works of art, books and documents. The systematic organization of these materials and specimens came to be seen as a microcosm of the world and by extension a visual expression of the divinely manufactured universe. By the early seventeenth century such collections, often contained in a specially made cabinet or *Kunstschrank*, had come within the reach of the middle classes and others. The contents of a typical example include shells, coral and pearl jewellery, an agate cup, and a tankard and cup of ivory, characteristically Baroque examples of the type of virtuoso art object, or *Kunststück*, made for such art cabinets (pls 2.65 and 2.66). The making of objects in elephant ivory, either carved or turned on a 'rose engine' lathe into a series of complex shapes, was both a professional practice and a normal

part of the education of princes. The form of such lathe-made objects reflected the God-given geometry of the universe but in addition, being entirely machine-made, they symbolized man's mastery over nature through mathematics and mechanics (pl.2.67). But the painting of the cabinet is also a 'vanitas', a reminder, as the baby's skull shows, that such earthly riches and fruits of ingenuity are fleeting in the face of death.

Materials could also have other meanings. Many of the most exotic were believed to have the capacity, very useful at the time, to detect poison, including Saxon soapstone, the newly invented ruby glass (see pl.1.15) and rhinoceros horn, which also had the sexual connotations it still carries in some cultures today (pl.2.68). Amber, mysteriously found washed up on the seashore, but in fact the fossilized sap of prehistoric trees, was

2.67 Ivory cup, Philipp Sengher. Florence, 1681. The entire cup, including the figure, is made on a lathe. (cat.37)

2.68 Rhinoceros horn beaker, maker unknown. Germany, c.1645. An erotic scene is hidden underneath the base of the beaker. (cat.36)

linked by the ancient Greeks to the sun god Apollo (see pl.1.49). For some royal collectors certain materials also had a national meaning, symbolizing overseas territories in which they had an interest. A tureen made of Icelandic obsidian entered the Danish royal *Kunstkammer* as an example of the 'various Diamonds from the North, as Rubies, Sapphires, Emeralds, garnets, Topaz, Amethysts, Crystals, Jasper and Obsidians' (pl.2.69). Its iconography symbolized the Danish victory over Sweden in the Great Northern War.

2.69 Tureen in Icelandic obsidian, Hartwig Holst, the mounts with the mark of Jens Komløv Pedersen. Copenhagen, 1725 (cat.31)

By the end of the seventeenth century the idea of the all-embracing *Kunstkammer* as a universal microcosm had begun to be replaced by art, scientific and natural history collections arranged according to aesthetic or historical criteria. This trend was especially evident among the princes in Germany, newly embarked on a wave of palace building made possible by years of peace. Augustus the Strong of Saxony, who had closely studied the example of Louis XIV, distributed among the pavilions of his newly built Baroque parade and performance ground, called the Zwinger, the scientific collections, the prints and drawings collection and the library. In the adjacent electoral palace he created the Green Vault, a set of Baroque showrooms for the decorative arts (excluding porcelain) and jewellery,

2.70 Agate vase with cameos, Pierre Ladoireau and workshop. Paris, 1687–9 (cat.30)

2.71 Vase, Johann Melchior Dinglinger, Johann Christian Kirchner. Dresden, Germany, 1719–21 (cat.32)

which was finished in 1729. In this he extended the idea of the small treasury of the type built by Louis XIV at Versailles (pl.2.70), by combining objects inherited from his predecessors as well as the products of the court manufactory in a carefully modulated environment. Museum-like in its systematic arrangement, it was also a calculated demonstration of the power and wealth of its creator, not only in its design and the number of objects, but as a demonstration of Saxony's natural riches in minerals and precious and semi-precious stones (pl.2.71).

The sequence began with the room of Renaissance and modern French bronzes, shown against oak panelling and dominated by equestrian bronzes of Louis XIV and Augustus the Strong. Next came a small room of ivories, lined with lacquer imitating marble. The room next door, decorated with mirrors and red lacquer, contained 370 pieces of mostly modern white silver. It was succeeded by a room of silver-gilt objects, lined with mirrors and bright green lacquer. Three hundred standing cups and other pieces were shown on 250 wall brackets and eight tables. The next space, the Hall of Precious Objects (*Pretiosensaal*), was the most spectacular of all (pl.2.72). Under a Renaissance vault, many hundreds of objects were shown on carved gilt brackets, seemingly infinitely replicated by the mirror-lined walls. Objects made of alabaster, lapis lazuli, agate, jasper, chalcedony and serpentine, along with shells, ostrich eggs and rock crystal, were carefully and systematically arranged by material to aid their study. In the corner was a room protected by an iron grille, filled with the small jewelled and enamelled products of Augustus's court workshops. But from this point on the room scheme raised the political temperature, with dynastic portraits in the window embrasures in the hall of precious objects, and next door a room with a set of cupboards containing, according to tradition, secret treaties and other similar material, on the doors of which were the arms of the territories of the royal house, including Poland and Lithuania.

The last room, designed to be the knock-out blow, was dedicated to jewellery and jewelled objects, most of it commissioned by Augustus himself. The wall cases contained sumptuous parures of the elector's personal jewellery, while at the centre were three *Kunststücke*, complex masterpieces by the court jeweller Johann Melchior Dinglinger. The gold tea and coffee set, adorned with enamels, lapis lazuli and ivory, had already played a role in matters of state, having been sent with much other precious material to Warsaw for the crowning of Augustus as the king of Poland in 1701, in order to help gain the support of the Polish nobility. The 'Court of the Great Moghul', representing in miniature the lavish birthday celebrations of an imaginary Asian ruler, was a vision of wealth and absolute power, embodied not only in its subject but also in the jewels and other precious materials from which it is made (pl.2.73). The Obeliscus Augustalis, created some 20 years after these works, was a *Kunststück* in architectural form, celebrating the power of the elector and king, constructed on a complex iconographical programme centred on a portrait enamel backed by trophies and surmounted by the elector's bonnet and the joint crown of Poland and Lithuania. It is a translation of an exterior obelisk carried out in a range of precious and other materials in a manner recalling the treatment of the Roman Baroque interior.

2.73 Court of the Great Moghul, Johann Melchior Dinglinger, Georg Christoph Dinglinger and workshop, Georg Friedrich Dinglinger, gold, silver, partially gilded, enamel, emeralds, pearls, lacquer painting. Dresden, 1701–8 (Grünes Gewölbe, Staatliche Kunstsammlungen Dresden)

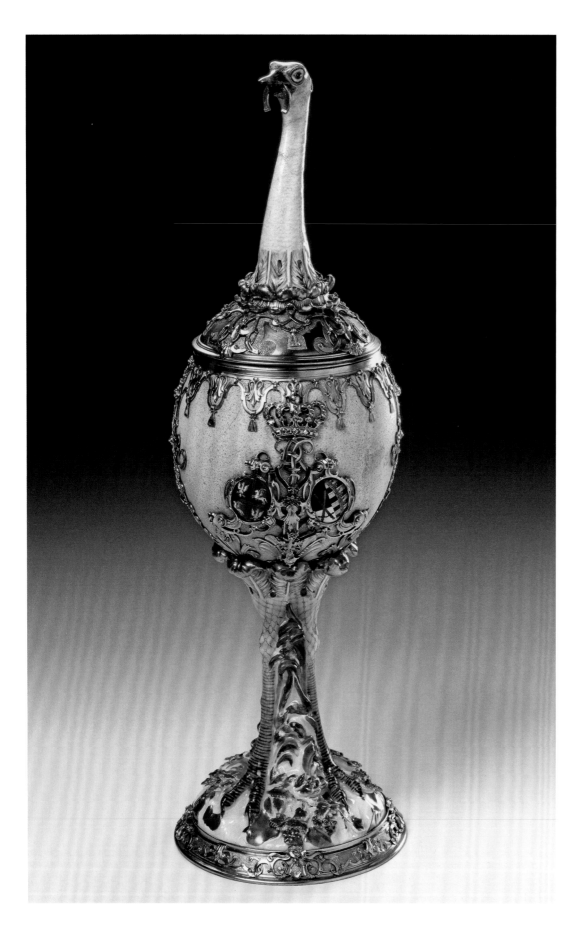

2.74 Ostrich egg cup, mark of Benjamin Herfurth and Johann Joachim Kändler. Dresden, 1734 (cat.47)

2.75 Lidded cup, probably mark of Wolfgang Howzer (metalwork). China (cup), 1630–40 and probably England (mounts), 1660–70 (cat.43)

2.76 Clock, Adriaan van den Bergh (movement) and Hans Coenraadt Breghtel (case). The Hague, 1650–75 (cat.28)

Magic Materials from Across the Sea

Among the collections from the Green Vault is an ostrich egg cup made to celebrate Augustus the Strong's second accession to the throne of Poland in 1734 (pl.2.74). Its tautological design, in which there is an interplay between the object's form and its material, is in a *Kunststück* tradition going back to the sixteenth century. But its exotic materials also say something else, for neither the porcelain nor the egg are from across the sea but are local Saxon products, the porcelain coming from the Meissen factory and the egg from a bird in the royal menagerie at Schloss Moritzburg. In one sense, the Court of the Great Moghul really had come to pass in Saxony.

Such a transfer was the logical conclusion of a fascination with cultures and products from outside Europe, and from Asia in particular, that accelerated in intensity in the early sixteenth century with the opening up of the trade routes to both the east and the west. By the mid-seventeenth century, with the expansion of the Dutch and English trading companies, Asian products, often made specifically for export, had ceased to be the unique preserve of the treasury and *Kunstkammer* and were becoming articles of trade and fashion. Chinese and Japanese porcelain took the lead (pl.2.75). 65 pieces of porcelain are recorded in the inventories of Charles I of England in 1649–51, while in 1681 Louis XIV ordered a porcelain service running to 1,508 pieces.[26] Also exported was Chinese and Japanese lacquer and Chinese and South Asian textiles and silver filigree. The fashion for filigree prompted extraordinary feats of skill by European makers in response (pl.2.76).

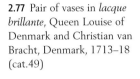

2.77 Pair of vases in *lacque brillante*, Queen Louise of Denmark and Christian van Bracht, Denmark, 1713–18 (cat.49)

2.78 Tulip vase on a wooden stand, Adrianus Koeks. Delft, before 1694 (vase), England or The Netherlands, probably 1700–50 (stand) (cat.44)

2.79 (*opposite*) Tea-table, makers unknown. Java, altered in England, *c*.1680, in the Duchess of Lauderdale's private closet at Ham House, London. The set of japanned chairs was made in the 1670s–80s in London. (cat.48)

Significantly, the demand for porcelain for the decoration of interiors was well in advance of the available imported materials, prompting the manufacture of imitations in tin-glazed earthenware, beginning in Delft in the 1640s (pl.2.78). The yearning for Delftware led to the setting up of factories elsewhere with the assistance of Dutch workers. The miniature palace of the Trianon de Porcelaine in the gardens of Versailles, built in 1670 for Louis XIV's mistress Madame de Montespan, was externally decorated in blue and white earthenware tiles in the Delft style. From the 1670s interiors in France, England, Holland and Germany were arrayed with porcelain and furnished with lacquer chests, cabinets and tables, moving an English economist to note that 'From the greatest gallants to the meanest cookmaids nothing is thought so fit to adorn their … closets like China and lacquered ware'.[27] Much lacquer, like the Javanese table of the Countess of Dysart (pl.2.79), had to be adapted for European use, but the demand for local versions, albeit made in painted varnish rather than true lacquer, was clearly indicated by the publication in 1688 of John Stalker and George Parker's *A treatise on Japanning and Varnishing … Together with an hundred distinctive patterns for japan-work, in imitation of the Indians*, aimed at both amateurs and professionals. Amateur lacquering and japanning could become a hobby at the highest social level, as the work done in the Danish court demonstrates (pl.2.77). The rage for

imitation lacquer even found its way into ceramics, decorating Meissen coffee pots made in red stoneware in the Chinese style (pls 2.80–2.81).

From about 1690, complete rooms were created in a mixed exotic style now called *chinoiserie*, in which the hundreds of pieces of porcelain were shown against mirrors or lacquer panels painted with 'Chinese' scenes (pl.2.83). At the palace of Oranienburg outside Berlin, named in honour of a Dutch queen, the porcelain in the Japanese Gallery of about 1695 is

displayed on prominent gilt-wood pyramidal stands carved in the fashionable Berlin acanthus style, backed by mirrors.

In the Porcelain Cabinet in the sister palace of Charlottenburg, created some ten years later, the porcelain and lacquer panels have become purely decorative highlights in a classical scheme carried out in gilt wood, beneath a painted ceiling (see pl.5.84). The mixed stylistic origin of such environments is exemplified by the turban-shaped lacquered vases that appeared among the massed architecturally disposed porcelain and Delft displays of Augustus the Strong's Japanisches Palais (pl.2.82).

2.81 Coffee pot, Meissen porcelain factory. Meissen, 1710–13 (cat.45)

2.80 Coffee pot, Meissen porcelain factory. Meissen, 1710–13 (cat.46)

2.82 Vase in the form of a turban, Martin Schnell. Dresden, 1715–21 (cat.50)

2.83 (*below*) Design for a chimney wall with lacquered panels and porcelain, Daniel Marot, etching and engraving. The Netherlands, *c.*1700 (Cooper-Hewitt Museum)

2.84 Dress fabric with 'bizarre' pattern, maker unknown, silk damask brocaded with coloured silks. Spitalfields, London, *c*.1708 (V&A:711-1864)

2.85 (*opposite*) The Haiyantang (Calm Sea Palace), one of the European pavilions at Yuanming Yuan, after Yi Lantai, engraving. Beijing, *c*.1786 (cat.26)

The appeal of these imported goods (and their imitations) lay not only in their sophisticated and fine materials but also in their novel decorative language and approach to design:

Among us the Beauty of Building and Planting is placed chiefly in some certain Proportions, Symmetries or Uniformities … but their [the Chinese] greatest Reach of the Imagination is employed in contriving Figures, where the Beauty shall be great and strike the Eye, but without any order or disposition of Parts, that shall commonly or easily be observ'd.… And whoever observes the Work upon the best *Indian* gowns, or the Painting upon the best Skreens or Purcellans, will find their Beauty is all of this kind [that is] without Order.[28]

The freedom allowed by a concept of beauty without order fed into the mainstream of Baroque design, most especially in the field of flat pattern in wallpapers and textiles, including the fantastical 'bizarre' silks (a modern term) whose overlapping layers of diagonally disposed asymmetrical ornament may be indebted to Japanese design (pl.2.84).

The impulse towards the exotic that lay behind *chinoiserie* was also a major factor in the creation of perhaps the best-known architectural expression of the Baroque in Asia, the western-style pavilions, with their fountains and gardens, in the Yuanming Yuan, the Summer Palace at Beijing, made for the Emperor Qianlong in 1747. Designed by the resident Jesuit artist Giuseppe Castiglione, the overall planning of the scheme was evidently inspired by European palace models, although much of the detail and ornament introduced Chinese elements (pl.2.85). The resulting mixture was a Chinese fantasy of Europe, designed as a display space for the emperor's numerous western gifts, which included tapestries in the *chinoiserie* style. But what was the main impulse? The emperor may have been trying to match the wonders of Versailles. He may also have been seeking to mirror the Chinese-style structures in Europe. What is clear, however, is that both the Chinese emperor, as the 'Son of Heaven', and the ruler of France, descendant of the Sun King, were laying claim to the whole world and using the Baroque style to do so.

CHAPTER 3

PERFORMANCE AND PERFORMATIVITY

Baroque Art and Design for the Theatre

Joanna Norman

The popularity of the Baroque style, across and beyond Europe, lay in its flexibility, its adaptability and its capacity to move onlookers. The style could effortlessly accommodate new materials, was employable in every conceivable situation and responded promptly to the ever-growing aspirations of its patrons. The performative impact of the Baroque was an especially powerful tool in the hands of expert practitioners. This chapter considers how Baroque art and design could engage with its audiences wherever it encountered them, not only in the royal palace but also in the performative art and design made for the theatre, the urban square and the high altar.

In July 1747 a select audience gathered in the Teatro Argentina in Rome to attend a 'dramatic composition' to

3.1 *Musical Celebration held in the Teatro Argentina, Rome, to celebrate the marriage of the Dauphin of France*, Giovanni Paolo Panini, oil on canvas. Rome, 1747 (Musée du Louvre)

celebrate the marriage of Louis, Dauphin of France, to Maria-Josefa of Saxony. Cardinal de la Rochefoucauld, the French ambassador to the Holy See, had rented what was usually a public theatre for the occasion and arranged for the temporary installation of 'the most charming paintings, and splendid rich decorations … and every other corresponding ornament for a royal celebration' in the royal French and Saxon colours of blue and red, illuminated with 1,000 candles.[1] With music by the Neapolitan Niccolò Jommelli and a libretto by Flaminio Scarselli, Professor of Eloquence at Bologna University and Secretary of the Bolognese Embassy in Rome, the work presented a sung 'conversation piece' between the gods, celebrating the virtue of Maria-Josefa and the bright future of France embodied in the Dauphin and his dynastic marriage. The work was performed three times, to audiences that included such eminent figures as the king of England, other foreign princes and ambassadors, 21 cardinals and even, at one of the performances, the pope himself (pl.3.1).[2]

As represented in a painting by Giovanni Paolo Panini, this most elaborate *festa* characterizes the visual experience of the Baroque theatre as it had developed over the course of the seventeenth and eighteenth centuries. Glittering candlelight, spectacular illusionistic sets and lavish costumes were all employed in conjunction with texts and music to produce ephemeral spectacles of magnificence and marvel. Far from mere entertainment, however, the theatre served as an arena of absolute control, a rigidly ordered space for the performance of a *Gesamtkunstwerk* in which these elements were carefully employed to manipulate audiences into participating in highly politicized dramatic events serving real aims of cultural politics and diplomacy.[3] In a world of constantly shifting political alliances, the theatre provided ruling élites with a means of fashioning their own identity and presenting themselves to the outside world and posterity, both through the theatrical events themselves and through their recording and transmission in print.[4]

This conscious deployment of theatre and spectacle for political purposes, while neither new nor exclusive to the Baroque, reached fresh levels of technical, artistic, literary and musical sophistication during the period. In addition, with the development of a new theatrical form, opera, and the establishment of the opera house, a new permanence and validity were accorded to the theatre, finding their greatest expression in the theatres built by the Bibiena family in the early to mid-eighteenth century. Typical of the Baroque, there were important regional and national variations. While Italy remained the most important source and influence on Baroque

theatre throughout much of Europe, Louis XIV's France presented an alternative vision, and perhaps the most consistent conscious programme of cultural policy in relation to the Baroque theatre, in the development and patronage during his reign of a new and distinctively French form, the *tragédie en musique* ('tragedy in music').

A multiplicity of theatrical genres existed in seventeenth-century Europe, including popular genres of physical theatre such as farce and *commedia dell'arte*, performed by troupes of travelling players on makeshift open-air stages, as well as 'sacred theatres' organized by religious bodies such as the Jesuits at key moments in the Church year, designed to divert but also to overawe and control the common populace through the use of visual spectacle (see Chapter Four). However, it was in the realm of dance and music drama, primarily the preserve of courts and other ruling elites, that the most sophisticated forms of entertainment took place. In England, the highly learned form of the masque, which reached its apogee in the 25-year-long collaboration between Inigo Jones (d.1652) and Ben Jonson (d.1637), was performed by members of the Stuart court supported by professionals. Such allegorical works as *Coelum Britannicum* (1634) employed erudite language together with music, lavish costumes and scenography to glorify the court itself, presenting it as a model for heaven, with the king himself dancing at the centre of an ideal microcosm.[5] In Italy, the celebration of significant political events such as diplomatic visits or dynastic births, marriages or coronations with a series of festivities, ranging from tournaments and jousts to theatrical performances, allowed courts to engage in a kind of cultural and festive diplomacy, transmitting messages to each other through their choice of subject matter and competing in lavishness and magnificence. It was as a result of these inter-court rivalries that a number of important developments had occurred in the first half of the seventeenth century which would help to standardize Baroque theatre. In Mantua, opera had been developed, thanks largely to the composer Monteverdi (d.1643) and the poet Striggio (d.1630) under the patronage of Duke Vincenzo Gonzaga, in direct competition with the earlier Florentine tradition of *intermezzi* or *intermedi*, sung and danced interludes, accompanied by spectacular effects and performed between the acts of straight drama; in Parma, the Teatro Farnese, built by Aleotti in 1618–28, thought to be the first permanent theatre equipped with sliding wings, was deliberately conceived in order to surpass the technology of the Teatro Mediceo in the Uffizi, built by Buontalenti in 1586.

It was, however, not as part of court life but in the commercial city of Venice that Baroque theatre developed as a result of the establishment of this new operatic genre. Opera was not immediately successful at the courts, which preferred the more participatory entertainments mentioned above, but it was perfectly suited to a republican city that was also a great tourist centre thriving on the Venetian myth of magnificence, luxury and spectacle. This was particularly true during the Carnival season, which ran from 26 December to Shrove Tuesday – the day before Lent began – and served as a period of festivity, entertainment and excess before the privations and fasting that Lent would bring. The rapid rise of opera in Venice is shown by the fact that four new theatres were established in the city between 1637 and 1641, specifically for the production of opera, all under private ownership and each with a capacity of 2,000–3,000. The Venetian theatre rejected the form of the court theatre, with its open banks of seating and fluid relationship between stage and auditorium, both regarded as performative zones, in favour of the commercial playhouse or box theatre, which imposed a strict separation between stage and auditorium with tiers of individual boxes for spectators lining the walls from floor to ceiling. This form was naturally far better suited to the mercantile ethos of Venice, as each box could be sold or rented out for a season, serving both as an effective means of social control by separating those in the boxes from those standing in the parterre, and as a means of generating income.[6] The commercial climate of this great city also had a significant effect on the musical development of opera: the huge choruses and large orchestras that characterized court entertainments, impressing audiences through sheer scale, were wholly unsuitable to a tightly-run financial enterprise needing to limit its outgoings. Instead, organized by musical impresarios, Venetian opera developed as a showcase for virtuosic singers, whose popularity could make or break a production and guarantee the success or failure of a theatre. This context also greatly encouraged the proliferation of new works: unable to rely on court patronage, theatres had to compete with each other and satisfy the paying public's desire for new and entertaining works, in order to earn the revenue necessary to sustain the actual theatres but also to maintain the economic stability of the city itself.

It was also primarily in Venice that perspectival sets and spectacular machinery were developed, under the control of Giacomo Torelli (1608–78). At the Teatro Novissimo, which opened in 1641 with a performance of *La Finta Pazza* ('The Feigned Madwoman'), acclaimed for its four appearances of gods descending to the stage in machines during the production, Torelli improved on the technology that had been so ground-breaking in Parma some years before. The new

mechanism operated sliding wings: by attaching canvas flats to a wheeled undercarriage mounted on runners beneath the stage, one set of wings could be pushed on-stage through slits in the floor while another was pulled off. Torelli also had an innovative central winch mechanism installed under the stage to operate all the sets of wings simultaneously, as can still be seen in surviving theatres such as that at Český Krumlov in the Czech Republic. This allowed the whole stage set to be changed in only a few seconds. Not only did this create far greater possibilities for scenic variety, but it made the scene changes an integral part of the spectacle, as they took place in full view of the audience, who marvelled at the rapid transformation of the stage into a completely different setting. This variety was increased by the use of certain generic types of set, including ruins, paradise, inferno, a temple square, a seascape, mountains and crags, which could be varied by lowering backdrops at different points on the stage to create 'long', 'medium' and 'short' scenes.[7]

Central-point perspective, to which the arrangement of several pairs of wings receding towards a backdrop naturally lent itself, was used to create the illusion of infinite stage depth. This, however, was problematic: first, the scale needed to create such false perspective meant that performers were limited to using the front of the stage for fear of ruining the illusion were they to move further back, their persons being wholly out of proportion with the fictive scene represented.[8] Secondly, such perspectival and symmetrical sets favoured a privileged viewer seated in the optimum location in the auditorium from which the entire effect could best be appreciated. This was entirely fitting for a court theatre, where it was wholly desirable that the privileged figure of the ruler should be the only one able to appreciate the spectacle in its entirety, and it also served to direct the audience's attention towards the ruler as the real focus of the event. It was not ideal, however, for the public context of Venice, in which paying spectators were subject to poor sightlines and distorted effects from the boxes lining the often flat walls of the theatres (pl.3.2).

In combination with perspectival sets, much of the visual illusion produced on stage was created by spectacular machines and special effects of various kinds. With the establishment of permanent theatres, built with space above and below the stage specifically to house the necessary machinery, the capacity for these effects became much greater. A set of seventeenth-century designs in Parma, probably produced for the Teatro Farnese, shows the scale and complexity of such machines. Among others, there are designs for a 'machine to carry eight people, which is closed at the beginning and gradually opens

Teatro Grimani
a S. Giovanni Grisostomo

in a circle to form the rays of the sun' (pl.3.3). This clearly strove for an effect similar to that suggested by Francesco Carini Motta, ducal architect at the Gonzaga court, in his 1676 treatise on scenography, which included details of cloud machines, musical effects and lighting, with clouds being lit internally, using torches to create the effect of the sun.[9] In addition to machines appearing in the upper zone of the stage, there were others such as wave machines, which operated at stage level, either from the rear of the stage, as proposed by Nicola Sabbattini in his *Pratica di fabricar scene e machine ne' teatri* (1638), or rising from trapdoors in the stage floor to create popular effects for marine scenes.[10] Other special effects such as rain, wind and thunder were generally produced off-stage. A slatted drum with a piece of canvas stretched over it was used to create the effect of wind, while dried peas were poured into a tall thin box studded with pieces of metal to imitate the sound of rain. The thunder machine comprised a long wooden box set in a seesaw-like contraption and attached to a pulley, used to lift one end of the box, which would then cause stones inside to roll around, projecting the threatening sound of thunder from above the stage, where it was situated.[11]

The visual impact of these machines, combined with illusionistic sets, was clearly spectacular: John Evelyn, attending the opera in Venice in 1645, praised the 'variety of scenes painted and contrived with no less art of perspective, and machines for flying in the air, and other wonderful notions'.[12] It is, however, hard to judge the full scenic effect given the challenge of reconstructing Baroque theatre lighting. Auditoria were lit by candles, their light flickering in reflective mirror sconces, as well as by chandeliers (sometimes also used on stage), which could in some theatres be raised or lowered. Contemporary representations of theatrical performances, however, generally do not include these, as they hung very low, obstructing the view of the action. With regard to stage lighting, we are fortunate that some original lights survive from court theatres such as Český Krumlov and Drottningholm, which help to convey something of the impact that these would have had on the stage effect. The various ways of lighting the stage could be combined if needed: footlights at the front could be raised or lowered from beneath to lighten or darken the stage. Similarly, candles hung on brackets on the rear side of wings could be turned away from the stage to darken it.

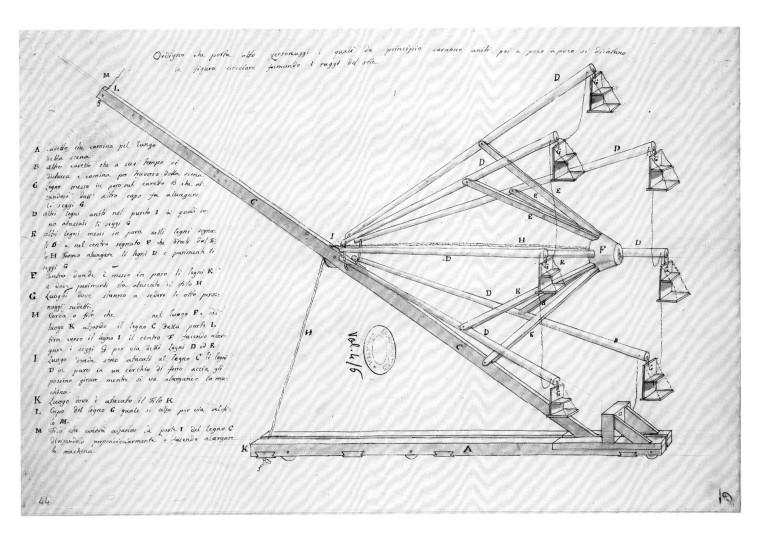

3.3 Design for a stage machine for the Teatro Farnese in Parma, artist unknown, pen, ink and wash over graphite. 1600–1700 (Archivio di Stato di Parma)

3.2 (*opposite*) *Teatro Grimani in Venice*, Vincenzo Coronelli, engraving. 1709 (Museo Civico Correr)

Theatre lighting was problematic (and perilous): lamps were cheaper than candles but were generally fuelled by animal fat, which filled the space with unpleasant smells and acrid smoke, not conducive to audiences' understanding or enjoyment of the entertainment.[13]

These conditions, in turn, affected the way that costumes and props were designed, as can be seen from the small number of Baroque theatre costumes surviving today. Costumes were, of course, an inherent part of the visual spectacle, and, particularly for smaller theatres, were often designed as multi-purpose garments that could be worn for different kinds of events, including ballet, opera and masquerades. Serving primarily to contribute to the visual interest and magnificence of productions through their variety and decoration, they were copiously adorned with cheap materials – metallic braid, paste jewels and gilt thread – to catch the light and create a rich effect.

Together with large numbers of costume designs, often annotated by designers with details of the fabrics and colours to be used, these few surviving costumes serve to highlight something of the splendid impression that they must have made on the Baroque stage. Male characters appeared dressed in short costumes derived from those of Roman heroes, this so-called 'Roman habit' (*habit à la romaine*) made up of a 'breastplate, plumed helmet, short skirt called a *tonnelet* and buskins' conveying the dignity and seriousness appropriate for such tragic and noble figures (pl.3.4).[14]

Conversely, decorum dictated that female characters should appear in rich, full-length and contemporary fashionable dress, which even, on occasion, extended as far as their hairstyles: in a 1670s production of *Alceste* in Paris, the hairstyle worn by the actress playing the part of Thétis was described as 'à la Sévigné', referring to the well-known contemporary epistolist Madame de Sévigné.[15] In addition, designers possessed a huge vocabulary of exotic or curious costumes, still popular from the days of the English masque (pl.3.5) and, particularly, the French *ballet de cour*. Among the many costume designs surviving from the seventeenth-century Parisian stage are a large number of designs of this sort, which catered to contemporary taste for the exotic: designs for Chinese or Turkish characters, some informed by real events such as the visit of the ambassador of the king of Siam to Versailles, others comic and absurd.[16]

3.4 Man's theatre costume, maker unknown. Italy, 1740–60 (cat.59)

3.5 (*opposite*) Design for the costume of a masquer Lord in the role of a star, pen and ink and watercolour heightened with gold and silver, Inigo Jones. London, 1613 (Devonshire Collection, Chatsworth)

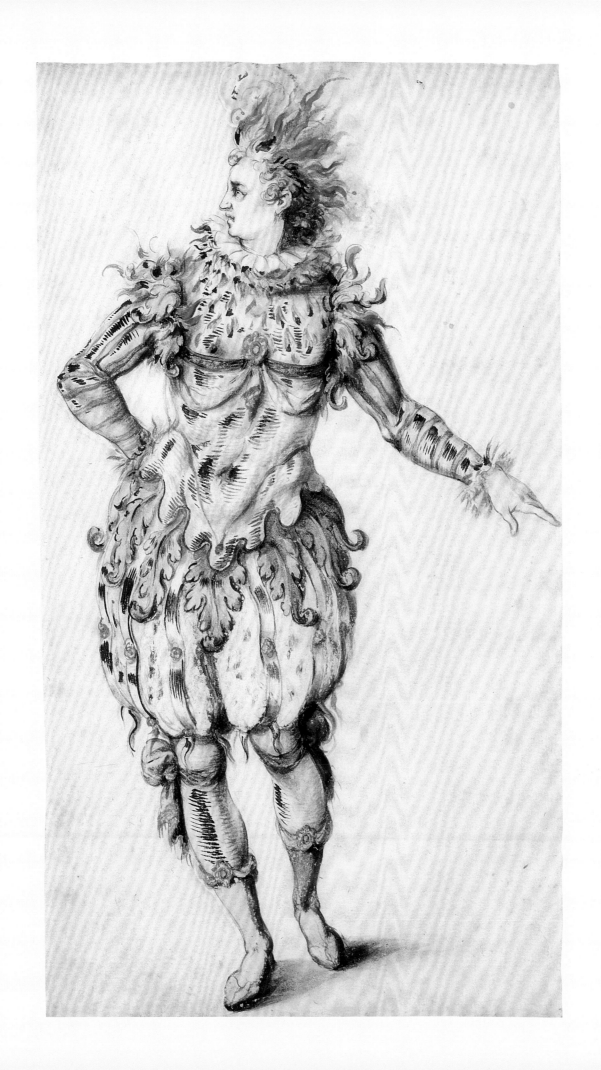

THE THEATRE AT ČESKÝ KRUMLOV

Joanna Norman

The castle theatre of Český Krumlov, located on the River Vltava in southern Bohemia, is a very rare case study of a Baroque court theatre that survives almost intact. Recently restored to its original state and retaining an exceptional quantity of stage sets, machinery, props and costumes, the theatre offers an unrivalled source of information about the life of a small but theatrically active court in mid-eighteenth-century central Europe.

Although a permanent theatre was first built in the castle in the 1680s, the current theatre and most of its fittings (pl.3.6) date from 1762–6, when Prince Josef Adam von Schwarzenberg refurbished the entire castle complex. For his theatre, by now a fairly standard element of many courts, Prince Josef brought architects, set designers and machinists from the imperial court of Vienna, the most important and fashionable centre in this part of Europe. Among them were Leo Maerkel and Johann Wetschel, set designers who may have trained with members of the Bibiena family in Vienna and who produced 13 complete sets in this style for Český Krumlov. Their sets follow the generic types established by the Bibiena, including the 'Columned Hall' (pl.3.7), which presents a symmetrical vision of Salomonic columns disappearing to a central vanishing point at the rear of the stage, while another backdrop presents a *scena per angolo*. The sets were operated with the traditional sliding wings system of winches and ropes beneath the stage, and annual performances in the theatre today using the same mechanism show the astonishing effect of an entire scene change achieved in only six seconds. In addition, a wave machine was installed at the back of the stage, four trap-doors in the stage allowed for spectacular appearances and disappearances, while other machines operated from above to facilitate the movement of 'heavenly' machines, and special effects machines were used from the wings to create rain, thunder and wind effects (pl.3.8). A small court orchestra was installed in a shallow pit in front of the stage, and played from one long, double-sided music stand, still in use today.

3.6 Two side wings from the 'Columned Hall' set, Leo Maerkel and Johann Wetschel. Český Krumlov, 1766

3.7 View of the interior and stage of the Castle Theatre, with the 'Columned Hall' set, painted by Leo Maerkel and Johann Wetschel. Český Krumlov, 1762–6

3.8 Wave Machine, Castle Theatre. Český Krumlov, c.1766

3.9 Cupid's bow and arrows, theatre props, maker unknown. Český Krumlov, 1750–1800 (cat.55)

Unfortunately, there are no visual records of performances taking place in the theatre but the large number and variety of texts, libretti and scores kept in the castle library imply that they were extremely varied in nature, with some works, such as Giuseppe Scarlatti's *Dove è amore è gelosia* of 1768, commissioned specifically for Český Krumlov. This idea is also supported by the theatre itself: the stage is, unusually, barely raked at all, suggesting that a large number of ballets were performed there by courtiers rather than professionals, while the numerous surviving costumes and props show a similar diversity, ranging from Roman-style and exotic opera costumes to *commedia dell'arte* masks and props (pl.3.9). Such diversity testifies not only to the varied interests and tastes of Prince Josef himself, but also to the sorts of entertainments performed for the diversion of the emperor on his occasional visits to Český Krumlov, through which the Schwarzenberg rulers demonstrated the magnificence of their own court but, more importantly, their loyalty and subservience to the emperor himself.

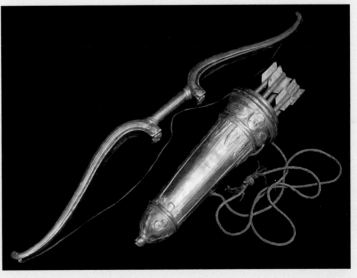

Ideas for the costumes of the allegorical figures who populated opera and drama were often taken from Cesare Ripa's *Iconologia*, first published in Rome in 1593 and the most influential source-book for such designs, republished in a number of languages and editions during the seventeenth century.[17] Other source-books included Bolzano's *Hieroglyphica*, published nine years after the *Iconologia*, Vecellio's *Habiti Antichi* (owned in its 1598 edition by Inigo Jones and used for his first masquing designs) and Callot's prints. Ballet was dominated by short costumes to facilitate ease of movement, although the gestures of the dancers were severely limited by the weight of the copious embroidery. These ballet gestures depicted in the surviving costume designs and prints formed part of a commonly understood but flexible language, codified to represent particular sentiments or moods, related to the codification of the representation of the passions by Charles Le Brun. Masks and props served as characters' allegorical attributes, such as Cupid's Bow and Arrows (see pl.3.9). Impressively gilded to catch the flickering candlelight, these props and accessories exploited the cheapness and light weight of *papier-mâché*, as costumes used cheap but visually impressive materials.

Even musical instruments could serve a dual aural and visual purpose. Anthropomorphic instruments were particularly appropriate for 'infernal' scenes populated by demons or dragons, for which the low, menacing sound of the bassoon would have been well suited (pl.3.11). More conventional musical accompaniment came from the orchestra, placed in front of the stage in a forerunner to the modern orchestra pit, and consisting of small numbers of string, woodwind, brass and continuo players, directed from the harpsichord. Often the instrumentalists who performed in the theatre were those who played in court orchestras such as Louis XIV's *24 Violons du Roi*, a small string ensemble that provided the music for opera and ballet as well as for the king's private entertainment, and which was emulated by Charles II in London, following his return from exile in France (pl.3.10).

3.10 Violin carved with the royal Stuart arms (rear view), attributed to Ralph Agutter. London, *c*.1685 (cat.54)

3.12 Costume design for Hercules in *Atys*, Jean Berain. Paris, 1676 (cat.58)

3.11 Bassoon in the form of a sea dragon, maker unknown. Italy, 1600–50 (cat.56)

The Theatre as a Permanent Building

The kind of theatre described above, technically equipped for rapid scene changes and numerous special effects, became the standard requirement for both public opera house and court theatre. The design was disseminated from Italy throughout Europe as opera took hold as the predominant genre of theatrical performance during the second half of the seventeenth century, and as the potential of the permanent theatre building began to be better understood both within and beyond Italy. In Rome, a city whose theatrical life depended on papal support, there were various attempts to build permanent theatres under the patronage of aristocratic families and individuals, most notably the Barberini, under Pope Urban VIII (1623–44), and Queen Christina of Sweden, whose Teatro di Tordinona opened in 1671 as a public venue, designed by Carlo Fontana. One of the most significant seventeenth-century permanent theatres in Italy was Francesco d'Este's Teatro della Spelta in Modena, the new ducal capital, built by Gaspare Vigarani in 1656 in a former granary. Unfortunately no visual record of it survives, but it was undoubtedly the most impressive theatre of its day, with a large stage fitted with the most up-to-date machinery, also designed by Vigarani. While its primary function was to serve as the setting for spectacular performances, its secondary but longer-lasting purpose was as a symbol of authority for the Este rulers, exiled from their native Ferrara in 1598; the theatre offered them a means of imposing their presence on their new ducal capital of Modena: the appropriation of a communal space for a court theatre served as an overt statement by Francesco d'Este that the city was now subject to the court, and that this court had the artistic and economic wherewithal to compete in the world of cultural politics on a European level.[18]

Meanwhile, in a Europe-wide wave of theatre construction, the early 1650s saw Philip IV of Spain restoring and enlarging the Coliseo theatre at the Buen Retiro palace in Madrid, while the Spanish viceroys of Naples and Milan built their own opera houses. Opera proved its adaptability to non-Italian contexts, spreading throughout the German-speaking lands and as far afield as Poland, while the Mantuan architect Giovanni Burnacini was commissioned to build a new imperial theatre 'with prodigious Machines' in Vienna.[19] In England, the theatre was revived at the Restoration although initially influenced by French rather than Italian inspiration, as a result of Charles II's exile in France. The Dorset Garden Theatre was built in London in 1671, specifically equipped with changeable scenery and lighting effects, and played host to embryonic forms of English opera such as Purcell's *The Fairy Queen*.

Louis XIV and Baroque Theatre in France

While Italy remained the dominant force in Baroque theatre design, exporting musical and design ideas through print as well as artists, musicians and 'machinists' to courts in the German-speaking and Spanish territories, France offered an alternative approach, which was not, however, entirely immune to Italian influence. Under the patronage of Cardinal Mazarin, there had been various attempts to introduce Italian opera into France, assisted by the exodus of Italian librettists, musicians and designers, including Torelli, from Rome to Paris at the death of Urban VIII. There was a clear nationalistic intention behind Mazarin's policy: that French practitioners would learn from these established Italian masters in order then to supersede them and produce a form of French opera that would serve as a cultural export and thereby increase France's status as the Continent's principal artistic centre. However, although individual works, including hybrid Italian–French spectacles, enjoyed some success, the policy did not entirely work. The critical French public found the music too discordant for its more conservative tastes, and was bored by a five-hour work sung in a language it did not understand. In addition, the complex and numerous scene changes so beloved of Italian opera were at odds with the strict conventions applied to French drama, such as the rule of the 'three unities', which dictated that time, place and action should be consistent within a dramatic work to ensure plausibility or *vraisemblance* and which placed an absolute primacy on text, unlike the Italian tradition which was concerned primarily with visual spectacle. Finally, attempts to import an Italian form in the politically volatile 1640s clashed with the anti-Mazarin and anti-Italian sentiment that erupted in the *Fronde*, the uprising of Louis's nobles against him, during which *castrati* singers were hounded and many Italian musicians and theatre professionals were forced into quick marriages with French brides or into gallicizing their names in order to survive. As at the early seventeenth-century Italian courts, French court audiences preferred participating in entertainments rather than watching them, and were particularly fond of the traditional *ballet de cour*. This kind of entertainment shared various similarities with the Florentine *intermezzi*, a series of dances by a cast of allegorical, grotesque or mythological characters, within a loose dramatic framework and danced by members of the court including the royal family.

Like his father before him, the young Louis XIV danced in these entertainments in a variety of roles, most notably in the *Ballet Royal de la Nuict* of 1653, his first appearance in the guise of Apollo. This magnificent spectacle, comprising 53 entries with over 250 costumes and ten changeable sets, was produced to mark the new political settlement that followed the *Fronde*. The performance took place over the course of a whole night each of its four parts representing a three-hour period with a series of varied and sometimes unrelated scenes. Louis's appearance came at the most dramatic moment: at dawn, he rose as Apollo, sun god and patron of the arts (pl.3.13). While it celebrated the end of civic troubles and ushered in a new era of peace and prosperity, the *Ballet Royal de la Nuict* also asserted the king's godlike status and absolute control over his subjects to ensure that such a rebellion could not happen again. Reinforcing this ground-breaking representation of the royal image, the *Ballet Royal de la Nuict* also marked the transition in French theatrical practice from hall floor to stage, placing Louis at the absolute centre of the spectacle and thus of the court.[20] It was a great success, lauded for the '*pompe superbe des habits*' and '*magnificence des machines*'.

APOLLON.   LE ROY.

3.13 Costume design for Louis XIV as Apollo, Henry Gissey or workshop. Paris, possibly 1654 (cat.63)

3.14 (*opposite*) *Charles XI of Sweden as Apollo Pythias*, David Klöcker Ehrenstrahl, Stockholm, 1670–71 (cat.62)

As with the opera, however, attempts to build a permanent theatre in Paris on the Italian model foundered. The Salle des Machines in the Tuileries was constructed to celebrate Louis XIV's 1659 marriage to Maria Theresa of Austria, the Spanish Infanta, as the city was ill-equipped with theatre buildings and court entertainments often took place in temporary structures. The permanent structures that did exist, such as the Palais Royal and Grande Salle of the Louvre, were not grand enough for a royal wedding. Originally intended to occupy the Palais Royal, but moved to a specifically built additional wing in the Palais des Tuileries, the *Salle des Machines* was designed to inaugurate not only the royal marriage, but also a new era of French magnificence and supremacy in the performing arts, for which it would offer the most impressive setting in Europe. Vigarani, the architect of Francesco d'Este's theatre in Modena, was brought specifically to Paris to carry out this work. The *Salle des Machines* certainly fulfilled these requirements in some physical aspects: surpassing the Modenese theatre, the *Salle des Machines* had the deepest indoor stage ever built, equipped, as the name implies, with the most up-to-date technological equipment for stage machines. Unfortunately, however spectacular it was visually, acoustically it was a disaster: partly as a result of the depth of the stage, nothing of the music or text could be heard. Inaugurated in February 1662 with the Italian opera *Ercole Amante* ('Hercules in Love'), interspersed as usual with ballets in which the king himself danced, the *Salle des Machines* was not used again until 1671 and only sporadically after that, and Louis refocused his theatrical attentions on the power of performance rather than its physical setting.[21]

Through the ministry of Colbert Louis XIV returned to the idea of creating a French national form of music drama that would challenge the supremacy of Italian opera.[22] Although the French *ballet de cour* continued to enjoy strong support, it was such an inherently French form that it could neither be exported nor could it rival the dramatic and musical appeal of Italian opera to audiences of other nationalities. The establishment of the state-run Royal Academy of Music in 1669 and the development of the *tragédie en musique* by Jean-Baptiste Lully and Philippe Quinault in the 1670s created such a national form; although it never managed to rival the enduring popularity of Italian opera across Europe, it served as an important instrument of cultural policy within France.

After the *Fronde*, the nobility's threat to the crown was perceived as a very real one, and the theatre offered a means of both controlling and diverting potentially troublesome courtiers, whose presence at such spectacles was virtually compulsory, while also glorifying the king and asserting his absolute authority through the chosen subject matter of the operas. Together with the other arts such as literature, painting and sculpture, which were also centrally controlled by Academies, music and opera formed an important element of the careful construction and presentation of the public image of Louis XIV, a crucial component of the so-called 'department of glory' (see Opera, p.156).[23]

After the failure of the *Salle des Machines*, French court performances generally took place at the Palais Royal or at Saint-Germain-en-Laye. Although the Academy of Music was housed in a wing of the Palais Royal, and Lully, its director, was protected by the king, it received no financial support from the crown, necessitating a considerable degree of reliance on the city of Paris as well as on Louis XIV's court for revenue. This meant that the works had to satisfy a paying public audience as well as one of courtiers, but it did also bring certain benefits: Lully was able to make use of his position to rehearse and première his *tragédies en musique* at court and then to perform them in Paris, using the same sets, machines and costumes that had been created for the court.[24] Although the Parisian theatres might remain inadequate in comparison with those in Italy and other Italian-influenced locations, their stage equipment nonetheless allowed for the spectacular effects that were popular with public French audiences, even if numerous set changes were not. In 1681 Jules Menéstrier categorized the different kinds of machines in use on the French stage in his *Des représentations en musique anciennes et modernes*, listing eleven types: 'celestial, sacred, military, rustic or pastoral, maritime, royal, civil, historical, poetic, magic, academic'. The *Gazette de France* reported in 1671 that a production of *Psyché* had included a grand finale in which all the gods and goddesses and the whole palace of Jupiter descended from above on a machine of enormous scale, impressing (and slightly alarming) courtiers and foreigners alike with its magnificent and diverse scenic effects. Machines created their own technical challenges, however, and were not always to audiences' tastes: in April 1695 Jean-Nicolas du Tralage described a 'maritime' machine in *Théagène et Chariclée* as follows:

Mlle Desmatins, playing Thetis, sits in a very large scallop shell carried on the narrow but round back of a dolphin: she comes on from one side of the stage and is only seen in profile, which has a very displeasing effect. One fears that at the slightest movement of the sea monster, the whole machine will overturn and the actress will be injured.... All that needs to be done is to have the seashell carried by two dolphins facing the audience: the spectacle would be more beautiful and without danger [pl.3.15].[25]

3.15 Design for the Chariot of Thetis in *Alceste*, Jean Berain and workshop, pen, ink and wash, Paris, 1674–8 (Musée du Louvre). The 'maritime' machine is similar to that criticized by Jean-Nicolas du Tralage in 1695, while Thetis wears a so-called *à la Sévigné* hairstyle

Opera

Joanna Norman

In its fusion of music, poetry, painting, lighting and engineering, opera can be seen as the archetypal Baroque art form. Conceived in Italy with the aim of recreating the ancient Greek form of music drama, it alternated recitative, a form of sung dialogue used to convey the plot, with arias, which provided the opportunity for virtuosic displays by the famous singers who, together with the visual spectacle of numerous set changes and fantastic machines, were the main attraction for audiences.

As it took root and evolved across Europe, however, opera began to lose its dramatic integrity. Arias increased in length and elaboration to become mere showcases for singers, while plots became increasingly outlandish and entangled to justify the ever more technologically

complex and awe-inspiring machines that its novelty-seeking audiences demanded.

In response to this, and wishing France to supersede Italy as the primary cultural centre, Louis XIV and his minister Colbert promoted efforts to create a form of French opera with real dramatic cohesion in which text, music and machines would be of equal importance, which would suit the French language and taste, but also be exportable to other countries. The Royal Academy of Music was therefore established in 1669 'to represent in public operas and representations in music and in the French language, the same and similar to those of Italy'. In 1673 the librettist Philippe Quinault and the Italian-born violinist and composer in charge of the Académie, Jean-Baptiste Lully, produced the

3.16 Dream scene from Lully's *Atys*, watched by the French court, Jasper van der Borght and Jérome Leclerc, wool and silk tapestry. Brussels, *c*.1700 (Schloss Charlottenburg)

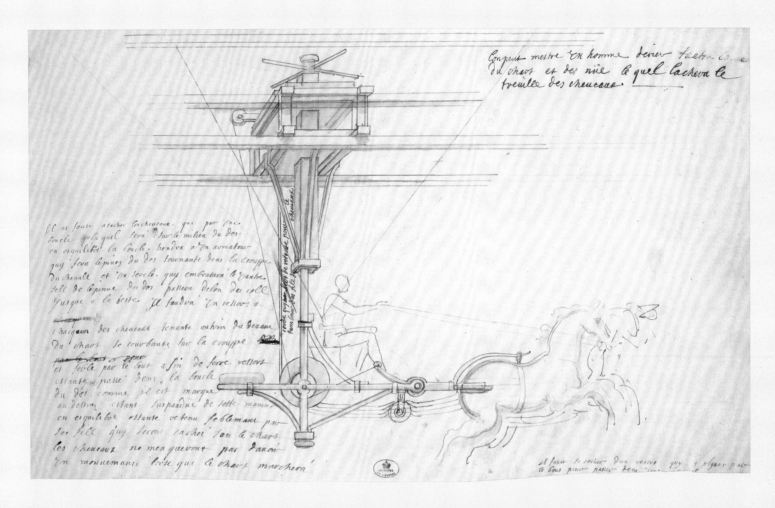

(handwritten French annotations surrounding the drawing)

3.17 Design for the chariot of the sun, for *Phaéton*, Jean Berain, graphite. Paris, 1683 (Archives Nationales, Paris)

3.18 Frontispiece to Handel's opera *Rinaldo*, engraving. London, 1711 (V&A)

first *tragédie en musique*, or 'tragedy in music': *Cadmus et Hermione*. This placed a greater importance on the text than did Italian opera, with Quinault consciously imitating the great French tragedians Corneille and Racine. It also differed musically, merging the contrasting styles of recitative and aria into a more fluid and continuous style of singing better suited to the French language.

The *tragédie en musique* served perfectly as an element of the cultural propaganda machine of Louis XIV. The dramatic plots, taken from mythology or epic poetry, could symbolize the life of the king, while the prologues preceding the operas overtly praised him. This could on occasion backfire, however: in 1677 *Isis* scandalized Paris with its plot based on the infidelities of the god Jupiter, assumed by audiences to refer to Louis XIV's supposed infatuation at that time with Isabelle de Ludres and the consequent severe displeasure of his *maîtresse en titre*, Madame de Montespan.

Performed both at court and in the city, the *tragédie en musique* had to please very different audiences. *Atys*, first performed in January 1676, was repeated several times at court and became known as 'the king's opera', but in the city, although praised for its beautiful sets, magnificent costumes and highly inventive scenes, it was thought insufficiently spectacular (pl.3.16). In contrast, *Phaéton*, with its sophisticated machine representing the fall and death of the central character at the end of the work, was less pleasing to the king but immensely popular in Paris, and became known as 'the people's opera' (pl.3.17).

However successful it might have been in France, however, the *tragédie en musique* failed to appeal to other audiences. Despite criticism for the terrible diction and acting ability of its frequently caricatured, quarrelsome performers, Italian opera remained popular across Europe. Even in London, hitherto more receptive to French than Italian influence, audiences were so impressed by George Frideric Handel's *Rinaldo*, performed when he visited the city in 1711, that he was made director of the Royal Academy of Music at the King's Theatre, Haymarket, in 1720, thus inaugurating a period of musical activity in London that produced some of the finest Baroque operas, still very much part of the repertoire today (pl.3.18).

Although Italian opera itself may have been unsuccessful in France, Italians retained the principal positions of designers and machinists in Paris. Torelli, the initial favourite, was exiled as a result of his direct involvement in the overly lavish entertainment at the château of Vaux-le-Vicomte, which led to the disgrace of Louis XIV's minister Nicolas Fouquet; thereafter it was Vigarani, from Modena, who served as principal designer and machinist. Only in 1680 did a Frenchman, Jean Berain, take over as Designer of the King's Bedchamber and Cabinet, where his tasks included producing 'all kinds of drawings, perspectives, figures and costumes … for plays, ballets, running at the ring and carousels'.[26] Despite having emerged from French rather than Italian tradition, utilizing the standard set types with which French audiences were familiar and conforming to Corneille's principle of only one set per act, Berain acknowledged the absolutist emphasis on precedence by continuing to design sets in the style of Torelli, focused on the central privileged viewpoint of the king, an arrangement that must, by the end of the seventeenth century, have looked rather outmoded.[27] He was not so successful as a machinist, however: his machines for Lully and Quinault's *Proserpine* in 1680 were so inadequate that Lully was forced to call on the services of Ercole Rivani, a Bolognese machinist lauded for his 'surprising machines' and 'very particular invention'.[28] After the French court's permanent move to Versailles, however, and in particular towards the end of the century, Louis XIV's interest in theatre waned and there was little innovation, with productions generally recycling earlier designs and machines and audiences expressing boredom at the lack of new ideas. France's Baroque phase of theatrical glory was over, and it was once more Italy that provided fertile ground for innovation and ideas that would be influential across Europe and beyond.

The Galli Bibiena Family

Towards the end of the seventeenth and particularly in the first half of the eighteenth century, by which time opera had become a fully established and codified genre across much of Europe, the physical building of the Baroque theatre reached full fruition and new levels of sophistication, principally as a result of the rise and spread of the Galli Bibiena dynasty. This family of architects and designers (mostly of and for theatres) originated from Bologna; they were trained in and taught the *quadratura* manner of painting, particularly popular in the region of Emilia-Romagna, where the walls of palaces, villas and even some churches were often decorated with fictive vistas depicting staircases, gardens or landscapes.[29] In the last years of the seventeenth century the brothers Francesco and Ferdinando Galli Bibiena established themselves by producing stage sets for a number of theatres across Italy, including those at Bologna, Parma, Venice, Turin, Rome and Naples. It was, however, Francesco's call to Vienna in 1699, to build the imperial opera house, that really paved the way for the phenomenon of the family's success across much of Europe.

Vienna already had a strong theatrical tradition, thanks largely to a series of dynastic marriages between emperors and Italian princesses, most notably Eleonora di Gonzaga who, when she married Emperor Ferdinand III in 1651, brought with her the best singers and musicians from her native Mantua as well as the theatre architect Giovanni Burnacini.[30] When Giovanni's son Ludovico inherited his father's position, one of his earliest projects was to construct a theatre on the Cortina (now Josefsplatz), which accommodated 2,000 spectators and 1,000 performers. The theatre opened in July 1668 in the presence of the young Empress Margherita, with a production of *Il Pomo d'Oro* (The Golden Apple), a celebration of the Habsburg family: one of the most spectacular theatrical entertainments of the Baroque, far surpassing the productions in the Teatro della Spelta and the Salle des Machines and using 23 sets which were apparently changed 50 times during the course of the performance. The opening scene alone set the tone for the rest of the spectacle. It represented the apotheosis of Emperor Leopold I, depicted on a rearing horse above a heap of trophies, at the rear of a perspectival set of Corinthian columns. In among these columns were flat pieces of scenery representing 12 equestrian statues of the lesser rulers of the Holy Roman Empire and the personification of Austrian Glory, who appeared riding a winged horse above putti crowning the emperor with an enormous laurel wreath.[31] The work ended with the eponymous golden apple being given not to one of the three goddesses as related in classical myth, but to Margherita

3.19 *The Theatre of the Glory of Austria and Apotheosis of Leopold I*: set design for the Prologue to *Il Pomo d'Oro*, Matthäus Küsel after Ludovico Burnacini, engraving. Vienna, 1668 (Kunstbibliothek)

herself, represented as both the most beautiful woman in the world and also the wisest in her decision to marry Leopold. Burnacini's work in this and in similarly impressive productions laid Vienna's foundations as an important theatrical centre, thereby also opening up a new geographical area of competition in inter-court cultural politics (pl.3.19).[32]

Burnacini's theatre was destroyed in the siege of 1683, and Emperor Leopold I commissioned Francesco Galli Bibiena to construct a suitably magnificent replacement for the regular performance of Italian opera in the former 'Grossen Comoedi Sall' of the Hofburg imperial palace. A 1704 engraving shows the splendour of the auditorium with its illusionistic painted ceiling and hugely prominent two-storey imperial box occupying the whole of the rear wall. This expression of imperial authority built into the permanent fabric was a new and highly significant departure: previously, the ruler's seat or dais had been on the parterre level and had often been movable, to allow him both the best possible experience as a spectator and to dance in the court ballets that often ended performances. The creation of the imperial box definitively broke with the tradition of the temporarily constructed theatre with portable seating, but also with the tradition of the ruler as performer: from henceforth, the Baroque ruler was to be an elevated and privileged spectator, in direct geographical opposition to the stage, and thus even more the focus of audience attention than before (pl.3.20).[33]

The success of this first commission proved to be the start of a long relationship between the imperial family and the Bibienas, during which various members of the dynasty worked on a range of sacred and secular architectural projects, catafalques, set designs and festive celebrations including fireworks, in addition to their principal theatrical duties.[34] In 1709, Francesco was appointed Theatrical and Festival Engineer by Emperor Joseph I; at Joseph's death his succession by Charles VI brought with it the appointment of Francesco's brother Ferdinando, who had designed the decorations for the emperor's marriage (when he was Charles III of Spain) in Barcelona in 1708, and who subsequently served him as court painter.[35] In turn, when Ferdinando returned to Italy for health reasons in 1716, he left in his place a son, Giuseppe, who was joined in 1723 by his brother Antonio, made Second Theatrical Engineer in 1727.[36] In this practice of family collaboration, in both artistic and practical senses, combined with their itinerancy, the Bibienas were a typical Baroque dynasty, and these factors largely account for their rise and rapid domination of the world of the theatre, as they were able to retain existing court posts while simultaneously travelling to secure others. By creating and imposing a homogeneous 'Bibiena style', rather than operating as individual artists, they were able to maintain a monopoly by offering up whichever family member might be available, the patron being reassured that the end result would nonetheless conform to the marque. It is precisely this adoption of a dynastic style that makes it so difficult to identify individual hands in the huge numbers of 'Bibiena family' drawings that still survive.

The Bibiena family contributed more to Baroque theatre than their virtual monopoly over designs and constructions for courts across Europe. They continued to use central-point perspective, which was often preferred by patrons, and created a series of stock sets that could be reused for appropriate generic settings: 'Palace, harbour, long gallery – short gallery, courtyard, chamber, prison, garden with parterre, garden of a different sort, large and small wood, wood with a military camp' (*Reggia, Marittima, Galleria lunga – galleria curta, Cortile, Camera, Carcere, Giardino con il perterre, Giardino in altro modo, Bosco lungo e curto, Bosco con campo attendato*). In these sets the Bibienas went further than their predecessors in employing the effect of accumulation to create the impression of depth, their designs representing endless staircases or ranges of Salomonic columns disappearing to infinity, intended to overawe the spectator.

However, their most ground-breaking invention, credited specifically to Ferdinando, was that of the 'angled scene' or *scena per angolo*, which was subsequently added to the stock repertoire of theatre designs. This broke entirely with the whole tradition of centralized perspective and the notion of the stage and auditorium as an integrally conceived single entity, by introducing an angled viewpoint that removed the concept of the privileged viewer and allowed a greater number of spectators to enjoy the effect of the stage illusion. It succeeded in both startling the viewer and drawing him in to the illusion.[37] The use of axial perspective had been reliant on a relatively deep stage providing space for the numerous sets of wings required to create the illusion of infinity;

conversely, the *scena per angolo* allowed an impression to be created of much greater depth but on a much shallower stage, and so was more practical and economical. The Baroque style was demanding on both artists and their audiences and the *scena per angolo* required viewers to use their imaginations to complete the expanse beyond what was suggested by the stage picture (pl.3.21).[38]

First employed in Bologna in 1703, the *scena per angolo* was described by the Bibienas in their publication *L'Architettura Civile* (1711), although with reference only to how to reproduce it on a flat surface (such as a painted backdrop) rather than in a series of backdrops and wings. This way of conceiving stage space as a shallow stage with entirely diagonal viewpoints was a radical challenge to the seventeenth-century style of Torelli, and it is notable that it was primarily in Italy and Central Europe that the *scena per angolo* was successful, the more conventional symmetrical style of Torelli remaining preferred in France and among its cultural satellites, such as Sweden.[39]

3.21 Design for a stage set with the hall of a palace opening to a garden, Antonio Galli Bibiena. 1728 (cat.57)

Vienna and Beyond: Theatre as Physical Statement

The Viennese connection, as testified by the Bibiena family's keenness to maintain their role there, was an extremely important one, as it opened up access to the patronage associated with the German-speaking courts, where the family were most active outside Italy. These relatively small courts, such as Dresden, Mannheim and Munich, played out their inter-court rivalries in the realm of the theatre just as their other European contemporaries did. The theatre building itself served as a manifestation of magnificence and economic might, a permanent testimony to the rulers responsible for its construction. Unfortunately most of these theatres have been destroyed by fire or bombardment; however, visual and textual records enable us to gain an impression of the originals. The court theatre at Mannheim, for example, built for the Elector Palatine by Giuseppe and Antonio's brother Alessandro (1737–41, destroyed in 1795), was considered by the English musicologist Charles Burney to be 'one of the largest and most splendid theatres of Europe, capable of containing five thousand persons'.[40]

One court theatre that does survive in almost its original state, giving a splendid indication of the magnificence of these Bibiena theatres, is the court opera house in Bayreuth (pl.3.22).

Commissioned from Giuseppe Galli Bibiena for the marriage of the Margrave's daughter Elisabeth Friederike Sophie to Duke Carl II Eugen of Württemberg, the opera house was inaugurated in September 1748 after nearly four years of construction. The significance of this marriage raised Bayreuth's status from that of a relatively obscure principality, and increased the pretensions of the ruling couple, who modelled their theatre on nothing less than that of the imperial court itself, employing the nephew of the Viennese theatre designer to carry out the work.[41] Having left his post at the Viennese court, since Italian opera was no longer such a popular entertainment under the rule of Maria Theresa, Giuseppe Galli Bibiena had worked briefly in Dresden in 1747 (his fame had spread there through the marriage of the Habsburg Archduchess Maria Josefa to the Saxon Prince Frederick Augustus), had come to Bayreuth later that year and had established his son Carlo as court scene painter.[42] Theatrical life in Bayreuth flourished at this time thanks to the personal interest of the Margravine Wilhelmine, who composed operas and wrote various libretti, some of which still survive; but, even with this in mind, the theatre far outclasses the status of the Bayreuth court in sophistication and grandeur. It was equipped with the standard stage machinery, but also included a

3.22 *View of the auditorium and margravial box of the court opera house*, Bayreuth, designed by Giuseppe Galli Bibiena 1744–48. Painting by Gustav Bauernfeind, gouache on paper. 1879 (Neues Schloss Bayreuth)

3.23 (*opposite*) Model of the new public theatre in Bologna, Giovanni Battista Martorelli and Antonio Gambarini, after Antonio Galli Bibiena. Bologna, 1756 (cat.51)

mechanism to raise the auditorium floor to the level of the stage to allow court balls to take place.[43] The form of the theatre was consciously modelled on that of Vienna, indicating the lofty pretensions of the ruling couple, while the iconography of the ornate interior decoration and the magnificent margravial box celebrated the advent of a new era of peace under their rule.[44] The inscription on the box links the ruling pair's names with that of Giuseppe Galli Bibiena: this was a mutually beneficial collaboration between aristocratic patron and Baroque artist, each deriving acclaim from the association.[45] The theatre served as the location for the most elaborate court ritual to take place, the splendid double staircase leading up to the margravial box providing the setting for the official entrance of the ruling couple as a kind of triumphal entry, thus leaving the audience in no doubt whatever as to who were the real performers in this event.

The Bibiena not only built court theatres but also public ones, and the survival of the Teatro Comunale in Bologna reminds us that a public theatre could be as much a status symbol for a city as it was for a court, as a means of communal self-representation (pl.3.22).[46] Bologna was the second city of the Papal States (at this point governed by a Bolognese pope, Benedict XIV, 1740–58), the home of the first European university, and had a reputation for producing both theatre

architects and musicians, so it is perhaps surprising that the theatre should not have been built until such a late date. The design process was also notoriously problematic: having offered his services to his native city unsolicited, Antonio Galli da Bibiena secured the commission only several years later, having won a public competition for the construction 'of a theatre, which the city is lacking' equipped 'with the greatest number of scene changes' (there were 12 in the opening performance of Metastasio and Gluck's *Trionfo di Clelia*).

Having won the commission, Antonio nearly lost it again, following general uproar at the projected expense to the public purse of his unpopular design, only keeping it by agreeing to modify some of what were perceived to be the more unpalatable aspects of his design. He scaled down the supposedly over-lavish decoration of the interior, deemed by some to be too luxurious to be appropriate for a rich but bourgeois city, and lessened the extreme curve of the bell-shaped auditorium in response to heavy contemporary criticisms, made on both design and acoustic grounds.[47] This was despite the architect's claims that the bell-shape actually enhanced the acoustics, as had been the case in the Teatro Filarmonico in Verona, built by Francesco for the Accademia Filarmonica in 1732, a building which survives, but not in its original state. This was highly praised precisely for its marvellous acoustics, as was fitting for a theatre whose musical director at the time was Antonio Vivaldi. Francesco's notes accompanying his plans for Verona give clear and detailed instructions on how the auditorium should be fitted out in wood to create a 'sounding' instrument, and indicate how important acoustics were to the Bibienas (pl.3.24).

The location of the theatre in the heart of the university quarter and Antonio's unexecuted ideas for its façade reveal both the architect's and the city's intentions: that the theatre would serve not in isolation, but would join other institutions such as the *Istituto delle Scienze*, the *Accademia Clementina* and the *Biblioteca Dotti*, to create an integrated and regenerated artistic and academic hub in the city centre.[48] Although the façade was never completed to Antonio's design, the theatre nonetheless served to testify to the importance of Bologna as a cultural centre, and in particular as the city that had produced the most important and sought-after family of theatre architects and designers in Europe.

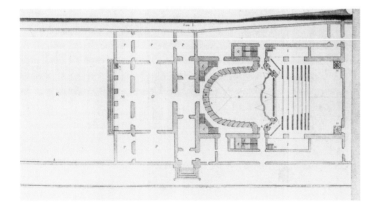

3.24 Ground plan of the Teatro Filarmonico in Venice, designed by Francesco Galli Bibiena, engraving, Francesco Zucchi after Saverio Avesani. Verona, 1731 (Biblioteca Civica, Verona)

Conclusion

The state of the theatre towards the close of this period, the time when the Baroque style was widely popular, can be seen in Francesco Battaglioli's painting of the finale of the performance of *Nitteti* in Madrid in 1756 (pl.3.25). Organized by Farinelli, the famous *castrato* and musical impresario who had been summoned to the Spanish court in 1737, this was one of the last spectacles to take place in the Coliseo del Buen Retiro, which was equipped with a very deep stage to accommodate illusionistic sets. Unabashed in the face of ever more strident criticism of productions relying on machine effects, the Coliseo not only had a pit full of machines and an on-stage spring, but the stage also had rear doors opening on to the gardens behind, enabling spectators to enjoy even more spectacular effects, such as firework displays and cavalcades of 40 riders, which would take place outside but were experienced by the audience as if they were at the rear of the stage. Such incredible, vastly expensive spectacles had helped Farinelli to create a carefully crafted mythology around the Spanish king, Ferdinand VI, which had been carried across Europe in the tales told by visitors to the Spanish court, a mythology which would, however, no longer serve under the new ruler Charles III on his accession in 1764. As were many Baroque theatres, the Coliseo was abandoned, the lavish sets and costumes discarded in favour of different novelties just as contemporary theory and practice of music were moving in a different direction, towards the reforms of Gluck and the early operas of Mozart. However, the influence of the Baroque theatre was not as limited as might be expected from such an ephemeral art form, always subject to the whims of rulers and impresarios and to changing fashions. The Bibiena family's innovation of the *scena per angolo* was to prove ground-breaking for the subsequent two centuries of theatre design, in its establishment of the stage as an entirely separate zone from that of the viewer, and in its breaking of the reliance on centralized perspective, while the heritage of Baroque theatre can still be seen today, not only in the revival performances of Baroque operas and in theatre building that still follows what is predominantly a Baroque form, but perhaps most of all for the unabated appetite among producers and audiences for the harnessing of new technologies and new materials to create ever more lavish and spectacular stage effects.

3.25 *Act III, Scene X of Metastasio's Nitteti,*
with music by Nicolò Conforto, performed at
the Buen Retiro Palace, Madrid, Francesco
Battaglioli. 1756 (cat.52)

Urban Festival

Elaine Tierney

On 29 May 1660, London rejoiced. Recently returned from exile on the Continent, Charles II entered the city for the first time in 17 years, presenting delighted spectators with a 'pageant whose brilliance outshone all else within living memory.'[49] The diarist John Evelyn's record of the day is particularly evocative, providing a veritable roll-call of early modern urban festival, comprising:

> …a Triumph of above 20,000 horse & foote, brandishing their swords and shouting with inexpressible joy: The ways straw'd with flowers, the bells ringing, the streets hung with Tapissry, fountaines running with wine: The Mayor, Alderman, all the Companies in their liver[ie]s, Chaines of Gold, banners; Lords & nobles, Cloth of Silver, gold & velvet every body clad in, the windos & balconies all set with Ladys, Trumpets, Musick & [myriads] of people flocking the streetes & was as far as Rochester, so as they were 7 hours in passing the Citty, even from 2 in the afternoone 'til nine at night.[50]

Evelyn's description of this royal entry is hardly unique. Throughout Europe, significant days were marked with a similar mix of civic pageantry, conspicuous display, acclamatory crowds, ringing bells and free-flowing wine. Important ritual events, such as coronations, state funerals, royal or ambassadorial entries, took place in the Baroque city; major military victories, royal births, birthdays and marriages were occasions for court and civic dignitaries to organize festivities, ranging from processions with magnificently attired participants, fireworks displays and public theatricals to tournaments on foot and grand equestrian carousels.

Space

The Baroque city was the principal site for celebrations of this kind: its landmarks, processional routes, squares and open spaces were dressed to best effect on such special occasions. Buildings were adorned with costly textiles, hangings and pictures; throughways were made more hospitable with flowers, straw and gravel; and purpose-built structures, such as platforms, stages, scenic apparatus and triumphal arches, temporarily became part of the urban landscape.

Baroque festival architecture was ephemeral, and to understand its impact we must interpret the significance of its physical, urban setting. As we have seen with theatre design,

the Baroque city was planned to reinforce the political theory of absolutism, its spaces, buildings and projects carefully executed to achieve particular effects in relation to specific ideological agendas (see The Festivities of Augustus the Strong, p.178). As architectural historian Henry A. Millon has argued, seventeenth- and eighteenth-century urban architecture was active, seeking to engage and encompass existing spaces and structures; its new developments were built to 'incorporate adjacent buildings, dominate open spaces, [and] to order urban distribution'.[51] Although specific components of this 'new urbanism', including paved public spaces and wide, straight avenues, had been introduced in earlier periods, seventeenth- and eighteenth-century strategies were directed at an ever more comprehensive imposition of order on the urban environment.

The Square

These trends are certainly evidenced by the history of the Baroque city square, which became more ordered and scenographic as it evolved from late Renaissance examples such as Michelangelo's reordered Campidoglio in Rome (from 1568); the Piazza della Signoria (1594) and Piazza dell'Annunziata (1608), both in Florence; and the Piazza dei Cavalieri in Pisa (1596). Some squares, such as the Place Royale in Paris, were completely enclosed, with buildings running along each of the four sides; others, including the Campidoglio and Place Louis-le-Grand, were enclosed on just three sides, leaving the remaining aspect open to seek the effect of the imaginary 'fourth wall' formed by the proscenium arch in a theatre.[52]

In all cases, these regularized, paved open spaces were intended to show secular and ecclesiastical monuments to best effect. Harmonized façades, strong use of linear and axial perspectives and felicitously placed fountains and columnar forms such as obelisks guaranteed squares that were orderly and visually cohesive. As a statement of royal power, order and urban architecture, the Baroque square was unequalled, exemplifying what Michael Webb has termed 'a new ideology of building, in which one man imposes his will on public space'.[53]

The definitive personification of the absolutist power of the Baroque square was probably the French *place royale*. The early precedents, such as the Parisian Place Royale (1606–12) and the Pont Neuf *terre-plein* (1614), already displayed the defining characteristics of the fully evolved type, with the square designed to frame a large-format bronze statue of the reigning

3.26 Inauguration of the equestrian statue of Louis XIV in Place Louis-le-Grand, from the almanac of 1700, artist unknown, engraving. Paris, 1700 (Bibliothèque Nationale de France)

monarch. In many ways, the ultimate royal 'showcases' were the Place des Victoires (1686) and Place Louis-le-Grand (now Place Vendôme) in Paris (pl.3.26).[54]

The latter was dominated by François Girardon's equestrian statue of Louis XIV, which depicted the king costumed *à la romaine*, combined in typical Baroque fashion with a fashionable full-bottomed wig. The fame and impact of the antique gilt-bronze statue of Marcus Aurelius, for much of its later history regarded as a representation of Constantine and erected as the centrepiece of Rome's Campidoglio, created a reputation for equestrian statues as prime symbols of power and military prowess: 'The equestrian tradition, connoting the noble warrior … [was] understood as the appurtenance of royalty' (pl.3.27).[55]

This combination of square and equestrian statue proved highly influential. As it was the largest bronze sculpture in Europe at the time, images of Girardon's statue were circulated with remarkable effect by means of contemporary prints, drawings and paintings. Six reproductions in miniature also survive, providing an unrivalled record of the monument, which was destroyed in September 1792 at the height of the French Revolution. Such representations fall into a category termed by Peter Burke as the 'media of persuasion', objects responsible for publicizing Louis's image and communicating the rhetoric around his image of kingship.[56] In the mid-1680s, the king's superintendent of buildings, Louvois, instituted a 'statue campaign', which saw sculpted representations of the king, mostly equestrian, installed at the centre of many major towns and cities, including Aix, Besançon, Bordeaux, Caen, Dijon, Grenoble, Le Havre, Limoges, Lyons, Marseilles, Montpellier, Pau, Poitiers, Rennes, Tours and Troyes.[57] Thus replicated, the *place royale* was intended to 'speak a common cultural and political language that derived from the new absolutist style developed in Paris and Versailles, tethering distant provinces to the seats of royal power' (pl.3.27).[58]

Further afield, Girardon's image of Louis was adapted to represent other monarchs. In one such case, the head is replaced by that of Maximilian II Emanuel, Elector of Bavaria (1662–1726) (pl.3.28). Likewise, Andreas Schlüter took Girardon's monument as his model when producing an imposing equestrian statue of Frederick-William, Great Elector of Brandenburg (cast in 1708), now standing before Schloss Charlottenburg near Berlin.[59]

Significantly, the city squares that displayed these images were not closed or restricted spaces. The sculptures were actors and the squares were stages for performances for socially diverse audiences, not 'democratic' auditoria, but spaces shaped by the competing interests and experiences of the people who used them.

The Piazza Navona in Rome was one such contested space. At the beginning of the seventeenth century, the square accommodated a heterogeneous mix of Roman nobility (including the influential Pamphili family), merchants, artisans, the predominantly Spanish congregation of S. Giacomo and a weekly food market. This changed in 1644 when Giovanni Battista Pamphili was elected pontiff, becoming Pope Innocent X. As San Juan has argued, the piazza's subsequent redevelopment underscored the Pamphili family's social ascent from 'private noble family' to 'an institution of the church'.[60]

Reflecting this change in fortunes, the Piazza Navona was reconceived as a space for aristocratic leisure. From being a vast, somewhat incoherent marketplace, by the time of Innocent's death in 1655 the piazza had become an orderly,

3.27 Equestrian statue of Louis XIV, François Girardon. Paris, *c*.1695 (cat.60)

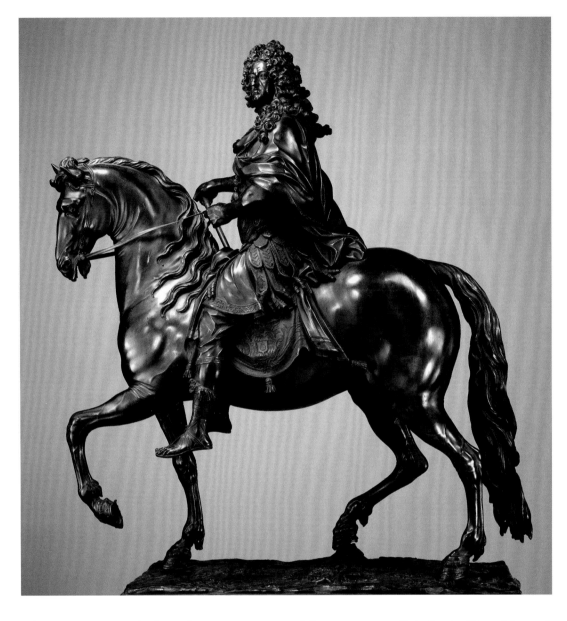

3.28 Equestrian statue of Maximilian II Emanuel, after Martin Desjardins, bronze. Germany, *c.*1710 (Bayerisches Nationalmuseum)

coherent city square. And yet, these improvements did not meet with universal approbation. Building Bernini's *Fountain of the Four Rivers* and refashioning the Palazzo Pamphili necessitated high levels of taxation at a time when basic foodstuffs, such as grain, were scarce and expensive. The diarist Giacinto Gigli recounts the grievances of ordinary Romans, who attached pasquinades to the fountain's masonry, a practice more readily associated with the mutilated statue of Pasquino which was set up nearby:

> While the pieces of Obelisk were conducted through the city, the people said many things, and that it was not the time to make this expense while there was the need to provide grain, and various words were attached to these stones, and one in particular said this: 'We want something other than obelisk and fountains, bread we want, bread, bread, bread.'[61]

Rebuilt, the Piazza Navona became a different kind of city stage: a place where the *theatrum mundi* encountered the theatre and the performative and spectacular characteristics of Baroque art and design. Giovanni Paolo Panini's *Preparations for Festivities in Piazza Navona* (pl.3.29) depicts the construction of a magnificent fireworks display, held in 1729 to celebrate the birth of the French Dauphin (see Fireworks, p.172).[62] Despite the fact that fireworks displays almost always took place at night, the scene is in daylight, and shows the extent to which even the preparatory stages of major urban festivals attracted huge public interest. The painting also functions as a social panorama: groups of genteel spectators watch as workmen put the finishing touches to the occasion's scenic apparatus and firework machines, while, on the left-hand side, a ragtag bunch of urchins are reprimanded by an officious-looking gentleman with a stick.

3.29 *Preparations for the festivities to celebrate the birth of the Dauphin in Piazza Navona in 1729*, Giovanni Paolo Panini. Rome, 1731 (cat.61)

FIREWORKS

Elaine Tierney

Fireworks displays enhanced public celebration throughout seventeenth- and eighteenth-century Europe. Like other forms of early modern spectacle, such displays were intensely political, marking events of national and international importance.

Notably, the fireworks had an extremely well defined military aspect. Technological treatises, such as *La Pyrotechnie de Hanzelet Lorraine* (Paris, 1630) and Casimir Siemienowicz's *Complete Art of Artillery* (Amsterdam, 1650), demonstrate the extent to which military and display fireworks resembled one another; artillery technicians produced explosives both for the battlefield and for celebration. As this gouache of an entertainment near Warsaw illustrates, designed displays often made explicit reference to their warlike origins, taking the form of mock battles, or, as in this instance, mimicking military manoeuvres (pl.3.30).

Unlike most modern events, Baroque fireworks were elaborately staged. High-profile artists and designers were commissioned to devise suitable scenic apparatus. In Rome in 1662, the francophile Cardinal Antonio Barberini employed Bernini, working alongside Giovanni Paolo Schor and the celebrated *fuocarola* Marcello Gondi, to produce *fuochi spettacolari* in Rome on the birth of a son and heir to Louis XIV. Bernini's striking design transformed the church of SS. Trinità dei Monti, and the piazza below it, into a rough-hewn mountain. The display's apparatus took almost three months to build and install, giving some sense of the scale of the occasion.

In addition to constituting impressive feats of engineering, large-format props and scenery also enforced important social and political agendas. This is certainly true of the display for the coronation of James II, played on the River Thames in front of the Palace of Whitehall on 24 April 1685. As a contemporary engraving shows (pl.3.32), it included all the trappings of royalty (the king's cipher, an imperial crown, a Louis XIV-style sun), as well as alluding to symbolic devices from Cesare Ripa's *Iconographia*, a widely referenced compendium of allegorical and emblematic figures.

3.30 *Fireworks at the Camp near Warsaw under the reign of Augustus II*, artist unknown. Probably Saxony or Poland, *c.* or after 1732 (cat.68)

3.31 *Fireworks at SS. Trinità dei Monti, Rome, to celebrate the birth of the Dauphin of France*, Dominique Barrière after Giovanni Paolo Schor, engraving. Rome, 1661 (Kunstbibliothek, Berlin)

PATER PATRIÆ

MONARCHIA

3.32 *A Representation of the fireworks upon the River of Thames over against Whitehall at their Majesties Coronation*, John Collins and William Sherwin after Francis Barlow, engraving. London, 1685 (Guildhall Library)

With ever more lavish production values, the French fireworks drama married pyrotechnic effects and narrative with spectacular consequences. *Les plaisirs de l'isle enchantée*, based on an episode from Ariosto's *Orlando Furioso* and performed over three days at Versailles in 1664, exemplified this tradition (pl.3.33). The 25-year-old Louis XIV was cast as the poem's hero, Ruggiero, with his courtiers playing knights-in-arms. Held captive by the evil sorceress Alcina, the knights were released only on the third and final day of the festivities, by means of a magic ring placed on the finger of Louis/Ruggiero. Simultaneously, the palace of Alcina was demolished by fireworks detonated within its walls.

Once the smoke cleared on the scene's charred remains, courtly spectators could not have doubted the occasion's real agenda, with the destruction of the fictional palace of Alcina restoring to sight the château of Versailles and the material basis of Louis's power in the 'real world'.

With their unique combination of sound and coloured light effects, fireworks were used thus to overwhelm spectators and articulate the relationships between ruling powers and society at large.

3.33 Destruction of the Palace of Alcina, from the third day of *Les plaisirs de l'isle enchantée*, Israël Silvestre, engraving. Paris, 1664 (The British Museum)

Processions

Processions routed through Baroque cities were integral to correct observation of special occasions. Participants, including royalty, corporate government, guilds, livery companies and local dignitaries, dressed in their finest clothing and moved through the city, stopping at significant symbolic locations *en route*. These were marked by purpose-built temporary structures such as triumphal arches, platforms for dramatic performance or *tableaux vivants*, and colossal figurative devices. Processions invariably took place under the public gaze. As Watanabe-O'Kelly has remarked, their 'efficacy' depended on 'the fact they are witnessed by the people'. That is: 'The monarch must be seen to be crowned, the bride must be exhibited to her husband's people, [and] the heir must be seen to walk behind his father's coffin.'[63]

With their highly visual aspect, recurrent royal and civic processions fulfilled an important ritual function, providing an unspoken commentary on the relations between central and municipal government. The procession after a royal entry was a public demonstration of unity, with local and national power-brokers brought together to be seen to be working in unison towards a common goal. Likewise, the procession before the new monarch's coronation was intended to be a highly visible act of legitimatization, showing off the support of political élites and encouraging the hallmarks of popular support in the form of exultant cries and noisy huzzahs.[64]

In some instances, the intensely public aspect of these performances was even used to promote other events. In 1662, in preparation for *Le Grand Carrousel*, Louis XIV issued a royal edict ordering participants to file through the city along pre-appointed routes over the three days before the main event. This gave ordinary Parisians, who would not be in attendance at the *Carrousel* itself, ample opportunity to see the flower of the French nobility in their finery and, by inference, to be overawed by the resources at the disposal of the French crown.[65]

Since each procession represented a symbolic journey, processional routes actively reshaped how participants and observers experienced their urban environment. By emphasizing specific landmarks, the routes were tailor-made to promote a particular point of view. In Paris in the 1680s, the route taken by official ambassadorial entries was altered to meet new ideological ends. Rather than culminate in the Place Royale in the east of the city, entries were redirected to the recently inaugurated Place de Nos Conquêtes (later Place Louis-le-Grand) in the west. The *Galerie des Glaces* at Versailles, started in 1678, had similar functions. Such changes in royal ceremonial were intended to communicate to an international audience France's ascendancy as the major European power, as embodied in the triumphal architecture of the Place de Nos Conquêtes.[66]

In some circumstances, processions were deliberately designed to heighten emotional response. Nothing was left to chance in the organization of the Pope-Burning processions, patronized by the Whig Green Ribbon Club, which were held annually in London between 1679 and 1681, 'carefully prepared to excite the whole of London'. Massed spectators watched as representative effigies were paraded in a torch-lit procession through the city before being ceremoniously thrown on top of a bonfire. Even the choice of date, 17 November, was loaded with meaning. As the anniversary of Elizabeth I's accession to the throne in 1558, it had become, in conjunction with Gunpowder Treason Day on 5 November, a rallying point for assertive English Protestantism, anti-Catholic feeling and xenophobic tensions.[67]

Cressy aptly terms these processions 'living tableaux as political cartoons', with the basic format adapted and elaborated to provide commentary on current affairs. The 1681 Pope-Burning procession used its processional route and pageantry to bridge the gap between history and the political moment. Beginning at Whitechapel, the procession finished at Smithfield with a huge bonfire and fireworks. As the place where heretics had been burnt during the reign of Mary I (r.1553–58), this site resonated with memories of the Catholic persecution of English Protestants. Its choice – and the use of a fire festival – functioned as a reminder of past atrocities, but, more significantly, this event was also a warning for the future, against the accession of the Catholic James, Duke of York.[68]

Spectacle

Festival occasions actually were, and were intended to appear as, expensive performances. Lavish production values and conspicuous expenditure were designed to heighten the status of the persons, ideologies or institutions being celebrated. And yet, precise estimates of the monetary costs of festival activity are very hard to arrive at. Many individual events had more than one source of funding, with contributions from corporations, government, the royal household, state departments and wealthy individuals. Even the better-documented events are subject to inaccurate estimates, incomplete or lost records and unspecified costs. In response to this, recent studies of early modern festival have tended towards the 'local' – either by interrogating individual events, or by taking account of festival activities in a single locality over a relatively short period of time.[69]

It is, however, clear that design strategies for urban festival were both multimedia and interdisciplinary. Elaborate out-of-doors performances were, inevitably, collaborative, bringing together the professional expertise and experiences of a huge variety of artists, designers, and technical experts. In his overview of early modern fireworks displays, Salatino acknowledges the 'vast marshalling of intellectual, aesthetic, and economic resources, as well as the sheer labor' that made early modern spectacle possible.[70]

High-profile occasions, such as coronations and royal entries, were central to the repertoire of many of the key practitioners of the Baroque style including Rubens, Nicodemus Tessin the Elder, Bernini, David Klöcker Ehrenstrahl, Martin Schnell and Johann Melchior Dinglinger, who were variously commissioned to devise props, scenic apparatus and temporary triumphal architecture.

Such major figures were, however, not working in isolation. Take, for example, the fireworks display held to celebrate the coronation of James II on 24 April 1685. As a contemporary engraving clearly illustrates (see Fireworks, pl.3.32), the event combined large-format scenic apparatus and sophisticated pyrotechnic effects. Contemporary documentation attributes the display's scenic devices to a broad multi-skilled workforce encompassing several master carpenters, their assistants, wheelwrights, blacksmiths and painters, while artillery technicians from the Government Office of Ordnance were responsible for making the fireworks and supervising their detonation on the night. There were also the trades associated with transporting the materials and guarding the display apparatus once *in situ* on the River Thames in front of the Palace of Whitehall.[71]

Such interdisciplinary work-practices are also registered in the huge variety of artefacts produced. As a kind of designed performance, open-air spectacle was a composite of purpose-built stages and platforms; large-format props and scenery; textiles and costume; smaller, hand-held props; and sound and light effects. And, like other forms of Baroque design, urban festival was intended to appeal to the senses. Official accounts stressed magnificence, itemizing the conspicuous quantities of luxury goods used – silver, gold, silk, velvet, gemstones and jewellery. One such narrative, describing Augustus the Strong's entry into Krakow before his coronation as king of Poland, exemplifies this tradition, emphasizing the occasion's 'trappings and splendid decorations':

> The drums, trumpets, tabors and other instruments were sounded merrily at this entry. Twenty pairs of camels laden with gold and silver were also led in. There were 24 led horses with saddles and saddle-cloths decorated most wonderfully with silver, gold and gemstones. The king's costume was so rich that its equal cannot be found in Europe. The cavalcade, right up to the baldaquin, was very splendid.[72]

The testament of surviving objects can tell a somewhat different story. The unrivalled collection of costumes and props used during Saxon court spectacle in Dresden proves a fascinating case-study, revealing the wide range of objects produced, the materials used, and the involvement of high-profile craftsmen. In the summer of 1709, preparations were well under way for an elaborate programme of festivities to celebrate the arrival of Augustus the Strong's brother-in-law, King Frederick IV of Denmark. Reflecting the heterogeneous nature of early modern court festival, this included a tournament on foot, a Ladies' Running at the Ring (or *Damenringrennen*), a Carousel of the Four Continents, a fireworks display, a themed banquet and a procession of classical gods and goddesses.

Just as the ballet dancers in the theatres were provided with lightweight props, processional objects and materials could be made to appear more costly and magnificent than they really were. For the Carousel of the Four Continents, the workshop of the leading court jeweller, Johann Melchior Dinglinger, produced a series of props that were intended to mimic luxury materials, primarily gold and precious stones. In reality, Augustus's imposing 'Apollo' sun mask was chased gilded copper (see The Festivities of Augustus the Strong, p.178), while the emblematic shields and sun-shaped ornaments worn by the royal horse were gilded copper, embossed before being punched and embellished with paste jewels (pl.3.35).[73]

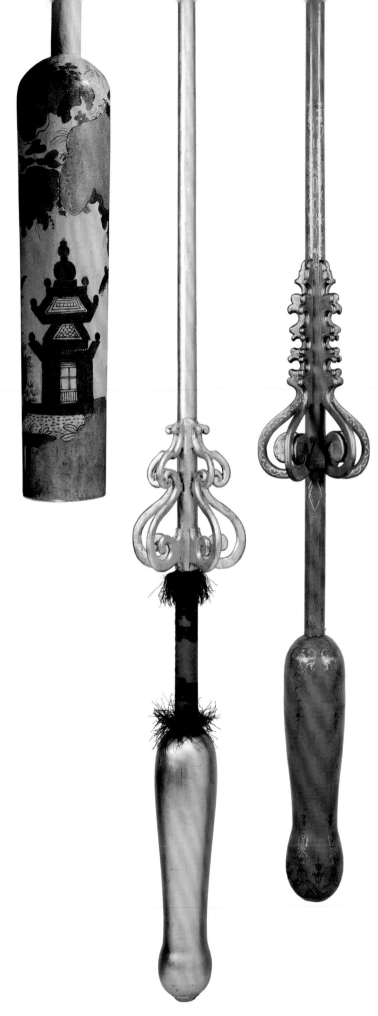

For the ladies' carousel, or *Damenringrennen*, the court's most gifted lacquerist, Martin Schnell, made colour-coded lances carried during the tournament, with gold leaf, bronze, red boluses, coloured lacquer, fringing and silk velvet applied to a wooden shaft. In recognition of their value, these lances were reused in 1719, when Augustus's only son, Frederick Augustus, married Maria Josefa, daughter of the emperor (pl.3.34).[74]

Significantly, many surviving objects can be compared and contrasted with highly finished representations of major court festivals. Johann Samuel Mock's gouaches illustrate the procession before the Carousel of the Four Continents (see The Festivities of Augustus the Strong, p.178), and in this example, the emblematic shield carried by an attendant to the King of the Americas is clearly identifiable by its apple motif (pl.3.42). By teasing out the relationships between existing three-dimensional objects and officially produced images, we can begin to have a better idea of the agendas behind festival and, as we shall see, the ways in which it was commemorated in two-dimensional manuscript and print objects.

3.34 Carousel lances, used in the Running at the Ring at the Dresden Carousels of 1709 and 1719, Martin Schnell. Dresden, 1709–19 (cats 71–3)

3.35 (*opposite*) One of a pair of horse ornaments in the form of suns, maker unknown. Dresden, before 1709 (cat.70)

THE FESTIVITIES OF AUGUSTUS THE STRONG

Claudia Schnitzer

Under the rule of Augustus the Strong, festive culture in Dresden achieved new heights. For the elector-king, both the festivities themselves and their splendid accoutrements functioned not merely as 'courtly pleasures' but served real social, political and ceremonial goals.

From the beginning of his reign, Augustus devoted his energies to preparing and evaluating his festivals, which became increasingly lavish and complex. The festival documentation, which survives, ensured a visual record of these ephemeral events.

For the very first carnival of his reign, in 1695, the young elector organized magnificent masked courtly events and himself played Alexander the Great in the Carousel of the Four Kingdoms. Shortly afterwards, the Procession of the Gods took place for the night-time Running at the Ring, in which – a particularity of Augustus's festivities – court ladies also participated (pl.3.36). For himself he chose a role referring to his accession to power: Mercury, the god of trade and the gods' messenger, who opened the procession.

Augustus celebrated the visit of Frederick IV of Denmark in June 1709 with a whole month of festivities: in addition to a firework display, several hunts and a foot combat, high points included a repeat of the Procession of the Gods, the Ladies' Running at the Ring and the Carousel of the Four Continents, as well as a 'Peasants' Tavern'. This time Augustus appeared as the sun god Apollo. For this role he commissioned the court jeweller, Dinglinger, to make him a gilded sun mask with his own features, which thereby functioned rather less as a disguise than as a means of glorifying him as a god.

3.36 *Countess Werthern in the Ladies' Running at the Ring,* held on 6 June 1709 in Dresden, attributed to Johann Samuel Mock, Dresden, 1710 (cat.67)

3.37 Sun mask of Augustus the Strong, Johann Melchior Dinglinger, embossed and gilded copper. Dresden, 1709 (Rüstkammer, Staatliche Kunstsammlungen Dresden)

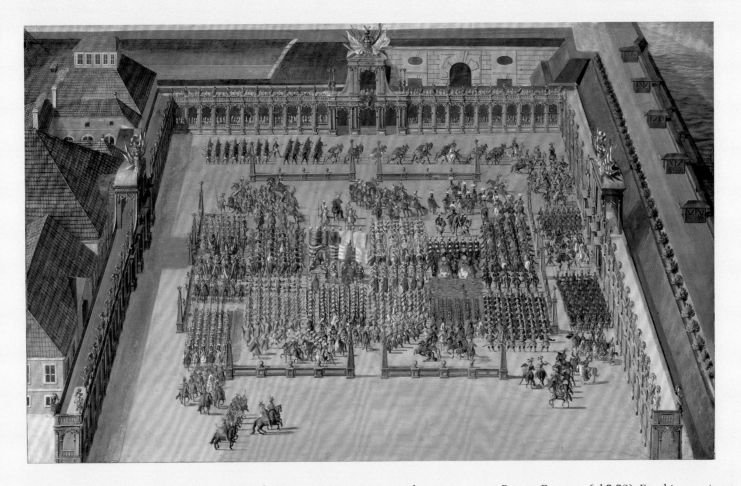

3.38 *Entry of the Four Quadrilles*, for the Carousel of the Four Continents, held in Dresden on 19 June 1709, attributed to Johann Samuel Mock. Dresden, after 1709 (cat.65)

3.39 *Banquet given by the King and Queen for Prince Frederick Augustus and Archduchess Maria Josefa at the Dresden Residenz*, 3 September, 1719, attributed to Antoine Aveline after Raymond Leplat. Paris, before 1728 (cat.149)

One of Augustus's innovations was the Ladies' Running at the Ring, held in the building that preceded the Zwinger, when 24 ladies in chariots had to aim their lances through the centre of a ring. The same 'amphitheatre' was used for the Carousel of the Four Continents, a highly significant event, as is confirmed by the survival of 170 gouaches of it.

The culmination of Augustus's festivities was the so-called Festival of the Planets, held in September 1719 for the marriage of Prince Frederick to Maria Josefa, daughter of the Holy Roman Emperor (pl.3.39). For this prominent political and dynastic event, Augustus had a suitable state apartment furnished in the palace, and, over the course of an entire month, and in a wide range of locations, presented a veritable 'Encyclopedia of Courtly Festival Forms'. The festivities were inaugurated by Apollo (the sun) with a dramatic firework display on the banks and waters of the Elbe, its subject the saga of the Argonauts. An armoured tournament was held on the Old Market in honour of Mars. Jupiter was the patron of the Carousel of the Four Elements, held in the Zwinger and deemed one of the most splendid equestrian entertainments of the Baroque. A water hunt took place on the Elbe, under the auspices of Diana (the moon), while Mercury led to a fair on the theme of international trade in the Zwinger. The Ladies' Festival in the Grosse Garten was dedicated to Venus, goddess of love. The grand finale was Saturn's mining festival, held in the Plauenschen Grund in the south-west of the city, in which a parade of miners and ironworkers displayed their most important manufacturing processes, highlighting the economic strength of the country, founded on its mineral resources. At the same time, a firework display presented the 'happy position of the stars', in which the circle of the seven planets welcomed the crowned monogram of Augustus, the 'earthly god'.

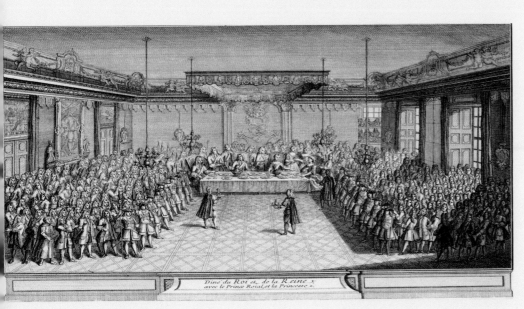

3.40 *The Proclamation of the Peace of Münster on the Grote Markt, Antwerp,* attributed to Maximiliaen Pauwels, oil on canvas. Antwerp, 1648 (Koninklijk Museum voor Schone Kunsten)

Temporary and Triumphal Architecture

Massive temporary architecture is one of the more striking features of Baroque urban festival: palaces, pavilions, temples, triumphal arches, their designs revealing a rich tradition of European festival architecture that included Roman triumphal arches, stages for outdoor theatre and the temporary stands and amphitheatres built for tilting and tournaments in the Middle Ages. By the early seventeenth century, temporary structures had become heavily inscribed with recondite systems of emblem and allegory, devised by leading poets and scholars and reflecting and emphasizing a particular occasion's overriding social and political agendas.[75] This was particularly true of triumphal arches constructed for entries, which, in McGowan's words, provided those occasions with their 'principal source of symbolism and decoration'.[76]

Like much of the ephemeral paraphernalia associated with festival, such architecture was not built to last. The structures were made out of canvas, wood and plaster, and painted to imitate more durable materials such as precious metal, marble, jasper and porphyry.[77] But, as Panini's painting of the Piazza Navona demonstrates, temporary architectural features were, in part, designed to interact with the permanent and monumental (pl.3.29). In this instance, Bernini's *Fountain of the Four Rivers* was flanked by two pavilions that are entirely in keeping with the piazza's dominant architectural motifs.[78]

Elsewhere, large-format figures, painted on board, were affixed to temporary structures, and imitations of the statues and carved reliefs that adorned contemporary buildings and monuments were set up representing classical virtues, allegorical entities and individuals with local historical significance.

Rare surviving examples in Antwerp's Vleehuis Museum give us some sense of the scale of temporary festival architecture. The earliest, a painted figure on wooden board representing *Pax*, was made as part of the city's celebration of the Peace of Münster in 1648 (pl.3.41). Contemporary representations by the engraver Wenceslaus Hollar and the painter Maximiliaen Pauwels show the figure *in situ* (pl.3.40). By herself Pax is more than two metres tall, but, as both images illustrate, she merely formed the pinnacle of the imposing temporary portico attached to Antwerp's town hall.[79] Although an isolated example, *Pax* is still a useful indicator of the massive scale on which temporary structures were conceived: something that is not always obvious from contemporary descriptions or representations.

3.41 *Allegorical Figure of Pax*, Erasmus II Quellin, oil on chased wood. Antwerp, 1648 (Museum Vleeshuis, Antwerp)

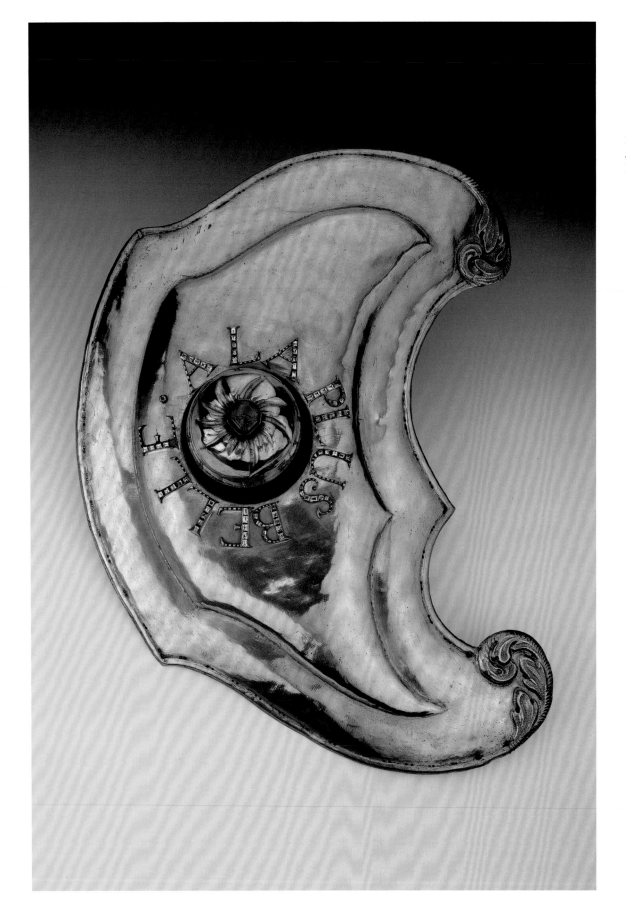

3.42 Carousel Shield,
Johann Melchior
Dinglinger. Dresden, 1695
(cat.69)

3.43 *Duke Christian von Sachsen-Weissenfels as the King of the Americas* in the Carousel of the Four Continents, Dresden, 1709, attributed to Johann Samuel Mock. Dresden, after 1709 (cat.66)

Costume and Textiles

Attending the procession before Charles II's coronation, the diarist and naval official Samuel Pepys made a statement by wearing his finest velvet coat, 'the first day that I put it on, though made half a year ago'.[80] Since spectators felt as obliged to dress up as did the participants, costume and textiles were integral to these performances. Participants and bystanders, attired in luxurious silks, velvets and gold and silver lace, were set against an appropriately lush backdrop, with residents on processional routes obliged, at the behest of civic proclamations, to decorate the façades of their homes with richly embroidered tapestries and painted hangings.

Some of this clothing may be termed 'ritual'. By wearing robes of office, an individual stated his place in the corporate hierarchy, while guild livery designated professional affiliations. Francis Sandford's *History of the Coronation of James II* emphasized another kind of significant clothing. In fine-grained detail Sandford described the special costume and paraphernalia associated with the coronation ceremony, approximating the hushed awe surrounding objects with a semi-sacred, ritual function.[81]

For non-ritual events, such as public theatricals, foot tournaments and grand equestrian carousels, clothing was no less important. Typical were the outlandish and wilfully exotic costumes worn by Saxon aristocrats during Augustus the

Strong's Carousel of the Four Continents. In Johann Mock's gouache, Duke Christian von Sachsen-Weissenfels is shown decked out in multicoloured feathers as King of the Americas (pl.3.43). It is worth noting that his costume imitated the fanciful ensemble worn by the Duc de Guise for Louis XIV's *Grand Carrousel* in Paris in 1662.

French influences were also evident in Stockholm in 1672, when the 17-year-old Charles XI attended his accession carousel wearing pageant armour modelled after the costume worn by Louis in 1662 (pl.3.14). It seems more than likely that the artists responsible for designing the 1672 carousel had access to the lavishly illustrated volume published by Charles Perrault (1670) to commemorate the French hastiludes.[82] Not unlike imitations of Girardon's equestrian statue, emulating Louis's dress declared the wearer's political ambitions. Augustus the Strong's choice of costume for his son's marriage to the emperor's daughter in 1719, '*un habit tel que le Roy de France defunt a porté dans les grandes ceremonies, telles que son marriage*', articulated the nature of his dynastic aspirations.[83] Likewise, the 1672 accession carousel was a watershed moment in Swedish history, and the imitation of French court culture expressed the expectations invested in the teenage king. In Rangström's words, 'Hopes and dreams were depicted' during the three days of festivities 'with the capital city of the new great power in Europe as their stage'.[84]

In an unexpected twist of fortune, Charles XI's pageant armour is still preserved in the Royal Armoury in Stockholm. The importance of the occasion was duly reflected by the large quantities of finest quality textiles withdrawn from the Royal Wardrobe and documented in the inventories, including *ponsou* (poppy-coloured) and *couleur de feu* velvet, silk and gold brocade, 'tafft roial', silver and gold braid and elk-skin for the skirts (pl.3.44).[85] A dizzying array of court artists and designers were responsible for the king's costume: his Roman-style pageant armour was made by the court sculptor Nicolaes Millich; his garments are attributed to the tailor Tolle Baillie; the buskins on his feet to the cobbler Jacob Schwartzkopf; while the *plumier* Daniel Balliet is credited with putting finishing touches to the helmet.[86]

Fancy dress was not just restricted to two-legged participants: horses, ridden by important people and tethered to the royal carriage, were also decked out in magnificent textiles. Velvet caparisons made for Queen Christina's coronation in Stockholm in 1650 were sumptuously embroidered with gold and silver thread, while Charles Le Brun's imposing portrait shows the Chancellor Séguier perched precariously on top of a heavily draped horse, as one of his young attendants shelters him with an extravagantly fringed palanquin. Painted to commemorate Séguier's presence at Louis XIV's official entry into Paris with his new bride in August 1660, the portrait shows a preponderance of lush and exotic textiles contributing to the atmosphere of aristocratic leisure (pl.3.45). Elsewhere, similar sumpter cloths were draped across lead horses, mules and donkeys, in royal and ambassadorial processions. A fascinating example, currently in the collections of Skokloster Castle, is associated with the Swedish ambassador Count Nils Bielke, and was probably used during his official entry into Paris in the 1680s (pl.3.46).[87]

3.44 Carousel armour, sword and helmet of Charles XI of Sweden, Nicolaes Millich (helmet and armour), Tolle Baillie (gown), Jacob Schwartzkopf (boots). Elements of the costume armour were re-used from the ballet costume the king wore two years earlier (see pl.3.14). Stockholm, 1672 (cat.64)

3.45 *Chancellor Séguier at the Entry of Louis XIV and Queen Maria Theresa into Paris, 26 August, 1660*, Charles Le Brun, oil on canvas. Paris, 1660 (Musée du Louvre)

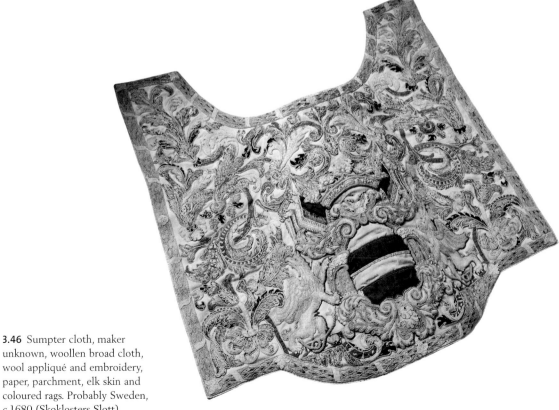

3.46 Sumpter cloth, maker unknown, woollen broad cloth, wool appliqué and embroidery, paper, parchment, elk skin and coloured rags. Probably Sweden, *c*.1680 (Skoklosters Slott)

Spectators

The audience for urban festival was determined by the nature of a particular event. Public processions, civic spectacles and fireworks displays were, in theory at least, seen by large, socially diverse crowds. In November 1697, John Evelyn estimated that over 200,000 people gathered to watch the fireworks display marking the Peace of Rijswijk in London's Piccadilly.[88] Other events had an intentionally semi-public aspect. As Watanabe-O'Kelly rightly contends, Louis XIV could have staged the 1662 *Grand Carrousel* 'away from the eyes' of all but a few, choosing instead to build an amphitheatre in the Tuileries with seating for thousands, and thereby accommodate more than just the very highest nobility.[89]

By contrast, entertainments exclusively for courtiers, such as the grand carousel to entertain Queen Christina of Sweden on her arrival in Rome, were well hidden from the public gaze. These were staged in purpose-built auditoria and amphitheatres constructed in the courtyards of urban palaces. Lauri and Gagliardi's colossal oil painting of the carousel suggests the political dimensions of spectatorship on these occasions, with the location and comfort of seating used as a tool of social differentiation – much as in the modern theatre or the contemporary development of the imperial box in the opera house. At Christina's carousel at the Palazzo Barberini, elaborately dressed boxes accommodated the guest of honour and her closest advisers, while the less exalted sat in plain, covered balconies attached to the palazzo's façade. Finally, the comparatively lowly, as seen to the right, made do with rows of tiered benches, which were uncovered and left to the mercy of the elements (see pl.2.2).

Other contemporary visual sources concur by acknowledging the hierarchies that applied to festival audiences. Bartholomäus Wittig's painting of a *Volksfest* in front of the Rathaus in Nuremberg contrasts a largely proletarian crowd 'on the ground' with more fashionably dressed spectators, positioned above the fray at the town hall's windows. Similarly, an anonymous depiction of festivities in Rome for the birth of the Spanish heir, Don Carlos, shows humble spectators in the street, with their betters installed in the windows of surrounding buildings or sitting in purpose-built viewing boxes attached to the façades, which were so commonly employed on such occasions (pl.3.47).

Similar structures were even built with commercial gain in mind, to sell a better view to willing spectators. In 1660, an entrepreneurial pair of Parisians, Deschamps and Dancerains, applied for official permission to build 'echauffaux' on the route taken by Louis XIV and his new bride, Maria Theresa, during their *entrée*.[90]

Notions of prestige and view are also key in Smuts's pithy analysis of early seventeenth-century royal entries in London. Smuts argues that for spectators to be guaranteed a continuous and coherent view of a procession they had to be participants.[91] Quality of view was certainly conflated with honour and status in 1661, when the entourages of the French and Spanish ambassadors came to blows over how their respective coaches were placed during the Swedish ambassador's formal entry.[92] In this instance, proximity to the main event asserted social standing, highlighting the significance of one's perceived vantage point.

For almost everyone else, the experience of urban festival was, at best, fragmentary, subject to the exhilaration and inconvenience of being an individual in a very large crowd. With this in mind, who can blame Samuel Pepys, who, with a 'great deal of company', stood on the 'leads' (roof) of his friend Mr Bowyer's house in an effort to get the best possible view of the fireworks display celebrating the coronation of Charles II in 1661?[93]

Urban festival invariably constituted a form of sensory overload. Massed spectators, on the ground and above, were deliberately engaged by special sound and light effects. André Félibien, chronicler of Louis XIV's elaborate *fêtes*, coined a rather felicitous expression when he described an entertainment held at Versailles in 1668 as '*agréable désordre*' (agreeable disorder). On this occasion, courtiers were 'ambushed' by fireworks concealed on the periphery of a horseshoe-shaped arena. In Félibien's account, the surrounded courtiers were stunned, with some falling, in shock, to the ground.[94] On even the regular performances, features such as festive ordnance, music, loud cries of acclamation, bonfires, bells, fireworks and illuminations reiterated the fact that something out of the ordinary was happening.

At present, scholars have yet to engage fully with the vital role played by this kind of factor in making, or 'designing', festival, the experiences that resist ready quantification: quality of view; spectator fatigue; discomfort; and the incidental, accidental or unexpected experiencing of events.

3.47 *Festivities held in Piazza Navona to celebrate the birth of Don Carlos, Infante of Spain,* artist unknown, oil on canvas. Rome, 1662 (Akademie der bildenden Künste, Vienna)

Festival Print

The existence and persistence of festival literature throws new light on the audience for early modern spectacle, intimating that events had audiences beyond the precisely local and physically present. These absent audiences mattered and it is arguable that the documentation and dissemination of a record of a festival were as vital as the event itself. These texts varied from scanty pamphlets to elaborately illustrated publications of record. Part of the latter tradition, Félibien's *Les plaisirs de l'Isle enchantée* ('The Pleasures of the Enchanted Isle') detailed festivities held at Versailles in 1664, its elegant prose punctuated by Israël Silvestre's handsome engravings. And, as has been noted, some volumes even blurred the line between 'mass-produced publication and one-off art object', being printed on vellum and hand-coloured or illuminated.

Devised to present an occasion in the best light, festival literature was the textual embodiment of an event's principal preoccupations and political agendas. Texts were often printed before an event, providing spectators with a guidebook that extrapolated and explained the occasion's complex symbolic content:

> Festival books present the festival already pre-packaged, already interpreted. The iconography is spelled out for us, the political pretensions of the ruler are underlined. The festival itself will vanish, but this interpretation will last as long as books are read. Festival books are therefore not simple records of a festival, but another element in it.[95]

Conclusion: Festival as Designed Experience

As carefully designed experiences, Baroque urban festivals were used to articulate the power relationships between state and civic institutions and society at large. The deliberate use of props, scenery, and sound and light effects was intended to enhance the prestige of the event, ideology, or persons being celebrated. In this respect, early modern festival can be read as a form of media manipulation, tailor-made to reflect an occasion's rationale.

Festival's importance for the ruling élite can be, in part, explained by the absence of an effective 'police force'. Instead, early modern cities relied on non-professionals to enforce the law, with bands of citizens organized into militias and watches, and charged with keeping the peace. These *ad hoc* arrangements did not always ensure effective policing, with militias and watches often criticized for being undisciplined, lazy and, on occasion, corrupt.

Read in this context, festival must be seen as an effective social and political mechanism. In their design, festivals exploited a range of materials and visual effects, and successful spectacles were much more than frivolous diversions for the urban populace – they were complex interactions between designed elements; politically informed agendas; location; and spectator response.

3.48 (*opposite*) Set of six altar candlesticks and altar cross, Antonio Arrighi. Rome, 1750. Shown on the altar of the Chapel of St John the Baptist in the church of S. Roque, Lisbon, (cat.108)

The High Mass

Nigel Llewellyn

The performative potential of the Baroque style was exploited in ways that blurred the elusive lines drawn in seventeenth- and eighteenth-century culture between secular and religious experience. Performance was as important a question in the sacred spaces of chapels and churches as it was in the supposedly secular worlds of the square (so often the venue for religious processions) and the theatre. Indeed, many of these designed performances[96] were liminal, in that they crossed between the two domains and touched on social issues and personal experiences both secular and religious. In their capacity to engage powerfully with audiences of all kinds and integrate with other media, works of art in the Baroque style were especially appropriate for these kinds of situations. For example, the carved and painted wooden sculptures carried during Holy Week, on saints' days and on high days and holy days were known throughout Christendom, but especially in cultures such as that of southern Spain, where the traditions were codified and subject to theocratic and municipal interest[97] (see Religious Processions, p.254).

Within the holy spaces of church interiors and chapels the most compelling Baroque performances were the dramatic displays of multimedia visual art that took place on the occasion of the High Mass. To understand the challenge that these occasions presented to the many kinds of designers and makers involved, we need to start by rehearsing the nature and purpose of this complex ritual. What is the Mass?

Central to the Christian faith is the belief that Jesus Christ is the 'Saviour', that he undertook to sacrifice himself in order to save humankind from its sinful condition. The sacrifice was both bodily, in the form of execution by crucifixion at the hands of his Jewish enemies with the compliance of the Roman state, and spiritual. The bodily sacrifice was foreseen both through prophecies in Scripture and more directly in Christ's own words, recorded by several of the gospel-writers as having been uttered at the Last Supper.[98] This meal was taken by Christ and his disciples to mark the Jewish feast of Passover, and it signalled the opening of the final chapter in the dramatic last stages of Holy Week, leading directly to Christ's death on the cross (his bodily sacrifice) on the afternoon of the following day (Good Friday).

The Last Supper was described as a simple meal during which Christ invested the core ingredients – bread and wine – with symbolic significance, as representing his own flesh and

blood. The chief account is given by St Matthew, who quotes Christ as uttering the words: 'Take, eat; this is my body.... Drink ye all of it. For this is my blood ...' (XXVI 26–7). Furthermore, the Gospels include Christ's prophecy that he was soon to be betrayed and sacrificed, but that his bodily presence among his followers should be maintained in symbolic form by their partaking of a ritual consumption of bread and wine.

By imparting this revelation, the Gospels set out what later theologians identified as Christ's 'Institution of the Mass', a scene that is told and retold in countless representations of the Last Supper. This was often seen as an alternative, or sometimes a supplement, to the more dramatic moment, often selected by artists and patrons, when at the same meal Christ announces his impending betrayal, an announcement denied by all of the disciples except, of course, Judas Iscariot.

The ritual taking of bread and wine is therefore central to the Christian faith. The term 'Mass' is often used to describe this ritual and occurs across Europe. Despite its having been in use for almost 2,000 years, the origin of the word is much disputed. It perhaps originates in the Latin verb *mittere*, to send, with significant connotations of *commission* or *dismissal*, as those who celebrate and participate in the ritual are sent out into the world after it ends. Since the Reformation of the sixteenth century, the word 'Mass' has been associated especially with the Roman Catholic Church, and its meaning has been extended from the central business of taking bread and wine to cover the whole service, the way it is conducted (that is, its liturgy), and the particular forms of words and music that are used. In most orders of service the lengthy ceremony is divided into stages, sections or numbers such as the Preface, the first part, including the *Kyrie*; the Offertory, when donations of money or alms and certain prayers are conjointly offered; and the *Sanctus*, the part that includes the setting of the Latin words 'Holy, holy, holy', sung, chanted or spoken. Some Protestant denominations recognized a set pattern – the term 'canon' was used – for the section of the ceremony running from the *Sanctus* to the Eucharist – the actual partaking of the bread and wine in symbolic or physical form.

Other terms were applied to variants of the ritual among the numerous Christian denominations, and carry additional theological overtones: for example, 'Eucharist' itself comes from the Greek meaning 'thanksgiving'. Yet others use the term 'The Lord's Supper', referring directly to the Last Supper, and, most commonly in many Protestant churches, the term 'Holy Communion' is used, implying communal participation in the particular sacrament that represents an act of collective thanksgiving (pl.3.49).

In terms of its physical location in a place of worship, the ritual of the Mass takes place at a table-top in the church or chapel on which the sacrificial ritual substances are prepared and which typically forms the upper surface of the altar.

3.49 *Charles II of Spain in adoration of the Holy Sacrament*, Claudio Coello, oil on canvas. Madrid, 1685–90 (Monasterio del Escorial, Madrid)

As do and did many pagan religions, early Christianity accorded a central role to a sacrificial table, on the flat top of which a sacrifice might actually take place or be acted out. As we will see in Chapter Four, Baroque altars were subject to particular rules and constraints and indeed, across Western Christendom, were a topic of dispute.

After the Council of Trent, when the Roman Catholic Church adopted a whole new set of theological and liturgical strategies in response to the criticisms of Protestant Christians, the management of the High Mass was rearranged. As the ritual was understood and practised in the period when the Baroque style was current, the altar was both the setting for the dramatic re-enactment of the institution of the Mass and the station for the distribution of the symbolic materials of bread and wine, which would allow the devout to participate in the sacrifice.

The exact theological nature of the bread and wine presented and taken at Mass was the subject of a great deal of debate and even of conflict. According to the principles reconfirmed by the edicts of the Council of Trent and adopted throughout the orthodox Roman Catholic world, the bread and wine are transformed at the moment of consecration, through the sacred agency of the ordained officiating priest, who is, of course, the leading actor in the performance that lies at the heart of the High Mass. The belief that the bread and wine actually become the flesh and blood of the Saviour is a Roman doctrine describing a process called transubstantiation. After transubstantiation, it is believed that only the appearances (the 'accidents') of the natural bread and wine are perceived by the human eye. In contrast, one of the central tenets of the ritual as it was developed in the Protestant churches was an insistence on the continuing *symbolic* reality of the bread and wine, dismissing the Roman emphasis on magical transformation as mischievous and corrupting of scriptural understanding and the integrity of both officiating priests and communicants. The theological position taken to resolve the apparent contradictions around the nature of the host – the name given to the bread eaten in the ritual – was that Christ is really present at the Mass but that his presence cannot be grasped by the natural senses of mortal humankind. The emphasis on the magical reality of transubstantiation, reaffirmed so passionately in Counter-Reformation teaching, is one of the most important elements in the Roman High Mass and has a directly determining impact on the works of art that were designed and made for it.

To help us grasp how the visual culture of the Baroque High Mass functioned, we need to reconstruct a sense of the spiritual and temporal setting for what was a multimedia performance intended to appeal through all the senses to the intellect, the heart and the very soul with the uttermost profundity.

Although the core ritual and the central symbolism remained unchanged, different kinds of Masses took place at different times of the day, during the liturgical year, and on different kinds of occasion. In some contexts, the Mass was less of a public performance than a private or near-private devotion. Different cycles of liturgy also applied in secular and monastic churches. But the Easter High Mass was when the devout across the Christian world were under solemn injunction to attend the Mass and engage in an annual spiritual renewal, particularly if they were irregular in their attendance at other times in the year.

The High Mass was a lengthy and impressive religious performance invariably conducted at the extreme east end of the church, which was, in most cases, an attenuated, longitudinal space. So, for most witnesses, the Mass was seen from a distance, sometimes a considerable one, with the details of gesture and word hard to glimpse or hear. But other onlookers and participants, especially priests and social elites, were stationed much closer. So two kinds of visual communication were required: the officiating priests and their assistants needed to employ large-scale gestures; and visual artists and designers needed to employ the kinds of effects that would work well over long distances. In addition, minute and exact references and gestures were needed for those seeing the rituals from close up. As with so many aspects of the Baroque liturgy, spiritual demands were integrated with social hierarchies, and in many Baroque churches and chapels the rich and powerful owned and occupied pews and galleries that gave them direct, uninterrupted and relatively intimate opportunities to witness the Mass at close quarters. Their social prestige was matched by their privileged access to the ritual.

As we have seen, Baroque designers of performances in theatres and in public spaces had to help their audiences contend with contested viewpoints and poorly lit or polluted atmospheres. To communicate over long distances the ritual essences of the High Mass, across the heads of a throng of participants and through the dense incense-filled air, the officiating priest was marked out for his audience by his vestments, full-length, with deep sleeves to allow him to make strong gestures, and richly embroidered with ornament known as orphrey and other holy signs, both to communicate symbolic messages and to catch the eye. In the complete set, there were six key visible vestments worn by the officiating priest: the amice, the alb, the girdle, the maniple, the stole and the chasuble. The amice and alb were always worn as a pair and in

3.50 Priest's chasuble rear view from the Chapel of St John the Baptist in the Church of S. Roque, Lisbon, Francesco Giuliani and Filippo Salandri. Rome, 1744–9 (cat.112)

some churches known together as the 'apparel'; the amice was draped across the shoulders and adorned with embroidered ornament, while the alb, which was of fine white material, was left hanging long. The amice originally enveloped the head and neck as a symbolic 'helmet of salvation', but by the Baroque period it had been reduced to a smaller garment covering the shoulders, and played a purely symbolic role. The chasuble, plain or coloured (called, for example, in German *Messgewand*, or 'mass-garment'), was a garment that helped define the ritual; it was sleeveless, covered the torso and shoulders, and was worn over the alb and the stole (pl.3.50). The latter was mostly emblematic and awarded to a deacon at his ordination as a full priest; it was ordinarily worn over the left shoulder, but over both shoulders at the Mass. The effect was enhanced by the maniple (literally 'handful'), which was a strip of fabric usually about two feet in length, but sometimes, inconveniently, very much longer, worn hanging from the left wrists of priests, deacons and sub-deacons at the Mass. The outfit was completed by the girdle worn round the waist. The theoretical origins of the maniple are unclear: it is perhaps a reminiscence of the napkin used by a priest symbolically or actually to wipe away the tears he sheds for the sins of his flock, or it may derive from the fabric of the ropes used to tie Christ's hands at the mocking, scourging and judgement that continued the Passion cycle subsequent to the Last Supper.

Priests wore various recognizable items of apparel: for example, the square cap (beret or *biretta*), carefully colour-coded to match the ecclesiastical hierarchy (black, purple or red for priests, bishops and cardinals); however, the officiating priest who was celebrating the Mass wore a dedicated and specific uniform. The priest who was the celebrant was the leading player in the dramatic performance of the Mass: he had to be ordained, since deacons were forbidden to pronounce absolution (the declaration of God's forgiveness of sins), or a blessing, or to consecrate the eucharistic Sacrament. Deacons could support but not lead.

The ritual significance of the gestures that the priest had to make – blessing, welcoming, and so on – were of such importance that the hands had to be kept free for as much of the ceremony as possible. The wide sleeves of the tunic-shaped robe known as a dalmatic, as worn by deacons at the Mass,

3.51 Missal cushion from the Chapel of St John the Baptist in the church of S. Roque, Lisbon, Francesco Giuliani and Filippo Salandri. Rome, 1744–9 (cat.111)

3.52 *Virgin of the Immaculate Conception*, from Patriarchal Missal *In conceptione B: Mariae Virginis*, artist unknown, miniature painting on vellum. Italy, 1700–1800 (Treasury of Sé Cathedral, Lisbon)

would not have been practical for the celebrant, who also had to discard his cope, the rich vestment much used in other ceremonies. For these practical reasons, the officiating priest was often less splendidly robed at the High Mass than were his colleagues. The complex texts that the priest used had to be rehearsed and memorized as fully as possible; the officiant did not have hands free to support a book. When the holy texts changed, as they so often did over the course of the liturgical year, the lines of words had to be held up before the priest by an assistant or written out for easy access on a so-called altar card (in Italian *cartagloria*). In the Roman Church, the words of the liturgy or office for the seven canonical hours of the Church day were set out in a bound volume called the breviary. These books gave easy access to a selection of key and useful texts, such as the words of psalms, particular prayers (or collects) and sections of text for reading out aloud from Scripture or from the authorized lives of the saints. Some breviaries were fully illustrated with narrative and figurative miniatures and richly decorated with ornament. Less grand was the Missal (the word itself meaning Mass-book) or standard prayer-book, often placed on a dedicated cushion (pls 3.51, 3.52).

John V's chapel at São Roque

Nigel Llewellyn

Around 1700 the fortunes of the ancient Atlantic kingdom of Portugal were transformed by the opening up of extensive diamond- and gold-mining operations in the imperial territory of present-day Brazil. The new wealth dramatically increased the disposable income of the Portuguese crown and had a cultural impact that was even greater than the general economic effect on the country.

As did absolutist monarchs across Europe, in Portugal the greatest royal patron of the day, John (or João) V, treated his empire as his personal possession and spent the wealth generated by colonial exploitation as if it were his own. John was immensely devout, and, working through his minister at the Vatican, he sought actively to secure favour with the papacy, with various ends in view such as the award of the title 'Most Loyal', to match the similar designations such as 'Most Christian' enjoyed by other kings as well as the creation of a Portuguese cardinalate. So it was that John channelled vast sums of money into ambitious purchases of religious art, mostly in the Baroque style and much of it imported directly from Rome, the centre of the Catholic luxury trade.

In 1742, a new project of unparalleled ambition was launched, the commissioning from Rome of a complete side chapel, dedicated to

St John the Baptist and the Holy Spirit, to be installed within Lisbon's main Jesuit church of S. Roque (pl.3.53). This is a unique survival of the highest historical and artistic importance, since John's lavish patronage is fully documented throughout. Not only was the architectural fabric of the chapel imported from Italy, including a fully articulated set of decorative claddings for walls, vault and floor; in addition, all the internal decorative and liturgical fittings that were required for

3.53 Model for the Chapel of St John the Baptist in the Chapel of S. Roque, Lisbon, Giuseppe Palmes with Giuseppe Voyet, Giuseppe Focchetti and Gennaro Nicoletti, after Luigi Vanvitelli. Rome, 1742–4 (cat.105)

3.54 (*left*) Stole, Francesco Giuliani and Filippo Salandri. Rome, 1744–9 (cat.113)

3.55 Altar card: Central Canon, Antonio Vendetti after Luigi Landinelli and Lorenzo Morelli. Rome, 1744–9 (cat.121)

Mass to be celebrated throughout the Church year were also ordered – furnishings, silverware for the altar (the whole ensemble was blessed by the pope before it left Rome in 1749), decorative hangings for the walls and vestments for the priests. Complete sets of vestments were supplied in appropriate colours for all the Church festivals.

The immediate beneficiaries of all these expensive commissions were the long-established and highly enterprising applied and decorative artists operating in Roman workshops in the immediate ambience of the papal court, the epicentre of Roman Catholic politics and culture. All the specialist crafts were employed in this massive enterprise, and despite being spread around the workshops of a number of different makers and designers the work still took several years to complete.

Luigi Vanvitelli, later the architect of the Neapolitan palace at Caserta, designed the chapel, which was installed off the north nave aisle close to the main sanctuary, flanked at

3.56 (*right*) Great candlestick, Giuseppe Gagliardi and Leandro Gagliardi. Rome, 1749 (cat.107)

S. Roque by large subsidiary altars displaying stunning sets of reliquaries. The plan and decoration of the chapel were orthodox but lavish, the walls being articulated by fluted three-quarter columns and lined with thin sheets of decorative marbles of various colours and patterns. The expenditure was scrupulously recorded in the royal accounts. The chapel and its furnishings are an extraordinary example of how Baroque artists and patrons created magnificent settings for the performance of religious ritual.

3.57 (*below*) *Antependium* from
the Chapel of St John the Baptist
in the church of S. Roque, Lisbon,
Francesco Giuliani and Filippo
Salandri. Rome, 1774–9 (cat.125)

The priest was himself entirely clad in vestments that were
appropriate in terms of colour to the relevant point in the
liturgical calendar. These clothes obscured the natural body of
the priest, to reduce as far as possible any association between
him and the sub-lunar or corporeal world. The vestments
of the Mass were reserved: carefully preserved in the sacristy,
scrupulously maintained, worn only on the appropriate
occasion and removed immediately afterwards.

In really ambitious sets of vestments, the clothing worn by
the priests was integrated with the decoration of the altar and
the church, to allow the priest to blend seamlessly but also
mysteriously and dramatically into the architectural setting of
the holy space. For example, at S. Roque in Lisbon (see John
V's Chapel at S. Roque, p.194), each set of vestments included
an ornamental *antependium*, or altar frontal (pl.3.57), and a
dorsal (sometimes dossal), a curtain-like fabric of full length,
which hung behind the priest and the altar, across a chapel
door or to screen off an exit during the sacrament. The
embroidered fabrics of these ornamental surfaces matched
precisely the vestments being worn by the officiating priest and
his helpers. As the agents of the divine, the priests became
indistinguishable from the sacred space of the church itself.

3.58 Pair of cruets and salver from the Chapel of St John the Baptist in the church of S. Roque, Lisbon, Antonio Gigli. Rome, 1749 (cat.123)

The Baroque theme of the total integration of visual effect in different media was not restricted to the inanimate substances of works of art.

Cleansing and disposal were essential aspects of the ritual of the High Mass and required a number of dedicated utensils. These functions constrained design and also determined the kinds of materials used. The term 'host' (from a Latin word meaning sacrifice) was often applied to the bread or bread-like wafer representing Christ's body, and such was the potency of this sanctified material and of the wine that accompanied it, miraculously transformed into the blood of Christ, that at the end of the ceremony all remaining traces had to be disposed of, every crumb and drop consumed and all the utensils cleansed and dried (pl.3.58). 'Drink ye all of it', St Matthew has Christ demand of the Apostles (XXVI 27). This ceremonial cleansing or ablution was a necessary precaution in the world of the Baroque, where the forces of good and evil were understood to be playing out an endless competition for power and where holy materials had to be kept from falling into the hands of evil-doers and the forces of darkness.

3.59 Bell from the Chapel of St John the Baptist in the church of S. Roque, Lisbon, Antonio Gigli. Rome, 1749 (cat.116)

The items and ritualized stages that supported these cleansing duties included the *lavabo*, or basin, where the celebrant washed his hands prior to the consecration of the host, a moment of particular solemnity that would be marked by the sounding of a bell (pl.3.59). The ablutions using jugs, other vessels and cloths would take place perhaps at an aumbry, the recess where the sacred vessels could be kept, or alternatively at a small table (in English 'credence') erected near the altar (pl.3.60). Also used at the altar itself would be

3.60 Ablution set: ewer and basin from the Chapel of St John the Baptist in the church of S. Roque, Lisbon, Vincenzo I Belli. Rome, 1747 (cat.115)

a corporal, a fine linen cloth upon which the consecrated elements could be carried and covered against spillage, and for the wine and the host there was a chalice, specially dedicated for use at the Eucharist, and a paten, a metal plate in gold or silver, similarly dedicated to eucharistic purpose, which was often designed to be placed over the chalice (pls 3.61, 3.62).

To contain the host prior to its dedication and consecration there was a pyx, a receptacle that took a number of forms, sometimes hanging over the altar, in which case it might take the shape of a dove symbolizing the Holy Spirit, sometimes taking a more conventional box- or chest-like form. Close variants of the pyx were other containers with similar purposes called tabernacles or sometimes *ciboria*, kept on the altar and reserved for the Blessed Sacrament.

3.61 Chalice and paten from the Chapel of St John the Baptist in the church of S. Roque, Lisbon, Antonio Gigli. Rome, 1749 (cat.109)

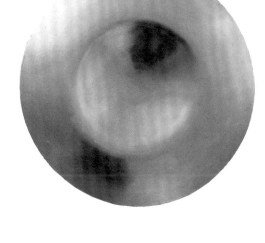

3.62 Chalice veil from the Chapel of St John the Baptist in the church of S. Roque, Lisbon. Francesco Giuliani and Filippo Salandri. Rome, 1744–9. This was placed over the paten when resting on the chalice, to protect it. (cat.110)

The German word for pyx is *Monstranz*, from the Latin
word 'to show', which reminds us of a complex double
function for these vessels: they are intended both to preserve
and reveal, to safeguard but also to advertise to the assembled
throng the host, which is inserted there by the celebrant, who
turns and displays it (pl.3.63). What might also be shown in
vessels of this type were other traces or morsels of holy matter,
not those intended for miraculous transubstantiation into
the very flesh of the Redeemer but matter that represented
the physical traces of his saints. For monstrances were also a
standard type of reliquary, that is, a receptacle for the
preservation and containment of holy material: for example,
the body parts of saints, or materials that were claimed to have
been in direct contact with Christ (parts of the True Cross),
or with his apostles and saints, or items otherwise invested
with miraculous powers.

Other kinds of metalwork in use at the High Mass were
solely symbolic in their functions, for example, the altar cross,
set in the centre and flanked by candles (pl.3.48). The cross
of course was the sign of Golgotha, the place of sacrifice that
had produced the body and blood of Christ, which was
commemorated through the Mass itself. Dealing with the
candles and assisting in other ways at the altar was an acolyte or
server who supported the officiant. Specially blessed on Easter
Eve and placed on the Gospel or liturgical north side of the
altar until the following Ascension Day was the Paschal Candle,
around which the celebrant and his assistants would have had
to manoeuvre during the High Mass held on Easter morning.

3.64 Thurible from the Chapel of St John the Baptist in the church of S. Roque, Lisbon, Leandro Gagliardi. Rome, 1750 (cat.117)

It was not only visual signs that were relied on to stimulate the senses of celebrant and congregation, for the High Mass was a potent synaesthetic performance: sound and aroma were also employed alongside objects designed to excite the sense of sight. To the side of the high altar stood an assistant responsible for the manipulation of the thurible or censer, a complex receptacle for hot coals ready to react with aromatic incense spooned from a boat to create perfumed clouds of steam and smoke at certain key moments in the ritual (pl.3.64). It was the claimed lack of scriptural authority that made Protestants sceptical about such practices, but in the Roman High Mass these dramatic effects were exploited to the full. The censer was swung on a set of chains about one metre in length, the heat contained at a safe distance from the assistant. The movement of the metal links and the sound they made would attract the notice of the congregation as their eyes were arrested by the coloured smoke and their nostrils caught by the heady aroma that was given off. The machine was loaded by means of long-handled tongs and a dish. Regarded as the finest of the spices used in incense-burners was the gum-resin known as frankincense (*olibanum*, of the genus 'Boswellia') (pl.3.65).[99]

Conclusion

The High Mass is perhaps the most demanding ritual for Baroque artists and designers in the context of the sacred space; but, as we have seen, the performative quality of the Baroque style was an aspect of its adaptability and flexibility. Baroque art could create illusions and weave mysteries in theatre and square as well as it could in a church. But the High Mass was not, of course, the only kind of religious ritual that deployed works of Baroque art and design as performative props and aids to devotion. As we shall see in the next chapter, the potential of the style to move and persuade was fully exploited in all corners of all sacred spaces.

3.65 Incense boat and spoon from the Chapel of St John the Baptist in the church of S. Roque, Lisbon, Leandro Gagliardi. Rome, 1750 (cat.118)

CHAPTER 4

POWER AND PIETY

Sacred Spaces
Nigel Llewellyn

The Baroque style was a powerful agent in the communication of ideas and emotions to crowds of spectators wherever they were, whether thronging streets or packing theatres. Its capacity for performance and display was matched by its effectiveness in engaging the minds and souls of individual beholders at their pious exercises. These devotional needs were accommodated in the art and design of Baroque sacred spaces such as the sanctified ground of churches and chapels, and in religious events and services held both in towns and villages and in the countryside. Furthermore, a great deal of sacred Baroque art was displayed in the home. The extraordinary metalwork and textile art that spoke to the assembled crowds at High Mass were created by teams of artists who also applied their skills to building vast ecclesiastical spaces and decking them out in imagery using an astonishing range of different materials and media. In its luxurious complexity and psychological impact the Baroque style was a potent aid to piety; since its effects touched the very souls of individual onlookers, it engaged in issues that were both immediate and familiar and that had an eternal outcome for the salvation of the devotee. This chapter considers the

4.1 Interior of the Church of S. Francisco de Assis, Salvador da Bahia. Brazil, 1708–55

powerful impact of the Baroque style on church art and design as well as its role in pious exercises.

As we have seen, there were many confessional and doctrinal alternatives within seventeenth- and eighteenth-century Christendom, yet what all the churches had in common was the need for a policy on the designing, manufacture and use of sacred art. The churches with claims to universal authority, such as the Roman Catholic and the Orthodox faiths, had agreed, promoted and imposed standards and rules relating to religious art. These same organizations however recognized and accommodated devotional, regional and cultural differences. For example, some Catholic churches erected in Portuguese India were clearly influenced in their layout by Hindu temples, while in Mexico, religious images were sometimes modelled out of corn pith.[1] No less telling examples could be drawn from every quarter of Europe: communion kerchiefs were decorated with Baroque ornament for the Calvinist church at Valka in Hungary in 1729.[2] The cult of saints, which was criticized by the Protestant churches but strongly promoted by Roman Catholics, was an especially powerful force in encouraging local and individual identities. The religious orders, pursuing their mission to bring salvation to the new worlds being opened up by European colonialism and trading activity (pl.4.1), exploited the full potential of religious imagery by implying or stating linkages and identifications between the indigenous gods and their images and the Western canon of saints (pl.4.2).[3]

Near the top of the Catholic hierarchy was the image of the Blessed Virgin Mary, often in her personification as the 'Immaculate Conception' (see The Virgin of the Immaculate Conception p.208). As Whistler has pointed out, following King John IV's dedication of Portugal to the cult of the Virgin of the Immaculate Conception in 1646, the devotion became so popular in Portugal's Brazilian territory that, by the early nineteenth century, some 20 per cent of all Brazilian parishes were dedicated to her.[4] The Franciscan order developed an especially close identification with the cult. Popular in Baroque Portugal and its possessions was the image of the Franciscan saint known as St Anthony of Padua, who was actually born in Lisbon. Images abounded of St Francis Xavier, whose burial place was in the Portuguese possession of Goa. Every country and region and town had its own traditions and logic to identify its particular saints, who could be figured in Baroque imagery and conjured in the mind's eye as intercessionary agents in the course of individual and communal devotion. (see The Cult of Saints, p.230)

The conventions about the depiction of saints were maintained by a complex combination of informal tradition and

formal decision-making. As we have seen, the most important Western clients of the Baroque style, the Roman Catholic Church, responded to the challenge of Protestantism by debating and then adopting a complex and far-reaching code, the Canons and Decrees of the Council of Trent – referred to as 'Tridentine' after the north Italian city of Trento – where a great church council had sat in deliberation over almost 20 years.[5] The Tridentine code was implemented across the Roman Catholic provinces and dioceses as priests under the leadership of their bishops undertook their duties caring for the souls of their congregations.[6] The priesthood was instructed that 'by means of the stories of the mysteries of our redemption portrayed in paintings and other representations the people are instructed and confirmed in the articles of faith ... [and] that great profit is derived from all holy images'.[7] In addition to this general reaffirmation of the legitimacy of images, a number of the decisions taken at Trent had a direct bearing on the construction and fitting out of places of worship and the manner in which the visual arts should henceforth be employed in relation to pious practices and the liturgy (or order of worship). Through the period when the Baroque style was fashionable and indeed the dominant style in precisely this area of artistic production, churches and chapels were expected to display art in the form of images that functioned in particular and prescribed ways. The imagery on display in sacred spaces had to avoid false doctrine and it had to be instructive, not disorderly, unbecoming or confusing. Church images had to conform to the reformulated and restated Catholic doctrines about the intercessory powers of the saints and the veneration of relics. In short, images had to be used in legitimate ways, a topic that had been disputed passionately across Christendom for centuries. In fact, the Tridentine decrees made reference to patristic decisions of the Second Council of Nicaea.

A key point – on which Catholics were especially sensitive because of the telling criticisms that had been directed at them from many Protestant quarters – was that the material reality of a religious image should never itself become the object of worship. The images were not themselves the gods that were worshipped. Their role was to generate veneration for the prototypes they represented. The post-Tridentine position on church art was that paintings and sculpture, and the other applied and decorative arts, should continue to narrate stories about the sacred mysteries and the miracles of the saints and should continue to decorate the walls of churches and chapels. However, this art had to be designed and executed to be clear in its purpose and avoid distracting viewers from the imagery's primary, devotional role.

In the immediate aftermath of Trent some artists and patrons applied the new rules about church art with radical strictness, but this was a quite short-lived phase in the history of Christian art. The analysis of the Baroque that has been offered in the earlier chapters of this book proves that the style was less concerned simply with clarity of expression and transparent story-telling and more concerned with emotional engagement and complexity of response. Indeed, some have regarded the development of the Baroque style, which in a number of important ways represents a rejection of the purest Tridentine ideology, as a sign of the erosion of the political and spiritual certainty of the immediate post-Trent church. It is demonstrably true that sacred art in the Baroque style soon became accepted as orthodox and that it contributed effectively to a multi-levelled and multi-sensory experience of sacred spaces that was typical of the devotional lives of contemporaries. There is also a great deal of evidence that sensory experience through the medium of complex and powerful art was sufficiently highly valued to challenge orthodoxy, and not only in the visual arts. In church music, the increased size of musical forces in the seventeenth century had to be accommodated by reorganized ecclesiastical spaces. When musicians played and sang from the west end of a church, the congregation – habitually facing eastwards towards the high altar – would turn to listen, a move that represented a partial disassociation of music from ritual, which was entirely against the spirit of the Tridentine reforms.

4.2 *Virgin and Child*, maker unknown (probably Chinese). Probably The Philippines, *c*.1700–20 (cat.7)

THE VIRGIN OF THE IMMACULATE CONCEPTION

Nigel Llewellyn

The Gospel accounts of Mary, the mother of Jesus, tell us little, leaving a scriptural vacuum that was filled by Catholic reformers with numberless cults, images and devotions. With her earthly husband, Joseph, and her son she is the third member of an earthly trinity representing an exemplary, Holy Family. Joseph almost always appears as a kindly old man, but the variety of representations of Mary is legion, many developed in response to global missionary practice with a global currency and recognized across the Catholic world.

The doctrine of the Virgin of the Immaculate Conception (now defined as 'conceived without the stain of original sin' and not concerned with virginity or otherwise) was championed by the Franciscans and by many powerful lay Catholics: it presents Mary in her aspect as the queen of heaven and earth, crushing evil underfoot. Two versions of this image, both by Italian artists for Spanish royal patrons – one from the 1620s, the other from the 1760s – illustrate the type. Reni's version appeals to a broad audience of viewers in the prettiness of its colouring and in the simplicity of expression on the faces of the three main figures. The Madonna's hand gesture signifies prayer and her girlish locks stream in the solar breeze (pl.4.3).

4.3 *The Virgin of the Immaculate Conception*, Guido Reni, oil on canvas. Italy, 1627 (The Metropolitan Museum of Art, Victor Wilbour Memorial Fund, 1959)

4.4 *The Virgin of the Immaculate Conception*. Indo-Portuguese, probably Goa, 1750–1800 (cat.127)

4.6 *The Virgin of the Immaculate Conception*, Giambattista Tiepolo, Aranjuez. 1767 (cat.88)

How exactly Mary was graced by immaculacy was long debated by theologians; some cited a passage from *Revelation* which described '[the] woman clothed with the sun and the moon under her feet and ... a crown of twelve stars'. In Tiepolo's version, she exudes reserved authority, seemingly free of physical constraints, unheeding of the supporting cherubim, the unique epitome of freedom from original sin as required of the Mother of Christ. In a typical Tiepolo visual joke, several of the twelve stars are hidden behind her head. The serpent with an apple in its mouth (an allusion to original sin) makes an iconographic link with another Marian cult popular in the Baroque, the Virgin as Woman of the Apocalypse. Tiepolo's image deals in immensity: the space dominated by the picture and the heavens dominated by the figure of Mary (pl.4.6).

Other figures of the Virgin of the Immaculate Conception were in handier sizes, some fit for personal or domestic contemplation. Canvases can be worked to permit a picture of almost any size, but other materials circumscribe the dimensions of the image. For example, tusks of ivory limit the carver to relatively small images, such as those made in Goa and the Philippines for the European market that exploited iconographic traits similar to the ones we see in the painted versions. But Mary could not only present a powerful image as the queen of heaven and earth; she could be exemplary on almost every level. Wooden statues of her could be borne aloft in street procession. Some versions were almost doll-like in their design, with attached headdresses using real hair, and exquisitely embroidered and bejewelled robes.

All humankind could identify with Mary as a mother; half of humankind with her as a woman, sister or daughter. Baroque artists developed different images of Mary to play all of these roles. It was this remarkable adaptability and universality of identification that made images of the Blessed Virgin Mary so central to the canon of Baroque imagery.

4.5 *The Virgin of the Immaculate Conception*, maker unknown. Portugal, *c.*1760 (cat.87)

Spaces Dedicated to the Sacred

Christians were surrounded by Baroque art. Sacred imagery was displayed not only in homes but in every kind of public space, from wayside shrines to ecclesiastical buildings of all sizes and shapes, among them enormous constructions on a titanic scale such as the Vatican Basilica of St Peter. This is a complex in which the church has to be understood as just one part of a much larger total entity, encompassing the square across which visitors approach the basilica, along with the astonishing programme of scenographic, external and internal decoration. St Peter's is an extraordinary example of the key qualities in the Baroque style (as explored in Chapter Two). It is a carefully designed functional space, intended to gather together and process enormous crowds of pilgrims and visitors to the Vatican, which operated as an early modern princely court as well as a shrine, and fulfilled a number of other functions. On a daily basis through the Church year and for special events such as Holy Years or papal investitures, the piazza beyond the west façade was a site for processions involving the kinds of artistic devices and media discussed in Chapter Three. These performances were arranged with the formality and dignity that, across Europe, were habitually accorded a head of state, with liveried servants, uniformed guards, flags, lantern-sets in precious metals and ceremonial equipment of all kinds (pl.4.7).[8] Small, portable altars and shrines were carried to be displayed to onlookers. These were invariably richly ornamented to catch the eye and were sometimes decorated with elaborate scenes of martyrdom played out by a complete cast of saints and villains and with angels in attendance.[9] This art was sacred in name only and shared its aesthetic values with secular works in the Baroque style.

Religious processions were often organized to move from church spaces to particular landmark structures erected in town or country. Ceremonial columns had been erected since ancient times and considerable numbers of commemorative crosses were set up across the medieval world. The tradition did not end with the Reformation: the monument to the Great Fire of London is an interesting transitory Protestant version of this type. In the Baroque, plague columns were set up in Austria (pl.4.8), Bavaria and in the Czech lands (Telč, Teplice, Valeč, Olomouc) to mark pledges given by rulers making a votive

4.7 Ceremonial mace made for a cardinal, Giovanni Giardini. Rome, 1691–6 (cat.76)

4.8 Plague Column, Vienna, Matthias Rauchmiller, Johann Bernhard Fischer von Erlach, Paul Strudel, Tobias Kracker, Johann Bendel. 1683–93

4.9 Basilica of S. Maria della
Salute, Venice, Baldassare
Longhena. 1681

4.10 (*opposite*) Sanctuary of Bom
Jesús do Monte, Braga. Portugal,
1722–80s

offering in return for relief from the plague.[10] The most striking Baroque church in Venice, S. Maria della Salute ('Health'), has exactly this function (pl.4.9).

Across Catholic Christendom the Baroque style was employed for a genre of sacred art that was related to processional art, adapting an idea that had been developed in the Renaissance to create holy, outdoor spaces intended to remind pilgrims of Christ's sacrifice at Jerusalem and often located on hilltops, the so-called Sacri Monti. For these, Baroque designers used architecture and decoration to create spaces that owed more to the theatre and other forms of popular culture than to conventional church art. In the Alpine region, the holy mountains were typically set up in wild and remote places and comprised a set of chapels, spaced a little way apart from one another, each with a tableau of carved and painted figures playing out a scene from the Passion cycle.[11] A contemporary recorded that the Sacro Monte at Varallo attracted the people of Piedmont in the form of 'infrequent

cavalcades … munificent in the gifts they leave … sometimes as many as ten thousand visitors … in a single day'[12] (see The Stations of the Cross and Popular Piety, p.216).

In Iberia, the most extraordinary project of this kind was the development of the sacred mountain at Braga, in northern Portugal, not a remote mountain but on the fringes of an ancient city (pl.4.10). The development of the Bom Jesús do Monte pilgrimage site included architectural works and large numbers of specially commissioned sculptures, whose iconography conformed to a programme drawn up in accordance with Jesuit doctrine. A new design was agreed for Braga in 1722 and in the following year a gateway was erected with a Latin inscription claiming that the site was 'Jerusalem restored and rebuilt'. The visitor's journey starts with the conventional Passion subject of the 'Wounds of Christ', which was set at the foot of a cascading stairway adorned with fountains representing the Five Senses. And then, with a typical late Baroque convergence of the devotional, the allegorical, the

scriptural and the philosophical, the visitor encountered statues representing pagan deities such as Diana and Mercury. In time, voices of disquiet were raised against these pagan incursions and late in the eighteenth century a pragmatic solution was agreed: they were not removed but simply renamed – for example, Orpheus became Solomon. A near-contemporary elision of the secular and the religious occurs in a comparable scheme by the great Bohemian sculptor Matyas Bernhard Braun (b.1684). Between 1715 and 1720 he worked on a complex scheme at the Von Sporch country house at Kuks, where the patron's unorthodox ideas about moral improvement were pictured in Braun's statues of the Beatitudes, the Virtues and the Vices (pl.4.11).

Some of the sacred art produced for domestic spaces was of very grand conception, for example, an altar from Dresden (pl.4.12) which, although of extremely modest size, uses highly precious materials in a composition including all the components that one might expect to encounter on a much larger Baroque altar: the architectural frame, ornamental putti, the cresting with the name of Jesus in a star-burst setting, a picture of the Redeemer, the cross and a mass of other symbolic and figurative material. A comparable ratio of ornament to figuration is found in a picture from the New World where the devotional subject – the Holy Family with attendant angels – is set into a carved and decorative frame of such elaboration that it risks dominating the picture itself (pl.4.13).

4.11 Statues of Virtues and Vices, copies after the originals by Matyas Bernhard Braun, Kuks Castle. Czech Republic, 1712–15

4.12 Miniature house altar, maker unknown. Germany, c.1710 (cat.128)

4.13 (opposite) *Holy Family with Angels*, artist unknown, Cuzco School. Cuzco, 1700–1800 (cat.130)

THE STATIONS OF THE CROSS AND POPULAR PIETY

Nigel Llewellyn

On a summer's day in 1749 central Rome was packed to bursting with a sweating crowd of more than 100,000 pilgrims. Under the watchful eye of Pope Benedict XIV and the college of cardinals, the fountains were stopped and the markets were closed. On a temporary stage set up before the church of S. Giacomo degli Spagnuoli stood an aged Franciscan dressed in chains and a crown of thorns, beating himself with a scourge. Shouting 'Penitence' and 'to Hell', he exhorted the onlookers to repent, and they responded with great moans of 'Mercy! Mercy!'

This figure was Leonard of St Maurice (1676–1751, canonized 1867), who had worked among students and convicts and whose ministry helped prepare the city for the Holy Year of 1750. Leonard's mission focused on the setting up of series of small shrines in a narrative sequence marking the stages on Christ's final journey (the *Via Crucis* or Way of the Cross) through Jerusalem to Calvary. These 'Stations of the Cross' displayed images that exploited theatrical and artistic devices to encourage acts of public, communal devotion, often highly

emotional in mood (pl.4.15). The Franciscans were put in charge of the cult and Leonard evidently established almost 600 series of 'Stations': the popularity of the idea benefited Baroque artists across the Roman Catholic world. Series were set up both around the interiors of churches and along processional routes, very often linking urban and rural environments.

In 1731, the pope had confirmed the correct number of Stations as fourteen in a narrative sequence adapted from the original points of meditation for pilgrims, long established on the *Via Dolorosa* (Way of Sorrows) in Jerusalem: 'His First Fall' (No.3), 'His Third Fall' (No.9), and so on. Within the narrative (Station No.6) was the story of St Veronica (pl.4.16), the compassionate woman who wiped Christ's suffering brow as he passed, an act that miraculously left the imprint of his face on her cloth (a relic long kept at St Peter's, Rome). Encouraged by his success, in 1749 Leonard established a famous and influential set of Stations in the Roman Coliseum, regarded then as a site of early Christian martyrdom. These are

4.14 Passion Shrine from the Via Crucis, O Aleijadinho, Congonhas do Campo, Minas Gerais. Brazil, 1796–9

4.15 *Second Station of the Cross*, Giandomenico Tiepolo, oil on canvas. Venice, *c.*1747 (Oratory of the Crucifix, Church of S. Polo, Venice, Italy)

4.16 (*above right*) *St Veronica*, Francesco Mochi, marble. Rome, 1629–32 (St Peter's Basilica, Rome)

4.17 *St Luitgard*, Matyas Bernhard Braun. 1710 (Charles Bridge, Prague)

each marked with a simple stone plaque bearing the sign of the cross. At the entrance, pilgrims are advised that 'Kissing the sacred cross will bring an indulgence of one year and twelve days', the period in purgatory remitted for those taking part in the devotion.

These images are part of the visual culture of popular piety in the Baroque age, as are pilgrimage churches, holy mountains, wayside crosses, the statuary shrines on the Charles Bridge at Prague (pl.4.17), or the Angels with the Instruments of the Passion, designed by Bernini for the Castel Sant'Angelo Bridge in Rome. They encouraged a public but personal engagement between the devotee and the passionate drama being played out in the imagery displayed. An interesting and contemporary Protestant parallel might be drawn with J.S. Bach's *Passions*, musical settings of the words of the evangelists St John and St Matthew that also appealed to vernacular audiences, retold a familiar narrative and exploited drama, emotion and meditation.

Church Interiors

Despite the great quantity of sacred art made for domestic spaces and processional performances, the most important commissions were for church interiors. Not all churches with significant amounts of Baroque art were designed, built and decorated as part of a single, coherent plan of work. Indeed, there is no single type of the Baroque church. Even when a rich and long-lived patron was involved, church-building was a lengthy project and easily disrupted by chance, ill-health, natural disaster and the vagaries of political change. Rare exceptions to this rule are some smaller churches or buildings that enjoyed particular favour and dedicated attention, such as the Vienna Karlskirche. Churches had to fulfil many varied functions and were set up on different kinds of sites, although there was no universal rule for their layout. Some were erected on fresh sites, with sufficient space to permit the architect to propose a plan of their choice, but for a city church to be free-standing was unusual (pl.4.18). Others were built on the footprints left by previous buildings and were required to replicate or acknowledge their shape. The practical need to conform with the footprint of a previous building often encouraged architects to use the traditional cruciform basilican ground plan, which was employed across the Christian world. In this form, long naves and side aisles accommodate the congregation, provide processional spaces and give convenient access to side chapels, of which there are sometimes as many as four or five on each side. The crossing of this longitudinal axis by the transepts provides a substantial open space in front of the devotional focus of the church, which is at the far east end beyond the crossing. An enormously influential variant of this basic design was the ground plan of the Gesù, the headquarters church of the Jesuit order in Rome, started in the later sixteenth century by Vignola, consecrated in 1584 and available in the seventeenth century to be decorated by some of the most distinguished practitioners of the Baroque style (pl.4.19). Anyone pausing in the piazza outside and studying the contours of the austere façade can, in fact, glean a good basic understanding of the interior space. What confronted the Baroque artists entering the church was a lengthy but broad open nave with no aisles but with side chapels deeply recessed into the nave walls, interconnected to offer something of the parallel longitudinal potential of a conventional plan. The transept is an equally ingenious adaptation, no deeper than the nave chapels but very deep from east to west and creating an enormous open space in the centre of the building.

4.18 Model for the church of St Mary-le-Strand, maker unknown after James Gibbs. London, after 1717 (cat.25)

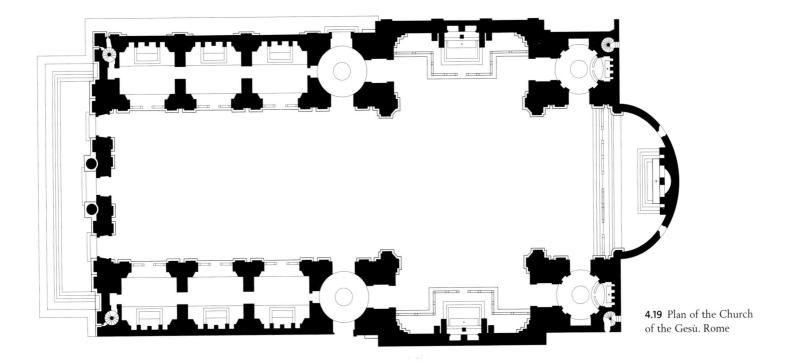

4.19 Plan of the Church of the Gesù. Rome

The different classes of church building had different functions that determined their design and decoration. The adaptability of the style meant that all these types, from quite humble parish churches to the grandest cathedrals, could be decked out, either wholly or partially, with lavish Baroque interiors. Such decorative projects could powerfully express the interests of their patrons, whether these were ecclesiastical bodies, élite families or semi-civic bodies such as confraternities. Most parish churches were under diocesan authority but some were collegiate churches, which retained parish duties but were ruled by chapters of canons under a dean. More specialist were the abbey churches set up at monastic houses ruled by abbots, some with large permanent or pilgrimage congregations as well as their monastic residents (see The Benedictine Abbey at Melk, p.220). In the cathedrals were the thrones of the bishops who ruled the dioceses and often controlled vast wealth.

As with the scheme of decoration on buildings of all types and periods, the designers of Baroque churches had a number of issues to keep in balance in planning their decorative programmes. Traditional solutions were refreshed, for example, by using the four triangular areas of wall and ceiling at the base of crossing domes – called pendentives – for pictures of the Four Doctors of the Church or the four Evangelists with their symbols (the angel, the lion, the ox and the eagle).[13] The high-arching areas at the far east end, usually behind and above the high altar, as were other domes and ceilings, were especially suited to heavenly scenes of triumph and ascension, vision and adoration and were populated by angels and miraculously transported saints. The subjects of pictures and statuary positioned at less lofty altitudes, and so more visible to onlookers, tended towards the narrative, the contemplative and the socially directive – scenes of martyrdom and scriptural exegesis, images of the Sacred Heart or of saints in sacred discourse, the heraldic emblems and the name of the local lord, the current pope or the patrons of the chapel.

The patrons, priests, designers and artists engaged in commissioning and providing sacred art for these buildings sought to balance innovation and appropriateness, or what in early modern discourse was called 'decorum'. Decorum was a concern both within and without the building. In the posthumous collection of varied writing by and associated with Sir Christopher Wren, known as *Parentalia*, there are comments on the steeple of the London City church of St Mary-le-Bow, which was under construction in 1671–80:

[it is a] peculiar kind of building, which has no fixed Rule to direct it, if we are to consider it only as a part of some other building, it can be esteemed no other than a delightful Absurdity: But if either considered in itself, or as a Decoration on a whole City in prospect, not only to be justified, but admired ... [it] is beyond Question as perfect as human Imagination can contrive or execute....[14]

THE BENEDICTINE ABBEY AT MELK

Eric Garberson

This portrait of Abbot Berthold Dietmayr (pl.4.20), who reigned at Melk from 1700 to 1739, suggests the visual richness of life in a Baroque monastery. As in countless portraits since the Renaissance, the abbot stands before an elaborate architectural backdrop hung with rich drapery and enormous tassels. Although inconsistent in viewpoint and scale, this fictive architecture, like the real architecture of the monastery itself, provides an appropriate setting. Here Abbot Berthold wears the robes of the Rector of the University in Vienna, a post he assumed in 1706, while the mitre and staff on the richly draped table refer to his ecclesiastical authority as abbot. The prominently displayed plan for the rebuilding of the church proclaims his interest in architecture and his role as the rebuilder of the monastery. This role was further demonstrated by the display of his coat of arms, seen here on the back of the throne, on parts of the building constructed during his rule.

Similar portraits, of past abbots and other important men, were prominently displayed to document the monastery's history and to demonstrate its political connections. Other pictures, accumulated over the centuries, also hung throughout or were grouped in galleries like that in the abbot's quarters at Melk. As in the Middle Ages, richly decorated manuscripts continued to be produced, but now primarily for ceremonial or commemorative purposes. One such manuscript (pl.4.21), containing well-wishes and poems of praise, was presented by the community to Abbot Adrian Pliemel upon his election in 1739. It is decorated with emblems, a typically Baroque form of imagery, often also employed as architectural decoration, that combines text and image to produce a composite meaning. Here a giant sunflower, marked with an 'A' for Adrian and taken from the abbot's coat of arms, makes a witty play on his name (Pliemel = Blümel, or small flower). Bending protectively over the monastery, it channels rain from a cloud bearing the figures of five patron saints. The crowning phrase, 'from this watering it sprouts anew', conveys the community's hopes for prosperity under the new abbot's rule. Similar imagery was also created for circulation outside the monastery, such as the engraving reused as the frontispiece to a 1747 volume publicizing the Melk library. The personification of Wisdom, holding a quill and surrounded by other implements of scholarship, looks up at a medallion portrait of Abbot Berthold held by a genius trumpeting the fame of the monastery, seen in the distance poised majestically on the bluffs above the Danube (pl.4.22). The emblem of a bee landing on a flower illustrates the programmatic statement, 'from these studies my nourishment'.

In the main rooms of the monastery, such as the library (pl.4.23), architecture and decoration function together to convey the values of the community while also providing an appropriate setting for the institution's daily and ceremonial life. Here the richly inlaid furnishings house uniformly bound books in the most up-to-date manner and create an overall effect of magnificence in keeping with the rank of its patron, Abbot Berthold. The allegorical fresco on the ceiling proclaims that the goal of monastic learning is the attainment of divine wisdom and the Christian virtues that such wisdom guarantees.

4.20 *Abbot Berthold Dietmayr*, attributed to Jan Kuptezky, oil on canvas. After 1706 (Stift Melk)

4.21 *Festschrift für Abt Adrian Pliemel*, manuscript, 1739 (Stift Melk)

4.22 (*far right*) View of Melk Abbey, Austria, designed by Jakob Prandtauer, 1702–36

4.23 Library with ceiling frescoes by Paul Troger, Melk Abbey. Austria, 1731–2

4.24 Font house from Ringsaker Church, Lars Jenssen Borg. Norway, 1704 (cat.91)

The Sacraments

An important aspect of decorum in relation to church decoration involved matching particular functions to particular areas of the building. This principle can be illustrated if we take as our starting point the canon of the Sacraments, the devotional practices reserved to the Catholic priesthood, many of them reflected in church layout and decoration.[15] At the first stage of the spiritual journey, the soul of the individual is welcomed into the faith at Baptism, marked by the pouring on of water, and a ritual that was often given a separate space, either a baptismal chapel or sometimes even a separate building. Because it employed sanctified water, the rite always required a dedicated vessel, the font itself. To conserve the sanctity of the font, ornamental and symbolic covers were often provided, for example, Grinling Gibbons's highly naturalistic composition in wood for All Hallows by the Tower, showing fruit and foliage being managed by two winged angels and topped off by an eagle.[16] For the baptism, embroiderers supplied a white chrisom (garment) to be worn by the child. Where there was no room for a separate architectural space, a font-house could serve. These were originally quite numerous in Lutheran Norway, where they were placed near church entrances. In fact, across Christendom, the ceremony tended to be carried out near places of entrance. Holy Communion and Baptism were the only two sacraments recognized by the Lutheran church and their use of font-houses with matching

4.25 Font from Ringsaker Church, Lars Jenssen Borg. Norway, 1704 (cat.92)

fonts (pls 4.24, 4.25) gave symbolic emphasis to the ritual, perhaps to balance the emphasis that the altar, even in a Lutheran church, gives to the Communion.[17] In the Catholic Church and in some Protestant churches too, the rite of Confirmation, that is, the marking of the soul with the seal of the Holy Spirit, was the essential precursor for participation in the Eucharist or mass by the partaking of Communion, discussed in Chapter Three.

Among Catholics, the sacrament of Penance required the penitent individual to make a confession, heard by the priest, who then pronounced absolution. Since the transaction was secret, special areas had to be set aside within the public spaces of the church. St John Nepomuk, a martyr to the cause of confessional secrecy, is often portrayed with his finger to his lips and urging silence, sometimes under the Latin motto *Tacui*. At the church of S. Maria Maddalena in Rome a remarkable set of life-size allegorical figures in the nave, carved by a team of sculptors *c*.1700, personify aspects of this ritual such as 'Humility', 'Simplicity', and 'Secrecy' with her finger to her lips. The Catholic reformers revised and revived the sacrament of Penance and defended its practice and the significance of the confessional as a means of emphasizing the key role of the priest. Furthermore, the sacrament presented interesting opportunities for artists and designers.[18] Baroque churches were supplied with elaborately carved and decorated wooden confessional boxes, often in sets and typically allowing the priest to deal with two clients together, one to each side. Inlaid and rich exotic woods were often used (see pl.1.29).

Using holy oils to anoint someone on the verge of death – the sacrament of Extreme Unction – usually took place away from the church and was not generally an occasion for the creation of visual art, although it was a subject for painters. The sixth sacrament is Ordination, the act of induction to the priesthood, which happens on certain set days in the year, famously among Catholic deacons, in acts of group worship, in the vast open spaces of the crossing of St Peter's. Finally, there is Matrimony. Each sacrament is a channel for imparting grace and all derive ultimately from Christ's instructions as set out in the Gospels.[19]

One of the most important of all church functions was commemoration, and the construction of tombs and monuments of all kinds was a major preoccupation for Baroque artists. Some Baroque churches are densely packed with commemorative art, especially the floors, marking the places of burial. The carved ledger stones, inlaid with *pietra dura*, that pave the nave floor at St John's Co-Cathedral in Valletta, Malta, represent one of the most extraordinary displays of Baroque art and design anywhere (pl.4.26).[20]

4.26 Floor of St John's Co-Cathedral and detail of marble tombstones inlaid in the floor. Valletta, Malta, early seventeenth to eighteenth century

4.27 Chandelier, given to the Riddarholm Church, Stockholm, by Queen Hedvig Eleonora in memory of King Charles X of Sweden, Andreas I Wickert. Augsburg, *c.*1650 (cat.98)

Many church spaces were turned over to commemorative use: chapels and aisles housed lofty wall tombs; smaller painted and carved epitaph monuments hung between windows and some side chapels were entirely given over to their function as family mausolea. Some were privately owned spaces, with access often denied to the public by wrought-iron grilles, and they were lavishly equipped with furnishings and lighting (pl.4.27).

The more elaborate Baroque funeral monuments display complex mixtures of imagery. First, they use architectural motifs and frames to draw the attention of onlookers and give the monument its distinct place among the confusion of sacred images typical of so many Baroque churches; secondly, there is figure sculpture to represent the deceased by means of an effigy, or the family or other mourners, and there are allegorical figures to personify the good qualities of the person commemorated – virtues such as Faith, Wisdom or Fortitude.

Thirdly, the social élites across the Baroque world used heraldic devices on their funerary monuments to set out their social rank and to confirm their blood lineage. Finally, there were monumental inscriptions that gave biographical information or contemplative or moralizing commentary in the form of epitaphs. The preliminary drawing for a wall tomb (pl.4.28) shows all the key elements in a composition that was repeated with minimal variants in thousands of Baroque monuments. The subject is shown in contemporary dress reclining in a meditative fashion and attended by putti. Below, above and behind her is an imposing architectural framework, which supports at its very peak a cartouche for an heraldic emblazon, also supported by angels, this time with trumpets to suggest the fame of the individual. Below, and thus easy to read, is a panel of inscription in a decorated frame. A variant on the standard form of the recumbent or semi-recumbent effigy, and one

4.28 Design for the monument to Dorothy, Lady Brownlow, in St Nicholas's Church, Sutton, William Stanton. London, *c.*1700 (cat.93)

4.29 Funerary chapel of Henri de Bourbon, Prince de Condé, Pierre-Paul Sevin. France, 1683 (cat.94)

4.30 Figure of 'Fama' from the Funerary Achievement of Pontus Fredrik de la Gardie in Västerås Cathedral, attributed to the workshop of Burchardt Precht. Sweden, 1692–3 (cat.96)

which swung in and out of fashion among Baroque artists but had its particular champions among the designers of papal tombs, was the kneeling effigy (pl.4.31). This seems to have been regarded not as unique to but especially appropriate for devout senior churchmen and it allowed unrivalled engagement between the sculpted effigy and the spectator.

Monuments were permanent constructions that created an image for the deceased, but in their permanence they should not be separated from other elaborate manifestations of visual culture, produced to mark every stage in the Baroque death ritual. Much of this apparatus was ephemeral so does not survive, but there are representations in the form of drawings, paintings and engravings showing how complete chapels and large church spaces were decked out with temporary architecture on occasions such as state funerals (pl.4.29). Sometimes, the knightly paraphernalia was carried at funerals and then set up over the grave as a kind of permanent commemorative marker (pl.4.30). A long-standing variant on the funeral monument, and one with continuing currency

4.31 Bozzetto for the tomb of Pope Alexander VII, Gianlorenzo Bernini. Rome, c.1669–70 (cat.95)

in the Baroque period, was the chantry, a space in Catholic churches set aside and endowed for memorial activities, especially the Requiem Mass, the repetition of which aimed to bring comfort to the soul in purgatory. Commemoration was a holy rite; it reaffirmed social rank and gave an opportunity for didactic and moralizing reflection on individual qualities, a mix of secular and religious functions typical of sacred Baroque spaces.

The churches themselves were divided into areas for the congregation and reserved areas for the priesthood. The choir was a liminal area between priest and people with its north or cantoris side (for the cantor, or precentor) dedicated to the voice that led the worship and its south side for the officiating cleric (decani, the dean's side). Further east lay the high altar itself and usually to the north and east of that was located the sacristy, a kind of storage area, annexe and parish office, often equipped with its own altar at which small-scale worship might take place but used mainly for storing valuable holy property. This was under the charge of a sacristan (in English, often contracted to sexton); in really important Baroque churches the functions of the sacristy would be taken on by an even more secure Treasury. Here would be kept the valuable liturgical equipment and other precious possessions, especially the reliquaries, when they were not in use in a service.

THE CULT OF SAINTS

Nigel Llewellyn

The cult of saints was one of the most divisive of all the many theological and administrative disagreements between the Catholic and Protestant wings of western Christianity. Catholic reformers emphasized the exemplary qualities of saints' good works and cited their miracles as signs of God's grace, his direct involvement in the world of sinners. Furthermore, in 1634 the Vatican significantly strengthened the criteria that led to the canonization of individual candidates for sainthood. In their teaching, Catholic priests emphasized the intermediary role that saints played between individual worshippers and the deity. But Protestants remained suspicious of any intermediaries between the individual believer and his or her God, and were concerned that the unwary or the ill-educated might pray directly to a saint, as if praying to God, and thus inadvertently commit idolatry. Protestant sceptics were also able to cite plenty of evidence of corrupt practice in relation to canonization, falsified accounts of miracles and idolatrous responses to imagery.

In art, figures of saints ranged from top-quality carved marble sculpture for royal chapels to simple woodcuts for pilgrims that were produced by Baroque artists in thousands of copies. Especially popular were the newly created saints from the missionary orders. Prominent amongst these were the Jesuits, established in 1540 to become a powerful tool of Catholic renewal through pious prayer and education.

The visual representations of these new saints were carefully controlled by the Church and swiftly became an artist's stock-in-trade. Three of the key saints were canonized in 1622, at the very moment when art historians have traced the emergence of a definable Baroque style. The Basque St Ignatius of Loyola (c.1491–1556) appears in his dark robes as a thoughtful, bearded figure. His fellow student St Francis Xavier (1506–52) became a missionary, a scenario which gave ample opportunity for the depiction of exotic settings for his teaching and miracle-working (pl.4.32). Francis ministered (and was eventually buried) in the East:

4.32 *The Death of St Francis Xavier,* Carlo Maratta, oil on canvas. Rome, *c.*1679 (Church of the Gesù, Rome)

Portuguese India, the East Indies, Japan and finally China. St Philip Neri (1515–95) was a Florentine, but his ministry is closely identified with the city of Rome and its vulnerable young men, who were supported by the Congregation of the Oratory that he founded in the 1570s (pl.4.34). A key moment in Philip's personal pilgrimage was the ecstatic vision of divine love he was said to have experienced while at prayer in the Roman catacomb of St Sebastian in 1544.

In Central Europe, the figure of St John Nepomuk, a canon of Prague, was enormously influential, giving rise to countless church and altar dedications (pl.4.33). Catholic reformers, keen to emphasize the essential role of the priesthood in spiritual life, embellished an ancient legend that John had been martyred by drowning for refusing to divulge the secrets of the confessional. The first to be canonized from the New World was the Dominican reclusive Rosa of Lima (1586–1617, canonized 1671), whose fame was such that an image of her was carved in Rome for export to Peru (pl.4.35). The popularity of these saints, and their imagery, are inextricably linked to the development of the international Baroque.

4.35 *The Death of St Rosa of Lima,* Melchiorre Caffa, marble. Rome, 1665 (Church of S. Domingo, Lima)

4.33 Interior of the Church of St John Nepomuk (Asamkirche), Munich, Egid Quirin Asam and Cosmas Damian Asam. 1733–46

4.34 *St Philip Neri,* Alessandro Algardi, marble. Rome, 1636–8 (Sacristy, Church of S. Maria in Vallicella, Rome)

Piety and Relics

The Counter-Reformatory cult of saints gave renewed impetus to the production and veneration of the holy vessels that would store, protect and sometimes also display the bodily relics associated with intercession, votive offering, the annual calendar and other ecclesiastical functions. There is a paradox built into the dual functions of some reliquaries, designed both to contain something precious and to show it off. The reliquaries made in the Baroque period fall into a number of standard types (pl.4.36). Some take the form of treasure chests or caskets totally enclosing the precious material; these are usually quite simple in shape, although often luxuriously decorated. A second type closely echoes the pattern of the monstrance, taking the form of a complex metal object, probably decorated with precious stones or enamel, standing on a small foot and displaying a morsel of sacred material in a glazed upper section. A third type of reliquary is anthropomorphic, shaped, for example, like a hand or a head and containing a saint's finger or skull. A final, much rarer group has a distinctive figurative or narrative component (pl.4.37).

4.36 Reliquary, Giuseppe Borgiani. Rome, possibly 1751–2 (cat.101)

4.37 (*opposite*) Reliquary of the Cradle of Christ, Giuseppe Antonio Torricelli, Cosimo Merlini the Younger and grand-ducal workshops, after Giovanni Battista Foggini. Florence, 1697 (cat.102)

4.38 Monstrance, Johannes Zeckel, Augsburg. Germany, 1705 (cat.103)

The extreme piety that was the public face of the late Medici court in grand-ducal Florence is the context for the remarkable investment in the reliquary art produced there around 1700 under the artistic leadership of the architect and designer Foggini. No expense was spared to produce exquisite jewel-like reliquaries, which fall into several of these standard types. They both safeguard and display the holy treasures in the grand-ducal collection; many of them make especially inventive use of *pietra dura*, a Florentine specialism (see Chapter Two). Some of the materials used to make this extraordinary collection of reliquaries were found near to Florence, for example, the chalcedony and jasper mined at Volterra used to make the clouds and the figure of Christ on the reliquary of S. Emerico (1717). Other materials were imported: red Sicilian agate, yellow Sicilian jasper, red Bohemian agate and Casertino flint.[21] Some reliquaries were historiated with appropriate narrative tableaux and carved figures set into their displays of ornament and bejewelled richness. Foggini's design for the reliquary of the Cradle of Christ, executed by Torricelli and other specialists, takes the form of the actual fragment that it purportedly conserves (pl.4.37).

The monstrance – made to display the Host symbolic of the transubstantiated body of Christ – became more and more significant within the hierarchy of liturgical precious objects, sometimes reaching remarkable levels of luxurious complexity. One of the most splendid was the Bemposta monstrance, made in the 1740s for the Portuguese crown by Ludowice, who provided a typical combination of symbolism, narrative and a jewelled setting. His design juxtaposes personifications of Faith, Hope and Charity with Eucharistic symbols and narrative medallions showing the Passion cycle. Zeckel's monstrance has fewer jewels but uses ears of wheat and grapes to signify the Eucharistic bread and wine (pl.4.38). These frame the Last Supper, when the Mass was instituted. Above, angels support a baldacchino to honour the Holy Spirit, hovering in the form of a dove. The curved holder in the centre, used to support the edge of the host and to hold it up to view, may well have produced echoes of the crescent moon at the foot of figures of the Blessed Virgin Mary in her personification as the Virgin of the Immaculate Conception. The Host partaken of at the Eucharist is seen as the body of the redeemer, incarnated and born, miraculously, in the immaculate person of his earthly mother.

Not all reliquaries or monuments acted as shrines and not all shrines were commemorative. In fact, the term 'shrine' covers a bewildering array of objects and functions (pl.4.39). They can

4.39 Shrine, maker unknown, Trapani. Sicily, *c.*1650 (cat.129)

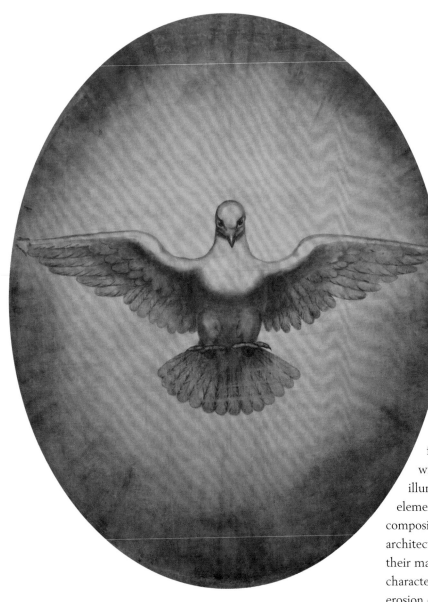

be areas within a building, perhaps at or around a saint's tomb or enclosing an altar over a grave. Alternatively, shrines can be caskets for relics. Some shrines take the form of jewels to be worn on the person. One of the greatest of all shrines in western Christendom, radically redesigned and equipped by artists using every known device in the Baroque armoury, was the unique area at the east end of the Vatican Basilica of St Peter's, a space filled by Bernini with the *Cathedra Petri* or The Throne of St Peter (pls 4.41, 4.42). This takes the form of a great symbolic sculpted and wrought throne, with, carefully positioned above and behind it, an illuminated image of the dove of the Holy Spirit, the third element in the Holy Trinity. The theatricality of Bernini's composition is reminiscent of the lively tradition of temporary architecture within Baroque churches, constructions that left their mark on permanent architecture. One of the most characteristic tendencies of the sacred art of the Baroque is the erosion of distinctions between categories we might expect to be immutable, for example, the permanent and the temporary in architecture. The *theatrum sacrum* theme was powerfully manifested in the central European tradition of side-wing altars, which vary in size and design and which lead up to a high altar with an altarpiece painting that can be removed and replaced according to liturgical need and the changing church calendar.[22] Truly temporary were the constructions used in funerary rites, the so-called *castra dolorosa* – for example, the one constructed for Eisenstadt in 1748 which had 15 candles set on five steps leading up to a canopied platform; or the remarkable, global reach of the funerary arrangements made for John V of Portugal in 1751, which included the erection of temporary *castra* in several European capitals as well as in Brazil and India.[23]

4.40 Model for the dove of the Holy Spirit, attributed to Giovanni Paolo Schor after Gianlorenzo Bernini. Rome, 1666 (cat.85)

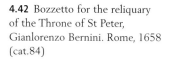

4.42 Bozzetto for the reliquary of the Throne of St Peter, Gianlorenzo Bernini. Rome, 1658 (cat.84)

4.41 *The Throne of St Peter* designed by Gianlorenzo Bernini in St Peter's Basilica, Rome, François Spierre, after a drawing by Giacinto Gimignani and Lazzaro Morelli. France, 1666 (cat.86)

Congregations

The nave, being the body or the people's part of the church, was the area from which the congregation heard the words urged on them from the pulpit. Seats for congregations were rare in Baroque churches. The most remarkable, and one of the best documented, Baroque pulpits is that from the Jesuit church at Leuven, now in Brussels Cathedral (pl.4.44).[24] Dated 1699, it was carved in oak in a form that was explored in a series of preparatory studies, for example, for the figures of Adam and Eve in Paradise. The architectural and structural form of the pulpit is entirely subsumed by a dense covering of fictive drapery, figure carving, symbolic signs and ornament. It is impossible to imagine that it did not somewhat overshadow the person of the preacher. The work, known as the *Chaire de la Verité*, seems to manifest the oft-stated Protestant grievance that Catholic imagery gave priority not to the Word but to the Image.

Of all aspects of Baroque church furnishing, the altar, in its many different manifestations, received more attention than any other category from patrons, artists and onlookers. All the main Christian denominations employed altars primarily at the Eucharist, although several of the Protestant sects adopted a very modest policy towards embellishment and decoration. Even so, many Lutheran altarpieces from north Germany and Scandinavia show a flowering of Baroque ornament (pl.4.43). The Norwegian example has remarkable acanthus wings that display the German style of 'gristly' or auricular Baroque ornamentation discussed in Chapter Two.[25] The winged design follows earlier South German models and like them is sculpted rather than painted, with the figure of God accompanied by angels surmounting the whole.

4.43 Altarpiece from Vestby Church, attributed to Torsten Hoff, carved, painted and partially gilded wood. Norway, 1725 (Norsk Folkemuseum)

4.44 (*opposite*) Pulpit made for the Jesuit Church in Leuven, now in the Cathedral of St Michael and St Gudula, Hendrick Frans Verbruggen. Brussels, 1696–9

The Crucifixion as the largest, central scene has given way to an image of the Last Supper, a subject that is common to Lutheran altarpieces since it represents the institution of the Eucharist, celebrated at that same altar.[26] The Crucifixion scene appears above and over that is a third scene depicting the Resurrection. This triumvirate of motifs, their placing and their size, reflects a theological focus on the commemorative nature of Eucharistic celebration. In this instance the central carving of the Last Supper is flanked on the left by the figure of Moses, who instituted the law by acting as God's agent for the prescribing of the Ten Commandments, and on the right by St John the Baptist. This interplay between 'Law' and 'the Gospel' was also typical of Lutheran altarpieces.[27] The figure of Moses is present through a process of association between the manna sent from heaven by God as the prophet led the Israelites out of Egypt (Exodus 13–18), and the taking of the Host. Moses stands to prefigure the Last Supper. St John the Baptist – understood to be both the last of the Prophets and the forerunner of Christ – forms a crucial link between the Old and New Testaments, a role reinforced here by the unusual depiction of him with angel's wings symbolic of his status as God's 'messenger'.

The engravings used as sources for images of the Last Supper and Passion narratives in Protestant altarpieces came chiefly from the Netherlands and transmitted imagery created by sixteenth- and seventeenth-century Catholic painters, both Italian and Flemish. The Catholic origin of these images appears not to have troubled the Lutheran patrons, a reminder that it was not the imagery *per se* that they objected to, but the devotions to which such images might be directed and subject. Many Protestant altarpieces display inscriptions to remind the viewer that the function of religious imagery is to illustrate the Word of God. An unusual post-Reformation English triptych featuring the disciples on its outer doors is accompanied by the following cautionary verse, which could be taken to stand for all such images: 'Regard not these pictures but follow the Lord/As did these Apostles in life and in word'.[28] The saints are presented not as intercessors but as exemplars of virtue. Despite the lively animation in the carving of the Vestby altarpiece no appeal is being made to the eye as the means of revelation. In this instance, the visual language of the Baroque is concentrated solely in the ornamental motif of the wings. A work such as this raises the central question for the sacred arts of the Baroque: what can be said about the effects of this visual art on the mind and soul of the onlooker?

Power and Sacred Art

Jane Eade

Bernini's masterpiece *The Ecstasy of St Teresa* (1647–52) is perhaps the quintessential image of Baroque religious art, where the realms of heaven and earth meet in the vision of the saint (see The Cornaro Chapel, p.96). The point when St Teresa is pierced by God's love in the form of his angel's flaming dart is both an instant in historical time and a moment whose reverberation is eternal. Within the context of the chapel for which it was carved, an analogy is being drawn with the historical sacrifice of Christ and its living memorial in the liturgy of the Mass. Almost 20 years after his *St Teresa*, Bernini produced his marble altarpiece of the *Blessed Ludovica Albertoni*, the terracotta model of the effigy for which is still extant. In this instance we are witness not to a vision but to the throes of death. The sculptures of Teresa and Ludovica show the main protagonists in ecstasy, (pls 4.45, 4.46) presenting divine knowledge as a form of passionate union. The erotic character of this particular dynamic floods the religious art of

4.45 Model of the head of St Teresa, for the Cornaro Chapel, attributed to Gianlorenzo Bernini. Rome, 1640–55 (cat.82)

4.46 Bozzetto for the altarpiece of the Blessed Ludovica Albertoni, Gianlorenzo Bernini. Rome, c.1671–4 (cat.83)

the Baroque, and it is what led in the late eighteenth century to a view of the style as decadent and even licentious. By the nineteenth century the Swiss historian Jacob Burckhardt could comment of Bernini's *St Teresa* that 'one forgets mere questions of style at the shocking degradation of the supernatural'.[29]

The Passions

Yet spirituality requires a body, and it is in the Baroque portrayal of the saintly human figure that the attempt to display the paradox of divine immanence and transcendence is at its most visceral. The highly sensual appeal of the visual arts in this period has a parallel in contemporary debate about the 'passions'. This is the seventeenth-century term for what we would class as emotions and desires, and it continues to be useful not least because it reminds us how much more 'theologically engaged' and 'morally dangerous' these states were considered to be in this period.[30] The term 'passion' has its roots in the Greek *pathe*: a combination of passivity and suffering that had its most powerful expression for Christians in the Passion of Christ. In appealing to our instincts for compassion (*compassio*, or 'suffering with') and empathy (*empatheia*, or 'feeling in'), artists relied on the fact that 'seeing' embraces more than the eye. In our responses to works of art it is empathy, involving the whole person, that bridges the gap between image and onlooker, and as the Renaissance theorist Alberti famously wrote, it is empathy that enables us to 'mourn with the mourners, laugh with those who laugh, and grieve with the grief-stricken'.[31] The physiological basis of this connection in the nervous system has been underpinned by recent work in cognitive neuroscience.[32]

Encouraging viewers to identify their own sensations with a visual representation is a strategy that is not unique to the Baroque.[33] However, the emotional character of knowledge was the subject of a sophisticated debate in this period and it was an idea expressed in works of art that are especially demanding of the senses. The subtlety of discussion about the passions undermines both the stereotypical view of early modern thought as riven by a thoroughgoing dualism between mind and body, and of Baroque art as appealing exclusively to the emotions (where these are characterized as physiological, non-cognitive and involuntary feelings).[34]

Passions were understood in general to be appetites of the soul that represent things as attractive or harmful, and hence as objects of desire or aversion. Although typologies differed, St Augustine of Hippo (354–430) and St Thomas Aquinas (*c*.1225–74), two key thinkers whose writings were particularly influential in the seventeenth century, both produced models of the human soul in which the 'passions' of the body (such as desire, fear, pleasure and sorrow) were movements both of a lower animal, or 'sensitive' soul, and potentially of the acts of the will known as 'affections' that belonged to a higher, rational or 'intellective' soul.[35] An appropriate example of an affection would be religious feeling. Augustine had grouped all forms of

passions under the single rubric of 'love'.[36] This love is expressed by his successor Aquinas in terms of motion and rest:

> For the activity of a cognitive power is fulfilled when the things apprehended are in the knower, whereas the activity of an appetitive power is fulfilled when the lover is drawn by what is loved. And so cognitive activity resembles rest, whereas the activity of an appetitive power resembles movement.[37]

Motus in Aquinas, following Aristotle, refers not simply to 'movement' but to any kind of process or state of 'becoming'.[38] The dynamic of conversion, or 'turning' towards is expressed in the devotional arts of the Baroque by a powerful sense of kinetic energy, mirroring an interior yearning for the repose of union.

The possession of a free and active will in orienting the passions was a crucial aspect of classical Christian psychology. The need for these potentially destructive and combustible movements of the soul to be 'tamed, outwitted, overruled, or seduced' relates to a wider concern in this period with the relationship between knowledge and control.[39] It permeates philosophy, advice and conduct literature, treatises on painting, musical theory, and writings on prayer. The passions were understood to be inscribed on the body in 'facial expressions, blushings, trembling and postures'.[40] In 1668 the French painter and art theorist Charles Le Brun gave his celebrated lecture *Conférence sur l'expression générale et particulière*, which attempted to codify how the internal movements of the soul were manifested by the body, such as the state of Rapture (pl.4.47).[41] In appealing to the passions and affections painters and sculptors relied on a conception of knowledge to which feelings were central.

In the Christian mystical tradition the need to direct the passions to good ends in order to contribute to a virtuous life expressed itself in an immense literature on the 'discernment of spirits',[42] the most famous of which were the *Spiritual Exercises* of St Ignatius of Loyola, founder of the Society of Jesus.[43] Although the notion that the ideology of the Society resulted in a distinctively 'Jesuit style' in the arts has long since been undermined, the artistic contribution of the order (both as practitioners and patrons) is nevertheless remarkable, as the provenances of many of the works in this exhibition indicate.[44] Moreover, as these works demonstrate, the spread of the visual language of the Baroque from Rome to all continents was in large part a consequence of the Society's missionary activity. What is crucial in this context, however, is the dynamic of the

4.47 *Rapture*, Charles Le Brun, black chalk. Paris, (Musée du Louvre)

Exercises themselves and Ignatius's belief that what motivates assent in the acquisition of knowledge is longing.[45]

Heavily reliant on the senses (especially sight), the *Exercises* comprise a series of contemplations based on visualizing narrative scenes from the New Testament. Imaginative exercises such as the 'Composition of Place' and the 'Application of the Senses' – in which the exercitant is invited to 'see in imagination' the persons and circumstances of the event, 'to hear what they are saying', 'smell the infinite fragrance and taste the infinite sweetness of the divinity', and to 'apply the sense of touch, for example, by embracing and kissing the

place where the persons stand or are seated' – are designed to connect the realm of the divine with the concrete experiences of the person meditating.[46] The sustained visualization required draws the senses from their habitual worldly state of flux and disarray, and directs them to a specific, contemplative end. Despite the concern of the *Exercises* with internal, mental imagery, they nevertheless had an impact on the way in which people both created and responded to devotional works of art.[47] They emphasized the morally affective nature of the visual in a way that was more 'systematic, sequential and experiential than had been attempted before'.[48]

The Altarpiece

A good example of the Baroque appeal of the passions is the monumental altarpiece of the Virgin of Sorrows which was made for the chapel of S. Lucía, the earliest of the Jesuit *hacienda* complexes in Central Mexico (pl.4.49). As we have seen, two of Mary's most popular seventeenth-century personifications were the Virgin of Sorrows and the Virgin of the Immaculate Conception. The feast of the Seven Sorrows, or the *Mater Dolorosa*, is an ancient one and has its roots in the first line of the medieval hymn on the Crucifixion, *Stabat Mater Dolorosa* ('the Sorrowful Mother was standing'). Originally celebrated on the Friday before Palm Sunday, in 1668 a feast day (15 September) was granted to the Servite order for the honouring of Mary's *compassio* or fellow-suffering.

The majestic scale and rich gilding of the Mexican altarpiece is in keeping with accounts of the chapel's sumptuous interior, which contained 'gold, silver and expensive cloths', including

'Chinese silks and velvets'.[49] The arched, portal-shaped frame encloses a two-tiered structure derived from Renaissance prototypes. The twisted Salomonic columns are named after those in St Peter's, Rome, thought to derive from the temple of Solomon, the form of which Bernini revived in his design for his baldacchino in the same church (see pl.2.4). Both decorative and symbolic, Salomonic columns are an exemplary Baroque idiom. The altarpiece includes individual painted panels within a semicircular arch that present the sorrowful episodes in the Virgin's life, and frame the free-standing Neapolitan sculpture of the Madonna within a tabernacle.[50] Some of these images are based on Jerónimo Nadal's illustrated *Annotations and Meditations on the Gospels*, which St Ignatius himself had urged Nadal to compile as a guide to prayerful meditation in the tradition of the *Spiritual Exercises*.[51] To be read from left to right and from bottom to top, the images from Nadal comprise: the circumcision of the child Jesus; the flight into Egypt; Jesus taking leave of his mother; their meeting on the road to Calvary; the Passion; and the entombment.

The traditional 'first sorrow' of the prophecy of Simeon (Luke II: 33–35), that Mary's own heart would be pierced by a sword, is replaced here by the unusual subject of the circumcision. A particular devotion of the Jesuit order, it represented the moment when Jesus was named, and consequently the dedication of the Society, whose monogram, IHS, comprises the first three letters of the Saviour's name in Greek. It is also the moment when the name of Jesus is first associated with his blood, evoking the coming Passion and perhaps also the martyrdom of the saints. The usual image of Mary at the foot of the cross is also replaced in this cycle by Jesus's blessing of his mother. Between the topmost panels of the altarpiece, where a Crucifixion scene would ordinarily be, there is an Italian painting of St Lucy, patroness of the *hacienda*, which is known to have replaced an earlier sculpture.[52] Surmounting the Virgin's head is a flaming heart spiked with seven swords, a reference to Simeon's prediction. In the dramatic sculpture by the Brazilian O Aleijadinho (pl.4.48) the swords actually pierce the Virgin's body, an allusion not only to the intensity of her pain but suggestive of her role as co-redeemer.[53]

4.48 Virgin of Sorrows, O Aleijadinho. Brazil, 1791–1812 (cat.89)

4.49 (*opposite*) Altarpiece of the Virgin of Sorrows, artist unknown. Mexico, *c*.1690 (cat.90)

While the painted images take us on a narrative journey, it is the central figure of the Madonna, facing outward, who engages our immediate attention. One way of directing the passions is to appeal to the human disposition to love things that we perceive as being like us. As we contemplate these images of the Virgin our bodies respond by feeling something of her distress. The use of mixed media helps to blur the boundary between the real and represented, enabling a closer sense of recognition and identification. The Virgin's head and hands are sculpted in wood and mounted on an armature covered by cloth. Glass eyes and tears are used in order to make her anguish as vivid and lifelike as possible, just as ivory and glass are used alongside painted pine wood in the bust by José de Mora of 1670–80 (pl.4.50). Playing on the gap between reality and painted representation in this way in order to manipulate a viewer's emotions encouraged the kind of unchecked, instinctive responses – such as tears – that religious teachers like Ignatius of Loyola believed could provide a conduit for grace. Indeed, it appears that it is precisely the quality of figurative realism and the ability to communicate pathos that in part led to the acceptance and refashioning of European art across other continents.[54]

Painted Garlands

The relationship between seeing and knowing is the focus of a Flemish image of the *Holy Sacrament in a Flower Garland* (pl.4.51), attributed to the Jesuit brother Daniel Seghers (1590–1661). The motif of the flower garland derives from the paintings of the Madonna in a wreath of flowers created by Jan Breughel the Elder, to whom Seghers had been apprenticed.[55] Despite the seventeenth-century popularity of the painted garland, which came to surround all manner of images both sacred and secular, those that display the Eucharist are relatively rare.[56] It is apparently the first time that the body of Christ is represented as the central subject of a painting by the motif of a white, wheaten wafer. There is a curious fittingness to this symbolism, given that, as a genre, still life is defined by its exclusion of the human form. Yet this is precisely what makes the image so startling: it is about the Passion of Christ but has no figurative content.[57]

The painting makes a direct appeal to the senses, especially sight but also taste, touch and smell. The blowsy roses and heavy ripe fruit invite the viewer to contemplate touching, smelling and eating. One can almost feel the silkiness of the rose petals, the dry ears of corn, the pulpy fleshiness of a ripe peach, the coolness of the chalice and the raised quality of its chased metal surface. Alongside the marvelling at flowers and plants out of season, and at new and exotic varieties, went a religious attention to their symbolic potential. For the Jesuits especially, books of prayers developed the notion 'that flowers (and nature as a whole) revealed profound religious truths'.[58] Despite the thorns and other spiky plants symbolic of the Passion, the painting is dominated by the wild-looking roses at the base, flowers that carried complex, often contradictory symbolism. The rose could represent love and spring but also the blood of the martyr and even death itself.[59] The open-ended nature of floral symbolism is especially pertinent in the context of paintings like these, in which the garland may be interpreted both as a warning against sensual pleasure and an illustration of God's bounty.

4.52 *Cupid*, artist unknown
after Anthony van Dyck. Oil on
canvas, probably 1630–1700
(National Gallery in Prague)

During the conservation of this painting it became apparent
that there are animals painted behind the bouquets in the
foreground. The lion on the right (St Mark) is balanced on the
left by an ox (St Luke). The winged head of an angel in the
centre represents St Matthew. The position of the head suggests
that the picture was hung with the spectator's eye level with
the lower half of the painting, so that his or her gaze was
drawn upwards as to an altarpiece. A painting representing
St Matthew as a cherub (modelled after a copy of a Cupid by
Van Dyck) (pl.4.52)[60] may be intended as a reference to the
Eucharist as 'Bread of Angels' (Psalms 78: 25), which is the
inscription (*ecce pane aeng*) partly visible on the niche in
another painting of this subject by Jan van Kessel (pl.4.53).
The angel's gaze is balanced at the top of the painting by the
head of an eagle (St John) surmounting the cartouche.[62] An
ancient symbol of power and victory, and from the Middle Ages
of Christ's ascension, the eagle was also renowned for its acute
vision and was used to represent sight in seventeenth-century
allegories of the five senses.[63]

To portray the body of Christ as a wafer, held aloft at the
moment of consecration or adoration, stresses its miraculous
nature. As we have seen in relation to the High Mass, according
to the Catholic doctrine of transubstantiation, the consecration
is the moment when the elements of bread and wine are
changed into the substance of Christ's body and blood (while
maintaining the 'accidents' of their natural appearance). This
type of Eucharistic awareness, in which just to gaze upon the
Host was likened to actual consumption, reached its apogee in
contemporary devotions such as the Forty Hours or
Quarant'Ore, in which continuous prayer was made for 40
hours before the Blessed Sacrament.[64] Elaborate illuminations
were constructed for this devotion, with the monstrance
containing the Eucharist placed at the deepest point of a
brilliantly lit theatre: an example of what have been referred
to as Baroque 'special effects'.[65] Exactly the same sense of
kinaesthetic space operates in the garland paintings, in which
the wafer is painted as shining out from the darkness like the
moon in the night sky, its whiteness picked up by the luminous
sheen given to the flower petals and fruit skins.

Like the theatres of the Forty Hours, these paintings are
supremely aware of their own artistry. The very detail and
precision with which the natural world is depicted – is 'represented' – drives a wedge between visual contemplation and
tactile knowledge. Ultimately what we are most aware of is the
artifice of painting. This self-consciousness as 'art' is what made
it possible for these images to traverse the boundary between
the Church and the secular context of the collector's cabinet,
or *Kunstkammer* (see pl.2.66).[66] The subject was first painted
by Breughel for Cardinal Federico Borromeo, Archbishop of
Milan, and their correspondence and Borromeo's other writings
provide a highly illuminating insight into the relationship
between novelty, artistry, commerce and spiritual benefit.[67]
The consummate craftsmanship and pictorial illusionism of
these pictures attracted royal patrons and benefactors from all
over Europe, both Catholic and Protestant.[68] The equivocal
symbolic potential of these images is borne out by the cost of
the garland, which could command more than 20 times the
amount of money paid for the 'narrative' centrepiece.[69]

4.53 *Still Life of Flowers and Grapes* encircling a monstrance in a niche, Jan van Kessel, oil on copper. Probably Antwerp, 1670 (National Galleries of Scotland)

4.54 *The Kunstkammer of Prince Vladislaus Sigismundus Vasa, future king Vladislaus IV of Poland*, Etienne de la Hyre, oil on canvas. Probably Antwerp, 1626 (Royal Castle, Warsaw)

4.55 *The Penitent Magdalen*, maker unknown (possibly Swiss). Probably France, *c.*1660–75 (cat.177)

The Magdalen

A painting by Etienne de la Hyre showing *The Kunstkammer of Prince Vladislaus Sigismundus Vasa, future king Vladislaus IV of Poland* of 1626 (pl.4.54) includes a representation of a *Madonna and Child in a Floral Garland* by Jan Breughel the Younger (1601–78) and Henrik van Balen (1575–1632) just visible behind a representation of Rubens's *The Drunken Silenus supported by Satyrs*.[70] Just in front of the Rubens panel is a portrayal of the penitent Mary Magdalen, another devotional image commonly commissioned for display within the context of a private collection. The Magdalen was one of the most popular saints of the post-Reformation period; the most familiar image of her is, as here, semi-naked in a grotto. However, the legend of her conversion was also a favoured subject for painters and a small, gem-like painting, whose scale and setting suggest that it was for domestic use, shows the saint in a luxurious dressing room at precisely this moment (pl.4.55).

The highly reflective finish of this object is arrived at using the technique of *Amelierung*: painting and engraving in gold and silver foils on the reverse of clear glass followed by layers of lacquer. Then areas of the picture are backed with tinfoil to create an illusion of liquid brilliance. The highly ornate metal frame, integral to the object, is decorated using the same technique. The deep red wall-hanging that forms the backdrop of the image shimmers like running water, an effect heightened by the viewer's own movements in front of the painting. The small scale and the richness of the materials suggest that this object was intended to be viewed at close range by a single person, an intimacy in viewing that links it to miniature painting and jewellery. The visual tendencies of the Baroque are most often associated with the monumental and grandiose, yet this picture of the Magdalen demonstrates that the sense of movement and drama is just as compelling in miniature. The play on the mutable qualities of glass, and the appeal of precious stones, make it easy to see why reverse painted glass was popular for small devotional objects, such as domestic altars, reliquaries and crucifixes. The work can be compared with the Baroque predilection for mirrors and other furniture with highly reflective surfaces such as silver and lacquer.

The Magdalen's eyes are raised heavenward and her lips slightly parted in a characteristic pose of religious ecstasy, recalling Le Brun's drawing of *Rapture* (see pl.4.47). Just as the roses in the garland paintings could express contrary meanings, so here virtue and vice are both constellated in a mirror. On the wall beside the Magdalen's head, catching the force of the sun's illumination, is the mirror that symbolizes her reflected self as *imago Dei* ('the image of God'), a central doctrine of Augustinian theology.[71] On the floor, amid the hastily discarded jewels, a second, cracked mirror warns against vanity and the sensual world's potential for deception. The radiance of the sun, visible in fine brushwork across the dress, just illuminates the edges of the pedestal case supporting the clock and we are given the sense that the timeless and the time-bound meet in the person of the saint. At first sight no one would mistake this small painting for anything other than a Catholic devotional image. Yet a second glance is complicated for the viewer by the tensions apparent in two unusually insistent motifs: the power of the sun and the notion of reflection.

The saint sits like Danaë in her shower of gold, yet it is precisely this solar iconography that clouds the characterization of her as a saintly type. The prevalence of the sun motif and laurel crown (found intermittently on the dress and echoed in the frame), combined with the colours of the French court, suggest a reference not only to divine omniscience but to the person of Louis XIV as 'Apollo' and 'the Sun King'. The figure of the Magdalen is therefore cast – both literally and metaphorically – in a new light. It may be that the saintly figure here is intended as an allegorical portrait of one of the king's mistresses, a notable feature of the court portraiture of this and earlier periods.[72] Like the passions themselves, it is an equivocal description.

4.56 (*opposite*) *Time and Death*, probably by Caterina de Julianis. Naples, probably before 1727 (cat.97)

Piety and Wax

The combination of small scale and richly worked ornament reminds us of a more ubiquitous paradox in the making of devotional objects: while they are intended to encourage meditation on poverty, they are themselves often fashioned from highly crafted materials greatly prized and of great monetary value. Not all devotional objects have such a rich decorative appeal, however. Some, like the wax sculpture of *Time and Death* in the V&A collection, are startlingly gruesome in their focus on the flesh and its corruption (pl.4.56). The authorship of this extraordinary work is unclear: it is, perhaps, partly by the celebrated wax modeller Gaetano Zumbo or Zummo (1656–1701), famous for *teatrini* like this, or by a follower, Caterina de Julianis, a Neapolitan nun (active *c*.1695–1742).[73] It is probably a copy of a work commissioned from Zumbo by the Medici family.[74] Like the Flemish flower garlands and the painting of Mary Magdalen, wax tableaux occupy the same theoretical space that produced the

Kunstkammer or cabinet piece and evidence how much sacred Baroque art was deployed beyond the sacred spaces of the church. While tableaux on this theme were commissioned by the Medici for their private collection, there is some evidence that the V&A version was at one time housed in the sacristy of a Neapolitan church.[75]

The Goncourt brothers said of Zumbo's *teatrini* that he mitigated their power by giving his sculptures 'almost the appearance of toys'.[76] Yet the small scale of this *teatrino di morte* enriches its symbolic function, which is the passage of the Christian man through his life on earth to a world beyond. Emotionally demanding of the viewer, it represents a synthesis of art forms in being both sculpted and painted and forming an architectural setting. Framed in a box like a miniature stage set, *Time and Death* forms part of a small corpus of similarly constructed waxworks of both religious and secular subjects. The macabre nature of this work is comparatively rare, however, and provides a counterpoint to the more familiar Neapolitan

RELIGIOUS PROCESSIONS

Marjorie Trusted

Processions have a long history. In the Old Testament David danced before the Ark of the Covenant in procession to Jerusalem, and the ancient Romans instituted triumphal processions after military victories. From the medieval period onwards wood figures of Christ on a donkey, known as *Palmesels*, were wheeled through German towns on Palm Sunday. During the Baroque period religious processions were particularly important events in Italy and the Iberian Peninsula, and in Central and South America. They were much valued by the Church in Spain; a late sixteenth-century writer commented that they could 'draw out afflictions from the soul, and … demonstrate Christian zeal over and against the damnation of heretics'.

Religious processions in Spain took place during Holy Week (*Semana Santa*). In the days leading up to Easter images of Christ, the Virgin and the apostles were taken on floats through many towns and villages, including Murcia, Valladolid and Seville. These images, called

pasos, from the Latin *passus*, suffering, were usually made of painted wood (pl.4.58). Scenes of the Passion were depicted, such as the Garden of Gethsemane and the Crucifixion. The figures were usually owned by penitential confraternities, who accompanied the floats and often carried them. Physical stamina was required, and the exertion was often part of a penitential act by the members of the confraternities, who were generally hooded and cloaked to conceal their identities. The images were both physically and emotionally moving, and stirred the people who watched them or

4.57 *Christ of the Earthquakes*, artist unknown, oil on canvas. Cuzco, *c*.1730–60 (Banco de Crédito del Peru, Casa Goyeneche)

4.58 (*left*) Processional figure of Judas Iscariot from the *paso* of the Agony in the Garden and Capture of Christ, Andrés Solanes. Valladolid, 1629–30 (cat.75)

4.59 *Transferral of the image of the Virgin of Guadalupe to the new sanctuary, 1709,* Manuel de Arellano. Mexico, 1709 (cat.74)

walked with them. The Spanish art historian Martí y Monso remarked of the strong emotional reaction they caused in spectators: 'the beauty of [the] … figures is more evident to most of the public, who spontaneously and impulsively admire them as works of art, venerate them as divine representations, or rejoice before the realism of those figures'. Often music and fireworks accompanied the processions, and in some cities, such as Valladolid, members of the confraternities carried candles, while others flagellated themselves. Wigs and costumes could be added to the carved figures, making them more lifelike and at the same time more theatrical.

The feast of Corpus Christi was a more joyous affair, when silver processional monstrances housing the Eucharist, known in Spain as *custodias,* were paraded through the streets. These could be several metres high, often ornamented with small scenes of the Last Supper and figures of saints. Sacramental plays sometimes performed alongside these processions gave dramatic force to the images.

Other religious processions celebrated particular images, especially miraculous ones. In Peru a figure of the crucified Christ was carried out into the streets during a series of earthquakes in 1650 in Cuzco, and apparently caused them to cease. It was consequently revered and used as a processional object to ward off future earth tremors (pl.4.57). In Mexico and elsewhere in Hispanic America processional images could be made of comparatively light materials such as corn paste, pressed on to a wood armature, given a gesso surface and painted. The lighter weight made them more portable.

Secular processions were immensely important during this era: monarchs and consorts were welcomed into cities, and ambassadors into their new posts. King Charles II of Spain's wife, María Luisa of Orleans, was welcomed with an elaborate *entrada* of painted niches representing the different kingdoms ruled by Spain along her route into Madrid in 1680. The Marquês de Abrantes, who had been appointed as the Portuguese ambassador to Rome in 1712, made a glittering ceremonial entrance with a train of 120 carriages the following year, when he was received by Pope Clement XI.

tradition of miniature sculpted *praesepi* or Christmas cribs. *Time and Death*, and sculptures like it (for example pl.4.60 of *The Judgement of the Damned)*, are didactic objects intended as *memento mori*. The sense of horror provides a way of focusing the imagination on death as a kind of 'visual homeopathy'.[77] The author of this piece is likely to have been familiar with contemporary devotional manuals such as the often reprinted *L'Huomo al Punto; Cioé, L'Huomo in Punto di Morte* by the Jesuit Daniello Bartoli (1608–85). First published in Rome in 1667, this book recommends detailed visualization of the corruption of the body in the tomb as a spiritual exercise.[78]

The remarkable ability of wax to mimic human skin and hair is at the root of its visual power. This fleshy, visceral quality is what has given the medium such an ancient association with portraiture and with the commemoration of the dead.[79] A new, scientific interest in the body is discernible in this sculpted group, making *Time and Death* a very different object from the *Judgement* wax. The figure of Time is rudely pink, in stark contrast to the various shades of yellowing, bloodless skin and dark brown rotting flesh that surround him. This realism in depicting the human anatomy introduces a tension that could be interpreted as part of a shift in the explanation of the nature of the body from theology to natural science.[80] It is an instance of the Baroque looking at the body 'within' in order to render the physical manifestation of the passions more accurately. 'Truth', *ingegno* ('talent') and 'marvel' are terms that frequently appear in early first-hand accounts of such works and suggest that for contemporary audiences an appreciation of these objects was centred on their artistry, their skill in execution, and their witness to reality as much as for their religious message.[81] A virtuosity in simulating the 'truth' of the material world had the paradoxical function of making such images more effective transmitters of supernatural power. They are illusions, yet are intended to convey the workings of the senses (and, by extension, of spiritual vision) as essentially trustworthy. The universal view that the art of the Baroque appeals exclusively to the senses over and against the intellect is a phantom. That the passions function cognitively is demonstrated by the self-awareness of Baroque visual language, the double gesture to the image *qua* image as well as to what it represents, displaying a deliberate manipulation of the senses for positive spiritual and intellectual ends.

MORS IMPIORVM·PESSIMA

mortuus est Diues Epulo, et se
...lue est in inferno. Luc. ...

CHAPTER 5

THE PALACE

Michael Snodin

The middle years of the seventeenth century witnessed the start of a 100-year-long surge of palace building unmatched before or since. All over Europe, absolutist régimes, from Russia to Portugal, built or renovated palaces as their main centres of power while minor princes, noblemen and prelates busily set out, at their own levels, to do the same. Emulation was the driving force, as Frederick the Great of Prussia noted: 'There is not one of them, down to the youngest son of a youngest son from an appanaged line, who does not preen himself upon some resemblance to Louis XIV; he builds his Versailles; he has his mistresses; he maintains his standing armies' (pl.5.1).[1] Such palace building was closely conditioned by political events and their economic outcomes. While France led the way with Versailles and other royal palaces, and was soon emulated in northern Europe and Scandinavia, it was not until after 1700, following the expulsion of the Turks from Hungary and an economic revival, that palace building really took off in central and eastern Europe.

These Baroque creations, with their seemingly endless sequences of dazzling rooms and vast scale, have established for us what a palace should be. But, rather surprisingly, of all the forms of Baroque building, the palace is now, perhaps, the most difficult for us to understand fully. The magnificence is undeniable, and its central aim, the glorification of the ruler, still relatively easy to grasp. Even in a republic like France, the spell can still work, as the millions of tourists visiting the

great complex of Versailles confirm. But such palaces can too often seem to be, borrowing William Hazlitt's description of Fonthill Abbey, 'a desert of magnificence, a glittering waste of laborious idleness',[2] as the real meaning of all the pomp and expense has passed away along with the ancient concept of princely magnificence and the system of absolute power that both promoted and embodied it.

Princes could point to Aristotle, as well the ancient Roman architect Vitruvius and his Renaissance follower Leon Battista Alberti, in claiming that expensive display or magnificence was a virtue, indeed almost a duty:

> Men of publick Spirits approve and rejoice when you have raised a fine Wall or Portico, and adorned it with Portals, Columns and a handsome Roof, knowing you have thereby not only served yourself, but them too, having in this generous Use of Wealth, gained an addition of great Honour to yourself, your Family, your Descendants, and your City.[3]

In Cesare Ripa's *Iconologia*, an influential illustrated catalogue of emblematical figures, the personification of Magnificence holds a plan of a 'sumptuous building', as she also did in the ceiling painting of the teenage Louis XIV's new bedchamber in the Louvre, created in the 1650s. But there Magnificence, significantly, shared the canvas with Magnanimity, her necessary corollary. A similar pairing lay behind the design of the

5.2 *Louis XIV and his court arriving for the consecration of the Hôtel des Invalides, 26 August 1706,* Pierre-Denis Martin, oil on canvas. Paris, after 1706. The Invalides, begun in 1676, was designed by Jules Hardouin Mansart (Musée Carnavalet)

buildings put up for old soldiers and sailors by the monarchs of the seventeenth and eighteenth centuries, such as the Hôtel des Invalides in Paris and the Royal Hospital for Seamen at Greenwich. Not for nothing were these great domed structures modelled on magnificent royal palaces, for they not only displayed the power of the monarchy but also its benevolent attitude to those who served it. This adoption of palatial magnificence in public buildings prompted an English commentator to observe that the Invalides 'has the Air of a Palace, as the Louvre has that of an Hospital, tis a foundation becoming the soul of a military prince' (pl.5.2).[4]

For Louis XIV, who showed as keen an interest in the creation of the Invalides as he did in that of Versailles, the external magnificence of both buildings contributed to his personal glory and thus that of France. The same drive for *gloire* through magnificence lay behind the majestic design, rich materials and allusions to military victories in the interiors of Versailles. But within the royal court, magnificence also played another part. In absolutist France, the higher court aristocracy had no real role in the state administration and were excluded from the professions. Relaxation, amusement, conversation and the royal rituals (and occasional military campaigns) were the whole business of such a society. Status, for which the only reward was fame and honour, crucially depended first on the king's favour and secondly on the degree of display. Some have argued that the maintenance of magnificence was crucial, since it set the bar for the maintenance of social status: any reduction could mean a catastrophic loss of position. A duke must look like a duke, and it is certainly true that the king strove to outdo the court in magnificence. According to Norbert Elias, the 'prestige consumption' that this system promoted was actively encouraged by the king, who wanted the aristocracy to spend its money on goods and its energies on personal rivalry rather than getting together to oppose his control.[5] But other historians have maintained that court ceremonial and its trappings were, to quote Jeroen Duindam, 'a performance of devout adherence to hierarchies terrestrial and celestial. It instituted and reinforced the compact between the ruler and the highest officers of the household and the state.'[6] The ruler was just as much a prisoner in the gilded cage as was the court. In such a society, reading the signs was vital: 'A man who knows the court is master of his gestures, of his eyes and of his face; he is profound, impenetrable; he dissimulates bad offices, smiles at his enemies, controls his irritation, disguises his passions, belies his heart, speaks and acts against his feelings.'[7]

5.3 *Vincennes* or *July* from the tapestry series
called *The Royal Residences* or *The Months*.
Paris, 1670–1700 (cat.131)

Versailles

Versailles, the main French stage for this court society, was the most famous and influential of all European Baroque palaces. Its enormous setting encompassed both the town in front and the great gardens and park behind. Their radiating plans focused the whole scheme on the palace itself and more particularly on the King's Bedchamber, the *Chambre du Roi*, within it. The holy of holies, it was the still centre of a national system of representation of the monarch through his setting and person. We are reminded of Louis's self-representation as Apollo, the ancient god of the sun, the light of which 'shines on those other stars which surround it like a court'.[8] The vast buildings and their landscape settings were planned around the movement and spectacle of the ceremonial ritual that revolved around the king, the whole of whose life at court was lived in public, including going to bed and getting up (the *lever* and *coucher*).

Of the 2,100 horses stabled at Versailles in 1705, 300 were for hunting in the forest beyond the formal garden, the original reason for the royal presence. Hunting was not simply a diversion from other business; it was thoroughly ritualized and courtiers vied for the honour of putting on and taking off the king's boots (pl.5.3).[9] Even when the king was not present, the rituals were acted out: courtiers bowed before Rigaud's royal portrait in Louis's Throne Room (see The Portrayal of Absolutism, p.30) and doffed their hats before the laid royal table.[10] Recent commentators have highlighted the similarities between such court rituals and gestures and those of the church,[11] which in some ways were less formal than those of the palace; while one was allowed to turn one's back to the altar, one could never do so to the king.

As with many other palaces, Versailles was more than a setting for royal ritual. After being made the chief royal residence in 1682 it housed the centre of government and accommodated those nobles required to reside at court. In 1744 some 10,000 people, including servants, lived in the château. But Versailles also had another function. It was the central expression of the highest forms of French national culture and as well as being a venue for music, theatre and other more ephemeral events it was the main showplace for the products of the royal academies of painting, architecture and music. In its very architecture and design, Versailles was the most prominent manifestation of the royal project to establish the dominance of French culture across Europe.

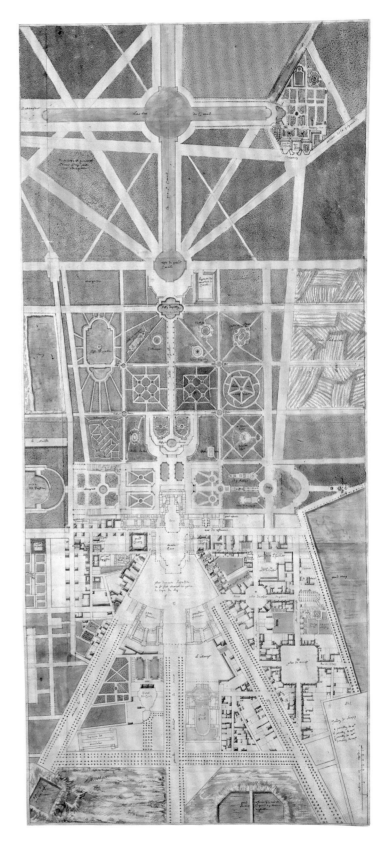

5.4 Plan of the château, gardens and environs of Versailles, artist unknown, Versailles, 1687 (cat.134)

From Town to Country

The idea of the fully developed Baroque palace, and its accompanying gardens, had been adopted across most of Europe by the early eighteenth century. Its architectural language and form, in the mixed style that has been called Late International Baroque,[12] was derived from two main sources: the urban palaces of Italy, and the domestic castles or châteaux of rural France. But two other starting points should also be noted: first, the Escorial outside Madrid, a vast Renaissance palace-cum-monastery built by Philip II of Spain from 1563, which not only set a precedent with its enormous size, but also provided an example of the uniform classical treatment of great structures; secondly, the reconstructions on paper of examples of ancient Roman architecture, suggesting ways in which buildings could relate to the landscape. Most notable of these was Pietro da Cortona's drawing of the 1630s of his palace-like vision of the ancient hillside sanctuary of Fortuna Primigenia at Palestrina near Rome, created when the architect was actually working on a modern palace in the same location.[13]

But such wide landscape-embracing plans were impossible in most urban settings, and Italian town palaces had long been built around relatively small enclosed courtyards. Since the early Renaissance, their sheer façades, often rising straight from the street, had been testing grounds for the handling of the language of classical architecture in a modern context. The sculptural vigour of urban palace façades of the Italian Baroque was anticipated by the late Mannerist palaces of the later sixteenth century in Genoa, which attracted Rubens's recording pencil and in the form of engravings helped to spark imitations across northern Europe in the 1620s and 30s. But the façades of most Italian Baroque palaces were crucially different from these richly decorated Genoese examples in their monumental treatment of classical architecture, exemplified by Borromini's palace for the Jesuit headquarters, the Propaganda Fide, and Bernini's Palazzo Chigi in Rome, designed in 1664. The front of the latter, with its giant pilasters above a plain basement and windows set closely in between, became a standard palace façade treatment in Italy and beyond (pl.5.5). Bernini's two unbuilt schemes for the Louvre (see Chapter Two, pp.88–9), which would have produced the most impressive city palace in

5.5 Palazzo Chigi, Rome, the façade designed by Gianlorenzo Bernini, engraving from *Il Nuovo Teatro delle fabriche et edificii in prospettiva di Roma moderna*, Giovanni Battista Falda. Rome, 1665 (Private Collection)

Europe, were also significant because the daringly curved façade of the east front in the first scheme became the starting point of a number of later town and country palaces (see pl.2.15). Perhaps even more influential was Bernini's later scheme, which demonstrated for the first time how to handle a monumental classical design along a very long façade.

The Roman Baroque courtyard model (and the Louvre schemes) inspired city palaces across northern and central Europe, often designed by Italians. In Vienna, the Kaunitz-Liechtenstein palace was designed by Enrico Zuccalli, court architect to the elector Max Emanuel of Bavaria, and Domenico Martinelli, formerly the professor of architecture in the Accademia di S. Luca in Rome. Directly derived from the Palazzo Chigi, it inspired many imitations. Perhaps the most impressive of all such buildings were the royal palaces in Stockholm, Berlin and St Petersburg. In the Swedish capital, Nicodemus Tessin the Younger combined Roman examples and Bernini's second Louvre design with a scenographic setting of ramps and stairs exploiting the dramatic site (pl.5.6). In Berlin, Andreas Schlüter synthesized the Stockholm model and the

Louvre scheme in his creation of a great palace for the new kingdom of Brandenburg-Prussia, combining Roman palace façades with entrances in the form of ancient triumphal arches. In St Petersburg, the exterior of Bartolomeo Francesco Rastrelli's Winter Palace, although built after 1750, still shows the monumentality of Roman High Baroque, but tempered by a lively use of colour.

The remarkable exception to the courtyard palace in Rome was the Palazzo Barberini, designed by Carlo Maderno, Bernini and Borromini and finished in 1633 (see pl.2.2). Designed in an H-shape, with access through ground-floor arcades to the garden behind, its plan of a recessed centre with wings was a reflection of the Renaissance 'villa suburbana' as developed by Andrea Palladio. But it was France, where plans with a ceremonial centre and advancing wings had long been the norm, that saw the development of the opened-up palace capable of infinite extension, a design idea that was to have an impact all over Europe. The most notable French example was of course Versailles. As it grew in size and grandeur, especially after becoming the permanent royal residence, the sheer

5.6 Royal Palace, Stockholm,
Nicodemus Tessin the Younger.
1697–1760

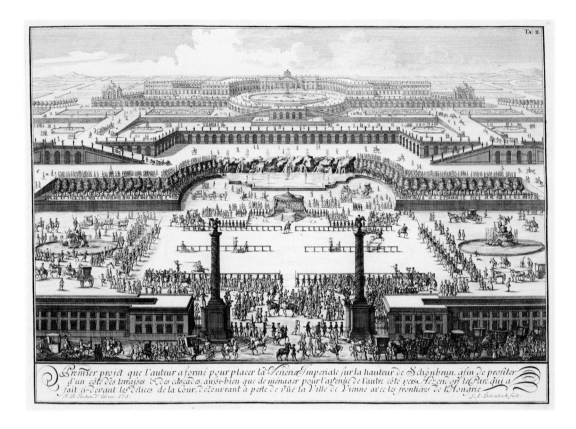

combined scale of the palace and gardens arrested the attention of rulers across Europe, most especially those who were in direct political rivalry with France. Some simply took on some of its elements. At Het Loo, the summer residence of Louis's great rival William III, stadholder of the Netherlands and king of England, and Queen Mary, the interiors designed by Daniel Marot reflected the latest French ideas, as did William III's court etiquette, although the relatively modest exterior was in the local style.

Some of the biggest rival schemes were never realized, such as the ideal palace at the centre of Paul Decker's sumptuous and influential book of engraved designs, the *Fürstliche Baumeister* ('The princely architect', 1711). When the summer palace of Schönbrunn outside Vienna eventually came to be built it was still very large, but was a modest reflection of Johann Bernhard Fischer von Erlach's staggering initial scheme of 1693 (pl.5.7). Blenheim Palace, made for the victorious Duke of Marlborough and thus as much a national monument as a house, was a calculated riposte to Versailles in its scale and dramatic massing (not unlike Decker's vision), but not in its dimensions (see pl.1.9). At Karlsruhe from 1715, such absolutist iconography was carried to extremes. Its centralized plan placed the palace at the centre of a circle from which 32 streets radiated across the town to the surrounding countryside (pl.5.8). It was not until after the death of Louis XIV that

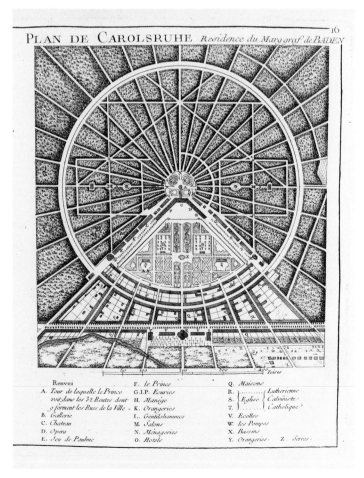

palaces and gardens began effectively to match his vision for
Versailles. Even though it is built around a series of courtyards,
the sheer size of Luigi Vanvitelli's palace at Caserta for the
king of the Two Sicilies, with its 1,200 rooms, produced a front
which communicates a sense of infinite length, linked through
open arches in its centre to a long vista into the hillside
gardens. As Prince Eusebius Liechtenstein had expressed it:
'If a building is to be magnificent it must be long and the
longer the nobler. For a great row of evenly spaced windows
one after the other makes for the greatest effect and
splendour.'[14] But it was at Peterhof and the Catherine Palace at
Tsarskoe Selo outside St Petersburg, both completed by
Bartolomeo Rastrelli, that the Versailles example was most
nearly rivalled, at any rate in terms of scale (pl.5.9).

The majesty and dignity required of these huge official
structures often precluded the variety in plan and elevation that
was characteristic of much late Baroque palace design, especially
in central Europe and in northern Italy. Such variety was better
suited to smaller official palaces, like those of the German
electors, or palaces with lesser official roles, such as suburban
summer retreats or hunting lodges. This was certainly the case
with the palace at Stupinigi near Turin, a very grand hunting
lodge designed by Filippo Juvarra for the kings of Savoy. Its
extraordinary geometrical plan is based on diagonals. The effect
on the ground is to create a stupendous entry to the raised
dome over the central *salone*.

In Vienna, such experimentation was given a major boost by
a burst of palace building prompted by the Emperor Leopold's

action to corral the aristocracy in Vienna, much as Louis XIV had done at Versailles. Matching the new town palaces were villa-like retreats or 'garden palaces' on the outskirts, which became a fruitful ground for architectural invention. While one of the designs by Fischer von Erlach included a diagonal ground plan anticipating that of Stupinigi, others were derived from Louis Le Vau's château of Vaux-le-Vicomte, with its central domed oval saloon and attached apartments (see Chapter Two). Vaux-le-Vicomte also helped to inform the planning of the most elaborate of the Viennese garden palaces, the Upper Belvedere, the summer palace of Prince Eugene of Savoy, the Duke of Marlborough's comrade-in-arms, designed by Lukas von Hildebrandt (see Centres of Diplomatic Power, c.1700, p.18). Its varied silhouette, which has been likened to an assembly of military tents, allowed the creation of long wings of rooms *en enfilade* centred on a raised middle section containing the great marble saloon. But the real clue to the meaning of the Upper Belvedere lay in its monumental staircase, which let visitors pass up to the marble saloon or, crucially, down through the ground floor and to the terraced gardens on the slope of the hill below. For all its sumptuous interior it was more a garden pavilion than a palace and as such was in the tradition of *maisons de plaisance* or 'pleasure palaces' in gardens designed as retreats from the ceremonies of the court, initiated by the rituals at Versailles and Marly.

Gardens and Palaces

Just as there was no single Baroque palace style, there was no single style associated with the gardens that accompanied them. They did, however, share some common characteristics (see The Baroque Garden, p.276). There was an unprecedentedly close connection between the Baroque palace and garden in terms of planning and in detail; for the first time gardens and houses were designed to work together to create a unified effect. At Versailles, as we have seen, town, palace and garden were laid symmetrically around a central axis. The garden axis alone was some eight kilometres long; the whole scheme was so large that it could, at the time, be fully appreciated only on paper. It was closely related to contemporary examples of urban planning and to the geometric fortifications then being built around French border towns by the great military engineer the Marquis de Vauban. Such likenesses were not of course accidental. They were technically related – just as the fireworks in the gardens were created by the artillery, so the great earthworks that turned the land into a succession of banks and levels were laid out using the techniques of military surveyors and carried out by thousands of troops drafted in to undertake the task. But at another level they also had the same purpose, for the Versailles scheme, whose alignment of avenues and hunting routes eventually set the course of long-distance roads, was not only a visual demonstration of the king's material domination of nature but also of his control of territory.[15]

The layout at Versailles was the biggest and most influential example of a style of formal gardening that had emerged in France in the mid-seventeenth century, chiefly through the work of the royal gardener André Le Nôtre. The notion of a pleasure garden, designed as a logical continuation of the architectural space of the palace, had been pioneered in his gardens at the château of Vaux-le-Vicomte. At Vaux, Le Nôtre abandoned the squares, rectangles and circles of the Renaissance garden in favour of a scheme of long avenues, developed from the Italian examples of the sixteenth century. Also taken from Italy was the use of statuary and fountains and of *parterres de broderie*, low-hedged plots filled with textile-like patterns realized in flowers or contrasting coloured materials. At Vaux these included crushed brick and slate. But in spite of the formal design, Le Nôtre's gardens employed systems of perspective and changing levels that enabled different views to unfold.

The enormous size of Versailles permitted a wide range of such effects, which changed as the garden developed over time.[16] In the earliest fully completed phase, the terrace nearest the palace contained the parterres, a coloured carpet designed to be seen from the windows of the royal rooms above, but later altered to hold fountains. Next, below the terrace, came the bosquets within a grid pattern of avenues. Each bosquet had a different theme and character and was, in effect, an outdoor room, invisible until entered, carved out of a dense mass of closely clipped trees. The effects were strongly architectural, often theatrical and were brought to dramatic life by water. There were jets and cascades and *buffets d'eau* that imitated in greenery and falling water the great silver buffets of the palace. The *Salle de Bal* was a fountain in the form of a Roman amphitheatre. The *Théâtre d'Eau* presented the fanning perspectives of a Renaissance theatre, filled with arching water jets. Beyond the bosquets and the *Jardin* stretched the *Petit Parc* with its huge cross-shaped Grand Canal, surrounded by woods pierced by diagonal avenues. The canal was furnished with boats and miniature warships and even a 'little Venice', a tiny fortified seaport, in which to dock them. Beyond the *Petit Parc* lay the *Grand Parc*, a hunting forest cut through with radiating avenues to allow the hunters (often carried in coaches) to gain access to their quarry.

At the head of the canal and facing the palace was the most important of all the Versailles fountains, representing Apollo in his chariot rising from the waves. It was part of what came to be developed as a programme of sculpture and painting, both inside and outside the palace, relating to the sun god, as a guide of 1674 put it: 'since the sun was the emblem of Louis XIV and poets fuse the sun and Apollo, everything at Versailles was related to that Greek god'.[17] The iconographical programme was determined by the Academy of Inscriptions and *Belles-lettres*, which advised Colbert on the state cultural programme. The figures on the Apollo fountain looked up to the Fountain of Latona, whose sculptural groups described an episode in the god's life. In the Grotto of Thetis by the side of the palace, enlivened by water tricks and lined with rock crystal, mirrors and shells, Apollo rested from his labours attended by the Muses, as the king rested at Versailles. On the new garden façade of the palace were figures of the months, arranged according to the sun's path. An ambitious and only partly executed scheme for a group of statues on the terrace included a large globe, four abduction subjects relating to the elements and 24 statues designed by Charles Le Brun representing the seasons, the elements, the four times of day, the four parts of the world, 'the four poems' and the four humours of men. According to Le Brun's biographer the programme was intended to refer to 'the union of linkage which composes the universe', which at that time was commonly still believed to revolve around the sun.[18]

Use and Meaning

In the painted views of the garden and *Petit Parc*, the ways in which the scenes are peopled throw much light on how Versailles and more particularly its gardens were seen and used. In one group of views the gardens are shown with a cast of fashionably dressed figures elegantly conversing and promenading, sometimes accompanying the king as he was pushed in his Bath chair (pl.5.10). We are reminded of the guides to the gardens written, remarkably, by Louis himself, in which the visitor is ordered to walk, turn, enjoy a particular view, fountain or statue and walk on, stop, turn, look, turn again and walk (or at one point take a boat). When Mary of Modena, the queen of James II of England, was taken round by Louis in 1689, she was served with a large collation at two stops, even though their route was shorter than the full eight kilometres.[19] The guided route prevented the visitor missing the chief sights, and would have meant that water could be saved by turning the fountains on only as needed, but it was also a formal, almost choreographed process, paralleling the ritualized movement of people in the ceremonials inside the palace. With its room-like bosquets, straight lines and confined routes, it was like an outdoor version of the palace itself. For visitors, however, it was not simply a stage for courtly behaviour, for in looking at the gardens and palace they were absorbing a particular set of messages of which the imagery of the Sun King was only the most obvious. Both gardens and palace were a calculated demonstration of the superiority of French arts and manufactures, not just in terms of design but also on a technical level. In the gardens, the impressive machinery needed to raise enough water for the huge fountain jets was as interesting to visitors as the artistry and high finish in the bosquets and subtle progression of successive viewpoints.

Another set of painted views of the gardens, made to decorate the *Grand Trianon*, shows them in a different mode. The settings, real enough, are unchanged. But they are peopled with disporting classical deities – almost as if the fountains have come alive. This is the other, imaginary Versailles, visited by Apollo and the gods (pl.5.11). The paintings recall the Versailles-like palace interiors in Jean Le Pautre's prints that formed the settings for classical stories – Versailles and indeed the whole French court design initiative was, after all, an attempt to rival the splendours of ancient (and modern) Rome. But the gardens were something more, being not only a setting for court ritual, and an expression of royal and national power, but also a dream-world, a place of enchantment that most famously came to life in a series of fêtes and *divertissements*, including the 1664 fête *Les plaisirs de l'isle enchantée* ('The

5.10 (*opposite*) *View of the Bassin d'Apollon and the Grand Canal in the gardens of Versailles*, Pierre-Denis Martin, oil on canvas. Paris, 1713 (Musée national des châteaux de Versailles et de Trianon)

5.11 *Bosquet of the Arc de Triomphe*, Jean Cotelle, gouache. Paris, 1693. The flying putti are seen bearing the nuptial toilet service of Venus. (Musée national des châteaux de Versailles et de Trianon)

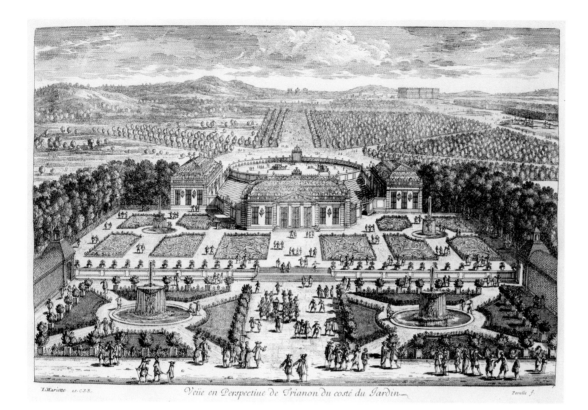

Pleasures of the Enchanted Isle'), which took place in the newly refurbished gardens (see Fireworks, p.172).

At the edges of the *Petit Parc*, and reached via the Grand Canal, lay two permanent diversions from the formality of the main garden. The *Ménagerie* resembled a tiny, elegantly furnished château, from an upper level of which the birds and animals could be viewed. The *Trianon de Porcelaine*, built in 1670 on the site of the village of Trianon, was an exclusive *maison de plaisance*, functioning as a retreat from the court for the king and his official mistress, Madame de Montespan. Access was strictly controlled, courtiers' wives being favoured over their husbands. Also known as the *Pavillon de Flore*, its fragrant gardens were a showcase for the royal flower collections, presented as perfect specimens. According to the duc de Saint-Simon, 'All of the compartments in each of the parterres were changed every day, and I have seen the king and the entire court driven out of the garden, although it is vast and built in terraces overlooking the Canal, because the scent of tuberoses hung so heavy in the air.'[20] The rarest scented plants were reserved for the *Cabinet des Parfums*, 'an extraordinarily built little palace commissioned so that several hours of the day might be whiled away here during the hot summer months'.[21]

The Trianon announced its informal nature through its plan of five pavilions and its exotic style. Each pavilion was roofed with coloured tiles; the exterior walls were also tiled in blue and white. In addition to a number of small rooms for eating, the Trianon contained two apartments, one dedicated to Diana, the other the *appartement des amours*. Record drawings of the beds (see pl.5.69) and a scene set in the Trianon, in which flying putti bear flowers in from the garden, show that these rooms were fitted out in a style significantly more luxurious and comfortable than the formal spaces of the main palace (see The Montespan Fan Painting, p.314). In 1687 the frivolous *Trianon de Porcelaine*, with its roofs crested with cupids and birds, was torn down and replaced by the much larger *Trianon de Marbre*, called the *Grand Trianon*, still standing today. Its construction not only marked the coming into favour of a new mistress, Madame de Maintenon, but a shift towards classical architecture in the gardens in keeping with Versailles's establishment as the seat of government. But by then Louis XIV had created at Marly, five kilometres from Versailles as the crow flies, a new *maison de plaisance* almost on the scale of a château. Set in a valley carved into a series of terraces and pools, the *Pavillon du Roi* had 12 pavilions set before it to house his guests. Admittance to the uniquely relaxed atmosphere of Marly was by invitation only, and the king used access to it as an instrument of control over his court (pl.5.13).

The French formal garden, as developed by André Le Nôtre at Versailles and elsewhere, had a profound effect on palace gardens across Europe. In 1701 the Elector Max Emanuel of

5.13 *Perspectival view of the château and gardens of Marly*, Pierre-Denis Martin, oil on canvas. Paris, 1723 (Musée national des châteaux de Versailles et de Trianon)

Bavaria summoned Le Nôtre's pupil Charles Carbonet and, later, Dominique Girard from Paris to create the gardens at the summer palace of Nymphenburg, outside Munich (pl.5.14). In addition to bosquets, canals and parterres, the gardens also contained developments of the small pleasure palace pioneered at Versailles, a type that became usual after about 1700.

There was the Badenburg, a small Baroque bathing palace that contained a banqueting hall, a bathing hall and a bedroom. The adjacent Pagodenburg tea-house had a Baroque exterior and silk- and lacquer-lined rooms. The Magdalenenklause, built from 1725 onwards, was a gothic 'hermitage' apparently in ruins, in the tradition of such buildings in monasteries. It was

fitted out with a chapel to St Mary Magdalen modelled on a Baroque garden grotto, a private oratory and three cell-like living rooms that included space for a bed. Very different from the sensual attractions of the *Trianon de Porcelaine* at Versailles, this was a royal retreat where the elector could go for solitary religious and philosophical meditation and the quiet appreciation of nature. Sometimes, the decorative elements in such gardens in the French style were actually French or were obtained from France. At Nymphenburg the elector's heir had his own French-made child's garden carriage, which in winter could be used inside the palace (see The Baroque Garden, p.276). At Hampton Court, where the gardens were designed

5.14 *Festivities in the gardens of Schloss Nymphenburg*, Ignaz Biedermann. Germany, 1727 (cat.136)

under the supervison of the French Huguenot émigré Daniel Marot, the ironwork was made by another French Huguenot, Jean Tijou (pl.5.15). But the Baroque was an international style; in the French-style gardens at the Holländisches Palais in Dresden, the sculpture included work from the Venetian studio of Antonio Corradini (pl.5.16).

Perhaps the most powerful agent in the spread across Europe of the French formal garden of the Le Nôtre type was A.J. Dezailler d'Argenville's *La Théorie et la Pratique du Jardinage*, first published (anonymously) in 1709, translated into English in 1712 by the Baroque architect John James as *The theory and practice of gardening: wherein is fully handled all that relates to fine gardens, commonly called pleasure-gardens, as parterres, groves, bowling-greens etc....* While D'Argenville's illustrations

presented Le Nôtre's ideas in a formulaic way that made them all too easy to copy, his text advocated an approach to design based first on a proper understanding of the site, and then a consideration of variety, diversity and composition, observing that 'the gardens that afford the greatest Variety, are the most valuable and magnificent'.[22] Significantly, in this 'variety', programmes of directed imagery of the type found at Versailles are completely absent, but magnificence is all. His most elaborate proposal is a Versailles-like scheme that combines a conventional canal fountain with a 'Group of Figures, as Neptune with Tritons', and at the end of the central avenue is a cascade: 'A termination of this kind is certainly the most magnificent that can be'.

5.15 Mask from the Fountain Garden Screen at Hampton Court, Jean Tijou. England, *c.*1690 (cat.132)

5.16 *Apollo flaying Marsyas,*
sculpture from the gardens of the
Holländisches Palais in Dresden,
Antonio Corradini. Venice,
1710–50 (cat.133)

THE BAROQUE GARDEN

Luke Morgan

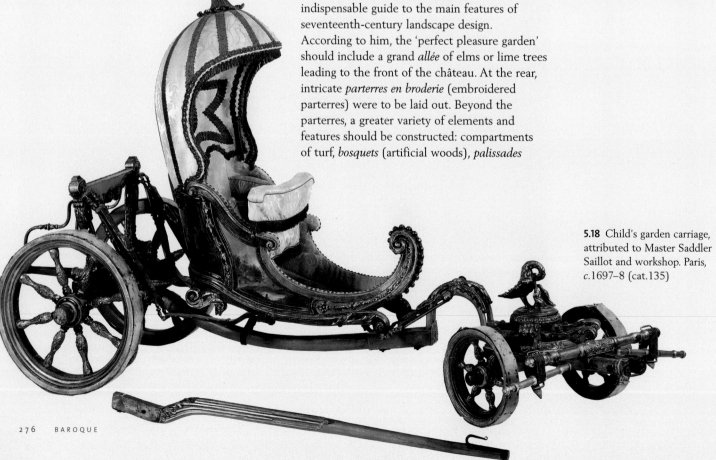

5.17 *Trompe l'oeil* arch in the gardens of the Château de Rueil, Israel Silvestre after Jean Lemaire, engraving. (Bibliothèque Nationale de France)

There are nearly as many versions of the Baroque garden as there are gardens. As a changeable medium in which the natural elements can never be wholly 'fixed', garden design is peculiarly resistant to stylistic naming. Whether or not there was a single concept of the 'Baroque garden' remains an open question, yet the period did produce gardens that shared certain features, if not a coherent and unified style in the sense sometimes used in the histories of the other visual arts.

An important point of difference between the gardens of the Baroque and of the Renaissance is that the former were conceived on a much grander scale. The gardens of André Le Nôtre were designed for horse and carriage rather than the solitary walker (pl.5.18). The dimensions of the Baroque garden in France were both real and virtual: in his *Le Jardin de Plaisir* (1651), André Mollet recommended the erection of 'perspectives of painted canvas' at the

extremities of the *allées* (avenues), thus artificially extending the garden still further. Illusionistic effects of this kind sometimes themselves assumed gargantuan proportions. At the Château de Rueil, for instance, Cardinal Richelieu commissioned a full-size painted *trompe l'oeil* triumphal arch from Jean Lemaire for a wall of his garden (pl.5.17).

Mollet's succinct text is, in fact, an indispensable guide to the main features of seventeenth-century landscape design. According to him, the 'perfect pleasure garden' should include a grand *allée* of elms or lime trees leading to the front of the château. At the rear, intricate *parterres en broderie* (embroidered parterres) were to be laid out. Beyond the parterres, a greater variety of elements and features should be constructed: compartments of turf, *bosquets* (artificial woods), *palissades*

5.18 Child's garden carriage, attributed to Master Saddler Saillot and workshop. Paris, *c*.1697–8 (cat.135)

5.19 *Bird's Eye view of the palace and gardens of Het Loo*, Pieter Schenk, engraving. Amsterdam, c.1698 (V&A:E.1572-1900)

(hedges) and more *allées*. Every one of the *allées* should, in turn, terminate in a statue or fountain, the chief subjects of which were mainly mythological. Although there were variations, the layout described by Mollet formed the basic pattern of many gardens of the period, from Versailles and Het Loo (pl.5.19) in the seventeenth century to Caserta (pl.5.20) in the eighteenth.

If, in the Renaissance, gardens were conceived as benign collaborations of art and nature, in the century of Louis XIV gardens became unmistakable expressions of power over nature and important instruments of 'self-fashioning', not to mention self-aggrandisement.

5.20 Gardens of the royal palace of Caserta, Luigi Vanvitelli, 1752–80

5.21 *The Triumph of Divine Providence and the fulfilment of her ends under the Papacy of Urban VIII*: record of the ceiling of the *salone* of Palazzo Barberini in Rome, workshop of Pietro da Cortona. Rome, *c*.1640 (cat.139)

Inside the Palace

The interior of the palace was the main stage for the enactment of princely ceremony and etiquette. Since the sixteenth century the accommodation of princes and their élites had been laid out in the form of an apartment, a suite of linked rooms usually including a bedchamber, a private closet and other smaller rooms, with one or more antechambers for attendants or visitors. In the seventeenth century, the earlier compact apartment was developed into the extended state apartment. As state apartments were usually for individuals (not couples), a Baroque palace or great house often had more than one: at Hampton Court, based on the French model, there were state apartments for King William and Queen Mary, each reached by its own monumental staircase. The north wing of the Palazzo Barberini in Rome had an apartment for Cardinal Francesco Barberini and apartments in the south wing for his brother Taddeo (who headed the secular side of the family) and his wife, all joined to the great central *salone* or hall. At Würzburg, as at other palaces of electors of the Holy Roman Empire, an apartment stood ready to receive the emperor (pl.5.22). The Duke and Duchess of Lauderdale had separate apartments in the French style, created in the 1670s on different floors, at Ham House, built some 50 years earlier. At Hampton Court the two royal bedchambers had a private link. It was unusual for the royal couple to share an official bedchamber, as they did at Rosenborg Castle in Copenhagen.

The detailed layout and functioning of Baroque state apartments varied according to different styles of ceremony. The French system, for instance, was different from the Imperial system practised in the Holy Roman Empire and in Spain. This had been developed in the sixteenth century from the ceremonies of the Burgundian court. But across the Baroque world, state apartments had a number of features in common. They were usually laid out *en enfilade*, with all the rooms linked by doorways set in a straight line, although for everyday practical purposes they were often also supplied with other forms of access via a network of concealed doors and back stairs and passages. Such linear planning was not only visually impressive; it also served to control and reinforce, through the ordering of space and the setting of clear boundaries, a ceremonial ritual and system of etiquette based on rank and degrees of access to the ruler or élite person. The concept of an enfilade was not in itself new, but its development in the seventeenth century promoted a unity of architectural treatment based on the design and placing of windows, doors and chimneypieces, and by extension the development of 'architectural' furniture: tables set against the wall with matching pier glasses and candlestands, and the formal arrangement of seating around the walls. By the same token, the linear emphasis of the enfilade, coupled with centralized and symmetrical planning, created a link between palace and garden characteristic of the Baroque, with avenues

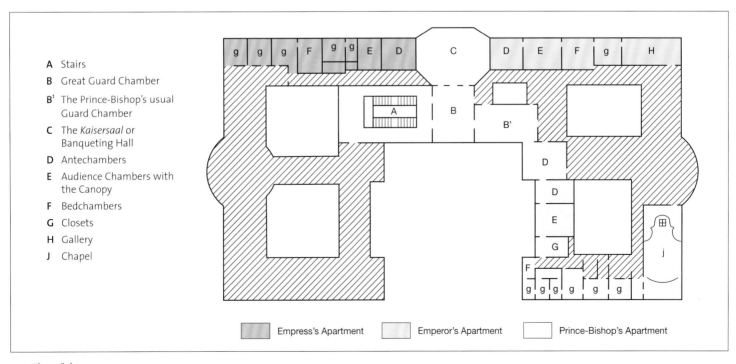

A Stairs
B Great Guard Chamber
B¹ The Prince-Bishop's usual Guard Chamber
C The *Kaisersaal* or Banqueting Hall
D Antechambers
E Audience Chambers with the Canopy
F Bedchambers
G Closets
H Gallery
J Chapel

Empress's Apartment   Emperor's Apartment   Prince-Bishop's Apartment

5.22 Plan of the state apartments in the Würzburg Residenz *c.*1750

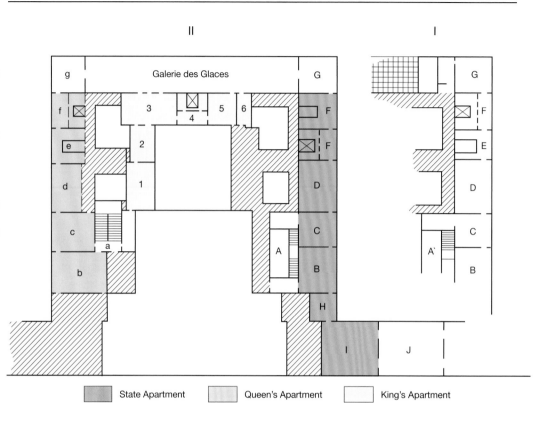

I **THE KING'S APARTMENTS UNTIL 1682**

A: The King's or Ambassador's Stairs; **B:** *Salle de Vénus*; **C:** *Salle de Diane*; **D:** *Salle de Mars* or *Salle des Gardes*; **E:** *Salle de Mercure* or *Antichambre* with the Throne; **F:** *Salle d'Apollon* or *Chambre du Lit*; **G:** *Grand Cabinet*, giving on to a smaller Closet and Bedchamber looking onto the Terrace.

II **THE APARTMENTS AFTER 1701**

A: The King's Stairs; **B:** *Salle de Vénus*; **C:** *Salle de Diane* or Billiard Room; **D:** *Salle de Mars* or Concert and Ballroom; **E:** *Salle de Mercure* or *Chambre de Parade ou du Lit*; **F:** *Salle d'Apollon* or *Chambre du Trône*; **G:** *Salle de la Guerre* giving on to the Great Gallery; **H:** *Salle de l'Abondance*; **I:** *Salon d'Hércule*; **J:** Ante-Chapel; **a:** The Queen's Stairs; **b:** The Great Guard Chamber; **c:** The Queen's Guard Chamber; **d:** *Antichambre*; **e:** *Grand Cabinet* with the canopy; **f:** *Chambre de la Reine* with the State Bed; **g:** *Salon de la Paix* giving on to the Great Gallery.

1: The King's Guard Chamber; **2:** *Antichambre* or *Salle du Grand Couvert* where the King ate in public; **3:** *Antichambre de l'Œil de Bœuf*, composed of the old *Antichambre des Bassans* and the King's old Bedchamber; **4:** *Chambre du Roi* until 1701; the *Salon ou le Roi s'habille*; **5:** The *Grand Cabinet* or *Cabinet du Conseil*; **6:** *Cabinet des Termes* giving on to the Backstairs and private closets, used mainly for keeping the King's collections of pictures and precious objects.

Galerie des Glaces

State Apartment Queen's Apartment King's Apartment

and vistas lined up with the internal spaces. But the desire for the enfilade could also produce some curious results, as in the Palazzo Borghese in Rome, where it was imposed in 1670–71 on a pre-existing set of rooms, causing the alignment of the doors to drift off the linear and form an angle as the enfilade progressed.[23] The enfilade of this city palace culminated in a *prospettiva* to the distant countryside that passed through the windows of a building opposite.

Although Versailles is often seen as the great exemplar of palace planning, the internal arrangements there were in fact rather idiosyncratic and determined by the addition of structures to the original small hunting lodge, especially after its adoption as the chief royal residence (pl.5.23). When the *Galerie des Glaces* (Hall of Mirrors) was completed in 1684 the old state apartment *en enfilade* (*Grands Appartements*) was reversed in direction and adopted an entirely ceremonial role, coinciding with the king's decision to take up permanent residence. Louis's new living apartment, comprising a guard chamber, *Grand Couvert* (for dining in public), antechamber,

bedchamber and cabinet, was not *en enfilade*, although the new bedchamber, the *Chambre du Roi*, was at the symbolically important dead centre of the palace. A state bedchamber remained, but was shifted by one room down the enfilade, retaining its role as a purely symbolic space. It had never been occupied by the king, who had actually slept in a smaller private room next door.

Almost every aspect of the design of the state apartment was linked to a carefully modulated system of etiquette, even including the more practical functions of life, such as eating and sleeping. All over Europe, after about 1660, the sequence of a state apartment usually began with the stairs to the *piano nobile* on the first floor. Thereafter the purposes and names of the rooms were determined by local custom,[24] although most apartments began with a room or hall for the guards and concluded with a bedchamber and a cabinet or closet and other more private rooms. In between, there were often antechambers used for dining and a number of rooms for holding audiences.

Eating

Eating was a movable activity, depending on the level of ceremony (see Dining at Court, p.288), and the idea of a single room dedicated to eating did not fully emerge until the eighteenth century. At Ham House the Marble Dining Room of the 1670s, where the family ate, also functioned as the central salon of the house, between the two apartments.[25] It was hung with leather, which did not retain the smell of food (pl.5.24).

The medieval tradition of ceremonial banqueting continued in the Baroque period, where it was part of the complex world of court performance. In Dresden in 1719, during the ceremonies and celebrations for the marriage of the emperor's daughter, the Archduchess Maria Josefa, to Prince Frederick Augustus of Saxony, the son of Augustus the Strong, the royal couples dined in the presence of the court in the first room of the state apartment. They were seated under an honorific canopy, but not on a raised dais, which was usual elsewhere (see The Festivities of Augustus the Strong, p.178). For a wedding banquet in Parma in 1714 the arrangements were

5.24 Detail of leather panels from the Marble Dining Room at Ham House, maker unknown. The Netherlands, *c*.1675 (cat.155)

similar, but a dais was used (pl.5.25) and in an ante-room next door was a huge display buffet of silver and gold plate.

Although buffets had begun as practical adjuncts to eating, by the Baroque period they were mainly for display, their practical function, if any, being limited to the service of drinks. The importance of the buffet as a demonstration of wealth and status is shown not only by its becoming part of the standard official equipment of English ambassadors going abroad (pls 5.26–28), but also by their placement away from eating rooms. At the Dresden wedding of 1719 the buffet was in its own room on the route to the state apartment. In the new city palace of the kings of Prussia in Berlin, the enormous buffet was housed in an architectural setting opposite the silver throne in the great centrally placed *Rittersaal* or Knights' Hall (pl.5.29).[26]

5.25 *Wedding banquet for Elizabeth Farnese and Philip V of Spain, held in Parma in 1714,* Ilario Spolverini, oil on canvas. Parma, 1714 (Palazzo del Municipio, Parma)

5.26 The Macclesfield wine set: fountain, cistern and cooler, from the buffet of Thomas Parker, 1st Earl of Macclesfield, mark of Anthony Nelme. London, 1719–20 (cat.157)

5.27 Pair of covered cups and salvers, from the ambassadorial buffet of Robert Benson, 1st Baron Bingley, mark of Philip Rollos. London, 1714 (cat.158)

5.28 Ewer and Basin, from the ambassadorial buffet of John Churchill, 1st Duke of Marlborough, mark of Elie Pacot. Lille, 1711–12 (cat.159)

5.29 *The silver buffet in Berlin*, Martin Engelbrecht after Eosander von Gothe, engraving. Frankfurt, 1717 (Kunstbibliothek, Berlin)

5.30 Spice box with nutmeg grater, mark of David Tanqueray. London, 1715 (cat.153)

5.31 Plan for a silver dish and pair of cruets, Nicolas-Ambroise Cousinet, pen, black ink, grey wash. Paris, *c.*1702 (Nationalmuseum, Stockholm)

5.32 Profile for a silver dish used for fish or fruit, Nicolas-Ambroise Cousinet, pen, black ink, grey wash and watercolour. Paris, *c.*1702 (Nationalmuseum, Stockholm)

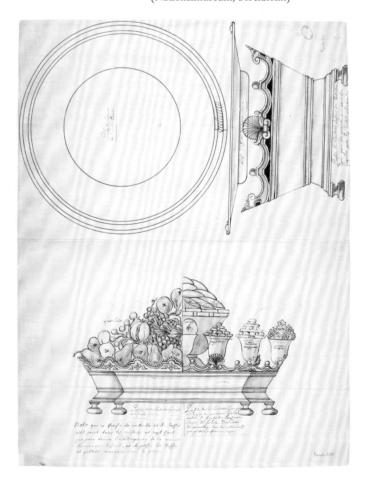

5.33 Table centrepiece, as arranged for the savoury course (*left*), and for the dessert course (*right*), David Willaume the Younger and Anne Tanqueray, London, 1731–2 (cat.160). The silver dishes and cutlery in the foreground are not part of the centrepiece itself

Eating in public was not however limited to great occasions of state. Louis XIV ate ceremonially every day, after 1690 in the *Salle du Grand Couvert*, watched by the court arranged by rank. Following ancient custom, his presence was symbolized by a boat-shaped vessel called a *nef*, but other things on the table were often brand new, for this period saw the invention of much of the table equipment used today, including matching sets of cutlery, soup tureens and condiment sets. For as the buffet became separate from the process of eating, so the tables

themselves came to be less loaded with food and more an area for the display of sets of costly silver. These innovations mostly emerged from French court circles, but were quickly observed and copied elsewhere, together with the adoption of the multi-course meal *à la française* (pls 5.31, 5.32). Many of these new kinds of silverware were devised to be used at less formal tables, including the centrepiece or *surtout*, which could be modified to serve both the savoury and dessert courses (pl.5.33).

DINING AT COURT

Philippa Glanville

'One must let the Germans eat and drink. This is the only way to win their friendship & their esteem. It is an absolute necessity to maintain a hospitable table' – the Marquis de Villars, writing to Louis XIV on negotiating with Max Emanuel of Bavaria

Lavish entertaining expressed Baroque theatricality. Rooms for dining were decked with paintings and aromatic shrubs, although no fresh flowers appeared on the table. The setting glittered with many candles, their flames reflected from mirrors and gilded plate on side tables. Dining was competitive, expressing the taste of the host and perceived as a kind of mock warfare. Diplomats sent descriptions home, listing temporary décors, goldsmiths' work and the number of dishes. Striking effects were valued. Artists designed dessert tables with parterres of out-of-season fruit or elaborate sugar sculptures (trionfi); in Dresden, the Italian court artist Giovanni Nosseni devised sugar sculptures after Giambologna's small bronzes for Johan Georg's wedding in 1607.

Concepts of civility and decorum drove innovations; a personal plate, knife, fork and spoon became the norm, as recommended by

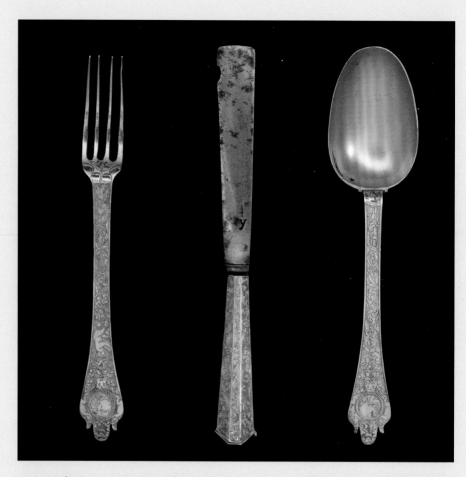

Antoine de Courtin in 1672 (pl.5.34). Menus emphasized clarity of flavours, simplicity of ingredients and more liquid soups, which required deeper bowls and tureens, as well as sauce-boats and condiment sets; all of these were evolved by French goldsmiths for Louis XIV and emulated across Europe (pl.5.35). Silver was supplemented with imported porcelain; salad was served in Japanese porcelain, because vinegar in the dressing stained precious metals. And at a Guildhall dinner in 1714, George I was offered a choice of four soups in silver gilt dishes, whereas his son was served a more modest two, in 'China'.

Drinking had extraordinary status at the German and Scandinavian courts; costly vessels were fashioned for ceremonious toasting, and stables, hunting lodges, grottoes, yachts and mines each had a dedicated toasting vessel. In Kassel, 352 elaborate cups were listed in Landgraf Moritz's inventory in 1613, a quarter of them gifts. For their electoral dinners, the electors each brought to Frankfurt personal rarities made

5.34 Knife, fork and spoon set, maker unknown. London, 1670–75 (cat.151)

5.35 Tureen and dish (the accompanying ladle not shown), mark of Claude II Ballin. Paris 1713–4 (tureen), 1714–5 (dish and ladle) (cat.152)

5.36 *Banquet for the Embassy of Viscount Castlemaine to the Pope* (detail), Arnold von Westerhout, engraving. Rome, 1687 (V&A:A.12.3)

5.37 (*right*) Goblet, attributed to the workshop of Friedrich Winter. Silesia (now Poland), 1695–1709 (cat.40)

of horn, ivory or hardstones to display on buffets, although this tradition of display had vanished in France by 1700. In the Dresden Residenz, a buffet celebrated the mineral riches of the region: a mounted figure rolled out from a silver-covered mountain, carrying a silver gilt cup for the toast.

By 1700, as wine connoisseurship developed, the sparkling clarity of lead crystal glass replaced precious metals for drinking; glass revealed the colour and quality of the wine (pl.5.37). Most wines were served chilled, in the newly devised single-bottle wine cooler or in large coolers, sometimes paired with a cistern and fountain for rinsing glasses (pl.5.38). In Brandenburg and Dresden, red glass, technically difficult and expensive to make, was adopted to serve the newly fashionable champagne.

Out-of-season vegetables such as asparagus or exotic hothouse fruit were intended to impress. Lady Mary Wortley Montagu admired the pineapple she was served in snow-bound Hanover

5.38 Wine cooler, marks of Paul de Lamerie and Paul Crespin. London, 1727–8 (cat.154)

in February 1718. Ice-cream, a popular novelty, demonstrated the ruler's control over nature and the skill of his confectioners. A new emphasis on fruit, salads, puff pastry and confections of cream and fruit demanded specialized serving equipment, such as a set of low geometric silver dishes made by Elie Pacot of Lille. Porcelain for dessert, presented in pyramids and flanking a centrepiece, was recommended by German and French cookery books in the 1690s (*Die wol unterwiesener Kochinn*, 1697, and Massialot's *Le Cuisinier royal*, 1698).

We can recreate the visual narrative of dinners of ceremony through illustrated accounts, such as the Roman embassy of James Castlemaine (pl.5.36). Stewards kept records of the etiquette, table décor and even the food and drink consumed; the French, Spanish, Danish and Wittelsbach courts are particularly well recorded. However, it is harder to penetrate the private world of princely dining *à l'hermitage* in Copenhagen, or in a Chinese garden pavilion by the lake at Max Emanuel's Nymphenburg, or during a hunt in one of the German principalities.

Meeting the King

In France the centre of the élite presence was the bedchamber, and splendid bedchambers in the French style duly appeared in other countries. Central to the bedchamber was the representative bed, often the most expensive piece of furniture in the palace and very frequently intended for show alone (see The State Bedchamber, p.296). But the range of functions fulfilled by the king's bedchamber, as the *Chambre du Roi*, in French court ritual was not on the whole repeated elsewhere. In Spain, Germany and England, for instance, people had very limited access to it, but in Versailles the royal bedchamber was the setting for a wide variety

5.40 *Inauguration of the Order of St Louis in the King's Bedchamber at Versailles*, 1693, François Marot. Paris, *c*.1710 (cat.162)

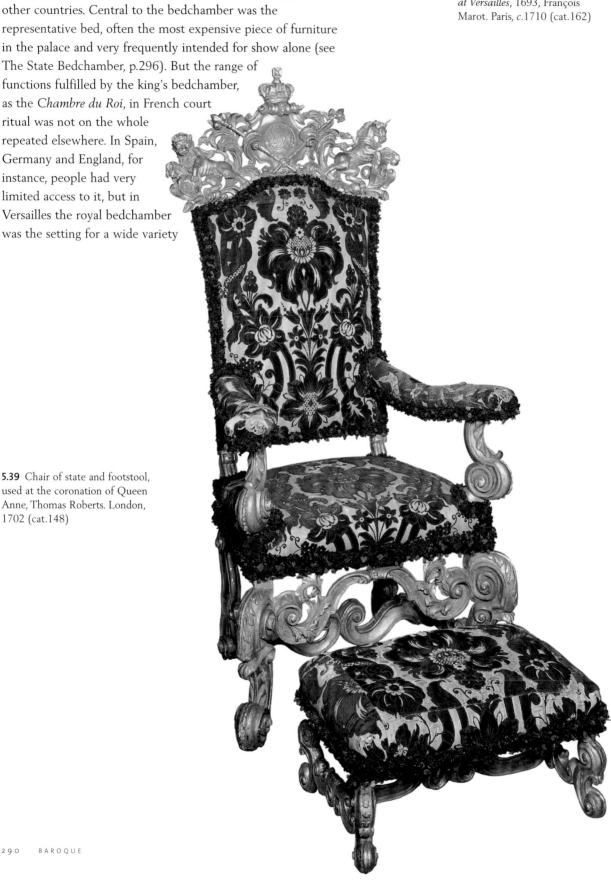

5.39 Chair of state and footstool, used at the coronation of Queen Anne, Thomas Roberts. London, 1702 (cat.148)

of functions in addition to sleeping, including the daily ritual of *lever* and *coucher* and smaller public meals (*petit couvert*), as well as some of the most important official events, such as the reception of ambassadors and the awarding of official orders (pl.5.40). In the imperial system the audience function of the Versailles bedchamber was taken by the audience chamber (or throne room) in the state apartment. It was marked by a chair or throne raised on a dais and covered by a canopy, often separated from the rest of the room by a railing (pl.5.39). The magnificent throne room in the state apartment at Versailles was purely symbolic, like the state bedchamber next door. For important receptions, when the king actually sat on the great silver throne, it was moved to the *Galerie des Glaces* and placed at the top end on a platform, reached by a set of temporary steps, sometimes flanked by huge silver candelabra. The Versailles throne inspired a number of others, including that of the newly created king of Prussia, which was placed opposite the great buffet in Berlin (pl.5.29).

5.41 *Frederick I of Prussia* seated on his silver throne, Samuel Theodor Gericke. Berlin, 1713 (cat.149)

5.42 (*opposite*) *Private Audience of the Archduchess Maria Josefa* in the State Bedchamber of the Dresden Residenz, Quirin Fonebonne after Raymond Leplat, etching and engraving. Paris, before 1728 (Kupferstich-Kabinett, Staatliche Kunstsammlungen Dresden)

Visits by foreigners could highlight these different systems of court ceremony. When Cardinal Francesco Barberini visited Louis XIII in the Louvre in 1625, he was surprised to be received by the king seated in a bed, surrounded by a balustrade. But sometimes different systems could be accommodated, as during the wedding celebrations in Dresden in 1719.[27] An enormously important dynastic and political event, it prompted the creation of a completely new state apartment at the electoral Residenz for the formal reception. The apartment had two adjacent and parallel enfilades, one finishing in the state bedchamber (in the French style), the other in the audience chamber (in the imperial style). The new princess passed through four older chambers before reaching the dining chamber at the head of the new apartment (see The Festivities of Augustus the Strong, p.178) where she was welcomed by the king and queen. They then went through the ante-rooms and crossed the audience chamber, before reaching the adjacent state bedchamber. After a conversation of the two couples they went back to the audience chamber, where the court attended the princess. Although the bed was in the latest French style, the room lacked the usual French bed platform and balustrade that would have separated the court from the two royal couples. Excluded from the room itself, the members of the court looked on through the doorways, the women from one, the men from the other (pl.5.42). At the ducal court in Modena, guests were received in the imperial style in the audience chamber, or in the bedchamber as in France, as diplomacy required.[28]

At such receptions, the physical movement through the state apartment and people's positions within the rooms played a key role in conveying messages of hierarchy and precedence. Italian etiquette books,[29] which assume the host to be a cardinal, reveal a system of great complexity based on the relative importance of the guest to the host. Guests were met by the host at a place in direct relationship to their rank, counting from the audience chamber. Thus a cardinal might be met in the guard chamber or *sala*. Ambassadors would be treated according to rank: those from Bologna would be met in the middle of the inner ante-room, but those from the Grand Duke of Tuscany would be favoured by being met in the middle of the outer ante-room, which followed on from the *sala*. Within the audience chamber apparently tiny details counted for much. The arrangement of furniture was crucial, the most favoured position being that facing the door.

1. Le Roy.
2. La Reine.
3. Le Prince Royal.
4. La Princesse Royale.
5. Les Officiers de la Cour.
6. Les Dames de la Cour.

Chambre du Lit de l'Appartement de parade du Roy,
Où sa Majesté et la Reine ont receu la première visite de la Princesse Royale après son arrivée
et Entrée Solemnelle, et réception dans la Ville et Château de Dresden, le 19 Aoust 1719

Once seated, the person of higher rank began the conversation. A similar system applied when the guest left: a cardinal would accompany another cardinal to his coach and the host would turn once the coach began to leave. The Tuscan ambassador would also be taken to his coach, but the host would turn before the coach left. But rules could be broken. In Modena in the 1650s, as Alice Jarrard has shown, Francesco d'Este's sense of his growing status caused him to modify the usual codes appropriate to a duke. The French royal ambassador was specially honoured by being met by the duke not only outside the ceremonial area of the baldacchino but four steps beyond the end of the throne carpet.[30]

The special emphasis given to the bedchamber in French court ritual required that the space be physically subdivided. As we have seen, at the Louvre during the reign of Louis XIII, a balustrade divided the bed from the rest of the room, and the bed itself was placed in an alcove. Within the balustrade the floor was raised like a stage. When Cardinal Chigi came to the state bedchamber at Fontainebleau in 1664 to read out the

pope's apology to Louis XIV (prompted by a diplomatic dispute), he did so seated within the balustrade (pl.5.43). The ceremony was witnessed within the balustrade by the chief officers of state – all nobles – and outside it by the cardinal's retinue. For the installation of new knights of the order of St Louis, the king stood outside the balustrade (see pl.5.40).

Position, precedence and gesture were also central to the daily ritual of *lever* and *coucher* that took place in the *Chambre du Roi*. In the *lever*, the king was woken by his valet, who slept at the foot of the bed. Six different groups of family and courtiers then entered in turn. First, while the king was still in bed, came the *entrée familière*: the legitimate children and grandchildren of the king (the 'children of France'), legitimate princes and princesses of the blood as well as doctors and the first valet and page. Next was the *grande entrée*, the chief officers of the *chambre* and the *garderobe*, including the Lord Chamberlain and Chief Gentleman of the Bedchamber, who laid out the king's robe. The king got up. Then came the *première entrée* of the king's readers, the supervisors of the

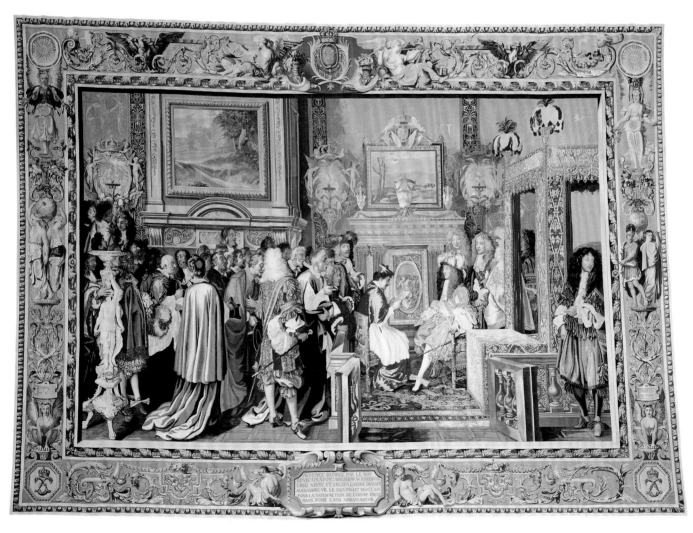

5.44 Armchair, Nicolas Lefèvre.
Paris, 1680 (cat.164)

entertainments and festivities, and others. The king put on his shoes. Next came the *entrée de la chambre*, consisting of the rest of the officers of the *chambre*, together with the Grand Almoner, ministers and secretaries of state, state councillors, the Marshal of France and others. The king picked up his robe and his nightshirt was removed by the *maître de la garderobe* and the first servant of the wardrobe, the first pulling the right sleeve, the second the left. The Lord Chamberlain, or one of the king's sons if present, brought the shirt for the day. The king put it on, the first valet holding the right sleeve, the first servant of the wardrobe the left. The king then rose from his armchair and the *maître de la garderobe* helped him complete dressing.

Two more entries completed the ritual. The fifth was for gentlemen and ladies of the nobility who stood high in the king's favour. But most sought after was membership of the last and sixth, which was through a back door. It was open to the king's legitimate and illegitimate sons and their families, sons-in-law, and a select further group, including such powerful figures as the superintendent of buildings.[31] Differences in rank were not only expressed by being seated as opposed to standing, but also through the types of seat furniture used. At the bottom was the *tabouret*, a special type of small stool (mainly used by women), then a chair with a back, and finally a chair with a

5.43 (*opposite*) *Audience of Cardinal Chigi in the King's Bedchamber at Fontainebleau*, from the tapestry series *The History of the King*, Atelier of Jean Mozin, Gobelins Workshops, after Charles Le Brun. Paris, 1672–6 (cat.4)

back and arms. Their correct use was governed by a complex code. In the tapestry, Cardinal Chigi is shown seated in a chair without arms, the king in an armchair. This may have been done to allow the tapestry to make a strong political point, for records of the actual event tell us that the king showed the cardinal particular favour. Not only did Louis advance halfway across the chamber to meet him, but he allowed him to sit in an armchair exactly like his own. The seating code determined that in the presence of the king everyone stood except for the dauphin (the king's eldest son), his wife, the king's legitimate daughters and grandchildren and princesses of the blood, who could sit on *tabourets*. In the presence of the dauphin, his wife and the king's sons and daughters sat in armchairs, while the grandchildren, princes and princesses of the blood, cardinals, duchesses, foreign princesses and *grandes despagnes* sat on *tabourets*. The rest, namely dukes, foreign princes and *grands despagnes*, and ladies and gentlemen of quality, all stood. In the presence of princes and princesses of the blood (who were outside the direct royal line and therefore ranked below the king's grandchildren) almost everyone could sit in an armchair.[32] In such circumstances the right to use a *tabouret* was highly prized; those who had it were known as *femmes assises* (sitting women) or even *tabourets*.

In spite of the strongly ritualized character of French court ceremony, much of which had been newly introduced by Louis XIV, life at Versailles was in other respects more open than at many other courts, in which access to the ruler was far more limited and the more private rooms of the palace less accessible. As with the formal ceremonies, this was also promoted by the king, who had a strong belief that making himself accessible at court and visible to the public favoured peace and harmony.[33] The state rooms at Versailles lacked the boundaries imposed elsewhere and could be visited by anyone correctly dressed (and the necessary sword could be hired). The king could be seen every day on his journey through the state apartment to attend Mass in the chapel when, according to the duc de Saint-Simon, 'anyone could talk to him if he wished, but less distinguished persons had to clear the captain of the Guards first'.[34] From 1682 thrice-weekly evening *appartements* took place in which the king and queen and the royal family gambled or played cards, billiards and other games in the state apartment in the company of the entire court. Informal as these occasions might seem, they were of course part of a closely timed and controlled routine that governed the whole of court life.

THE STATE BEDCHAMBER

Tessa Murdoch

State beds are first mentioned in fourteenth-century France as used for laying out the body of a deceased monarch, bishop or nobleman. By the early seventeenth century, beds were placed in alcoves, an idea promoted by the celebrated Parisian hostess Madame de Rambouillet. The alcove (from a Spanish word of Arabic origin) provided a compact space which was easy to heat.

The space around the bed, known as the *ruelle*, was often divided from the rest of the room by an arch and balustrade. A 1650s French engraving shows a lady with her admirer and an attendant seated at the foot of a grand bed (pl.5.46). The host or hostess might also receive visitors while lying in bed or at toilet. In 1682, the Danish king's official mistress Sophie Amalie Moth was painted in her bedroom (pl.5.45). Seated at her dressing-table, she rinses her fingers in a basin of water held by her page. Her dressing-table is covered in a sumptuous Venetian lace toilet-cloth. The silver mirror and toilet box are flanked by two-handled covered

gold cups with matching footed salvers, similar to those issued to Lord Bingley, English ambassador to Spain, in 1714. Her grand bed is in an alcove, perhaps derived from a print by Jean le Pautre. The velvet bed hangings are green (the colour of Venus, goddess of love), trimmed with gold and silver lace; the lining is golden silk with silver trimmings.

Under Louis XIV access to the royal state bedchamber was strictly controlled. The French king turned getting up and going to bed into a daily theatrical event. The state bedroom was also a stage for significant royal events. In 1645 the young Louis XIV's bedroom at the Château of Fontainebleau was the setting for the signing

5.45 *Sophie Amalie Moth in a Bedchamber*, Horatius Paulijn, oil on canvas. Copenhagen, 1682 (Gisselfeld Kloster, Denmark)

5.46 (*left*) Frontispiece to *La Pretieuse ou le mystère des ruelles*, Michel de Pure, engraving. Paris, 1656 (Bibliothèque Nationale de France)

of the marriage contract between King Vladislas IV of Poland and Princess Louise Marie de Gonzaga. The young king witnessed the event with his brother and mother from inside the balustrade that separated them from the crowd of courtiers. In 1693 the inauguration of the new order of chivalry of St Louis took place in the king's bedroom at Versailles. In 1698, William III's ambassador to Versailles, the Earl of Portland, noted that, among the many favours shown to him, the French king presented him with a candle at the royal *coucher* (going to bed).

French court etiquette promoted the harmonious design of every element of the interior of the state bedroom. The printed engravings of Jean Berain and Daniel Marot (pl.5.48) spread the idea beyond France, while French beds found their way to the rest of Europe. An example from the collection of Nils Bielke (pl.5.47) was, according to tradition, given to him when he was in Paris as Swedish Ambassador by Louis XIV.

5.47 State Bed, possibly given by Louis XIV to the Swedish Ambassador, Nils Bielke. Paris, before 1682 (cat.165)

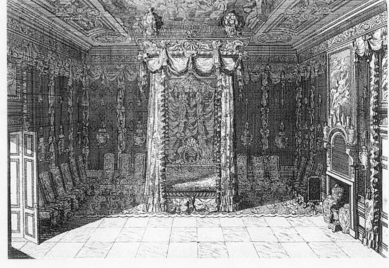

5.48 *Design for a State Bedchamber*, Daniel Marot, engraving. *c.*1702 (V&A:E.5914-1905)

The Power of Design

The relative informality of the *appartements* evenings could not have disguised the powerful messages of control and royal power expressed in every aspect of the visual language of the state apartment's design, including its architectural form, decoration and the fixed and movable furnishings. The whole long progress, from the great Staircase of the Ambassadors through the state apartment and *Galerie des Glaces* before reaching the king, was designed to overawe and perhaps even terrify (pl.5.50): such seems to have been the case when the Turkish ambassador was reportedly unable to complete his journey until he changed his breeches.[35] The scale and the magnificence of the rooms, filled with marble, gold, luxurious textiles and enormous pieces of solid silver furniture, were backed up by a carefully calculated decorative programme celebrating the character, glories and conquests of the Sun King. On the staircase the ambassador would have met the king in marble, in the form of a bust right in the centre of the ascent (pl.5.49). On the walls painted figures in modern dress representing the nations of each continent looked over draped balustrades, flanked by huge panels depicting French military victories. On the ceiling, figures of the gods, the muses, the arts, the months and the continents were linked to scenes of great recent events, all shown in Roman dress and reflecting French superiority. At the centre were figures of Care and Strength, Magnificence and Authority.

5.49 *View of the Staircase of the Ambassadors*, Louis de Surugue de Sergis after Jean-Michel Chevotet. Paris, *c.*1720 (cat.137)

5.50 *Louis XIV receiving the Persian ambassadors in the Galerie des Glaces at Versailles*, attributed to Nicolas de Largillière. Paris, 1715 (cat.145)

The painted decorations on the ceilings of the state apartment were inspired by those of Pietro da Cortona at the Palazzo Pitti in Florence (see pl.2.35). While the Pitti ceilings relate the history of the Medici dynasty as far back as the ancient gods, the Versailles decorations focus entirely on the king himself, connecting his history and qualities to the ancient gods and heroes. The king is loving and loved (Venus), a hunter and navigator, developing distant trade for the benefit of his people (Diana), victorious and peace-loving (Mars), a protector of the arts and sciences (Mercury), magnificent and magnanimous (Apollo), a dispenser of justice and pious provider (Jupiter) and thrifty and reserved (Saturn).[36]

At the other end of the state apartment, in the *Salon de la Guerre* (War Drawing Room) at one end of the gallery, the king in a stucco relief tramples his enemies while two figures of fame trumpet his victories and two chained prisoners crouch beneath (pl.5.51). On the ceiling France sits surrounded by Victories and flanked lower down by Rebellion and Discord and her foreign enemies: Germany, Holland and Spain. The ceiling of the gallery itself is an enormous celebration of the 30 main events of the king's reign up to 1676, starting, in the centre, with his assumption of personal rule in 1661. As with the list of subjects covered by the *histoire médallique* (see The Medallic History of Louis XIV, p.66), they include not only international

events like the victories and peace treaties, but also national ones like the abolition of duelling and the creation of the police. At the other end of the gallery was the *Salon de la Paix* (Peace Drawing Room), celebrating victorious France's magnanimity and Christian Europe at peace.

The system of controlled access and protocol inside the palace was prefigured by what happened outside. At Versailles, only certain people were allowed to take their coaches into the inner courtyard, which gave them the privilege of entering the great stairs without setting foot outside the building. In some cases, for instance in many Italian city palaces, and at the Residenzes in Dresden and Würzburg and the palace of Caserta, the entrance to the stairs was effectively inside the palace. The way in which coaches were used shows that the extravagant display of symbolism and allegory marking their exterior decoration was not mainly for the public in the streets but a crucial part of palace culture, designed not only to be seen in the context of the palace itself, but also to be a sort of substitute palace when on the move. Their floors, inlaid using the Boulle technique of wood, engraved brass, pewter and tortoiseshell, and their wall linings and ceiling canopies were matched only by the most luxurious rooms that a palace could provide. For the occupants of such a coach, arrival at the great staircase must have seemed an almost seamless transition.

5.51 *Salon de la Guerre*, château of Versailles, the room designed by Charles Le Brun, with a relief of *Louis XIV on Horseback riding in Triumph over his enemies* by Antoine Coysevox. The state appartment is seen to the left, the *Galerie des Glaces* to the right. Paris, 1678–86

Staircases and Galleries

When the king of the Two Sicilies saw the model of the proposed stairs and chapel at Caserta (pl.5.52) he was reportedly overcome with an emotion 'fit to tear his heart from his breast'.[37] Staircases, calculated to make a huge initial impression, were often the most exciting and complex spaces of the Baroque palace, both in terms of architectural design and of the messages they could convey through painting, sculpture and architectural decoration. They presented great opportunities for architectural invention given the design constraints of the palace, not only because they could be more architectonic in their treatment, being a transitional space between the exterior and interior, but also because they occupied spaces outside the restrictive enfilade.

The staircase at Versailles, demolished in 1752, was not only the most famous example, but also the most imitated in its overall form as well as in detail, as shown by the examples at Hampton Court, Het Loo and Caserta. But it was relatively restrained in its spatial design, and matched in its decoration the classical treatment and the rich and brightly coloured marble, paint, plaster and gilt metal of the state apartment. Just as the treatment of those rooms was inspired by the Palazzo Pitti in Florence, so the illusionistic figures on the stairs were inspired by Italy, not by a staircase but rather by the wall

paintings in the Sala Regia of the Quirinal Palace in Rome.[38] Italy was, however, the ultimate source of many of the more complex examples of Baroque palace staircases, such as that of the summer palace of Drottningholm outside Stockholm, begun by Nicodemus Tessin the Elder in 1665 and at that stage adorned with vigorous fleshy plasterwork cartouches by the northern Italians Giovanni and Carlo Carove. When, however, the stair decoration came to be finished by Tessin's son in the 1680s, it made direct reference, in its painted decoration and marble finishes, to Versailles.

Among the most dramatic Baroque palace staircases are those by Balthasar Neumann at Würzburg and Luigi Vanvitelli at Caserta. They adopted the imperial or double-return form, in which the drama of the ascent is increased by having to double back to see the top. In both cases the journey begins in a low vaulted vestibule entered from the centre of the building. The stairs rise towards light, made all the more dramatic at Caserta by being tightly enclosed. They culminate in an open vestibule leading straight on to the palace chapel and at right angles to two immensely long enfilades. At Würzburg they lead to a guard chamber (the White Hall) decorated in unpainted plaster, and then, with another turn, to the huge, richly painted Imperial Hall giving access to the two state apartments. While such a staircase could be effectively buried within a building as

5.52 Staircase and upper vestibules of the royal palace of Caserta, designed by Luigi Vanvitelli. Caserta, 1756–9 (cat.138)

5.53 *Ideal view of the staircase of Schloss Weissenstein at Pommersfelden,* designed by Johann Lukas von Hildebrandt, 1713–16, engraving by Salomon Kleiner. Germany, 1728 (Stiftung Schloss Weissenstein)

immense as Caserta, at Würzburg it occupied much of the central block. At the smaller palace of Schloss Weissenstein at Pommersfelden the huge stairs filled the whole of the projecting central section. Behind it lay the Imperial Hall (pl.5.53).

The elaboration and the strong architectural treatment of the imperial halls were possible because they stood outside the apartment. The same was true of the great galleries that sometimes formed the principal and most significant room of the Baroque palace. Their large scale and multi-purpose nature as picture galleries, assembly rooms and occasional throne rooms often made them the main stage for the display of princely power (see The Gallery, p.310). By the same token, the marble-topped tables, cabinets and other pieces of furniture that they contained were few but monumental (see pl.2.37).

Into the Apartment

In 1717 Nicodemus Tessin the Younger put together in manuscript a 'treatise on the decoration of interiors, for all kinds of royal residences, and others of distinction in both town and country'.[39] Intended for his architect son, and based on his travel notes, most especially in France and Italy, and his work as the Swedish royal architect, as well as books, prints and other sources, it casts a rare light on the visual language of contemporary palace decoration and furnishing, not only revealing what had been most characteristic of Baroque palace decoration since its beginning in the mid-seventeenth century, but also showing the hierarchies within interior design and the relative status of its constituent elements. Tessin's view of palace decoration was based on a profound understanding of the direct link between magnificence and political and, by extension, economic power – the latter largely derived from his observations in France.

While the main aim of the decoration of palaces and great houses was splendour and magnificence, differing levels of splendour and dignity could be conveyed by both design and the use of materials. For Tessin, the most magnificent decoration displayed the union of the three arts of painting, sculpture and architecture. On this aspect of Baroque design, Tessin believed, the great palace galleries, most notably that at Versailles, were second only to the great churches of Rome.[40] The gallery in the royal palace in Stockholm, modelled on that at Versailles, signalled its higher status than the rooms at the summer palace of Drottningholm, which had ceilings carried out in paint alone.[41]

Although the more private rooms of a palace were of a lower status, and thus on a less majestic scale, they were still required to be opulent, if more intimate and comfortable. They were also more subject to the vagaries of fashion. For the serious, architecturally minded observers of palatial milieux they could sometimes offend. When Christopher Wren twice visited 'the palace, or if you please the Cabinet of Versailles' in 1665, before the creation of the king's state apartment, he observed:

not an Inch within but is crowded with little curiosities of Ornaments: the Women, as they make here the Language and Fashions, and meddle with Politicks and Philosophy, so they sway also in Architecture; Works of Filgrand [filigree], and little Knacks are in great Vogue; but Building certainly ought to have the Attribute of the Eternal, and therefore the only thing uncapable of new Fashions.[42]

5.54 *Madame de Montespan,*
said to be above a gallery at
Clagny, after Henri Gascar. Paris,
1679–85 (cat.170)

5.55 Mirror with painted
decoration, probably Antoine
Monnoyer. Probably London,
1710–20 (cat.144)

The contrast between the different approaches to public and private is well shown in an imaginary painted scene of Madame de Montespan reclining on a luxurious canopied day-bed. The decoration that surrounds her typifies the private rooms of the apartment, while behind it are seen the public spaces of a great vaulted gallery formally furnished with cabinets on stands (pl.5.54).

Tessin's treatise is divided into three sections: first, 'fixed' or architectural decoration, secondly paintings and sculpture ('movable decoration'), and thirdly furniture and furnishings ('movable decoration, of all sorts of furniture').[43] The first section deals with vault and ceiling treatments and with wall treatments in paint, marble, and the most expensive and most recent innovation (and fashionable craze), mirrors large enough to cover walls (pl.5.55). Tessin takes particular notice of the glass over the chimneypiece in the *Chambre du Roi* at Versailles, installed in 1684 and perhaps one of the first examples of that use. He then treats ceiling cornices, doors, windows and chimneypieces, the last the most important architectural feature in most rooms. Floors played a very important part in underlining status, especially in France. Tessin notes the grading of quality in marble floors, and the need for them to echo the ceiling pattern. The marble in those at Versailles came from different parts of France, with the most precious being used nearest the king's apartments. Fine wooden parquetry floors laid in patterns also had a high status and were used throughout the great state apartment and the queen's apartment at Versailles, except for the guard chambers. But the finest and rarest floors used marquetry in the so-called Boulle technique, more commonly used on furniture or for the floors of grand coaches, as we have seen.[44]

The second section of Tessin's treatise deals with the display of art, or 'movable decoration', both ancient and modern. Art collecting had long been the pursuit of kings, but by the seventeenth century pictures by the great masters had become a precious and even more prestigious commodity. Rulers eagerly set out to build up their collections, preferably by acquiring another collection *en bloc*, as Charles I of England did when he bought the Duke of Mantua's paintings in 1627. At the same time there was a shift in ways of displaying art in the palace. It now appeared in public rooms as well as the more private rooms, a development that laid the ground for the creation of the modern art gallery. In Modena, paintings were introduced into the new ducal apartment created in 1647, and were given special prominence by being hung against red velvet trimmed with gold.[45] The new *camera di parata* or Room of Display was at once a reception space (for the display of the duke) and a place to display the 'true marvels of Painting', hung on the walls and set into the ceiling. The impact of one such painting, a virtuoso depiction by Correggio of the Adoration, known as *Night*, is described in a guide book: 'when the curtain that covered this great treasure was drawn, the thirsty wayfarers quickly genuflected'.[46] But tastes and customs varied across the Baroque world. Tessin observes that the part played by ancient sculpture and other fragments in the state apartments of Italian palaces was carried out in Versailles by its famous solid silver furniture, at any rate until it was melted down in 1689.

5.56 Clock, designed for the Small Gallery at Versailles, probably Jean Berain the Younger after Jean Berain the Elder. Paris, *c*.1699 (cat.146)

Furnishing the Apartment

The word furniture (*meubles*), as used in the title of the last part of Tessin's treatise, meant not just tables and chairs, but rather the unified treatment of a scheme of decoration through the use of an ensemble of matched furnishings. The wider-scale adoption of this concept (*ameublement*) coincided with the emergence of the all-powerful court designer with a finger in every pie. Examples included the Versailles *Galerie des Glaces* with its silver furniture and ceiling paintings designed by Charles Le Brun, the bedchambers of Daniel Marot designed to the last detail – including the arrangement of the chairs against the walls (see The State Bedchamber, p.296) – and the Stockholm interiors masterminded by Tessin himself. Many of the types of furniture and furnishings described by Tessin in 1717 were strikingly modern. They had been introduced only since about 1650 – mainly in France – and were characterized by a marked increase in comfort and convenience. They included the ancestors of the modern upholstered armchair and sofas, desks and the useful combination of table, candlestands and often a mirror (pl.5.57). Tessin does not mention other innovations, including clocks as furniture, commodes and bookcases (pl.5.56).[47] Candlestands, or *guéridons*, helped with

5.57 Table and pair of candlestands, attributed to Pierre Gole and workshop, Mathieu Lespagnandelle (carving) and David Dupré (gilding). Paris, *c*.1671 (cat.140)

5.58 Candlestand with 'Indian' figure, maker unknown. Probably Venice, *c.*1675 (cat.156)

the new forms of lighting, candelabra and chandeliers hung with reflective rock crystal and glass (pls 5.58, 5.59). 'Nothing can exceed', Tessin wrote, 'the effect of a beautiful apartment well lit with white candles' (pl.5.60).[48] In 1695 the *Galerie des Glaces* at Versailles was lit by 7,000 candles.[49] But Tessin's long experience meant that he could also track changing fashions in furnishing. By 1717 the incredible array of enormous candlestands, plant pots, tables and other pieces of solid silver furniture that adorned the king's state apartment had been melted down to pay for the wars, encouraging imitations in gilt and silvered wood and replacements in the Boulle technique, which for all its glamour did not involve the use of precious metals. On the tables of patriotic noblemen, according to the duc de Saint-Simon, the melted table silver was replaced with the fine faience of Rouen.[50]

5.59 One of a pair of candelabra, Christoffer Merker, Stockholm, 1684 (cat.141)

5.60 *Ball celebrating the return of Louis XIV and his queen from Strasbourg,* from the royal almanac for the year 1682, engraving. Paris, 1682 (Bibliothèque Nationale de France)

Textiles

Central to the creation of an *ameublement* was the use of textiles. This is hard to appreciate today, when the palaces have so often been stripped of their original furniture and wall hangings and the tapestries and upholstery, where they survive, have faded. Of the 19 chapters in Tessin's last section, 12 are on textiles or textile-based furniture, most importantly tapestries and beds. Tapestry had been the most expensive and prestigious form of furnishing for centuries and during the Baroque period court-based workshops were established, notably at the French royal Gobelins manufactories near Paris (see The Gobelins Workshops, p.124), which produced great propagandist subjects for the king.[51] Tapestries were especially useful for making grand statements in large public rooms and continued to be used as an impressive wall decoration: in the Dresden Residenz in 1719 the three pre-existing great halls were filled with tapestry, but not the new state apartment that followed.

The appeal of earlier tapestry had lain in its function as a rich but movable wall covering, a transportable luxury travelling with the court from residence to residence. When courts became less peripatetic in the Baroque period, the useful movable quality of textiles continued to be a factor, allowing apartments and their furnishings and decorations to be changed according to the season. In northern European palaces tapestries were often left in place throughout the year, but in central and southern Europe they seem to have been put away in the summer. Other forms of textile were also used in the same seasonal way. In Italy, there were often separate apartments for summer and winter, but in the summer Queen Christina's winter *ameublement* of crimson damask was covered over with green taffeta, partly to guard against dust coming through the open windows of her Roman palazzo.[52] At Versailles, according to Tessin, the winter *ameublement* of the state apartment was sometimes of green and sometimes of red velvet, both with fringes and braids in gold. In the summer it was changed for an *ameublement* in brocade with floral patterns in gold and silver and coloured silks with metal lace fringes.[53] The changes to the seating furniture were managed with slip covers. The throne room at Versailles, which according to Tessin was almost indescribably rich, was permanently fitted out with 18 pilasters in cloth of gold set against a backing of red velvet. In winter, the velvet walls were hung with paintings by Guido Reni, Van Dyck, Rubens and Valentin de Boulogne. In summer these were exchanged for huge hangings embroidered in high relief in gold, silver and silk, all on a silver ground (pl.5.61). The throne dais, carpet and hanging *portières* over the door were treated in the same way, but in lower relief.[54]

5.61 Drawing of an embroidered wall hanging from the King's Audience Chamber at Versailles, artist unknown. Paris, *c*.1687 (cat.147)

The handling of such textiles, including the custom of hanging contrasted fabrics in vertical strips, the use of gathered drapery and the very great emphasis on deep and complex fringes (made by specialist *passementiers*), was aimed at producing effects that were not only rich but also what has been aptly described as 'lively and frothy',[55] now perhaps best understood through contemporary representations. A similar approach was taken in the design of dress, not only for women, but also for men, with their huge wigs and elaborate ribbons (pls 5.62, 5.63). The combined effect of dress and decor must have been nothing short of astonishing. 'It was a fine silken thing which I spied walking th'other day through Westminster-Hall, that had as much Ribbon on him as would have plundered six shops, and set up Twenty Country Pedlars; all his body was dres't like a May-pole or a Tom-a Bedlam's Cap'.[56]

5.62 Mantua, maker unknown. London, *c.*1708 (cat.142)

5.63 Costume of Charles X of Sweden, maker unknown, broadcloth, silver brocade, embroidery. France or Sweden, 1654 (Livrustkammaren)

The Gallery

Reinier Baarsen

As a room type, the gallery is neither an invention of the Baroque nor is its potential as an architectural expression of that style immediately apparent. Essentially a long, narrow room, opening up with windows along one or both sides, it is characteristically decorated in a unified, rhythmic manner, without a pronounced sense of direction. In Britain, long galleries are a notable feature of the Elizabethan 'prodigy houses', but they are absent from most Baroque country houses, including such iconic ones as Sir John Vanbrugh's Castle Howard. The Baroque apartment did not include a gallery.

And yet, in some of the greatest palaces and town houses of the European Baroque the gallery was the principal room, serving as the supreme symbol of the owner's dynastic, political and cultural aspirations. It could acquire this position because it was the largest room in the house, and precisely because it was not part of any particular person's apartment. The best-known example is the *Galerie des Glaces* at the

5.64 The *Galerie des Glaces* at the château of Versailles, Jules Hardouin Mansart, decorated by Charles Le Brun. 1678–84

5.65 Detail of the ceiling of the *Galerie des Glaces* showing the king armed on land and sea, Charles Le Brun, château of Versailles. Paris, *c.*1684

5.66 (*opposite*) Gallery in the Palazzo Colonna, designed by Gianlorenzo Bernini and others. Rome, 1661–1703

Château of Versailles, completed in 1684. It is pierced by great French windows overlooking the gardens laid out by André Le Nôtre. On the opposite wall, these are reflected by mirrored recesses of equal size – a stupendous innovation at the time. The ceiling, designed and painted by Charles Le Brun, glorifies the person and reign of Louis XIV, the Sun King (pl.5.64). Although along its walls were set out large silver vases containing orange trees, and splendid furniture of silver and hardstones, it was in the main kept empty. The entire court could congregate here and watch the king pass through. Only rarely, such as on the occasion of the reception of the Siamese ambassador in 1686, was the great silver furniture from the king's state apartment amassed in the centre of the gallery to create a décor of unparalleled splendour (pl.5.67).

The *Galerie des Glaces* is terminated at either end by an antechamber, the *Salon de la Guerre* on the king's side and the *Salon de la Paix* on the queen's. The visitor coming from either of the two apartments turns the corner, which, in these rooms, greatly heightens the gallery's Baroque, climactic effect. This idea was taken from the greatest Italian Baroque gallery, that of the Palazzo Colonna in Rome (pl.5.66). Its central space was constructed from 1661, painted by Giovanni Paolo Schor and others with a huge fresco glorifying Marcantonio Colonna, the hero of the battle against the Turks fought at Lepanto in 1571. The idea of incorporating the two antechambers was conceived by Gianlorenzo Bernini in 1674. One was created within an adjoining building, and its higher floor level was retained, turning it into a raised throne-room. Of seminal importance to the representation of the Colonna, the gallery housed the family's collection of classical sculpture. The display of works of art was a primary function of the Baroque gallery. In each anteroom there was a grandiose cabinet, a veritable 'gallery within a gallery' (pl.5.68), and in the early eighteenth century a series of splendid gilded side-tables and stands was made for the three rooms that together make up this eminently theatrical *Gesamtkunstwerk*.

Bedchambers

The most extragavant textile displays were applied to beds and their matching sets of upholstered furniture. Although the standard type of French bed (developed in the early seventeenth century) was essentially a four-poster curtained box of simple outline, it allowed an extensive display of costly textiles and lavish trimmings in gold and silver. Tessin described the bed in the *Chambre du Roi* at Versailles, which was of this standard type and hung with brocade with gold flowers on a silver ground, as 'extremely pretty'. But the 'very magnificent' state bed in the state apartment, set on a marquetry floor behind a silver balustrade, was an 'angel bed' (*lit d'ange*) with hangings of silver and gold lace with coloured silks.[57] The curtains of angel beds were suspended from a 'flying tester', a canopy that covered the whole bed and was suspended at its outer end from the ceiling. The open design of angel beds not only made them suitable for use in the summer, but also gave the greatest opportunity to show off the upholsterer's art in the bed covering and back and, more especially, in the curtains when they were drawn up. Angel beds seem to have had a special appeal to foreign observers of French fashions. Certainly Tessin, a great lover of extravagant upholstery, was careful to record the two spectacular angel beds in the *Trianon de Porcelaine* just before their removal in 1687 (pl.5.69). But French upholsterers did not have a monopoly on dramatic beds, as Giovanni Paolo Schor's bed for the Colonna palace shows (pl.5.70). In one extraordinary design for an angel bed Tessin attempted to synthesize much of what he admired, if only on paper, with solid silver sculptural elements copied directly from Italian design drawings and drapery inspired by France (pl.5.71). Also derived from French angel beds were those in the Anglo-Dutch style as developed by Daniel Marot, adorned with vigorously carved crestings and head-boards. Tessin disapproved of such beds '*all'Angloise*' because of their carvings in bad taste and textiles that departed from French norms.[58]

5.69 Bed in the *Chambre des Amours* at the *Trianon de Porcelaine*, Nicodemus Tessin the Younger, pencil. Paris, 1687 (Nationalmuseum, Stockholm)

5.70 State bed of Maria Mancini Colonna for the birth of her first-born son, Pietro Santi Bartoli after Giovanni Paolo Schor, engraving. Rome, 1663 (Kunstbibliothek)

5.71 Design for a silver bed with Cupid and Psyche, attributed to Nicodemus Tessin the Younger. The figures of Cupid and Psyche are painted on the silk headboard. Paris, before 1717 (cat.161)

THE MONTESPAN FAN PAINTING

Sarah Medlam

In the winter of 1670–71, Louis XIV created for his current *maîtresse en titre*, Madame de Montespan, an elegant entertaining complex in the gardens of Versailles known as the *Trianon de Porcelaine*. The central, single-storey pavilion contained a salon and two bedrooms. This painting shows, albeit imaginatively, its richly decorated interior, as well as Madame de Montespan herself. She appears to be 'offered' as a gift, suggesting that the painting was made for her. The artist seems to have been asked to create a masque-like, teasing fantasy, laughingly combining aspects of a group portrait of Louis XIV and his legitimate family painted in 1670 as Olympian gods (pl.5.72) with the kind of royal parade of luxury illustrated in the tapestry of *The Visit of King Louis XIV to the Gobelins*, which records a visit made in 1667 (see p.124).

Madame de Montespan demonstrates her own considerable powers as the king's favourite and the effective queen of fashion. Having removed the suggestive *déshabillé* for which she was renowned (see pl.5.54), she sits bare-breasted, her gown discarded over the jewel cabinet. Around her are examples of the most luxurious furnishings available at court at the time. No exact parallels for individual objects have been identified, but the silver, giltwood and ebony pieces incorporate the fashionable motifs of figure supports, fat paw feet and swags of bursting foliage held up by ribbon ties that appear on furniture associated with the court, which she may have seen and coveted (see p.122).

The gambolling *putti* who act as chorus and orchestra, underlining the overall theme of love, may offer a clue to more exact dating. On 21 April 1674 Madame de Montespan became the undisputed chief mistress when Louise de la Vallière finally retired to a convent. On 5 July, her children by Louis were brought to live at Versailles, following their legitimization in 1673.

5.72 *Family of Louis XIV in mythological guise*, Jean Nocret, oil on canvas. Paris, 1670 (Musée national des châteaux de Versailles et de Trianon)

5.73 Extended fan leaf depicting Mme de Montespan in the *Trianon de Porcelaine*, artist unknown. France, possibly 1674 (cat.163)

The small figure in the bath is distinguished by the services of the putti, his special status also signalled by the laurel branches held above his head. It seems likely that this figure is the duc de Maine, four years old in 1674. That summer also saw lavish entertainments at Versailles, all revolving around Madame de Montespan. At this time, she was so confident of her power that a little teasing of her royal lover was

allowable – perhaps by the commissioning of this most intimate of images.

Small gouache paintings such as this one are generally described as fan leaves and were indeed painted on parchment or vellum prepared for fans, though this example was painted on the fan arc and surrounding areas at the same time and may always have been intended as a decorative picture.

Beyond the Bedchamber

The high status and exclusive nature of the bedchamber and the dressing room, closet or cabinet beyond made them a setting for the latest and most luxurious fashions. While silver furniture was a rarity in the other state rooms, silver dressing tables, mirrors, candlestands and wall sconces as well as the equipment for the fireplace (pls 5.74–5.76) marked out the bedchamber as the most exclusive place of all. Large silver dressing sets, which included equipment for breakfast as well as for make-up, not only played a practical role in a woman's semi-public *levée* but were also prominent symbols of dynastic marriage (pl.5.77). On the same principle of exclusive access, the novel and expensive upholstered chairs, armchairs and day-beds were more common in the *ameublement* of the bedchamber and the rooms beyond than in the more formal state rooms (pl.5.78).

5.75 Pair of andirons, from Knole, Kent, made for the 5th Earl of Dorset, maker unknown. England, *c*.1670–77 (cat.167)

5.74 (*opposite*) Table, mirror and pair of candlestands in the King's Bedchamber at Knole, Kent, made for the Countess of Dorset, mark of Gerrit Jensen. London, 1676 (stands), 1680 (table) (cat.166)

5.76 Fireplace in the Queen's Bedchamber at Ham House, London, with fire pan, bellows, tongs, brush and shovel, maker unknown. England, c.1675–9 (cat.168)

5.77 Toilet service with the arms of William and Mary, Robert Collombe, Ferry Prevost, Philippe Regnault, Hans Coenraadt Breghtel. Paris, 1669–78 (cat.169)

5.78 Day-bed, attributed to
Thomas Roberts. London,
1705–10 (cat.173)

5.79 *Louis XV and the Regent, Philippe II, Duke of Orléans, in the Study of the Grand Dauphin at Versailles*, artist unknown. Paris, *c.*1720 (Musée national des châteaux de Versailles et de Trianon)

5.80 The Queen's Closet at Ham House.
Richmond upon Thames, 1670s

5.81 Wall panel from Montagu
House, with scenes of the loves
of Apollo, Charles de Lafosse,
Jacques Rousseau, Jacques
Parmentier and Jean-Baptiste
Monnoyer, probably after Daniel
Marot. London, *c*.1690 (cat.171)

Into the inner sanctum of the closet was packed a level of
furnishing and luxury unseen outside, and carried out to the
particular taste of the owner. The richly decorated 'Queen's
Closet' at Ham was equipped with an alcove (with a low dais)
containing chairs for sleeping (pl.5.80). But the closet was
also the site of influential experiments in furniture and interior
decoration. Closets pioneered walls of mirror and lacquer as
well as decorations in the new light style of grotesque
ornament that came into fashion at the end of the seventeenth
century (pl.5.81). They also introduced new types of carcase
furniture decorated in luxurious forms of wood and metal inlay

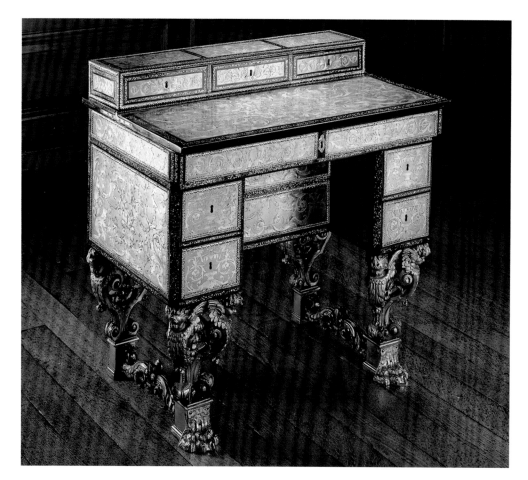

5.82 Desk, attributed to Pierre Gole. Paris, *c.*1670 (cat.175)

5.83 Display shelf for ceramics, maker unknown. England, *c.*1695 (cat.176)

(pls 5.82, 5.85). As Tessin noted,[59] these replaced the movable cabinets on stands that had been the leading type of display furniture for most of the seventeenth century (see pl.2.44).

While many such cabinets on stands were for display only, others contained collections of rarities, a natural role for closets and other private rooms. At Versailles the king's private treasure rooms pioneered the display of precious objects set on brackets and displayed against mirrors. In central Europe, rooms for the display of porcelain were often placed beyond the bedchamber, including the example at Charlottenburg and the astonishing *Spiegelkabinett* (Mirror Cabinet) at Pommersfelden, a glittering treasure box which is as much a display of mirrorwork and inlay as it is of porcelain (pls 5.83, 5.84, 5.86). Also beyond the bedchamber at Charlottenburg was the royal chapel. The way in which the contents of these cabinets and their decoration combined to form a single overwhelming impression was in direct descent from the total works of art of the Roman pioneers of the Baroque some 60 years earlier.

5.84 The Porcelain Cabinet at Schloss Charlottenburg, with ceiling paintings by Anthonie Coxie. 1706

5.85 Desk, maker unknown. Paris, *c.*1700 (cat.172)

5.86 The *Spiegelkabinett* at Schloss Weissenstein, designed by Ferdinand Plitzner. Pommersfelden, 1714–18

Notes

1. The World of the Baroque Artist

1. Palazzo Spada Collection no.161, oil on canvas; the work and its acquisition are discussed by Haskell (1980).
2. For a later, cosmopolitan, and somewhat sceptical reflection on operatic *argomenti* see Algarotti (1755), trans. in Strunk (1981).
3. The best general account of the intellectual history of these ideas remains Podro (1982). New critical editions were edited by Kemp (1995, 2000).
4. Downes (1996).
5. Between the accession of Urban VIII (Barberini) in 1623 and the death of Clement XIV (Garganelli) in 1774, fifteen different dynasties held the papacy; many were bitter rivals.
6. For the later Stuart works of renewal see Jardine (2002).
7. Portrait in National Maritime Museum, Greenwich, London.
8. Buckley (2004) relies on secondary sources: a definitive biography and cultural history are still awaited. For Italo-Swedish cultural links in this period see also Kent (1999), pp.187ff.
9. Voltaire (1764), p.186.
10. Cañeque (2004).
11. Hughes and Thake (2003).
12. Bernini, Rubens and Velasquez were among a good number of Baroque artists who were honoured as *Cavalieri*.
13. See several of the essays in Part I of Black (2005). This transnational code appears not to have extended beyond Christendom, witness the bestial scenes that followed the relief of Vienna in 1683; see Stoye (2006).
14. For a survey of the debate over the so-called early modern military revolution see Black (1994) and subsequent publications by the same author.
15. Fraser (2006).
16. For the cultural consequences of Swedish military endeavours in this period, see Kaufmann (1995), especially chapter 10.
17. Ellis (2004); coffee houses opened in Paris in the early 1670s.
18. See Pereira (1986), pp.159–170; idem (1970), pp.29–36; Chicó (1956).
19. Atwell (1982), pp.68–90; Souza (1986); Gruzinski (2002); Daniles and Kennedy (2002).
20. The literature on colonial expansions during this period is very extensive; for a recent survey of an important theatre see Pearson (2005), with important essays on the Portuguese trade focused on Goa.
21. Galleria Sabauda, Turin, see Roli (1977), plate 176A.
22. Words by Christopher Fishburn, 1683, see Wood (1995), p.215.
23. Measures 254 x 310 mm, now in North Carolina Museum of Art at Raleigh (no. 52.9.157), see Lo Bianco (1985), pp. 116–17 (cat.37).
24. See, for example, Mancini (1621), ed. Marucchi (1956).
25. See, for example, Murillo's *Virgin of the Rosary* (1650, Louvre).
26. Bilinkoff and Greer (2002).
27. There has been an important re-appraisal of the relationship between the Jesuits and the Baroque and other visual arts over recent years; the leading scholar in this field, G.A. Bailey, has shown that there is no single, consistent 'Jesuit' style; see Bailey, *Art of the Jesuit Missions* (1999).
28. Portrait of Ashmole, cited by Potter (2006).

29. Tobias Smollett describing a procession in Florence in 1765, see Smollett, ed. Felsenstein (1981), pp. 214–223.
30. Evangelisti (2007); Hills (2004).
31. The Arcadian movement in Roman literature, *c.*1700, for which see Johns (1993).
32. Bellori's 'Idea' appears as a prefatory essay to his collection of artists' *Lives* published in Rome in 1672, see extracts conveniently published in Harrison, Wood and Grainger (2000), p.96; Galileo's treatise was *Sidereus Nuncius*, 1610.
33. Koyré (1957), p.90.
34. Palazzo Spada collection no.95, oil on canvas, acquired by Virgilio Spada (1596–1662) in 1645.
35. Palazzo Spada Collection no.153, *Allegory of Astronomy*, oil on canvas, by G.B. Magni, called Il Modenino (*c.*1592–1674), painted *c.*1644.
36. Koyré (1957), p.222.
37. George Berkeley (1685–1753), Bishop of Cloyne, author of *An Essay towards a new Theory of Vision* (1709).
38. Koyré (1957), p.223.
39. Koyré (1957), p.225.
40. The sequence in the Vatican Pinacoteca shows Saturn, Mars, the Moon, Jupiter, Venus, the Sun, Mercury, a Comet; see Roli (1977), pp.117ff and plates 196A–F. The commission is documented in a letter from E. Manfredi, for which see Fantuzzi (1771), p.319.
41. See Kurz (1988), no.538.
42. Voltaire (1764), p.47.
43. Voltaire (1764), p.27.
44. Reported by Walpole (1786).
45. Cumberland (1724).
46. Wind (1938–9), pp.123–4.
47. For a convenient presentation of Jonathan Richardson's ideas on history painting from his *Essay on the Theory of Painting* and *The Science of a Connoisseur*, see Harrison, Wood and Grainger (2000), pp. 326–35.
48. Richardson (1719), pp.59 and 64.
49. Anderson (1998), p.58, quoting Bamford (1873), p.72.
50. Potter (2006), p.296 (quoting from Museum Tradescantianum, p.35).
51. Potter (2006), p.172, quoting De Beer (2000), ii, pp.132–3.
52. A standard commonplace in art criticism, from the early modern period through succeeding generations.
53. His social compassion is discernible in the *Acts of Mercy*, New York, Metropolitan Museum of Art.
54. Fleming (1961), pp.23–5.

2. The Baroque Style

1. Blunt (1982); Blunt (1973), pp.5ff; Kurz (1960), pp.414ff; Kurz (1963), pp.15ff.
2. Wölfflin, trans. Murray (1964); see also Blunt (1982), p.19.
3. De Beer/Evelyn (1955, rev. 2000), vol.II, p.261.
4. Summerson (1980), p.62.
5. Blunt (1979, repr. 2005).
6. Tarkiewicz, Vol. III (1974), p.327.
7. Notably in Vincenzo Scamozzi's set of an ideal city for *Oedipus Rex* (1585) at the Teatro Olimpico, Vicenza.
8. Made in 1627–8, now in the Royal collection, Stockholm. Conforti and Walton (1988), Ad. Cat.viii; Schädler (1985), p.45.
9. Fagiolo dell'Arco (1997), pp.528–31.
10. Bimbenet-Privat (2002), vol.2, pp.71–3; Gruber (1992), p.97.
11. See Gruber (1992), pp. 95–155; Hauglid (1950); Nelson (1995).
12. Griffiths (1998), pp.133–9.
13. Campbell (2008), pp.129–30.
14. Pepys's Diary, 11 April 1669, quoted in Esterly (1998), p.81.
15. Pereira (2000), p.150.
16. Mandroux-França (1973), Marie-Therese, 'Information artistique et "mass-media" au XVIIIe siècle: la diffusion de l'ornement gravé rococo au Portugal', *Bracara Augusta*, vol.27, no.64, p.76.
17. Fuhring (2003), pp.421–30. I am indebted to Peter Fuhring for alerting me to the prints in the castle.
18. Palmer (2003), Rodney, '"All is very plain, upon inspection of the figure": the visual method of Andrea Pozzo's *Perspectiva Pictorum et Architectorum*', in Palmer and Frangenberg (2003), pp.156–213.
19. Jackson and Jaffer (2004), p.88.
20. Fuhring (2006), pp.92–5.
21. Mandroux-França (1989), pp.35–43.
22. Snickare (2002), p.61.
23. Snickare (2002), pp.183–5.
24. One of the most spectacular surviving state gifts is that of the twelve saddles, harnesses and accompanying guns, given (with the horses) in 1673 to Charles XI of Sweden by Louis XIV; Rangström (1992), cat.245.
25. These included the series of volumes of prints called the *Cabinet du Roi*, begun in 1665. They depicted monuments, royal residences and picture collections, historical events and natural history.
26. Mitchell (2007), pp.11–43.
27. Jackson and Jaffer (2004), p.243.
28. William Temple writing in 1685: Temple (1692), p.99.

3. Performance and Performativity

1. 'vaghissime picture, e superbi ricchi apparati ... et ogni altro corrispondente ornamento per una festa Regia'; from the *Diario Ordinario*, quoted in Tirincanti (1971), pp.242–4.
2. Savage (1998), p.633.
3. Savage (1998), p.632.
4. Fenlon (2004), p.50. The most lavish sixteenth-century Florentine festivities were those of 1589, signalling a shift in Medici dynastic alliances away from Spain and towards France, with Europe-wide consequences.
5. Parry (1996), pp.178–9.
6. Hill (2005), pp.187–9.
7. Ogden (1978). The Teatro Novissimo and other Venetian theatres followed the Teatro Farnese in using this kind of mechanism. Previously only a small number of changes had been possible by such means as *periaktoi*, the first recorded changeable scenery (1543): three-sided prisms which could be swivelled to face the audience in different ways; see Clarke and Crisp (1978), p.13.
8. Both Sebastiano Serlio and Lenne de Sommi in his *Dialogo III* had acknowledged this problem in their sixteenth-century writings; see Polovedo (1982), pp.6–7. See also Muller and Muller (2005), p.676, for the suggestion that children may even have been used in English masques to lessen the disruption on the effect of the perspective.
9. 'Ordigno che porta otto personaggi i quali da principio saranno uniti poi a poco a poco si dilastano in figura circolare formando i raggi del sole'. For Carini Motta see Yans (1982).
10. Reus and Lerner (2001), p.85. Wave machines survive at Český Krumlov and Drottningholm theatres.
11. Reus and Lerner (2001), p.86; Küster (2003), pp.180–81.
12. Quoted in Clarke and Crisp (1978), p.27.
13. Hyatt Mayor (1945), p.25; Slavko (2001).
14. The wardrobe accounts in Český Krumlov list several expenses for trimmings of 'embroidered Roman costumes'; see Cichrová (1993), p.57.

15. De la Gorce (1982), p.66.
16. Ericani (1982), pp.95–9.
17. Gruber (1994), p.39.
18. Jarrard (2003), p.7.
19. Jarrard (2003), p.73–4.
20. Gruber (1994), p.38.
21. Cole (1962), pp.224–5; Coeyman (1990), p.23.
22. Gruber (1994), pp.34–6.
23. De la Gorce (1982), pp.17–18.
24. Bjurström (1961).
25. De la Gorce (1986), pp.15–16. Sets and machinery were judged in relation to antiquity: Greco-Roman texts judged the originality of a designer to be gauged not only by his subject-matter but by his means of representing it. Ménestrier, quoted in De la Gorce (1982), p.65 ; Tralage, quoted in De la Gorce (1982), pp.65–8.
26. Quoted in De la Gorce (1986), p.16.
27. Bjurström (1961), p.236.
28. De la Gorce (1986), p.19. This collaboration did not last long, however, as Rivani demanded an exorbitantly high annual salary for his services. Daniel Cronström, the Swedish ambassador, referred to Berain as a 'meilleur décorateur que machiniste'.
29. Lenzi and Bentini (2000), p.37.
30. Keil-Budischowsky (1993), pp.353.
31. Keil-Budischowsky (1993), pp.354–6.
32. Keil-Budischowsky (1993), pp.354–9, for a detailed description of the iconography of *Il Pomo d'Oro*.
33. Küster (2003), pp.67–70: previously rulers were generally seated in the front row of the parterre level, as shown in prints of performances in Dresden and Vienna.
34. See Lenzi and Bentini (2000), pp.258–9, for fireworks. Sketchbooks in the Staatliche Graphische Sammlung, Munich, include various designs for catafalques; the RIBA also holds a highly finished design by Giuseppe Galli Bibiena for a monument to Prince Franz Ludwig of Neuberg, Archbishop of Mainz (d. 1732), for the Augustinerkirche (RIBA Library Drawings and Archives Collections, London, SC3/1).
35. Hyatt Mayor (1945), pp.9–10.
36. Knall-Brskovsky (1984), pp.231–2.
37. Lenzi and Bentini (2000), pp.39–40.
38. Ogden (1978), p.3.
39. Bjurström (1963), pp.233–6.
40. Quoted in Corneilson (1997), p.63, fn. p.79.
41. Krückmann (1998), p.69.
42. Tipton (2000), p.368; Lenzi and Bentini (2000), p.320.
43. Tipton (2000), p.369. It was partially altered in the nineteenth century and replaced entirely in 1961.
44. Krückmann (1998), pp.75–7.
45. Hyatt Mayor (1945), p.12.
46. Küster (2003), p.86.
47. Lenzi (1975), pp.1–2. At this point the taste towards Neoclassicism and Enlightenment did not help Antonio's case, Baroque architecture and design no longer being as widely popular as it had been; it was particularly criticized by Francesco Algarotti in his *Saggio sopra l'opera in musica* (Livorno, 1763), as quoted by Lenzi.
48. Ugolini (1998), p.42.
49. Halfpenny (1959), p.19.
50. De Beer (1955), III, p.246, 29 May 1660.
51. Millon (1999), Introduction, pp.19–31 (p.19).
52. Mignot (1999), pp.316–17; Webb (1990), p.67; Girouard (1985), pp.128–9; Zucker (1955), pp.8–9.
53. Webb (1990), p.67.
54. Webb (1990), pp.84–8; Mignot (1999), pp.328–9; Ziskin (1994), pp.147, 151–2; Burke

(1992), pp.92–7; Mumford (1989), pp.395–6.
55. Hargrove (1989), p.11.
56. Burke (1992), p.13.
57. Burke (1992), p.93; Callisen (1941).
58. Ziskin (1994), pp.151.
59. Baer and Baer (1995), pp.4–5.
60. San Juan (2001), p.197.
61. Gigli (1958), p.323, cited and translated in San Juan (2001), p.197.
62. Arisi (1961), p.143; Arisi (1986), p.336; Bowron (1994), Bowron and Rishel (2000), pp.417–18; Wynne (1986), pp.81–2.
63. Watanabe-O'Kelly (2002), p.15.
64. Watanabe-O'Kelly (2004), pp.5–6; Strong (2005), pp.347–9; Mulryne and Goldring (2002), Introduction, pp.4–5.
65. Watanabe-O'Kelly (2002), p.19.
66. Ziskin (1994), p.151.
67. Williams (1958), p.105; Cressy (1989), pp.175, 179–82, 204–6; Harris (2005), pp.81–2, 186–8, 265, 285–7; Hutton (1994), pp.252–3, 25–7.
68. Cressy (1989), p.179; Harris (2005), pp.286–7.
69. See, for example, the following recent anthologies of festival studies: Mulryne and Goldring (2002); Mulryne, Watanabe-O'Kelly and Shewring (2004), Watanabe-O'Kelly and Bèhar (1999).
70. Salatino (1997), p.14.
71. National Archives, Kew, W/O 51-29, 5 March 1684/5; National Archives, Kew, W/O 51-30, 6 May 1685.
72. 'Die Trommeln/Trompeten/ Paucken/und an den Musiken/haben bey dieser Entree sich lustig hören lassen. Es sind auch 20. Paar mit Gold und Silber beladene Cameel gefürhret worden. Von denen Hand-Pferden waren 24. mit Sätteln und Schabracken/mit Silber/Gold und Edelgesteinen aufs herrlichste gezieret. Der Königl[iche] Habit ist so reich gewesen/daß in Europa dergleichen nicht zu finden. Die Cavalcade, biss an den Baldachin ist sehr prächtig gewesen.' Translation in Mulryne, Watanabe-O'Kelly and Shewring (2004), pp.438–9.
73. Gaehtgens (2006), pp.101, 248; Schaal (1992); Siebel (2004), p.250.
74. Siebel (2004), p.250; Gaehtgens (2006), p.251.
75. Strong (1984), pp.7–8, 26–7, 44–50; McGowan (2002), p.27.
76. McGowan (2002), p.37.
77. Jarrard (2003), pp.12, 24, 27; McGowan (2002), p.38.
78.Wynne (1986), p.82; Bowron and Rishel (2000), p.418.
79. Van Der Stock (1993), pp.315–17.
80. Latham and Matthews (1970) II, pp.81–2, 22 April 1661.
81. Sandford (1687), pp.36–7, 40–1.
82. Rangström (1994), p.110; Rangström (2004), p.295.
83. '...an ensemble/outfit like the one worn by Louis XIV on important occasions, such as his wedding'. Quoted in Gaehtgens (2006), p.257.
84. Rangström (1994), p.109.
85. Rangström (1994), p.109.
86. Rangström (1994), p.109.
87. Dahlin (1988), p.42.
88. De Beer (2000) v, pp.277–8, 2 December 1697.
89. Watanabe-O'Kelly (2002), p.19.
90. Archives Nationales, Paris, K 1000, no.299.
91. Smuts (1989), p.66.
92. Latham and Matthews (1970) ii, p.187, 30 September 1661; *Calendar of State Papers (Domestic)* XLIII, p.105, no.12, 3 October 1661.
93. Latham and Matthews (1970) ii, pp.86–7, 23 April 1661.
94. Félibien (1679), p.41.
95. Watanabe-O'Kelly (2002), p.23.
96. Verdi Webster (1998) passim.
97. Trusted (1995), pp.55–69; Verdi Webster (1998).
98. Matthew XXVI, 18–29; Mark XIV, 17–25; Luke XXII, 14ff, and less detailed in John XIII.
99. Groom (1981).

4. Power and Piety
1. Mather (1980).
2. Emoke (2002), no.137.
3. Bilinkoff and Greer (2002).
4. Whistler (2001), pp.92–4.
5. Wittkower (1999), vol.1, pp.1–3, introduces these issues with exemplary authority and clarity.
6. For a recent authoritative summary see Wright (2005).
7. The key words are conveniently available in translation in Holt (1963), vol.2, pp.64–5.
8. A remarkable set of processional lanterns in the Museu Nacional de Arte Antiga, Lisbon, nos. 508–511.
9. For example, the Portuguese processional shrine of St John the Evangelist, 1720–50, made in Lisbon and standing some two metres high; see Alegria et al. (1991), pp.250, 253.
10. Similar to the process described in Chapter One as the context for Fanzago's votive column in Naples.
11. See the splendid illustration in Wittkower (1999), p.67.
12. Kubler (1990), pp.413ff.
13. For example, the illustration of the Cappella Paolina at S. Maria Maggiore, Rome, in Wittkower (1999), p.9.
14. Wren (1750), p.315, quoting a 'Critical review of Buildings' dated 1734.
15. The Bolognese painter G.M. Crespi (1665–1747) undertook a series of paintings of the sacraments for Cardinal Ottoboni to give a sense of popular religious practice; the camparison with Poussin's earlier philosophical sets on the same iconography is instructive.
16. Oughton (1979), plate, p.162.
17. Personal communication from colleagues in Norway: Marie Fongaard Seim, Arne Bugge Amundsen and Henrik von Achen.
18. Artus Quellin's design in the Kgl. Kobberstiksammlung, Royal Museum, Copenhagen (illustrated as plate 2 in Berge (1997).
19. See Roli (1977), plates 164a–d and 165a–c, and discussion on pp.105ff; pictures are in the Staatliche Kunstsammlungen, Gemäldegalerie Alte Meister, Dresden.
20. The literature on Baroque Malta is extensive; there is a full bibliography in Hughes and Thake (2003).
21. For an interesting comparative project by an artist working on reliquaries abroad see Sciberras (1999), pp.392–400.
22. Bourke (1963), p.76.
23. Agghazy (1959), plate 145, and Smith (1955); Giuseppe Vasi engraved a number of these constructions, for example the Castrum for Ferdinand VI of Spain in 1759; see Scalabroni (1981), cat.422.
24. Bozzetti are at the Fine Arts Museum, Brussels.
25. Hauglid (1950), vol.3, p.323.
26. For other post-Reformation examples see Koener (2004). The catalogue given in Sandner et al. (1993), pp.337–66, shows how rare this subject was before the Reformation.
27. Christie (1973), vol.1, p.293.
28. The Cornwall (or Cornewall) family triptych, dated 1588, from St Mary's Church, Burford, Shropshire. See Eade (2005), pp.5, 10.
29. Burckhardt (1855), quoted by Downes in Turner (1996), vol.14, p.262. Many authors, including Downes, have reflected on the relationship between sacred and historical time in Bernini's sculpture of St Teresa, a particularly comprehensive example being Portoghesi (1999).
30. See Dixon (2003), p.18. Susan James cites Descartes as an example of a seventeenth-century thinker who used the terms 'passion' and 'emotion' interchangeably. However, Dixon argues that he does so using 'passion' in an unusually broad sense as equivalent to all perceptions, whereas 'emotions' refer to the agitation of the 'animal spirits' in the body, that is, the restricted sense of 'passion' as usually defined. Dixon (2003), p.11.
31. Alberti, *De Pictura*, 2.41, quoted by Onians (2008), p.44.
32. See especially Freedberg (2007) and Onians (2008).
33. See for example Michael Baxandall's moving discussion of Passion groups in Baxandall (1980).
34. Dixon has demonstrated that the overarching category of the 'emotions' is a modern invention, as is the tendency to view them as bodily states opposed to rational thought.
35. See Table 3, 'Aquinas' model of the soul', Dixon (2003), p.36.
36. For how this was taken up by seventeenth-century authors see James (1997), p.6.
37. Aquinas, *Summa Theologica* 1a.81.1, quoted by Dixon (2003), pp.35–6.
38. I am indebted to Gerard J. Hughes SJ for clarifying this for me.
39. For a discussion of the philosophy in relation to advice literature see James (1997), pp.2f.
40. James (1997), p. 4.
41. Le Brun confused a Thomist theory of the 'concupiscible' and 'irascible' passions with the 'simple and mixed' passions of Descartes's late work *Les Passions de l'âme* (1649). See Montagu (1994), p.18. Montagu defends this identification, while Dixon argues that Aquinas's definition of the passions as 'movements of the lower part of the soul towards a sense-good or away from a sense-evil' is not the same as Descartes's theory in which 'the animal spirits acted on the soul to cause the passions'. See Dixon (2003), p.27 and note 7.
42. See the entries in Viller (1995). The best recent theological study of the tradition of discernment is McIntosh (2004).
43. Published in 1541, the *Exercises* are intended to facilitate a dynamic process of individual encounter with the divine in the form of a thirty-day retreat (where the 'days' can be of unequal length). Each retreatant is accompanied by a guide, for whom Ignatius's text was intended as a handbook.
44. The idea of a 'Jesuit style' in the arts was decisively refuted by the Jesuit scholar Joseph Braun (1857–1947). For a survey of this debate see Bailey, 'Le style jésuite n'existe pas', in O'Malley (1999). Evonne Levy has recently returned to the subject in a revisionist account that argues for an interpretation of Jesuit art as 'propagandist'. See Levy (2004).
45. Ignatius asks the exercitant to pray for *id quod volo*, 'that which I desire'. See Marsh (2006), pp.7–19.
46. Translation from Puhl (1951), pp.54–5. For a detailed examination of the 'Application of the Senses' see Endean (1990), pp.391–498.
47. As John Onians notes in discussing Aristotle, when we 'see' in imagination 'we are simply working with things we have seen before, either as themselves or in combination with something else' (Onians (2008), p.22). As far as I am aware the only author to link the experience of imaginative vision in the *Spiritual Exercises* to our responses to works of art is Norman Bryson, who in a remarkable essay compares the Ignatian cathexsis of vision to 'the excessive focus and brilliance' of the kitchen paintings of Juan Sánchez Cotán (1561–1627). See Bryson (1990), pp.63ff.
48. Bailey (2005), p.125.
49. A 1678 inventory of chapel contents required seven folios. See Konrad (1980), pp.268–9.
50. According to an eighteenth-century document this sculpture came from Naples. See Clara Bargellini's article on this object in Rishel with Stratton-Pruitt (2006), p.364.
51. Nadal (1593).
52. Rishel with Stratton-Pruitt (2006), p.364.
53. In a fascinating article Amy Neff traces references to Mary's childbearing on Calvary as part of her 'compassio'; Neff (1998).
54. See especially Bailey (1999), pp.192f.
55. The first documented flower garlands around images of the Madonna were commissioned for the collection of Federigo Borromeo, Archbishop of Milan (1564–1631), for the picture gallery in the Ambrosiana. For the history of these commissions, and of the genre in general, see Freedberg (1981).
56. I am currently aware of twelve examples. It is possible that some of the undated images were commissioned to celebrate the quatercentenary of the feast of Corpus Christi in 1664.
57. Hosts were often stamped with a cross, or the letters IHS, and from the twelfth century there appeared crucifixion scenes and the depiction of Christ as a lamb. Close inspection of this painting reveals an image of Christ crucified embossed on the wafer. For the practice of stamping hosts see Rubin (1991), p.39.
58. Goody (1993), p.174.
59. Goody (1993), p.156.
60. The copy of the Van Dyck from which the cherub's head (or a version of it) has been lifted is now in the National Gallery in Prague. It has probably been taken from an engraving, as the image is in reverse. Illustrated in Slavíček (2000), p.139. For the original see Barnes (2004), p.403.
61. Freedberg has noted a reliance on the 'charming' in the devotional techniques of the art of Catholic Reform: see Freedberg (1981), p.133.
62. The V&A painting can be compared to another work of the same subject by Jan Gillemans I (1618–75), which displays a similar chalice and includes the four evangelists in a cameo of a Last Supper scene (sold at Christie's, London, 15 April 1992, lot 134). I am indebted to Fred Meijer for bringing this painting to my attention.
63. For example 'Sight' in the series by Adriaen Collaert, after Marten de Vos, of 1575 (Albertina Museum, Vienna), illustrated in Segal (1990), p.149.
64. See Weil (1974).
65. Klein (2004), p.39.
66. I owe this insight to a work of Stoichita (1997).
67. Jones (1988).
68. Philip IV of Spain had a predilection for the flower pieces of Seghers and in 1662 Louis XIV bought a substantial collection of paintings that included a flower piece by him. Charles I was particularly fond of still life paintings and owned works by both Seghers and De Heem. Frederik Hendrik, Prince of Orange, and his wife Amalia van Solms particularly liked Seghers's floral garlands and received three such paintings from him.
69. According to Houbraken, in around 1650

the painter Jan Davidsz de Heem (1606–83/4) was paid the astonishing sum of 2,000 guilders for a cartouche of fruit and flowers, reputedly the highest sum ever paid for a painting in the Dutch Golden Age. See Loughman (1999), p.94.

70. Royal Castle, Warsaw. Illustrated in Wheeler (1995).

71. Dixon (2003), p.31.

72. For French as well as English examples see MacLeod and Marciari Alexander (2001). The Neoplatonic associations of allegorical portraiture are discussed in an illuminating essay by Stewart (1974).

73. Cagnetta (1977), p.498. Cagnetta attributes the work to Caterina de Julianis on the basis of private documents in his possession.

74. Zumbo's anonymous biographer records that the artist executed four works for the Medici in Florence. One of these, known as *La Corruzione I*, is housed in the zoological museum of La Specola in Florence and is remarkably similar to the V&A composition. See Lightbown (1964), p.489.

75. On the basis of private papers in his possession, Cagnetta states that this piece was at one time in the sacristy of S. Severo al Pendino in Naples, disappearing during the bombing in 1944. See Cagnetta (1977), p.498.

76. Goncourt (1894), p.140, quoted by De Ceglia (2007), p.9.

77. Morgan (1998), p.63.

78. Bartoli (1930). The association with this piece in particular is made by Lightbown (1964), p.494.

79. The literature on wax as a modelling material is notoriously thin. However, the Getty Research Institute has recently published an excellent edited volume including a translation of Julius von Schlosser's *Geschichte der Porträtbildnerei in Wachs* of 1910–11. See Panzanelli (2008).

80. Jonathan Sawday has analysed this shift in relation to the Renaissance culture of dissection, and suggests that early anatomists encountered the body as an entity akin to the discovery of a mysterious continent. The curious were on a voyage of *discovery* of the body in the tradition of the sixteenth-century physician Vesalius, as opposed to the *invention* of a Cartesian body. See Sawday (1995).

81. De Ceglia (2007), p.10.

5. The Palace

1. Blunt (1982), p.271.

2. Hazlitt (1856), p.284.

3. Fraser-Jenkins (1970), vol.33, pp.162–70; see also Thomson (1993). For Louis XIV and magnificence see Burke (1992).

4. Bold (2001), vol.44, pp.136–44.

5. Elias (1983), but for other views see Adamson (1999) and Blanning (2007).

6. Adamson (1999), p.178.

7. Elias (1983), p.105, quoting Jean de La Bruyère.

8. Blanning (2007), p.429, quoting from the instructions of Louis XIV to the Dauphin, 1661.

9. For '*botter*' and '*débotter*' see Blanning (2007), p.399.

10. Burke (1992), p.7.

11. Adamson (1999), p.28.

12. Blunt (1982), p.72.

13. Merz (1993), vol.56, pt.3, pp.409–50; Millon (1999), p.436.

14. Blunt (1982), p.189.

15. See Mukerji (1997).

16. See Lablaude (1995).

17. Walton (1986), p.80.

18. Walton (1986), p.85.

19. There are six versions of the manuscript guide, produced between 1689 and 1705. Hoog (1992); Thacker (1972), vol.1, no.1, pp.49–69.

20. Hyde (2005), p.154, n.74.

21. Lablaude (1995), p.104.

22. Hunt and Willis (1975), p.125.

23. Waddy (1990), pp.112–16.

24. Baillie (1967), vol.101, pp.169–99.

25. Thornton (1978), p.283.

26. Keisch (1997).

27. Waddy (1990), p.9.

28. Jarrard (2003), p.120.

29. Waddy (1990), p.5.

30. Jarrard (2003), p.120.

31. Elias (1983), pp.83–4.

32. Brocher (1934), p.28.

33. Sabatier (1999), p.435.

34. Hoog and Saule (2005), p.31.

35. Blanning (2007), p.430.

36. Sabatier (1999), p.142.

37. Millon (1999), p.483.

38. Sabatier (1999), p.146. The decorations were by Agostino Tassi and Giovanni Lanfranco, 1616–17.

39. Waddy (2002).

40. Waddy (2002), p.101.

41. Waddy (2002), p.31.

42. Soo (1998), pp.103–4.

43. Waddy (2002), pp.64–5: 'Premiere Partie dela Decoration Immobile; Seconde Partie, dela Decoration Mobile; Troiseime Partie, dela Decoration Mobile, en toutes sortes des Meubles.'

44. Waddy (2002), p.150.

45. Jarrard (2003), p.128.

46. Jarrard (2003), p.130.

47. See Thornton for these innovations in furniture. 'Guéridon' seems at first to have been the name given to black servants (Thornton (1981), p.390).

48. Waddy (2002), p.266.

49. Thornton (1981), p.388, note 3.

50. See Saule and Arminjon (2007).

51. See Campbell (2008).

52. Waddy (2002), p.236.

53. Waddy (2002), p.233.

54. Waddy (2002), p.231.

55. Thornton (1981), p.132.

56. Ribeiro (2003), p.87, quoting John Evelyn's *Tyrannus or the Mode, in a Discourse of Sumptuary Lawes* (1661).

57. Waddy (2002), p.244.

58. Waddy (2002), p.248.

59. Waddy (2002).

Summary Catalogue

Edited by Antonia Brodie
and Joanna Norman

Note: the following list is correct at the time of going to press.

Style
INTRODUCTION

1. (pl.2.1)
Figure of a camel made from
Baroque pearls
Maker unknown, probably Frankfurt am Main, Germany, before 1706
Baroque pearls with cold-painted gold, enamel, silver and silver gilt mounts set with emeralds and diamonds, h 12.3cm
Grünes Gewölbe, Staatliche Kunstsammlungen Dresden, VI 116

Provenance
Acquired from Privy Councillor Georg Freiherr von Rechenberg. Mentioned in: Specification 1706, fol.37v, no.10; Pretioseninventar 1725, fol.14r–14v; Inventar Pretiosenzimmer 1733, fols 407–409, no.27

Bibliography
Villa Hügel (1986), no.567; Syndram and Weinhold (2000), no.25

The terms *barrueco* (in Spanish) and *barocco* (in Portuguese) were coined in the Iberian Peninsula in the second half of the sixteenth century to describe the irregularly shaped pearls brought to Western Europe by sea as exotic rarities. The term 'Baroque pearl', which derived from this, is still in use today. Only much later would the term be used as a style or period label.

From the sixteenth century expensive pendants were produced in gold, enamel and precious stones incorporating these monstrous pearls. This particular kind of ornament, which brought art and nature together in a meaningful way, experienced a revival in late Baroque jewellery work. Augustus the Strong, elector of Saxony and king of Poland, was probably the keenest collector of these kinds of precious objects, with the result that the Green Vaults now hold the largest collection (57 pieces) of these figures 'with a body made from a pearl'. Many figures were acquired by Augustus shortly after 1700 from the Huguenot jeweller Guillaume Verbecq, who was resident in Frankfurt. This camel, however, came instead from the collection of Privy Councillor Georg Rechenberg. The enamel painting on the base depicts a Moorish woman between chests of precious jewels, thus alluding to the trade in exotic luxury goods. In the camel's travelling bag, executed in the finest enamel decoration, are three tiny gold bottles. (UW)

2. (pl.2.2)
Carousel for Queen Christina of Sweden
held in the courtyard of Palazzo Barberini,
Rome, 1656
Filippo Lauri (1623–94) and Filippo Gagliardi (1606/08–59), Rome, 1656–9
Oil on canvas, h 231cm, w 340cm
Museo di Roma, MR5698

Provenance
Barberini Collection; C. Sestieri; acquired by the City of Rome, 1959

Bibliography
Fagiolo (1997), no.A.16; Fagiolo dell'Arco (1997), pp.383–6; Walker (1999), pp.52–3, 64–9, fig.13; Bösel and Frommel (2000),

no.V.13; Leone et al (2002), no.IV A9; Küster (2003), no.57

The Joust of the Carousels represented in the painting took place in the Cavallerizza courtyard of Palazzo Barberini on the penultimate night of Carnival, 28 February 1656. For this occasion the recently built Baroque palazzo, depicted towering on the right of the scene, became the main theatre for Roman festivities. The Barberini re-established the pre-eminence of their family with these extravagant celebrations in honour of Queen Christina of Sweden, the Catholic convert who had moved to Rome several months previously. The joust was only one event of a month of 'Barberini festivities'.

The painting is by Filippo Gagliardi, an architect and painter who decorated the architecture and sets for the event, and by Filippo Lauri, described by critics as 'a noble genre painter [*bambocciante*]' who reproduced skilfully and meticulously the facial expressions of the numerous figures. The lavish staging in the courtyard necessitated the destruction of several adjoining houses to make room for the joust and the stands of boxes. The most prominent and richly decorated stand is that reserved for the queen, whose figure appears barely sketched out. The representation of the magnificent night-time festivity remains faithful to the detailed description of the event left by Count Galeazzo Gualdo Priorato. The Joust of the Carousels marked a shift away from those previously held in Rome, such as the Joust of the Saracen, organized in 1634 in Piazza Navona by Cardinal Antonio Barberini, in its derivation from a North European model. (ER)

THE FIRST GLOBAL STYLE

3. (pl.2.63)
Cabinet
Domenico Cucci (*c.*1635–1705), Gobelins Workshops, Paris, 1679–83
Cabinet of pine and oak veneered with ebony, set with *pietra dura* plaques and with gilt bronze mounts; stand of carved, gilded and painted wood, h 299cm, w 196cm, d 65cm
Duke of Northumberland, Alnwick Castle

Provenance
Louis XIV of France; inventory of the Garde Meuble de la Couronne 1728 (no.372); sold at the Louvre 3 February 1751; Robert Fogg; purchased 3rd duke of Northumberland 19 April 1822

Bibliography
De Serre (1930); Lunsingh-Scheurleer (1987); González-Palacios (1986), pp.19–60; Pradère (1989), pp.53–6; Verlet (1990–94) III, pp.106–9; Baxter (1992); Demetrescu (1996); Koeppe and Giusti (2008), pp.46–8

The cabinets are the only survivors of the furnishings of Versailles from before 1700, representing, in their impressive luxury, the many lost pieces of furniture supplied to the château. The two cabinets cost 16,000 *livres*. Cucci was brought to Paris from Florence by Louis XIV as part of his programme to enliven the luxury trades. The king appointed him director of the new Gobelins Workshops, which included not only cabinet-makers but also hardstone workers, metal-workers, tapestry weavers and embroiderers. In his lifetime, he was as much known for his gilt-bronze as for his furniture.

Each cabinet is made in three horizontal sections, on an open stand carved with ox legs, a design derived from the animal-legged frames of Italian marble tables. The two stands appear to have been carved by different hands, with differences in the thickness of the legs and in the carving of the giltwood swags. The *pietra dura* panels are of flat mosaic except for the main door panels, which are also carved in three dimensions. The stone-cutters whom Cucci brought from Florence with him included at least one who specialized in both techniques, Ferdinando Megliorini.

After Fogg sold the cabinets to the duke of Northumberland in 1822, the stands were repainted and regilded and the plinths added by Morel & Hughes. (SM)

4. (pl.5.43)
Audience of Cardinal Chigi in the King's
Bedchamber at Fontainebleau
Paris, 1665–80
Atelier of Jean Mozin (1665–80), Gobelins Workshops, after cartoons by Charles Le Brun (1619–90).
Tapestry in wool and silk with gilt-metal-wrapped thread, h 374cm, w 579cm
Inscribed: AVIENCE DONNÉE PAR LE ROY LOVIS XIV. A FONTAINEBLEAV AV CARDINAL CHIGI NEVEV ET LEGAT A LATERE DV PAPE ALEXANDRE VII. LE XXIXJVILLET MDCLXIV. POUR LA SATISFACTION DE L'INIVRE FAITE DANS ROME A SON AMBASSADEVR; on left border: LVD.VS XIIII / AN.O 16[72]; on right border: LVD.VS XIIII / AN.O 1676
Mobilier National, GMTT 98-1, on loan to Musée national des châteaux de Versailles et de Trianon, V 3847

Bibliography
Meyer (1980); Campbell (2008), pp.374–89

This tapestry is the seventh piece of the third series of the *History of the King* series, begun at Colbert's orders in 1664 to the designs of Le Brun, which portrayed significant political, military and civil events of Louis XIV's reign. This particular subject referred to a dispute between the Pope and the French king, which had occurred in Rome in 1662 and which had resulted in French troops occupying Avignon (then under papal command). Following a peace treaty signed in Pisa in February 1664, the Pope sent his nephew, Cardinal Chigi, to render a formal apology to Louis XIV, which took place in the King's Bedchamber at the palace of Fontainebleau. Differences between written accounts of the event and the scene portrayed in the tapestry were intended to highlight the humiliation of the papal legate: while in reality it seems that he was allowed to be seated in an armchair like the king, Le Brun shows him seated on a chair without arms, thus placing him at a lower social level. Other historical inaccuracies include the comte d'Harcourt, seen behind the legate, still wearing his hat, as would not have been permitted in the presence of the king. Although it appears that Le Brun did not represent the actual furnishings of Fontainebleau in the tapestry, the cabinet behind the king bears similarities to one listed in the Inventaire général de la Couronne, while the silver guéridon on the left is very close to a drawing (now in the Louvre) for four guéridons which were delivered to the Garde-Meuble in 1668. There are significant differences between Le Brun's cartoon, in the Louvre, and the tapestry as executed, in which the architecture of the room was simplified and the bed became more prominent. (JN)

5. (pl.2.62)
Candelabrum made for the Royal Chapel
Jean-François Cousinet (b. *c*.1666), Stockholm, 1695
Cast, chased and embossed silver; feet altered, h 51.3cm, w 41.7cm, d 15cm
Embossed with the arms of Sweden and the monogram of Charles XI
The Royal Collections of Sweden, HGK *kyrksilver* 34

Provenance
Commissioned by Charles XI of Sweden for the Chapel of the Royal Palace, Stockholm, dedicated 4 November 1695

Bibliography
Hernmarck (1948), pp.49–50; Grate (1994), no.16; Nationalmuseum (2003), no.234

This three-branched altar candlestick was executed by Jean-Francois Cousinet for the chapel (destroyed by fire in 1697) of the Royal Palace in Stockholm. Cousinet, a French silversmith who had been received as a master in the Paris guild in 1686, was summoned to work for the court of Charles XI of Sweden, where he was active between 1694 and 1711. In 1707 he delivered a baptismal font, also for the royal chapel, one of very few pieces of solid silver furniture to survive from this period. These two works are perhaps the most significant indicators of Tessin's attempts to import the French Baroque style into Sweden; it has been suggested that Tessin was himself involved in the design of the candelabrum. The base bears, on one side, the crowned monogram of Charles XI, between palms and laurels, and on the other side, the arms of Sweden. The lion feet are not original, as can be seen from holes underneath the volutes of the base, intended for the original claw feet supports. They were probably added in the eighteenth century, in keeping with a change in fashion: designs for candelabra made for the Riddarholm Church, Stockholm, by Carl Hårleman in the 1730s follow a similar style to that of Cousinet, but with lion feet instead of the claw feet mentioned in an inventory of 1697. (JN)

6. (pl.1.35)
The Child Jesus as the Good Shepherd
Maker unknown; Indo-Portuguese, probably Goa, 1675–1750
Carved ivory with traces of polychromy, h 43cm, w 15cm, d 8cm
V&A: A.58–1949

Provenance
Given by Dr W.L. Hildburgh, 1949

Bibliography
Collin (1984); similar examples in Estella Marcos (1984), cats 562–73; Theuerkauff (1984), pp.224–5; Estella Marcos (1997), cats 135–9

Christ is shown as a child dressed as a shepherd, and perched on top of the mount, his chin resting on his right hand, asleep. Three leafy branches fan out from the back of the group; in the central branch is a half-length relief of God the Father holding an orb in his left hand, and blessing with his right, and above him the dove as the Holy Spirit. Below is a mount with a fountain, from which sheep are drinking. This is flanked by St Joseph and the Virgin. Beneath, St Mary Magdalen reclines beside a crucifix, reading a book. The mountainside is dense with animals, including lions, rabbits, dogs and sheep.

This distinctive composition is unique to Goan

ivories, and recurs again and again; many examples have survived. The clustered figures, and certain important iconographic types taken from Indian art, such as the fountain, showing the plentiful effusion of nature's blessings, had deep-rooted ritual value, and seem to have been re-applied in a Christian context. The combination of the Christ Child in the guise of a shepherd with saints, a fountain, vegetation and animals suggests the richness of the natural world. Ivory carving had a long tradition on the Indian subcontinent, and elaborate works of art were made, particularly as diplomatic gifts, often presented to Western rulers. Most of the raw ivory would have been exported from Mozambique in East Africa. Goa was the second base in India to be established by the Portuguese, having been conquered by Alfonso de Albuquerque during the reign of Manuel I of Portugal, initially in 1510, and reconquered in 1512. Portugal was interested first and foremost in trade, and the discovery of India was motivated by a desire to dominate trade-routes. But the Christian settlers and missionaries were also keen to convert the native populace to Christianity, and religious images in ivory were commissioned to assist in this. Some were exported to Europe, but others evidently remained and were used for evangelical purposes. From the sixteenth century onwards, the four main missionary orders (Augustinians, Jesuits, Dominicans and Franciscans) built churches and aimed to convert the inhabitants of India. Despite the control of the Church over subject matter, the iconography of Indian art also permeated Christian ivories; the most obvious and at the same time strangest instance of this is the *Child Jesus as the Good Shepherd*. (MTr)

7. (pl.4.2)
Virgin and Child
Maker unknown; probably the Philippines, 1700–20
Carved and partially gilded ivory, h 24.5cm
V&A: 1459–1902

Provenance
Given by Robert R. Storks Esq. of The Elms, St Margaret's on Thames, 1902

Bibliography
Longhurst (1929), vol.2, p.111, pl.89; Estella Marcos (1984), vol.1, fig.211 and vol.2, no.416; Clunas (1996), p.15, fig.6

This partly gilded ivory statuette is unsigned and undated, but its style suggests it was probably made in the early eighteenth century, almost certainly by a Chinese sculptor in the Philippines for the Spanish market. Ivory is a rare, exotic and luxurious raw material, but this Virgin was probably made not primarily as a work of art, but as a devotional piece, to educate, convert, and help with prayers and worship. It was no doubt commissioned from the Chinese sculptor by a Spanish patron, such as a prelate, or a member of one of the orders, the Franciscans, Dominicans or Augustinians, all of whom were active in the Philippines. Perhaps designed to be exported back to the Iberian Peninsula, it may also have been used locally to maintain the Christian beliefs of the local population. Delicately carved, and distinctive in handling, its features are in many ways typical of Hispano-Filipino ivory Madonnas: rippling drapery, the striated and gilded hair of both the Virgin and Child, the heavy eyelids and thick fingers, and the idiosyncratic tuck in the robe at the back, a feature often seen in Hispano-Filipino ivories, the exact origin of which is unclear. The Virgin exposes her breast for the Child, while her feet

are hidden by the generous folds of the robe, perhaps because for the Chinese the feet were considered erotic. (MTr)

8. (pl.2.55)
Armchair
Maker unknown, probably made in London for export, *c*.1685–1700
Carved and turned walnut with caned back and seat (the caning probably replaced), h 134.8cm, w 65cm, d 42cm
Stamped 'ML' and 'IL' on the back face of the back right stile, next to the seat
Skoklosters Slott

Provenance
Recorded at Skokloster in an inventory of 1756

It is not always easy to be sure whether 'English chairs' found in Europe (and beyond) were exported from London or made locally in imitation of English prototypes. The use of stamped initials, however, was a distinctive London practice, so in this instance we are clearly looking at a London-made piece. The presence of two different pairs of initials may reflect the work of two different craftsmen, such as the turner and the carver. Many other comparable caned chairs, of varying elaboration, survive at Skoklosters Slott – probably a mixture of imports and Swedish imitations. This particular chair is from a group of six.

The spiral-turned back columns and the forward-facing front legs (unlike the angled legs of cat.9) are features suggesting that this chair was made before 1700. The flat, uncarved panels that frame the caning of the back are uncharacteristic of chairs surviving in Britain. They were perhaps largely confined to chairs made for export, although most of those were also more richly carved. (BK, LW)

9. (pl.2.57)
Chair
Maker unknown, London, *c*.1705–15
Carved walnut with caned back and seat, h 140.9cm, w 47cm, d 58.4cm
Stamped 'IK' on the back face of top and bottom rails of chair-back and of front stretcher
Label to companion chair (V&A, W.57–1952) on underside of middle stretcher inscribed: 'This Chair was bought by the/late Mr. Geo Forster of Barcus–/Close at the sale of Ld. Windsor's House/hold furniture at Newcastle in the/year 1785. It was one of a suit of/his Lordships Best Chairs, and [was]/[bou]ght again by tho. Rippon[?]/auctioned[?] […]/[…] Geo Forsters sale in the[?] […]'
V&A: W.57A–1952

Provenance
Possibly made for Thomas, 1st Viscount Windsor; probably his son Herbert, 2nd Viscount Windsor; George Forster of Barcus Close, County Durham; Thomas Rippon[?]; untraced until bequeathed to the V&A by Dr C.J.N. Longridge, 1952

In this late version of the English caned chair, the caned panel is no longer flanked by columns (see cat.8), but occupies the whole width of the tall back-frame. As in earlier examples, the carved and pierced cresting is echoed by the front stretcher.

Caned chairs were considered so ordinary that few have retained a specific history. The early record of this one, and its pair, is exceptional – but somewhat unclear. 'The year 1785' on the label may be a mistake for 1758, when the 2nd and last Viscount Windsor died. He did live at Barcus Close, a few miles from

Newcastle-upon-Tyne, so the chairs could well have been sold there after his death. They may have been made for his father, the 1st Viscount Windsor, perhaps around 1703 when he married. The original set probably comprised six or more chairs, and may have included a matching armchair now in the Treasurer's House, York.

Despite the chairs' history in north-east England, they were undoubtedly made in London, the centre of the English caned chair trade. The stamp 'IK' on the three carved elements probably represents an outworker carver who supplied these parts to the chair-maker. (LW)

10. (pl.2.58)
Chair with stamped leather covers
Maker unknown, Portugal, *c*.1720–40
Carved and turned walnut with embossed and incised leather back and seat trimmed with brass-covered pine domes (simulating nail-heads); oak seat rails and pine back-frame, h 136.5cm, w 58cm, d 50cm
Unidentified arms and crest in embossed leather back-cover
V&A: 789–1865

Provenance
Purchased from Señor Blumberg of Lisbon, 1865

This distinctive Portuguese chair-pattern is an idiosyncratic response to the 'English chair', in which embossed leather is substituted for the carved and caned panels of the seat and back. This type of chair is usually dated to the second half of the seventeenth century, but a much later date-span is proposed here, since the most closely related English caned precedents date from around 1715. The example in cat.9 has the same high arched top, repeated in the stretcher between the front legs. On this Portuguese chair the carved shell in the stretcher is echoed by a shell embossed in the leather at the top of the chair-back, making the relationship to the English prototypes all the clearer.

No directly dated examples of these Portuguese chairs are known, but a damask-covered armchair of very similar form, from the Convento dos Remédios, Braga, is dated 1733 (Museu Nacional de Arte Antiga, Lisbon, inv. no. 484 Mov). The coat of arms on the present chair, if it could be identified, might provide a further important clue to the dating of this type. (LW)

11. (pl.2.48)
Screen for the Council Room of Batavia Fort
Chinese craftsmen, Batavia (Indonesia), 1700–20
Carved, painted and gilded teak, h 297cm, w 231cm, d 60cm
Museum Sejarah Jakarta, Indonesia, 3724 D.L; 286/S/MSJ

Provenance
Made for the council room of Batavia Fort

Bibliography
Terwen-De Loos (1985), p.77 figs 41–2; Zandvliet (2002), no.12

This screen was made for the Council Room of the Dutch East India Company at Batavia Fort. Batavia, now Jakarta, was the headquarters of the Company in Asia from 1619, and was the capital of the Dutch East Indies, ruled by the Company from 1619 until 1800. The screen appears in a print depicting a Council meeting published in 1744 so must have been made before this date.

Batavian furniture was made predominantly by Chinese craftsmen who worked from a limited number of European pieces imported to provide examples. The bold scrolling acanthus leaves around the frame are common to Batavian furniture, and show the marriage of European and Chinese styles, but here the emblems of the Dutch East India Company are also incorporated into the carving. Beneath the crown which surmounts the cresting are, in the centre, the arms of Batavia, and on either side the six cities in which the Company had regional boards: Amsterdam, Rotterdam, Delft, Middelburg, Hoorn and Enkhuizen. In the central panel a classical warrior, probably Perseus, holding a shield bearing the head of Medusa, stands beneath a canopy.

Although the screen shows European influences in its decoration, its form is typically Indonesian. Screens of this kind, called a *schutsel* in contemporary inventories, were placed in front of doors providing privacy by concealing the room and its occupants when the door was open. (ABr)

12. (pl.2.38)
Title page for a set of friezes
Odoardo Fialetti (1573–1637) after a drawing by Polifilo Giancarli (active 1620–50) also called Polifilo Zancarli, Rome, 1628
Engraving h 14.8cm, w 47.3cm
Lettered: AL SIG CAVALIER/ CASSIANO DAL POZZO/ mio signore/ Humiliss servitore Gioseppe de Rossi/ D.D.D./ 1628/ Gio Jacomo de Rossi/ formis Romae alla Pace/ al insegna di Parigi/ Romae Superior/ licentia/ Poliphilus Giancarli/ Inventor/ Lucas Ciamberlanus Fecit
V&A: 17484

(pl.2.39)
Title page for a set of friezes
Claes Janz Visscher (1586–1652) based upon a drawing by Polifilo Giancarli (active 1620–50) also called Polifilo Zancarli, Amsterdam, 1636
Engraving
Lettered: VERSCHEYDEN AERDIGE/ MORISSEN/ van/ POLIFILO ZANCARLI/ geordineert/ ende/ Gedruckt by Claes Janss Visscher/ AD. 1636
V&A: E.1674:1–1888

(pl.2.40)
Title page for a set of friezes
After an engraving by Odoardo Fialetti (1573–1637) based upon a drawing by Polifilo Giancarli (active 1620–50) also called Polifilo Zancarli, Paris, 1646
Engraving h 22.5cm, w 52cm
Lettered: DIVERS DESSAINS/ de Frize de linvention/ d'O douard Fiolete/ propre aux Peintre Sculpteurs/ Menuisiers et autres/ A Paris chez Iean Boisseau Enlumineur/ du Roy pour les Cartes Geographiques En/ L'Isle du Palais a la Fontaine de Iouvence Royalle/ pres le Cheval de Bronze/ 1646
V&A: E.761–1927

(pl.2.41)
Title page for a set of friezes
William Vaughan (active 1664–72) after an engraving by Odoardo Fialetti (1573–1637) based upon a drawing by Polifilo Giancarli (active 1620–50) also called Polifilo Zancarli, London, 1672
Engraving h 9.9cm, w 28.2cm
Lettered: A/ Booke of Foldages/ designed by the famous Italian/ POLIFILO ZANCARLI/ Sould by John Overton at the/ White horse without Newgate/ 1672/ Gui Vaughan Sculp:
V&A: 28199.1
Bibliography
Kunstbibliothek (1939), no.558; Fuhring (2004), pp.73–4; Snodin (2006), p.13
The original design by Polifilio Giancarli was published in Rome in the early seventeenth

century. Its transmission and copying in France, The Netherlands and England, helped to spread the Italian Baroque style of scrolling acanthus ornament. By the time the design reached England, nearly half a century after the original, the design had become smaller and cruder in execution. (JN)

ART AND PERFORMANCE

13. (pl.1.55)
Sleigh with a figure of Diana
Gabriel Grupello (1644–1730) and workshop, possibly Düsseldorf, Germany, *c.*1710
Carved, gilded and later bronzed wood, upholstered in cloth, wooden runners studded with iron, h 185cm, w 235cm, d 108cm
Historisches Museum Basel, 1922.360.
Provenance
Elector Palatine Johann Wilhelm II
Bibliography
Kreisel (1927), p.162, ill.55B; Moser (1988); Fischer, Beisenkötter and Krebs (2002), pp.76–9; Wackernagel (2002), vol.1, p.86, fig.84, vol.2, pp.106–14; Belser (2003)
Courtly sleigh rides were an ideal opportunity for ostentatious displays of splendour by the princely houses of the Baroque era. Their magnificent vehicles were usually adorned with figures from classical mythology, or with the animals traditionally associated with the character traits and virtues they claimed to possess.

Stylistic comparisons have led to this Diana Sleigh being attributed to the workshop of the important Dutch-Italian sculptor Gabriel Grupello (or Gabriel de Grupello), who was born in Geraardsberg in Flanders on 23 May 1644 and died at Schloss Ehrenstein near Kerkrade on 20 June 1730. From 1695 until 1716, Grupello was sculptor to the court of the Elector Palatine Johann Wilhelm II in Düsseldorf.

The sleigh's iconographic ensemble, which includes the goddesses Fama and Diana as well as two tritons and various allusions to the chariots and battle-wagons of the ancients, coupled with the outstanding quality of the craftsmanship, indicate that this was a court sleigh of the very first order. It is thought to have belonged to the Elector Palatine Johann Wilhelm II and his second wife Anna Maria Luisa de' Medici.

The design of the ornamental wheels can be traced to a print of a carriage design by the Roman sculptor and architect Ciro Ferri. In this magnificent chariot the Earl of Castlemaine made his triumphal entry into Rome on 8 January 1687, having been appointed ambassador to the Vatican, and hence to Pope Innocent XI, by James II of England. (EB)

14. (pl.2.29)
Design for a silver basin with the Birth of Venus
Peter Paul Rubens (1577–1640), Antwerp, *c.*1632–3
Chalk and oil on oak, h 61cm, w 78cm
The National Gallery, London, NG 1195. Bought, 1885
Provenance
Collection of the Duke of Hamilton by 1830; bought (Clarke Fund), 1885
Bibliography
Martin (1970), pp. 187–93; Glanville (1996), p.29; Baker and Henry (2001), p.597; Fuhring (2001), pp.18–19, 28–9
This oil sketch or *modello*, together with an engraving of 1660 by Jacob Neeffs, is all that

survives relating to the silver ewer and basin made by the Antwerp silversmith Theodoor I Rogiers, to Rubens's designs, for King Charles I of England, as the inscription on Neeffs's engraving states. The engraving shows both the basin and ewer, for which no corresponding oil sketch is known, but whose main subject is the Judgement of Paris. The central part of the *modello* for the basin depicts the Birth of Venus, as related by Hesiod and the *Homeric Hymns*. Venus is shown arriving on the island of Cyprus, accompanied by three female figures who may represent Nereids, Horae or the Three Graces; blown into shore by Zephyrus and crowned by a cupid and a figure who has been identified as Persuasion. The outer rim shows Neptune and Amphitrite at the top, Cupid and Psyche at the bottom and swans, putti riding sea horses and Nerieds riding dolphins to the sides. The central part of the composition is closely related to Rubens's design for an ivory salt cellar made by Georg Petel, owned by Rubens himself and now in the Royal Collections of Sweden; it now appears in a rectangular sketch now in the Musée Bonnat, Bayonne. Similarly, the central part of the composition of the Judgement of Paris, according to Neeffs's engraving of the ewer design, also reappears in a painting on canvas of the same subject by Rubens, now in the Prado. (JN)

15. (pl.2.27)
The Descent from the Cross
Peter Paul Rubens (1577–1640), Antwerp, 1611
Oil on panel, h 115.2cm, w 76.2cm
The Samuel Courtauld Trust, The Courtauld Gallery, London, P.1947.LF.359
Provenance
?Jeremias Wildens, Antwerp (by 1653); ?Duc de Richelieu, Paris; Lord Methuen, Corsham Court, Wiltshire (by 1806); W. Warner; his grand-daughter Mrs E.C. Holloway, Cheltenham; bought by Viscount Lee of Fareham 1923; bequeathed by Viscount Lee in 1947 (with a life-interest to Viscountess Lee).
Bibliography
Borenius (1923–6), vol.1, no.33; Murray (1967), p.41, no.76; Held (1980), I, no.355, pp.488–91 and II, fig.351; Judson (2000), no.43b; Durante (2003–04), pp.54–61; Jaffé (2005), no.56, p.129
On 7 September 1611 Rubens was commissioned to paint a large winged altarpiece in Antwerp Cathedral for the Arquebusiers guild. *The Descent from the Cross* was selected as the subject from the central panel.

This unusually large and highly finished sketch is probably the *modello* which Rubens submitted to the guild to secure the commission. Its starting point was a far earlier drawing of the Descent (St Petersburg, Hermitage). The Courtauld sketch replicates its main features, including idiosyncratic details such as the man grasping Christ's shroud with his teeth.

However, Rubens was not quite satisfied. He reworked the composition, introducing several changes into both the oil sketch and the final work (revealed by x-radiography). These were intended to invest the Descent with greater energy and pathos, and to provoke a strong devotional response. More attention was focused on Christ's body, which was slightly removed from its cradling shroud. In addition, the emotive roles of Christ's mother and Mary Magdalen were heightened.

The central panel of the altarpiece was

installed in the Cathedral by 17 September 1612, where it remains today. Yet arguably the oil sketch gives a better sense of the dynamism and passion of Rubens' extraordinary composition. (CCam)

16. (pl.2.30)
Tankard with the *Drunkenness of Silenus*
Johann Baptist Weinold (d.1648) after designs by Peter Paul Rubens (1577–1640), Augsburg, *c.*1645–8
Carved ivory with enamelled silver gilt mounts, h 34.5cm
Marked BW in an oval with a pine cone
Skoklosters Slott, 371
Provenance
Mentioned in Skokloster inventory of 1793
Bibliography
Bengtsson (1995), no.43; Seelig (2001)
A large number of carved ivory drinking vessels mounted in silver or silver gilt exist, based on classical subjects taken from the paintings of Rubens. Rubens himself owned a salt cellar carved by Georg Petel after Rubens's own designs, which is now in the Royal Collections of Sweden. This tankard is one of a group showing the drunken Silenus in procession with satyrs and maenads, produced primarily in Augsburg. The iconography takes elements from various paintings by Rubens: the figure of Silenus from a painting in the Alte Pinakothek, Munich (also known in an engraving), the female satyr supporting him from the *Bacchanalia* (1614–15) now in the Pushkin Museum, Moscow, and the satyr and maenad couple from *Diana and her nymphs departing for the hunt* (1613–14) now in the Cleveland Museum of Art. A rare wax model by Petel relating to one of the earliest of these vessels on the Silenus theme survives in the Hamburger Museum für Kunst und Gewerbe. The Augsburg goldsmith Andreas I Wickert mounted a number of these tankards (including one in the V&A) during the 1630s, with minor variations on a standard model. Johann Baptist Weinold followed Wickert's model, but incorporated sections of enamel painting or ivory herm figures on the mounts; both are combined in this tankard. On the lid is an ivory putto figure, holding and crowned with bunches of grapes; the handle, also in the style of Wickert, is auricular with a female herm figure. In the earliest tankards the mounts and their decoration were entirely in silver or silver gilt; only those produced from the 1640s onwards, like this one, incorporated other elements. (JN)

17. (pl.2.31)
Ewer with *The Triumph of Neptune*
Massimiliano Soldani Benzi (1656–1740), Florence, Italy, *c.*1721
Cast bronze, h 79.7cm, w 37cm, d 28cm
V&A: A.18–1959
Provenance
Probably commissioned by Giovanni Battista Scarlatti, Florence; possibly in the collection in England of Baron George Bubb Doddington, Baron Melcombe; purchased by the V&A from Rosenborg and Stiebel Inc., New York, with its pendant (A.19–1959)
Bibliography
Lankheit (1962), pp.146–8; Pope-Hennessy (1964), vol.2, no.626; Honour (1965), pp.85, 89; Rosen (1974), no.84a; Snodin (1984), no.A3; Williamson (1996), pp.140–1
This is one of a pair of highly ornamented and purely ornamental ewers made for Senator Giovanni Battista Scarlatti by Massimiliano Soldani Benzi, the most renowned Florentine

bronze-worker in the late Baroque period. On one side of this monumental ewer the sea-god Neptune is depicted, surrounded by tritons blowing on conches, or fighting. On the other side a bearded triton rides a sea horse, also amidst tritons. A bare-breasted winged female figure forms the handle. Shell-like forms further enliven the surface, and four dolphins coil around the base. Hugh Honour noted that Sir Horace Mann, the British consul in Florence, was negotiating the purchase of some Soldani bronzes for George Bubb Doddington in 1759, and suggested that these could be the ones now in the V&A.

Charles Avery has recently discovered references to the ewers in Soldani's correspondence, some of which is in the Bodleian Library, Oxford. In 1722 Soldani evidently offered to cast further bronze versions for Senator Scarlatti, and in 1732 made the same suggestion to an Italian merchant resident in London, Giovanni Giacomo Zamboni. However, it seems unlikely that these were ever made. (I am grateful to Charles Avery for this information.)

The ewers were cast from wax models, and the moulds used in this process were later employed to create examples in coloured Doccia porcelain. Examples of these versions are now in the Museo Civico, Turin. (MTr)

18. (pl.1.21)
Louis XIV
After Hyacinthe Rigaud (1659–1743), Paris, after 1701
Oil on canvas, h 131cm, w 97cm
Musée national des châteaux de Versailles et de Trianon, MV 3563
Provenance
Château de Mesnières. Acquired by Louis-Philippe for Versailles in 1834
Bibliography
Constans (1980), no.5605; Ahrens (1990); Onfray (1997); Posner (1998); Rigaud original in Constans and Salmon (1998), no.3; Beaurain and Landry (2001); Perreau (2004), pp.102–4; Bertelli (2005)

The painting is a workshop copy of the large portrait of Louis XIV painted by Hyacinthe Rigaud in 1701 (Musée du Louvre; a second version at Versailles). Rigaud's original portrait was intended for Philippe d'Anjou, grandson of Louis XIV, who became king of Spain as Philip V on 16 November 1700 in accordance with the will of Charles II of Spain. When it was finished, however, Louis was so pleased with the painting that he decided to keep it, and displayed it in the throne room (*Salon d'Apollon*) at Versailles. The replacement portrait for Philip V (now at Versailles) was not sent to Madrid either, because of the outbreak of the War of the Spanish Succession of 1701–14.

Rigaud's workshop had to produce numerous copies of this work, considered the most important portrait of Louis XIV, because of its successful composition. The king is represented in his coronation robes, wearing the blue ermine-lined cloak decorated with golden fleurs-de-lis and the chain of the Order of the Holy Spirit, and with the sword of Charlemagne at his side. His hand rests on the sceptre; the French crown and the hand of justice are close by; in addition the king wears a large wig 'of majesty' and a lace collar as in the Bernini bust of 1665. Behind him is the throne and a column, symbolizing strength, its base decorated with an allegory of justice in low relief. Rigaud's portrait depicts a 'king of peace' founded on majesty, strength and justice. (NM)

19. (pl.2.25)
Charles II
Honoré Pelle (1641–1718), probably Genoa, Italy, 1684
Carved marble, h 128.9cm, w (base) 23cm, d 28.6cm
Inscribed: '1684 HONNORE PELLE, F' on the truncated right arm
V&A: 239–1881
Provenance
Given by Henry Durlacher Esq., 1881
Bibliography
Maclagan and Longhurst (1913), pp.33–4; Herding (1980), no.465; Whinney (1988), p.440; Boccardo (1989), pp.207–8, fig.214; Williamson (1996), p.135

This over-lifesize bust is a magnificent portrait of Charles II (1630–85), albeit almost certainly based on a painting or an engraving, rather than done from life. The king is shown with a flowing wig spilling over his shoulders, his head turned towards his right. His lace cravat and the drapery of his cloak appear windswept, their diagonal movement acting as a counterpoint to the turn of the head. Eric Maclagan remarked on the 'air of tragic weariness' in the restored monarch's gaze.

Little is known about the sculptor. Although born in France, Honoré Pelle was active in Genoa, and probably also spent time in Rome; this marble strongly suggests that he was inspired by Gianlorenzo Bernini, whose bust of Francesco d'Este in Modena is particularly close in style. A slightly smaller and earlier stone version of Pelle's *Charles II* is at Burleigh House, Stamford, signed and dated 1682. (MT)

ARCHITECTURE AND PERFORMANCE

20. (pl.2.11)
Elevation and plan of the façade of the Oratory and House of the Order of St Philip Neri, Rome
Francesco Borromini (1599–1667), Rome, 1638
Graphite on paper, h 40.4cm, w 33.8cm, including a restored strip of 3.5cm at right
The Royal Collection, RL 5594
Provenance
Probably collection of Cardinal Alessandro Albani, and purchased by George III in 1762; in the Royal Collection by about 1810
Bibliography
Blunt (1971), no.48; Connors (1980), no.41; Kieven (1993), no.10; Weston-Lewis (1998), no.81; Bösel and Frommel (2000), no.VIII.16

In 1637 Borromini succeeded Paolo Maruscelli as architect of the oratory of S. Filippo Neri, adjacent to the principal church of the Filippine order, S. Maria in Vallicella (the Chiesa Nuova). Maruscelli had already made detailed plans for the structure of the building, and though Borromini amended these substantially, his primary architectural contribution was the design of the façade. The provision of an elaborate façade for an oratory was in itself controversial, and it was thus consciously subordinate to that of the Chiesa Nuova – a little lower, and in brick rather than travertine.

The façade as begun in 1637 was of five bays on a shallow concave sweep, topped by a heavy entablature that continued the intermediate entablature of the Chiesa Nuova. In 1638 it was decided to move the order's library to the upper floor at the front of the complex, and this drawing records Borromini's amendments to the façade, enlarging the upper floor to give a squarish central block with a gable, and remodelling the flanking bays to integrate them with the five principal bays. Within the available space, less than 2.5m deep, Borromini achieved great visual movement by articulating the surface of each curved bay with a succession of dense mouldings and tiered planes, though the façade as executed omitted many of the decorative details seen here. (MC)

21. (pl.2.4)
Design for a capital and part of a column for the Baldacchino of St Peter's Basilica, Rome
Francesco Borromini (1599–1667), Rome, *c.*1625
Pen and ink with wash, over traces of black chalk or graphite, with much pinpointing, on discoloured paper, h 49.6cm, w 21.4cm
The Royal Collection, RL 5635
Provenance
Probably collection of Cardinal Alessandro Albani, and purchased by George III in 1762; in the Royal Collection by 1810
Bibliography
Blunt (1960), no.23; Blunt (1971), no.52; Kieven (1993), no.4; Kirwin (1998), pp.125, 160; Weston-Lewis (1998), no.58; Kahn-Rossi and Franciolli (1999), no.223; Bösel and Frommel (2000), no.XII.8; Barock im Vatikan (2005), no.53; Whitaker and Clayton (2007), no.126

Shortly after his election in 1623, Urban VIII commissioned Gianlorenzo Bernini to construct an enormous *baldacchino* in part-gilded bronze, 29m high, to stand at the crossing of St Peter's over the tomb of the saint. Bernini's own architectural experience was at that time minimal, and Francesco Borromini (who had been assisting Carlo Maderno in the completion of St Peter's) was pressed into service to produce finished drawings for the project.

This drawing studies the upper section of the right-hand columns of the Baldacchino, incorporating the Barberini emblems of bees, the sun, and branches of laurel. The twisting form echoes the ancient columns from the old basilica thought to have been brought by the Emperor Constantine from the Temple of Solomon in Jerusalem.

By September 1626 the columns had been cast in three sections, using bronze pillaged from the portico of the Pantheon, but the form of the canopy had not been finalized. A wood and papier-mâché mock-up of Bernini's initial design, culminating in a figure of the Risen Christ, stood in place until 1631, when it was replaced by another featuring volutes rising on the diagonals to a globe and cross. That version was cast in 1632, and work was completed the following year. (MC)

22. (pl.2.15)
Design for the east front of the Louvre, Paris
Gianlorenzo Bernini (1598–1680), Rome, 1664
Pen and ink on paper, h 16.4, w 27.7cm
Inscribed: Cav. Bernini; on verso: G.L. Bernino
The Samuel Courtauld Trust, The Courtauld Gallery, London, D.1984.AB.51.1
Provenance
Margaret Whinney; Anthony Blunt
Bibliography
Blunt (1982); Bradford and Braham (1991), no.9; Kieven (1993), no.30; Merz (1993); Hall (2007)

The project to redesign the Louvre was initially begun by the French architect Louis Le Vau, under the command of Louis XIV's minister Jean Baptiste Colbert. However, after construction on the east front had already begun, Colbert halted work and invited a number of architects, including Bernini and Pietro da Cortona, to submit their own designs for the royal palace. This drawing represents Bernini's first design for the east front, which presented a dramatically curving façade rising above a rusticated lower stage. The central drum was cased in a convex curve linked on either side by concave arcades to the side wings. The façade was to be an open loggia; this, however, provoked one of the principal criticisms of the design, namely that this openness was inappropriate for a royal palace for both aesthetic and security reasons.

Although Bernini revised his scheme, ultimately all his designs were rejected and the east front was instead executed to the designs of Claude Perrault and others. The attribution of this drawing to Bernini himself rather than his workshop or a later draughtsman was first proposed by Anthony Blunt and has been accepted by others including Elizabeth Kieven; Jörg Martin Merz, however, considered it insufficiently precise in its details for an architect's hand, preferring to class it as a copy related to the presentation drawing in the Louvre. (JN)

23. (pl.2.59)
View of the dome of the church of S. Carlo al Corso, Rome
Nicodemus Tessin the Younger (1654–1728), Rome, 1673
Pen and ink with wash on paper, letter-folded, watermark: saint, h 40.8cm, w 26.9cm
Inscribed: La Cuppola di S. Carlo Borromeo in Roma
Nationalmuseum, Stockholm, THC 2545
Provenance
Nicodemus Tessin the Younger (Catalogue of his collections printed in 1712); Carl Gustaf Tessin (ms inventory *c.*1732); Kongl. Museum (Lugt 1638); Nationalmuseum from 1866
Bibliography
Sirén (1914), p.XIX, 43; Laine and Magnusson (2002), p.71; Snickare (2002), pp.39–40, fig.11; Olin (2004), no.218; Strunck (2007) 2, p.335

The slender and confidently classical dome of the church of SS Carlo e Ambrogio al Corso in Rome was constructed in 1668–9 after a design by Pietro da Cortona. Its vigour, simplicity and vertical thrust contrast with the Mannerist decoration and comparative squatness of Cortona's earlier design for the dome of SS Luca e Martina. The drum is articulated by clustered pilasters flanked by free-standing Corinthian columns that frame the tall windows. In the attic, balusters and oval apertures with ornamental frames provide a harmonious transition between the drum and the ribbed roof.

The dome was much admired by contemporaries, among them the young Swedish architect Nicodemus Tessin the Younger, who arrived in Rome in the summer of 1673. In early August the heat prevented him from crossing the city to the Vatican, where he had begun measuring and drawing Bernini's newly finished Scala Regia. Instead, Tessin stayed in the neighbourhood of his lodgings near the Via del Corso where he drew the cupola of S. Carlo. He sent the drawing with a letter to his father, the court architect Nicodemus Tessin the Elder, in Stockholm, describing the dome as 'very beautiful', and particularly mentioning its '24 large columns' (letter 3 August 1673). The type of Roman Baroque classicism represented by Cortona's dome would be a major influence on Tessin's own works. (MO)

24. (pl.1.10)
Cabinet on a console table with a nocturnal clock and virginal
Giacomo Herman (d.1685) and Johannes Meisser (cabinet), Giovanni Battista Maberiani (virginal), Giovanni Wendelino Hessler (clock), Rome, cabinet 1669–75, virginal 1676, console table 1700–25
Poplar and walnut veneered in ebony, set with gouache panels, lapis lazuli and jasper with gilt bronze mounts; stand of carved and gilded wood with composite slab veneered in *verde antico* and *lumachella* marbles, overall h 286cm, w 172cm, d 72.5cm
Cabinet signed 'Johannes Meisser' on carcase under equestrian sculpture; clock engraved 'Gioann Wendelino Hessler; virginal signed 'Gio[van]ni Ba[tti]sta Maberiani
Cabinet and console table: Private Collection, Rome
Equestrian Statue: Collection Dr Gert-Rudolf Flick
Provenance
Commissioned by Pope Clement IX; recorded in 1669 as one of four cabinets by Herman shown to Cardinal Giacomo Rospigliosi at Palazzo del Qurinale, Rome; the console probably purchased 1955 by John Bowes Morrell and donated to the Assembly Rooms, York Conservation Trust; sold at Sotheby's London 4 December 2007, lot 60
Bibliography
González-Palacios (1984), I, p.55, pl.10; II, p.64, fig.108; Walker and Hammond (1999), p.2; London (2007), pp120–37; González-Palacios and Tavella (2007)

In 1669, the most celebrated Roman cabinet-maker of the day, Giacomo Herman, showed four cabinets to Cardinal Giacomo Rospigliosi, nephew of Pope Clement IX. This cabinet is almost certainly one of those four. The other three cabinets are closely similar and survive in Poland and Denmark: one in the Chapel of Loreto, Krakow, which may have been given to the King of Poland in 1683, one in Rosenborg Castle and one in Fredensborg Castle. It is likely that the cabinets were commissioned as diplomatic gifts.

All four cabinets originally incorporated a clock and virginals, and are decorated with *pietre dure* panels. Here, the panels depict scenes from the history of Rome and their splendour is reflected by mirrored slides that pull out on either side to create the effect of an even larger cabinet. The magnificent stand, with its bold sculptural carving, was made in the early eighteenth century to update this prestigious object.

Like the Fredensborg cabinet, the cabinet carcase is signed by Johannes Meisser of Freiburg. Very little is known about Meisser who was probably an assistant in Herman's workshop. The makers of the clock and virginal, however, are known to have carried out other important commissions in Rome.

Although the cabinet's origins are well documented, little is known about its more recent history. At some point the stand and cabinet were separated. The stand was acquired by John Bowes Morrell shortly after World War II and later donated to the York Assembly Rooms, where it stood until last year. The cabinet was sold at a London auction in 1972 by Mrs Baston, but where she acquired it is unknown. (AB)

25. (pl.4.18)
Model for the church of St Mary-le-Strand
Maker unknown, after designs by James Gibbs (1682–1754), London, *c.*1717
Carved and joined pearwood and boxwood, h 83cm, w 74cm, d 31cm
RIBA Library Drawings and Archives Collections, London, MOD/GIBB/2
Provenance
Presented by the Marquess of Exeter, 1980
Bibliography
Friedman (1984), pp.40–53, 311–12; Millon (1999), no.549 and p.182

In 1711 Queen Anne's government passed an Act of Parliament that fifty new churches 'in stone and other proper Materials' should be built in and around London, each to house 2000 parishioners; only twelve were eventually constructed. The position of this church at the centre of the Strand, on the ceremonial route from court and Parliament to the city and St Paul's Cathedral, made it a particularly important commission. Although initially a design by Thomas Archer was chosen, the commission was given to Gibbs in November 1714 after the death of the Queen forced plans to be modified; Gibbs then incorporated elements from Archer into his revised design. The model clearly reflects the four years Gibbs had spent studying with Carlo Fontana in Rome: its design is inspired by the Temple of Fortuna Virilis in Rome, while the portico recalls Pietro da Cortona's church of S. Maria della Pace as well as Christopher Wren's porches for St Paul's Cathedral. The V&A has a related drawing of 1714 for the east end steeple. Originally a bronze statue of Queen Anne, by the Florentine Giovanni Battista Foggini, was intended to stand on the dome of the portico, inspired by Fontana's initial designs for the monument to Queen Christina of Sweden in St Peter's in Rome; in 1715 this was replaced, however (as seen on the model), with a flaming urn. An earlier and cruder, fragmentary model for the church survives, also in the RIBA's collections, built to the same scale, which indicates that it was probably Gibbs's ideas for the surface treatment of the exterior that changed, rather than the basic idea. The present model shows the church as built and as illustrated in Gibbs's *The Book of Architecture* of 1728. The church was much criticised after construction for its perceived excess of exterior decoration. The model was given to the RIBA by the Marquess of Exeter, whose predecessors were the principal landowners in the parish until the early 20th century and who served as churchwardens for over 150 years. (CH, JN)

26. (pl.2.85)
The Haiyantang (Calm Sea Palace), one of the European pavilions at Yuanming Yuan
After drawings by Yi Lantai (active 1736–86), Beijing, 1781–6
Copperplate engraving, h 50cm, w 88cm
Inscribed in Chinese with the name of the palace and leaf number in the set
V&A: 29452:9
Bibliography
Berliner Festspiele (1985), pp.122–8; Jackson and Jaffer (2004), pp.343–5 and figs 26.6–7; Rawski and Rawson (2005), no.91

The Chinese Emperor Quianlong built a European-style palace with a series of pavilions, fountains and a maze, in the grounds of his summer palace outside Beijing, the Yuanming Yuan. The palace complex emulates European palaces such as Versailles while also presenting a Chinese fantasy of the exoticism of Europe. It was principally designed by two European architects resident at the Emperor's court, the Jesuits Giuseppe Castiglione and Michel Benoist. Construction was carried out in three phases; the *Haiyantang* or Calm Sea Palace was part of the second phase. This palace combined European and Chinese elements, such as the western-style gables and Chinese roof, built using Chinese building techniques. Its principal feature, however, was the fountain in front of the pavilion, with a scallop shell basin and six bronze figures of the animals of the Chinese zodiac on either side. This also functioned as a water clock, spouting water from one of the animals every two hours, and from all twelve together at noon. The pavilions continued the European theme inside: they housed the Emperor's collections of European furniture and precious objects, including a set of six Beauvais tapestries after designs by Boucher and sent from the French court. The Emperor commissioned the set of twenty engravings of the palace buildings and gardens from which this print comes, to commemorate and publicise it; they now serve, together with some architectural fragments, as the main visual record of the complex, which was largely destroyed in 1860. (JN)

MARVELLOUS MATERIALS

27. (pl.2.66)
A cabinet of curiosities
Johann Georg Hinz (d.1670), also called Hainz or Haintz, Hamburg, Germany, 1666
Oil on canvas, canvas h 114.5cm, w 93.3cm
Signed in the middle: Georg Hainz Altone/fecit A[nn]o 1666
Hamburger Kunsthalle, 435
Provenance
Auction coll. Johan von Bülow, Copenhagen, 19 April 1829, no.75; coll. Pius Warburg Hamburg until 1890; Hamburger Kunsthalle
Bibliography
Möller (1963); Battersby (1974), pp.93–5; Bastian (1984), no.56; Heinrich and Braun (1996), pp.8–24, 52; Sitt and Gassner (2008), pp.97, 99–101

This depiction of the shelves of a *Kunstkammer* highlights the art of collecting and the art of painting. A cup placed in the upper middle part of the picture recalls a splendid ivory cup, the so-called Loevenoern Goblet, made in 1665 by Joachim Henne. Surrounded by delicate glass objects, it is arranged prominently by Hinz as if seen from below, among precious natural curiosities.

The cup focuses on the sensory pleasures, and all the senses, excluding smell, are represented. Touch is given a lightly erotic interpretation with an idle bacchanal of putti and a pair of lovers. Taste is hinted at in the hunting scenes and toasts ('Let it go round about' and 'bring it to the others') engraved on two glass goblets on the highest shelf. Hearing is represented by the female musicians on the ivory tankard, their well-tempered play contrasting with the drunken Bacchus. On a casket set with jewels a small standing clock shows the passing of time. This *memento mori* message is reinforced with a human skull and one carved from coral. Other naturalia include exotic snail and nautilus shells. Pearls, between art and nature, are shown by Hinz on strings or worked into filigree drop earrings, brooches or medallions. The jewels signify both luxury and artistic skill, and display their brilliance as polished spheres, faceted or mounted in gold. Light entering through a window reflects the objects. Glass and light together embody sight, as at the base of the cup there are cut lenses for optical instruments.

The painting is full of antagonism: the luxurious nautilus shell is the antithesis of the functional lens. The *Kunstkammer* shelves also encourage the appropriate use of sensibility. Knowledge and the study of nature are inconceivable without findings based on sensory stimuli. This can be inferred from the medallions, one showing two Africans and the other showing the Danish king Frederick II (1559–88), thus promoting the politics of colonization in the service of trade and knowledge. Out of the symbol of decadence and finiteness at the centre of the painting, the play broadens with joy, death and redemption extending over the whole painting. The precious objects arouse yearnings which will be curtailed by death. (MS)

28. (pl.2.76)
Clock
Movement by Adriaan van den Bergh, case by Hans Coenraadt Breghtel (1609–75), The Hague, 1650–75
Silver, partially gilt, h 91.6cm, w 42.2cm, d 42.2cm
Clock is signed HCBreghtel Fecit Hagae; movement is signed 'Adriaen vanden Bergh Fecit Hagae'
V&A: 92–1870
Provenance
F. Davies, Bond Street, London; Christie's, 5 March 1869, lot 471
Bibliography
Lippincott (1999), no.189; Pijzel-Dommisse (2005), pp.14, 29

Conceived as a Temple of Life, the clock is surmounted by a figure representing Time. The eight-day movement strikes the hours on the cupola bell; three sides have dials; the front dial has an enamelled hour glass supported by gilded *putti*. Embossed plaques illustrating the Signs of the Zodiac (around the drum of the cupola), the Ages of Man and the Seasons (on the plinth) evoke the passage of time. Statuettes of classical deities on the cornice symbolize the months: Janus (January), Venus and Cupid (February), Mars (March), Apollo, Mercury and Saturn, Diana, and Jupiter. Reliefs of seasonal activities from the lives of the gods (on the plinth) include Diana bathing, illustrative of Summer. Scenes of instructing children, a young couple walking, men warming themselves by the fire and an elderly couple hobbling on sticks illustrate mortal life. The decoration of the frieze above picks up this theme: fishes evoke Winter; cornucopiae of flowers, Spring; Ceres' head, Summer; and bunches of grapes, Autumn.

Breghtel was born in Nuremberg in 1609. By 1640 he was an established silversmith in The Hague, supplying silver for the Stadholder's family in 1645. The sumptuous decoration of this clock demonstrates the techniques and quality of work characteristic of leading goldsmiths' workshops in this fashionable city. The richly embossed floral ornament decorating the sides is matched by exquisite silver filigree work adorning the pilasters and half columns and representing tiles on the cupola roof. The statuettes, half columns and plinth supports are gilded.

This showpiece was displayed in the goldsmith's workshop and was still there after his widow's death in 1682, when his son-in-law Adriaen van Hoecke took over. It was sold at auction in Amsterdam in 1715. (TM, JP-D)

29. (not illustrated)
Pair of salt cellars in the auricular style
Probably Thomas Bogaert (probably 1597-1652/3), Amsterdam, The Netherlands, 1638
Silver and silver gilt, h 18.4cm
Town-mark of Utrecht for 1638

In the collection of The Trustees of the 9th Duke of Buccleuch's Chattels Fund

Bibliography

Oman (1953), pl.18; Frederiks (1961), IV, no.58, pls 68, 69; ter Molen (1984)

On this pair of salts, human faces on sinuous serpent bodies support figures inspired by Ancient Roman sculpture. The combination of the fantastic and the classical shows Bogaert's debt to the creations of the Utrecht silversmith, Adam van Vianen. Adam and his brother Paulus developed a style of ornament which exaggerated and juxtaposed forms from the natural world. Its origins lay in the fantastical, frescoed designs uncovered in the 1480s in the ruins of the Emperor Nero's palace, in Rome. These designs were termed 'grotesques' by contemporaries, because they were found in what were mistakenly believed to be underground chambers, or grottoes. The van Vianens exploited the three-dimensional possibilities of these fantastical patterns, and were particularly inspired by organic animal forms of water and cave-dwelling species such as fish, serpents and snails, exaggerating the proportions of the mouth or the scales of their skin. This style has become known as 'auricular', a reference to the resemblance between its smooth, curving forms and the inside of a human ear. These characteristics are evident in the chasing around the broad rim of the salt bowls. The contemporary Dutch term for this style, however, was 'whims and drolleries' ('fratsen en snaeckeryen'), which suggests the fantastical winged serpents on the base. The figures that support the salt bowls derive from classical models. The woman removing a thorn from her foot is Venus, and Bogaert's prototype was probably the small bronze copies of the antique Roman statue which circulated in the late sixteenth and early seventeenth centuries. The gilding on the bowls of the salts is both decorative and functional. Not only does it give the bowls the appearance of sun-like flowers, but it protects the silver from the corrosive properties of salt. (KK)

30. (pl.2.70)
Agate vase with cameos

Vase assembled and mounted by Pierre Ladoireau (d. 1716) and his workshop, Paris, 1687–9

Carved agate and chalcedony mounted with enamelled gold set with cameos in agate, lapis lazuli, jasper and carnelian, h 26.5cm

Marks: inside base: crowned fleur-de-lis above initials PL separated by a star; incised A.; exterior of base: A surmounted by fleur-de-lis

Museo Nacional del Prado, Madrid 037

Provenance

Collection of the Grand Dauphin, inventory 1689, no.23 or 24; collection of Philip V of Spain, inventory 1746, no.120; inventory 1776, no.59

Bibliography

Angulo Íniguez (1989), pp.78–9, 239–40; Verlet (1963), p.152; Arbeteta Mira (2000), no. 6.25; Arbeteta Mira (2001), no.120; Castelluccio (2002), p.150

Philip V of Spain inherited part of an important collection of precious objects from his father, Louis, the Grand Dauphin of France, in 1712. Although some pieces in the collection were of ancient provenance, many of the objects were created or transformed during the seventeenth century. The present vase is a fine example of the French classicizing interpretation of Baroque style. Its pair was stolen in 1918.

The vase comprises two pieces of carved agate held together by a wide gold strip decorated with enamels and cameos. The foot and top edge are similarly decorated. The cameos, of diverse origins and dates, combine conventional representations of rulers and gods with idealized depictions of historic figures, including Mary Stuart, and the young Louis XIV and his parents. The mark inside the base is that used by the *fermier* or tax collector Jacques Léger between 1687 and 1691. The initials 'PL' are the personal mark of Pierre Ladoireau.

The importance of the vase lies less in the quality of the materials than in the skill of the goldsmith who assembled it. Ladoireau, silversmith and bronze caster to Louis XIV, designed complex furniture and furnishings in silver, brass and bronze for the Great Gallery and the Small Gallery at Versailles. He cast the bronze vases decorating the Trianon cascade and worked on pieces for the Dauphin at Marly. Ladoireau ran an extensive atelier, including a smelting workshop with 45 crucibles, and opened a shop in 1686. He traded with China and India, but, despite this extraordinary activity, very little of his work survives.

The gold decoration of the vase is typical of print-inspired Parisian metalwork of the late 1680s. The enamels follow French jewellery fashions, as seen in the designs of Gilles L'Egaré, published in 1663, and are a rare example of French courtly jewel work from the golden age of Louis XIV. (LAM)

31. (pl.2.69)
Tureen in Icelandic obsidian

Hartwig Holst (active 1713–27), the mounts by Jens Komløv Pedersen (1683–1750), Copenhagen, 1725

Carved Icelandic obsidian, lidded, set with hardstones, mother-of-pearl, paste and portrait miniatures with silver gilt mounts, h 22.5cm, l 31cm, d 16.6cm

Hallmark of Copenhagen 1724 and maker's mark

The Royal Danish Collections, Rosenborg Castle, Copenhagen, 10–188 a–b

Bibliography

Gundestrup (1991), vol.1, p.232; Hein (1995)

This tureen is a symbol of the Danish victory in the Great Northern War of 1700–20 that ended Swedish hegemony in Scandinavia. On the front, miniatures depict Frederick IV of Denmark-Norway and his second wife, Queen Anna Sophia. Their monograms are on the back. The watercolours decorating the obelisks on the lid show the portrait of Charles XII of Sweden, scenes from his invasion of Norway, and the monument commemorating his death at Frederikshald in 1718. The Lamb of God stands in the centre of the lid on the reverse of a glass paste intaglio of Christian V, the father of Frederick IV, that can be seen inside the lid. The miniatures are backed by inscriptions that praise the Lord's blessing of the pious ruler and his righteous cause.

In the 1680s Christian V renewed attempts to work the hardstones of Norway and Iceland, exploiting the mineral riches of his realm, both to honour God's creation and to show the ingenuity of man. Accordingly this tureen entered the Royal *Kunstkammer* as an example of the 'various Diamonds from the North, as Rubies, Sapphires, Emeralds, Garnets, Topaz, Amethysts, Crystals, Jasper and Obsidians'. As royal silver commissions were all unmarked, the heavy and clumsy tureen cannot have been ordered by Frederick IV. Rather, the sovereign bought it to promote the working of Icelandic obsidian. In the 1750s vast quantities were exported to China. (JH)

32. (pl.2.71)
Vase

Design and jewel work by Johann Melchior Dinglinger (1664–1731), enamel paintings by Georg Friedrich Dinglinger (1666–1720), stone-cutting attributed to Johann Christian Kirchner (1691–1732), Dresden, Germany, 1719–21

Carved Kelheim stone set with enamel and emeralds, with silver gilt mounts, h 54cm, w 20.4cm, d 20.4cm

Grünes Gewölbe, Staatliche Kunstsammlungen Dresden, V 136

Provenance

Pretioseninventar 1733, p.971, no.7

Bibliography

Von Watzdorf (1962), vol.1, pp.237–40; Kappel and Weinhold (2007), p.216

This vase, carved from a relatively soft limestone from Kelheim, was installed in the Green Vaults in February 1722, together with its pendant. The use of a restrained colour palette and rather severe forms, inspired by antiquity, is characteristic of the late style of the Dresden court jeweller Johann Melchior Dinglinger. Its iconography is also inspired by classical mythology. The carved decoration celebrates Faunus and the goat-legged Pan, reinforced through oval medallions containing profile portraits of these two gods of nature, both regarded as protectors of shepherds and farmers. The monochromatic *camaieu* enamel paintings are among the last works of the court enameller Georg Friedrich Dinglinger, and recall antique cameos. The architectonic base, which evokes a central-plan building, contains niches with herms in the form of Pan and Diana, the goddess of hunting. The silver-gilt mounts, sparingly set with precious stones, form lambrequins and garlands that wrap around the stone vases, lightening their severity. The knob of the lid is formed from a piece of jasper and is marked with the royal monogram 'AR' (Augustus Rex), which also appears on the neck of the vase. (UW)

33. (pl.1.28)
Breast jewel

Maker unknown, Portugal, 1700–25

Silver, partially gilt, and gold set with diamonds, h 12.9cm, w 17cm

Museu Nacional de Arte Antiga, Lisboa, 875 Joa

Provenance

Aquired by MNAA, 1936

Bibliography

Museu Nacional de Arte Antiga (1974), no.185; Alegria et al. (1991), no.87; Levenson (1993), no.40; D'Orey (1995), no.70

This large breast ornament (*devant de corsage*), triangular in composition and set with rose-cut diamonds, is finished at top and bottom with feathers in chased gold. The scrolling openwork volutes and vegetation surround a basket highlighted by a larger diamond, mounted in an articulated frame. The back of the piece in gilded silver reveals the impressive complexity of the composition and mount, the latter executed with great technical mastery. Surviving pieces of this form and quality are extremely rare.

The piece is a notable work of Portuguese jewellery of French, or more probably Italian, inspiration. It shows surprising similarities with a design from 1675 by Pietro Cerini of Rome now in the V&A, and exemplifies a type of erudite jewellery of high quality and great intrinsic value, used by great ladies to complement a refined *toilette*. (LO)

34. (pl.2.60)
Casket

Grand-ducal workshops (*Galleria dei Lavori*), probably after Giovanni Battista Foggini (1652–1725), Florence, *c.*1720

Ebony set with panels of *pietre dure*, lapis lazuli and semi-precious stones, and with gilt bronze mounts, h 30cm, w 44.5cm, d 38.6cm

The Vyne, The Chute Collection (The National Trust), NT/VYN/F/34i

Provenance

Possibly purchased in Florence by John Chute, 1741–5; first listed in the Ante Room (its present location) at The Vyne in 1776 as 'Curious cabinet with glass cover on a gold frame, leather cover'

Bibliography

Palais des Beaux-Arts (1973), pp.178, 183, no.144; Sutton (1982), no.65, fig.62; Jackson-Stops (1985), no.202; González-Palacios (1986), I, p.43; Giusti (1988), no.40; Jervis (2007), no.7, figs 6–7

This splendid casket, one of the most magnificent to have been manufactured in the Florentine workshops of the Medici, is typical of the designs of their director, G.B. Foggini. It incorporates the richest of raised *pietra dura* flowers, fruits and insects, semi-precious stones and elaborate gilt bronze mounts, with terminal figures of horned satyrs in the corners, and is supported upon grotesque feet. The panels of *pietre dure* are framed in lapis lazuli bordered by gilt bronze mouldings. The composition rises to a peak of elaboration on the lid. The workmanship is of the highest quality.

The casket may have been purchased by John Chute, who travelled widely from 1722 to 1754, and who stayed in Florence, 1741–5. A bill in the Chute papers from William Vile dated 1752 refers to 'repairing a Stone cabinett' at The Vyne. Accordingly, the casket's splendid Rococo carved giltwood stand and glass vitrine (not exhibited) have been attributed to him. In 1752, The Vyne, near Basingstoke, Hampshire, belonged to John Chute's elder brother, Anthony, so the casket may have been a fraternal present. It was listed at The Vyne in 1776 (but not in 1754).

Anna Maria Massinelli (Giusti, 1988) dates the casket to about 1720, whereas Jackson-Stops (1985) places it at the time of Chute's 1741–5 Florentine sojourn, on the basis of the conservatism of the Medici workshops, which were then still producing caskets in Foggini style. The actual circumstances of this casket's acquisition are unclear, so the earlier date is preferred here. (CRow)

35. (pl.1.49)
Amber Tankard

Maker unknown, probably Königsberg (now Kaliningrad), 1659

Carved amber with silver gilt mounts, h 22.9cm, w 18.5cm, d 15cm

1659 carved on panel under the handle

The Vicar and Church Wardens of St Mary's Church, North Mymms, Hertfordshire

Provenance

Gift of Dame Lydia Mews to St Mary's Church, North Mymms, 1751

Bibliography

Rohde (1937), no.119, pl.53; Tait (1991) 2, pp.155–6, figs 174–5

Amber is formed from fossilized tree resin. On account of its unique qualities, it has been admired, traded and collected for thousands of years. It is commonly found washed up on the Baltic coast. The former Prussian city of Königsberg (now Kaliningrad) became established as an important centre of amber carving by 1600, producing curious objects for court consumption. Around 26 amber tankards like this one survive, mostly in the *Kunstkammern* of northern Europe. The panels of this example are carved with full-length female figures personifying the Virtues, and in this it resembles a similar tankard in the Residenz in Munich. What makes this tankard exceptional, however, is the fact that it is dated 1659 on the rear panel under the handle. Its loan by the church at North Mimms to the British Museum in 1901 secured its preservation and it has been on public display ever since. (DT)

The loan of this object is subject to legal formalities.

36. (pl.2.68)
Rhinoceros horn beaker
Maker unknown, Germany, *c.*1645
Turned and carved rhinoceros horn with silver gilt mounts, h 14.2cm
Skoklosters Slott, 35

Provenance
Skokloster inventory 1728. Given to Carl Gustaf Wrangel by the prince-bishop of Friesing, Veit Adam von Gepeckh, in June 1648

Bibliography
Bengtsson (1995), no.7

Under the beaker is a scene of a loving couple, in keeping with rhinoceros horn's perceived property as an aphrodisiac. The knop is in the form of a cupid holding a bow and arrows, while the scene is a hunting scene around the body of the beaker. The beaker must be that which Carl Gustaf Wrangel is known to have received as a diplomatic gift from the prince-bishop of Friesing, Veit Adam von Gepeckh, in June 1648. (BK)

37. (pl.2.67)
Ivory cup
Philipp Sengher (active 1681–94), also called Filippo Senger, Florence, Italy, 1681
Turned ivory, h 30cm, w 14cm, d 10cm
Inscribed under the base: FIL. SENGER. TORN.DEL. S. O. D. DI.TOSCANA .INVENT. ('Filippo Senger tornitore del signor granduca di Toscana invenit': 'Filippo Senger turner to the Grand Duke of Tuscany designed this'). A further inscription inside the bottom of the bowl reads: ANCHE LA FIGVRA. E.FATTA AL TORNO .A. 1681 ('the figure was also turned in 1681'). Both inscriptions have an inked-in background.
V&A: 74-1865

Provenance
Purchased at the sale of the collection of James Alexandre, comte de Pourtalès, 7 rue Tronchet, Paris, 6 March 1865, lot 1543

Bibliography
South Kensington Museum (1868), p.31; Maskell (1905), pp.297–8, pl.LXV; Longhurst (1929), vol.2, pp.89–90, pl.LXXVI; Aschengreen Piacenti (1963), p.283; Von Philippovich (1982), pp.428, 431

This turned cup and cover is a fine example of a virtuoso work of art produced at one of the great European courts during the Baroque period. The artist, Philipp Sengher, was the ivory turner to the Grand Duke of Tuscany, Prince Ferdinando de' Medici, and worked in the grand ducal workshops in Florence. Sengher probably came from South Germany,

although no evidence has been found so far of his exact place of origin. He was employed by the court of Denmark, as well as that of Tuscany. Appointed as tutor in turning to the Grand Duke, he made a lathe for him in about 1679–81. He also served as a courtier, buying pictures and works of art for his ducal employer, and accompanying him on trips, as well as paying other artists on the duke's behalf.

Sengher was clearly a turner of ivory, rather than a carver, and it is interesting to see here that even the figurative element, the supporting putto, is turned, not carved, as indicated by the inscription. Such elaborate turned ivories were avidly commissioned and collected by European royalty and aristocrats in the seventeenth and eighteenth centuries. Examples from royal collections survive in the Bayerisches Nationalmuseum in Munich and at the Green Vaults in Dresden, as well as at the Palazzo Pitti in Florence, where Sengher himself worked. (MTr)

38. (pl.1.4)
Flintlock pistol with the head of a classical warrior
Jean Louroux, Maastricht *c.*1661–87
Carved ivory stock, blued and engraved steel barrel and lock with silver mounts, l 57.8cm, h 12.4cm
The stock signed *Louroux a Maestricht*; stamped *IB* on the underside of the barrel
Skoklosters Slott

(pl.1.5)
Flintlock pistol with the head of a Polish hussar
Michel de la Pierre, Maastricht *c.*1660–65
Carved ivory stock, blued and engraved steel barrel and lock with silver mounts. l 51.5cm, h 12cm
The stock signed DE LA PIERRE-A MASTRICHT; stamped *CMCL* on the underside of the barrel
Skoklosters Slott

Provenance
First recorded at Skokloster in 1710

Bibliography
Rijksmuseum (1974), no.74; similar examples in Puype and Roth (1996), vol.1, part 2, pp.480–537

About ninety of these extremely exclusive pistols with ivory stocks, of which each of these is one of a pair, are known. They probably belonged to the Swedish general Carl Gustaf Wrangel (1613–76), who is known to have ordered several pairs of cavalry pistols from a gunmaker in Utrecht, testifying to the fame of Dutch gunmakers. The first ivory-stocked pistol made in Maastricht was a wheellock, probably made around 1650; the group of ivory-stocked flintlock pistols to which these belong were probably all made between 1660 and 1690. Their pommels are in the form of the heads of dragons, classical warriors or contemporary soldiers such as Polish hussars, and may have all been carved by the same ivory carver, as yet unidentified, before being fitted with barrels and locks by Maastricht gunmakers. Although the pistols are fully operational, it seems highly unlikely that they were intended for use, given the expense of ivory, but rather as display pieces; this is further supported by the direction of the heads, clearly meant to be seen face-on as if the pistols were hung vertically. The fashion for collecting firearms had developed from the sixteenth century with the invention of the wheellock mechanism and continued to gain further popularity with the invention of the

flintlock, which made the guns lighter and less cumbersome. (BK, JN)

39. (pl.1.15)
Ruby glass beaker
Mounts by Tobias Baur (*c.*1660–1735), Glass: probably Nuremburg, 1660–1700; Mounts: Augsburg, 1675–1700
Wheel-engraved ruby glass with silver gilt mounts, h 21.5cm, diam 9cm flaring to 9.8cm
Marks (on mounts): for Augsburg, TB
The British Museum – Bequeathed by Sir Augustus Wollaston Franks, AF.3147

Provenance
Bequeathed by Sir Augustus Wollaston Franks, 1887

Bibliography
Harden (1968), no.258; Tait (1991), no.236; von Kerssenbrock-Krosigk (2001), no.137

Ruby-red glass, which is made with a precipitate of gold (gold chloride), was especially prized in Germany in the late seventeenth century. It was first produced consistently by Johann Kunckel, an alchemist who worked from 1678 for Frederick William, Elector of Brandenburg, Germany. By 1684 he had perfected the technique. Highly prized by the princely courts, ruby glass was also made in Bohemia as well as Southern Germany and was often mounted in precious metals. Here the surface has been treated like a semi-precious stone and engraved on the wheel with scrolls, fruit and birds. (AD)

40. (pl.5.37)
Goblet
Engraving attributed to the workshop of Friedrich Winter (d.1711), Hermsdorf near Petersdorf (Piechowice), Silesia (now Poland), 1695–1709
Glass, wheel-engraved (relief-cut with polished details), h 18.6cm; d (foot) 10.3cm; d (bowl) 8.5cm
Arms of the Abbey of Sedlitz (modern Sedlec, Bohemia) and its abbot, Jindřich Snopek
V&A: C.2&A–1961

Provenance
Oscar Dusendschon Collection, Geneva, sold Sotheby's London, 9 December 1960, lot 34; H.U. Kuester Collection, Chertsey, sold Christie's London, 25 February 1936, lot 49

Bibliography
Von Saldern (1994), no.44

Venetian-style glassware, which had dominated the market for centuries, went rapidly out of fashion during the second half of the seventeenth century. Elegant and often elaborate shapes thinly blown by Italian virtuoso glass-blowers made way for much simpler, heavier and sturdier forms, ideal for engraving. New types of glass, which could be blown thicker and were harder and more lustrous, were developed especially for this purpose, and, simultaneously, engraving and cutting techniques were improved. Central European rulers vied with each other to patronize this luxury industry, often spending considerable amounts of money to launch specialized experimental workshops.

In the heartland of Silesian glass-production, at Hermsdorf in the Hirschberger Tal, Friedrich Winter established an engraving workshop sponsored by the local ruler, Count Christoph Leopold von Schaffgotsch. This highly innovative workshop, founded in 1690–91, was among the first to use engravers' lathes powered by water. The engraver was thus enabled to cut deeper into the glass surface with greater ease and speed, thus encouraging a new style of decorating, called relief cutting

or *Hochschnitt*, in which the whole surface was engraved and the background of the decoration entirely cut away and polished, leaving the pattern in relief.

During the innovative years under Friedrich Winter's leadership, relief cutting was at its most sculptural. After Winter's departure in 1694, the style became gradually less extreme and the engraving less deep. The workshop continued working in this manner into the 1730s.

The engraved decoration of the V&A goblet includes the arms of the Abbey of Sedlitz and its abbot, Jindřich Snopek, crowned by a mitre and two bishop's staffs. The surrounding ornamental strapwork is reminiscent of formal garden design of the period. It includes C-scrolls and stylized acanthus leaves, which can also be seen on the base of the bowl and on the stem. (RL)

41. (pl.1.27)
'Bucchero' vase
Maker unknown. Vase: Mexico, 1600–1700; mounts: Florence, *c.*1700
Earthenware with silver filigree mounts, h 20cm, w 20cm, d 15cm
Museo degli Argenti, Palazzo Pitti, Firenze, Bg.1917 (II) n.24

Provenance
Medici collection

Bibliography
Mosco and Cavazza (2004), pp.173–4

The vase, dating from the seventeenth century, shows both its Mexican origins and its subsequent adaptation to European taste through its elegant silver filigree mounts, executed around 1700 when the object entered the collection of Grand Duke Ferdinando de' Medici.

The fashion for 'bucchero' vases emerged simultaneously in seventeenth-century Spain and Portugal, whence it was exported to many European courts. It spread to Tuscany probably as a result of the long journey through the Iberian Peninsula made by Cosimo III in 1668–9. It is known that 'bucchero' ceramics were well represented at the Medici court: a large number were received as a diplomatic gift from Portugal around 1696.

This type of red clay was used primarily in Central America in the manufacture of ceramics, its use dating from before the arrival of the Spanish and Portuguese conquistadors. Mexican artisans continued to produce these types of ceramics, which were appreciated not only for their unusual material but also for their considerable dimensions, far greater than those possible with the firing techniques known to European ceramicists at that time. (CCal)

42. (pl.1.26)
Extended fan leaf depicting an imagined interior of a shop selling export wares
Artist unknown, possibly The Netherlands, 1680–1700
Gouache on paper, mounted on a wooden panel, h 26.3cm, w 43.6cm
V&A: P.35–1926

Provenance
Given by Sir William Lawrence, Bt

Bibliography
Jackson and Jaffer (2004), fig.1.4

Originally made as a fan leaf, its corners were later extended to create a small-scale painting. The scene depicted seems to represent an imagined interior of a shop selling export wares, including lacquered furniture, Chinese porcelain and redwares, Indian chintzes and small devotional figures of the Virgin and Child. This range of objects in different media suggest that the shop must be a European fantasy (they would not have been sold together like this in China, for example), a thesis further supported by the depiction of female shoppers in a fantastic mix of Turkish or Persian costume. The accuracy with which the wares themselves are represented, however, suggests that the artist was familiar with these kinds of objects. It has therefore been proposed that it may represent a loose depiction of an importer's shop in a European centre such as Amsterdam. This is further supported by the peculiar perspective which seems to imitate the Chinese style of painting, and by certain similarities with other Dutch fans of the period which also place real objects within imagined interiors to create exotic and fantastic scenes. (JN)

43. (pl.2.75)
Lidded cup
Metalwork probably by Wolfgang Howzer (active 1652–88); cup, China, 1630–40; mounts, probably England, 1660–70
Hard-paste porcelain cup with silver gilt cover and mounts, h 30.6cm, w 32cm, d 16cm
Marks: WH above a cherub
V&A: M.308–1962
Provenance
Temple family at Stowe until 1848; Christie's, 15 August 1848, lot 108; bequeathed by Claude D. Rotch
Bibliography
Glanville (1996), pp.115–16; Snodin and Styles (2001), fig.1

Originally made as a holder for writing brushes, this cup was personalized by its English owner by commissioning silver-gilt mounts that reflected status and ownership. The goldsmith has made an unusual effort to complement the decoration on the porcelain, copying the image of the flowers, the Chinese table and the incense burner on the elaborate silver-gilt cover. The greyhound handles and hound finial probably represent a family heraldic crest, perhaps that of the Arkinstall family of Cambridgeshire described as 'on a mount vert a greyhound sejant'. Later acquired by the dukes of Buckingham and Chandos, the cup adorned one of the drawing room closets at Stowe, Buckinghamshire, until 1848.

The maker's mark WH has been attributed to Wolfgang Howzer, goldsmith of Zurich, who was apprenticed to his father and gained his freedom in 1652. Howzer worked in London in the 1660s and made communion plate for St George's Chapel, Windsor, and for Bishop Cosin's private chapel at Bishop Auckland, County Durham. The earliest London-made silver by Howzer bears other makers' marks, but, after 1664, a letter of recommendation from Charles II to the London Goldsmiths' Guild enabled Howzer to register his own mark. He subsequently became 'Embosser in Ordinary' to the king. Similar handle mounts with hounds, also marked WH but with a scallop, embellish a ruby glass cup of about 1660 from the collection of Baron Fairhaven at Anglesey Abbey. A pair of Japanese Arita porcelain bowls of about 1665 in the J. Paul Getty Museum display the same marks as the present cup. (TM)

44. (pl.2.78)
Tulip vase on a wooden stand
Vase: Delft, The Netherlands, before 1694
Adrianus Koeks (active 1687-1701); 'Greek A' Factory
Stand: England or The Netherlands, probably 1700–50; possibly after Daniel Marot (1661–1752)
Tin-glazed earthenware, painted blue and white; on carved wooden stand; Vase: h 103cm, w 50cm, d 50cm; Stand: h 61cm, w 52cm, d 52cm
Crowned arms and monogram WMRR (Wilhelmus Maria Rex Regina) of William and Mary; marked AK for Adrianus Koeks
The Royal Collection, RCIN 1082.1
Provenance
Made for Queen Mary's Water Gallery at Hampton Court
Bibliography
Lane (1949); Wilson (1972); Archer (1984); Ayers (1994); Aken-Fehmers (2007)

The fashion for collecting oriental porcelain and for commissioning European ceramics which imitated oriental wares was enthusiastically taken up by Queen Mary at Het Loo and Honselaarsdijk and, after she and William III came to the British throne in 1689, at Hampton Court and Kensington Palace. This vase is one of four pairs and one single piece surviving from her Water Gallery at Hampton Court, where she had a suite of private apartments, including a 'Delft-Ware Closett', a 'Looking Glass Closett', a 'Marble Closett' and a 'Bathing Closett' with an adjoining dairy. The Water Gallery was where Queen Mary's extensive collection of porcelain and Delftware was displayed; engravings by Daniel Marot possibly relating to it give some indication of the massed architectural displays that were popular in palace porcelain cabinets at this time. This vase can be dated by the inclusion of the interlinked initials of the king and queen to before her death in 1694, after which the Water Gallery was abandoned and later destroyed by William III; its decoration also incorporates Tudor roses, Scottish thistles, Irish harps and French *fleurs-de-lis*. Its spouts show that it was designed to hold flowers, possibly tulips; Mary's interest in plants, as well as porcelain, would have had the chance to develop in The Netherlands, the principal importer of exotic goods to Europe. Although this stand, in the Dutch auricular style, is not original to the vase, it is very probable that the vase would have had a stand of some kind, just as vases, candle holders and orange trees stood on stands in the *Galerie des Glaces* at Versailles for the reception of the King of Siam. (JN)

45. (pl.2.81)
Coffee pot
Meissen porcelain factory, Meissen, Germany, 1710–13
Red stoneware (Böttger stoneware), black glazed and painted in unfired lacquer colours, h 15.3cm, w 12.8cm, d 6.8cm
V&A: C.160&A–1937
Provenance
Bought from H.E. Bäcker
Bibliography
Cassidy-Geiger (2004); Kopplin (2004)

For the stoneware body and shape see cat.46. Much Böttger stoneware was left plain, but a great deal was decorated, whether by polishing, wheel engraving, faceting, painting in enamels or gold, or painting in lacquer colours over a black glaze – often but not always in imitation of Asian lacquer – as here. Black-glazed wares were among the very first Meissen productions displayed and offered for sale in 1710 at the Leipzig Easter Fair, held to promote Saxony's industries and luxury goods, when they were described in the *Leipzig Gazette* as 'lacquered like the most beautiful Japanese products'. The lacquer painting is traditionally attributed to the workshop of the Dresden court lacquerer Martin Schnell, who was paid for work at or for the Meissen factory between 1711 and 1715. Very little of the lacquer decoration on Böttger stoneware can be attributed to Schnell himself, however, and the style and quality of the work vary enormously. The decoration here imitates Japanese *maki-e* (literally 'sprinkled picture') lacquer. At least some of the designs on these black-glazed wares were based on European 'Japanning' pattern books and Chinese woodcuts. Decoration of Böttger blackwares ceased in 1713, leaving very large stocks of undecorated wares at the factory. There is growing evidence that the very earliest Meissen wares were little if ever used, but were primarily intended for display. Certainly, the unsold 'useful' Böttger stonewares transferred from Meissen to Augustus the Strong's 'Japanese Palace' in 1733 would have been set upon brackets in tiered ornamental displays rather than put to practical use. (HY)

46. (pl.2.80)
Coffee pot
Meissen porcelain factory, Meissen, Germany, 1710–13
Red stoneware (Böttger stoneware), h 16cm, w 13cm, d 7.1cm
Inscriptions: '132 R' painted in black
V&A: C.26:1&2–2006
Provenance
'Japanese Palace', Dresden; sold from the Royal Saxon Collections, Rudolphe Lepke, Berlin, 12 October 1920, lot 95 or 96; thence private collections by descent; accepted by H.M. Government in lieu of inheritance tax and allocated to the V&A, 2006
Bibliography
Boltz (2000); Cassidy-Geiger (2004)

The coffee pot is made in the red stoneware body that the Meissen factory produced from its foundation in 1710 until 1713, when commercial manufacture of porcelain was achieved and production of stoneware was run down or discontinued. Both materials were developed by the alchemist Johann Friedrich Böttger, who had been arrested by Augustus the Strong, elector of Saxony and king of Poland, and ordered first to transmute gold, and then to make porcelain. In 1707 he succeeded in making a red stoneware similar to the Chinese redwares from Yixing, which were much sought after in Europe, and in the following year he became the first European to make 'true' or 'hard-paste' porcelain of the East Asian type. Most Böttger stonewares – described in factory documents as 'red porcelain' or 'Jasper porcelain' – were made in plaster moulds, often with integrally formed relief decoration, as here. Many of the vessel shapes derive from European metalwork, and the design of these has traditionally been attributed to the Dresden court goldsmith Johann Jakob Irminger, who is known to have made design models in hammered copper for the factory. This coffee pot, however, has much in common with English Huguenot silver, and may combine elements from French silver prototypes, now lost, with a spout and scrolled strut derived from Yixing stoneware and Chinese porcelain respectively. The mark is an inventory number for the 'Brown Saxon' wares at the 'Japanese Palace', Dresden, to which some of the factory's unsold stocks of stonewares were transferred in 1733. (HY)

47. (pl.2.74)
Ostrich egg cup
Metalwork by Benjamin Herfurth (1684–1759), porcelain by Johann Joachim Kändler (1706–75), Dresden, Germany, 1734
Ostrich egg with enamelled porcelain, gold and silver mounts, h 42.6cm, diam 13.5cm
Monogram of Augustus III as king of Poland; inscription on reverse, on enamelled medallion: 'Im Vier/und dreisigsten Nach/Siebzehn hundert Iahr,/Da Pohlens Oberhaupt/AVGVST der III war,/Fiel hier in MORIZBURG/diss schoene Straussen Ey:/Trinck aus und Wunsch/dem Herrn und/Churhaus Gluck dabey!/den XXVI Aprill/MDCCXXXIV'
Grünes Gewölbe, Staatliche Kunstsammlungen Dresden, III 224
Provenance
Mentioned in Inventar Pretiosenzimmer 1733, p.43, no.61 (as a later entry); in Inventar Kaminzimmer 1818, p.59, no.41
Bibliography
Schmidt and Syndram (1997), no.685; Kappel and Weinhold (2007), pp.277–8; Bock (2005), no.165

According to its inscription, the cup dates from shortly after the coronation of Elector Frederick Augustus II of Saxony as king of Poland (as Augustus III) on 17 January 1734, and serves as a remarkable commemoration of this event. The monarch's insignia are emblazoned on the breast of the ostrich: below the crowned monogram, the Saxon-Polish arms appear together with the ornaments of the Golden Fleece and the Polish Order of the White Eagle.

In its unusual combination of materials the cup fuses tradition and modernity. It alludes to the *Kunstkammer* founded in 1560, which in 1595 contained fourteen of these exotic natural history specimens, half of which were made into silver-gilt drinking vessels in the form of ostriches. The vessel also impressively highlights the achievements of the porcelain factory founded in 1710 at Meissen, in which Johann Joachim Kändler worked from 1731, using his outstanding artistic talents to bring the art of porcelain to unprecedented heights. Kändler often visited nearby Moritzburg, to study from nature the exotic animals kept there, which included ostriches. Surviving work records indicate that in June 1734 he manufactured a 'Cup in the form of an Ostrich Egg'. The toast, inscribed in enamel, identifies the imposing vessel as a 'welcome' cup, which was used for particular festivities, possibly at Schloss Moritzburg itself. (UW)

48. (pl.2.79)
Tea table
Maker unknown, Java; altered in London, *c.*1680
Carved, lacquered and gilded teak with carved, turned and ebonized wood additions, h 74cm, w 89cm, d 50cm
Ham House, The Dysart Collection (purchased by H.M.Government in 1948 and transferred to The National Trust in 2002), NT/HH 149 1948
Provenance
In the Duchess of Lauderdale's private closet in 1683
Bibliography
Thornton (1978), fig.216; Thornton (1980), fig.88; Bowett (2002), pp.23, 156

The duchess of Lauderdale's inner sanctum at Ham, known as the Duchess's Private Closet, still contains many of her small cabinet paintings and family portraits. The inventory of 1683 shows that its furniture was mainly Oriental or japanned. The following were listed: 'Two cases of Shelves for bookes, Japanned/One Table of the Same./One Scriptore [fall-front writing desk] of walnut tree./One Cedar table./One Japan box for sweetmeats & tea./One Tea table, carv'd and guilt'.

One can easily imagine the duchess and her friends seated on the japanned backstools, clustering around the 'Tea table, carv'd and guilt', presumably this Javanese red, black and gilded low table. The table was provided with an ebonized English stand about 1680 to raise its height to that suitable for Western seating. Very similar, also with a scalloped top, but unaltered, and at its original height, is a rather bigger Javanese table at Dyrham Park, Gloucestershire (NT), acquired by William Blathwayt, William III's Dutch-speaking Secretary at War. There is also a similar, smaller, and unaltered Javanese low table or tray of the same date in the Duchess's Private Closet at Ham. These Javanese pieces would have been imported via the East India Company or the Dutch equivalent, the VOC. The latter is perhaps more likely, given the Dutch trading station in Jakarta, then known as Batavia. (CRow)

49. (pl.2.77)
Pair of vases

Queen Louise of Denmark (1667–1721) and Christian van Bracht (*c*.1637–1720)
Denmark, 1713–18
Carved wood with *lacque brillante* – japanned with tiny flecks of metal, h 30.3/30.5cm, diam 13.2/13.4cm
The Royal Danish Collections, Rosenborg Castle, Copenhagen, 32–244/32–245

Provenance
Given as a present to Frederick IV of Denmark

Bibliography
Rosenborg Castle (2005), no.463

In 1669 Christian van Bracht moved from Amsterdam to Copenhagen, where he founded a dynasty of court lacquerers whose members were active into the 1760s. One of his specialities was *lacque brillante*, a technique in which tiny flecks of metal are strewn into the varnish to give a glittering effect. Japanning became a fashionable pastime. Queen Louise, the wife of Frederick IV, who presented her husband with these two vases, was a pupil of van Bracht. The vases belong to a set of seven also comprising one red, two green, and two blue and white, which was inventoried in the Marble Room at Rosenborg Castle in 1718.

The form and colour of the vases clearly derive from Oriental porcelain. The set topped a cabinet on a stand together with two sets of Oriental ceramics, one white with green and gilt foliage, the other blue and white with pierced decoration. This formal mass array was matched by the cabinet itself, which was decorated with *chinoiserie* scenes in exotic woods and tinted bone on a ground of pale boxwood. In 1718 the Marble Room functioned as a semi-private passage between the king and queen's shared bedroom and the Audience Chamber of Frederick IV; a fitting place in which to exhibit a personal gift from a devoted wife to her unfaithful husband. In 1724 Frederick IV furnished his Audience Chamber with a set of furniture in multicoloured *lacque brillante*. By then the technique had become a hallmark of the Copenhagen court. (JH)

50. (pl.2.82)
Vase in the form of a turban

Lacquer-painting by Martin Schnell (1675–1740?), Dresden, 1715–21
Limewood, turned, carved and painted, h (with lid) 45cm, diam 29cm
Kunstgewerbemuseum, Staatliche Kunstsammlungen Dresden, Inv.-Nr. 46 996

Provenance
In the Palais zu Alt-Dressden, 1721; probably from the Porzellansammlung Dresden, 1945

Bibliography
Reichel (1978); Auer, Arnold and Arnold (1995), no.420; Kopplin (1998), no.16

The vase belongs to a group of 15 that were mentioned in the 1721 inventory of the 'Holländisches Palais', later called the 'Japanisches Palais', in Dresden, but it is not clear whether this vase in the Turkish style was exhibited in this palace, which was decorated mainly with objects from East Asia or in *chinoiserie* style. It is thought that this group of Turkish-style vases might have originally stood in the Taschenbergpalais or the so-called 'Türkisches Palais', where a Turkish room was installed until 1718. Being one of the major military powers in the Holy Roman Empire, Saxony had for many years been heavily involved in the struggle with the Turks. In 1683 the elector of Saxony Johann Georg III joined the famous Polish king Jan Sobieski with 11,000 troops and helped to defeat the Turks in the battle of Kahlenberg, thereby saving Vienna. *Turcomanie* was more than just a fashion in Dresden; it was mixed with fascination and respect for the mighty Ottoman Empire, which was still many years from becoming the 'sick man of Europe'. (AVDG)

The Theatre

51. (pl.3.23)
Model of the new public theatre in Bologna

Giovanni Battista Martorelli and Antonio Gambarini (1734–87), after designs by Antonio Galli Bibiena (1697–1774), Bologna, 1756
Carved, painted and gilded wood, h 89cm, w 192cm, d 62cm
Archivio Storico della Fondazione Teatro Comunale di Bologna

Bibliography
Lenzi (1975); Ugolini (1998), pp.74–84; Millon (1999), no.450; Lenzi and Bentini (2000), no.85a; Küster (2003), no.34

Antonio Galli Bibiena was appointed to design a new public theatre for the city of Bologna in 1755, having won the commission in public competition. The project had been conceived as early as 1747, the ruling senate deciding that the city needed a replacement for the inadequate and outmoded public 'salone delle feste' in the Palazzo del Podestà, particularly following the destruction by fire of the private theatre of Palazzo Malvezzi two years previously.

The model marks an important point in the design process for the theatre. In 1756, building work was suspended amid concerns over rising costs and Antonio was invited to submit his designs, in the form of architectural drawings and this model, for discussion by Bolognese nobles and citizens. Criticized for a supposed inefficient use of space, excessively ornate interior decoration, brick rather than wood construction and faulty acoustics caused by the 'bell-shaped' auditorium and deep proscenium, Antonio was forced to modify his scheme in order to retain the commission. These modifications can be seen in the *Pianta e spaccato per il nuovo teatro* of 1771. The model therefore serves both as a very rare survival of a design model for a theatre, which includes the original colour scheme and intended painted illusionistic ceiling, and as the only record of its architect's original intentions. (JN)

52.
Act III, Scene X of Metastasio's Nitteti, with music by Niccolò Conforto, performed at the Buen Retiro Palace, Madrid

Francesco Battaglioli (about 1710–96), Madrid, 1756
Oil on canvas, h 123.8cm, w 151.1cm
English Heritage, London

Provenance
Formerly at Marble Hill House

Bibliography
Bryant (1991), p.43; Urrea (1977); Torrione (2000); Küster (2003), no.112b

The Italian artist Francesco Battaglioli was employed at the Spanish court of King Fernando VI from 1754 to 1760 as stage painter for the royal theatres. The painting is thought to represent the final act of the opera *Nitteti*, written for the Spanish king with a libretto by Pietro Metastasio and music by Niccolò Conforto, first performed in the Coliseo del Buen Retiro on 23 September 1756. It provides a visual record of the huge dimensions of the lost theatre, exaggerated even further here by the artist. Another painting by Battaglioli, also formerly at Marble Hill House, represents a scene from the opera *Didone Abbandonata*, also performed at the Spanish court. Copies of both works exist in the collection of the Real Academia de Bellas Artes de San Fernando, Madrid, while two further paintings by Battaglioli, thought to depict the opera *Armida Placata* (once also thought to be the subject of this painting) are in the Opéra Garnier in Paris. The Madrid paintings were first attributed to Battaglioli by Jesús Urrea in 1977 on stylistic grounds. Those in Paris had previously been classified as 'school of Bibiena', the latter's influence evident in the scenery represented, with its retreating arches of Salomonic columns.

The two English Heritage paintings may have belonged to Farinelli, the famous castrato singer, musical impresario at the Spanish court. This is suggested by an inventory in the Archivio di Stato di Bologna of works auctioned after Farinelli's death and a contemporary account by Giovenale Sacchi, which mention 'certain pictures, where Francesco Battagliuoli expresses scenes from Niteti, and Dido, and Armida … in the said pictures everyone admires the magnificence of those scenes'. (JN)

53. (pl.3.6)
Two side wings from the 'Columned Hall' set

Johann Wetschel (1724–73) and Leo Maerkel, Bohemia, 1766–7
Tempera on wood, CK 8840/18: h 301.9cm, w 108cm, d 2.5cm; CK8840/19: h 253cm, w 82cm, d 2.5cm
The Castle of Český Krumlov, The National Institute for the Protection and Conservation of Monuments and Sites, CK 8840/18 and 19

Provenance
Made for the 'Columned Hall set for the theatre of Český Krumlov Castle

Bibliography
Jiri (1958), pp.71–95; Ptáčková et al (1993); Jiri (1994), pp.12–26; Zdenka (2001); Slavko (2004), pp.197–212

These side wings form one side of the seventh and eighth rows of flats from the set for a 'Columned Hall', used in the Castle Theatre at Český Krumlov. This aristocratic family theatre, originally founded in 1680–2 by Johann Kristian Eggenberg, was rebuilt and equipped with new machinery and stage decorations in 1765–7 by Josef Adam Schwarzenberg.

The wings are painted to resemble two interior Salomonic columns with Corinthian capitals, with a male figure wearing an antique tunic alongside. The reverse of the wing is undecorated and built up by transversal rods. The stage at Český Krumlov is equipped with stage-changing machinery which enables the front six rows of flats and backdrop to be moved simultaneously; these last two rows of flats, however, are fixed, with struts to support them. With a change of backcloth and the inclusion of the eighth row of flats, the 'Column Hall' stage set can also be transformed into the 'Temple' set. (KC)

54. (pl.3.10)
Violin

Attributed to Ralph Agutter (active 1670–1710), England, *c*.1685
Pine belly, sycamore back, sides and neck, and ebony fingerboard, h 58.5cm, w 20.5cm, d 3.8cm
Carved with the royal arms and mottoes of the House of Stuart
V&A: 34–1869

Bibliography
Baines (1998), pp.16–17; Dilworth (1999)

The back of this instrument is carved with an elaborate scroll pattern and emblazoned with the royal Stuart coat of arms used by Charles II and James II, indicating that it was made for the royal household some time before 1688, when William III added the lion crest. The peg box has a carved female head at the top and an *amorino* or cherub at the back. The base of the instrument is decorated with a female figure tuning a lute. The fingerboard may be original, but the tuning pegs and bridge are probably later replacements.

Although the instrument bears no date or label, it is very similar to a violin made by Ralph Agutter (Private Collection) in 1686. Both have virtually identical peg boxes and carved head finials, and the 1686 violin has a narrow strip of carved flowers and cupids running along its back. A number of bowed instruments are decorated with inlay, but these two are among the very few with carved backs. Agutter's workshop was in the Strand, London, and only a short distance from Grinling Gibbons's establishment in Bow Street. Although the carving on this instrument cannot with any certainty be attributed to Gibbons or his workshop, it is characteristic of the highly elaborate scrolled patterns in which he excelled, especially in the interiors of Hampton Court Palace, Middlesex, and Petworth House, Sussex. (JY)

55.
Cupid's bow and arrows

Maker unknown, Český Krumlov, Bohemia, 1750–1800
Gessoed and gilded papier-mâché, Bow: l 91.5cm, w 8.5cm; Quiver: l 54cm, w 14cm
The Castle of Český Krumlov, The National Institute for the Protection and Conservation of Monuments and Sites, Bow CK 10 113, Quiver CK 10 116

Provenance
Made for the theatre of Český Krumlov castle

Bibliography
Zdenka (2001), p.6; Vlnas (2001), nos I/2.97, I/2 104; Droguet and Jordan (2005), p.49

The bow and quiver form one of three identical sets in the collection of the Český Krumlov castle theatre. The gessoed and gilded bow comprises two square-section swan-necked pieces joined by a cylindrical grip. The bowstring is of golden tinsel cord. Theatre props were often made of papier-maché, as can be seen in surviving examples designed by Louis-René Boquet.

The quiver has a flat ungilded back and a hazel-nut-shaped tip. The face is decorated with palmettes and channelling in relief. The feathered ends of gilt wood arrows protrude from the semi-circular slot at the top of the quiver. (KC)

56. (pl.3.11)
Bassoon in the form of a sea dragon
Maker unknown, Italy, 1600–60
Wood (poplar), tongue of metal, bocal of brass (not original), total l 141.2cm, diam 5.9cm flaring to 10.7cm, max wall thickness 0.9cm
The Metropolitan Museum of Art, The Crosby Brown Collection of Musical Instruments, 1889 (89.4.881a,b)
Provenance
Acquired by Mary Elisabeth Brown 1880–90
Bibliography
Heyde (2007) 1; Heyde (2007) 2

This whimsical instrument is in the form of a sea dragon and was probably built as a stage prop and noise maker for underworld scenes. It is equipped with six finger holes and a metal pipe or bocal to accommodate a double reed. Composed of two chiseled-out halves glued together, its body is carved with fish scales painted sea-blue, while the dragon's head and the fins are gilded. Its provenance prior to its acquisition by Mary Elisabeth Brown sometime between 1880-90 remains unknown, but a similar instrument in the shape of a horned water serpent was acquired in Italy by the Cincinnati Art Museum in 1919. Both of the now hollow instruments may have been equipped with a tube system, later removed, which originally enabled them to be truly playable.

The sea dragon shows signs of much wear, poor repairs, and some loss of wood. Prior to its purchase by Mrs Brown, the instrument received uninformed restorations perhaps in an effort to make it playable. Damage to the gilding was touched up with bronze paint, the original blue-green paint was darkened, and later most of its surface was amateurishly painted with black wash. The bocal was added by a restorer who estimated its original length and diameter and at some point its neck was broken off and repaired. Despite this history of repair and losses, the instrument still documents the symbolic use of sound and forms to heighten drama and provides early evidence of a tradition of monster-headed instruments that continued into the nineteenth century. (HH)

57. (pl.3.21)
Design for a stage set with the hall of a palace opening to a garden
Antonio Galli Bibiena, Italy, 1728
Pen and ink, h 45.7cm, w 63.8cm
Inscribed: 'Apartamenti serenni che corrispondono a Reggi giardini'
RIBA Library Drawings and Archives Collections, London, SC 3/4
Provenance
Presented by Sir John Drummond Stewart, 1838–9
Bibliography
Jeudwine (1968)

The Bibiena family, famous across Europe from the end of the seventeenth century up to the middle of the eighteenth century, held a virtual monopoly over theatre design and construction thanks to their collective approach to their commissions. Their groundbreaking concept of the *scena per angolo* was first published in Ferdinando Galli Bibiena's *L'Architettura Civile* of 1711, after which it entered the theatre designer's repertoire. It broke with the established tradition of centralized perspective, by shifting the vanishing point and the view of the set as perceived from the auditorium. This not only disrupted the previously popular concept of a continued centralized perspective allowing the auditorium to continue the illusion on stage, but it also created a more radical disjuncture by removing the notion of the privileged viewer. Whereas perfectly symmetrical sets, with seemingly endless theatre flats disappearing into infinity, could be best appreciated from only one place in the auditorium (the ruler's seat or box), the *scena per angolo* privileged nobody and therefore allowed everyone to appreciate the illusion. It also benefited stage designers, as it could be produced with very few pieces of scenery, and was adaptable to even the shallowest of stages. This design is thought to have been produced by Antonio while he was working at the court of Vienna, assisting his brother Giuseppe; it typifies the emphasis on architecture on a massive scale often found in drawings by the Bibiena, with the central staircases breaking the symmetricality. The view to the left of a palatial interior seems to retreat into infinity, while the view to the right extends into a garden. (JN)

58. (pl.3.12)
Costume design for Hercules in *Atys*
Jean Berain the Elder (1640–1711), Paris, 1676
Pen, ink and watercolour on paper, h 37.5cm, w 23.5cm
V&A: S.1108–1982
Bibliography
de la Gorce (1986)

Atys was first performed in 1676 to the French court at Saint Germain-en-Laye, and later that year to the Parisian paying public, with a libretto by Philippe Quinault and music by Jean-Baptiste Lully. It became known as 'the king's opera' as it was so beloved of Louis XIV, being performed a number of times in his private rooms as well as to the entire court. The *dessinateur du roi*, Jean Berain, designed the costumes, which included the usual mix of classical figures such as Hercules and allegorical figures such as Sleep. The costume design represents Hercules in 'Roman' dress as was common for tragic or noble male heroes; he is identifiable as Hercules from his attributes of a lion skin and a club, and his stance is that of a ballet position. The character of Hercules appeared as a dancer in the prologue to the main part of the opera; such prologues were as important as the operas themselves as they openly praised the king (in contrast to the opera plots, which referred to him obliquely), and thus served as a significant part of the construction of mythologies around him. This design was not included in de la Gorce's survey of the large number of costume designs attributed to Berain and his studio; there is much work still to be done on the different hands often indiscriminately ascribed to Berain himself. (JN)

59. (pl.3.4)
Man's theatre costume
Maker unknown, Italy, 1740–60
Silk velvet with silver strip and thread embroidery, hessian under structure, h 165cm, w 82cm, d 82cm
V&A: S.92–1978
Provenance
Used at a private court theatre at Meleto Castle, Tuscany; possibly also used at the Ricasoli family theatre in Florence
Bibliography
Fowler (1982)

This rare example of a Baroque theatre costume is one of a group from the small private theatre at Meleto Castle, in Tuscany, which opened in 1741. Although the costumes date from the same period, they were not made specifically for Meleto, but were acquired later. Like many theatres in private houses, that at Meleto was hardly bigger than a standard room; the audience was very close to the performers and the candlelight shone equally on stage and audience. Thus while the silver embroidery would have caught the flickering light, fine detail would have been harder to appreciate; this enabled the maker to mix finely worked embroidery with bolder, more theatrical effects, such as the glass 'jewels' backed with cardboard.

For noble and tragic roles, Baroque opera and dance evolved a style of costume based on Roman military dress. Here, the chased breastplate and leather strip kilt have become velvet, adorned with silver metal padded embroidery. The velvets and metal threadwork, braids and fringing are obviously expensive, although the costume is built on to hessian to give substance and structure and the 'jewels' (mostly missing) are cardboard-backed glass. The costume is cut not from a single length of fabric, but a length patched together – possibly recut from another garment. The gold metal strip embroidery is finely executed and is certainly the work of professional embroiderers, maybe even ecclesiastical vestment makers. Although the fabrics are worn, they have survived surprisingly well on the inside of pleats and areas where the material has been covered. (SW)

The Square

60. (pl.3.27)
Equestrian statue of Louis XIV
François Girardon (1628–1715), Paris, *c.*1695
Cast bronze, h 102cm, w 98cm, d 50cm
Inscription on the edge of the cloak: GIRARDON IN. ET FEC.
Paris, Musée du Louvre, department des sculptures, MR 3229
Provenance
Acquired by the Royal Administration in 1784 and installed in the *salles des Antiques* at the Louvre
Bibliography
Francastel (1928), no.54, pp.27, 81; Souchal (1977–93), vol.2, pp.55–6; Martin (1986), pp.104–5, fig.49

Many statues were commissioned by municipal or regional institutions to honour Louis XIV. The first statues of him in Paris portrayed him on foot and were executed for the Hôtel de Ville and for the place des Victoires, by Martin Desjardins, unveiled in 1686. Further statues were erected in Tours in 1693 and Pau in 1697.

Louis wanted an equestrian statue like that of Henri III on the Pont-Neuf, or Louis XIII on the place Royale (now place des Vosges). He commissioned one from Bernini but did not like it, so in 1679 appointed Girardon to plan a statue for the front of the Louvre colonnade. At the end of 1685, Girardon received a commission for a huge equestrian statue for the planned place Louis-le-Grand (now place Vendôme). On 31 December 1692 the Swiss caster Balthasar Keller cast the horse and its rider in one single operation. The statue was placed on its pedestal in 1699; however, as early as 1695 the king had also ordered a bronze reduction of the sculpture. Girardon kept another example of this in his own collection, which is probably this statue.

Four equestrian statues were commissioned in 1686, including one by Martin Desjardins erected in Lyons in 1713, during the king's lifetime. The remaining three were erected during the Regency, after Louis's death. The statue originally intended for Nantes, cast by Antoine Coysevox in 1687, was finally unveiled in Rennes in 1726. Statues were unveiled in Dijon, by Etienne Le Hongre, in 1724 and in Montpellier, by Mazeline and Hurtrelle, in 1718. The projects for Toulouse and Aix-en-Provence were never realized. (GB-B)

61. (pl.3.29)
Preparations for the festivities to celebrate the birth of the Dauphin in Piazza Navona in 1729
Giovanni Paolo Panini (1691–1764), Rome, 1731
Oil on canvas, h 107cm, w 248cm
Inscribed: I.P. PANINI 1731
National Gallery of Ireland, Dublin, NGI 95
Provenance
Commissioned by Cardinal Melchior de Polignac; de Polignac family by descent; 3rd Lord Ashburton; 4th Lord Ashburton sale Christie's, London 3 June 1871, lot 31; purchased by National Gallery of Ireland
Bibliography
Arisi (1961), no.85; Arisi (1986), no.211; Wynne (1986), no.95; Kiene (1993), p.107; Arisi (1993), p.82; Bowron and Rishel (2000), no.264, p.418

This painting chronicles the installation for an elaborate fireworks display to celebrate the birth of a son and heir to Louis XV in September 1729. Arranged by the French ambassador, Cardinal Melchior de Polignac, these festivities did not take place until November, a testament to the scale of De Polignac's vision and ambition. The artist Pier Leone Ghezzi transformed Piazza Navona, using papier mâché arches, trophies and columns to evoke the square's distant past as the circus of the Roman emperor Domitian.

To ensure a suitably splendid record of his efforts, in 1729 De Polignac commissioned for the king a painting of preparations for the event, now in the Louvre. This 1731 copy, believed to be a personal memento for De Polignac, is virtually identical to the Louvre's painting in size and format, but with numerous small compositional variations. Curiously, the Palazzo Altemps, De Polignac's official residence in Rome, can be seen on the far right of the composition – impossible from Panini's vantage point at the centre of the square.

Giovanni Paolo Panini, or Pannini, a leading painter of Roman festival, had an unerring eye for detail. His precise rendering of architecture and festival apparatus was enlivened by animated groups of figures, often comprising identifiable personalities. Here De Polignac stands towards the centre of the composition wearing a black tricorn hat, red stockings and the Order of the Holy Spirit. To his right is the exiled Stuart royal family, then resident in Rome: James 'The Old Pretender' and his two sons, Princes Charles Edward and Henry Benedict Stuart. (ET)

62. (pl.3.14)
Charles XI of Sweden as Apollo Pythias
David Klöcker Ehrenstrahl (1628–98), Stockholm, 1670–71
Oil on canvas, h 107cm, w 84.5cm
Unsigned
Nationalmuseum, Drottningholm, NMDrh 179
Provenance
Commissioned by the Swedish Queen Dowager Hedvig Eleonora (mother of Charles XI) 1670; delivered by the artist to Countess Ebba Brahe 1671; Drottningholm Palace
Bibliography
Strömbom (1943), p.303; Sjöblom (1947), pp.98–9, pl.17; Johannesson (1968); Gunnarsson (1976), no.401, p.68, no.24; Rangström (1992), no.227; Rangström (1994), pp.74, 76; Olin (2000), pp.81–2, 86, fig.22; Lindell (2001), nos 184, 626, pp.44, 193, 196–7; Palazzo Ruspoli (2003), p.197, no.76

The court painter David Klöcker Ehrenstrahl was the dominant portraitist in Sweden during the latter half of the seventeenth century. He was well schooled in the use of symbols in art and royal protocol. In this painting the Swedish King Charles XI is depicted as Apollo, a role that clearly relates to the language of symbols surrounding the French autocrat Louis XIV.

The painting is not only a portrait symbolically depicting a monarch in the guise of an ancient god. The costume really existed and was worn by Charles XI in a ballet on his fifteenth birthday, 25 November 1670, when he played the part of Apollo. In the painting the god (king) has just descended from heaven and is shown at the moment when he takes an arrow from the quiver, in order to kill the dragon Pythias.

The portrait was commissioned by the mother of Charles XI, Queen Dowager Hedvig Eleonora. She, her son, the painter Ehrenstrahl and the two architects Nicodemus Tessin the Elder and the Younger formed a core of influential individuals who shaped the representation of royal milieux during the period known in Sweden as the Age of Greatness. (E-LK)

63. (pl.3.13)
Costume design for Louis XIV as Apollo
Henry Gissey (1621–73) or workshop, Paris, possibly 1654
Graphite, watercolour, bodycolour and gold paint on vellum, h 60.4cm, w 22.5cm
Inscribed: APOLLON. LE ROY.
The Royal Collection, 13071
Provenance
In the Royal Collection by the early twentieth century
Bibliography
Blunt (1945), no.72; Christout (1967), pp.72–7; related drawing in Christout (1987), no.30; Roberts (2002), p.417

Although Louis XIV did not officially use the figure of the sun god Apollo as his emblem until 1661, he first introduced the idea in the *Ballet Royal de la Nuict* of 1653, in which he first appeared in the role on stage. This drawing seems to show the king's costume for the same role a year later in the ballet *Les Noces de Pelée et de Thétis*, when he was fifteen. The king is shown in a ballet pose and holding a pair of castanets. His costume is clearly one of great richness, with silk, gold brocade, precious stones and a headdress of ostrich feathers; the decoration is in the form of tiny suns, reinforcing the Apollo theme. The costume seems to be identical to that of another drawing attributed to Gissey or his workshop in the Institut de France; the more finished quality of this drawing, as well as the use of gold leaf and vellum, however, all suggest that it is a presentation drawing rather than a design; it was common practice to produce such record drawings, which were often presented to patrons. Henry Gissey (or Henri de Gissey) was *dessinateur ordinaire du Cabinet du Roi*, in which post he was later succeeded by Jean Berain, and as such was responsible for designing costumes for the frequent and popular *ballets de cour* held at the French court. A number of drawings attributed to him or to his workshop are in various collections including the V&A. (JN)

64. (pl.3.44)
Carousel armour, sword and helmet of Charles XI of Sweden
Helmet and armour possibly designed and made by Nicolaes Millich (about 1630–99), gown made by Tolle Baillie, boots made by Jacob Schwartzkopf, Stockholm, 1672
Sword: gilded brass hilt, steel blade, l 68.5cm, blade l 52.9cm; scabbard: silk velvet on leather; helmet: gilded leather and ostrich feathers; armour: breast plate and backplate of gilded brass, skirt of gilded brass sewn to leather strips, undergown of linen, silk velvet and silk brocade with gold and silver lace trimming, buskins of leather with gilding and applied brass decoration, h 90cm
Marks: a sun on the sword blade
Livrustkammaren, Stockholm, Sword 2215; Helmet 06/6732; Armour 262
Provenance
Worn by Charles XI of Sweden during the Carousel of 1672
Bibliography
Ehrenstrahl (1685); Rangström (1992), nos 231–2; Rangström (1994); Gerstl (2000), p.134, pl.IX; Rangström (2002), no.212

The accession to the Swedish throne of the 17-year-old Charles XI in 1672 was celebrated with a carousel partly modelled upon the Parisian carousel of 1662. Four quadrilles, representing different nations, took part in the games. The king himself commanded the quadrille representing the Geats, an ancient Scandinavian people, but he and all his knights were dressed *à la romaine*, presenting Sweden as a great power akin to Imperial Rome. One source of inspiration for the carousel equipment was Andrea Mantegna's painting *The Triumph of Caesar*; another was Emanuele Tesauro's history *Del regno d'Italia sotto i barbari epitome*, published in 1664.

In addition to the king's armour in gilded brass, some other unique objects survive from his quadrille: two saddles associated with the armour, three Roman insignia, horns and fasces. The three main artists of Charles's court, the architect Nicodemus Tessin the Elder, the painter David Klöcker Ehrenstrahl and the sculptor Nicolaes Millich, contributed to the carousel. Ehrenstrahl documented the whole carousel in his illustrated publication *Certamen Equestre*, and also supervised the production of the participants' equipment. The craftsmen responsible for the equipment have all been identified in the palace archives. (LR)

65. (pl.3.38)
***Entry of the Four Quadrilles,* for the Carousel of the Four Continents, held in Dresden on 19 June, 1709**
Attributed to Johann Samuel Mock (1687–1737), Dresden, Germany, after 1709
Gouache and graphite on paper, h 58.9cm, w 91.6cm
Kupferstich-Kabinett, Staatliche Kunstsammlungen Dresden, Ca 199, fol. 6
Provenance
Mentioned in the Kupferstich-Kabinett inventory of 1738, addendum 1747
Bibliography
Gaehtgens et al. (2006), no.179.2

The Carousel of the Four Continents was a prestigious festival display in honour of King Frederick IV of Denmark in which – as with the ladies' Running at the Ring (cat.67) – hosts and guests actively took part together. Frederick IV presided over the Quadrille of the Europeans wearing a Roman-style carousel costume; Augustus the Strong appeared as chief of the African Quadrille, while dukes Johann Georg and Christian von Sachsen-Weissenfels led the Asian and American quadrilles respectively. After their entrance into the wooden amphitheatre, competitors from all four quadrilles had to follow a pre-arranged course, aiming various weapons at targets called quintains. Augustus had ordered that the four quadrilles should march into the arena from opposite directions: Europe opposite the palace; Asia through the indoor riding-hall; America through the fortification opposite the riding-hall and finally Africa from the fireworks ground through the newly revealed gate. In total, 170 large-format gouaches document this spectacular carousel. (CSc)

66. (pl.3.43)
***Duke Christian von Sachsen-Weissenfels as the King of the Americas* in the Carousel of the Four Continents**
Attributed to Johann Samuel Mock (1687–1737), Dresden, Germany, after 1709
Gouache on paper, h 58.9cm, w 91.4cm
Kupferstich-Kabinett, Staatliche Kunstsammlungen Dresden, C 5760 (Ca 197, fol.54)
Provenance
Mentioned in the Kupferstich-Kabinett inventory of 1738, addendum 1747
Bibliography
Schnitzer (1999), pp.156–7, 163–4

The cousin of Augustus the Strong is identified as the King of the Americas by his tall, elaborate headdress of coloured feathers, crowned with a crescent moon, and by his feather-trimmed carousel costume. He is accompanied by four footmen, similarly dressed as Native Americans and bearing his carousel equipment: a lance, a shield, a spear and a javelin. To ensure that the carousel would have a consistent level of magnificence, Augustus ordered that the costumes and decorations of all the carousel participants should be dictated by their rank. Consequently the leaders of the four quadrilles appeared in more elaborate carousel costumes than the general competitors, called avanturiers. This also applied to the heraldic shields which Augustus provided: while the aventuriers carried shields of base metal painted with their devices, the kings were supplied with expensive and splendid gilded presentation shields. Like the painted shields, three of these, including that of the King of the Americas (cat.69), were reused, having been made originally for a carousel in 1695. Only the Danish guest of honour received new equipment: namely, the surviving helmet and shield which make up the 'Eagle Garniture'. (CSc)

67. (pl.3.36)
Countess Werthern in the Ladies' Running at the Ring
Attributed to Johann Samuel Mock (1687–1737), Dresden, Germany, 1710
Gouache on paper, h 58.4cm, w 91.6cm
Kupferstich-Kabinett, Staatliche Kunstsammlungen Dresden, Ca 198 fol. 14
Provenance
Mentioned in the Kupferstich-Kabinett inventory of 1738, addendum 1747
Bibliography
Gaehtgens et al. (2006), no.176.2

The ladies' Running at the Ring formed the climax of the month-long festivities to honour Frederick IV of Denmark. For the competition, three racing lanes were marked out in the wooden stadium on the site of the modern-day Zwinger, and furnished with target rings. In the centre lane a lady in a chariot tried to pass a lance through the ring; on either side a knight on horseback also tried to pierce the ring with a lance. Their strikes were counted up and added, as a gallant gesture, to their lady's score. Twenty-four ladies, each accompanied by a charioteer, two knights on horseback and six on foot, took part in the courtly competition. Every lady drew by lot not only her three gentlemen, but also a pastel colour – Countess Werthern, for instance, drew *incarnat* (flesh-colour) – which was used as the principal colour for the group's clothes, decorations and chariot. For at least one of the ladies, however, it was not merely a question of luck: the *Mätresse* or official mistress of Augustus the Strong, Countess Cosel, 'drew' the popular *couleur de rose* (rose pink), and was escorted by no less significant knights than the Danish king as her charioteer and Augustus as one of her mounted knights. (CSc)

68. (pl.3.30)
Fireworks by night at the Camp near Warsaw under the reign of Augustus II
Artist unknown, probably Saxony or Poland, about or after 1732
Gouache on paper, h 57cm, w 85.9cm
Inscibed centre bottom 'Feu d'artifices, au Camp de Varsovie, sous le Regne du Roi Auguste second'
Kupferstich-Kabinett, Staatliche Kunstsammlungen Dresden, Ca 194 fol.118
Provenance
Dresden Royal Collections
Bibliography
On the Camp of Czerniaków: Marx (1976); Schmidt and Syndram (1997), nos 338–9

The image shows fireworks exploding behind an altar-like structure bearing the monogram of the Polish king Augustus II, A.II.R.P. (Augustus II Rex Poloniae), accompanied by a choreographed volley of rifle and cannon fire from the Polish artillery, recognizable by their green uniform with red facings. The inscription under the gouache, published here for the first time, suggests that it depicts the *Campement bei Czerniaków* organized by Augustus II from 31 July to 18 August 1732. This splendid military event – part manoeuvres, part parade – took place in the countryside between Warsaw and Wilanów. Polish, Lithuanian and Saxon soldiers from all army divisions participated. In 1730 Augustus organized in Saxony the *Zeithainer Lager*, manoeuvres for

27,000 men of the collective army. This formed the crowning glory of his extensive military reforms and served as a highly significant courtly and political event, to which he invited guests from across Europe. Similarly, the Polish Camp near Warsaw fulfilled an important role in marking the end of Polish military reform. In the centre of the camp was a royal enclosure with a two-storey Belvedere and a spectators' dais. In front of this was a battery of 19 cannons. Also in the foreground of the image, 12 cannons, already fired, can be seen with further cannons at the sides. The reflecting ponds and balustrades, however, do not appear in the plan of the Camp of Czerniaków which has survived in the Kupferstich-Kabinett (Inv. No. Sax.top. IV, 2.1). (CSc)

69. (pl.3.42)
Carousel shield
Johann Melchior Dinglinger (1664–1731), Dresden, Germany, 1695
Raised copper, gilded and with punched decoration and set with paste, velvet lining, h 48.9cm, w 37.3cm
Inscribed 'A LA PLUS BELLE'
Rüstkammer, Staatliche Kunstsammlungen Dresden, Inv.-Nr. N 168
Provenance
Inventar der Guten Schlittenkammer von 1708, p.107f, no.14
Bibliography
Nickel (1983); Grossman (1998), no.244

The shield belongs to a group of similar pieces made by Johann Melchior Dinglinger for the Procession of the Gods, held as part of the evening Running at the Ring entertainments on 7 February 1695. In this event Augustus the Strong played the role of Mercury, the messenger of the gods, who opened the procession.

This shield was used in two further festive parades held by Augustus the Strong. During the month-long state visit of the Danish king Frederick IV, Augustus organized the Carousel of the Four Continents, held on 19 June 1709 in a newly erected wooden amphitheatre (the forerunner of today's Zwinger). While the Danish guest of honour appeared in the guise of a Roman emperor as king of the Europeans, Augustus the Strong portrayed the King of the Moors. The shield was carried by an 'Indian' before the King of the Americas, played by Prince Christian von Sachsen-Weissenfels. Finally, on 15 September 1719, Augustus the Strong organized the Carousel of the Four Elements for the wedding celebrations of Crown Prince Frederick Augustus (II) and Archduchess Maria Josefa. For this event Augustus carried the shield himself as the head of the Quadrille of Fire.

The simple decoration of the asymmetrically curved shield consists of embossed scrolling leaves at each end and an apple, made from two beaten hemispheres soldered together, placed in a central hollow. A large, red glass (paste) jewel is placed in a box setting on the apple in place of a blossom. Around the apple, glass (paste) jewels or rock crystals spell out 'A LA PLUS BELLE' ('To the most beautiful'), referring to the golden apple of Paris. The inside of the shield is lined with red velvet and has two handles. (HS)

70. (pl.3.35)
Pair of horse ornaments in the form of suns
Johann Melchior Dinglinger (1664–1731), Dresden, 1709
Embossed and gilded copper set with rose-cut rock crystal or quartz stones, backed with polished silver foil; the stones in round chest settings of copper, partly lace settings (large stones), partly screw settings (small stones); mounted with a foot-plate to be screwed to the riding equipment; L454: h 18.5cm; diam sun 15–15.5cm; footplate l 5.8cm, w 2.3cm; L455: h 18.7cm, diam sun 15.2–15.4cm; footplate l 5.6cm, w 2.3cm
Rüstkammer, Staatliche Kunstsammlungen Dresden, L 454 and L 455
Provenance
Worn by the horse of Augustus II, for the Entry of the Gods and Night-time Running at the Ring in Dresden, 1709
Bibliography
Seibel (2004), pp.27–9, 243, cat.7.10

These two small sun ornaments are part of a set of parade riding equipment belonging to Augustus 'the Strong'. The original design of this repeatedly reworked set recalls a sketch in the king's own hand. The various phases of manufacture of the riding equipment mark the high points of his reign. He used it for the solemn entry for his Polish coronation in Krakow in 1697, and again in 1709 for a grand celebration in Dresden. This carousel was prompted by the military success of Tsar Peter I against King Charles XII of Sweden, who in 1706 had defeated Augustus in the Nordic War. With his ally, King Frederick IV of Denmark, as guest of honour, Augustus organized courtly events including an Entry of the Four Continents and an Entry of the Gods.

Taking Louis XIV as his role model, Augustus appeared as the sun god Apollo in the Entry of the Gods for the night-time Running at the Ring. For this self-fashioning he ordered from the workshop of his court goldsmith Johann Melchior Dinglinger a gilded copper sun mask bearing his own features and, as a new addition made for his coronation riding equipment, two small flaming sun ornaments with white stones, to serve as head and back ornaments for his ermine-coloured horse.

For the festivities held in Dresden in 1719 to celebrate the marriage of his son to one of the emperor's daughters, Augustus took the role of the head of the Quadrille of Fire in the Carousel of the Four Elements. For this event both of the 1709 horse ornaments were replaced with new suns with faces made from fire-red paste jewels. In this form, but renewed with blue silk velvet, Augustus's son Augustus III used the riding equipment for the entry to his Polish coronation in Krakow in January 1734. (JCB)

71. (pl.3.34)
Carousel lance
Martin Schnell (*c.*1675–before 1740), Dresden, Germany, probably 1709 and/or 1719
Wood, gilded over bole, gilt-bronze, gilt iron tip; gold thread fringe; silk velvet grip, l 243.5cm (tip l 28cm)
Rüstkammer, Staatliche Kunstsammlungen Dresden, R 286
Provenance
Probably used in the Running at the Ring at the Dresden Carousels of 1709 and 1719; Rüstkammer Dresden, Inventar der Guten Schlittenkammer 1785, p.125, no.280; Inventar der Guten Schlittenkammer 1793 p.41, no.163
Bibliography
Schnitzer and Hölscher (2000), no.54; Gaehtgens et al. (2006), no.192

This delicate, shiny, French-style gilded lance, with a blue silk grip, was carried by Augustus II, elector of Saxony and king of Poland, in the festivities held in 1709 in Dresden, either in his role as the sun god Apollo in the night-time Running at the Ring, or in the Ladies' Running at the Ring. He used it again in 1719 for his role as the head of the Quadrille of Fire in the Carousel of the Four Elements. Another gold-lacquered French lance belonging to the king survives in the Dresden Rüstkammer. Both belong to an extensive series of lances of similar carved form and decoration, made by the Dresden court lacquerer either in 1709 or 1719, or reworked in 1719. In keeping with the etiquette governing court production, the golden lances were reserved for the most important figures in courtly entertainments, in 1719 these being King Augustus II of Poland and his guest King Frederick IV of Denmark. Also mentioned in the Rüstkammer inventory are two 'Ladies'-Room-Lances of Gold Glaze', which were perhaps used by the favourite ladies in the Ladies' Running at the Ring. (JCB)

72. (pl.3.34)
Carousel lance
Martin Schnell (*c.*1675–before 1740), Dresden, Germany, 1719
Painted and lacquered wood, l 269.5cm (tip l 26.5cm)
Rüstkammer, Staatliche Kunstsammlungen Dresden, R 276
Provenance
Used in the Running at the Ring at the Dresden Carousel of 1719; Rüstkammer Dresden, Inventar der Guten Schlittenkammer 1717 ff. pl. 60–62, nos 72 and 73
Bibliography
Schnitzer and Hölscher (2000), no.52b

This delicate lance, painted orange and with gold Berainesque ornament, belongs to an extensive series of French-style lances made by Martin Schnell for the Running at the Ring tournaments organized in Dresden in 1709 and 1719. The pointed iron tip identifies it as a lance for use in the tournaments. Competing teams were distinguished by the colours of their lances and clothes. Many differently coloured lances, with a great variety of decoration in gold or silver, can be identified in the Rüstkammer inventories, and some survive. Ladies used smaller lances.

The Rüstkammer manual for the Running at the Ring held for the Festival of Venus, part of the wedding celebrations of the prince elector of Saxony held in Dresden in 1719, shows that 64 knights' lances – 18 in red and silver, 18 in green and gold, 18 in yellow and silver, 18 in blue and gold – as well as 36 ladies' lances – nine in each of the four colour combinations – were supplied.

In this event the electoral heir accompanied his bride dressed 'in the Roman style' in the colour 'cerise' (cherry red) with silver. This orange and gold lance cannot in fact be ascribed to any of the four main teams competing in the Festival of Venus, but its strapwork ornament points to Schnell's style of 1719. Indeed, for the Ladies' Running at the Ring of 1719 the participating 24 ladies and 72 knights used a large palette of *choisierten* (self-selected) colours (24 in total), but not, however, in combination with gold or silver. (JCB)

73. (pl.3.34)
Carousel lance
Martin Schnell (*c.*1675–before 1740), Dresden, Germany, probably 1709–19 but before 1733
Turned and carved lime wood, painted and gilded, grip lost, gilded iron tip with net, l 343.5cm (tip l 19.5cm; butt l 42cm; handle l 18cm), diam (max.) 10.5cm
Rüstkammer, Staatliche Kunstsammlungen Dresden, R 225
Provenance
Used in the Running at the Ring at the Dresden Carousel of 1719
Bibliography
Schnitzer and Hölscher (2000), nos 52–4; Siebel (2004), no.7.22; related objects in Gaehtgens et al. (2006), nos 188–92

This particularly long tournament lance for the Running at the Ring is among the most outstanding works produced by Martin Schnell, 'court lacquerer' to Augustus II, for the court festivities of 1719. Schnell strove to learn the technique, colours and ornament of Asian lacquer painting, and to introduce them to the king in various commissions. He created artistic pieces of furniture and display pieces for the king's state rooms as well as table decorations and numerous other furnishings and equipment for the famous court festivities at Dresden. Schnell also supplied tournament lances in *chinoiserie* style, suggesting that a courtly masquerade with an Asian theme was held, such as for the Entry and Carousel of the Four Continents in Dresden in 1709. The court jeweller also followed this trend, creating a Chinese-style weapon; a precious samurai sword with a real Japanese blade and Asian-looking (although rather gaudy) enamel decoration. The golden-brown to dark-brown decoration on this yellow-gold painted lance shows that Schnell took careful note of Asian examples, and produced sensitive but also rather stereotypical copies. We see elaborately composed rock formations, Far Eastern plants and animals, pavilions and a lady in a kimono with a parasol. Large areas of dark powdered pigment, loosely sprinkled and lacquered over, lend the landscape composition, reproduced with the realistic proportions of nature, an air of great refinement and reverence. (JCB)

Sacred Spaces

SPACE AND RITUAL

74. (pl.4.59)
Transferral of the image of the Virgin of Guadalupe to the new sanctuary, 1709
Manuel de Arellano (1691–*c.*1722), Mexico, 1709
Oil on canvas, h 176cm, w 260cm
Inscribed: Verdadero mapa del sitio en que se benera la milagrosa imagen de Nuestra Señora de Guadalupe de la ciudad de México Conforme se Zelebró la translación a su nuevo Santuario, el día 30 de abril de 1709…
Colección del Marqués de los Balbases
Bibliography
Museo de América (1999), no.3; Pierce et al. (2004), no.29; Rishel with Stratton-Pruitt (2006), VI–19

Arellano is the surname of several Mexico City painters not yet satisfactorily studied. The attribution of this painting to Manuel de Arellano, by Rogelio Ruiz Gomar, is so far the most likely. The long inscription identifies specific locations, as well as St Philip of Jesus, patron of the festivities, by number. A single letter, 'A', identifies a man walking before the viceroy with the phrase 'a good man called Juan', *un buen varón llamado J.a.* This has led to speculation that there might have been a Juan de Arellano.

This is one of the most notable city views painted in America. Besides commemorating an important event in the history of Mexico

City, when the miraculous Virgin of Guadalupe was moved to its new church, the painting is a map of the surrounding area, complete with compass, and a lively representation of the society of New Spain. Included are religious and civil authorities, groups in confraternities and parish associations, various classes, races, and ages. Participation in the festivities was wide-ranging: solemn walking in the procession, accompanying it with music as the Virgin stopped to face the city and spectators, parading as 'giants' representing the four continents, dancing in indigenous costume, riding allegorical floats, looking on from rooftops and the streets, enjoying the company of friends and family, and even swimming in the river during what is the warmest time of year in the Valley of Mexico. (CBa)

75. (pl.4.58)
Processional figure of Judas Iscariot from the *paso* of the Agony in the Garden and Capture of Christ
Andrés Solanes (d. 1635), Valladolid, Spain, 1629–30
Carved and painted wood, h 176cm
Museo Nacional Colegio de San Gregorio, Valladolid, inv. 511
Bibliography
Agapito y Revilla (1925); Fundacion Central Hispano (1999), pp.39–43; Museo Nacional de Escultura (2000), pp.39–43

Between 1629 and 1630 the sculptor Andrés Solanes earned different amounts of money for the *paso* or tableau of the Agony in the Garden and the Capture of Christ for Valladolid's Brotherhood of the True Cross. Records show the delivery and receipt of payment for this group. Recorded in the same account book are payments to other artists, including Jacinto Rodríguez, Martín López de Vallejo, Pedro Carrillo, Francisco García, who painted the figure of the Angel, and Gregorio Guijelmo, who decorated the rock for the same *paso*.

That so many artists were involved in creating the *paso* shows that the group once included more figures than it does today, in particular the figures of Christ and the Angel. Further proof of this is the way that the figure of Judas Iscariot points to something that is no longer there, clearly the person that the soldiers needed to capture.

The *Revelations* of the fourteenth century St Bridget of Sweden were a popular source of information about the life and passion of Christ for many artists. The *Revelations* provided details of the physical appearance of Judas which Solanes used to form this figure: Judas was short; red-haired and dressed in yellow the night Jesus was captured, yellow being the colour symbolically associated with treason.

There is a close stylistic similarity between the figure of Judas and that of Christ in the *paso* of the Agony in the Garden of Gethsemane. Not only do both have the same treatment of hair and beards carefully arranged in fine tufts stuck to the flesh, and clothes draped in ample and heavy volumes, but they also share a similar facial type. (JU)

ROME & THE PAPACY

76. (pl.4.7)
Ceremonial mace made for a cardinal
Giovanni Giardini (1646–1721), Rome, 1691–6
Cast and chased silver and silver gilt, h 109cm, w 25cm, d 25cm
Marks: crossed keys and umbrella (Bulgari Calissoni 43); basket of flowers (Bulgari Calissoni 363c)
V&A: 646–1906
Provenance
Presented to the Museum by Colonel W.F. Tipping, 1906
Bibliography
González-Palacios (1995); Montagu (1996), p.14; Lo Bianco (2005), no.172

This mace was made for an unidentified cardinal on his creation; it was a symbol of his authority, and was carried by a special bearer in ceremonial processions.

Originally, it would have incorporated his coat of arms, and at the top those of Pope Innocent XII who raised him to the cardinalate. After his death so beautiful and precious an object was not melted down, but later came into the possession of another cardinal who owed his position to Benedict XIV, and replaced the papal arms with those of Benedict. Subsequently it was acquired by Cardinal Carlo Oppizzoni in 1804. The preservation and reuse of such maces is not uncommon: the new owner would change the coat of arms to his own, and those of the pope to that of the pontiff to whom he owed his own elevation. He might also make further changes. In this case, while Oppizzoni put his own arms on the mace, he left those of Benedict XIV, probably because Oppizzoni was archbishop of Bologna, Benedict's native city, where his memory was still revered. Instead, he added an inscription referring to Pope Pius VII, and an image of St Peter (the first pope), each inappropriately surmounted by a cardinal's hat. Although the retention of Benedict XIV's arms by Oppizzoni seems logical, it leaves open the question of where the mace had been before 1804.

The Museum records state that the control mark of the silversmith Andrea Pini (1696–1710) is 'on the internal surface' of the arms of Benedict XIV (1740–58). This should mean that between these dates either Benedict's arms were worked on the same sheet of silver previously used for another pope's arms, or that changes were made to the structure of the top. Behind Oppizzoni's arms is said to be the monogram CCA.

Giovanni Giardini was the leading silversmith of his day, and published a famous book of designs for silver work. Nevertheless, the use of so Baroque a work in the early nineteenth century is remarkable testimony to the quality of this mace. Indeed, the ornamentation is quite restrained (more so than the two designs for maces in Giardini's book), with its three identical *putti*, scrolls and festoons of laurel. While one cannot exclude the possibility of alterations during the preceding century, it appears entirely coherent and perfectly proportioned, with a finely judged relationship of gilded to white silver, and of plane surfaces to ornamentation. (JM)

77. (pl.2.17)
View of St Peter's Square, Rome
Gaspar van Wittel (1652/3–1736) also called Gaspare Vanvitelli, Rome, 1715
Oil on canvas, h 56cm, w 109cm
Inscribed on central column: Gaspar Van Witel Roma 1715
Viscount Coke and Trustees of Holkham Estate
Bibliography
Briganti (1996), no.59; Laureati and Trezzani (2002), Kunsthistorisches version no.26; Barock im Vatikan (2005), Kunsthistorisches version no.44

The Netherlandish view painter Gaspar van Wittel worked for most of his life in Rome, where he was known as Gaspare Vanvitelli. He earned great success with his painted views of ancient and modern monuments of the city of Rome, selling them to Grand Tourists and local nobility and prelates. This view of St Peter's Square was particularly popular, with Van Wittel producing at least fourteen versions of it between 1684 and 1721, all based on a preparatory drawing, squared for transfer, now in the Biblioteca Nazionale di Roma, which was also published as an engraving in a tract by the hydraulic engineer Cornelis Meyer. The artist adopted a particular panoramic perspective in order to be able to show the church and its dome, both arms of Bernini's colonnade embracing the piazza with the obelisk at its centre, and the Vatican palace behind the colonnade to the right. He reused virtually the same viewpoint in all versions of the subject, and his composition was later followed virtually exactly by the artist Giovanni Paolo Panini in his own painted view of the piazza. Van Wittel's interest lay not only in depicting the space and architecture of the square, however, but in the everyday activities which took place within it: in this case the piazza contains a diverse range of figures including visitors to the basilica, horse-drawn carriages, bullock-drawn carts, nobles, soldiers, monks, beggars, donkeys and dogs. This painting, one of the later versions produced by the artist, is one of a series of five paintings of identical dimensions in the Holkham collection; of the others, four are also by Van Wittel. (JN)

78. (pl.1.44)
Pope Innocent X
Domenico Guidi (1625–1701), *c.*1690, after a model by Alessandro Algardi (1598–1654) of 1650, Rome
Cast bronze, h 97.5cm, w 87cm
V&A: 1088–1853
Provenance
Perhaps in the collection of Cardinal Giovanni Francesco Albani, Rome; and perhaps later sold from the collection of M. Magnan de la Roquette on 22 November 1841 and following days, Paris; purchased from John Webb, London, 1853
Bibliography
Museum of Ornamental Art (1853); South Kensington Museum (1868), p.3; South Kensington Museum (1881), pl.48; Maclagan and Longhurst (1932), p.160; Pope-Hennessy (1964), vol.2, p.626; Bershad (1970); Wittkower (1990), p.222; Montagu (1985), p.431, cat.156.D.1; Weston-Lewis (1998), no.29

This bust of Pope Innocent X is a pair to one of a later pope, Alexander VIII, also by Guidi; both are in the V&A's collection. Guidi's portrait of Innocent X is ultimately based on a terracotta model of 1650 by Alessandro Algardi, who was Guidi's master; this terracotta is now in the Museo Nazionale di Palazzo Venezia (formerly it was in the Palazzo Odescalchi) in Rome. Guidi's terracotta version of this prototype by Algardi is in the Palazzo Doria-Pamphili in Rome. Algardi's terracotta model, and several bronzes he cast from that model, differ from Guidi's portrayals of the pope, particularly in the drapery and details of the vestments. Guidi clearly adapted his master's portrait after both Algardi's and Innocent X's deaths. He was probably commissioned to make a posthumous bronze portrait of Innocent for the then reigning pope, Alexander VIII, to be paired with a portrait of Alexander himself, in about 1690 (the bust of Alexander is documented as being cast in April of that year). Innocent X had made the future Alexander VIII (then Pietro Ottoboni) a cardinal in 1652, and this may explain why the latter wanted his bust to be paired with that of his papal predecessor.

Guidi unusually cast and finished his own bronzes, and so this was probably produced under his supervision. The high quality of its surface can be seen in the details of the vestments, the low-relief birds and fleurs-de-lis encircled with foliate designs on the stole, and the subtle representation of the facial features. This sculpture is in the tradition of monumental bronze portraits of popes, such as the famous examples by Bernini and Algardi. The sweeping vestments and Baroque naturalism, while actually rooted in classical traditions of Roman imperial busts, give these portraits immense presence and power. (MTr)

THE TOTAL WORK OF ART

79. (pl.1.31)
Interior of St Peter's Basilica, Rome
Giovanni Paolo Panini (1691–1764) and his studio, Rome, 1730–42
Oil on canvas, h 149.8cm, w 222.7cm
Inscribed: Julio Paulo/ Pannini; also inscribed on cupola, ceiling of nave, sarcophagi above doorways and base of pillar to left
The National Gallery, London, NG 5362. Bought, 1942
Provenance
Du Cane Estates (Braxted Park, Essex) sale, London, 1942; bought from F.A.Drey, 1942
Bibliography
Levey (1957), pp.53–6; Arisi (1961), no. 134; Levey (1971), pp.172–5; Millon (1999), nos 7–9; Baker and Henry (2001), p.517; Bowron and Rishel (2001), nos 265, 277

Giovanni Paolo Panini and his workshop produced at least eighteen versions of this painted view of the interior of St Peter's Basilica in Rome. The first of these, by Panini himself and now in the Louvre, was commissioned in 1729 by the French Ambassador to Rome, Cardinal Melchior de Polignac, on the occasion of the birth of the French Dauphin (see also cat.61), and showed him among the visitors to the basilica. Panini depicted the church interior as if seen from the left of the main entrance, looking down the nave, with the Baldacchino seen at the crossing and the *Cathedra Petri* glimpsed through it in the apse. Subsequent versions of the composition, which used a similar but not necessarily identical viewpoint, have been classified by Michael Levey into three distinct groups, their dating determined by the construction date of the monuments they represent within the basilica. This particular version, therefore, can be dated to before 1742, as it does not include the monument to Maria Clementina Sobieski (wife of the 'Old Pretender', James III of England) by Pietro Bracci, erected in 1742 above the first doorway in the left aisle on the orders of Benedict XIV. Later versions show further changes, including the addition of figures to the monument to Innocent XII, added in 1746, and the insertion in 1754 of the sculptures of St Teresa and St Vincent de Paul in the niches of the columns of the central nave. (JN)

80. (pl.1.14)
Celebrations in St Peter's, Rome, for the Jubilee year of 1700
Johann Ulrich Kraus (1655–1719), Augsburg,

Germany, 1700
Print, broadside, h 48.5cm, w 42.7cm
Lettered: St Peters Haupt = Kirch in Rom (top right); Jubel-Jahr auf das 1700 Jahr (top left); Wahre Abbildung der Herzlichen grossen, künstlichen und prächtigen Kirch S. Petri in Rom, und was gestalten von Ihro Päpstlichen Heyligkeit Innocentio XII die guldene Porten mit dem Apostolischen Gnaden = Hamer…beschlossen und zugemauert worden; Cum Grat: et Privil.Sacrae Caesarae Majestatis. Joann.Ulrich Krausen sc: et Ex.
The British Museum, 1862.0208.317
Provenance
Acquired 1862
Bibliography
Hollstein XIX.292.B; Italian edition for different occasion in Tozzi (2002), no.IV.23
The main part of the broadside shows the crossing of St Peter's Basilica with Bernini's Baldacchino at the centre, as decorated for the Jubilee Year of 1700 during the pontificate of Clement XII. The crossing is filled with pilgrims, giving an indication of the massive scale of the basilica; temporary structures emerge from the crowds while banners hang from the cupola. A screen is set up blocking off the apse and the view of the *Cathedra Petri* to provide a temporary setting for the celebrations to take place. Below the main engraving smaller images show the ground plan of the basilica; the narthex with the Pope censing the door to the church before entering; St Peter's Square with Bernini's colonnade; the side and rear view of the church exterior; and the *Cathedra Petri*. The broadside also exists in an Italian edition, signed 'J.A. Graff i', produced for the canonisation of Lorenzo Giustiniani, Giovanni da San Facondo, Giovanni di Dio and Pasquale Baylon in 1690 during the papacy of Alexander VIII. (JN)

81. (pl.2.21)
View of the Cornaro Chapel in S. Maria della Vittoria, Rome
Attributed to Guidobaldo Abbatini (*c.*1600–56), Rome, *c.*1651
Oil on canvas, h 168.2cm, w 120cm
Staatliches Museum Schwerin, G 930
Provenance
Federico Cornaro Collection 1653; Sale Palazzo Cornaro a San Polo; sold by Finck before 1863
Bibliography
Lavin (1980), pp.77–140, 196–210; Marder (1998), pp.110–16; Bernardini and Fagiolo dell'Arco (1999), no.61; Millon (1999), no.65; Barock im Vatikan (2005), no.252
The Cornaro Chapel, designed and executed by Bernini from 1647 to 1651 in S. Maria della Vittoria, was commissioned by the Venetian cardinal Federico Cornaro, with the dual aim of commemorating the recently canonised visionary St Teresa of Avila and that of furthering his own aspirations for the papacy. This contemporary painting depicts the whole chapel, focusing on Bernini's sculpture of *The Ecstasy of St Teresa* above the altar, with the side *coretti* containing the sculpted figures of the members of the Cornaro family observing the event on either side. The painting serves as an important document of the chapel as it was when inaugurated in 1651 before various alterations were carried out, including the balustrade installed after Cornaro's death in 1659. The high level of finish of the painting, and of the detail with which it depicts the chapel, makes it unlikely that this was a *bozzetto* made during the preparatory process for its decoration. Instead, Irving Lavin suggested, and subsequent scholars have agreed, that the painting would seem to correspond with a mention in an inventory made at the death of Federico Cornaro of his collection, of a *modello* of the chapel, painted as a record rather than as a design for presentation. Although the artist is unknown, it has been suggested that it is likely that the painting was executed by a painter within Bernini's circle, possibly even Guidobaldo Abbatini, who painted the frescoed vault of the chapel; as yet, however, this attribution is unconfirmed. (JN)

82. (pl.4.46)
Model of the head of St Teresa, for the Cornaro Chapel
Attributed to Gianlorenzo Bernini (1598–1680), Rome, 1640–55
Terracotta, h 30cm, w 18cm, d 11cm
Museo Nazionale di Palazzo Venezia, Rome, inv 13270
Provenance
Acquired in 1949 from the Evangelista Gorga Collection, Rome
Bibliography
Bernardini and Fagiolo dell' Arco (1999), no.67; Barock im Vatikan (2005), no.257
This terracotta model for the head of St Teresa is one of very few surviving which relate to Bernini's work in the Cornaro Chapel. Its status, however, is disputed. The dimensions of the model and the measurements of and between its facial features are virtually identical to those of the marble sculpture in the chapel itself. This seems to exclude the possibility that it is a copy after the sculpture, as it would be almost impossible to produce something of such close dimensions given the shrinkage which occurs during the firing process. However, it also seems unlikely that it is a preparatory *bozzetto*, as this would not correspond with Bernini's usual working practice of producing sketch models rather than finished works like this, which presents the most precise details of St Teresa's face. The rather flat working of the clay has further suggested to scholars that the head cannot securely be attributed to Bernini. Instead it has been proposed that the head either represents a copy made for study or collecting purposes (although this fails to explain the dimensions in relation to the marble group) or that it may have been made during the design and production process, as a means of judging the lighting effects in the chapel. Questions of authorship similarly affect one of the other two terracotta models for the Cornaro Chapel, namely that of the angel and saint group in The Hermitage; the only model generally accepted as an autograph work for the commission is that of the members of the Cornaro family, now in the Fogg Art Museum. (JN)

83. (pl.4.46)
Bozzetto for the altarpiece of the Blessed Ludovica Albertoni
Gianlorenzo Bernini (1598–1680), Rome, *c.*1671–4
Terracotta, h 19.5cm, w 45cm, d 20cm
V&A: A.93–1980
Provenance
Probably by descent through the Altieri family in Rome to Principessa Christina Altieri; Theodoli-Bruschi family, Bologna; Heim Gallery, London; purchased by the V&A, 1980
Bibliography
Kosareva (1974), comparative pieces; Perlove (1990), p.17; Boucher (2001), no.55
The Blessed Ludovica Albertoni (1473–1533) was renowned for her acts of charity in Rome, and was officially beatified in 1671. In the same year her descendant, Cardinal Paluzzo degli Altieri, commissioned Bernini to enlarge his family chapel, where Ludovica was buried. The artist apparently undertook this work without requesting payment. This terracotta is a preparatory model for the finished marble. Ludovica is shown on her deathbed, but in ecstasy, experiencing a mystical union with Christ, her soul and body flooded with divine love. Her biographer reported that 'her face [was] aflame, but so cheerful that she seemed to have returned from paradise'. Her arched back and swirling drapery powerfully suggest her ecstatic fervour. The losses to the face, pillow, drapery and left foot probably occurred during the firing. A drawing for this work exists in the Museum der Bildenden Künste in Leipzig, and three other terracotta models are known (in the Hermitage, the Louvre, and a private collection). In addition a bronze version was auctioned at Sotheby's, London, on 7 July 2006, lot 80; its current whereabouts are unknown. The present terracotta seems to correspond most closely to the finished work. The theatricality and emotive power of the marble are seen here in embryonic form. (MTr)

84. (pl.4.42)
Bozzetto for the reliquary of the Throne of St Peter
Gianlorenzo Bernini (1598–1680), Rome, 1658
Terracotta and tinted stucco, h 58.4cm, w 29.2cm
The Detroit Institute of Arts, Founders Society Purchase, Ralph Harman Booth Bequest Fund, 52.22
Provenance
Possibly Chigi-Saraceni Collection, Siena; perhaps collection of Don Flavio Chigi in the Casino, Giardino alle Quattro Fontane or elsewhere; collection of Cardinal Mattei di Pergola; Conte Mattei di Pergola (Marches); C.A. de Frey, Lucerne, Switzerland; purchased from Dr Paul Drey, New York, 1952
Bibliography
Battaglia (1943), pp.244–9; Grigaut (1952–3); Grigaut (1953); Raggio (1983); Wittkower (1990); Avery (1997), pp.109–112; Darr, Barnet and Boström (2002), no.137; Barock im Vatikan (2005), no.81
Although the *Cathedra Petri* dates from the pontificate of Alexander VII, Urban VIII had commissioned Bernini, as early as 1630, to design a new altar in the Baptistery to house the most sacred relic of the wooden chair of St Peter. During his papacy, however, Alexander VII decided that it should be moved to the main apse of the basilica, where it would be framed by the great bronze columns of the Baldacchino to form the visual focus to the whole nave on entering the church. The work, one of Bernini's most ambitious attempts to create a *Gesamtkunstwerk*, involved a long and complex design process for which a number of drawings and, unusually, full-size sculptural models survive. This terracotta model shows the sculptor's design for the massive bronze throne-shaped reliquary at the heart of the work. The relief scenes depict the key scenes from the story of St Peter: the Miraculous Draught of Fishes; 'Feed My Sheep'; the Washing of the Feet and the Charge to Peter. The two standing angels executed in tinted stucco are the result of a later restoration; only their feet and wings are original. (JN)

85. (pl.4.40)
Model for the dove of the Holy Spirit
Attributed to Giovanni Paulo Schor (1615–74) also called Johann Paul Schor and Il Tedesco, after Gianlorenzo Bernini (1598–1680), Rome, 1666
Oil on canvas, h 222cm, w 178cm
Fabbrica di San Pietro in Vaticano
Bibliography
Fagiolo and Portoghesi (2006), p.175
The scenographic ensemble of the *Cathedra Petri* is illuminated by light piercing the window above the sculpted throne, containing the image of the Dove of the Holy Spirit. Rather than the window being executed in stained-glass, records in the Fabbrica accounts list the commission from Bernini to Schor to paint the work 'in oil with varnish on glass' (*Liste mestrue della Reverenda Fabrica di S. Pietro e giustificationi delle medesime, dell'anno 1666*, in AFSP, arm.42, E 7, c. 3v), while other records list payment for canvas bought specifically for the 'large window in the centre of the splendour of the Cathedra'.
The finished quality of the figure of the dove and the monochrome brush-strokes on the reverse of the canvas imitating the effect of the reflected light emanating from the Holy Spirit, which emerged when the work was conserved for exhibition in 2006, led Alfredo Maria Pergolizzi to conclude that it is most likely that this represents a presentation oil sketch for the design of the window, which was intended to be painted directly onto glass. Unfortunately this technique proved to be insufficiently hardy: records show that by 1770 it was already in need of repair. It was again replaced in 1801 before the current window was installed in 1911. (JN)

86. (pl.4.41)
The Throne of St Peter
François Spierre (1639–81) after a drawing by Giacinto Gimignani (1606–81) and Lazzaro Morelli (1608–90), France, 1666
Etching, h 79.2cm, w 51.7cm
Lettered: ALEXANDER VII PONT MAX / Cathedrum S. Petri in interiore templi fronte ingredientibus ab ipso limine, e regione aspectabilem, decntius collocavit exornavitq. Sancti Ecclesiae Doctores / Athanasius, Io. Christostomus, Ambrosius, Augustinius colossea statura unica aeris fusura expressi, thecam sustinent, qua includir. Angeli, nubes, radii, de Caelo, am / biunt. Spiritus Sanctus columbae specie supereminems opus coronat. Bastis ex Iaspide, vario, pretiosoq. Distincta lapide. Caetera ex aere auro superinducto A. S. MDCLXVI / Eques Io. Laurenz. Bernin Inv. Franciscus Spier Sculp.
The British Museum – Donated by Nan Ino Cooper, Baroness Lucas of Crudwell and Lady Dingwall, 1719.1208.2233
Provenance
Donated by Nan Ino Cooper, Baroness Lucas of Crudwell and Lady Dingwall
Bibliography
Battaglia (1943), p.180; Martinelli (1981), pp.22-3; Martinelli (1983–4); van der Wall (1987), pp.62–3, 169, R14; Bernardini and Fagiolo dell'Arco (1999), no.91; Barock im Vatikan (2005), no.84
Executed after a preparatory drawing by Giacinto Gimignani and Lazzaro Morelli now in the Biblioteca Apostolica Vaticana (Archivio Chigi 24924), Spierre's etching of the *Cathedra Petri* was produced shortly after its inauguration on 19 February 1666, to the orders of Pope Alexander VII. As its inscription indicates, the etching was intended to record

and publicise Bernini's work and thus glorify and immortalize Alexander VII as its patron. Spierre had already produced etchings of some of Bernini's previous works. The image and inscription document the whole sculptural ensemble within its architectural context. Four sculpted figures of the Doctors of the Church hold up the throne containing the relic of the original throne of St Peter itself, below the window depicting the Dove of the Holy Spirit, surrounded by a sunburst of rays and tumbling cherubic figures. The print is important evidence of the original appearance of this window, which does not survive in its original form. (JN)

FURNISHINGS

87. (pl.4.5)
The Virgin of the Immaculate Conception
Attributed to António Machado (d.1810), Lisbon, 1775–1810
Carved, painted, gilded and silvered pine, with glass eyes, h 235cm, w 85cm, d 65.5cm
Museu Nacional de Arte Antiga, Lisboa, 2475 Esc
Provenance
Acquired on the art market, 2005; collection of the architect Tertuliano de Lacerda Marques; originally in an unidentified church in Lisbon
Bibliography
Franco and Rodrigues (2006); similar example in Levenson (1993), no.94; Lisbon (2005), pp.356–9, cat.255
This figure, despite its late dating, is infused with the traditional aesthetics of Portuguese sculpture as well as those of *docere*, *delectare* and *movere* associated with Baroque imagery. The crescent moon, the cherubim and the serpent are all characteristic elements of the iconography of the Virgin of the Immaculate Conception; added to this is a sculptural dynamism in the drapery, giving the composition a sense of movement, torsion and pathos.

Both the scale and quality of the execution imply a significant commission, although details of this are as yet unknown. The suggestion that only a relatively large workshop would have been capable of producing it initially led the sculpture to be considered as related to the work of Joaquim Machado de Castro (1731–1822), the royal sculptor. Although it is true that much Lisbon-produced work does look back to Machado de Castro's workshop, it is nonetheless also true that the capital was an artistically vibrant centre, particularly in the period of reconstruction following the earthquake of 1755.

This piece can be attributed to António Machado, a student of the Rome-trained Baroque sculptor José de Almeida (c.1700–60), on the basis of stylistic similarities with his other works. Although it shows a clear debt to sculptures by Machado de Castro such as his *Charity* on the façade of the Basilica of Estrela, as with his *Venus and Cupid* at the Janelas Verdes fountain, nonetheless, the canon of the head, the definition of the lower part of the drapery of the Virgin's mantle, the morphology of her feminine hands and the scenographic effect of her agitated mantle, resembling a fluttering piece of cloth, clearly point to the work of António Machado. (MJVC)

88. (pl.4.6)
The Virgin of the Immaculate Conception
Giovanni Battista Tiepolo (1696-1770), Aranjuez, Spain, 1767

Oil on canvas, h 279cm, w 152cm
Museo Nacional del Prado, Madrid, P00363
Provenance
Commissioned for the convent church of S. Pascual Baylon in Aranjuez by Charles III of Spain
Bibliography
Whistler (1985); Whistler (1998); Courtauld sketch in Seydl (2005)
This was one of seven altarpieces commissioned by Charles III of Spain in March 1767 for the church of the new convent of S. Pascual Baylon at Aranjuez, the first major religious foundation set up by the king. The convent was a Franciscan institution and so the altarpieces depicted Franciscan saints or patrons or cults associated with the order, such as that of the Virgin of the Immaculate Conception. Within the scheme of the church, this painting was displayed as the altarpiece on the altar to the left of the high altar. The commission was a significant one in Tiepolo's artistic development as the first in which he had to carry out the entire decoration of an interior in a series of individual canvases rather than fresco painting. A presentation *modello* for the painting, made for approval by Charles III himself, is in the collections of the Courtauld Institute in London, comparison with the final painting showing the alterations made by the artist following the completion of the building of the church and subsequent modulations of lighting. The Virgin is represented in the altarpiece as a majestic and remote figure, trampling on the serpent of evil and standing on a crescent moon, both a symbol of chastity and a reference to the Biblical Woman of the Apocalypse. The series of altarpieces was installed in S. Pascual in 1770; however, they were very soon removed and replaced with paintings by the artist Anton Raphael Mengs and his followers, whose more academic style was preferred by the king. (JN)

89. (pl.4.48)
Virgin of Sorrows
Antônio Francisco Lisboa (1738–1814), called O Aleijadinho, Brazil, 1791–1812
Carved and painted wood, h 83cm, w 48cm, d 34cm
Museu de Arte Sacra de São Paulo – Organização Social de Cultura / Secretaria de Estado da Cultura / Governo do Estado de São Paulo – SP – Brazil
Provenance
Acquired in the antiques market by Heloisa and Haroldo Graça Couto; acquired by the Museu de Arte Sacra de São Paulo; registered by IPHAN 1963
Bibliography
Ribeiro de Oliveira (2002) no.37; Rishel with Stratton-Pruitt (2006), pp.50–1
The iconography of the Virgin of Sorrows or Mater Dolorosa was particularly popular in Counter-Reformatory Portugal and subsequently in Brazil, where a number of churches and images were dedicated to her cult. The name refers to the Seven Sorrows of the Virgin's life, represented by the seven swords which pierce her heart. This seated figure may have been made for a side altar or small chapel, although its origin is not known. It was first attributed to Aleijadinho, the principal sculptor of the Brazilian Baroque, in 1969 by Lygia Martins Costa and later supported by Myriam Andrade Ribeiro de Oliveira on stylistic grounds including the almond-shaped eyes, chiselled facial features and sharply diagonal shaping of the drapery. The sculpture is carved from more than one

block of wood painted in oils; the decoration on the hem of the Virgin's dress is a later addition. She originally would have had a crown of seven stars, representing the seven sorrows, or twelve stars, symbolizing the twelve tribes of Israel. (JN)

90. (pl.4.49)
Altarpiece of the Virgin of Sorrows
Artist unknown, Mexico; statue: Naples, Italy; painting of St Lucy: Italy; c.1690
Carved, painted and gilded wood, set with oil on panel and canvas, and with silver, textile and glass, h 615.5cm, w 425.3cm, d 74cm
Fundación Televisa A.C.
Provenance
Church of the Jesuit Hacienda of S. Lucía, Estado de México; Hotel Fundición, Zimapan, Hidalgo; Collection Borbolla, Cuernavaca, Morelos
Bibliography
Metropolitan Museum of Art (1990), no.146; Bargellini (1993); Rishel with Stratton-Pruitt (2006), no.VI–15
This is an altarpiece of 'Salomonic' type, so called because of its twisted columns, based on those thought to have come from Solomon's temple, which inspired Bernini. Such altarpieces were current between about 1650 and 1730. This particular design, with its arched frame and angels bearing symbols of the Passion, recalls descriptions of a lost altarpiece built by Tomás Juárez with paintings by Juan Correa for the Mexico City Jesuit church of S. Pedro y S. Pablo. This church is next to the college of the same name, which was supported by the profits of the hacienda of S. Lucía. It is likely that the altarpiece was made by the same workshop, since the authorities of the college supervised activities at the hacienda. The combination of sculpted figures with symbolic and narrative paintings provides a variety of topics for meditation. The Italian painting of St Lucy, at the top, replaces an original Crucifixion. The Virgin of Sorrows is from Naples, according to inventories. Some of the paintings are based on Jerónimo Nadal's *Annotations and Meditations on the Gospels*. The visual precedents, and the inclusion of imported and local works, testify to the capacity for integrating multiple elements by artists working for the Jesuits in seventeenth-century New Spain. (CBa)

91. (pl.4.24)
Font house from Ringsaker Church
Lars Jenssen Borg (c.1652–1710), made for Ringsaker, Norway, 1704
Carved and joined painted and gilded wood, h 309cm, w 223cm, d 183.5cm
Inscribed to the effect that the painting was paid for by Niels Nielsen Hedemark and his wife Maren Christensdatter in honour of God and the decoration of the church in 1713
Norsk Folkemuseum, NF.1941–0148
Provenance
Ringsaker Church, Hedmark, 1704–1865; Nordiska Museet, Stockholm, 1886–1938; deposited Norsk Folkemuseum, 1938
Bibliography
Hauglid (1950), pp.40, 43–4; Préaud (1999), no.2105
This font house, a small chapel where baptisms took place, was made for Ringsaker Church in Norway, a medieval stone church built in the second half of the twelfth century. The commission for the font house, and a pulpit and baptismal font, was given to Lars Jenssen Borg in 1704. The structure surrounding the font was an integral part of the church interior,

underlining the importance of the sacramental act. The outer walls are richly decorated with swirling acanthus leaves, characteristic of one of the main phases of the Baroque style in Norwegian woodcarving. The acanthus motif also appears in the ornaments over the entrance door flanking the crowned monogram of Frederick IV of Denmark and Norway. The Corinthian pilasters supporting the entablature and the balusters in the openings add a balancing and decorative effect to the composition. The whole design may have been inspired by a print for a baptismal chapel by Jean Lepautre. According to the inscription on the doors of the font house, the gilding and painting were paid for by the local magistrate Niels Nielsen Hedemark and his wife Maren Christensdatter in 1713. The font house was probably removed during a modernization of the church in 1865. It was bought in 1886 by Nordiska Museet in Stockholm, Sweden. In 1938 the font house was deposited at Norsk Folkemuseum – the Norwegian Museum of Cultural History in Oslo – and is now displayed in the museum's collection of church art. (MFS)

92. (pl.4.25)
Font from Ringsaker Church
Lars Jenssen Borg (c.1652–1710), made for Ringsaker, Norway, 1704
Carved, painted and gilded wood, h 120cm, diam 60cm
Ringsaker Church, Norway
Provenance
Ringsaker Church, Hedmark, 1704
Bibliography
Hauglid (1950), pp.43–4
According to a contract of 1704, the woodcarver Lars Jenssen Borg was commissioned to make a pulpit, baptismal font and font house for Ringsaker Church. This was one of Borg's many commissions for major church decorations in eastern Norway. His style and use of the acanthus motif had a significant impact on Norwegian carvers and carpenters. The supporting base of this baptismal font represents a little boy or putto. He carries the font basin on his head, supporting it with his left hand. The basin is richly decorated with flowers and ribbons. The figural font resembles a similar piece made by Borg for Hof Church in 1703. The original paint on the font from the early 1700s was later covered with brown paint, which was removed during the restoration of the church interior in 1959–65. The font was originally placed in a small font house in the church (see cat.91). It was probably removed during the modernization of the interior in 1865. The baptismal font is still in use in the church today. (MFS)

93. (pl.4.28)
Design for the monument to Dorothy, Lady Brownlow, in St Nicholas's Church, Sutton
William Stanton (1639–1705), London, c.1700
Pen, ink and wash on paper, h 32.7cm, w 22.2cm
V&A: D.1104–1898
Provenance
1 of 44 drawings bought from Mr. E. Parsons of Brompton Road, 28 May, 1898, for £3.10.0d. Previously sold at Messrs. Sotheby and Wilkinson's, 27 November, 1861, for £1.3.0d.
Bibliography
Physick (1968); Physick (1969), pp.52–3
This drawing, which was acquired by the V&A in 1898 as the work of Caius Gabriel Cibber

(1630–1700), was first attributed to William Stanton, one of a family of master-masons of Holborn, by John Physick in 1968. William Stanton and his son Edward produced several monuments to members of the Brownlow family between c.1679 and 1726, in Belton and Old Somerby churches, Lincolnshire. The church of St Nicholas was rebuilt in 1862 and although the monument survives, it is concealed behind an organ. It was described by John Aubrey in his 1718 *The Natural History and Antiquities of the County of Surrey* as a 'beautiful Marble Monument railed in, whereon lies, at full length, a Lady leaning on her left Arm, and by her three Children, two weeping, and one pointing to a Glory surrounded with Cherubims on a Curtain, on the Top two Cupids with Golden Trumpets; on each side two Urns, and on an oval Tablet underneath is the following Inscription: *Here lyes the body of Dame Dorothy Brownlowe, Wife of Sr.* William Brownlowe *of Belton in the County of* Lincoln, Bart. *eldest Daughter and Coheiress of Sir Richard Mason Knight & Clerk Controler of the Green-Cloath to King Charles and King James 2d. and of Dame Anne his Wife who departed this Life the 13 day of* January, *Anno Domini 1699/1700 in the 34 Year of her Age…'* (JN)

94. (pl.4.29)
Funerary chapel of Henri de Bourbon, Prince de Condé
Pierre-Paul Sevin (1650–1710), France, 1683
Gouache on paper, h 43.2cm, w 28.8cm
Inscribed: fondation du feu Mr Jean Perrault, président … la Chambre. P.P. Sevin fecit 1683. Décoration funèbre qui se fait tous les ans. Un service solemnel a la mémoire du déffunct S.A.S.Mr Henry de Bourbon premier prince du sang dans l'église des R.P. Jésuites de St-Louis.
Musée Carnavalet – Histoire de Paris, D.8554
Provenance
Acquired by the city of Paris for the Musée Carnavalet, in a public sale in Paris, 1977
Bibliography
Guilmard-Geddes (1978); Musée Carnavalet (1985), no.47; Chantrenne (2004)
The Church of St Louis was the Parisian centre of the Jesuits, and housed, in a chapel in the north transept of the church, a monument containing the hearts of the princes de Condé, including Henri de Bourbon. Although this latter died in 1646, the first commemorative service in honour of his life and death was not held until 1683, subsequently becoming an annual event. For this, temporary decorations were installed in the chapel (dedicated at that time to St Ignatius), covering the walls and most of the windows with black drapes, decorated with cartouches containing biblical figures and inscriptions. A canopy, decorated with Henri de Bourbon's arms, hung over the monument, draped with an ermine-lined cloak bearing the Condé crown. Allegorical figures represented the Virtues, while bas-reliefs focusing on death and war were displayed. Numerous candles and braziers illuminated the chapel.
Sevin's gouache, which differs in certain respects from engraved depictions of the event, shows two paintings on the side walls of the chapel, representing Louis XIII offering the model of the church to St Louis and St Louis embarking on the crusade. The altarpiece, which was actually a bronze relief of St Ignatius kneeling before the cross, has been replaced or covered with a painting of Louis XIII in prayer at mass. Sevin produced a number of gouaches for such catafalques in

this church and in the cathedral of Notre Dame, including a significant number for the funeral of the Grand Condé in 1687. (JN)

95. (pl.4.31)
Bozzetto for the tomb of Pope Alexander VII
Gianlorenzo Bernini (1598–1680), Rome, c.1669–70
Modelled terracotta, h 30.3cm
V&A: A.17–1932
Provenance
Purchased from Miss M.E. Elwes in London, 1932; probably in Miss Elwes's family since about 1860–70; according to family tradition, acquired in Spain
Bibliography
Maclagan and Longhurst (1932), p.159; Pope-Hennessy (1964), vol.2, no.639; Montagu (1989), pp.111–14 and fig.136; Avery (1997), pp.133, 254, fig.368
This is a preliminary sketch model for the marble figure of Pope Alexander VII on the tomb erected to him in St Peter's in Rome. Alexander VII originally commissioned the monument from Bernini for St Peter's, but the succeeding pope, Clement IX, wanted to place it in S. Maria Maggiore, opposite his own. After Clement IX's death, however, his successor, Clement X, revoked these plans, and reverted to the former idea of placing it in St Peter's.
The present model, which depicts the pope kneeling on a cushion, his hands clasped in prayer, and his papal tiara under the flowing cope, is an autograph work by Bernini. It conforms relatively closely to the finished monument, and relates also to one of the drawings for the tomb now in the Royal Collection at Windsor, which was apparently made for the earlier proposed monument in S. Maria Maggiore. The full-scale wood model with clay figures was completed in 1672, when Bernini received his final payment, but the actual monument was not finished until May 1678, when the pope's body was transferred to it. Bernini delegated all marble-carving for the tomb to assistants, who carried out this work from 1672 to 1678. The terracotta is therefore exceptionally important as a preparatory work by the master himself.
This summary sketch reveals much about Bernini's working methods. He modelled the head separately, so that he could experiment with its angle before positioning it on the body. Like the only other surviving terracotta model for the tomb, a figure of Charity, now in the Istituto delle Belle Arti in Siena, it exhibits tool marks, and even the suggestion of thumb- and fingerprints, indicating how the artist worked out his ideas. The hands are now missing, and there are surface cracks, but the rest of the model is comparatively intact. It is a remarkable testament to Bernini's handling of clay on a small scale in preparation for what was to be a magnificent monumental papal tomb. (MTr)

96. (pl.4.30)
Figure of 'Fama' from the Funerary Achievement of Pontus Fredrik De La Gardie
Attributed to the workshop of Burchardt Precht (1651–1738), Stockholm, 1692/3
Carved, painted, gilded and silvered wood and papier-maché, h 175cm, w 160cm
Västerås Cathedral, Church of Sweden, 101-0016:2
Bibliography
Sohlberg (1834), pp.57–8; Lindegren (1898), p.82, fig.71; Hahr (1923), p.55; Ekström

(1976), pp.169, 172, 241–2; von Corswant-Naumburg (1999), pp.210–12, 214, 297, 378
Count Pontus Fredrik De La Gardie died in October 1692. He had been a privy councillor and lord chief justice at the court of appeal in Tartu, now in Estonia. The count was buried in Riddarholmskyrkan, the royal burial church in Stockhom, with appropriate ceremonial. Before the bier in the funeral procession was carried the chief achievement – the count's coat of arms surmounted by three helmets. Hereditary nobles marked their elevated position by also carrying the coats of arms of the deceased's ancestors on the father's and mother's side. They could be shown on an achievement or be attached to the horses' caparisons. At Count Pontus Fredrik's burial the main achievement was accompanied for the first time by representations of Fama (reputation) and Tempus (time) holding caparisons showing respectively his fathers' and mother's ancestry. Each achievement was carried by two or three men, held high on a pole now removed. The Count was later buried in his mother's family's vault in Västerås Cathedral, the achievements being placed close to the magnificent monument of his mother's father, count Magnus Brahe.
The achievement, attributed to the Stockholm workshop of the court sculptor Burchardt Precht, clearly shows the impact of Roman Baroque. Precht was very familiar with the style through the court architect Nicodemus Tessin the Younger and via the study journey to Italy which they made together in 1687–88. His grounding in the north German carving tradition in Hamburg and Bremen, enabled him skilfully to translate the Italian forms from stone into wood. Precht and his workshop produced many pieces, notably for churches, the most important of which was after designs by Tessin. (JR)

97. (pl.4.56)
Time and Death
Probably Caterina de Julianis (active about 1695–1742), Italy, probably before 1727
Coloured and moulded wax, h 84cm, w 109cm, d 24cm
V&A: A.3–1966
Provenance
Probably the church of S. Severo al Pendino, Naples; disappeared 1944; from about 1944 in the collection of Armando Brasini; sold by his heirs to the V&A under the bequest of Dr W.L. Hildburgh, 1966
Bibliography
Lightbown (1967); Murrell (1971), pp.102–6; Pyke (1973), pp.73, 163; Cagnetta (1977), p.498
In a crumbling graveyard, the winged figure of Father Time seated on the left points to a clock, while a half-draped emaciated figure of a smiling beggar, seated on the other side of the clock, solicits alms; a papal tiara lies at his feet. One small discoloured and decaying corpse lies in front of Time, while another corpse with entrails revealed lies beside him, surrounded by rats, snakes and skulls. A dead youth is stretched out on the right, while on the extreme right the crowned skeletal figure of Death holding a spear looks on. Ivy trails over the surrounding stonework; the sloping ground gives a sense of theatricality to the whole. The painted background depicts decaying funerary monuments.
This highly realistic and dramatic wax tableau was a *memento mori*, intended to inspire thoughts on mortality. Until recently it was attributed to the wax sculptor Gaetano Giulio Zumbo or Zummo, but it has now been

convincingly reassigned to Caterina de Julianis. This artist was a Neapolitan nun who specialized in wax modelling. The piece was inspired by Zumbo's works, and the dead youth was in fact based on a figure of a dead bare-breasted woman in one of his wax compositions. Because the present work was intended for a church, this figure was transformed into a male subject. Coloured wax was the ideal medium for such morbidly realistic scenes, and the artist has been able to convey with astonishing illusionism the textures of stone, flesh and drapery. Wax figures could be formed from moulds, as well as modelled, and so copies and variations of compositions were easily made. A closely similar composition known to be by Caterina de Julianis is in the Chiesa dell'Immacolata in Catanzaro, previously in Bishop Emmanuel Spinelli's palace, and dating from before 1727. (MTr)

98. (pl.4.27)
Chandelier
Andreas I Wickert (1600–61), Augsburg, c.1650
Embossed and cast silver, chased and partially gilded, h 165cm, w 163cm, d 163cm
Inscribed upon shield: 'HERS/GEV' and on reverse 'DEO/ ET/ AETERNITATI/ SACRUM,/ IN MEMORIUM OPTIMI CONIUGIS,/ AUGUSTISSIMI SUECORUM QUONDAM REGIS,/ CAROLI GUSTAVI,/ TEMPLO RIDDERHOLMENSI/ MONUMENTUM HOCCE CONSECRAVIT/ HEDWIG ELEONORA, REGINA VIDVA/ ANNO DOMINI/ MDCLXIII'. Central rod a later replacement, marked with hallmarks of Stockholm masters Jonas Nyman and Gottfried Dubois and the year letter 'L' (1723)
The Office of the Marshal of the Realm of Sweden
Provenance
Given to the Riddarholm Church, Stockholm, by Hedvig Eleonora, Queen Dowager of Sweden, in memory of her husband Charles X, 1663
Bibliography
Andersson (1954); Hoos (1981), pp.90-92
The chandelier is constructed from a central silver gilt rod (a later replacement) cased within three openwork balusters, one above another, with six branches extending from each baluster. Each branch is formed from a human figure (male, on the lowest level; female, on the middle level; and putti on the uppermost level), whose lower bodies merge into acanthus tendrils. Putti figures also sit on the ends of the branches reaching up to the drip pans, which are in the form of flowers. The acanthus leaf and petal decoration, which is also continued on the openwork balusters, and the inclusion of touches of the auricular style, is characteristic of the silver produced in Augsburg at this time. At the base of the chandelier a putto is suspended holding a shield engraved with the crowned arms of Sweden and Holstein-Gottorp and the initials of Queen Hedvig Eleonora within a laurel wreath; the longer inscription on the reverse of the shield refers to the donation of the chandelier by the dowager queen to the Riddarholmskyrkan, the royal burial church of the Swedish monarchs, as a monument to her late husband. It was, however, originally a secular piece, and may possibly have been acquired in Germany at the time of the negotiations surrounding the Peace of Westphalia. A similar, but smaller, example, with more developed auricular forms, is in the Great Church (St Nicholas's Church) in Stockholm. (JN)

99. (pl.2.36)
Altar card
Johann Adolf Gaap (1664–1724) and Charles Germain (1677–1745), Rome, 1699
Gilt bronze and silver gilt set with lapis lazuli, hard-stones and miniature paintings on parchment, h 58cm, w 83cm
Provincia d'Italia della Compagnia di Gesù
Bibliography
Berliner (1952–3); Fagiolo and Madonna (1984), pp.174–5; Bernardini and Fagiolo dell'Arco (1999), no.141

According to the inventory of the Church of the Gesù for 1701, this magnificent altar card formed part of the altar furnishings for the side Chapel of S.Ignazio. This has led to the suggestion that it may have been designed by Andrea Pozzo himself, although there is no evidence to support this attribution.

The work was executed by a number of different craftsmen: the German silversmith Johann Adolf Gaap, who executed the figures of angels and the clouds of the sunburst; Filippo Ferreri, who provided the other metal elements and Charles Germain, from the celebrated family of French silversmiths, who was responsible for all the jewel work.

The altar card is one of three elements, of which only the central part is exhibited; the smaller flanking cards follow the same structure and also have jewels set into the lapis lazuli borders. The two angels which support the energized frame of the altar card, kneeling on clouds and holding the instruments of the passion (one a spear, the other a sponge), recall Berninian prototypes. The altar card is a remarkable survival given the spoliation of the Church of the Gesù in 1798-99, during which much of the church's silver, including parts of the statue of St Ignatius on this altar, was looted. (JN)

100. (pl.3.63)
Monstrance
Maker unknown, Portugal, 1725–50
Cast and chased silver gilt set with diamonds, emeralds, rubies, sapphires, topazes and garnets, h 76cm
Museu Nacional de Arte Antiga, Lisboa, 388
Our
Provenance
Patriarchal Palace of S. Vicente de Fora
Bibliography
Smith (1936); Couto and Gonçalves (1960); Palácio de Queluz (1987), no.326; Palácio Nacional da Ajuda (1988), no.25; Teixeira (1993), no.V12

With the suppression of the religious orders in Portugal in 1834, the convent properties next to the church of St Vincent in Lisbon became the palace of the Archbishop or Patriarch of Lisbon, from where this monstrance came. Like the majority of sacred works of art commissioned in the reign of John V, it is clearly inspired by the classicist current of the Roman Baroque. The stem of the monstrance is formed of a sphere symbolizing the universe surmounted by two putti emerging from the clouds holding a sunburst. The enrichment of the monstrance with precious stones reflects a key moment of artistic patronage inspired by royal example, and reveals the extent of Portuguese economic prosperity brought about by the fabulous quantities of gold and gems from Brazil that year after year came into Lisbon. (LO)

101. (pl.4.36)
Reliquary
Giuseppe Borgiani (1685–1769), Rome, possibly 1751–3
Cast and chased silver on carved and gilded wooden base, h (with base) 45.2cm, w (with base) 21.1cm
Marks: Crossed keys and umbrella (Bulgari Calissoni, 119?); G.B. (Bulgari Calissoni, 297a)
Santa Casa da Misericórdia de Lisboa / Museu de São Roque, Or 0042
Provenance
Made for the church of S. Roque
Bibliography
Vassallo e Silva (1992); Museu de São Roque (1997), no.234; Museu de São Roque (1998), no.50

This object, made of a sheet of repoussé silver attached to a wooden backing, is representative of the dominant type of Italian Baroque reliquary, of which those containing relics of the true cross are among the more common.

Made for the church of S. Roque, the reliquary has until now been ascribed to the silversmith Gaetano Smits; however, it is clear that the second letter of the maker's mark is a 'B', not an 'S', and the initials are enclosed in an oval, not a rectangle, identifying the maker as Giuseppe Borgiani.

Giuseppe was the son of the silversmith Michele Borgiani; he worked in his father's shop, and succeeded to his father's patent in 1733, some two and a half months before his father's death. He held various posts in the guild, but by 1764 he was described in their records as old and infirm.

As *assaiatore camerale*, on 8 January 1751 he assayed some of the reliquaries made for the chapel of St John the Baptist and the Holy Spirit in the church of S. Roque, the same church for which he made this reliquary. Five chalices that he made for Portugal still survive, two in Lisbon, in the collections of the Treasury of the Cathedral and the Museu Nacional de Arte Antiga, a third in the Museu Nacional de Soares dos Reis, Oporto and two in Vila Viçosa. (TLV)

102. (pl.4.37)
Reliquary of the Cradle of Christ
Giuseppe Antonio Torricelli (1659–1719), Cosimo Merlini the Younger (d.1736) and grand-ducal workshops, after designs by Giovanni Battista Foggini (1652–1725), Florence, 1697
Pietre dure, rock crystal, silver gilt, h 26.5cm, w 20cm, d 15 cm
Museo degli Argenti, Palazzo Pitti, Firenze, A.s.e. 1911, n.101
Provenance
Medici collection
Bibliography
Mosco and Casazza (2004), p.156

This reliquary was commissioned in 1695–6 by Grand Duke Cosimo III de' Medici and designed by Giovanni Battista Foggini, the artist in charge of the grand-ducal workshops. Originally there were two chalcedony angels on alabaster clouds and a *gloria* of silver clouds around the cradle, with cherubim and angel heads supporting a scroll bearing the inscription 'Gloria in excelsis Deo'.

As was common practice, the execution of the individual elements was assigned to various specialists active in the grand-ducal workshops. The goldsmith Cosimo Merlini the Younger executed the silver elements, of which the only surviving parts today are the four small angel heads on the corners of the agate base,

while the manufacture of the *pietra dura* parts was assigned to Giuseppe Antonio Torricelli, a true virtuoso in this technique.

In its extraordinary chromatic richness, the variety of materials used and the refinement of the techniques involved, as well as in the collaboration of highly specialized craftsmen, the work perfectly reflects the so-called style of Cosimo III. His rule saw an extraordinary flourishing in Florence of commissions for extremely high-quality devotional works, partly as a result of the strong religiosity of the Grand Duke himself, and partly thanks to the presence of first-rate artists such as Foggini and Massimiliano Soldani Benzi. (CCal)

103. (pl.4.38)
Monstrance
Johannes Zeckel (d. 1728), Augsburg, Germany, 1705
Silver and silver gilt set with glass, h 84.6cm, w 45.2cm, d 19.8cm
Maker's mark of Johannes Zeckel; town mark of Augsburg for 1705
V&A: M.3–1952
Provenance
Given by Dr W.L. Hildburgh, 1952
Bibliography
Finaldi et al. (2000), no.72

The word 'monstrance' comes from the Latin *monstrare*, to show. A monstrance displayed the Sacred Host, the consecrated bread which, in Roman Catholic belief, is the body of Christ. These vessels first appeared in 1264 after the institution of the feast of Corpus Christi; a monstrance was processed through the streets during the feast and subsequently placed on the altar for the service of Benediction. During the Counter Reformation, the Catholic Church placed greater emphasis on the Eucharist, and the design of new monstrances reflected this theology.

In the centre of this monstrance a representation of the Last Supper shows the disciples seated round the table at the institution of the Eucharist. Christ himself is present only when the host is placed inside the *lunula*, the window above. The sun's rays represent Christ's radiant presence, which is flanked by winged angels. The monstrance is surmounted by a canopy and imperial crown with orb and cross. The cornucopias at each side support wheat and vines, symbolizing the bread and wine of the body and blood of Christ. The monstrance is supported by the theological virtues: allegorical figures of Faith, Hope and Charity. The base is decorated with New Testament scenes of the Adoration of the Kings and the Crucifixion and the Old Testament scenes which foreshadow these events, Melchizedek offering bread and wine to God (Genesis 14:18) and Moses commanding the people to gather manna (Exodus 17:15–17).

Zeckel was active as a maker of sacred silver in Augsburg from 1691. There are several monstrances bearing his mark. (TM)

104. (pl.4.51)
Holy Sacrament in a flower garland
Attributed to Daniel Seghers (1590–1661), Antwerp, Belgium, c.1645–61
Oil on canvas, h 149cm, w 114cm
V&A: 4420–1857
Provenance
Purchased 1857
Bibliography
Kauffmann (1973), vol.1, pp.261–2, no.324; Couvreur (1967); Hairs (1998), pp.108–71

The son of a silk merchant, Seghers was

brought up as a Calvinist in Holland, but in 1611 enrolled in the Antwerp painters' guild. Converting to Catholicism, he entered the Jesuit order, took his final vows in 1625, and spent two years in Rome. Returning to Antwerp, he combined the profession of painting with a monastic vocation. His master Jan Brueghel had painted floral garlands encircling religious images for the reforming archbishop of Milan, Cardinal Federigo Borromeo. Seghers specialized in this genre, with the central motifs added by collaborators such as Thomas Bosschaert, Rubens and even Poussin. Such paintings reflect the garlanding of religious works on feast days, and reaffirmed the role of images as objects of veneration, in Catholic opposition to Calvinist iconoclasm.

The lower part of this garland is dominated by spiky plants, especially roses and thistles, hawthorn, blackthorn, rose-hips and raspberries. Above are grapes, stalks of wheat and corn, poppies, cornflowers and narcissus. Most allude symbolically to Christ's Passion and the Holy Sacrament, represented as a chalice with a nimbus. The eagle crowning the wreath – a motif of ancient Roman derivation – symbolizes the Resurrection, as do the butterflies. The parrot is a decorative accessory. In 1857 this work was acquired with a flower-piece of similar character by the Antwerp painter Jan Pauwel Gillemans (V&A, 4419–1857).

Seghers's paintings were presented to cardinals and senior clergy, nobles and monarchs, including Queen Christina of Sweden and Charles I of England, the emperor and the king of Spain. The humanist secretary of the prince of Orange, Constantijn Huygens, esteemed Seghers as 'painter of flowers, and flower of painters'. (ME)

105. (pl.3.53)
Model for the Chapel of St John the Baptist in the Church of S. Roque
Giuseppe Palmes, Giuseppe Voyet, Giuseppe Focchetti, Gennaro Nicoletti, Rome, 1744–7
Carved and polychromed walnut with gilded copper, h 140cm, w 93cm, d 86cm
Santa Casa da Misericórdia de Lisboa / Museu de São Roque, Mb 0326
Bibliography
Conceição (1827), pp.38–42; Viterbo and d'Almeida (1900), pp.75–7; Madeira Rodrigues (1988) 1, pp.28–31; Levenson (1993), no.106; Teixeira (1993), pp.260–62; Borghini and Vasco Rocca (1995), pp.113–23; Montagu (1996), pp.160–62, fig.237; de Seta (1998), pp.29–30; Millon (1999), p.566; Pimentel (2008)

The model of the Chapel of St John the Baptist was conceived in 1743, as part of the commission by John V of Portugal for the chapel from Rome. The chapel was designed by the architect Luigi Vanvitelli, although significant alterations were made by the Portuguese court to the original conception. Giuseppe Palmes, a cabinet-maker, made the model. Giuseppe Focchetti and Giuseppe Voyet executed the imitation marble painting, and Gennaro Nicoletti the miniatures in oil on copper.

The provenance of the model is described by the chronicler Frei Cláudio da Conceição: 'This model, of which His Majesty was very fond, was given to the architect of Obra de Mafra, Joao Frederico Ludovici, whilst in possession of the model, Jose Frederico Ludovice, Notary,... sold [it] to Joao Baptista Verde, who is the current owner.' According to Sousa Viterbo, this item, which had belonged to the Ludovice family for many years, was in 1882 given to the Museu Nacional de Belas Artes. In poor condition, it was restored in 1879 by Diodato Guedes and Sebastiao Ferreira d'Almeida. On 6 November 1879, the Museu de Belas Artes requested permission from the Provedor da Santa Casa da Misericórdia de Lisboa for the painter Silva Porto to visit the chapel 'in order to restore the paintings in the model of the said Chapel, in the possession of this Academy'. It is now thought that Sebastiao Ferreira d'Almeida did the two lateral paintings, and Silva Porto the central one.

After the Santa Casa da Misericórdia de Lisboa became responsible for the Chapel of St John the Baptist in 1892, interest in the model grew. This model differs from the chapel itself in several respects: the two platforms placed before the altar rail, the shape of the steps, and the paintings that represent the mosaic panels. (AM)

106. (not illustrated)
Confessional
Giovanni Palmini, Rome, 1742–4
Walnut and metal, h 85cm, w 81cm, d 44cm
Santa Casa da Misericórdia de Lisboa / Museu de São Roque, Mb 0349

Bibliography
Viterbo and d'Almeida (1900), p.97; Raul (1969–91), 5, p.35; Madeira Rodrigues (1988) 1, p.224

This is one of a pair of movable confessionals that could be attached to the balustrade or communion rail of the chapel of St John the Baptist. Carved in walnut by the Italian cabinet-maker and carver Giovanni Palmini, it exemplifies the elegant style of Roman carving of the period. The use of this type of confessional was widespread following the doctrinal standards set by the Council of Trent (1545–63) for the administration of the sacrament of Penitence and Confession.

Each confessional has, at the centre, a small opening or window, with a gilded metal grille, and, on the confessor's side, a small door. The penitent would kneel down outside the confessional facing the grille, while the priest would be seated sideways within, in order to listen to the penitent's confession. (AM)

The Silver of the Chapel of St John the Baptist at S. Roque
The colourful splendour of the marbles, mosaics, lapis-lazuli columns and gilt bronze on the walls of the chapel of St John the Baptist and the Holy Spirit is matched by the brilliant gilding of the liturgical objects. Like the chapel, the plate was made by the leading Roman workmen in the latest style, the *barochetto*, the majority ordered in 1744. Instructions were sent for the making of the most important pieces; costed drawings were prepared in Rome, and approved in Lisbon, though often subject to modifications.

Most of the liturgical plate still survives, providing the richest and most coherent assemblage of such work, made even more precious because so much of the treasure in Rome and the papal states was sacrificed to pay the indemnity to Napoleon demanded in 1797. Even in S. Roque several pieces, including the few vessels made of gold and the great ciborium and the throne for the exhibition of the Eucharist, disappeared before 1798, and other pieces were taken by the French in 1812.

John V commissioned two sets of most of the liturgical metalwork for this chapel, one in gilt bronze for everyday use, and one in silver gilt

for feast-days and special occasions. So Antonio Vendetti not only made a set of silver gilt mass cards (cat.121), but also produced a less elaborate set in gilt bronze. The cross and candlesticks by Arrighi, in gilt bronze and lapis-lazuli (cat.108), are usually to be seen on the altar of the chapel, while a spectacular set in silver gilt by Angelo Spinazzi and other silversmiths is now kept in the museum.

Such works were sometimes designed by a silversmith (in this case Spinazzi) but often by a sculptor or an architect. Sculptors might be called upon to model the figures, as Giovanni Battista Maini made the Corpus for Spinazzi's cross. Usually it is only by chance that the names of designers or sculptors are recorded, though we know that Vanvitelli's designs included the altar with its metal decoration. It is likely that sculptors collaborated in several of the works shown here, but there is rarely documentation to confirm this, still less to provide their names.

The other chapels in the church also required their own liturgical metalwork, such as the reliquary by Giuseppe Borgiani (cat.101). (JM, TLV)

107. (pl.3.56)
Great candlestick
Giuseppe Gagliardi (1697–1749) and Leandro Gagliardi (1729–1804), Rome, 1749
Silver gilt on gilt bronze base, h 285cm
Marks: crossed keys and umbrella; 2 Gs separated by a sun (Bulgari Calissoni 540); Signed: JOSEPHUS GAGLIARDUS ROMANUS INVENTOR FU[N]DIT ET FECIT
Santa Casa da Misericórdia de Lisboa / Museu de São Roque, MPr 1

Provenance
Ordered by John V of Portugal for the Chapel of St John the Baptist, S. Roque, Lisbon

Bibliography
Viterbo and d'Almeida (1900), pp.37–42; Madeira Rodrigues (1988) 1, pp.79–101; Alegria et al (1991), no.II 67; Levenson (1993), no.107; Borghini and Vasco Rocca (1995), nos 69, 91; Montagu (1996), pp.172–7, 179; Montagu (2004)

This is one of a pair of what were called *torcieri*; they are virtually identical apart from the Doctors of the Church seated on the bases, here Saints Jerome, Ambrose and Thomas Aquinas.

The basic design follows that invented by Angelo Spinazzi for the 'noble' set of silver gilt cross and candlesticks for the altar of the Chapel of St John the Baptist, greatly enlarged and with much added decoration. Changes were made after the model was shown in 1748, and further alterations were made later; Carlo and Pietro Pacilli provided most of the models, but they said that some of the changes and additions were made by Giovanni Battista Maini.

The pair of candlesticks consists of 296 pieces, each small element screwed on, with the screws on the inside so they would not be visible. After Giuseppe Gagliardi's death, the work was completed by his son Leandro, but many assistants were involved in the casting, and the subtle and infinitely varied working of the surface. The gilders said Gagliardi had told them the Portuguese ambassador wanted this done with the utmost perfection; their compliance with this wish has been revealed by recent cleaning.

The candlesticks are the most spectacular (and, despite the thinness of the casting, most expensive) of the pieces of silver made for the chapel, and arguably the finest surviving pieces

of Italian late Baroque silver, both sculpturally and technically. The extraordinary richness of the design is contained within a firmly articulated structure, and the lively vigour of the whole matched by the expressive vitality of the individual figures. (JM)

108. (pl.3.48)
Set of six altar candlesticks and an altar cross
Antonio Arrighi (1687–1776), Rome, 1750
Gilt bronze and lapis-lazuli, cross: h 164cm; candlesticks: h 119cm (x2), h 114cm (x2), h 106cm (x2)
Santa Casa da Misericórdia de Lisboa / Museu de São Roque, MPr 37–43

Provenance
Ordered by John V of Portugal for the Chapel of St John the Baptist, S. Roque, Lisbon

Bibliography
Viterbo and d'Almeida (1900), p.43; Madeira Rodrigues (1988) 1, pp.127–51

Antonio Arrighi made some of the most important silver for the chapel of St John, but, like most Roman Baroque silversmiths, he also worked in bronze. He supplied the chapel with the gilt bronze decoration of the altar with its gradine and the frame of the altarpiece, and this set of cross and candlesticks used on it for all but the most important occasions. It is possible that Vanvitelli provided drawings for the set, as he did for the altar and the tabernacle (also made by Arrighi), but models are included in the silversmith's account, approved in April 1750. Arrighi also set the small slabs of lapis-lazuli in the niches and the larger pieces in the bases and the cross; these had been cut and polished in the workshop of Cecilia Tedeschi, widow of the stone-worker Francesco.

The combination of gilt bronze and lapis-lazuli is typical of the Roman Baroque, but the profusion of cherub-heads, and the cherubim who frolic on the bases, are characteristic of the *barochetto*. The idea of figures seated in niches flanked by paired columns goes back at least to the Renaissance, as in Antonio Gentile's cross and candlesticks in the Vatican, drawn by Arrighi for the king of Portugal. The figures on the cross represent four Doctors of the Church. The four-sided bases of the candlesticks display a total of 24 figures, probably made up of two sets of the Apostles, though some figures lack any attributes, perhaps intentionally to avoid blatant duplication, but possibly the consequence of time and use. The workmanship is of high quality, with a profusion of well-chased decorative motifs. The seated figures, robust rather than elegant, offset the sweetness and charm of the ubiquitous cherubim, inserting a note of almost rustic strength into the courtly ensemble of the chapel. (JM)

109. (pl.3.61)
Chalice and paten
Antonio Gigli (active 1724–55), Rome, 1749
Silver gilt, h 29cm
Marks: crossed keys and umbrella; a lion (Bulgari Calissoni, 568)
Santa Casa da Misericórdia de Lisboa / Museu de São Roque, MPr 24

Provenance
Ordered by John V of Portugal for the Chapel of St John the Baptist, S. Roque, Lisbon

Bibliography
Viterbo and d'Almeida (1900), pp.30–31; Madeira Rodrigues (1988), 1, pp.153–4

The 'service for the Mass' was essential for the chapel of St John, and was among the objects requested from Lisbon in March 1744; the

payments run from April 1745, with the final payment on 8 December 1749.

Antonio Gigli might seem a strange choice for so large and important an order since, although he had a mark of his own, he was not a master of the guild. The silver in Lisbon demonstrates his competence: the modelling is strong and bold, the decoration is for the most part of more or less naturalistic vegetal forms, as well as the standard repertory of brackets, scrolls, cartouches, etc., with the ubiquitous cherub-heads, all modelled with considerable skill. The chalice follows a type that is usual for the period. The foot has a complex outline, with representations of the Instruments of the Passion between two high-relief cherub-heads, and surrounded by the eucharistic grapes and wheat. There are further Instruments of the Passion on the knop, and yet more appear on the calyx, alternating with cherub-heads in relief. The stem is composed of brackets and mouldings which throughout exert a firm control over the decoration, confining the various elements within their borders. (JM, TLV)

110. (pl.3.62)
Chalice veil
Made by Francesco Giuliani, and embroidered by Filippo Salandri, Rome, 1744–9
Gros de Tours (ribbed silk), lamé in silver gilt, embroidered in relief in gold thread, lined in taffeta and trimmed with gold thread, h 78cm, w 75cm
Santa Casa da Misericórdia de Lisboa / Museu de São Roque, MT 100
See commentary to cat.114.

111. (pl.3.57)
Missal cushion
Made by Francesco Giuliani, and embroidered by Filippo Salandri, Rome, 1744–9
Gros de Tours (ribbed silk), lamé in silver gilt, embroidered in relief in gold thread, lined in taffeta and trimmed with gold thread, h 51cm, w 41cm
Santa Casa da Misericórdia de Lisboa / Museu de São Roque, MT 30
See commentary to cat.114

112. (pl.3.50)
Priest's chasuble
Made by Francesco Giuliani, and embroidered by Filippo Salandri, Rome, 1744–9
Gros de Tours (ribbed silk), lamé in silver gilt, embroidered in relief in gold thread, lined in taffeta and trimmed with gold thread, h72cm, w 108cm
Santa Casa da Misericórdia de Lisboa / Museu de São Roque, MT 25
See commentary to cat.114

113. (pl.3.54)
Stole
Made by Francesco Giuliani, and embroidered by Filippo Salandri, Rome, 1744–9
Gros de Tours (ribbed silk), lamé in silver gilt, embroidered in relief in gold thread, lined in taffeta and trimmed with gold thread; bobbin lace in gold thread, l 256cm, w 30cm
Santa Casa da Misericórdia de Lisboa / Museu de São Roque, MT 87
See commentary to cat.114

114. (not illustrated)
Maniple
Made by Francesco Giuliani, and embroidered by Filippo Salandri, Rome, 1744–9
Gros de Tours (ribbed silk), lamé in silver gilt,

embroidered in relief in gold thread, lined in taffeta and trimmed with gold thread; bobbin lace in gold thread, l 100cm, w 30cm
Santa Casa da Misericórdia de Lisboa / Museu de São Roque, MT 86

Provenance
All ordered by John V for the Chapel of St John the Baptist, S. Roque, Lisbon
Bibliography
Viterbo and d'Almeida (1900), p.166; Madeira Rodrigues (1988), 1, pp.208–11, 214–18; Madeira Rodrigues (1988), 2, no.102–10; Madeira Rodrigues (1989), pp.214–15; Vasco Rocca (1990), no.90; Tassinari (2008)

This vestment set, perfectly unified in materials, technique and style, comprises all the traditional elements for dressing the celebrant and the altar for festive services. The set also includes two large door curtains, which are not exhibited. The 'roseate' vestments were used on the third Sunday in Advent (Gaudete) and the fourth Sunday in Lent (Laetare) to symbolize joy in the approaching celebration, interrupting the penitential atmosphere of the weeks on either side, conveyed by the purple vestments used during these periods. The pink textiles, illuminated by the silver gilt lamé ground and enriched by the delicate contrast of the yellow-gold embroidery, give a particular elegance and refinement to the whole set.

The set is characterized by the quality of its materials and by the impeccable precision of every aspect of its execution – from the gold embroidery to the lining, to the passementerie, to the lace. The ornament is astonishingly varied and exuberant: dense floral motifs, whimsical *chinoiserie*, classic acanthus volutes with fringed palms, elaborate cartouches enclosing lace motifs typical of French silks of the 1720s. This variety does not, however, compromise the stylistic unity of the ensemble.

The embroidery was carried out by Filippo Salandri, one of a family of distinguished Roman embroiderers. Benedetto Salandri collaborated in 1746 on the embroidery for two large altar frontals for the tomb of St Peter in the Vatican, while Carlo Salandri's works are documented for both Lisbon and Rome. Filippo, in particular, must have been an established and well-known artist-artisan in mid-eighteenth-century Rome, as Pier Leone Ghezzi, the celebrated caricaturist, drew him at work in a drawing of 1737 (Biblioteca Apostolica Vaticana, Ott. lat. 3116, f.105v).

Roman embroidery, the expression of a long tradition of high quality associated with the Baroque magnificence of the papal court, was greatly appreciated throughout eighteenth-century Europe, partly owing to its principal patron, Benedict XIV. The Portuguese turned to the Roman ateliers to provide textiles for the chapel of St John the Baptist, the favoured project of John V. Commissioned by the king in 1740, the chapel was constructed in Rome between 1742 and 1747. As with its other furnishings, the textiles, so central to eighteenth-century liturgical spectacle, used the taste, style and splendour of Rome as a model.

The project resulted in the creation of a considerable number of vestments, all embellished with embroidery in gold relief and in gold-coloured silk, including two sets (white and red) for solemn celebrations, five (white, red, green, purple and pink) for the celebration of feasts and five for daily use. Over 150 pieces of this ensemble survive today: a truly remarkable number, especially as the majority

remain in a good state of preservation, complete with their original lining and passementerie. Thanks to rich archival documentation, it is possible to identify not only the embroiderers, but also the tailors, weavers and even the merchants who provided the silk lamé, linings and passementerie for these vestments. For this reason in particular, they serve as important evidence for the study of historic textiles, an area of study in which most artists are anonymous.

In addition to the sacred vestments there were also lace-decorated undergarments and three tapestries. Between 1744 and 1749 several workshops dedicated themselves intensively to the project. The total cost of the textiles came to 33,798 *scudi* and 89 Roman *baiocchi*. In Rome on 29 August Filippo Salandri submitted a bill for the pink festive vestment set together with the red festive set also made by him: 'For the less rich vestments in crimson lamé embroidered in gold, and the other vestments in pink lamé also embroidered in gold the sum of 3589:4' (Lisbon, Bibl. Ajuda, Ms. 49-VIII-25, f. 26). The elements of the set that survive correspond to those listed in the inventory of 1784. (MTa)

115. (pl.3.60)
Ablution set: ewer and basin
Vicenzo I Belli (1710–87), Rome, 1747
Silver gilt, ewer: h 23cm; basin: w 53cm, d 42cm
Marks: crossed keys and umbrella; VB
Santa Casa da Misericórdia de Lisboa / Museu de São Roque, MPr 27–28

Provenance
Ordered by John V of Portugal for the Chapel of St John the Baptist, São Roque, Lisbon
Bibliography
Viterbo and d'Almeida (1900), pp.31–32; Madeira Rodrigues (1988), 1, pp.124–6

Before the Mass, water would be poured from the ewer over the priest's hands, and into the basin. The elegant and finely worked decoration of the basin includes a number of biblical scenes that do not have any obvious connection with water, washing or purification, and in some cases differ from those of the preliminary design (Papworth, no.75). Around the rim are seated figures of the Evangelists. Within the basin the horizontal reliefs represent *The Multiplication of the Loaves and Fishes*, and *Christ Giving the Keys to Peter*, while the vertical reliefs show *The Risen Christ Appearing to Mary Magdalen*, and *Christ's Charge to Peter ('Feed My Sheep')*. The latter is usually, but probably wrongly, interpreted as *John the Baptist Preaching*; certainly *Christ's Charge to Peter* is one of the scenes shown on the design drawing. On the ewer are medallions of Christ and the Virgin, two seated virtues (Innocence or Chastity, and possibly Religion), and below two putti, one of whom undoubtedly symbolizes Justice, while the other is accompanied by a lion, and probably symbolizes Fortitude.

These were ordered from Lisbon in 1744; Belli received his first recorded payment in July 1745, and delivered the completed work by August 1747. (JM, TLV)

116. (pl.3.59)
Bell
Antonio Gigli (active 1724–55), Rome, 1749
Silver gilt, h 20cm, d 9cm
Marks: crossed keys and umbrella; a lion (Bulgari Calissoni, 568)
Santa Casa da Misericórdia de Lisboa / Museu de São Roque, MPr 25

Provenance
Ordered by John V of Portugal for the Chapel of St John the Baptist, S. Roque, Lisbon
Bibliography
Viterbo and d'Almeida (1900), p.33; Madeira Rodrigues (1988), 1, p.152

The bell forms part of the same set as cat.109. It is used during the Mass to mark the most important points in the service. (JM, TLV)

117. (pl.3.64)
Thurible
Leandro Gagliardi (1729–1804), Rome, 1750
Silver gilt, h 31cm
Marks: crossed keys and umbrella (Bulgari Calissoni, 118); L.G beneath a star (Bulgari Calissoni, 541)
Santa Casa da Misericórdia de Lisboa / Museu de São Roque, MPr 21

Provenance
Ordered by John V of Portugal for the Chapel of St John the Baptist, S. Roque, Lisbon
Bibliography
Viterbo and d'Almeida (1900), pp.32–3; Madeira Rodrigues (1988), 1, pp.158, 160; Montagu (1996), pp.164–6

When on 1 October 1759 Pope Benedict XIV blessed the liturgical silver before its dispatch to Lisbon, the Portuguese ambassador presented him with Antonio Gigli's thurible and its accompanying incense boat and spoon, which Benedict then gave to the Metropolitan church of his native city, Bologna (see Borghini (1995), nos 72–3).

It was Leandro Gagliardi who was commissioned to replace them, repeating exactly the models used by Gigli, though the quality, while still high, could be judged as slightly lower than that of the originals. His account for making this and the accompanying incense boat is dated 8 April 1750.

The type of this thurible is typical of its period, and displays the bold modelling characteristic of Gigli's Mass service. (JM, TLV)

118. (pl.3.65)
Incense boat and spoon
Leandro Gagliardi (1729–1804), Rome, 1750
Silver gilt, boat: h 20cm, w 18cm; spoon: l 13cm
Marks: crossed keys and umbrella; L.G beneath a star (Bulgari Calissoni, 568)
Santa Casa da Misericórdia de Lisboa / Museu de São Roque, MPr 22

Provenance
Ordered by John V of Portugal for the Chapel of St John the Baptist, S. Roque, Lisbon
Bibliography
Viterbo and d'Almeida (1900), p.33; Madeira Rodrigues (1988), 1, pp.152, 158–9; Montagu (1996), pp.164–6

For the history of this piece, made by Gagliardi following a model by Antonio Gigli, see cat.117.

The conceit of representing the incense boat (*navicella* in Italian) as a boat is highly original – indeed, Antonio Gigli had first proposed a much more conventional design incorporating a far less obvious reference to a boat. As executed the boat, with a cherub-head at its prow, is guided by a figure of Religion, while the waves create a rhythmic pattern along the body of the vessel. The crossed scrolls that attach it to the stem are also an unusual feature of this remarkable object. (JM, TLV)

119. (not illustrated)
Ablution vessel

Antonio Gigli (active 1724–55), Rome, 1749
Silver gilt, h 10cm, d 17cm
Marks: crossed keys and umbrella; a lion (Bulgari Calissoni, 568)
Santa Casa da Misericórdia de Lisboa / Museu de São Roque, MPr 26

Provenance
Ordered by John V of Portugal for the Chapel of St John the Baptist, S. Roque, Lisbon
Bibliography
Viterbo and d'Almeida (1900), p.42; Madeira Rodrigues (1988), 1, p.152

An ablution vessel (or ablution cup) was used by the priest to wash his fingers when he had given communion, other than at the Mass. Gigli supplied three such vessels, two undescribed, and one 'large', which was presumably this, the only one to survive. In style it closely resembles the other silver made by him for the chapel of St John (see cat.109 etc). As on the handle of the bell (cat.116), the cherub-heads are finely modelled, full of life and expression, suggesting the intervention of a sculptor. (JM, TLV)

120. (not illustrated)
Candle snuffer
Antonio Gigli (active 1724–55), Rome, 1749
Silver gilt, h 12cm, w 8cm
Marks: crossed keys and an umbrella; a lion (Bulgari Calissoni, 568)
Santa Casa da Misericórdia de Lisboa / Museu de São Roque, MPr 30

Provenance
Ordered by John V of Portugal for the Chapel of St John the Baptist, S. Roque, Lisbon
Bibliography
Viterbo and d'Almeida (1900), p.33; Madeira Rodrigues (1988), 1, p.157

This forms part of the same service for the Mass as cat.109. (JM, TLV)

121. (pl.3.55)
Altar card: Central Canon
Antonio Vendetti (1699–1796), Rome, 1744–9
Silver and silver gilt, h 59cm, w 53cm
Marks: crossed keys and umbrella (Bulgari Calissoni 117a); spread-eagle (Bulgari Calissoni, 1071)
Santa Casa da Misericórdia de Lisboa / Museu de São Roque, MPr 18

Provenance
Ordered by John V of Portugal for the Chapel of St John the Baptist, S. Roque, Lisbon
Bibliography
Viterbo and d'Almeida (1900), p.34; Madeira Rodrigues (1988) 1, pp.110–22; Alegria et al. (1991), no.II 68; Montagu (1996), pp.166–9

This is the central altar card, the largest and most elaborate of the set of three. The text, more usually written on parchment (as it is in Vendetti's gilt bronze set), is engraved on a sheet of silver, imitating the folds of paper or parchment. The lettering was, as always, engraved by a specialist.

At the top, on either side, are seated Catholic Faith and the Church; the central relief of the *Institution of the Eucharist* is surmounted by the enthroned image of Faith with the dove of the Holy Spirit, and flanked by Hope and Charity (the three theological virtues); below sit the two priests, Melchizedek and Aaron, and at the bottom are the arms of the king of Portugal. The relief is surrounded by the eucharistic symbols of grapes and wheat, and the whole is enriched by cherubim, cherub-heads, and a wealth of festoons, foliage, shells and scrolls, almost masking the architectonic structure. The inventive imitation of paper, laced together, and the superabundance of the decoration, compensate for the fact that Vendetti's figures are sculpturally weaker than the best of the silver produced for the chapel of St John. Even Vendetti's supporters tended to be lukewarm in their praise of his abilities, and his enemies claimed that Lorenzo Morelli had worked the surface of these altar cards.

Vendetti's recorded payments run from September 1746 to December 1749; on 1 September 1748 the work was said to be nearly finished. (JM, TLV)

122. (not illustrated)
Burse
Made by Francesco Giuliani, and embroidered by Filippo Salandri, Rome, 1744–9
Gros de Tours (ribbed silk), lamé in silver gilt, embroidered in relief in gold thread, lined in taffeta and trimmed with gold thread, h 31cm, w 31cm
Santa Casa da Misericórdia de Lisboa / Museu de São Roque, MT 44
See commentary to cat.114.

123. (pl.3.58)
Pair of cruets and salver
Antonio Gigli (active 1724–55), Rome, 1749
Silver gilt, cruets: h 21cm; salver: w 27cm
Marks: crossed keys and umbrella (Bulgari Calissoni, 117a); a lion (Bulgari Calissoni, 568)
Santa Casa da Misericórdia de Lisboa / Museu de São Roque, MPr 11
Provenance
Ordered by John V of Portugal for the Chapel of St John the Baptist, São Roque, Lisbon
Bibliography
Viterbo and d'Almeida (1900), p.31; Madeira Rodrigues (1988) 1, pp.154–5, 157
These cruets for the wine and water used in the mass form part of the same service as cat.109. The bold relief decoration is very similar throughout the service, but the husk and berries decoration so prominent on the cruets is not present on the pieces described above. (JM, TLV)

124.
Ciborium
Antonio Gigli (active 1724–55), Rome, 1749
Silver gilt, h 34cm, d 15cm
Marks: crossed keys and umbrella; a lion (Bulgari Calissoni, 568)
Santa Casa da Misericórdia de Lisboa / Museu de São Roque, MPr 23
Provenance
Ordered by John V of Portugal for the Chapel of St John the Baptist, S. Roque, Lisbon
Bibliography
Viterbo and d'Almeida (1900), p.32; Madeira Rodrigues (1988), 1, p.153
This ciborium, for the conservation of the consecrated wafers of the host, forms part of the 'service for the Mass' made by Antonio Gigli (see cat.109). It was perhaps because its function, to hold the Body of Christ, was similar to that of a chalice (which contains his blood) that it follows much the same form, with the body of the vessel, unadorned except for its rim, held in a calyx decorated with the grapes as well as the wheat of the eucharist. (JM, TLV)

125. (pl.3.57)
Antependium
Made by Francesco Giuliani, and embroidered by Filippo Salandri, Rome, 1744–9
Gros de Tours (ribbed silk), lamé in silver gilt, embroidered in relief in gold thread, lined in taffeta and trimmed with gold thread, h 108cm, w 225cm; width of textile: 50cm (excluding selvage)
Santa Casa da Misericórdia de Lisboa / Museu de São Roque, MT 153
See commentary to cat.114.

Frame for the antependium
Agostino Valle (active 1726–48), Rome, 1748
Gilt bronze, h 110cm, w 221cm
Santa Casa da Misericórdia de Lisboa / Museu de São Roque, MPr 44
Provenance
Ordered by John V of Portugal for the Chapel of St John the Baptist, S. Roque, Lisbon
Bibliography
Madeira Rodrigues (1988), 1, pp.184–6
The principal decoration of this elegant frame consists of shells, a favourite motif of metalworkers of the *barochetto*; they appear in a quite similar form on the frame made by Antonio Arrighi for the mosaic above the altar. Almost nothing is known of Agostino Valle, a metal founder with an address at the Botteghe Oscure, who had provided gilded nails to the Pamphili in 1726. As well as this frame, he also made the cross with its rays set over the altar of the chapel of St John the Baptist and the Holy Spirit.

His first recorded payments for work in the chapel date from April 1745, and he submitted his account in 1748. In it he describes the material of this frame for the embroidered altar frontals as *rame* – strictly copper, but the word could also be used for bronze; the backing is brass, and there is a lime-wood core. The decoration is cast and fixed to the basic form of the frame, which was made by being drawn through shaped slots on a board, by the same technique as wire. The base below is cast, with a decoration of 'little flowers' and leaves, and a central cartouche.

The full account, while interesting for what it tells us of the techniques employed, is a salutary reminder of how much work and artistry went into what one might too easily dismiss as just an adjunct of the splendid embroidery. In a chapel as richly decorated as this, the least element is a fully considered work of art. (JM)

PRIVATE DEVOTION

126. (pl.4.50)
Virgin of Sorrows
José de Mora (1642–1724), Granada, Spain, c.1670–80
Carved and painted pine set with ivory and glass, h 48.35cm, w 49cm, d 29cm
V&A: 1284–1871
Provenance
Purchased from G. Bracho through M.R. Steel, 1871
Bibliography
Webb (1927), p.58, pl.14A (mistakenly attributed to Martínez Montañés); Trusted (1996), no.46, with earlier references; Williamson (1996), p.142; Anderson (1998), pp.48–9, 85–6, figs 56–7 (mistakenly attributed to Pedro de Mena); Lopez-Guadalupe Muñoz (2000)
Busts of the mourning Virgin, often known as *Dolorosas*, were produced in some numbers in Spain during the Baroque period. Often they were paired with a bust of Christ as Man of Sorrows, crowned with thorns, *Ecce Homo*. They embodied the story of the Passion: Christ's sufferings and the Virgin's pain. The author of this example, José de Mora, was active in Granada in the late seventeenth and

early eighteenth century. His handling of wood is particularly notable, seen here in the restrained facial expression, the finely carved veil, and the corkscrew ringlets, made from twisted wood shavings. The whole sculpture is made from several pieces of wood ingeniously fitted together. The face is a mask, behind which the tongue, teeth and eyes have been inserted, after which the back of the head and veil would have been set in place. The luminous quality of the eyes suggests that they may be made from painted ivory. Although some of the original polychromy has been repainted, the brilliant smalt blue is still evident. The work was once attributed to another Granada sculptor, Pedro de Mena, whose similar busts of the Virgin are known in several collections, churches and convents. Although stylistically the present work is undoubtedly by José de Mora, it must descend from Pedro de Mena's prototypes. Such busts were often placed in side-chapels, and were used for devotional purposes. (MTr)

127. (pl.4.4)
The Virgin of the Immaculate Conception
Maker unknown, Indo-Portuguese, India, probably Goa, 1750–1800
Carved ivory, h 46.5cm, w 14cm
Museu Nacional de Arte Antiga, Lisbon, Inv 405 Esc
Provenance
Paço de S. Vicente de Fora, Lisbon, 1913
Bibliography
Coutinho (1959); Távora (1983), pp.52–3; Estella Marcos (1997), Sousa (2008)
This magnificent sculpture carved from a single piece of ivory represents the Virgin, whose serene expression and clasped hands reflect an attitude of prayer. A short veil partially covers her long centrally-parted hair. She wears a belted garment that reveals one bare foot; her mantle falls in elegant and flowing folds. Her clothing shows a border characteristic of Indo-Portuguese production. The figure stands on a sickle moon above a sphere carved with six angel heads and clouds; the base is decorated with scrolling leaves.

Representations of Marian invocation undoubtedly form one of the most important groups of imagery of the Portuguese East, not only for the large numbers that survive, but also for the diversity and plasticity of the various interpretations. The image of the Virgin of the Immaculate Conception, disseminated by missionary religious orders, first the Franciscans, then the Jesuits, was undoubtedly one of the most popular subjects, which reflected, over the eighteenth century, a gradual move towards Western models. (MCBS)

128. (pl.4.12)
Miniature house altar
Maker unknown, Germany, c.1710
Silver gilt and gold set with enamel, precious and semi-precious stones, watercolour on paper and glass, h 17.4cm, w 9.5cm, d 3.4cm
Grünes Gewölbe, Staatliche Kunstsammlungen Dresden, VI 118
Provenance
Acquired at Easter Fair in Leipzig, 1730; mentioned in the Pretioseninventar 1725–33, fols 68v–69r; Inventar Pretiosenzimmer 1733, fols 701–3, no.456
Bibliography
Künstlerhaus, Vienna (1988), no.82; Schmidt and Syndram (1997), no.87; Kappel and Weinhold (2007), p.220

The Green Vaults possess relatively few pieces of sacred treasury art. In its construction from a predella, an altarpiece flanked by a pair of double columns on either side and with a baldachin and *gloria* hanging over it, the miniature architecture of this altar follows the typology of late Baroque altars. Even the furnishings were not forgotten, in the form of tiny candlesticks on either side of a central crucifix. The Christological iconography of the small altar is Protestant in character, representing the Entombment, Crucifixion and Resurrection, as well as the monogram 'IHS'. Augustus the Strong, who acquired this precious piece at the Leipzig Easter Fair in 1730, had already converted to Catholicism in 1697 in order to take the Polish throne; however, the population of Saxony remained predominantly Protestant. (UW)

129. (pl.4.39)
Shrine
Maker unknown, Trapani, Sicily, c.1650
Gilded copper, enamelled and set with coral, h 46.6cm, w 30.2cm
V&A: M.157–1956
Provenance
Hildburgh Bequest
Bibliography
Similar examples in Di Natale (2002), nos 13–17, and Di Natale (2003), nos II.8, II.33
This small shrine, made in Trapani, Sicily, was for domestic use in a private chapel. The central figure, thought to be St Rosalia, the patron saint of Palermo, suggests that the piece was made for a local Sicilian family. In the mid-1600s the veneration of the saints came under strict regulation from the Catholic Church. St Rosalia was admitted to the official list of Catholic Martyrs by the Jesuits in Rome in 1627, just decades before this shrine was made.

Craftsmen in Trapani were renowned for their skilled use of coral. The town guild, founded in the 1600s, regulated production and established a coat of arms, allowing the identification of the work of the Trapani masters. This shrine demonstrates a characteristic technique in which coral was cut into small shapes and inset into gilded copper, bronze or silver. Geometric and floral designs like those upon this example were used on secular and religious objects alike. The seventeenth century saw the increase in manufacture of objects decorated with coral for ecclesiastical use such as holy water stoups, monstrances and shrines. (SS)

130. (pl.4.13)
Holy Family with Angels
Artist unknown, Cuzco School, Viceroyalty of Perú, 1700–1800
Oil on canvas with gold highlights; carved, gilded and polychromed wood frame inlaid with mirror glass, h 140cm, w 100cm, d 20cm
Museo de América, Madrid, 1982/07/1
Bibliography
Museo de América (1983), p.23; Martinez de la Torre (1997), pp.131–2, 135, no.134; Casa de la Contratación (2003), pp.525/288; Arbeteta Mira (2006), p.206
This painting and its frame form a pair with a similar ensemble representing the Child Jesus carrying the cross. Here, in a colourful and intimate scene taken from popular iconography of the childhood of Jesus, Christ sleeps in his cradle, rocked by two angels, watched by Mary who is embroidering quietly. Joseph bends over to contemplate the baby.

There are flowers in the meadow and birds in the trees, details common to the Cuzco school of painting.

This subject, which occurs frequently in popular painting, derives from mystical writings, in particular Sister Maria de Jesús de Ágreda's *The mystical city of God*. According to legend this widely known work was dictated to the nun in supernatural circumstances. It was denounced as heretical by the Jesuit Rodrigo Valdes to the Lima Inquisition in 1699.

Several aspects of the painting reflect Mother Ágreda's text. The rustic landscape is a reference to the Holy Family's flight into Egypt. The birds and angels also have meaning, and may refer to passages where Mary and the Christ child are entertained by the singing of birds and angels.

The frame is made of pierced gilded wood inlaid with small mirrors, and decorated with a complex design of foliage, pomegranates and flowers topped by a small winged head. In the viceregal world the mirrors, extremely expensive imported articles, were used to display status, besides having a symbolic meaning. Mirrors were placed in retables and altarpieces and would have sparkled with reflected light from the sun and candles, symbolizing the divine light.

This work of art, created for private devotion, is an impressive example of viceregal domestic religiosity, outside fashion and often unorthodox, but alive to the physical world. (LAM)

The Palace and the Garden

131. (pl.5.3)
Vincennes* or *July*, from the tapestry series known as *The Royal Residences or The Months
Atelier Jean de la Croix (active 1662–1712) of the Gobelins Workshops, after designs by Charles Le Brun (1619–90) and others, Gobelins Workshops, Paris, 1670–1700
Tapestry woven in wool and silk, h 335cm, w 345cm
Remains of workshop mark lower right I.D.L. [the current reading L.D.L. is created by later restoration]
V&A: T.371–1977
Provenance
Sold from Collection Henry Say, Galerie Georges Petit, Paris, 30 November 1908, lot 32; Château de Fleury-en-Bière; purchased Sotheby's, London, 1 July 1977, lot 6
Bibliography
Fenaille (1903–23), pp.128–165; Adelson and Landini (1990); Bremer-David (1997), p.25

This tapestry is from a series representing twelve of Louis XIV's royal residences during different months of the year, with the king shown hunting with his retinue in the grounds of his châteaux. The composition puts these outdoor scenes into the background, with the foreground dominated by a display of abundance, both the bounty of nature and the luxury of court life. The textiles and other precious objects laid on the balustrade are known to have been drawn from Louis's treasury, and the animals and birds from his menagerie. The series was conceived and designed by Le Brun, but many artists collaborated by providing the details in which they specialized, such as floral arrangements.

The first set of *Les Maisons Royales* or *The Royal Residences* was made in the workshop of Lefebvre and Jans in 1668, and between then and 1713 the Crown commissioned seven complete sets of this popular subject, woven with gold thread. A number of other less lavish sets were commissioned by private individuals. The set of tapestries to which this example belongs, smaller in dimensions and in a border without royal emblems, was probably such a private order late in the seventeenth century from the workshop of Jean de la Croix. (CBr)

THE GARDEN

132. (pl.5.15)
Mask from the Fountain Garden Screen at Hampton Court
Jean Tijou (active 1660– *c.*1716), England, *c.*1690
Embossed wrought iron, h 60cm, w 78cm, d 17cm
Hampton Court Palace – Historic Royal Palaces, on long term loan to the Victoria and Albert Museum
Provenance
From the Fountain Garden Screen at Hampton Court Palace
Bibliography
Tijou (1693), pl.2; Gardner (1922), pp.77–81; Ayrton and Silcock (1929), pp.7–83; Harris (1960), ill.7; Murdoch (1982), p.25; Groom (1996); Thurley (2003), pp.229, 230, 234, 351–3

English architectural blacksmithing was revitalized by King William III and Queen Mary II's love of formal gardens. The ironworker Jean Tijou, a French Huguenot, excelled at the art of *repoussé* or embossed ironwork, hammering sheet iron into relief. His work at Hampton Court, St Paul's Cathedral, Kensington Palace and country seats including Chatsworth, Drayton House and Wimpole Hall had a lasting impact on a trade still shaped by medieval Gothic traditions.

Tijou's magnificent gated screen at Hampton Court, from which this mask comes, was originally erected in William and Mary's Great Fountain Garden. Twelve large panels of scrollwork, spaced with vertical pilaster sections, were enlivened with embossed acanthus leaves, sunflowers, masks, tasselled *lambrequins* (resembling drapery) and heraldic motifs, possibly painted steely blue and gilded. Details of the screen, including a flamboyant version of this mask, appear in Tijou's *A New Booke of Drawings* of 1693, the earliest English ironwork publication. Tijou was highly regarded by contemporaries, receiving an impressive £2,160 2s. 0 1/4d.for the screen.

During Queen Anne's reign the screen was re-erected at the south end of the Privy Garden, only to be moved in 1729 to the Pavilion Terrace. The panels, though not the gates, were removed to the Victoria and Albert Museum in 1861 for restoration. In 1900 they were returned to Hampton Court, where most were eventually replaced in the Privy Garden. Paint and gilding were added to the screen during recent restoration. Although no records of decoration to the screen survive from the 1690s, the diarist Ralph Thoresby recorded in 1712 'curious iron balustrades, painted and gilt in parts', a decorative scheme that reflected contemporary continental taste. (SL)

133. (pl.5.16)
Apollo flaying Marsyas
Antonio Corradini (1668–1752), Venice, 1710–50
Carved marble, h 220cm, w 100cm, d 57cm
V&A: A.6–1967
Provenance
Supplied to Augustus II for the palace gardens in Dresden after 1723; sold Dresden 31 May 1836 (buyer unknown); sold Messrs Foster & Son, London, 7 June 1843 (buyer unknown); at Easton Neston, Northamptonshire, by 1902; purchased by the V&A from the Old Clock House, Ascot, Surrey, under the Murray Bequest, 1967
Bibliography
Hodgkinson (1971); Cogo (1996), pp.245–7, fig.67

Marsyas unwisely challenged Apollo, the god of the Muses, to a musical contest, and lost. As a penalty he was flayed by Apollo. Here Marsyas is shown upside-down, while Apollo commences peeling off his skin. One putto sits by Apollo's lyre on the ground, while another looks over Apollo's shoulder. This is one of twelve life-size marble sculptures made by Corradini for the gardens in Dresden owned by Augustus the Strong, elector of Saxony and king of Poland. They were carved in Venice, where the sculptor was based, and exported to Saxony. Their Italianate forms lent the gardens the spirit of Versailles. They were dispersed in a sale in the nineteenth century; this is one of two groups now in the Victoria and Albert Museum. (MT)

134. (pl.5.4)
Plan of the château, gardens and environs of Versailles
Artist unknown, Versailles, France, 1687
Pen and ink with pencil and wash, h 126cm, w 57cm
Inscribed throughout giving the names of buildings, bosquets and fountains etc.
Nationalmuseum, Stockholm, THC 1
Provenance
Nicodemus Tessin the Younger (Tessin cat.1712, p.24); Carl Gustaf Tessin (inv. *c.*1732); King Adolf Fredrik; King Gustav III; Kongl. Museum; Nationalmuseum from 1866 (Tessin-Hårleman Collection)
Bibliography
Centre culturel suédois (1985), no.A.4; Nationalmuseum (1986), no.7; Dee and Walton (1988), no.1; Snickare (2002), p159-60; Olin (2004), no.486

This drawing of the palace, gardens and environs of Versailles can be dated to 1687, the date of the second visit to Versailles by Nicodemus Tessin the Younger. This is suggested by the existing fountains and bosquets which correspond to those mentioned by Tessin in his account of his visit. In addition, it is supported by the presence of the recently erected Grand Trianon, and by details of the north wing of the palace, including the project for a new chapel and a theatre (abandoned in 1688). The lower part includes the outbuildings which had been completed by this date, including the Royal Stables. The authorship of the drawing has been attributed to Francois d'Orbay on stylistic grounds, but not as part of the larger group of drawings to which it belongs. It would seem rather that Jean II Le Blond was involved in their production, although whether as draughtsman or as supplier to Daniel Cronström is unclear. A small separate piece of paper is joined to the sheet to show the *Escalier des cent marches* and the orangery below. Unusually, the draughtsman chose to use the plan of the first floor of the palace rather than the ground floor; this did however enable him to show both the Galerie des Glaces and the king's bedchamber, which forms the central point of the entire plan. It seems likely, given the probable dating, that Tessin commissioned the drawing himself while in Paris. (JN)

135. (pl.5.18)
Child's garden carriage
Attributed to Master Saddler Saillot and his workshop, Paris, *c.*1697–8
Carved, joined, painted and silvered wood, embroidered leather, later oil paintings, felt wheel rim covers, metal fittings formerly silvered, silk damask upholstery (after 1728, redone in the nineteenth century) trimmed with original silver braid, h 153cm, l 247.5cm, d 96cm
Bayerische Verwaltung der staatlichen Schlösser, Gärten und Seen, München, WAF A 25
Provenance
Probably ordered by Elector Max Emanuel of Bavaria for his first-born son Joseph Ferdinand
Bibliography
Kreisel (1927), p.29f; Wackernagel (2002), vol.1, pp.62–5, vol.2, pp.84–8

Carriages for children of aristocratic or princely families were intended to encourage leadership qualities. This carriage, probably used by the young prince Joseph Ferdinand, would have been pulled by a pair of sheep or goats, wearing blue velvet harnesses and
bridles with silver buckles, as mentioned in eighteenth-century inventories. Miniature carriages were often gilded, as this one was originally, and appear in contemporary paintings. The pelican group on the front of the carriage may symbolize parental love. The broad felt wheel-rim covers allowed the carriage to be used indoors or out, protecting marquetry floors or the fine gravel paths of parks. The elegant phaeton-like design of the carriage body is reminiscent of the Roman-style carousel-carriages so popular at Baroque court festivities.

The lack of heraldic insignia on this carriage suggests that it may have been produced speculatively by a Parisian luxury goods dealer. In Munich the carriage was painted blue and silver, the Bavarian court's colour scheme. In 1728 the 'little blue velvet Parisian garden carriage' used by Joseph Ferdinand's younger brother, Charles Albrecht, from around 1700, received the charming panel paintings and a new silvered volute on the roof.

The delicately ornamented body was manufactured from several wooden blocks as massive contemporary panelling. X-ray examination (kindly sponsored by the Messerschmitt Stiftung München) shows that the domed canopy of the carriage is constructed like a barrel. The undercarriage was made by a wheelwright and includes a number of innovative features. The perch or shaft is fitted with iron swan necks, developed simultaneously in Rome and Paris in the 1660s. The fore-carriage has a full wheel-plate. The carriage suspension is formed by elbow springs under the seat, which hook into the main braces of the richly carved hind standards, held by iron stays on the perch wings. (RW)

136.
Festivities in the gardens of Schloss Nymphenburg
Ignaz Biedermann (1670– *c.*1747), Starnberg, Germany, *c.*1727
Oil on canvas, h 71.5cm, w 165.3cm
Bayerisches Nationalmuseum, Munich, R 7834
Provenance
Acquired in 1902 on the art market in Munich
Bibliography
Straub (1969), Prochazka (1976), Schmid and Staudinger (1993)

On 17 August 1727 the Bavarian Elector Charles Albrecht organised the festivities for the birthday of his younger brother, Clement Augustus, the Elector and Archbishop of Cologne since 1723. Ignaz Biedermann, a painter from Starnberg, depicted these festivities held in the gardens in front of Schloss Nymphenburg, the summer residence of the Bavarian electors. Two separate tournament areas were prepared, one on each side of the Nymphenburg garden canal. On the canal there were two long lines of covered gondolas. From the boats, which were also used for dining, and from the spectators' stands on either side, the guests could watch the spectacle of two games of skill: a Ladies' Running at the Ring (on the left) and a Quintain (on the right). In the Quintain the tournament rider had to ride at a full gallop and hit a wooden figure with his lance, to the accompaniment of trumpets and trombones. As well as skill in the sport, elegant bearing and good riding were also rewarded. In the Ladies' Running at the Ring the lady sat raised up in a carousel carriage driven by a knight and drawn by two horses. The main aim of the race, among others, was to spear the heart of a cupid whilst driving past. The tournament was followed by a night-time illuminated target shooting, in which the black circle of a round target had to be hit using bows and arrows. Preparations for this event can be seen in the foreground of the painting. (AS)

THE STAIRCASE

137. (pl.5.49)
View of the Staircase of the Ambassadors
Louis de Surugue de Sergis (1686–1762) after a drawing by Jean-Michel Chevotet (1698–1772), Paris, *c.*1720
Engraving, h 36.8cm, w 63cm
Lettered: J.M. Chevotet Surugue / Vue interieure du Grand Escalier de Versailles Prospectus interioris majorum Scallarum Versalianarum/ Costé Oposé a l'entré Pars fores speclans
V&A: E.93–1901
Bibliography
Nolhac (1900); Revel (1958); Millon (1999), no.345u

The Staircase of the Ambassadors was perhaps the most famous and influential of all the individual parts of the palace of Versailles, possibly excepting the *Galerie des Glaces*. This engraving, published as part of a lavish book of prints about the staircase, serves as an important record of the grandeur of the staircase which was destroyed in 1752 to make way for new developments under Louis XV; although the intention was to rebuild it at a later date, this was never carried out. The lower part of the staircase was entirely executed in coloured marbles, as the Queen's Staircase, which still survives, would be some years later. On the first floor level painted panels by Charles Le Brun, Adam van der Meulen and others imitating tapestries, depicting Louis XIV's military victories were placed between pilasters and columns on bronze bases, alternating with fictive perspectives of visitors from the four corners of the globe leaning over fictive balustrades to admire the palace. The wall decoration was complemented, as can be seen from an engraving by Simonneau, by the illusionistic decoration of the vault, lit by natural light. At the centre of the lower stage of the staircase there was a fountain and at the upper level, the very centre of the whole ensemble, a bust of the king, with Hercules, Minerva and, most significantly, Apollo above, asserting the gloire of the king. One of the painted panels by van der Meulen and Le Brun survives at Versailles giving an indication of the scale and magnificence that the staircase must have had. (JN)

138. (pl.5.52)
Model for the staircase and vestibules of the royal palace of Caserta
Made by Antonio Rosz and his workshop after designs by Luigi Vanvitelli (1700–73), with wax reliefs by Tommaso Soldari (d. 1779) and decoration by Pietro Ferdacchini, Caserta, Italy, 1756–9
Carved and painted wood, h 124cm, w 377cm, d 128cm
Palazzo Reale Caserta
Bibliography
Palazzo Reale (1973); de Seta (1990); Millon (1999), no.177; de Seta (2000), pp.305–6

A number of architectural models for Vanvitelli's design for the royal palace at Caserta survive, including this one for the central staircase, vestibules and, in a separate part which attaches to it, the royal chapel (not exhibited here). Such models allowed the architect to test his designs and try out revisions, as well as serving as reference models for the craftsmen working on the project. They also functioned as presentation models, however, to be shown to the King of the Two Sicilies, who had commissioned the palace, models giving a 'better effect' than drawings and creating better publicity around an architectural project. This model took nearly four years to complete, including its decoration in oil which reproduced the intended colours of the marbles, and the wax statuettes by Soldari. It allows the whole inside area of the monumental staircase to be seen, by opening one of the side doors; it also shows the lower vestibules where coaches would disgorge their occupants at the foot of the staircase and the play of illusionistic arches on the upper vestibule, leading to the enfilades and, on one side, into the chapel. The model achieved its aims, however: the king was apparently overcome by emotion when it was presented to him. (JN)

THE GALLERY

139. (pl.5.21)
***The Triumph of Divine Providence and the fulfilment of her ends under the Papacy of Urban VIII:* record of the ceiling of the *salone* of Palazzo Barberini, Rome**
Workshop of Pietro da Cortona (1596–1669), Rome, *c.*1640
Oil on canvas, h 168cm, w 113cm
Galleria Nazionale d'Arte Antica di Roma, Palazzo Barberini, 1943
Provenance
Commissioned by Maffeo Barberini, Pope Urban VIII for the Palazzo Barberini; Vitale Bloch 1934
Bibliography
Scott (1991), pp.125–35; Kieven (1993), p.130; Lo Bianco (2004), pp.3–14; Barock im Vatikan (2005), no.152

Palazzo Barberini, in its architectural and painted decoration, represented a highly sophisticated manifestation of the power of the family of Pope Urban VIII. The ceiling paintings form the largest and most complex ensemble of any Roman palazzo, and liken the Barberini members to divinities. Ceilings were commissioned from both rising artists and those already under Barberini patronage, including Pietro da Cortona who painted the *salone grande*, the double-height room at the centre of the palace which was seen by all visitors. This painting of the ceiling design shows the geometrical framework of fictive architecture dividing the ceiling into a central panel depicting Divine Providence Enthroned with four outer sections, representing Faith, Hope and Charity, Religion, and Rome, bearing the attributes of papal keys and a tiara crowned with the Barberini arms. Mythological scenes fill the rest of the painted surface in a triumph of illusionism and abundance of tumbling figures, incorporating elements from earlier artists such as Michelangelo, Raphael, Correggio, Annibale Carracci, Alberti, Guercino, Domenichino and Lanfranco.

Although this painting was at one time thought to be the artist's *bozzetto* or model for the ceiling, its closeness to the ceiling as executed in every respect makes this an unlikely supposition. It seems more probable that in fact the painting represents a workshop copy of the ceiling design, possibly intended to serve as a diplomatic gift. (JN)

140. (pl.5.57)
Table and pair of candlestands
Attributed to Pierre Gole (*c.*1620–84) and his workshop; carving attributed to Mathieu Lespagnandelle (*c.*1616–89); gilding attributed to David Dupré, Paris, *c.*1671
Carved, gilded and silvered wood, brass and pewter marquetry, and gilt bronze. Table: h 90cm, w 100cm, d 80cm; candlestands: h 130cm, w 50cm, d 50cm
Knole, The Sackville Collection (The National Trust). Table: NT/KNO.F.125; candlestands: T/KNO.F.127 a-b
Provenance
Possibly acquired by Charles Sackville, later 6th earl of Dorset; Sackville family by descent; possibly listed in 'The Guard Room' at Knole in 1799: 'Two Stands inlaid with Brass – a Table dit[to]', but not listed in 1706 and 1730
Bibliography
Jackson-Stops (1977), p.1496; Lunsingh-Scheurleer (1980), p.386; Baarsen et al. (1988), pp.50–51; Drury (1991); Lunsingh-Scheurleer (2005), pp.168–72

Traditionally this rare and important Parisian furniture was given by Louis XIV to Charles Sackville, later 6th earl of Dorset, Charles II's special ambassador to the French court in 1669–70. The structural and sculptural elements of the table and the *torchères* relate to designs by Charles Le Brun for furniture at Versailles, and the fleurs-de-lis on the stretcher of the table may indicate royal patronage. The Knole group has been linked to a commission from Louis XIV in 1671 for two tables, four *torchères*, and eight *porte-carreaux* (low stools bearing cushions), all in silver and gold. As well as Gole, the carver Lespagnandelle and the gilder Dupré were mentioned in the 1671 document.

It is possible that part of this set ordered by Louis XIV (which included *torchères* of the four seasons: the Knole stands incorporate putti bearing sheaves of corn, and grapes) was given by the king to Sackville as a present. Sackville left Paris in 1670, however, the year before, and so the set may have come to Knole (by 1799?) in some other way.

The Knole group is certainly attributable to Gole and his workshop. The quality of the gilt bronze, brass and pewter tops of the table and its flanking stands is superb. They are comparable to designs attributed to Gole (e.g. the sketch for the floor of the grand dauphin's *Cabinet Doré* at Versailles, 1678–82, Musée des Arts Décoratifs, Paris). The brass and pewter metalwork of the writing desk at Boughton is very similar in conception, though less vigorous in design, being also attributed to Gole, and linked to the 1st duke of Montagu's diplomatic activities in Paris.

The Knole table and stands were over-gilded, probably in the nineteenth century. In 1991, the remarkably well preserved original silvering and water gilding were uncovered. This has revealed the subtlety of the mix: the silvering of the ribbons tied into bows beneath the apron of the table contrasts elegantly with the gilding of the frame. (CRow)

141. (pl.5.59)
Pair of candelabra
Christoffer Merker, Stockholm, 1684
Gilded bronze, faceted pearls and rosettes of rock crystal, h 47cm, w 36cm
Skoklosters Slott
Provenance
Included in the cash account book of 1684 of Nils Brahe (1633–99)
Bibliography
Thornton (1978), pp.268–78

This pair of candelabra or *girandoles*, designed to be placed on a pair of guéridons, comes from a garniture which also included a chandelier. Their maker, Merker, was a girdle maker in Stockholm, and was therefore allowed to produce other objects in gilded bronze. The pyramidal form of this type of candelabrum, usually with six candle branches radiating from the central stem, became standard in Paris by around 1670. Also particularly developed in Paris was the use of rock crystal in such candelabra and chandeliers; although expensive and difficult to work as a material, it was highly effective at reflecting light. This pair, although made in Stockholm, follow this standard Parisian model. By the time of their production, however, it was becoming more common in Paris to use clear glass instead of rock crystal, which by the end of the seventeenth century had almost entirely ceased to be used for such lighting. Nils Brahe, who acquired this garniture, was the son-in-law of the Swedish general Carl Gustaf Wrangel, having married his eldest daughter, and later inherited Skokloster Castle. (BK, JN)

142. (pl.5.62)
Mantua
Maker unknown, London, *c.*1708; stomacher 1720–30
Silk damask brocaded with silk and gold file; l 265.4cm, stomacher l 33.7cm
The Metropolitan Museum of Art, Purchase, Rogers Fund, Isabel Shults Fund and Irene Lewisohn Bequest, 1991 (mantua: 1991.6.1a,b; stomacher: 1991.6.2)
Provenance
Purchased 1991
Bibliography
Majer (1991)

The mantua (from the French *manteau*) first appeared in the early 1670s as an informal garment. Although worn over stays and probably sashed, the mantua's loose, unboned construction provided a welcome alternative to fashionable dress of rigidly-boned pointed bodice and heavily-pleated trained skirt. Despite the prohibition of the mantua at Versailles by Louis XIV, who disapproved of its 'undress', it gained widespread popularity. By 1700, the mantua became more formal and was distinguished by elaborate back drapery, evolved from an earlier fashion for pulling back the skirt.

This mantua is kimono-like in construction even though the fabric has been pleated and draped to fit the body, and the bodice fullness is further controlled by the girdle at the waist. Pinholes suggest stitching was used to secure the high bustle, the luxurious folds of which create the impression of having been drawn up spontaneously. The sleeve cuffs have taken on the large proportions of those on men's coats, and the thickly applied lace and fringes of the seventeenth century have been replaced by deep flounces of self-fabric.

The Eastern simplicity of the mantua's cut is combined with the brilliant colour and powerful asymmetry of a bizarre silk. Produced only between 1695 and 1720, bizarre silks were characterized by elongated diagonal patterns incorporating exotic, and at times abstract, motifs. These highly fashionable silks were available in limited quantities, and it is remarkable to have such an expansive quantity survive in its original usage. The dress itself is the only complete and unaltered early eighteenth-century mantua known to exist. (ABo)

143. (pl.2.37)
Console table
Maker unknown, Rome, c.1700
Carved and gilded pine with stone composite top veneered in breccia, h 85cm, w 176cm, d 89cm
V&A: W.35–1977
Provenance
Mayer Amschel Rothschild Collection, Mentmore Towers; acquired by H.M. Government for the nation, Mentmore Sale, 18–20 May 1977, lot 872
Bibliography
Colle (2000), pp.73–91
This table is characteristic of the exuberant late Baroque style found in Rome around 1700. At the centre of the apron is a female mask with headdress. The legs are set at an angle to the corners of the table and are formed from heavily carved 'S' scrolls, with winged, howling male masks, and heavily ribbed 'C'-scroll feet placed on blocks at the base. The back legs, where they are visible, are carved in the same way as the front, but left unadorned where hidden from view. Two stretchers link the front and back legs, with the front one placed at a lower level. They are both carved with howling, winged masks terminating in acanthus-leaf beards.

The scrolls are similar to those on the organ loft of S. Maria in Vallicella, Rome, built by Francesco Magli in 1698–9 to the designs of Camillo Rusconi. This highly theatrical version of Baroque was publicized by engravers like Filippo Passarini in *Nuovi inventioni d'ornamenti* (1698), and inspired by carvers like Giovanni Paolo Schor and Ciro Ferri, whose works included papal thrones and ambassadorial coaches. The original provenance of this table remains unknown, but it would most likely have been one of a pair from the state apartments of a Roman palazzo. It came to the V&A from Mentmore Towers, the Buckinghamshire residence of Mayer Amschel Rothschild, and is characteristic of the flamboyant tastes of a family whose collections included, in addition to more famous French items, some outstanding Italian pieces of furniture. (JY)

144. (pl.5.55)
Mirror with painted decoration
Probably painted by Antoine Monnoyer (1670–1747), probably London, 1710–20

Mirrored glass painted in oils with stained wood frame, h 186cm, w 158.5cm, d 6cm
Arms of Duncombe of Stocks (probably added later)
V&A: W.36–1934
Provenance
Given by the Hon. Mrs Blezard
Bibliography
Cornforth (1993)
The *Galerie des Glaces* or Hall of Mirrors at the Palace of Versailles, completed in 1684, fostered a taste for using looking-glass in European royal and aristocratic interiors. Glass was still made in small pieces and joins were concealed with decorative banding. As at Versailles, the illusion of extended space might reflect formal gardens seen from the windows opposite. Looking-glass played an important role in cabinets of porcelain or glass, multiplying images and providing a glimpse of the backs of these exotic treasures.

In about 1690, Mary II commissioned a looking-glass closet for her London palace in Kensington. It was decorated by Jean-Baptiste Monnoyer, known as Baptiste, a Huguenot refugee famous for flower paintings executed for Louis XIV at Versailles and Vincennes. The contemporary closet of Anne, Duchess of Monmouth and Buccleuch, at Moor Park, Hertfordshire, was similarly embellished with an overmantel glass painted with flowers by Jakob Bogdany. Much treasured, this was moved to Dalkeith Palace outside Edinburgh, where the duchess settled in 1700.

The V&A's painted glass was probably also intended as an overmantel. It is associated with Stocks House, Aldbury, Hertfordshire. The flower painting, including roses, honeysuckle and lilies, is lighter in character than the work of Jean-Baptiste Monnoyer and is attributed to his son Antoine, who was working in London from the 1710s. Such naturalistic depiction of flowers reflected growing interest in botany and the cultivation of rare floral specimens. The decorative strapwork echoes contemporary ironwork and reflects the ornamental prints of Daniel Marot. (TM)

145. (pl.5.50)
Louis XIV receiving the Persian ambassadors in the Galerie des Glaces at Versailles
Attributed to Nicolas de Largillière (1656–1746), Paris, 1715
Oil on canvas, h 70cm, w 153cm
Musée national des châteaux de Versailles et de Trianon, MV 5461
Provenance
Purchased 1898
Bibliography
Musée des Arts Décoratifs (1960), no.755 (tapestry); Constans (1980), no.1021; Garnier (1989), no.125; Constans (1995), no.1132; Milovanovic (2005), no.17; Salmon (2007), no.10, p.54
Mehmet Riza Beg, the ambassador of the Shah of Persia, was received formally in the *Galerie des Glaces* on 19 February 1715. As for the embassies from Genoa (1685) and Siam (1686), the throne was placed on a dais at the end of the gallery next to the *Salon de la Paix*. The ceremony was particularly sumptuous: according to the duc de Saint-Simon (*Mémoires*, IV, pp.631–3), Louis XIV wore a costume embroidered with pearls and diamonds worth 12.5 million *livres*; however, Saint-Simon also specified that the king's dress was 'of gold and black stuff', which does not correspond with the painting. Saint-Simon added that the king, who would die six and a half months later, seemed thinner and sickly,

bent under the weight of his clothes. The duc d'Anjou, the future Louis XV, and Philippe d'Orléans, the future regent, are depicted on the right and left of the king respectively, both, like him, wearing the blue sash of the Order of the Holy Spirit. The attribution of the painting is problematic: the name of Antoine Coypel has long been cited because Saint-Simon indicated that the painter had been present at the ceremony in order to paint it. This attribution is no longer tenable; on stylistic grounds, Xavier Salmon recently proposed a reattribution to Nicolas de Largillière. (NM)

146. (pl.5.56)
Clock, designed for the Small Gallery at Versailles
Probably Jean Berain the Younger (about 1674–1726) after Jean Berain the Elder (about 1640–1711), Paris, 1699
Graphite, pen and ink with wash on paper, h 83.5cm, w 43.7cm
Inscribed with explanations in pen and ink in the small plans to the right, corresponding to sections of the clock, starting from the bottom: 'Plan du premier socle marque A', and 'porte'/'porte', corresponding to doors back and front; above: 'plan de la corniche marqué B'; and top: 'plan du pied destaille en profil de tombeau marque C'. The face of the barometer is inscribed: 'tempeste/pluy frequente/pluy/chengent/beau temps/tres beau/tres sec'. Scale at the bottom: 11cm = 1 pieds (sic)
Nationalmuseum, Stockholm, THC 1135
Provenance
Nicodemus Tessin the Younger (Tessin cat.1712, p.12); Carl Gustaf Tessin (inventory about 1732, 4:3, 'Autre (pendule) proprement dessiné par Berain, avec la description'; inventory 1749, p.168); King Adolf Fredrik; Kungl. Biblioteket (Royal Library); Kongl. Museum (Lugt, 1638); Nationalmuseum from 1866 (Tessin-Hårleman Collection)
Bibliography
Weigert (1935); de la Gorce (1986), pp.48–9, 51, 156; Dee and Walton (1988), no.60
The drawing depicts a sumptuous clock in marquetry and ormolu designed by Jean Berain the Elder for the Small Gallery at Versailles and made 1693–6. The clock never reached the gallery (destroyed in the eighteenth century), and it is unclear whether it was a royal commission, or made speculatively. Berain demanded an excessive price for the clock and could not sell it; so in 1699 he offered it for sale at the Swedish court. This presentation drawing and a description, probably dictated by Berain, explaining the functions and iconography of the clock, and the difficulties involved in its development and manufacture, promoted the sale.

The clock was valued at 2,000 *livres* in the inventory taken after Berain's death. It later became the property of the dukes d'Aumont. In 1782, it was given a new mechanism, but after that date we lose trace of it.

The drawing shows one face of the clock, with female herms representing Dawn and Noon; Evening and Midnight are hidden. The smaller male herms on the upper level represent the four seasons (Winter and Autumn shown). The enamel clock face featured a *bas-relief* of Apollo and other ornaments on an enamel surface. The crowning feature is a blue enamel sphere with gold stars and the signs of the zodiac.

In his description, Berain excuses the poor quality of the drawing and the fact that it shows only one side, adding that it was drawn

by a young man. This is commonly thought to be Jean Berain the Younger, who was 25 at the time. (MO)

THE THRONE ROOM AND AUDIENCE CHAMBER

147. (pl.5.61)
Drawing of an embroidered wall hanging from the King's Audience Chamber at Versailles
Artist unknown, France, c.1687
Pen and ink, wash, watercolours and gouache on paper, graphite, h 66.7cm, w 49.1cm
Inscribed: 'Meuble Brodée dans la Sale d'Audience de l'Apartement à Versailles' (Carl Gustaf Tessin)
Nationalmuseum, Stockholm, THC 1554
Provenance
Probably Nicodemus Tessin the Younger; Carl Gustaf Tessin (inv. c.1732: '1 Meuble brodé dans la Salle d'Audience a Versailles. Dessein coloré'); King Adolf Fredrik; Kungl. Biblioteket; Kongl. Museum (Lugt, 1638); Nationalmuseum from 1866 (Tessin-Hårleman Collection)
Bibliography
Weigert (1932); Centre Culturel Suédois (1985), no.C13; Nationalmuseum, Stockholm (1986), no.17; Walton (1986), p.23, fig.21; Dee and Walton (1988), no.13; Saule (1996), p.77, fig.92; Laine and Magnusson (2002), pp.199–200; Saule and Arminjon (2007), no.17, fig.36, p.48
This drawing is a record of one of the set of large-scale embroidered wall-coverings displayed during summer in the *Salon d'Apollon* at Versailles, which usually served as an audience chamber. It was here that the throne was placed. The panels were embroidered with large quantities of gold and silver thread and also included relief plaques of silver. The Swedish architect Nicodemus Tessin the Younger saw the room in 1687, and, very impressed, remarked particularly on the three-dimensionality of the silver and gold embroideries: 'The magnificence of this piece is surprising: the furnishing is distinguished by embroidered gold pilasters in relief of up to three thumbs; the figures are almost life-size, with all the nudes in solid silver; and the rest is embroidered in gold in relief of up to four or five thumbs in some places, particularly the trophies at the bottom; the colours have been slightly mixed all across the embroideries so as to be able to distinguish them more clearly; the background is all embroidered in silver'.

This particular panel shows the enthroned figure of Peace under a canopy, surrounded by a garland of tulips, roses, peonies and other flowers. A little further down two putti are trying to set fire to a group of war trophies. The embroideries are all lost, and this drawing is among the few traces we have of them. (MO)

148. (pl.5.39)
Chair of state and footstool used at the coronation of Queen Anne
Thomas Roberts (active 1686–1714), London, 1702
Carved and gilded walnut upholstered in modern silk velvet with seventeenth-century fringing. Chair: h 173.5cm, w 88cm, d 98cm; footstool: h 29cm, w 65 cm, d 44cm
Crowned S stamped inside one rail of the footstool
Marquess of Salisbury, Hatfield House
Provenance
Used at the coronation of Queen Anne in 1702

Bibliography
Coleridge (1967); Beard (1997), p.141; Bowett (1999); Bowett (2002), pp.240–41

Although British monarchs were traditionally crowned in St Edward's Chair (used since the coronation of Edward II in 1308), each coronation also required a variety of chairs of state, to be used at different moments in the lengthy ceremony. This chair and footstool were made in 1702 by the royal chair-maker, Thomas Roberts. The frames were carved in a flamboyant Italianate manner, at a cost of £20 (including £3 for the footstool). The original upholstery work, by Richard Bealing, cost £4 4s 0d, using gold and blue brocade supplied by Anthony Ryland at a cost of £72, the trimmings by William Elliott, laceman. The current upholstery dates from the 1950s, and uses early seventeenth-century fringe.

The chair displays all the elements that had become standard for a chair of state by 1700 and that were to influence the design of thrones throughout the eighteenth and nineteenth centuries. It was oversized, giving dramatic emphasis to the sitter, the footstool having both necessary and emblematic functions. The back, widening to the cresting, was already a feature of such chairs. The carving of the broad cresting, rising above the crowned head of the monarch, is richly symbolic, including the lion and unicorn supporters, crossed sceptres and palms, flanking a crown above a cartouche with the queen's monogram. (SM)

149. (pl.5.41)
***Frederick I of Prussia* seated on his silver throne**
Samuel Theodor Gericke (1665–1729), Berlin, 1713
Oil on canvas, h 245cm, w 154cm
Stiftung Preussische Schlösser und Gärten Berlin-Brandenburg
Bibliography
Keisch and Netzer (2001), ill frontispiece, p.288; Saule and Arminjon (2007), pp.125-37

Frederick III, Elector of Brandenburg, was created Frederick I, King of Prussia in 1701, and immediately made moves to set himself up as an equal to other, more established, European monarchs. Already in possession of a number of pieces of silver furniture given by the House of Orange between 1646 and 1667, he commissioned further pieces following his coronation with which to furnish the state rooms of the Berlin palace, at that time being redesigned by Andreas Schlüter as an appropriate royal residence. Inventories of 1715–16 list Frederick's silver furniture, in Berlin and in his other palaces, as including 5 chairs, a sofa throne, 18 mirrors, 13 tables, 3 tea tables, 48 candlestands, 26 candelabra, 13 chandeliers, 9 chimney screens, as well as a large number of firedogs and other fire furniture. An unidentified throne is known to have stood in the *Rittersaal* in the Berlin palace opposite the great display of buffet plate. The silver throne depicted here appears as a symbol of authority in a number of portraits of the king, painted by various court painters including Samuel Theodor Gericke, who had been sent to Italy by Frederick to study under Carlo Maratta. As represented by Gericke, it is an imposing piece of furniture, with scrolling feet and arms and a highly elaborate cresting, bearing the Brandenburg arms in relief flanked by a pair of river gods and surmounted by a crown, held in the talons of two sculptural figures of the eagles of Brandenburg and Prussia. The throne is first inventoried in 1702, when it was in the former Secret Council Room; it is however possible that it may have been made before 1701, the royal arms being added after Frederick's coronation. None of Frederick's silver furniture survives, having been melted down from 1745 onwards. (JN)

DINING

150. (pl.3.39)
***Banquet given by the King and Queen for Prince Frederick Augustus and Archduchess Maria Josefa at the Dresden Residenz,* 3 September 1719**
Attributed to Antoine Aveline (1691–1743) after a drawing by Raymond Leplat (1663–1742), Paris, before 1728
Engraving and etching, h 24.2cm, w 34.4cm
Lettered: Diné du Roï et de la Reine/avec le Prince Roïal et la Princesse. Illegible pencil inscription
Kupferstich-Kabinett, Staatliche Kunstsammlungen Dresden, Mappe Festlichkeiten 1719, fol. 10 der Drucke
Bibliography
Das Königliche Denckmahl (1719), pp.41–2; Gaehtgens et al. (2006), no.213

The marriage of Crown Prince Frederick Augustus (II) in 1719 to Maria Josefa, daughter of the Holy Roman Emperor, was an occasion of the utmost political and dynastic importance for Augustus the Strong. In order to provide a suitably impressive setting for the reception of the bride on 2 September 1719, the king furnished a glittering sequence of state rooms after the French fashion on the second floor of the Dresden Residenz. The corner state room (Corner Dining Room) was the first room of the enfilade in the west wing of the Residenz. This was where the royal couple formally received the bride, and where, the following day, a public banquet took place, at which the royal party dined in the presence of nobles of the court as well as native and foreign guests. The royal table stood upon a velvet-covered podium under a canopy. The royal couple sat at the head of the table, flanked by the bride and bridegroom, one on either side. The service of the three-hour meal followed strict ceremonial conventions. (CSc)

151. (pl.5.34)
Knife, fork and spoon set
Maker unknown, London, 1670–75
Silver gilt with engraved ornament and armorials; spoon: l 20.4cm, w (max.) 4.7cm; fork: l 20cm, w 2.5cm; knife: l 19.8cm, w 2.5cm
Marks: TT below a coronet on spoon and fork, lower case 'y' and dagger on knife blade
V&A: M.325–1962
Provenance
Claude D. Rotch Bequest
Bibliography
Cokayne (1983), vol.1, p.193; Moore (1999), p.140; Brown (2001); Hindel and Herbert (2005), pp.50–51

Although four registered London silversmiths have the initials TT, the crowned TT mark has not survived in the records at Goldsmiths' Hall. The mark has been ascribed to Thomas Tysoe, but he was apprenticed in 1674 and would not have registered a mark until the 1680s.

The London cutler's mark on the knife blade can be attributed to either Joseph Surbut or William Boswell. Surbut was granted use of the 'y' mark in 1631 and Boswell in 1669. Boswell seems the more likely maker given the later date of the knife handle.

The trefid (three-sectioned) end of the fork and spoon handle became fashionable in the 1660s, evolving from earlier 'Puritan' spoons and French forms. The octagonal knife handle is typical of the mid to late seventeenth century, and the square-ended blade was developed in the 1650s, perhaps in response to the introduction of forks for food-spearing instead of knives.

The rich and finely engraved decoration was inspired by continental prints. The small roundels are engraved with classical scenes; that on the fork may depict Perseus and Andromeda. Scrollwork with stylized foliage and putti intermingle with homely vignettes of fashionable ladies, buglers and soldiers.

The coat of arms on the spoon and fork are those of Sir Robert Button of Tockenham Court, Lyneham, Wiltshire, and his wife Eleanor, daughter of William Compton of Hartbury, Gloucester. It has been suggested that the cutlery was made during Button's term of office as High Sheriff of Wiltshire in 1670. (AE)

152. (pl.5.35)
Tureen, dish and ladle
Attributed to Claude II Ballin (1661–1754), Paris; tureen: 1713–14; dish and ladle: 1714–15
Cast, embossed, chased and engraved silver gilt, tureen: h 20.5cm, w 22.5cm; dish: d 28.5cm; ladle: l 33.5cm, w 10cm
Marks: tureen: crowned V; dish and ladle: crowned X. Engraved with arms of Max Emanuel of Bavaria as governor of the Spanish Netherlands
Bayerische Verwaltung der staatlichen Schlösser, Gärten und Seen, München, Res.Mü. SK 1259–1261
Provenance
Acquired by Max Emanuel, Elector of Bavaria, while exiled in France
Bibliography
Musée national des châteaux de Versailles et de Trianon (1993), no.31; Bimbenet-Privat (2002), vol.1, p.234

The *pot à oille*, or tureen, and its dish both bear the arms used by Elector Max Emanuel from 1711 to 1714 as ruler of the Spanish Netherlands. An inventory entry shows that the receptacle was acquired by Max Emanuel in Paris in 1714. The knop of the lid, with the inscription 'M.E.C.I.B. 1705' (Max Emanuel Churfürst in Bayern 1705) is not original, probably coming instead from one of the silver objects bought by him in 1705 in Mons or Paris.

Both the tureen and its dish are covered with minutely detailed decoration in low relief, incorporating elements of both floral and *Laub- und Bandelwerk* ornament; the *pot à oille* also uses strapwork forms composed of flower stalks and slender pointed leaves. The *pot à oille* differs stylistically from a wine cooler of 1712–13, also in the Munich *Silberkammer*, which bears the mark of Claude II Ballin. The design of the tureen is altogether more malleable and less severe than that of the wine cooler, calling into question the attribution of the tureen, which bears no hallmarks, to Ballin.

The small size and circular footprint of the tureen follow that popular at the court of Louis XIV, derived from the container used for the Spanish soup *olla podrida*. Both the plasticity of the design and the lavish decoration of the piece, however, already herald the shift towards a taste for more massive lidded vessels as the principal focus of the table. (LS)

153. (pl.5.30)
Spice box with nutmeg grater
David Tanqueray (active 1708–30), London, 1714–15
Cast, raised and engraved silver, h 12cm, w 8cm, d 7cm
Engraved with cypher 'ES' under ducal coronet; Marks: London hallmarks for 1715, maker's mark
The British Museum – Bequeathed by Peter Wilding, 1969.0705.33
Provenance
Sold from the Earl of Lichfield sale Christie's (London) 26 November 1941, lot 94 for £270. Bequeathed by Peter Wilding
Bibliography
Tait (1972), Hayward (1959); similar examples in Hackenbroch (1963) and Hartop (1996)

This silver spice box opens with two hinged lids to reveal inner compartments and a removable central nutmeg grater. The floral knop of the grater forms that of the box itself. The box sits on four lion feet. Nutmeg was very fashionable at the end of the seventeenth century as well as being an important ingredient of punch and other warm alcoholic drinks.

The spice box is a French form and very unusual in English silver; it seems certain that it was introduced into England by Huguenot craftsmen. It was seemingly referred to as a salt box during the early eighteenth century, the internal compartments presumably serving to hold salt and pepper (different types of pepper being available at this time). Other existing versions are oval rather than rectangular (or precisely octagonal) in form or alternatively without the internal grater. A pair by Willaume in the Untermyer Collection shows the move by Tanqeray to create smoother surfaces decorated with unifying engraved decoration. David Tanqueray was the son of a weaver in Normandy and was apprentice to David Willaume, his mark being entered at Goldsmiths Hall in 1713. This is therefore one of his earliest works. The cypher 'ES' may refer to Elizabeth, Duchess of Somerset (1682-1722). (JN)

154. (pl.5.38)
Wine cooler
Paul de Lamerie (1688–1751) and Paul Crespin (1694–1770), London, 1727–8
Cast, chased and engraved silver, h 26.5cm, w 35cm, d 29.75cm
Engraved with the royal arms; marks: Paul Crespin overstriking Paul de Lamerie
V&A: M.1–1990
Provenance
Supplied by the Royal Jewel House to Philip Stanhope, 4th earl of Chesterfield, for his appointment as English ambassador to The Hague in 1728
Bibliography
Glanville (1990); Glanville (1996), p.39; Murdoch (2008), pp.106–7

Wine coolers intended for a single bottle were introduced in France in the late seventeenth century; the earliest London-made examples date from 1698. Coolers to the present design were first made by Paul de Lamerie for the 8th duke of Norfolk in 1723. In 1728 Crespin received a large order for plate for the use of Philip Stanhope, 4th earl of Chesterfield, as Ambassador to The Hague. Where appropriate, Crespin used sub-contractors to fulfil this order. De Lamerie already had moulds for coolers from the Norfolk commission and reused them to produce this piece and its pair, now in the National Museums of Scotland.

Chesterfield regarded the dinner table as central to diplomatic negotiations; within four months of his arrival at The Hague he added a 50-foot dining room to the ambassadorial residence.

This cooler and its pair are the earliest known surviving examples of eighteenth-century London silver to incorporate large areas of figurative chasing. The V&A example is chased with scenes representing the Four Elements in sculptural reliefs set against a diaper ground imitating a fine linen damask tablecloth. The matching cooler has scenes of the Four Seasons.

Crespin made his name in London in 1724 with a silver bath weighing over 6,000 ounces. Supported by dolphins, it was chased with scenes of Diana bathing and Perseus and Andromeda. John V of Portugal gave the bath to his mistress, the Abbess of the Convent of Odivelas, Madre Paula, born Paula Teresa da Silva. (TM)

155. (pl.5.24)
Leather panels from the Marble Dining Room at Ham House
Maker unknown, The Netherlands (Flanders), *c.*1675
Embossed, painted and gilded leather; 16 panels stitched together, h 228cm, w 188cm
Ham House, The Dysart Collection (purchased by H.M.Government in 1948 and transferred to The National Trust in 2002), NT/HH 169.1.1948

Provenance
Probably listed in 1677 in the ground-floor Marble Dining Room at Ham House

This section of painted and gilded leather, decorated with flowers, birds, insects and putti, is assumed to have come from the Marble Dining Room at Ham, so called because of its formerly black and white marble floor, which matched the surviving floor in the adjoining Great Hall.

Both the Marble Dining Room floor and the 1670s leather hangings were replaced by the 4th earl of Dysart in 1756, and it is his scheme – comprising new leather hangings and a decorative parquetry floor – that survives *in situ*. The original 1670s scheme is described in Thornton (1980), but not this fragment of leather. It is likely that it comes from the Marble Dining Room, and that it is one of the 'six peices of guilt leather hangings' (1679), which were also listed in 1677 and 1683. A bill of 25 April 1673 may refer to the installation of these panels: 'larkes [laths] & putting up the giltt Leather hanging – 8s 0d'.

Leather was a practical wall-covering for a dining room, given that textile wall hangings retained the smell of food, and was extremely fashionable at this date, sometimes replacing tapestries in summer. The fashion, and the manufacture, derived from Spain and the Spanish Netherlands. Antwerp inventories reveal the popularity of painted and/or gilded leather as a background for pictures in cabinet rooms, and both Spanish and Netherlandish leather hangings were exported. Leather hangings were luxury items; the Ham fragment is particularly richly decorated and is probably of Flemish manufacture. The fashion was long-lasting in England: Dyrham Park, Gloucestershire (NT), retains its Dutch or Flemish painted and gilded leather hangings of about 1695 in the Entrance Hall, and it is interesting that the 4th earl of Dysart replaced like for like, ordering his new Marble Dining Room hangings from John Sutton, 'Leather Gilder', London, in 1756. (CRow)

156. (pl.5.58)
Candlestand with 'Indian' figure
Maker unknown, probably Venice, *c.*1675
Carved, painted, ebonized, and partially gilded wood, h 125cm, w 38cm, d 38cm
Ham House, The Dysart Collection (purchased by H.M. Government in 1948 and transferred to The National Trust in 2002), NT/HH 79 1948 (as marked underneath the stand)

Provenance
One of a pair in the Great Dining Room at Ham House by 1677

Bibliography
Thornton (1980), pp.118–20, fig.105; Drury (1984), pp.39–40, pl.47C; Bowett (2002), p.124

The pair of stands, in the form of blacks wearing feather dresses, with quivers of arrows on their backs and bells on their wrists and ankles, was designed as an exotic form of *torchère* or *guéridon*. The circular tray held above their heads, on which candelabra would have been placed, is in the form of a tambourine. The modelling of the figures is of very high quality.

This type of anthropomorphic stand was highly fashionable in Northern Europe when this piece and its pendant were acquired by the Duke and Duchess of Lauderdale. The first mention of this pair in *situ* at Ham is in the 1677 and 1679 inventories, when 'Two Indian stands' were listed in the first-floor Great Dining Room (the present Round Gallery: the floor was removed between 1698 and 1725 to create a higher Entrance Hall). The pair was more precisely described in 1683 as 'Two blackamore stands'.

A similar *torchère* figure is depicted in an engraving of about 1675 by Jean Le Pautre. There is another pair of blackamoor *torchères* at Knole, Kent (NT), of about the same date and quality. Both the Ham and Knole pairs must have been made in the same place, as the figures, the tambourine trays and the gilded plinths are so closely related. Thornton and Drury described the Ham pair as Venetian, but this was doubted by Bowett, who stated that 'there is no reason' why they should not be English. The style of the giltwood plinths, however, seems to be North Italian, and figures of this kind were certainly made in Venice. In Florence, the Medici archives contain references from 1675 to 'blackamoor *torchères*', and a comparable Florentine pair, dated to the late seventeenth century, is in the Palazzo Pitti. Even so, the precise origin of these Ham and Knole blackamoor *torchères* remains uncertain. (CRow)

THE BUFFET

157. (pl.5.26)
The Macclesfield wine set

Wine cooler
Anthony Nelme (d.1723), London, 1719–20
Cast, chased, embossed, engraved and raised Britannia standard silver, h 76.8cm, w 109cm, d 72.5cm, weight 1552oz
Engraved with the arms of Thomas Parker, 1st earl of Macclesfield; Marks: leopard's head erased for Britannia standard silver; date letter for 1719–20; leopard's head crowned, for the London Assay Office; AN in monogram and e in a shaped punch for Anthony Nelme
V&A: M.27–1998

Wine cistern
Anthony Nelme (d. 1723), London, 1719–20
Britannia standard silver, raised, embossed, chased and cast, h 41cm, w 63.5cm, d 40cm, weight 357oz 16dwt
Engraved with the arms of Thomas Parker, 1st earl of Macclesfield; Marks: leopard's head erased for Britannia standard silver; date letter for 1719–20; leopard's head crowned, for the London Assay Office; AN in monogram and e in a shaped punch for Anthony Nelme
V&A: M.26–1998

Wine fountain
Anthony Nelme (d. 1723), London, 1719–20
Cast, chased, embossed, engraved and raised Britannia standard silver, h 71cm, w 40cm, d 50cm, weight 330oz 16dwt
Engraved with the arms and supporters of Thomas Parker, 1st earl of Macclesfield surmounted by baron's coronet; Marks: leopard's head erased for Britannia standard silver; date letter for 1719–20; leopard's head crowned, for the London Assay Office; AN in monogram and e in a shaped punch for Anthony Nelme
V&A: M.25:1-3–1998

Provenance
Supplied to Thomas Parker, 1st earl of Macclesfield

Bibliography
Shirley (1998) 1; Shirley (1998) 2

This is the only known surviving matching silver wine set of three pieces, and was supplied by Anthony Nelme for use by Thomas Parker, 1st earl of Macclesfield. The set weighs over 2,200 ounces and cost over £1,200. Such grandeur was usually associated with official ambassadorial entertaining. The fountain, cistern and cooler formed part of the buffet display in the new Dining Room at Macclesfield's Oxfordshire home, Shirburn Castle. The dining room at Shirburn was remodelled after 1716 with alcoves, still in situ, equipped with marble shelves for the display of silver. The silver wine cooler was placed on the floor, with the fountain and cistern on marble shelves above. The fountain contained water for rinsing wine glasses between refills, the cistern standing beneath the fountain tap caught the water tipped from the glasses, and the wine cooler, filled with ice, was used to chill both white and red wines.

Lord Macclesfield admired the Duke and Duchess of Marlborough's spectacular buffet displays at Blenheim Palace and Marlborough House, London. The Marlborough plate was inspired by European precedent. A temporary buffet was set up at Versailles in 1668 for a fête in honour of Louis XIV's mistress Madame de Montespan. The Berlin buffet, created between 1695 and 1698 by leading Augsburg goldsmiths for Elector Frederick II of Brandenburg, was displayed in the Knights' Hall (*Rittersaal*) of the Stadtschloss. In 1712, Augustus the Strong commissioned his architect to design a silver buffet for the State Apartments of the Residential Palace in Dresden. Most of the silver for this buffet was also made in Augsburg.

The design of the Macclesfield wine service derives from Daniel Marot's *Nouveaux Liure d'Orfeurerie* republished in The Hague in 1712. Marot trained under Berain at Versailles, but between 1694 and 1696 he resided in London where his design drawings were sought after by leading artists and craftsmen. His influence continued into the 1720s as the Louis XIV style remained prestigious in Britain after Louis's death in 1715. The lions' head masks, dolphin's head tap and bold gadrooned ornament are typical of silver supplied by leading Huguenot goldsmiths in London and may have been the work of Huguenot journeymen in Nelme's workshop. The higher silver content of the Britannia standard was well-suited to such cast sculptural ornament.

Lord Macclesfield enjoyed a meteoric career as a barrister. Called to the bar in 1691, his reputation was established through the Tutchin libel case in 1704. In 1710 he was appointed Lord Chief Justice and in 1718 became Lord Chancellor of England. George I gave him £14,000 to mark this appointment and this spectacular wine service reflects the royal patronage Macclesfield enjoyed. It was probably commissioned in 1718 but the Baron's coronets indicate that it was delivered before Macclesfield was elevated to an earldom in 1721.

All three pieces in the set are embellished with the Macclesfield coat of arms with their leopard supporters matching the fountain finial and the family motto *Sapere aude* (Dare to be wise). The coat of arms records that Macclesfield's mother and wife were both heiresses: *Quarterly, 1st and 4th, Gules, a chevron between three leopards' faces or, for Parker; 2nd and 3rd;, azure, a mullet between two bars and in chief two mullets argent for Venables; with an escutcheon in pretence, Sable, a bend between three spears heads or for Carrier.* The coat of arms is supported by *Two leopards reguardant proper each gorged with a ducal coronet gules.* Thomas Parker's mother was Anne Venables, of Nuneham, Cheshire, and he married his second cousin, Janet Carrier of Wirksworth, Derbyshire, in 1691.

Macclesfield's public life came to an end following impeachment in 1725 for corruption through the sale of masterships in Chancery. He was fined £30,000. (TM)

158. (pl.5.27)
Pair of covered cups and salvers, from the ambassadorial buffet of Robert Bensen, 1st Baron Bingley
Philip Rollos (*c.*1660–1715), London, 1713–14
Cast and chased silver gilt, Cup and cover: h 38cm, w 35.5cm, d 20.5cm; Salver: diam 40.4cm, h 13.5cm
Engraved with arms of Queen Anne, and AR; Marks: RO with a star above and below
V&A: M.30:1-3–2008; M.31:1-3–2008

Provenance
Delivered by Samuel Smythin to the Royal Jewel House between 26 Dec 1713 and 26 Mar 1714; made for Robert Benson, 1st Baron Bingley for his appointment as English ambassador to Spain; returned to Jewel House 1725; Ernest Augustus, Duke of Cumberland and Crown Prince of Hanover; by descent; Chrichton Bros 1924; Sir Philip Sassoon Bt; by descent; Marquess of Cholmondeley; Houghton sale, Christie's London 9 Dec 1994 lot 103; accepted by HM Government in lieu of Inheritance Tax and allocated to the Victoria and Albert Museum, 2008

Bibliography
Jones (1924); Tipping (1924); Jacobsen (2007)

These splendid and weighty objects and are some of the finest surviving examples of display silver for a buffet. It is unusual to find a pair of cups and covers which retain their matching salvers. Salvers were used from the 1620s as footed plates for dessert and as ecclesiastical standing patens. As stands for glasses in serving wine, they prevented drips from staining the table linen. By 1700, such salvers had acquired an additional ceremonial status, advertising court office. In this case, their association has ensured their preservation as a set.

A politician, businessman and diplomat, Robert Benson, 1st Baron Bingley, was appointed Ambassador Extraordinary to Spain in December 1713. An ambassador's silver, set out at official functions, symbolized his status and that of the English monarch that he represented. Bingley was granted 5893 ounces of silver and 1066 ounces of gilt plate as part of his ambassadorial allowance. The original scratch weights are visible on the bases of the salvers and the cups. The archives of the Jewel House indicate that their fashion and combined weight of 490 ounces cost just under £400. Bingley never visited Spain and returned most of the silver and silver-gilt including this set to the Jewel House in June 1725.

Philip Rollos was one of the leading goldsmiths working in London in the early eighteenth century. Recorded as a freeman of the Goldsmiths' Company in 1697, he was appointed to the Livery the following year. His workshop was at Bull Inn Court, The Strand. He served as Subordinate Goldsmith to William III and to Anne. Of foreign birth, Rollos is usually described as of Huguenot origin, but his place and date of birth and even his date of death are unrecorded. He was succeeded by his son of the same name. (TM)

159. (pl.5.28)
Ewer and basin, from the ambassadorial buffet of John Churchill, 1st Duke of Marlborough
Elie Pacot (1657–1721), Lille, France, 1711–12
Cast, embossed, chased and engraved silver; ewer: h 36cm, w 32cm; basin: d 73.8cm
Engraved with the arms of Bridgewater impaling Russell, over the arms of Marlborough. Marks: D, fleur-de-lis, L with trefoil, anchor and star flanked by EP
V&A: M.4&5–2007
Provenance
Commissioned by John Churchill, 1st duke of Marlborough; Sarah Churchill, Dowager Duchess of Marlborough; probably Scroop Egerton, 1st duke of Bridgewater
Bibliography
Murdoch (2007), 1

This spectacular ewer and basin were commissioned by John Churchill, 1st duke of Marlborough, from the Lille goldsmith Elie Pacot, during the War of the Spanish Succession. Silver was cheaper in Lille than in London and Churchill also acquired silver candlesticks by Pacot. Pierre Tiron, Pacot's son-in-law, was expert in casting and responsible for the ornamental cast medallions of Roman emperors and empresses and Minerva as goddess of war and patroness of the arts which decorate the rim of the basin and the ewer below the spout. These celebrate Churchill as inspired military leader and art patron.

The fine engraved cartouche on the basin surmounted by a ducal coronet, flanked by eagles and winged putti and punctuated with a trophy of arms, is attributed to Simon Gribelin, a specialist Blois-trained Huguenot engraver *en taille douce* who settled in London. Although reflecting the latest Parisian style, the ewer and basin were made to complement a pair of basins made in London to royal order in 1700–01. These basins were commissioned from the Rouen-born Huguenot goldsmith Pierre Harache for Marlborough's use as ambassador to The Hague. All the pieces formed part of the lavish buffet displayed on the sideboard in the dining room at Marlborough House, London, and at Blenheim Palace. (TM)

160. (pl.5.33)
Table centrepiece, as arranged for the savoury and dessert course

David Willaume II (1693–1761) and Anne Tanqueray (1691–1733), London, 1731–2
Cast and chased silver, h 28.5cm, weight 438.9 ounces (troy). All items except two casters have scratch weights totalling 405 ounces 7 pennyweights
Dishes and casters engraved with the arms of Cholmley Turner of Kirkleatham quartering those of his wife, Jane Marwood; tureen cover, caster stands and drip pans engraved with the crest of Turner; tureen engraved with crest, possibly that of 5th earl of Coventry. Marks: tureen and largest dish, AT in a lozenge with sun above and scallop shell below; smaller dishes, DW in a rectangle; no.4 unmarked modern replacement
Leeds Museums and Galleries (Temple Newsam House) No.2/1988
Provenance
Probably William, 4th earl of Coventry; Cholmley Turner; Jane Turner (née Marwood); William Metcalfe later Marwood, then by descent through the Marwoods of Busby Hall; sold Hurcomb's of Piccadilly, 1926 (£412 13s 0d); sold Sotheby's, 27 June 1963 (£4,000); S.J. Phillips Ltd; purchased 1988
Bibliography
Brett (1968), p.197; Glanville (1987), p.24; Lomax (1989); Lomax (1991); Lomax (1992), no.81; Rutherford (1992), no.20

The *surtout* or centrepiece became popular in England shortly after its first appearance in France around 1700. English inventories of the early eighteenth century described these objects as 'machines'. Lord Bingley, ambassador to Spain, was issued with one such in 1713, one of the earliest records of their use in England. Paul de Lamerie supplied a 'fyne polished surtout with cruets' to George Treby in 1720 and a 'ring with four branches, four buttons, four round saucers and a large Bason' to Lord Fitzwalter in 1728. A 'toureene' was issued to Lord Galway by the Jewel Office on his appointment as ambassador to Portugal in 1708.

The *surtout* had a dual function at dinner. The tureen, cruet stands and candlesticks were placed on the table for the service of the savoury. By replacing the cruet with caster stands, placing the large dessert dish over the tureen and attaching the smaller dessert dishes to the candlestick arms, the 'machine' was made ready for the dessert course.

The Kirkleatham centrepiece reflects the technical ability of its Huguenot goldsmiths. Their expertise is exemplified by the cast frame supported by four cast and chased double scroll feet and the hand-raised tureen, decorated with chased geometric, scrolled and foliated ornament. The caster bodies are decorated with strapwork, a Huguenot introduction. The foot of each caster is cast and then turned in the traditional French manner, as are the wires and finials. (PLR)

THE BEDCHAMBER

161. (pl.5.71)
Design for a silver bed with Cupid and Psyche
Studio of Nicodemus Tessin the Younger (1654–1728), Stockholm, before 1717
Gouache, silver and gold with support-lines in graphite on folded paper, h 42.9cm, w 27.5cm
Stamped with Lugt, 1638 (Kongl. Museum).
Watermark: Coat of arms with diagonal bands surmounted by a fleur-de-lis; letters CJ; letters CDG
Nationalmuseum, Stockholm, THC 1060
Provenance
Nicodemus Tessin the Younger; Carl Gustaf Tessin (ms inv. *c.*1730: '1 Beau Lit coloré avec

l'Histoire de Psiché au fond'); King Adolf Fredrik; Kungl. Biblioteket; Kongl. Museum (Lugt, 1638); Nationalmuseum from 1866
Bibliography
Thornton (1978), fig.120; Nationalmuseum (1986), no.61; Dee and Walton (1988), no.26; Snickare (2002), pp.146, 149, fig.65; Waddy (2002), p.255; Nationalmuseum (2003), no.22

This spectacular design for a silver bed with canopy was thought to record a bed designed by Charles Le Brun for Louis XIV in the 1660s. Probably, however, it depicts a design by Nicodemus Tessin from around 1717, when the architect was writing his *Treatise on Interior Decoration*. For this pioneering work, which remained unpublished until 2002, Tessin drew on printed sources, and notes and drawings made during long study trips in Europe. Some of the beds described are apparently Tessin's own inventions, and for this one he writes, 'I imagine that if the headcloth were made of different materials, and the nudes painted on silk, representing Cupid and Psyche with her lamp, this would do perfectly well. At the corners of the canopy there would be seated putti, large as life, holding plumes; two more should be below standing [and elevated] on light pedestals on either side of the headcloth, holding more plumes. These putti should be of solid silver.'

It is unclear whether the drawing follows the description or the other way around. Cupid and Psyche appear to be actually in the bed, awkwardly clinging to the headcloth, rather than decorating it. This confusing effect suggests that the artist was working from a description rather than composing it himself. The drawing does not show the bed slightly from above in the conventional manner, so it looks like a narrow bench-like sofa. The draughtsman has tried to compensate for this effect by shading the lower right pedestal.

The putti on the pedestals were based on a drawing of a day bed that Tessin acquired in Rome in the 1680s. The mix of late-seventeenth-century Italian and French elements is typical of his work. In this case, he probably provided a description and model drawings for a draughtsman in his studio. (MO)

162. (pl.5.40)
***Inauguration of the Order of St Louis in the King's Bedchamber at Versailles**, 1693*
François Marot (1666–1719), Paris, about 1710
Oil on canvas, h 51cm, w 76cm
Musée national des châteaux de Versailles et de Trianon, MV 2149
Provenance
Commissioned in 1710 and intended as a tapestry design for the Gobelins Workshops; Hubert; acquired by Louis-Philippe for Versailles in 1833
Bibliography
Constans (1980), no.3135; Constans (1995), no.3446; Constans and Salmon (1998), no.72; Milovanovic (2005), no.28

The painting depicts the creation of the first knights of the Order of St Louis. This military order was established by Louis XIV in 1693 to reward valorous soldiers. Unlike the Order of St Michael and the Order of the Holy Spirit, which each comprised 100 knights drawn from the nobility, membership of the Order of St Louis was open to commoners, and there were no limits placed upon the number of knights. This order, in particular its red sash, inspired Napoleon when he instituted the Legion of Honour in 1802.

In this painting by François Marot, the king

wears the blue sash of the Order of the Holy Spirit, and presents the decoration to various kneeling figures. These are hard to identify owing to the painting's status as a sketch for a tapestry that was never woven (part of the project to continue the series *The History of the King*). The event actually took place in the former King's Bedchamber (now part of the bull's-eye antechamber), but here the artist places it in the bedchamber of 1701, with the *Allegory of France* carved by Nicolas Coustou decorating its archivolt. Flanking the royal bed are two important paintings from the collection of Louis XIV: *David* by Domenichino (on the right) and *St John on Patmos* by Innocenzo da Imola (on the left), then attributed to Raphael. Both paintings are on display today in the *Salon d'Apollon* in the Palace of Versailles. (NM)

163. (pl.5.73)
Extended fan leaf depicting Mme de Montespan in the *Trianon de Porcelaine*
Artist unknown, France, possibly 1674
Gouache on two thicknesses of vellum, mounted on a copper sheet, with gold and silver highlights, h 28.5cm, w 48.6cm
V&A: P.39–1987
Provenance
Possibly commissioned by Mme de Montespan; sold Sotheby's, 6 July 1987, lot 81; purchased from Partridge Fine Arts Ltd, 1987
Bibliography
Cowen (2003), pp.84–5

This painting started life as a fan-shaped sheet of parchment (animal skin), prepared by scoring or pleating. The sheet was stuck on to a larger sheet, which in turn was mounted on to a thin, paper-covered copper panel. Some painting on the 'fan' section may have been undertaken before it was mounted. Microscopic investigation shows some trimming of, for example, gold highlights at the edge, while other areas of the 'fan' show more than one layer of paint, as if painted over after the enlargement. In the window area the paint layer appears continuous over both grounds. The fan area has been finished with a glossier glaze, which now shows craquelure and darkening not evident on the outer ground. It is likely that all the phases of work took place at almost the same time, with the painting as the intended product.

Fan painters (*éventaillistes*) could not join the painters' guild of St Luke and were debarred from selling pictures. By painting sheets that had clearly been designed as fans, they could claim the purity of their intention. Nonetheless, such small paintings are not uncommon. They must always have been particularly suitable for decorating the wooden panelling fashionable in Parisian hôtels and the smaller, private apartments at Versailles. (SM)

164. (pl.5.44)
Armchair
Nicolas Lefèvre, Paris, 1680
Carved, painted and gilded beech and walnut, upholstered in modern silk damask trimmed with original silk fringe, h 107cm, w 64cm, d 50cm
Nationalmuseum, Stockholm, Salsta Slott no.12
Provenance
Purchased by Nils Bielke, governor of Pomerania and Swedish ambassador to France; the Isabella Chamber, Salsta Slott
Bibliography
Thornton (1975); Centre Culturel Suédois (1985), pp.222–6; Stavenow-Hidemark (1985)

This carved, blue-painted and gilded armchair is part of a suite of furniture acquired by Nils Bielke, Swedish ambassador to Paris, in 1680. Bielke purchased several sets of chairs in Paris; a surviving receipt signed by Nicolas Lefèvre may refer to this set.

Bielke served as Sweden's ambassador to France from 1678 to 1682. In 1687 he was appointed governor general of Pomerania, and the suite of furniture was probably first installed at his residence in Stettin. At the time Bielke was a successful politician and military commander. His downfall, however, was in forging too close a friendship with Sweden's enemy, France, unlawful minting and financial self-interest. Even though charged with high treason, and forced to return to Sweden, he remained a wealthy man. He lived out his life in style at Salsta Castle in Uppland, where, some time between 1705 and 1720, the furnishings acquired in Paris were installed in the state bedroom.

The state bedroom at Salsta has been referred to as the Isabella chamber. The Parisian chairs were upholstered in bone-white, so-called Isabella-coloured, silk damask, trimmed with a purple and white silk bell-fringe. Remaining today are six fauteuils, four armchairs, and five back-stools. In the room there was also a carved and gilded day-bed upholstered in the same way, and a great bed with Isabella silk damask hangings and coverlet. The chamber walls were hung with Isabella silk damask and brocatelle borders, once violet with gold-coloured ground.

The bell-fringe is original. The upholstery was restored in 1928, using a silk damask of the same colour and pattern acquired from Italy. The Isabella Chamber was last restored in the 1970s. In 1982 the Salsta Castle collection was acquired by the National Museum of Fine Arts. (HK)

165. (pl.5.47)
State Bed
Maker unknown, probably Paris, before 1682
Painted wood frame with silk velvet hangings with applied decoration and embroidery, h 375cm, w 205cm, d 155cm
Nationalmuseum, Stockholm, NMK 1/1914

Provenance
Probably commissioned by Nils Bielke, 1682

Bibliography
Nationalmuseum (1915); Hernmarck (1954); Thornton (1978), pp.34–5

The Bielke state bed was acquired by the Nationalmuseum in 1914 and has been considered a highlight of the collection ever since. The successful purchase was made at auction with financial help from the Friends of the Nationalmuseum, the Bielke family and the owner of the auction house Bukowski.

In addition to the high quality of the bed, and its innovative design, the textiles are unusually well preserved. This is probably because the bed was displayed for only a limited time while owned by the Bielke family, when it was housed at Tureholm in Södermanland.

The rich bed hangings are made of red velvet with embroidery and applied decoration in white and green silk. The pattern is in the style of Jean Berain, who worked as a designer for Louis XIV.

According to tradition, the bed was given to the Swedish ambassador Nils Bielke by the French king in 1682. This is no longer considered probable; the bed was more likely to have been commissioned by Bielke himself. (CRob)

166. (pl.5.74)
Table, mirror, and pair of candlestands in the King's Bedchamber at Knole, Kent
Gerrit Jensen (d.1715), and others, London, stands: sheet silver marked 1676, table: sheet silver marked 1680
Embossed and chased sheet silver with oak carcase; the mirror glass has been replaced; table: h 78.7cm, w 101.6cm, d 73.6cm; mirror: h 193cm, w 104cm; candlestands: h 112cm
All four pieces are decorated with a countess's coronet above FDHP; Marks: on table, TL or TJ above a scallop between two pellets; on stands, London hallmark for 1676
Knole, The Sackville Collection (The National Trust), mirror: NT/KNO.F.153, table: NT/KNO.F.151, candlestands: NT/KNO.F.152 a–b

Provenance
Made for the countess of Dorset about 1680, and in the King's Bedroom at Knole probably before 1730 (not listed in the 1706 inventory)

Bibliography
Gore House (1853), no.92; Jackson (1912), vol.2, p.858; 25 Park Lane (1925), no.746; Jourdain (1952), p.44, fig.22; Penzer (1961), pp.85–8; Palais des Beaux Arts (1973), nos 133–5; Jackson-Stops (1985), no.129; Beard (1986), p.487; Schroder (1988), pp.117–19; Bowett (2002), pp.126–8; Saule and Arminjon (2007), p.205, fig.197

This is one of only three sets of silver furniture in British collections retaining all its components: table, looking-glass, and candlestands. A set in the Royal Collection (RCIN 35298–300), given to Charles II by the Corporation of London, and another formerly in the collection of the dukes of Buckingham (private collection) also survive. All silver furniture was extravagant, but pieces like these made of sheet silver, hammered out from the back, finished, polished, and mounted on a wooden carcase, were less expensive than solid silver, yet still spectacular.

The set was supplied by Gerrit Jensen for £407 5s. in 1680. Jensen was widely employed by the crown and the aristocracy, and is most famous for pieces with Boulle or 'seaweed' marquetry, though he also sold expensive mirror glass. He supplied the glass for the silver looking-glass and table of 1699 attributed to Andrew Moore in the Royal Collection (RCIN 35301 and 35302). The shape of the Knole looking-glass is very similar to RCIN 35301, but the form and decoration of the bolection frame are more old-fashioned.

The looking-glass, the front of the table, and the tops of the stands bear the coronet and cipher of Frances Cranfield, countess of Dorset, who married twice: first Richard Sackville, 5th earl of Dorset, then, in 1679, Henry Powle. The cipher probably reads FDHP for Frances Dorset and Henry Powle.

The stands are marked 1676, and the table 1680–81. The table also has a maker's mark, interpreted as TL, or TJ (for Thomas Jenkins). The depiction of *Apollo and Marsyas* on the table top may derive from Antonio Tempesta's edition of Ovid's *Metamorphoses* published in Amsterdam in 1606, and was possibly executed by foreign *émigrés*. The discrepancy in date marks may be explained by the reuse of older silver on the stands. The looking-glass is unmarked and undated. (CRow)

167. (pl.5.75)
Pair of andirons, made for the earl of Dorset
Maker unknown, England (London), *c.*1670–before 1677
Embossed silver, and iron, h 63.5cm
Engraved with the arms of Sackville impaling Cranfield beneath an earl's coronet
Knole, The Sackville Collection (The National Trust), NT/KNO/S/1 a&b

Provenance
Made for the 5th earl of Dorset, before 1677; possibly in the Drawing Room (now Reynolds Room) since 1730: '2 Silver Andirons/2 Dogs w.th Silver Knobs' (the accompanying fire dogs, not exhibited, have knob finials)

Bibliography
Jourdain (1952), p.45, fig.23; Penzer (1961), p.181, fig.11; Schroder (1988), p.120

Andirons – iron bars slotted into the decorative fronts – supported large logs, which were burnt in the country rather than coal. Silver was favoured as the decorative element as it would have shimmered as it reflected the flickering fire.

This is one of the two finest and most decorative pairs of silver andirons of this approximate date at Knole. The other pair, surmounted by flaming urns, dates from about 1680. Both pairs share the same footprint and similar decoration in the French style.

The maker of this pair is unknown, but he must have been a superb designer and craftsman with an established *atelier*. The putti are graceful and well modelled, and show the influence of François Duquesnoy, famous for his sculpted infants. Beneath the plinths on which the putti stand are shields engraved with the arms and coronet of Richard Sackville, 5th earl of Dorset, a great patron of silversmiths, whose arms adorn numerous pieces of silver at Knole. Here, the Sackville arms impale Cranfield, for Lady Frances Cranfield, daughter and heiress of Lionel Cranfield, 1st earl of Middlesex, whom Sackville married in 1637.

These andirons have a developed iconography. One putto holds a shovel and an apple (a symbol of Venus), while the other holds a bellows and grapes (symbolic of Bacchus). The putti are clearly cupids, given that the head of Venus within a circular niche, supported by pairs of putti issuing from acanthus leaves, appears at the centre of the base of each andiron. The sides of the andirons have recumbent grotesque bearded satyr terms, beneath grotesque masks, and terminating in lion's paw feet. The rest of the decoration consists of spirited renderings of garlands, fruit, and winged *amorini*. (CRow)

168. (pl.5.76)
Bellows, tongs, brush and shovel, from the Queen's Bedchamber at Ham House, London
Maker unknown, England, *c.*1675–9
Wood and leather with embossed silver mounts. Bellows: l 51.4cm; tongs: 81.5cm; shovel: l 82cm; brush: l 63cm
The bellows has an unidentified SS silversmith's mark
Ham House, The Dysart Collection (purchased by H.M.Government in 1948 and transferred to The National Trust in 2002). Bellows: NT/HH 468 1948; tongs: NT/HH 136 1948; shovel: NT/HH 135 1948; brush: NT/HH 87 1948

Provenance
From the Queen's Bedchamber, Ham House, possibly since 1679

Bibliography
Macquoid and Edwards (1924), p.86, fig.44C; Thornton (1980), pp.147–8, fig.126; Jackson-Stops (1985), no.135, pp.210–11; Schroder (1988), p.118; Thornton (1998), pl.216, pp.107, 110

In 1672 the duke of Lauderdale married his lover, Elizabeth, *suo jure* countess of Dysart, and together they transformed Ham, a villa on the Thames near Richmond. In 1678, Evelyn described it as 'indeede inferiour to few of the best Villas in Italy itselfe. The house furnishd like a greate Princes'. What must have seemed particularly princely was the silver fireplace furniture, of which Evelyn famously wrote in *Mundus Muliebris or The Ladies Dressing Room Unlock'd and her Toilet Spread* (1685): 'the chimney furniture of plate for iron's now quite out of date'.

This set may well have been in the Queen's Bedchamber since 1679, when the inventory lists 'One Broome and one bellowes garnisht with silver', which were hanging from 'two silver hooks'. The inventory also lists a firepan, firedogs and a grate all 'garnisht with silver'.

The engraved cipher, beneath a ducal coronet, on the front of the bellows, has been interpreted as the JEL monogram of the duke and duchess of Lauderdale, but the cipher appears to read EDL for Elizabeth [countess of] Dysart [duchess of] Lauderdale [or Elizabeth, Duchess of Lauderdale]. The silver-mounted firegrate in the Queen's Bedchamber bears the same monogram.

The elaborate embossed silver mounts of the bellows indicate awareness of the kind of acanthus-based arabesque design that was disseminated via Roman engravings. Seventeenth-century silver-handled iron fireplace implements also survive in the Danish Royal Collection. The 1677, 1679, and 1683 Ham inventories reveal that the main rooms at Ham all had silver fireplace furniture, and several silver-mounted firepans still survive, including an exquisite small-scale example in the Green Closet (a cabinet room for pictures and miniatures), which is complete with a filigree fender and silver detachable 'feet'. (CRow)

169. (pl.5.77)
Toilet service with the arms of William and Mary
Candlesticks by Robert Collombe (1633–1711) 1669–70; Ferry Prevost; Philippe Regnault 1670–71; Hans Coenraadt Breghtel (1608–75) 1678, Paris, 1670–8
Embossed and engraved silver gilt; 23 pieces: Mirror: h 61.5cm, w 53.5cm, d 40cm; Ewer: h 21.5.cm, w 23cm, d 11.2cm; Basin: h 40cm, w 46.5cm, d 34cm; Candlesticks: h 18cm, w 12.7cm, d 12.7cm; Mug: h 13.8cm, w 14cm, d 10.1cm; Lidded bowl: h 7.6cm, w 14.5cm, d 11cm; Powder flasks: h 15cm, w 7.2cm, d 7.2cm; Octagonal boxes: h 7.5cm, w 12cm, d 17cm; Circular boxes: h 4.8cm, w 7cm, d 7cm; Oval boxes: h 4.1cm, w 7.5cm, d 5.8cm; Jewel casket with pincushion: h 11cm, w 17.2cm, d 11.8cm; Square caskets: h 9cm, w 23.5cm, d 20.1cm; Oval footed salvers: h 7.2cm, w 28.6cm, d 23.8cm; Circular footed salver: h 7.8cm, w 19.5cm, d 19.5cm; Snuffer: h 3.7cm, w 17.5cm, d 5.5cm; Snuffer tray: h 6cm, w 22cm, d 17.3cm
Some pieces engraved with the arms and monogram of William and Mary
The Trustees of the Chatsworth Settlement

Provenance
Possibly a wedding present to William of Orange and Mary Stuart in 1677

Bibliography
Dennis (1960), no.284; Treasures (1979), no.149; Blair (1997), p.111; Bimbenet-Privat (2002)

This silver-gilt toilet service is one of three in the Devonshire Collection today. A fourth, dating from about 1685, was sold at auction in 1958. Its earliest pieces are two candlesticks by Robert Collombe dated 1669–70. The majority of the 23 pieces bear the mark of Ferry Prevost and the Paris wardens' mark for 1670-71, the same date as the covered bowl by Philippe Regnault. In 1678, three boxes were made in The Hague by Hans Coenraadt Breghtel, presumably to make pairs of Prevost's octagonal, round and oval boxes.

Apart from the snuffers and snuffer tray, the pieces either bear the arms of Mary Stuart when Princess of England, Scotland and Ireland and/or the joint monogram or arms of William and Mary of Orange. William Cavendish, 4th earl (later 1st duke) of Devonshire was instrumental in the Glorious Revolution of 1688 and it has long been believed that the toilet service was a gift from the king and queen, in recognition of this support.

Until the nineteenth century, the bulk of the family's collections was kept in London. In October 1696 a Plate Room was constructed by Joel Lobb at Devonshire House on Piccadilly. Payments to Lobb for travelling crates and to the Mansfield carrier, however, show that plate did move between the 1st duke's properties.

A serious theft at Devonshire House in July 1788 saw the deposit of three cases of plate, including this toilet service, with the Bank of England. The plate was still there in 1810, explaining the toilet service's absence in inventories of that period.

The toilet service was listed at Chatsworth in 1828 and 1868 but returned to Devonshire House by 1892 where it most probably remained until March 1917. It was then deposited with the London, County & Westminster Bank in one of 11 cases of plate, likely removed in response to increased German bombing raids. In 1921, the plate was retrieved from the bank and taken to Chatsworth where all four toilet services were listed ten years later. Described as 'the most complete and oldest Parisian toilet service known' by Bimbenet-Privat, it remains at Chatsworth, displayed in the 1st duke's State Bedchamber. (HO)

THE CABINET AND CLOSET

170. (pl.5.54)
Madame de Montespan, said to be above a gallery at Clagny
After Henri Gascar (c.1634–1701), Paris, 1679–85
Oil on canvas, h 143cm, w 112cm
Galleria degli Uffizi, Soprintendenza per il Patrimonio storico artistico ed etnoantropologico e per il Polo museale della città di Firenze, inv.1890 no.2837

Bibliography
Musée des arts décoratifs (1960), no.521; Thornton (1978), fig.20; Lunsingh-Scheurleer (2005), fig.126; Saule and Arminjon (2007), p.39

This painting of Mme de Montespan is a slightly trimmed copy of an original by Henri Gascar which formerly belonged to the marquise herself, and which is now in a private collection. The *maîtresse en titre* of Louis XIV is shown reclining on an elaborately canopied daybed, in a private space above a gallery, traditionally said to be at Clagny, the château given to her by the king in 1685. It is more likely, however, that the interior is fictionalised rather than representing a real space; nonetheless, the furnishings are certainly indicative of those used in private spaces,

compared with more public rooms. In Mme de Montespan's space at the top of the steps, which can be sealed off from the outside world by drawing the canopy curtains, the furnishings are the most lavish and comfortable, with rich fabrics covering the daybed, ostrich plumes (seen in the original but not in this trimmed version) surmounting the canopy, and oriental cushions on the floor. In contrast, the view through the open curtain shows a vast open space with monumental and almost severe furnishings. At the centre of the right hand wall, a large canted mirror is hung between the tall windows above a matching table, flanked by two enormous lacquered cabinets on stands, on which massed displays of oriental porcelain are arranged. Upholstered stools line the walls, while the only pieces of furniture in the centre of the room are solid silver vases and baskets, overflowing with flowers, sitting on the ground. Although details of the commission for the original painting are not known, the composition, with its profusion of flowers and cupids, as well as the semi-naked figure of the king's mistress, would seem to suggest a main theme of love and luxury. (JN)

171. (pl.5.81)
Wall panel from Montagu House, with scenes of the loves of Apollo
Painted by Charles de Lafosse (1636–1716), Jacques Rousseau (1626–93), Jean-Baptiste Monnoyer (1634–99) and Jacques Parmentier (c.1658–1730) probably after designs by Daniel Marot (c.1661–1752), London, c.1690
Oil on canvas, h 223.7cm, w 177.5cm
In the collection of The Trustees of the 9th Duke of Buccleuch's Chattels Fund

Provenance
Commissioned by Ralph, 1st Duke of Montagu for Montagu House, London. Later moved to Boughton, Northamptonshire

Bibliography
Jackson-Stops (1980); Baarsen et al. (1988), no.22

This panel comes from a set of five now at Boughton House but formerly at Montagu House, the London residence built by Ralph, Earl (and later 1st Duke) of Montagu, which was destroyed in 1845–52. The panels must represent the entire wall coverings of a cabinet or closet, as their colouring and subject matter would also seem to suggest. Two drawings by Daniel Marot in the V&A, annotated with indications of the colours to be used, are clearly preparatory designs for this particular panel, as is evident from the iconography of the central narrative scene. The left hand part of the drawing and panel represent Apollo and Daphne, at the moment of Daphne's metamorphosis into a laurel tree. The right hand part has been misread as an alternative version of the Apollo and Daphne story but actually depicts a lesser-known episode, namely the love of Apollo for the youth Cyparissus, who, distraught at having accidentally killed a sacred stag (seen in the background of the scene), was transformed by Apollo, at his own request, into a cypress tree. The subject matter of the other panels in the set is equally amorous: the other double panel shows *Diana and Endymion and Diana Bathing*, while the single panels show *Jupiter and Io, Venus and Adonis* and the *Triumph of Galatea* respectively. The painting is clearly a team effort; the mythological scenes are likely to be by Lafosse and the fruit and flower baskets and garlands by Monnoyer. The V&A design drawings, however, suggest that the decorative scheme of central narrative panels

with vertical grotesques (recalling, albeit on a much smaller scale, the painted panels on the Staircase of the Ambassadors at Versailles) was conceived by Marot himself. The diaper pattern forming the background of the panel was originally carried out in silver, now oxidized, which would have made the coloured grotesques and central narrative panels seem as if they were floating in air. (JN)

172. (pl.5.85)
Desk
Maker unknown, Paris, c.1700
Carcase of pine and walnut; veneered with brass, clear horn with painted paper behind, ebony, stained bone, tortoiseshell, copper and mother-of-pearl; mounts and escutcheons of brass; watered silk lining to the interior cupboard, h 78cm, w 119.5cm, d 71.2cm
V&A: 372–1901

Provenance
Given by Mrs J.A. Bonnor

Bibliography
Himmelheber (1976); Ronfort (1991); Wilk (1996), pp.74–5; Wilson (2008), pp.90, 92–3

The desk has seven drawers and a cupboard with a fall-front door at the centre. It stands on eight legs of striking, S-shaped form. It is veneered in a *contre-partie* veneer of brass, inlaid with marquetry composed of a variety of colourful materials which are largely unfaded. The marquetry panels on the back, sides and front depict lively scenes of musicians, animals, fruits and flowers within a strapwork frame. As Ronfort has established, several distinctive features of the marquetry, including the obelisk on the fall-front door and elements of the scenes on the top and sides, suggest that this piece was made in the same workshop as a group of desks, clocks and boxes with comparable marquetry designs, often on a ground of brass, dated to between about 1680 and 1700. Many of these are in public collections, including the British Royal Collection and the J. Paul Getty Museum. A box in the V&A (1022–1882) is also part of this group.

This item may have originally had a matching *gradin*, a freestanding shelving unit which stood on top of the desk, usually along its back edge (see cat.175). These provided a system for filing papers, but are rare survivals. (CSa)

173. (pl.5.78)
Day bed
Attributed to Thomas Roberts (active 1686–1714), London; the silks probably woven in Italy, 1705–10
Carved and gilded beechwood and pine, upholstery of appliquéd damasks and brocades, with silk and metal-thread embroidery, the backs lined with harateen (a worsted cloth with watering), h 121.5cm, l 198cm, w 69cm
Viscount De L'Isle MBE DL from his private collection at Penshurst Place, Kent

Bibliography
Bowett (2002), p.249

The day-bed, with six chairs and an easy chair *en suite*, retains its original upholstery. Matching wall panels also survive. Sets of seat furniture that included a day-bed and easy chair were supplied for bedrooms or dressing-rooms – rooms that combined grandeur with privacy and ease.

The upholstery was originally a vivid combination of colours, patterns and weaves. The ground (preserved unfaded behind the gilded mouldings) is a silk, woven in Italy, in stripes of bright yellow with a scrolling damask pattern, alternating with stripes in chiné

technique with spiky motifs in red and white and green and white. This is further embellished with appliqué motifs in damasks and brocades, outlined with applied cords and braids – in the manner of French beds of the period, like that in the collection of the J. Paul Getty Museum (79.DD.3.1–16).

The suite has been attributed to Thomas Roberts, chair-maker to the royal household from 1686 until 1714. The tightly scrolled legs and curving stretchers are similar to seat furniture supplied by him, although both elements were also found on French and German chairs of the period. Engravings by Daniel Marot show similar hard-edged upholstery. Tradition associates the suite with Leicester House in London, although no documentary evidence of this survives. A single day-bed of similar design was at one time at Grimsthorpe Castle, Lincolnshire. (SM)

174. (pl.2.44)
Cabinet on a stand
Attributed to Pierre Gole (c.1620–84), Paris, 1660–71
Carcase of pine and oak; fruitwood feet; drawers of walnut and oak; veneers of ivory, stained bone, horn, tortoiseshell, padouk, barberry, snake wood, sycamore, hornbeam, satinwood; ebony mouldings; escutcheons and mounts of brass, h 126cm, w 84cm, d 39cm
V&A: W.38–1983

Provenance
Probably made for Henriette Anne, duchesse d'Orléans, for the Palais-Royal, Paris

Bibliography
Lunsingh-Scheurleer (1984); Pradère (1989), pp.44–51; Riccardi-Cubitt (1992), p. 86; Wilk (1996), pp.66–7; Lunsingh-Scheurleer (2005), pp.108–10; Wilson et al. (2008), pp.98–9

Cabinets on a miniature scale like this are rare, and this is the only known example veneered with ivory, a luxurious and expensive import. Because the top is low, it is veneered with marquetry like the front and sides. The backs of the legs, however, hardly visible when the piece was positioned against a wall, are veneered economically with walnut. The central door opens to reveal a nest of drawers veneered with woods, rather than ivory. When first made, much of the wood marquetry would have been much brighter. Now, only the leaves of green-stained bone retain their original intense colour.

Pierre Gole supplied the king with a group of ivory furniture in 1664. This cabinet was probably made for Henriette Anne Stuart (daughter of Charles I of England and Henrietta Maria of France). In 1661, she married the duc d'Orléans, brother of Louis XIV. They took up residence in the Palais Royal, and in the inventory drawn up on her death in 1670, a cabinet of this form and decoration was described in the *cabinet blanc* (white cabinet). (CSa)

175. (pl.5.82)
Desk
Attributed to Pierre Gole (c.1620–84), Paris, c.1670
Carcase of oak; carved and gilded legs; veneers of pewter, brass, ebony and mother-of-pearl; gilt bronze mounts, h 88.5cm, w 89cm, d 55.3cm
In the collection of The Trustees of the 9th Duke of Buccleuch's Chattels Fund

Provenance
Possibly the desk delivered by Gole to Louis XIV at Versailles in 1672. By tradition given by Louis XIV to the 1st duke of Montagu

while ambassador to the French court

Bibliography
Lunsingh-Scheurleer (1980); Pradère (1989), pp.47–8; Murdoch (1992), pp.119–20, pl.70; Bowett (2002), pp.212–13; Lunsingh-Scheurleer (2005), pp.183–90; Wilson et al (2008), pp.106–7

Lunsingh-Scheurleer was the first to attribute this piece and cat.174 to Pierre Gole. Although there has yet been no study of the materials and construction of furniture attributed to this maker, his style and marquetry patterns are distinctive. This desk is notable for its combination of a veneered carcase supported by a giltwood base (see cat.172 for an alternative approach). The side stretchers on the base are carved with fleurs-de-lis, usually associated with royal commissions.

Desks with lockable drawers for storage and a superstructure for filing papers (the *gradin*, which stands at the back of the desk top) were at this date a relatively recent development. This desk is reputed to have been a gift from Louis XIV to Ralph, 1st duke of Montagu, who was English ambassador to the French court in the late seventeenth century. Louis commissioned a number of pieces of furniture from Gole, who became *ébéniste du roi* in 1656. The desk is said to have returned with the duke to Britain, where he resided at Montagu House in Bloomsbury and Boughton House, which he remodelled in the French taste. (CSa)

176. (pl.5.83)
Display shelf for ceramics
Maker unknown, England, *c*.1695 or 1718–24
Carved and turned gilded pine, h 72cm, w 78cm
Cipher and arms of Lady Elizabeth (Betty) Germaine after 1718
Charles Stopford Sackville

Provenance
Lady Betty Germaine; Lord George Sackville 1769; by descent

Bibliography
Thornton (1984), no.109, pp.86–7; Bowett (2002), p.24; Murdoch (2007), 2

A unique survival, these shelves reflect the taste of Sir John Germaine's two wives, Lady Mary Mordaunt and Lady Betty Berkeley, the successive owners of Drayton House, Northamptonshire.

Drayton, the seat of the Mordaunt family since about 1500, passed to Sir John Germaine through his first marriage to Mary, daughter of the 2nd earl of Peterborough, following her scandalous divorce from the 7th duke of Norfolk. Mary continued to call herself 'duchess' after her divorce and remarriage. Together the Germaines collected quantities of Oriental porcelain, which decorated almost every available surface at Drayton.

This is one of five similar sets of shelves now at Drayton. Surviving bills testify to Mary's purchase of 'a hanging shelfe' in 1695 and further 'Japaned' and 'Cabinett' shelves in 1697. One of the sets of cabinet shelves retains her duchess's coronet. The others bear the armorials of Lady Betty Germaine, Sir John's second wife, as a widow. These shelves may have been purchased by Lady Mary, and later altered, or more likely were a later commission to match Lady Mary's original set. The inventories of 1710 and 1724 list '2 gilt hanging Shelves' in the Spangled Room, and a further set in 'my Lady's Dressing Room' in 1724.

When first gilded, the shelves, with their elaborate backs of pierced acanthus scrollwork and finely worked engraved gesso surface, provided a suitable setting for the gleaming blue and white porcelain framed by the four barley-twist columns at the front and half-columns at the back. (TM)

177. (pl.4.55)
The Penitent Magdalen
Maker unknown, possibly made by Swiss craftsmen in France, *c*.1660–75
Verre églomisé – clear glass gilded, etched and lacquered on the reverse and backed with foil, chased gilt bronze frame, w 53cm, h 61cm
V&A: 146–1879

Provenance
Robinson Collection; purchased 1879

Bibliography
Mérot (1990), p.114; Thornton (1984), p.64; discussion of technique and comparative objects in Ryser and Salmen (1995)

This brilliant, jewel-like image depicts the conversion of Mary Magdalen, a medieval legend painted by a number of artists in the seventeenth century, including Caravaggio, Rubens and Artemisia Gentileschi. The saint's eyes are raised in ecstasy toward the light that streams in from the left, the billowing drapery and discarded jewels suggesting sudden physical movement. Exceptionally in an image of the Magdalen there are two mirrors: one by the saint's head, catching the divine illumination, represents self-knowledge and wisdom; a second, cracked mirror lying on the floor amid the discarded jewels, is an allusion to the perils of vanity and self-deception. The sun as symbolic of spiritual insight is conflated in this object with references to Louis XIV as *Roi Soleil*, making what appears to be an image of divine revelation into something more complex. It may be that the figure of the saint is also intended as an allegorical portrait of one of the king's mistresses, a popular seventeenth-century conceit.

Intended for private devotion, this glittering image places the saint in an unusually sumptuous interior and was probably intended to be hung in a similar setting. The reflective qualities of glass, combined with the visual appeal of precious stones, made reverse painted glass popular for small devotional objects. Historically, however, such techniques have tended to be viewed as an inferior type of enamelling, hence the original cataloguing of this object as a ceramic in 1879. (JE)

Bibliography

25 Park Lane, London, *A Loan Exhibition of English Plate* (exhib. cat., 1925)
Adamson, John (ed.), *The Princely Courts of Europe 1500–1750* (London, 1999)
Adelson, Candace, and Roberta Landini, 'The "Persian" carpet in Charles Le Brun's "July" was a 16th-century Florentine table tapestry' in *CIETA Bulletin* 68 (1990), pp.53–68
Agapito y Revilla, Juan, *Las cofradias, las procesiones y los pasos de Semana Santa en Valladolid* (Valladolid, 1925)
Agghazy, Maria G., *A barokk szobrászat Magyarországon. (Mvészek, mesteremberek ... Mıemlékek)* (Budapest, 1959)
Ahrens, Kirsten, 'Honori praevia virtus: une interpretation de l'architecture a l'arrière-plan du portrait officiel de Louis XIV peint par Rigaud en 1701' in *Gazette des Beaux-Arts* vol.115, no.1456–7 (May/June 1990), pp.213–26
Ahrens, Kirsten, *Hyacinthe Rigauds Staatsporträt Ludwig XIV: typologische und ikonologische Untersuchung zur politischen Aussage des Bildnisses von 1701* (Worms, 1990)
Aken-Fehmers, Marion S. van, et al., *Delfts aardewerk: geschiedenis van een nationaal product* (Zwolle, 2001)
Aken-Fehmers, Marion S. van, *Vazen met tuiten: 300 jaar pronkstukken/Vases with spouts: three centuries of splendour* (Zwolle, 2007)
Alberti, *De Pictura*, 2.41, quoted by Onians (2008), p.44
Alegria, José Augusto, et al., *Triomphe du baroque* (Palais des Beaux-Arts, Brussels, exhib. cat., 1991)
Algarotti, Francesco, *Saggio sopra l'opera in musica* (Livorno, 1763), trans. in Strunk (1981)
Alm, Göran, et al., *Barockens Konst* (Lund, 1997)
Amarger, Arnaud, et al., *La Galerie des Glaces, Histoire et Restauration* (Dijon, 2007)
Anderson, J.A., *Pedro de Mena, Seventeenth-Century Spanish Sculptor* (Lewiston, NY, 1998)
Anderson, M.S., *War and Society in Europe of the Old Regime, 1618–1789* (London, 1998)
Andersson, Aron, 'Augsburg Silver Furniture in Sweden' in *Connoisseur* vol.134 (November 1954), pp.194–6
Androssov, Sergei, 'Italienische Gartenplastik des 18. Jahrhunderts in Russland und Deutschland: Analogien und Parallelen' in *Sitzungsberichte Kunstgeschichtliche Gesellschaft zu Berlin* vol.41–2 (October–July 1992–4), pp.6–10
Angulo Íñiguez, D., *Catálogo de las alhajas del Delfin* (Madrid, revised edition 1989)
Arbeteta Mira, Letizia, 'Las Alhajas del Delfin, un tesoro dinastico?' in *Reales-sitios* vol.37, no.144 (2000), pp.38–55
Arbeteta Mira, Letizia, *El tesoro del Delfin: alhajas de Felipe V recibidas por herencia de su padre Luis, gran Delfin de Francia* (Museo del Prado, Madrid, exhib. cat., 2001)
Arbeteta Mira, Letizia, *Magos y Pastores: Vida y arte en la América Virreinal* (Museo de América, Madrid, exhib. cat., 2006)
Archer, Michael, 'Dutch Delft at the court of William and Mary' in *International Ceramics Fair & Seminar*, 1984, pp.15–20
Archer, Michael, *Delftware: the Tin-glazed Earthenware of the British Isles : a Catalogue of the Collection in the Victoria and Albert Museum* (London, 1997)
Arisi, Ferdinando, *Gian Paolo Panini* (Piacenza, 1961)
Arisi, Ferdinando, *Gian Paolo Panini e i fasti della Roma del '700* (Rome, 1986)
Arisi, Ferdinando, *G.P. Panini* (Soncino, 1991)
Arisi, Ferdinando (ed.), *Giovanni Paolo Panini, 1671–1765* (Milan, 1993)
Arnold, Ulli, and Werner Schmidt, *Barock in Dresden: Kunst und Kunstsammlungen unter der Regierung des Kurfürsten Friedrich August I von Sachsen und Königs August II von Polen, genannt August der Starke, 1694–1733, und des Kurfürsten Friedrich August II von Sachsen und Königs August III von Polen, 1733–1763* (Staatliche Kunstsammlungen, Dresden, exhib. cat., 1986)
Arnold, Ulli, *Die Juwelen Augusts des Starken* (Munich, 2001)
Aschengreen Piacenti, Cristina, *Il Museo degli argenti a Firenze* (Milan, 1968)
Aschengreen Piacenti, Cristina, 'Documented works in ivory by Balthasar Permoser and some documents related to Filippo Senger' in *Mitteilungen des Kunsthistorischen Instituts in Florenz* vol.4, no.10 (February 1963), pp.273–85
Atwell, W.S., 'International Bullion Flows and the Chinese Economy, 1530–1650', *Past and Present*, XCV (1982)
Auer, Arnold and Arnold, *Im Lichte des Halbmonds. Das Abendland und der türkische Orient* (Staatliche Kunstsammlungen Dresden, exhib. cat., 1995)
Avery, Charles, and David Finn, *Bernini. The Genius of the Baroque* (London, 1997)
Avery, Charles, 'Lord Burlington and the Florentine Baroque Bronze Sculptor Soldani: New documentation on the Anglo-Florentine art trade in the age of the Grand Tour' in Corp, Edward T. (ed.), *Lord Burlington – The Man and His Politics. Questions of Loyalty* (Lewiston, NY, 1998), pp.27–47
Avery, Charles, '"Sculpture gone wild": Bernini and the English' in Grell, Chantal, and Milovan Stanic (eds), *Le Bernin et l'Europe: du baroque triomphant à l'âge romantique* (Paris, 2002), pp.161–78
Ayers, John, 'The ceramics surviving at Hampton Court: A brilliant and various collection' in *Apollo* vol.140, no.390 (August 1994), pp.50–54
Ayrton, Maxwell, and Malcolm Silcock, *Wrought Iron and Its Decorative Use* (London, 1929)
Baarsen, Reinier, et al., *Courts and Colonies: the William and Mary Style in Holland, England, and America* (New York, 1988)
Baarsen, Reinier, *17th-century Cabinets* (Amsterdam, 2000)
Bacou, Roseline, 'Cartons et dessins de Le Brun pour l'Escalier des Ambassadeurs, au Musée du Louvre' in Hoop-Scheffer, Hasselt and White (eds), *Liber amicorum Karel G. Boon* (Amsterdam, 1974), pp.13–27
Bailey, G.A., '"Le style jésuite n'existe pas": Jesuit Corporate Culture and the Visual Arts', in O'Malley, J.W., G.A. Bailey et al. (1999)
Bailey, G.A., 'The Jesuits and Painting in Italy, 1550–1690' in Mormando (1999)
Bailey, G.A., *Art of the Jesuit Missions in Asia and Latin America 1542–1773* (Toronto and London, 1999)
Bailey, G.A., 'Italian Renaissance and Baroque painting under the Jesuits and its legacy throughout Catholic Europe', in O'Malley, J.W., and G.A. Bailey (eds) (2005)
Bailey, G.A., *Art of Colonial Latin America* (London, 2005)
Baillie, Hugh Murray, 'Etiquette and Planning of the State Apartments in Baroque Palaces', *Archaeologia* vol.101 (1967)
Baines, Anthony, *Catalogue of Musical Instruments in the Victoria and Albert Museum. Part II: Non-keyboard instruments* (London, 1998)
Baker, Christopher, and Tom Henry, *The National Gallery Complete Illustrated Catalogue, with a supplement of new acquisitions and loans 1995–2000* (London, 2001)
Bamford, P.M., *Fighting Ships and Prisons: the Mediterranean Galleys of France in the Age of Louis XIV* (Minneapolis, 1873)
Bargellini, Clara, *El retablo de la Virgen de los Dolores* (Mexico City, 1993)
Barnes, Susan J. (ed.), *Van Dyck, A Complete Catalogue of the Paintings* (New Haven, CT, and London, 2004)
Barock im Vatikan: Kunst und Kultur im Rom der Päpste II, 1572–1676 (Kunst und Ausstellungshalle der Bundesrepublik Deutschland, Bonn, exhib. cat., 2005)
Bartoli, D., 'L'Uomo al Punto', in Faggi, A. (ed.), *Collezione di Classici Italiani*, vol.I (Turin, 1930)
Bastian, Karin, *Georg Hinz und sein Stilllebenwork* (Hamburg, 1984)
Battaglia, Roberto, *La cattedra Berniniana di San Pietro* (Rome, 1943)
Battersby, Martin, *Trompe-l'oeil. The Eye Deceived* (London, 1974)
Baumstark, von Herzogenberg and Volk (eds), *Johannes von Nepomuk: 1393–1993* (Bayerisches Nationalmuseum, Munich, exhib. cat., 1993)
Baumstark, Seling and Seelig (eds), *Silber und Gold: Augsburger Goldschmiedekunst für die Höfe Europas* (Bayerisches Nationalmuseum, Munich, exhib. cat., 1994)
Baxandall, Michael, *The Limewood Sculptors of Renaissance Germany* (New Haven, CT, and London, 1980)
Baxter, Clare, 'A pair of pietra dura cabinets at Alnwick: the history of their acquisition' in *Apollo* vol.135, no.364 (June 1992), pp.350–52
Bazin, Germain, *Aleijadinho et la sculpture baroque au Brésil* (Paris, 1963)
Bazin, Germain, *The Baroque* (London, 1968)
Beard, Geoffrey (ed.), *Dictionary of English Furniture Makers, 1660–1840* (Leeds, 1986)
Beard, Geoffrey, *Upholsterers and Interior Furnishings in England, 1660–1820* (New Haven, CT, 1997)
Beaurain, David, 'La fabrique du portrait royal' in Gaehtgens, Thomas W., et al. (eds), *L'art et les normes sociales au XVIII siècle* (Paris, 2001), pp.241–60
Beauvais, Lydia, *Charles Le Brun: 1619–1690* (Paris, 2000)
Beier, A., et al. (eds), *The First Modern Society. Essays in English History in Honour of Lawrence Stone* (Cambridge, 1989)
Belser, Eduard J., *Der barocke Rennschlitten Amrhyn-Göldlin: Ins Licht gerückt – Aus der Sammlung des Historischen Museums Luzern* (Lucerne, 2003)
Bencard, Mogens, 'The Glass Cabinet at Rosenborg Palace' in *Journal of the History of Collections* no.3 (1991), pp.1–12
Bencard, Mogens, *Silver Furniture. Catalogue of silver furniture in the Rosenborg Castle* (Copenhagen, 1992)
Bengtsson, Anders (ed.), *Silver och smycken på Skokloster: utställningskatalog 1995* (Bålsta, 1995)
Berge, Willem, 'Sculptors on the move: Thomas Quellin Denmark', *Church Monuments*, XII (1997), p.37
Berliner Festspiele, *Europa und die Kaiser von China 1240–1816* (Martin Gropius Bau, Berlin, exhib. cat., 1985)
Berliner, Rudolf, 'Johann Adolf Gaap. Fragmente zur Biographie eines deutsch italienisches Metallkunstler' in *Münchner Jahrbuch der bildenden Kunst* nos 3–4 (1952–3), pp.233–55
Bernardini, Maria Grazia and Maurizio Fagiolo dell'Arco, *Gian Lorenzo Bernini: regista del barocco* (Palazzo Venezia, Rome, exhib. cat., 1999)
Bershad, D., 'A series of papal busts by Domenico Guidi' in *Burlington Magazine* vol.112, no.813 (December 1970), pp.805–10
Bertelli, Sergio, and Judith Landry, 'The sovereign's naked leg: on regal knees' in *FMR* no.4 (January 2005), pp.31–46
Bessone, Silvana, *Le Musée National des Carosses, Lisbonne* (Paris 1993)
Bimbenet-Privat, Michèle, *Les Orfèvres et l'orfèvrerie de Paris au XVIIe siècle* (Paris, 2002)
Bimbenet-Privat, Michèle, 'Le mobilier d'argent de Louis XIV et son impossible diffusion' in Coquery, Emanuel (ed.), *Rinceaux et Figures: L'ornement en France au XVIIe siècle* (Saint-Remy-en-l'Eau, 2005), pp.112–23
Bjurström, Per, *Giacomo Torelli and Baroque Stage Design* (Stockholm, 1961)
Bjurström, Per, *Feast and Theatre in Queen Christina's Rome* (Stockholm, 1966)
Black, Jeremy, *European Warfare, 1660–1815* (London, 1994)
Black, Jeremy (ed.), *Warfare in Europe 1650–1792* (Aldershot, 2005)
Black, Jeremy, 'Was there a Military Revolution in Early Modern Europe?' in *History Today* 58 (7), July 2008
Blair, Claude (ed.), *The History of Silver* (London, 1997)
Blanning, Tim, *The Pursuit of Glory, Europe 1648–1815* (London, 2007)
Blinkoff, J., and Allan Greer, *Colonial Saints. Discovering the Holy in the Americas* (London, 2002)
Blunt, Anthony, *The French Drawings in the Collection of His Majesty the King at Windsor Castle* (Oxford and London, 1945)
Blunt, Anthony, 'Supplements to the Catalogues of Italian and French Drawings' in Schilling, Edmund, *The German Drawings in the Collection of Her Majesty The Queen at Windsor Castle* (London, 1971), pp.45–239
Blunt, Anthony, *Art and Architecture in France, 1500 to 1700* (Harmondsworth, 1973)
Blunt, Anthony, *Some Uses and Misuses of the Terms Baroque and Rococo as applied to Architecture* (Oxford, 1973)
Blunt, Anthony, *Borromini* (London and Cambridge, MA, 1979, revised 2005)
Blunt, Anthony (ed.), *Baroque and Rococo Architecture and Decoration* (London, Toronto, Sydney, New York, 1982)
Blunt, Anthony, and Hereward Lester Cooke, *The Roman Drawings of the XVII and XVIII Centuries in the Collection of Her Majesty The Queen at Windsor Castle* (London, 1960)
Bobone, Augusto, *A Capela de S. João Baptista* (Lisbon, 1901)
Boccardo, P., *La Scultura a Genova e in Liguria* (Genoa, 1989)
Bock, Sebastian, *Ova struthionis. Die Straußeneiobjekte in den Schatz-, Silber- und Kunstkammern Europas* (Heidelberg, 2005)
Bold, John, 'Comparable Institutions: The Royal Hospital for Seamen and the Hôtel des Invalides', *Architectural History* (2001), vol.44
Boltz, Claus, 'Steinzeug und Porzellan der Böttgerperiode' in *Keramos* 167/168 (April 2000), pp.3–156
Borenius, Tancred, *A Catalogue of the pictures etc at 18 Kensington Palace Gardens, London, collected by Viscount and Viscountess Lee of Fareham*, 2 vols (London, 1923–6)

Borghini, Gabriele, and Sandra Vasco Rocca, *Giovanni V di Portogallo (1707–1750) e la Cultura Romana del suo Tempo* (Rome, 1995)
Borsi, Franco, *L'architettura del principe* (Florence, 1980)
Bösel, Richard, and Christoph L. Frommel, *Borromini e l'universo barocco: catalogo* (Milan, 2000)
Bottineau, Yves, and Olivier Lefuel, *Les Grands Orfèvres de Louis XIII à Charles X* (Paris, 1965)
Boucher, Bruce (ed.), *Earth and Fire: Italian Terracotta Sculpture from Donatello to Canova* (V&A, London, and Museum of Fine Arts, Houston, exhib. cat., 2001)
Bourke, John, *The Baroque Churches of Central Europe* (London, 1963)
Bowett, Adam, 'The English "Horsebone" Chair' in *Burlington Magazine* vol.141, no.1154 (May 1999), pp.263–70
Bowett, Adam, *English Furniture: 1660–1714, from Charles II to Queen Anne* (Woodbridge, 2002)
Bowett, Adam, 'The engravings of Daniel Marot' in *Furniture History* vol.43 (2007), pp.85–100
Bowron, Edgar Peters, 'Review: *Pannini* by Michael Kiene' in *Burlington Magazine* vol.136, 1091 (February 1994), pp.117–18
Bowron, Edgar Peters, and Joseph Rishel (eds), *Art in Rome in the Eighteenth Century* (Philadelphia, 2000)
Bradford, William, and Helen Braham, *Master Drawings from the Courtauld Collections* (London, 1991)
Braham, Allan, and Peter Smith, *François Mansart* (London, 1973)
Brassat, Wolfgang, 'Monumentaler Rapport des Zeremoniells: Charles Le Brun's *Tenture de l'histoire du Roy*' in Berns, Jorg-Jochen, and Thomas Rahn (eds), *Zeremoniell als hofische Asthetik in Spatmittelalter und Fruher Neuzeit* (Tübingen, 1995)
Brauer, H., and Rudolf Wittkower, *Die Zeichnungen des Gian Lorenzo Bernini*, 2 vols (Berlin, 1931)
Bremer-David, Charissa, *French Tapestries and Textiles in the J. Paul Getty Museum* (Los Angeles, 1997)
Brennan, Michael G., *The Sidneys of Penshurst and the Monarchy 1500–1700* (Aldershot, 2006)
Brett, Gerard, *Dinner is Served: A History of Dining in England, 1400–1900* (London, 1968)
Briganti, Giuliano, *Gaspar Van Wittel e l'Origine Della Veduta Settecentesca* (Milan, 1996)
Brocher, Henri, *Le rang et l'étiquette sous l'ancien régime* (Paris, 1934)
Brouzet, David, 'Jean-Baptiste et Pierre-Denis Martin peintres des Maisons royals' in *Estampille L'objet d'art* no.328 (October 1998), pp.64–82
Brown, Peter (ed.), *British Cutlery: An Illustrated History of Design, Evolution and Use* (Fairfax House, York, exhib. cat., 2001)
Brown, Stewart J., and Timothy Tackett (eds), *Enlightenment, Reawakening and Revolution 1660–1815*, The Cambridge History of Christianity, vol.7 (Cambridge, 2006)
Brunner, Henry, *The Treasury in the Residenz Munich* (Munich, 1975)
Brusatin, Manlio, and Gilberto Pizzamiglio, *The Baroque in Central Europe: Places, Architecture and Art* (Venice, 1992)
Bryant, Julius, *Marble Hill House, Twickenham* (London, 1991)
Bryson, Norman, *Looking at the Overlooked. Four Essays on Still Life Painting* (London, 1990)
Buckland, Frances, 'Gobelins tapestries and paintings as a source of information about the silver furniture of Louis XIV' in *Burlington Magazine* vol.125, no.962 (May 1983), pp.271–83
Buckland, Frances, 'Silver furnishings at the court of France, 1643–1670' in *Burlington Magazine* vol.131, no.1034 (May 1989), pp.328–36
Buckley, Veronica, *Christina Queen of Sweden: the Restless Life of a European Eccentric* (London, 2004)
Bulgari Calissoni, Anna, *Maestri argentieri gemmari e orafi di Roma* (Rome, 1987)
Burckhardt, J.C., *Der Cicerone: eine Anleitung zum Genuss der Kunstwerke Italiens* (1855), quoted by Downes (1996)
Burden, Michael (ed.), *The Purcell Companion* (London, 1995)
Burke, Peter, *The Fabrication of Louis XIV* (London and New Haven, CT, 1992)
Bursche, Stefan, *Tafelzier des Barock* (Munich, 1974)
Cagnetta, François, 'La vie et l'oeuvre de Gaetano Giulio Zummo' in Piacenti (1977), vol.2, pp.489–501
Callisen, S.A., 'The Equestrian Statue of Louis XIV in Dijon and Related Monuments', *Art Bulletin* XXIII, 2 (June 1941), pp.131–40
Campbell, Marian, *Decorative Ironwork* (London, 1997)
Campbell, Thomas P. (ed.), *Tapestry in the Baroque: Threads of Splendor* (New Haven, CT, and London, 2008)
Cañeque, A., *The King's Living Image in Colonial Mexico. The Culture and Politics of Viceregal Power* (London, 2004)
Careri, Giovanni, and Ferrante Ferranti, *Il Barocco nel Mondo* (Paris, 2002)
Casa de la Contratación, Seville, *España y América. Un océano de negocios* (exhib. cat., 2003)
Casciu, Stefano, *La Principessa saggia: l'eredità di Anna Maria Lusia de' Medici elettrice palatina* (Livorno, 2006)
Cassidy-Geiger, Maureen, '"a wholly new style of porcelain ...": Lacquer-Style Production at the Meissen Manufactory' in Cassidy-Geiger, Maureen, and Letitia Roberts (eds), *Schwartz Porcelain: The Lacquer Craze and its Impact on European Porcelain* (Munich, 2004), pp.73–81
Cassidy-Geiger, Maureen (ed.), *Fragile Diplomacy: Meissen Porcelain for European Courts ca. 1710–63* (New Haven, CT, and London, 2007)
Castelluccio, Stéphane, *Les Collections royales d'objets d'art: de François Ier à la revolution* (Paris, 2002)
Centre Culturel Suédois, Paris, *Versailles à Stockholm: dessins du Nationalmuseum, peintures, meubles et arts décoratifs des collections suédoises et danoises* (Paris, 1985)
Chandra, L. (ed.), *India's Contribution to World Thought and Culture* (Madras, 1970)
Chantrenne, Damien, 'Des projets inédits concernant les pompes funèbres du Grand Condé par Pierre Paul Sevin, 1687' in *Histoire de l'art Paris* no.54 (June 2004), pp.59–72
Chicó, Mario Tavares, 'Gilt-carved work retables for the churches of Portuguese India', *Connoisseur* (February 1956)
Chong, Alan, and Wouter Kloek (eds), *Still Life Paintings from the Netherlands 1550–1720* (Swolle, 1999)
Christie, Sigrid, *Den Lutherske Ikonografi I Norge Inntil 1800*, 2 vols (Oslo, 1973)
Christout, Marie-Françoise, *Le Ballet de cour de Louis XIV, 1643–1672, mises en scène* (Paris, 1967)
Christout, Marie-Françoise, *Le ballet de cour au XVIIe siècle/The ballet de cour in the 17th century* (Geneva, 1987)
Cichrová, Kateřina, The Wardrobe of the Chateau Theatre in Český Krumlov in Pleskačová, Jana, Miroslava Přikrylová and Věra Ptáčková (eds), *The Baroque Theatre in the Chateau of Český Krumlov. Miscellany of papers for a special seminar* (Český Krumlov, 1993), pp.56–64
Cirillo, Giuseppe and Giovanni Godi, *Il mobile a Parma fra barocco e romanticismo, 1600–1860* (Parma, 1983)
Clarke, Mary, and Clement Crisp, *Design For Ballet* (London, 1978)
Clifford, Timothy, *Designs of Desire: Architectural and Ornament Prints and Drawings 1500–1850* (Edinburgh, 1999)
Clunas, Craig, *Chinese Carving* (London, 1996)
Coccioli-Mastroviti, Anna, 'Struttura e organizzazione spaziali del palazzo e della villa bolognesi nella trattistica, negli scritti dei viaggiatori stranieri, nelle guide' in Erer, Maria-Luisa (ed.), *Arte lombarda* no.143 (2005), pp.59–66
Coe, Ralph T., 'Small European Sculpture' in *Apollo* vol.96, no.130 (December 1972), pp.514–23
Coeyman, Barbara, 'Theatres for Opera and Ballet during the Reigns of Louis XIV and Louis XV' in *Early Music* XVIII, 1 (February 1990), pp.23–37
Cogo, Bruno, *Antonio Corradini: Scultore Veneziano 1668–1752* (Este, 1996)
Cokayne, George Edward (ed.), *The Complete Baronetage*, 5 vols (reprinted Gloucester, 1983)
Colbert, Jean-Baptiste, *Lettres, instructions et mémoires de Colbert* (Paris, 1861–82)
Cole, Wendell, 'The Salle des Machines: Three Hundred Years Ago' in *Educational Theatre Journal* XIV, 3 (October 1962), pp.224–7
Coleridge, Anthony, 'English Furniture Makers and Cabinet-Makers at Hatfield House – I: c.1600–1750' in *Burlington Magazine* vol.109, no.767 (February 1967), pp.63–70
Colle, Enrico, *Il mobile barocco in Italia: arredi e decorazioni d'interni dal 1600 al 1738* (Milan, 2000)
Collin, F., 'The Good Shepherd Ivory Carvings of Goa and their Symbolism' in *Apollo* vol.120, no.978 (September 1984), pp.170–75
Conan, Michel (ed.), *Baroque Garden Cultures: Emulation, Sublimation, Subversion* (Washington, 2005)
Conceição, Frei Cláudio da, *Gabinete Histórico* vol.11 (1827)
Conforti, Michael, and Guy Walton, *Royal Treasures of Sweden, 1550–1700* (Washington, 1988)
Connors, Joseph, *Borromini and the Roman Oratory* (London, 1980)
Constans, Claire, 'Evocation de l'appartement de Madame de Maintenon' in *Revue du Louvre* no.3 (1976), pp.197–207
Constans, Claire, *Château de Versailles: catalogue des peintures* (Paris, 1980)
Constans, Claire, *Les Peintures Volume II: Musée National du Château de Versailles* (Paris, 1995)
Constans, Claire, and Xavier Salmon, *Splendors of Versailles* (Mississippi Arts Pavilion, Jackson, exhib. cat., 1998)
Contardi, Bruno, 'L'altare di San Luigi Gonzaga in Sant'Ignazio' in Battisti, Alberta (ed.), *Andrea Pozzo* (Milan, 1996), pp.96–119
Cooke, Edward S. (ed.), *Upholstery in America and Europe from the Seventeenth Century to World War I* (New York, 1987)
Corneilson, Paul, 'Reconstructing the Mannheim court theatre', *Early Music* XXV (February 1997)
Cornforth, John, 'Looking Glass Mysteries' in *Country Life* vol.187, no.42 (21 October 1993), pp.72–4
Coutinho, Bernardo Xavier, *Nossa Senhora na Arte* (Porto, 1959)
Couto, João, and António M. Gonçalves, *A ourivesaria em Portugal* (Lisbon, 1960)
Couvreur, Walter, 'Daniël Seghers' Inventaris van door hem Geschilderde Bloemstukken' in *Gentse Bijdragen tot de Kunstgeschiedenis en de Oudheidkunde* vol.20 (1967), pp.87–158
Cowen, Pamela, *A Fanfare for the Sun King: Unfolding Fans for Louis XIV* (London, 2003)
Cressy, David, *Bonfires and Bells: National Memory and the Protestant Calendar in Elizabethan and Stuart England* (Stroud, 1989)
Cumberland, Richard, *Origines gentium antiquissimae...* (London, 1724)
Dahl, Ilse, *Das Barocke Reitermonument* (unpublished doctoral thesis from Düsseldorf University, 1935)
Dahlin, Anki, *Textil på Skokloster* (Skokloster, 1988)
Daniles, C., and Kennedy, M., *Negotiated Empires. Centers and Peripheries in the Americas, 1500–1820* (London, 2002)
Darr, Barnet and Boström, *Italian Sculpture in the Detroit Institute of Arts*, 2 vols (Detroit, 2002)
De Beer, E.S. (ed.), *The Diary of John Evelyn*, 6 vols (Oxford, 1955, rev. 2000)
De Ceglia, Francesco, 'Rotten Corpses, a Disembowelled Woman, a Flayed Man. Images of the body from the end of the C17th to the beginning of the C19th. Florentine wax models in the first-hand accounts of visitors', *Perspectives on Science* 14, no.4 (2007)
Dee, Elaine Evans, and Guy Walton, *Versailles: The view from Stockholm* (Cooper-Hewitt Museum, New York, exhib. cat., 1988)
DeJean, Joan, *The Essence of Style* (New York, 2005)
Delaforce, Angela, *Art and Patronage in Eighteenth Century Portugal* (Cambridge, 2002)
de la Gorce, Jérôme, 'Un aspect du merveilleux dans l'opéra français sous le règne de Louis XIV: les chars marins', in Schnapper (1982)
de la Gorce, Jérôme, *Berain, dessinateur du Roi Soleil* (Paris, 1986)
del Pesco, Daniela, *Il Louvre di Bernini nella Francia di Luigi XIV* (Naples, 1984)
de Mesa, J., and T. Gisbert, *Monumentos de Bolivia* (La Paz, 4th edn 2002)
Demetrescu, Calin, 'Domenico Cucci le plus baroque des ébénistes de Louis XIV' in *L'Estampille l'objet d'art* no.306 (October 1996), pp.58–79
Dennis, Faith, *Three Centuries of French Domestic Silver: Its Makers & Its Marks* (New York, 1960)
de Serre, J., 'Cabinets from Louis XIV Collection' in *Country Life* vol.68, no.1753 (23 August 1930), p.34
de Seta, Cesare, 'Architecture in miniature' in *FMR* 42 (February 1990), pp.81–96
de Seta, Cesare, *Luigi Vanvitelli* (Naples, 1998)
de Seta, Cesare, *Luigi Vanvitelli e la sua cerchia* (Palazzo Reale, Caserta, exhib. cat., 2000)
Detroit Institute of Arts, *Twilight of the Medici* (Florence, 1974)
Diamantmuseum Antwerp, *Een eeuw van schittering: diamantjuwelen uit de 17de eeuw/A Sparkling Age: 17th-century Diamond Jewellery* (Antwerp, 1993)
Dilworth, John, 'Early English sophistication' in *The Strad* vol.110, no.1307 (March 1999), pp.264–71
Di Natale, Maria Concetta, *Il corallo Trapanese*

nei secoli XVI e XVII (Brescia, 2002)
Di Natale, Maria Concetta, *Materiali preziosi dalla terra e dal mare* (Palermo, 2003)
Dixon, Thomas, *From Passions to Emotions: the Creation of a Secular Psychological Category* (Cambridge, 2003)
D'Orey, *Five Centuries of Jewellery: National Museum of Ancient Art, Lisbon* (London and Wappingers Falls, 1995)
Downes, Kerry, 'Baroque', in Turner, Jane (ed.), *Grove Dictionary of Art*, vol.14 (London, 1996)
Droguet, Vincent and Marc-Henri Jordan, *Théâtre de Cour – Les spectacles à Fontainebleau au XVIIIe siècle* (Paris, 2005)
Drury, Martin, 'Italian Furniture in National Trust Houses' in *Furniture History* vol.20 (1984)
Drury, Martin, 'Diplomat's prize' in *Country Life* vol.185, no.40 (3 October 1991), pp.54–5
Durante, Stephanie-Suzanne, et al., *Peter Paul Rubens: a Touch of Brilliance. Oil sketches and related works from the State Hermitage Museum and the Courtauld Institute Gallery* (Munich and London, 2003–4)
Eade, Jane, 'The Triptych Portrait in England, 1575–1646', *The British Art Journal* VI, no.2 (2005)
Ehrenstrahl, David Klöcker, *Certamen equestre..., Das grosse Carrosel und prächtige Ring-Rännen nebst dem, was sonsten Fürtreffliches zu sehen war, alss der durchleuchtigste groszmächtigste König und herr Carl der Fÿlfftte, die Regierung seines väterlichen Erb-Köningreichs Anno M.DC.LXXII: den XVIII. den Decembris in seiner königlichen Residentz zu Stockholm antratt* (Stockholm, 1685)
Ekström, Gunnar, *Västerås Domkyrkas Inventarier genom tiderna* (Västerås, 1976)
Elias, Norbert, *The Court Society* (Oxford, 1983)
Ellis, Markman, *The Coffee House: a Cultural History* (London, 2004)
Emoke, László, *Hungarian Renaissance and Baroque Embroideries*, Museum of Applied Art (Budapest, 2002)
Endean, Philip, 'The Ignatian Prayer of the Senses', *Heythrop Journal*, XXXI (1990)
Entwisle, E.A., *A Literary History of Wallpaper* (London, 1960)
Ericani, Giuliana, 'L'*Impero della China* sulla scena e nella festa veneziana tra Sei e Settecento' in Schnapper (1982), pp.95–104
Eriksen, Roy (ed.), *Contexts of Baroque: Theatre, Metamorphosis, and Design* (Oslo, 1996)
Estella Marcos, Margarita M., *La escultura barroca de marfil en España: las escuelas europeas y las coloniales*, 2 vols (Madrid, 1984)
Estella Marcos, Margarita M., *Ivories from the Far Eastern Provinces of Spain and Portugal* (Monterrey, 1997)
Esterly, David, *Grinling Gibbons and the Art of Carving* (London, 1998)
Evangelisti, Silvia, *Nuns: a History of Convent Life 1450–1700* (Oxford, 2007)
Faggi, A. (ed.), *Collezione di Classici Italiani*, vol.I (Turin, 1930)
Fagiolo, Marcello, and Maria Luisa Madonna, *Roma 1300–1875. L'arte degli Anni Santi* (Palazzo Venezia, Rome, exhib. cat., 1984)
Fagiolo, Marcello, Bruno Adorni and Maria Luisa Madonna, *Barocco romano e barocco italiano: il teatro, l'effimero, l'allegoria, numerosi documenti* (Rome, 1985)
Fagiolo, Marcello, *La Festa a Roma dal Rinascimento al 1870*, 2 vols (Palazzo Venezia, Rome, exhib. cat., 1997)
Fagiolo, Marcello, and Paolo Portoghesi, *Roma Barocca: Bernini, Borromini, Pietro da Cortona* (Museo Nazionale di Castel Sant'Angelo, Rome, exhib. cat., 2006)
Fagiolo dell'Arco, Maurizio, *La festa barocca* (Rome, 1997)
Fantuzzi, G., *Memorie della vita del generale Conte L. Marsili* (Bologna, 1771)
Félibien, André, *Relation de la feste de Versailles. Du 18 juillet mil six cens soixante-huit* (Paris, 1679)
Fenaille, Maurice, *État général des tapisseries de la manufacture des Gobelins, depuis son origine jusqu'à nos jours, 1600–1900* (Paris, 1903–23)
Fenlon, Iain, 'Music and Festival', in Mulryne, Watanabe-O'Kelly and Shewring (2004), pp.47–55
Finaldi, Gabriele, et al., *The Image of Christ* (London, 2000)
Fischer, Beisenkötter and Krebs, *Dem Volk zur Schau – Prunkschlitten des Barock. Württembergisches Landes-museum* (München, 2002)
Fleming, John, in *Connoisseur* (August 1961)
Fowler, James (ed.), *Images of Show Business from the Theatre Museum, V&A* (London, 1982)
Francastel, Pierre, *Girardon, par Pierre Francastel: biographie et catalogue critiques, l'oeuvre complète de l'artiste reproduite en quatre-vingt-treize héliogravures* (Paris, 1928)
Franco, Anísio, and Ana Duarte Rodrigues, 'Nova aquisição para o Museu de Arte Antiga: Nossa Senhora da Conceição do Laboratório de Machado de Castro' in *Revista de História da Arte*, II (2006), pp.242–3
Fraser, Antonia, *Love and Louis XIV: the Women in the Life of the Sun King* (London, 2006)
Fraser-Jenkins, A.D., 'Cosimo de Medici's Patronage of Architecture and the Theory of Magnificence', *Journal of the Courtauld and Warburg Institutes* vol.33 (1970)
Frederiks, J.W., *Dutch Silver: Embossed Ecclesiastical and Secular Plate from the Renaissance until the End of the Eighteenth Century*, 4 vols (The Hague, 1952–61)
Freedberg, David, 'The Origins and Rise of the Flemish Madonnas in Flower Garlands', *Münchener Jahrbuch der Bildenden Kunst* XXXVII (1981)
Freedberg, David, 'Empathy, Motion and Emotion' in Herding and Krause Wahl (2007)
Friedman, Terry, *James Gibbs* (New Haven, CT, 1984)
Fuhring, Peter (ed.), *Design into Art. Drawings for Architecture and Ornament. The Lodewijk Houthakker Collection* (London, 1989)
Fuhring, Peter, *Ornament in prent: zeventiende-eeuwse ornamentprenten in de verzamelingen van het Rijksmuseum/Ornament in print: seventeenth-century ornament prints in the collections of the Rijksmuseum* (Amsterdam, 1998)
Fuhring, Peter (ed.), *Rubens, Silver Ewer and Basin* (Brussels, 2001)
Fuhring, Peter, 'Jean Barbet's "Livre d'Architecture, d'Autels et de Cheminées": drawing and design in Seventeenth-century France' in *Burlington Magazine* vol.145 (June 2003)
Fuhring, Peter, *Ornament Prints in the Rijksmuseum II: the Seventeenth Century* (Amsterdam, 2004)
Fuhring, Peter, *Designing the Décor: French Drawings from the Eighteenth Century* (Lisbon, 2006)
Fundación Central Hispano, Madrid, *Gregorio Fernandez 1576–1636* (exhib. cat., 1999)
Gaehtgens, Thomas W., et al., *Splendeurs de la Cour de Saxe: Dresde à Versailles* (Château de Versailles, exhib. cat., 2006)
Galeries nationales du Grand Palais, Paris, *Un Temps d'exubérance: les arts décoratifs sous Louis XIII et Anne d'Autriche* (exhib. cat., 2002)
Gallingani, Daniela (ed.), *I Bibiena, una famiglia in scena: da Bologna all'Europa* (Florence, 2002)
Garcia Saiz, Concepción, *La pintura colonial en el Museo de América* (Madrid, 1980)
Gardner, J. Starkie, *Ironwork part III: The Artistic Working of Iron in Great Britain from the Earliest Times* (London, 1922)
Garnier, Nicole, *Antoine Coypel: 1661–1722* (Paris, 1989)
Gerstl, Doris, *Drucke des höfischen Barock in Schweden: der Stockholmer Hofmaler David Klöcker von Ehrenstrahl und die Nürnberger Stecher Georg Christoph Eimmart und Jacob von Sandrart* (Berlin, 2000)
Gigli, Giacinto (ed. Ricciotti, Giuseppe), *Diario Romano 1608–1670* (Rome, 1958), trans. in San Juan (2001)
Gilberto (1992)
Girouard, Mark, *Cities and People: a Social and Architectural History* (New Haven, CT, and London, 1985)
Girouard, Mark, *Life in the French Country House* (London, 2000)
Giusti, Annamaria (ed.), *Splendori di Pietre Dure, L'Arte di Corte nella Firenze dei Granduchi* (Palazzo Pitti, Florence, exhib. cat., 1988)
Giusti, Annamaria (ed.), *Arte e manifattura di corte a Firenze: dal tramonto dei Medici all'impero (1732–1815)* (Livorno, 2006)
Glanville, Philippa, *Silver in England* (London, 1987)
Glanville, Philippa, 'The Chesterfield Wine Coolers' in *National Art Collections Fund Review* vol.87 (1990), pp.103–8
Glanville, Philippa (ed.), *Silver* (London, 1996)
Goldstein, Claire, *Vaux and Versailles: The Appropriations, Erasures and Accidents That Made Modern France* (Philadelphia, 2007)
González-Palacios, Alvar, 'Bernini as a furniture designer' in *Burlington Magazine* vol.112, no.812 (November 1970), pp.719–22
González-Palacios, Alvar, *Il tempio del gusto: Roma e il Regno delle Due Sicilie: le arti decorative in Italia fra classicismi e barocco* (Milan, 1984)
González-Palacios, Alvar, *Il tempio del gusto. Il Granducato di Toscana e gli stati settentrionali: le arti decorative in Italia fra classicismi e barocco*, 2 vols (Milan, 1986)
González-Palacios, Alvar, 'Giovanni Giardini: New Works and New Documents' in *Burlington Magazine* vol.137, no.1107 (June 1995), pp.367–76
González-Palacios, Alvar and Mario Tavella, *A Magnificent Roman Baroque Cabinet by Giacomo Herman* (London, 2007)
Goody, Jack, *The Culture of Flowers* (Cambridge, 1993)
Gore House, London, *Catalogues of Specimens of Cabinet Work and of Studies from the Schools of Art exhibited at Gore House, Kensington* (exhib. cat., 1853)
Gough, S. (ed.), *Treasures for the Nation* (British Museum, London, exhib. cat., 1988)
Gould, Cecil, *Bernini in France: an Episode in Seventeenth-century History* (London, 1981)
Graham, Clare, *Ceremonial and Commemorative Chairs in Great Britain* (London, 1994)
Grate, Pontus (ed.), *Le Soleil et l'Étoile de Nord: La France et la Suède au XVIIIe siècle* (Nationalmuseum, Stockholm, and Galeries Nationales du Grand Palais, Paris, exhib. cat., 1994)
Graves, Alun R., *Tiles and Tilework of Europe* (London, 2002)
Griffiths, Antony, *The Print in Stuart Britain 1603–1689* (London, 1998)
Grigaut, P., 'Two bozzetti by Gian Lorenzo Bernini' in *Bulletin of the Detroit Institute of Arts* vol.32, no.3 (1952–3), pp.61–5
Grigaut, P., 'A bozzetto for St Peter's Cathedral' in *The Art Quarterly* no.16 (1953), pp.124–30
Groom, Nigel, *Frankincense and Myrrh: a study of the Arabian incense trade* (London, 1981)
Groom, Suzanne, *Gilding Report on the Fountain Garden Screen* (unpublished, Historic Royal Palaces Agency, 1996)
Grossman, G. Ulrich (ed.), *Von teutscher Not zu höfischer Pracht, 1648–1701* (Germanisches Nationalmuseum, Nuremberg, and Cologne, exhib. cat., 1998)
Gruber, Alain, 'The Ballet Royal de la Nuict: a masque at the court of Louis XIV', *Apollo* vol.386 (March–June 1994), pp.34–40
Gruber, Alain (ed.), *The History of the Decorative Arts: Classicism and Baroque in Europe* (New York, London, Paris, 1992)
Gruzinski, S., *The Mestizo Mind. The Intellectual Dynamics of Colonization and Globalization* (London, 2002)
Guiffrey, Jules, *Comptes des bâtiments du roi sous le règne de Louis XIV* (Paris, 1881–1901)
Guiffrey, Jules, *Inventaire général du mobilier de la couronne sous Louis XIV (1663–1715) publié pour la première fois sous les auspices de la Société d'encouragement pour la propagation des livres d'art* (Paris, 1885–6)
Guilmard-Geddes, Laurence, 'Les pompes funèbres des Condé aux Jésuites de Paris. Deux gouaches inédites de Pierre-Paul Sevin', in *Bulletin du musée Carnavalet* (1978), 2, pp.5–16
Gundestrup, Bente (ed.), *The Royal Danish Kunstkammer 1737*, 2 vols (Copenhagen, 1991)
Gunnarsson, Torsten (ed.), *David Klöcker Ehrenstrahl* (Nationalmuseum, Stockholm, exhib. cat., 1976)
Hackenbroch, Yvonne, *English and other silver in the Irwin Untermyer collection* (London, 1963)
Hackenbroch, Yvonne, and Maria Sframeli, *I Gioielli dell'Elettrice palatina al Museo degli argenti/The jewels of the Electress Palatine in the Museo degli argenti* (Florence, 1988)
Hahr, August, *Västerås domkyrka* (Västerås, 1923)
Hairs, Marie-Louise, *Les Peintres flamands de fleurs au XVIIe siècle* (Tournai, 1998)
Halfpenny, Eric, '"The Citie's Loyalty Display'd" (A literary and documentary causerie of Charles II's Coronation "Entertainment")', in *The Guildhall Miscellany* 10 (1959), pp.19–35
Hall, Michael, 'Gianlorenzo Bernini's third design for the east façade of the Louvre of 1665, drawn by Mattia de Rossi' in *Burlington Magazine* vol.149, no.1252 (July 2007), pp.478–82
Harbison, Robert, *Reflections on Baroque* (London, 2000)
Harden, Donald (ed.), *Masterpieces of glass: a selection* (British Museum, London, exhib. cat., 1968)
Hargrove, June, *The Statues of Paris: An Open-air Pantheon* (Antwerp, 1989)
Harris, Ann Sutherland, 'Studio di Bernini, disegno per un orologio' in Béguin, Di Giampaolo and Malgouyres, *Disegni della Donazione Marcel Puech al Museo Calvet di Avignone* (Naples, 1998), p.162
Harris, Eileen, *Going to Bed: The Arts and Living* (London, 1981)
Harris, John, *English Decorative Ironwork from Contemporary Source Books 1610–1836*

(London, 1960)
Harris, Tim, *Restoration: Charles II and his Kingdoms, 1660–1685* (Harmondsworth, 2005)
Harrison, Charles, Paul Wood and Jason Grainger (eds), *Art in Theory 1648–1815. An Anthology of Changing Ideas* (Oxford, 2000)
Hartop, Christopher, *The Huguenot legacy: English silver 1680–1760, from the Alan and Simone Hartman Collection* (London, 1996)'
Haskell, Francis, *Patrons and Painters: a Study in the Relations between Italian Art and Society in the Age of the Baroque* (1963; rev. edn New Haven, CT, 1980)
Hauglid, Ruar, *Akantus: Fra Hellas til Gundbrandsdal* (Oslo, 1950)
Hayward, J.F., *Huguenot Silver in England 1688–1727* (London, 1959)
Hazlitt, William, *Criticisms on Art, and Sketches of the Picture Galleries of England: With Catalogues of the Principal Galleries* (London, 1856)
Hein, Jørgen, 'Manufacturing and engraving glass' in Krog, Ole Villumsen (ed.), *Royal Glass* (Copenhagen, 1995), pp.44–6
Hein, Jørgen, 'Curiosités à Rosenborg' in *Connaissance des Arts* no.592 (March 2002), pp.90–101
Heinrich, Christoph, and Michael Braun, *Georg Hinz: das Kunstkammerregal* (Hamburg, 1996)
Held, Julius, *The Oil Sketches of Peter Paul Rubens: a critical catalogue* (Princeton, NJ, 1980), 2 vols
Hempel, Eberhard, *Baroque Art and Architecture in Central Europe: Germany, Austria, Switzerland, Hungary, Czechoslovakia, Poland. Painting and sculpture, seventeenth and eighteenth centuries. Architecture, sixteenth to eighteenth centuries* (Harmondsworth, 1965)
Henriques, Ana de Castro, *Museu Nacional de Arte Antiga. Guide* (Lisbon, 2004)
Herding, K., *Pierre Puget* (Berlin, 1980)
Herding, K., and A. Krause Wahl (eds), *Wie sich Gefühle Ausdruck verschaffen: Emotionen in Nahsicht* (Berlin, 2007)
Hernmarck, Carl, *Kunglig prakt från barock och rokoko* (Malmö, 1948)
Hernmarck, Carl (ed.), *Mästerverk i Nationalmuseum konsthantverk: en konstbok från Nationalmuseum* (Stockholm, 1954)
Hernmarck, Carl, *The Art of the European Silversmith 1430–1830* (London, 1977)
Heyde, Herbert, 'Two European wind instruments in the shape of a dragon' in *Music in Art: International Journal for Music Iconography* vol.32, no.1–2 (2007), pp.133–41
Heyde, Herbert, 'Gli strumenti musicali zoomorfi e teatrali in Italia nel tardo Rinascimento e nell'epoca barocca' in Falletti, Meucci and Rossi-Rognoni (eds), *Meraviglie sonore. Strumenti musicali del barocco italiano* (Galleria dell'Accademia, Florence, exhib. cat., 2007), pp.81–93
Hildebrand, Josephine, and Christian Theuerkauff (eds), *Die Brandenburgisch-Preußische Kunstkammer* (Berlin, 1981)
Hill, John Walter, *Baroque Music: Music in Western Europe, 1580–1750* (New York, 2005)
Hills, Helen, *Invisible City. The Architecture of Devotion in Seventeenth-Century Neapolitan Convents* (Oxford, 2004)
Hilton, Lisa, *Athénais. The Real Queen of France* (London, 2002)
Himmelheber, Georg, 'Puchweiser, Boulle und die Boulle-Möbel für München' in Glaser, Hubert (ed.), *Kurfurst Max Emanuel: Bayern und Europa um 1700* (Bayerisches Nationalmuseum, Schloß Lustheim, exhib. cat., 1976), vol.1, pp.250–63
Hindel, Keith, and John Herbert, *London-made Knives and their Marks: the Collections of the Worshipful Company of Cutlers of London* (London, 2005)
Hodgkinson, Terence, 'Two garden sculptures by Antonio Corradini' in *Victoria and Albert Museum Bulletin* vol.4, no.2 (April 1968), pp.37–49
Hollstein, F.W.H. (series ed.), *German engravings, etchings, and woodcuts, ca. 1400–1700*, XIX (Rotterdam, 1976)
Holt, E.G. (ed.), *A Documentary History of Art* vol.2 (New York, 2nd edn 1963)
Honey, W.B., *European Ceramic Art* (London, 1952)
Honour, Hugh, 'Florentine baroque bronzes in an English private collection' in *Connoisseur* vol.159, no.640 (June 1965), pp.85–9
Honour, Hugh, *Chinoiserie: the vision of Cathay* (London, 1961)
Honour, Hugh, *Goldsmiths and Silversmiths* (New York, 1971)
Hoog, Simone, *Manière de montrer les Jardins de Versailles, par Louis XIV* (Paris, 1992)
Hoog, Simone, and Béatrix Saule, *Your Visit to Versailles* (Versailles, 2005)
Hoos, Hildegard, *Augsburger Silbermöbel* (unpublished doctoral thesis from Johann Wolfgang Goethe Universität, Frankfurt am Main, 1981)
Hoos, Hildegard, 'Augsburger Silbermobel: Prunkvolle Ausstattung höfischer Gemächer/Augsburg silver furniture: splendid furnishings from courtly rooms' in *Weltkunst* LVII/12 (15 June 1987), pp.1691–5
Hsia, R. Po-chia (ed.), *Reform and Expansion 1500–1660*, The Cambridge History of Christianity, vol.6 (Cambridge, 2007)
Hughes, Q., and C. Thake, *Malta: The Baroque Island* (Valletta, 2003)
Hunt, John Dixon, and P. Willis, *The Genius of the Place, The English Landscape Garden 1620–1820* (London, 1975)
Hunt, John Dixon, and Erik de Jong (eds), *The Anglo-Dutch Garden in the Age of William and Mary/De Gouden eeuw van de Hollandse tuinkunst* (London, 1988)
Hunt, John Dixon, and Michael Conan, *Tradition and Innovation in French Garden Art: Chapters of a New History* (Philadelphia, 2002)
Hutton, Ronald, *The Rise and Fall of Merry England: the Ritual Year 1400–1700* (Oxford, 1994)
Hyatt Mayor, Alpheus, *The Bibiena Family* (New York, 1945)
Hyde, Elizabeth, *Cultivated Power: Flowers, Culture and Politics in the Reign of Louis XIV* (Philadelphia, 2005)
Impey, Oliver R., *Chinoiserie: the impact of Oriental Styles on Western Art and Decoration* (Oxford, 1977)
Irwin, John, and Katharine B. Brett, *Origins of Chintz: with a catalogue of Indo-European cotton-paintings in the Victoria and Albert Museum, London, and the Royal Ontario Museum, Toronto* (London, 1970)
Jackson, Anna, and Amin Jaffer, *Encounters: the Meeting of Asia and Europe 1500–1800* (V&A, London, exhib. cat., 2004)
Jackson, Charles James, *An Illustrated History of English Plate*, 2 vols (London, 1912)
Jackson-Stops, Gervase, 'William III and French Furniture' in *Furniture History* vol.7 (1971), pp.121–6
Jackson-Stops, Gervase, 'A Courtier's Collection – The 6th Earl of Dorset's Furniture at Knole, I & II' in *Country Life* vol.151, nos 4170 and 4171 (2 & 9 June 1977), pp.1495–9, 1620–2
Jackson-Stops, Gervase, 'Daniel Marot and the 1st Duke of Montagu' in *Nederland Kunsthistorisch Jaarboek Bussum, Amsterdam* 31 (1980), pp.244–62
Jackson-Stops, Gervase (ed.), *The Treasure Houses of Britain. Five Hundred Years of Private Patronage and Art Collecting* (National Gallery of Art, Washington, exhib. cat., 1985)
Jacobitti, Gian Marco, and Anna Maria Romano, *Il Palazzo reale di Caserta* (Naples, 1994)
Jacobsen, Helen, 'Ambassadorial plate of the later Stuart period and the collection of the Earl of Strafford' in *Journal of the History of Collections* vol.19, no.1 (May 2007), pp.1–13
Jaffé, David (ed.), *Rubens: A Master in the Making* (The National Gallery, London, exhib. cat., 2005)
James, Susan, *Passion and Action: The Emotions in Seventeenth-Century Philosophy* (Oxford, 1997)
Jardine, Lisa, *On a Grander Scale: the Outstanding Career of Sir Christopher Wren* (London, 2002)
Jarrard, Alice, *Architecture as Performance in Seventeenth-Century Europe: Court Ritual in Modena, Rome and Paris* (Cambridge, 2003)
Jenkins, David (ed.), *The Cambridge History of Western Textiles* (Cambridge, 2003)
Jervis, Simon Swynfen, 'Echoes over Two Centuries. Two newly acquired Italian Tables at the V&A' in *Country Life* vol.177, no.4581 (6 June 1985), pp.1590–96
Jervis, Simon Swynfen, 'Pietre Dure Caskets in England' in *Furniture History* vol.43 (2007), pp.245–65
Jeudwine, Wynne, *Stage Designs* (Feltham, 1968)
Jiri, Hilmera, 'Zamecke divádlo v Českem Krumlove in *Zpravy pamatkove pece* no.18 (1958), pp.71–95
Jiri, Hilmera, The Chateau Theatre at Český Krumlov in *Czech Theatre* no.7 (1994), pp.12–26
Johannesson, Knut, I polstjärnans tecken in *Lychnos-bibliotek* vol.24 (1968), pp.103–7
Johns, Christopher, *Papal Art and Cultural Politics. Rome in the Age of Clement XI* (Cambridge, 1993)
Jones, E. Alfred, 'The Duke of Cumberland's English plate' in *Burlington Magazine* vol.44, no.250 (January 1924), pp.40–2
Jones, Jennifer, *Sexing la Mode. Gender, Fashion and Commercial Culture in Old Régime France* (Oxford, 2004)
Jones, Pamela M., 'Federico Borromeo as a Patron of Landscapes and Still Lifes: Christian Optimism in Italy ca.1600', *Art Bulletin* LXX, no. 2 (1988)
Josephson, Ragnar, 'Karl XI och Karl XII som esteter' in *Karolinska förbundets årsbok* (1947), pp.11–12
Jourdain, Margaret, *Stuart Furniture at Knole* (London, 1952)
Judson, J. Richard, *The Passion of Christ*, Corpus Rubenianum Ludwig Burchard VI (Turnhout, 2000)
Kagan, R.L., *Urban Images of the Hispanic World 1493–1793* (New Haven, CT, 2000)
Kahn-Rossi, Manuela, and Marco Franciolli, *Il giovane Borromini: dagli esordi a San Carlo alle Quattro Fontane* (Museo Cantonale d'Arte, Lugano, exhib. cat., 1999)
Kappel, Jutta, and Ulrike Weinhold, *Das Neue Grüne Gewölbe*, Museum Guide (Dresden, 2007)
Karsten, Arne, 'Triumph und Trauma: das Grabmal fur Alexander VII Chigi: 1655–1667' in Bredekamp, Horst and Volker Reinhardt (eds), *Totenkult und Wille zur Macht: die unruhigen Ruhestatten der Papste in St Peter* (Darmstadt, 2004), pp.197–210
Kauffmann, C.M., *Catalogue of Foreign Paintings [in the V&A]: Vol.1 Before 1800* (London, 1973)
Kaufmann, Thomas DaCosta, *Court, Cloister, & City: the Art and Culture of Central Europe, 1450–1800* (London, 1995)
Keil-Budischowsky, Verena, 'Barocke Bühnendekorationen für den Wiener Kaiserhof' in *Kunsthistorisches Jahrbuch Graz* XXV (1993), pp.353–64
Keisch, Christiane, *Das grosse Silberbuffet aus dem Rittersaal des Berliner Schlosses* (Berlin, 1997)
Keisch, Christiane, and Susanne Netzer, *'Herrliche Künste und Manufacturen': Fayence, Glas und Tapisserien aus der Frühzeit Brandenburg-Preussens 1680–1720* (Berliner Kunstgewerbemuseums, exhib. cat., 2001)
Kent, Neil, 'Gustaf III and Italian Culture' in West (1999)
Kiene, Michael, *G.P. Pannini: Römische Veduten aus dem Louvre* (Paris, 1992, Brunswick, 1993)
Kieven, Elisabeth, *Von Bernini bis Piranesi: Römische Architekturzeichnungen des Barock* (Graphische Sammlung, Staatsgalerie, Stuttgart, exhib. cat., 1993)
Kimball, Fiske, *The Creation of the Rococo* (Philadelphia, 1943)
Kirchberg, Ulrike, *Zwischen zwei Welten – König Johann von Sachsen* (Schloß Weesenstein, Müglitztal, exhib. cat., 2001)
Kirwin, William Chandler, *Powers matchless: the Pontificate of Urban VIII, the Baldachin, and Gian Lorenzo Bernini* (New York, 1998)
Klein, Norman M., *The Vatican to Vegas: a History of Special Effects* (New York, 2004)
Klingensmith, Samuel John, *The Utility of Splendor: Ceremony, Social Life, and Architecture at the Court of Bavaria, 1600–1800* (Chicago and London, 1993)
Knall-Brskovsky, Ulrike, *Italienische Quadraturisten in Österreich* (Vienna, 1984)
Knothe, Florian, *The Manufacture des meubles de la couronne aux Gobelins under Louis XIV: a Social, Political and Cultural History* (unpublished doctoral thesis, University of London, 2008)
Koener, Joseph Leo, *The Reformation of the Image* (London, 2004)
Koeppe, Wolfram and Annamaria Giusti (ed.), *Art of the Royal Court: Treasures in Pietre Dure from the Palaces of Europe* (New Haven, CT, 2008)
Das Königliche Denckmahl, Welches Nach geschehener Vermählung [...] Friedrich Augusti, Mit [...] Maria Josepha, [...] In [...] Dreßden, [...] 1719 gestifftet worden (Frankfurt, 1719)
Konrad, Herman W., *A Jesuit Hacienda in Colonial Mexico: Santa Lucia 1576–1767* (Palo Alto, CA, 1980)
Kopplin, Haase and Balla, *'Sächsissch Lacquirte Sachen': Lackkunst in Dresden unter August dem Starken* (Museum für Lackkunst, Münster, exhib. cat., 1998)
Kopplin, Monika, 'All Sorts of Lacquered Chinese on a Black Glaze – Lacquer Painting on Böttger Stoneware and the Problem of Attribution to Martin Schnell' in Cassidy-Geiger, Maureen, and Letitia Roberts (eds), *Schwartz Porcelain: The Lacquer Craze and its Impact on European Porcelain* (Munich, 2004), pp.83–90
Kosareva, Nina, 'A terracotta study by Gianlorenzo Bernini for the statue of the Blessed Ludovica Albertoni' in *Apollo* vol.100, no.154 (December 1974), pp.480–85
Koyré, A., *From the Closed World to the Infinite Universe* (Baltimore and London, 1957)
Kräftner, Johann (ed.), *Baroque Luxury*

Porcelain: the Manufactories of Du Paquier in Vienna and of Carlo Ginori in Florence (Munich, Berlin, London, New York, 2005)
Krapf, Michael, *Triumph Der Phantasie: Barocke modelle von Hildebrandt bis Mollinarolo* (Österreichische Galerie Belvedere, Vienna, exhib. cat., 1998)
Kreisel, Heinrich, *Prunkwagen und Schlitten* (Leipzig, 1927)
Kreisel, Heinrich, *Die Kunst des deutschen Möbels, I: Von den Anfängen bis zum Hochbarock* (Munich, 1968)
Kreisel, Heinrich, *Die Kunst des deutschen Möbels, II: Spätbarock und Rokoko* (Munich, 1970)
Krückmann, Peter, *Paradies des Rokoko, I: Das Bayreuth der Markgräfin Wilhelmine* (Munich, 1998)
Krügel, Katharina, *Der sächsische Barockbildhauer Johann Benjamin Thomae (1682–1751): ein Beitrag zur Geschichte der sächsiche Barockplastik* (Dresden, 1990)
Kubler, George, 'Sacred Mountains in Europe and America', in Verdon and Henderson (1990)
Kunst- und Ausstellungshalle der Bundesrepublik Deutschland, Bonn, *As Grandes Coleções: Museu Nacional de Arte Antiga Lisboa* (exhib. cat., 1999)
Kunstbibliothek, Berlin, *Katalog der Ornamentstichsammlung der staatlichen Kunstbibliothek Berlin* (Berlin and Leipzig, 1939)
Künstlerhaus, Vienna, *Ecclesia triumphans Dresdensis* (exhib. cat., 1988)
Kurz, Otto, 'Barroco: 'Storia di una parola', *Lettere Italiane*, XII (1960)
Kurz, Otto, 'Barocca, Storia di un concetto' in *Barocco Europeo e Barocco Veneziano* (Florence, 1963)
Kurz, Otto, *Catalogue of Bolognese Drawings of the XVII and XVIII Centuries ... at Windsor Castle*, 1955 (2nd edition, Bologna, 1988)
Küster, Ulf (ed.), *Theatrum mundi: die Welt als Bühne* (Munich, 2003)
Lablaude, Pierre-André, *The Gardens of Versailles* (London, 1995)
Laine, Merit and Börje Magnusson (eds), *Travel notes, 1673–77 and 1687–88/Nicodemus Tessin the Younger* (Stockholm, 2002)
Landwehr, John, *Romeyn de Hooghe, the Etcher: Contemporary Portrayal of Europe, 1662–1707* (Leiden, 1973)
Lane, Arthur, 'Daniel Marot: Designer of Delft vases and of gardens at Hampton Court' in *Connoisseur* vol.123, no.511 (March 1949), pp.19–24
Lankheit, Klaus, *Florentinische Barockplastik: die Kunst am Hofe der letzten Medici, 1670–1743* (Munich, 1962)
Latham, Robert, and William Matthews, *The Diary of Samuel Pepys, a New and Complete Transcription* (London, 1970)
Laureati, Laura, and Ludovica Trezzani, *Gaspare Vanvitelli e le origini del vedutismo* (Chiostro del Bramante, Rome, and Museo Correr, Venice, exhib. cat., 2002)
Lavin, Irving, *Bernini and the Unity of the Visual Arts* (New York, 1980)
Lavin, Irving, *Past-present: Essays on Historicism in Art from Donatello to Picasso* (Berkeley, 1993)
Lenzi, Deanna (ed.), *Pianta e Spaccato del Nuovo Teatro di Bologna offerto al nobil'uomo ed eccelso Sig. Senatore Conte Girolamo Legnani da Lorenzo Capponi in Bologna, 1771* (Bologna, 1975)
Lenzi, Deanna, and Jadranka Bentini (eds), *I Bibiena: una famiglia europea* (Venice, 2000)
Lenzi, Clerici-Bagozzi and Beaumont, *Meravigliose scene, piacevoli inganni: Galli Bibiena* (Palazzo comunale, Bibiena, exhib. cat., 1992)
Leone, Rosella, et al., *Il Museo di Roma racconta la città* (Palazzo Braschi, Museo di Roma, exhib. cat., 2002)
Levenson, Jay A., *The Age of the Baroque in Portugal* (National Gallery of Art, Washington, exhib. cat., 1993)
Levenson, Jay (ed.), *Encompassing the globe: Portugal and the world in the 16th and 17th centuries* (Washington, 2007)
Levey, Michael, 'Panini, St Peter's, and Cardinal de Polignac' in *Burlington Magazine*, 99 (February 1957), p.54
Levey, Michael, *The seventeenth and eighteenth century Italian schools* (London, 1971)
Levy, Evonne, *Propaganda and the Jesuit Baroque* (Berkeley, 2004)
Liefkes 1997
Liefkes, Reino, *Glass* (London 1997)
Lightbown, Ronald W., 'Gaetano Giulio Zumbo – I: The Florentine Period', *Burlington Magazine* vol.74, no.106 (1964)
Lightbown, Ronald W., 'Time and Death: a new relief by Zumbo' in *Victoria and Albert Museum Bulletin* vol.3, no.1 (January 1967), pp.39–44
Lindell, Ingrid (ed.), *Face to Face. Portraits from Five Centuries* (Nationalmuseum, Stockholm, exhib. cat., 2001)
Lindegren, Agi, *Mariakyrkan i Westerås* (Stockholm, 1898)
Lino, Raul, et al., *Documentos para a História da Arte em Portugal*, 12 vols (Lisbon, 1969–91)
Lippincott, Kristen, *The Story of Time* (Queen's House, Greenwich, exhib. cat., 1999)
Lisbon, Palácio do Correio Velho Leilão de Antiguidades, auction 150 (2005)
Lo Bianco, Anna, *Pier Leone Ghezzi pittore* (Palermo, 1985)
Lo Bianco, Anna, *Pietro da Cortona's Ceiling: National Gallery of Ancient Art at Palazzo Barberini* (Rome, 2004)
Lo Bianco, Anna, and Angela Negro, *Il Settecento a Roma* (Palazzo Venezia, Rome, exhib. cat., 2005)
Lomax, James, 'A Centrepiece for Temple Newsam' in *National Art Collections Fund Review* (1989), pp.115–18
Lomax, James, 'Silver for the English Dining Room, 1700–1820' in *A King's Feast* (Kensington Palace, London, exhib. cat., 1991), pp.124–5
Lomax, James, *British Silver at Temple Newsam and Lotherton Hall: A catalogue of the Leeds Collection* (Leeds, 1992)
Longhurst, Margaret H., *Catalogue of Carvings in Ivory*, 2 vols (V&A, London, 1926–9)
Lopez-Guadalupe Muñoz, Juan Jesus, *José de Mora* (Granada, 2000)
Loughman, John, 'The Market for Netherlandish Still Lifes, 1600–1720', in Chong and Kloek (1999)
Lunsingh-Scheurleer, T.H., 'Pierre Gole, ébéniste du roi Louis XIV' in *Burlington Magazine* vol.122, no.927 (June 1980), pp.378–94
Lunsingh-Scheurleer, T.H., 'The Philippe d'Orléans ivory cabinet by Pierre Gole' in *Burlington Magazine* vol.126, no.975 (June 1984), pp.333–9
Lunsingh-Scheurleer, T.H., 'A la recherche du mobilier de Louis XIV' in *Antologia di Belle Arti* 27–28 (1987), pp.38–49
Lunsingh-Scheurleer, T.H., *Pierre Gole, ébéniste de Louis XIV* (Dijon, 2005)
Lutteman, Helena, 'Rubens i elfenben' in Cavalli-Bjorkman, Gorel (ed.), *Rubens i Sverige* (Stockholm, 1977), pp.131–40
Mabille, Gérard, 'Les surtouts de table dans l'art français du 18ième siècle' in *L'Estampille* 126 (1980), pp.62–73
McGowan, Margaret M., 'The Renaissance Triumph and its Classical Heritage' in Mulryne and Goldring (2002), pp.26–47
McIntosh, Mark, *Discernment and Truth: Meditations on Christian Contemplation and Practice* (New York, 2004)
Maclagan, Eric, 'A Bust of Charles II by Honoré Pelle' in *Architectural Review* (August 1913), pp.33–4
Maclagan, Eric, and Margaret Longhurst, *Catalogue of Italian Sculpture* (V&A, London, 1932)
MacLeod, Catharine, and Marciari Alexander, Julia (eds), *Painted Ladies: Women at the Court of Charles II* (New Haven, CT, and London, 2001)
Macquoid, Percy, and Ralph Edwards, *The Dictionary of English Furniture*, 3 vols (London, 1924)
Madeira Rodrigues, Maria João, *The Chapel of Saint John the Baptist and its Collections in São Roque Church, Lisbon* (Lisbon, 1988)
Madeira Rodrigues, Maria João, *Museu de São Roque. Tecidos* (Santa Casa da Misericórdia de Lisboa, exhib. cat., 1988)
Madeira Rodrigues, Maria João, *La chapelle de Saint Jean-Baptiste et ses collections en l'Eglise Saint Roch, à Lisbonne* (Inapa, 1989)
Majer, Michele, 'Recent Acquisitions: A Selection 1990–1991' in *Metropolitan Museum of Art Bulletin* New Series, vol.49, no.2 (Autumn 1991), p.54
Mancini, Giulio, *Considerazioni sulla pittura* (1621, ed. Marucchi, 1956)
Mandroux-França, Marie-Thérèse, 'Information artistique et "mass-media" au XVIIIe siècle: la diffusion de l'ornement gravé rococo au Portugal, *Bracara Augusta*, XXVII, no.64, 1973
Mandroux-França, Marie-Thérèse, 'La patriarchale du roi Jean V de Portugal' in *Colóquio Artes* no.83 (December 1989), pp.34–43
Marder, Tod A., *Bernini and the Art of Architecture* (New York, 1998)
Mariage, Thierry, *The World of André Le Nôtre* (Philadelphia, 1999)
Marie, Alfred, *Naissance de Versailles* (Paris, 1968)
Marsh, Robert R., 'Id Quod Volo: the Erotic Grace of the Second Week', *The Way, Journal of Christian Spirituality* 45, no.4 (October 2006)
Martí y Monso, J., *Estudios Históricos-Artísticos relativos principalmente á Valladolid* (Valladolid and Madrid, 1898–1901)
Martin, Gregory, *The Flemish School, circa 1600–circa 1900* (London, 1970)
Martin, Michel, *Les monuments équestres de Louis XIV: une grande entreprise de propagande monarchique* (Paris, 1986)
Martinelli, Valentino, *Bernini. Disegni* (Florence, 1981)
Martinelli, Valentino, 'Il disegno della Cattedra berniniana di Giacinto Gimignani e Lazzaro Morelli per l'incisione dello Spierre del 1666' in *Prospettiva* nos 33–6 (April 1983–January 1984), pp.219–25
Martinez de la Torre, Cruz and Paz Cabello Carro, *Museo de América* (Brussels, 1997)
Marx, Harald, 'Johann Samuel Mock und das "Campement bei Czerniaków" 1732' in *Jahrbuch der Staatlichen Kunstsammlungen Dresden* no.10 (1976/1977), pp.53–87
Maskell, A., *Ivories* (London, 1905)
Massinelli, Anna Maria, *Hardstones: The Gilbert Collection* (London, 2000)
Mather, Christine, *Baroque to Folk: an exploration of the links between the fine arts of the baroque and the emerging folk arts of the colonies of the Iberian Peninsula/De lo barroco a lo popular: una exploración de la relación entre el arte barroco y la aparición de las artes populares en las colonias de la península ibérica* (Santa Fe, 1980)
Mérot, Alain, *Retraites mondaines – Aspects de la décoration intérieure á Paris, au XVIIe siècle* (Paris, 1990)
Merz, Jörg Martin, 'Stuttgart Architectural Drawings: Exhibition Review' in *Burlington Magazine* vol.135, no.1089 (December 1993), pp.843–4
Merz, Jorg Martin, 'Das Fortuna-Heiligtum in Palestrina als Barberini-Villa', *Zeitschrift für Kunstgeschichte* (1993), vol.56, pt.3
Metropolitan Museum of Art, New York, *Mexico: Splendors of Thirty Centuries* (New York, 1990)
Meyer, Daniel, *L'histoire du Roy* (Paris, 1980)
Meyer, Daniel, *Gli arazzi del Re Sole/Les tapisseries de l'Histoire du Roi/The Tapestries of the Sun King* (Palazzo Vecchio, Florence, exhib. cat., 1982)
Mignot, Claude, 'Urban Transformations' in Millon (1999), pp.315–31
Millon, Henry A., 'Bernini-Guarini: Paris-Turin: Louvre-Carignano' in *'Il se rendit en Italie': Studi in onore di André Chastel* (Rome, 1987), pp.479–94
Millon, Henry A., *The Triumph of the Baroque. Architecture in Europe 1600–1750* (National Gallery of Art, Washington, exhib. cat., 1999)
Milovanovic, Nicolas, *Louis XIV, le Roi-Soleil: Trésors du château de Versailles* (Shanghai Museum, exhib. cat., 2005)
Mitchell, David, 'The Influence of Tartary and the Indies on Social Attitudes and Material Culture in England and France, 1650–1703', in *A Taste for the Exotic: Foreign Influences on Early Eighteenth Century Silk Design, Riggisberger Berichte* 14 (2007)
Mojser, Miklos, *Baroque Art in Central Europe – Crossroads* (Budapest, 1993)
Möller, Lise Lotte, 'Georg Hintz' Kunstschrank-Bilder und der Meister der großen Elfenbeinpokale' in *Jahrbuch der Hamburger Kunstsammlungen* no.8 (1963), pp.57–66
Mollet, André, *Le Jardin de Plaisir* (Paris, 1981)
Montagu, Jennifer, *Alessandro Algardi*, 2 vols (New Haven, CT, 1985)
Montagu, Jennifer, *Roman Baroque Sculpture. The Industry of Art* (New Haven, CT, 1989)
Montagu, Jennifer, *The Expression of the Passions. The origin and influence of Charles Le Brun's Conférence sur l'expression générale et particulière* (New Haven, CT, and London, 1994)
Montagu, Jennifer, *Gold, Silver and Bronze: Metal Sculpture of the Roman Baroque* (New Haven, CT, 1996)
Montagu, Jennifer, 'Gagliardi versus Sampaijo, the case for the defence' in *Antologia di belle arti. Studi romani* nos 67–70 (2004), pp.75–92
Moore, Simon, *Cutlery for the Table: a History of British Table and Pocket Cutlery* (Sheffield, 1999)
Morales, Alfredo J. (ed.), *Filipinas, puerta de Oriente: De Legazpi a Malaspina* (Museo San Telmo, San Sebastián, and Museo Nacional del Pueblo Filipino, Manila, exhib. cat., 2003)
Morgan, David, *Visual Piety: A History and Theory of Popular Religious Images* (Berkeley, Los Angeles and London, 1998)
Morgan, Luke, 'The Early Modern *Trompe-L'Oeil* Garden' in *Garden History* 33, no.2 (Autumn 2005), pp.286–93
Morgan, Luke, *Nature as Model: Salomon de Caus and Early Seventeenth-century Landscape Design* (Philadelphia, 2006)
Mormando, Franco (ed.), *Saints and Sinners.*

Caravaggio and the Baroque Image (Boston College, Mass., exhib. cat., 1999)
Mosco, Marilena, and Ornella Casazza, *The Museo degli Argenti: Collections and Collectors* (Florence, 2004)
Moser, Dietz R., *Maskeraden auf Schlitten* (Munich, 1988)
Mosser, Monique, and Georges Teyssot, *The Architecture of Western Gardens* (Cambridge, MA, 1990)
Mukerji, Chandra, *Territorial Ambitions and the Gardens of Versailles* (Cambridge, 1997)
Muller, Frans, and Julie Muller, 'Completing the picture: the importance of reconstructing early opera', *Early Music* XXXIII, 4 (2005), pp.667–81
Mulryne, J.R., and Elizabeth Goldring (eds), *Court Festivals of the European Renaissance: Art, Politics and Performance* (Aldershot, 2002)
Mulryne, J.R., Helen Watanabe-O'Kelly and Margaret Shewring, *Europa Triumphans: Court and Civic Festivals in Early Modern Europe* (Aldershot, 2004)
Mumford, Lewis, *The City in History: Its Origins, Its Transformations, and Its Prospects* (San Diego, New York and London, 1989)
Murdoch, Tessa, *Huguenot Artists, Designers and Craftsmen in Great Britain and Ireland, 1680–1760* (unpublished PhD thesis, Westfield College, University of London, 1982)
Murdoch, Tessa (ed.), *Boughton House: The English Versailles* (London, 1992)
Murdoch, Tessa, 'Ducal splendour: silver for a military hero. The Elie Pacot ewer and basin made for John Churchill, 1st Duke of Marlborough' in *Silver Studies: The Journal of the Silver Society* no.22 (2007), pp.5ff
Murdoch, Tessa, 'Les Cabinets de porcelaines' in Pignon, Corinne (ed.), *Pagodes et dragons, Exotisme et fantaisie dans l'Europe rococo 1720–1770* (Paris, 2007), pp.42–50
Murdoch, Tessa (ed.), *Beyond the Border: Huguenot Goldsmiths in Northern Europe and North America* (Brighton, 2008)
Murray, Peter, *Catalogue of the Lee Collection* (London, 1967)
Murrell, V.J., 'Some aspects of the conservation of wax models' in *Studies in Conservation* no.16 (1971), pp.95–109
Musée des arts décoratifs, Paris, *Louis XIV: faste et décors* (exhib. cat., 1960)
Musée Carnavalet, Paris, *Saint-Paul – Saint-Louis: les Jésuites à Paris* (Paris, 1985)
Musée national du château de Versailles, *Charles Le Brun 1619–1690: le décor de l'escalier des ambassadeurs à Versailles* (Paris, 1990)
Musée national des châteaux de Versailles et de Trianon, *Versailles et les tables royales en Europe: XVIIème–XIXème siècles* (exhib. cat., 1993)
Museo de América, Madrid, *Arte colonial en el Museo de América* (Madrid, 1983)
Museo de América, Madrid, *Los Siglos de oro en los virreinatos de América 1550–1700* (exhib. cat., 1999)
Museo Nacional de Escultura, Valladolid, *Pasos Restaurados* (Valladolid, 2000)
Museu Nacional de Arte Antiga, Lisbon, *O Trajo Civil em Portugal* (exhib. cat., 1974)
Museu de São Roque, Lisbon, *Esplendor e devoção: os relicários de S. Roque* (Lisbon, 1997)
Museu de São Roque, Lisbon, *Ourivesaria e Iluminura, Século XIV ao Século XX* (Lisbon, 1998)
Museum of Ornamental Art, London, *Catalogue of the Museum of Ornamental Art* (London, 1853)
Nadal, Jerónimo, *Evangelicae Historiae Imagines*, 1593
Nationalmuseum, Stockholm, *Meddelanden från Nationalmuseum Nr 39: Statens Konstsamlingars tillväxt och förvaltning 1914* (Stockholm, 1915)
Nationalmuseum, Stockholm, *Christina, drottning av Sverige: en europeisk kulturpersonlighet* (exhib. cat., 1966)
Nationalmuseum, Stockholm, *Kung Sol I Sverige* (exhib. cat., 1986)
Nationalmuseum, Stockholm, *Silver: makt och prakt i barockens Sverige* (exhib. cat., 2003)
Neff, A., 'The Pain of Compassio: Mary's Labor at the Foot of the Cross', *The Art Bulletin* LXXX, no.2 (June 1998)
Nelson, Marion (ed.), *Norwegian Folk Art: the Migration of a Tradition* (New York, London, Paris, 1995)
Nickel, Helmut, 'Über einige Inventionsstücke zum Großen Aufzuge des Caroussell-Rennens der Vier Weltteile zu Dresden im Jahre 1709' in *Waffen- und Kostümkunde* vol.2, no.25 (1983), pp.81–94
Nolhac, Pierre de, 'L'escalier des Ambassadeurs', in *Revue de l'art ancien et moderne* (1900), pp.55–68
Norberg-Schulz, Christian Norberg, *Baroque Architecture* (London, 1986)
Ogden, Dunbar H., *The Italian Baroque Stage: Documents* (Berkeley, CA, 1978)
Olin, Martin, *Det Karolinska porträttet: ideologi, ikonografi, identitet* (Stockholm, 2000)
Olin, Martin and Linda Henriksson (eds), *Architectural Drawings. I, Ecclesiastical and Garden Architecture: Nicodemus Tessin the Younger* (Stockholm, 2004)
O'Malley, J.W., G.A. Bailey, et al., *The Jesuits: Cultures, Sciences, and The Arts 1540–1773* (Toronto, 1999)
O'Malley, J.W., and G.A. Bailey (eds), *The Jesuits and The Arts 1540–1773* (Philadelphia, 2005)
Oman, Charles, *The Golden Age of Dutch Silver* (London, 1953)
Oman, Charles, *Caroline Silver 1625–1688* (London, 1970)
Onfray, Michel, 'Ein Schauspiel narzisstischer Spiegelungen/The mirrors of Narcissus at the theatre' in *Parkett* no.50–51 (1997), pp.6–22
Onians, John, *Neuroarthistory: from Aristotle and Pliny to Baxandall and Zeki* (New Haven, CT, and London, 2008)
Ottomeyer, Hans, and Peter Pröschel, *Vergoldete Bronzen: die Bronzearbeiten des Spätbarock und Klassizismus* (Munich, 1986)
Ottomeyer, Hans, and Michaela Völkel, *Die öffentliche Tafel: Tafelzeremoniell in Europa 1300–1900* (Kronprinzenpalais, Berlin, exhib. cat., 2002)
Oughton, *Grinling Gibbons & the English woodcarving tradition* (London, 1979)
Palácio Nacional da Ajuda, Lisbon, *A Linguagem dos Nossos Ourives* (exhib. cat., 1988)
Palácio de Queluz, Queluz, *William Beckford & Portugal: a viagem de uma paixão 1787, 1794, 1798* (exhib. cat., 1987)
Palais des Beaux Arts, Brussels, *Treasures from Country Houses of the National Trust and the National Trust for Scotland* (exhib. cat., 1973)
Palazzo Reale, Naples, *Mostra Vanvitelliana. Catalogo dei documenti e dei modelli* (exhib. cat., 1973)
Palazzo Ruspoli, Rome, *Cristina di Svezia. Le collezioni reali* (exhib. cat., 2003), p.197, no.76
Palmer, Rodney, ' "All is very plain, upon inspection of the figure": the visual method of Andrea Pozzo's *Perspectiva Pictorum et Architectorum*' in Palmer and Frangenberg (2003), pp.156–213
Palmer, Rodney, and Thomas Frangenberg (eds), *The Rise of the Image: Essays on the History of the Illustrated Book* (Aldershot and Burlington, VT, 2003)
Panofsky, Erwin, 'The Ideological Antecedents of the Rolls-Royce Radiator' in Lavin, Irving (ed.), *Three Essays on Style* (London, 1995), pp.129–66
Panzanelli, Roberta (ed.), *Ephemeral Bodies. Wax Sculpture and the Human Figure* (Los Angeles, 2008)
Papworth, John Woody, 'On Artistic Ecclesiastic Decoration, as exhibited in a Collection of Designs made about the middle of the last century' in *Weale's Quarterly Papers on Architecture* vol.1 (1843–1844), pp.1–32, plates 67–73
Parry, Graham, 'Experimenting with the Baroque at the court of Charles I', in Eriksen (1996), pp.173–84
Parry, J.H., *The Spanish Seaborne Empire* (Berkeley, CA, 1990, 2nd edn)
Paulsen, Åshild, *Magnus Berg, 1666–1739: en kunstner ved kongens hoff* (Oslo, 1989)
Pearson, Fiona (ed.), *Virtue and Vision. Sculpture and Scotland 1540–1990* (Edinburgh, 1991)
Pearson, M.N., *The World of the Indian Ocean, 1500–1800* (London, 2005)
Penzer, N.M., 'The Plate at Knole' in *Connoisseur* vol.139 (April 1961), pp.84–91, 178–84
Pereira, José, 'The Plan of the Hindu Temple and its Impact on the Baroque Church', in Chandra (1970)
Pereira, José, 'The Art Historiography of Baroque India', *Indica* (Bombay) XXIII, 1986
Pereira, José, 'Baroque India', *The Neo-Roman Religious Architecture of South Asia: a Global Stylistic Survey* (New Delhi, 2000)
Perlove, Shelley Karen, *Bernini and the Idealization of Death: The Blessed Ludovica Albertoni and the Altieri Chapel* (Philadelphia, 1990)
Perreau, Stéphan, *Hyacinthe Rigaud 1659–1743, le peintre des rois* (Montpellier, 2004)
Physick, John, 'Tracing the work of William Stanton' in *Country Life Annual* (1968), p.88
Physick, John, *Designs for English Sculpture 1680–1860* (London, 1969)
Piacenti, C. (ed.), *La ceroplastica nella scienza e nell'arte. Atti del I Congresso Internazionale 1975* (Florence, 1977)
Pierce, Donna, et al., *Painting a New World: Mexican Art and Life 1521–1821* (Denver Art Museum, exhib. cat., 2004)
Pijzel-Dommisse, Jet, *Haags goud en zilver: edelsmeedkunst uit de Hofstad* (Gemeentemuseum, The Hague, exhib. cat., 2005)
Pimentel, António Filipe, 'Modelo da Capela de São João Baptista' in *Catálogo Museu de São Roque* (Lisbon, 2008)
Podro, Michael, *The Critical Historians of Art* (New Haven, CT, and London, 1982)
Polovedo, Elena, 'Spazio scenico, prospettiva e azione drammatica nel teatro barocco italiano' in Schnapper (1982)
Pope-Hennessy, John, *Catalogue of the Italian Sculpture in the Victoria and Albert Museum*, 3 vols (London, 1964)
Portoghesi, Paolo, 'The Birth of the Baroque in Rome' in Millon (1999)
Posner, Donald, 'The genesis and political purposes of Rigaud's portraits of Louis XIV and Philip V' in *Gazette des Beaux Arts* vol.131, no.1549 (February 1998), pp.77–90
Potter, Jennifer, *Strange Blooms* (London, 2006)
Pradère, Alexandre, *French Furniture Makers: the Art of the Ebéniste from Louis XIV to the Revolution* (London, 1989)
Préaud, Maxime, *Inventaire du fonds français: graveurs du XVIIe siècle. Tome 12, Jean Lepautre* (Paris, 1999)
Prochazka, Ethel, 'Wer war Ignatius Bidermann? Zu einem Gemäldezyklus im Bayerischen Nationalmuseum' in *Weltkunst* vol.46, no.20a (October 1976, special issue), pp.2002–3
Ptáàkovà, Vefia, et al. (eds), *The Baroque Theatre in the Chateau of Český Krumlov* (Prague, 1993)
Puhl, Louis J., *The Spiritual Exercises of St Ignatius* (Chicago, 1951)
Puype, J.P., and R. Roth, *The Visser collection: Arms of the Netherlands in the Collection of H.L. Visser* (Zwolle, 1996)
Pyke, E.J., *A Biographical Dictionary of Wax Modellers* (Oxford, 1973)
Raggio, Olga, 'Bernini and the Collection of Cardinal Flavio Chigi' in *Apollo* vol.117, no.255 (May 1983), pp.368–79
Rangström, Lena, *Riddarlek Och Tornerspel: Tournaments and the Dream of Chivalry* (Stockholm, 1992)
Rangström, Lena, 'Karl XI's karusell 1672: en manifestation med europeiska rotter och influenser, transformerad till stormaktstidens Sverige/Charles XI's carousel in 1672: a manifestation with European origins and influences, transformed to the period of Sweden as a great power' in *Livrustkammaren* (1994), special issue, pp.105–14
Rangström, Lena, *Modelejon Manligt Mode 1500–1800* (Livrustkammaren, Stockholm, exhib. cat., 2002)
Rangström, Lena, 'Certamen Equestre: the Carousel for the Accession of Karl XI in 1672' in Mulryne, Watanabe-O'Kelly and Shewring (2004), II, pp.292–7
Rawski, Evelyn S., and Jessica Rawson (eds), *China: the Three Emperors 1662–1795* (Royal Academy, London, exhib. cat., 2005)
Reichel, Friedrich, 'Die Türkenmode und Ihr Einfluß auf die sächsische Kunst. Eine kulturgeschichtliche Skizze' in *Beiträge und Berichte der Staatlichen Kunstsammlungen Dresden 1972–1975* (1978), p.151
Reichel, Friedrich, 'Betrachtungen zu einem Königs-Bildnis' in *Dresdener Kunstblatter* vol.38, no.2 (1994), pp.43–6
Reus, Klaus-Dieter, and Lerner, Markus, *Faszination der Bühne: Barockes Welttheater in Bayreuth, Barocke Bühnentechnik in Europa* (Bayreuth, 2001)
Revel, Jean-François, 'L'escalier des Ambassadeurs', in *Connaissance des Arts*, 74 (1958), pp.71–7
Ribeiro, Aileen, *Dress in Eighteenth-century Europe 1715–1789* (London, 1984)
Ribeiro, Aileen, *Dress and Morality* (London, 2003)
Ribeiro de Oliveira, Myriam Andrade, Olinto Rodrigues dos Santos Filho and Antônio Fernando Batista dos Santos, *O Aleijadinho e sua oficina: catálogo das imagens devocionais* (São Paulo, 2002)
Riccardi-Cubitt, Monique, *The Art of the Cabinet: including a Chronological Guide to Styles* (London, 1992)
Richardson, Jonathan, *The Science of a Connoisseur* (London, 1719)
Rijksmuseum, Amsterdam, *Muskets and Pistols* (exhib cat., 1974)
Rishel, Joseph J., with Suzanne Stratton-Pruitt, *The Arts in Latin America, 1492–1820* (Philadelphia Museum of Art, exhib. cat., 2006)
Roberts, Jane (ed.), *Royal Treasures. A Golden Jubilee Celebration* (London, 2002)
Rohde, Alfred, *Bernstein, ein Deutscher Werkstoff* (Berlin, 1937)

Roli, Renato, *Pittura Bolognese 1650–1800 dal Cicagni al Gandoli*, Fonti e Studi per la Storia di Bologna e delle Province Emiliani e Romagnole (Bologna, 1977)

Ronfort, Jean-Nerée, and Jean-Dominique Augarde, 'Le maître du bureau de l'Electeur' in *L'Estampille l'objet d'art* no.243 (January 1991), pp.42–75

Rose, Giles, *A Perfect School of Instructions for The Officers of the Mouth* (London, 1682)

Rosen, Susan F., *The twilight of the Medici. Late Baroque art in Florence, 1670–1743* (Detroit Institute of Arts and Palazzo Pitti, Florence, exhib. cat., 1974)

Rosenberg, Jakob, Seymour Slive and E.H. ter Kuile, *Dutch Art and Architecture, 1600 to 1800* (London, 1991)

Rosenborg Castle, *Guide* (Copenhagen, 2005)

Rosenborg Castle, *Kongernes Rosenborg* (Copenhagen, 2006)

Rubin, Miri, *Corpus Christi: The Eucharist in Late Medieval Culture* (Cambridge, 1991)

Rutherford, Jessica, *Country House Lighting 1660–1890* (City Art Gallery, Leeds, exhib. cat., 1992)

Ryser, Frieder, and Brigitte Salmen, 'Amalierte Stuck uff Glas/Hinder Glas gemalte Historien und Gemäld', *Hingerglaskunst von der Antike bis zur Neuzeit* (Murnau, 1995)

Sabatier, Gérard, *Versailles ou la figure du roi* (Paris, 1999)

Salatino, Kevin, *Incendiary Art: the Representation of Fireworks in Early Modern Europe, Bibliographies and Dossiers*, The Collections of the Getty Research Institute for the History of Art and the Humanities, 3 (Los Angeles, 1997)

Salmon, Xavier, *Imagens do Soberano*, (São Paulo, 2007)

San Juan, Rose Marie, *Rome: A City Out of Print* (Minneapolis, 2001)

Sandford, Francis, *The History of the Coronation of James II* (London, 1687)

Sandner, Ingo, et al., *Spätgotische Tafelmalerei in Sachsen* (Dresden, 1993)

Saule, Béatrix, *Versailles Triomphant: une journée de Louis XIV* (Paris, 1996)

Saule, Béatrix, and Catherine Arminjon, *Quand Versailles était meublé d'argent* (Château de Versailles, exhib. cat., 2007)

Savage, Roger, 'A dynastic marriage celebrated' in *Early Music* vol.26, no.4 (November 1998), cover, pp. 632–5

Sawday, Jonathan, *The Body Emblazoned. Dissection and the Human Body in Renaissance Culture* (London and New York, 1995)

Scalabroni, Luisa, *Giuseppe Vasi 1710–82* (Rome, 1981)

Scarisbrick, Diana, *Jewellery in Britain 1066–1837* (Norwich, 1994)

Schaal, Dieter, 'The Dresden Carousel of 1709' in Rangström (1992), pp.416–17

Schädler, Alfred, *Georg Petel (1601/02–1634): Barockbildhauer zu Augsburg* (Munich and Zurich, 1985)

Schmid, Emanuel, and Ulrike Staudinger, '"Die Kurfürstin ließ Katzen und Mäuse braten..." Tafelfreuden am Münchner Hof: Die Anständige Lust' in Zischka, Ottomeyer and Bäumler (eds), *Eßkultur und Tafelsitten* (Münchner Stadtmuseum, Munich, exhib. cat., 1993), pp.82–84, ill.3

Schmidt, Werner, and Dirk Syndram, *Unter einer Krone: Kunst und Kultur der sächsisch-polnischen Union* (Staatliche Kunstammlung, Dresden, and Royal Castle, Warsaw, exhib. cat., 1997)

Schnapper, Antoine (ed.), *La Scenografia Barocca* (Bologna, 1982)

Schnitzer, Claudia, *Höfische Maskeraden. Funktion und Ausstattung von Verkleidungsdivertissements an deutschen Höfen der Frühen Neuzeit* (Tübingen, 1999)

Schnitzer, Claudia, and Petra Hölscher, *Eine gute Figur machen: Kostüm und Fest am Dresdner Hof* (Kupferstich-Kabinett, Dresden, exhib. cat., 2000)

Scholten, Frits (ed.), *Goudleer Kinkarakawa: de geschiedenis van het Nederlands goudleer en zijn invloed in Japan/redactie* (Groningen, 1989)

Scholten, Frits, 'Rubens' werkplaats-academie of "de ghemeynschap die onse Consten van Schildry ende Belthouwery t'samen hebben"' in *Nederlands kunsthistorisch jaarboek* vol.55 (2004), pp.34–53

Schroder, Timothy, *The National Trust Book of English Domestic Silver, 1500–1900* (New York, 1988)

Sciberras, Keith, 'Ciro Ferri's Reliquary for the Oratory of S. Giovanni Decollato in Malta' in *Burlington Magazine* vol.141, no.1156 (July 1999), pp.392–400

Sciberras, Keith, *Roman Baroque Sculpture for the Knights of Malta* (Malta, 2004)

Scott, John Beldon, *Images of Nepotism. The Painted Ceilings of Palazzo Barberini* (Princeton, NJ, 1991)

Seelig, Lorenz, 'Zwei Augsburger Humpen mit der Darstellung des Trunkenen Silen nach Peter Paul Rubens' in Eikelmann, Schommers and Seelig (eds), *Studien zur europaischen Goldschmiedekunst des 14. bis 20. Jahrhundert: Festschrift fur Helmut Seling zum 80. Geburtstag am 12. Februar 2001* (Munich, 2001), pp.51–74

Segal, Sam, *Jan Davidsz de Heem und sein Kreis* (Utrecht and Braunschweig, exhib. cat., 1991)

Segal, Sam, *Flowers and Nature: Netherlandish Flower Painting of Four Centuries* (The Hague, 1990)

Seling, Helmut, *Die Kunst der Augsburger Goldschmiede, 1529–1868: Meister, Marken, Werke* (Munich, 1980)

Seydl, Jon L., *Giambattista Tiepolo: Fifteen Oil Sketches* (Los Angeles, 2005)

Sframeli, Maria, 'The gems of Anna Maria Luisa de' Medici, Electress Palatine' in Luchinat, Cristina Acidini (ed.), *Treasures of Florence: the Medici Collection 1400–1700* (New York, 1997), pp.199–220

Shirley, Pippa, 'A service for wine' in *Magazine Antiques* vol.153, no.6 (June 1998), pp.876–81

Shirley, Pippa, 'The Macclesfield wine set' in *Silver Society Journal* no.10 (Autumn 1998), pp.112–14

Siebel, Sabine, *The Glory of Baroque Dresden: the State Art Collections Dresden* (Mississippi Arts Pavilion, Jackson, exhib. cat., 2004)

Sirén, Osvald, *Nicodemus Tessin d.y's studieresor i Danmark, Tyskland, Holland, Frankrike och Italien* (Stockholm, 1914)

Sitt, Martina, and Hubertus Gaßner (eds), *Spiegel geheimer Wünsche. Stillleben aus fünf Jahrhunderten* (Hamburg, 2008)

Sjöblom, Axel, *David Klöcker Ehrenstrahl* (Malmö, 1947)

Slaviček, Lubomír, *Flemish Paintings of the 17th and 18th Centuries* (Prague, 2000)

Slavko, Pavel, *The Castle Theatre in Český Krumlov* (Český Krumlov, 2001)

Slavko, Pavel, The Castle Theatre in the State Castle in (Český Krumlov in *The World of Baroque Theatre: A compilation of Essays from the Český Krumlov Conferences 2002, 2003* (Český Krumlov, 2004)

Slive, Seymour, *Dutch Painting, 1600–1800* (New Haven and London, 1995)

Smith, Robert, *Os Mausoleus de D. Joao V nas quatro partes do mundo* (Lisbon, 1955)

Smollett, Tobias (ed. Felsenstein, F.), *Travels through France and Italy*, letter XXVII (Oxford, 1981)

Smuts, Malcolm, 'Public Ceremony and Royal Charisma: the English Royal Entry in London, 1485–1621', in Beier (1989), pp.65–93

Snickare, Mårtin (ed.), *Tessin: Nicodemus the Younger: Royal Architect and Visionary* (Stockholm, 2002)

Snodin, Michael, *Rococo: Art and Design in Hogarth's England* (V&A, London, exhib. cat., 1984)

Snodin, Michael, and John Styles, *Design and the Decorative Arts: Britain 1500–1900* (London, 2001)

Snodin, Michael, *The V&A Book of Western Ornament* (London, 2006)

Sohlberg, Lars Gustaf, *Historisk Beskrifning öfver Domkyrkan i Westerås* (Västerås, 1834)

Sonnemann, Rolf, and Eberhard Wächtler (eds), *Johann Friedrich Böttger: Die Erfindung des Europäischen Porzellans* (Leipzig, 1982)

Soo, L.M., *Wren's 'Tracts' on Architecture and other Writings* (Cambridge, 1998)

Sørensen, Bent, 'Pannini and Ghezzi: the portraits in the Louvre: Musical performance at the Teatro Argentina' in *Burlington Magazine* vol.144, no.1193 (August 2002), pp.467–74

Sotheby's, London: Sale of Important Italian and Continental Furniture, 4 December 2007

Souchal, François, *French Sculptors of the 17th and 18th Centuries: the Reign of Louis XIV: illustrated catalogue*, 4 vols (Oxford, 1977–93)

Sousa, Maria da Conceição Borges de, *Presença portuguesa na Asia* (Lisbon, 2008)

South Kensington Museum, *Inventory of the Objects in the Art Division of the Museum at South Kensington Vol. I, For the Years 1852 to the end of 1867* (London, 1868)

South Kensington Museum, *The South Kensington Museum – Etchings and Works of Art in the Museum* (London, 1881)

Souza, G.B., *The Survival of Empire: Portuguese Trade and Society in China and the South Seas, 1630–1754* (Cambridge, 1986)

Stavenow-Hidemark, Elisabet, 'The Isabella Chamber at Salsta: a Swedish state bedroom in the French taste' in *Furniture History* vol.21 (1985), pp.193–202

Stein, Fabian, *Charles Le Brun: La tenture de l'Histoire du Roy* (Worms, 1985)

Stewart, J. Douglas, 'Pin-ups or Virtues? The Concept of the "Beauties" in Late Stuart Portraiture', in *English Portraits of the Seventeenth and Eighteenth Centuries* (Los Angeles, 1974)

Stoichita, Victor I., *The Self-aware Image: an Insight into Early Modern Meta-painting* (Cambridge and New York, 1997)

Stoye, John, *The Siege of Vienna* (2nd edn, London, 2006)

Straub, Eberhard, *Repraesentatio Maiestatis oder churbayerische Freudenfeste. Die höfischen Feste in der Münchner Residenz vom 16. bis zum Ende des 18. Jahrhunderts* (Munich, 1969)

Strömbom, Sixten, *Svenska kungliga porträtt i Svenska porträttarkivets samlingar. Del I. Gustav I – Karl XII* (Stockholm, 1943)

Strong, Roy, *Art and Power: Renaissance Festivals 1450–1650* (Woodbridge, 1984)

Strong, Roy, *Feast: A History of Grand Eating* (London, 2002)

Strong, Roy, *Coronation: A History of Kingship and the British Monarchy* (London, 2005)

Strunck, Christina, *Berninis unbekanntes Meisterwerk, Die Galleria Colonna in Rom und die Kunstpatronage des römischen Uradels* (Munich, 2007)

Strunck, Christina (ed.), *Rom: Meisterwerke der Baukunst von der Antike bis heute. Festgabe für Elisabeth Kieven* (St Petersburg, 2007)

Strunk, Oliver, *Source Readings in Music History* (New York, 1981)

Summerson, John, *The Classical Language of Architecture* (London, 1980)

Sutton, D. (ed.), *Souvenirs of the Grand Tour* (Wildenstein & Co. Ltd Gallery, London, exhib. cat., 1982)

Syndram, Dirk, and Ulrike Weinhold, *...und ein Leib von Perl: die Sammlung der barocken Perlfiguren im Grünen Gewölbe* (Dresden, 2000)

Tait, Hugh, 'Huguenot silver made in London (c.1690–1723). The Peter Wilding Bequest to the British Museum, part 2' in *Connoisseur* vol.181 (September 1972), pp.25–36 and pls 9–10

Tait, Hugh (ed.), *Five Thousand Years of Glass* (London, 1991)

Tait, Hugh, *Catalogue of the Waddesdon Bequest in the British Museum, The Curiosities* (London, 1991)

Tarkiewicz, Wladyslaw, *History of Aesthetics* vol. III (The Hague, Paris, Warsaw, 1974)

Tassinari, Magda, *Colecção de tesxteis (Capela de S. João Baptista)*, *Catàlogo do Museu de S. Roque, Santa Casa da Misericórdia de Lisboa* (Lisbon, 2008)

Távora, Bernardo Ferrão de Tavares e, *Imaginària luso-oriental* (Lisbon, 1983)

Teixeira, José de Monterroso, *Triunfo do Barroco* (Fundação das Descobertas, Centro Cultural de Belém, Lisbon, exhib. cat., 1993)

Temple, William, *Miscellenea, the Second Part; in Four Essays, the Second Essay: upon the Gardens of Epicurus* (London, 1692)

ter Molen, J.R., *Van Vianen: een Utrechtse familie van Zilversmeden met een Internationale Faam*, 2 vols (Rotterdam, 1984)

Terwen-De Loos, J., *Het Nederlands-koloniale meubel: studie over meubels in de voormalige Nederlandse koloniën Indonesië en Sri Lanka* (Franeker, 1985)

Tesori reali di Danimarca, 1709: Federico IV a Firenze/Royal Treasures from Denmark, 1709: Frederik IV in Florence (Museo degli argenti, Palazzo Pitti, Florence, exhib. cat., 1994)

Thacker, Christopher, '"*La Manière de montrer les Jardins de Versailles*", by Louis XIV and others', *Garden History* vol.1, no.1(September 1972)

Theuerkauff, Christian, 'Gabriel Grupello: an exhibition at Düsseldorf' in *Apollo* vol.93, no.112 (June 1971), pp.460–69

Theuerkauff, Christian, *Elfenbein Sammlung Reiner Winkler* (Munich, 1984)

Thomson, David, *Renaissance architecture: Critics, Patrons, Luxury* (Manchester and New York, 1993)

Thornton, Peter, 'The Parisian *Fauteuil* of 1680' in *Apollo* vol.101, no.156 (February 1975), pp.102–7

Thornton, Peter, *Seventeenth-century Interior Decoration in England, France, and Holland* (New Haven, CT, 1978)

Thornton, Peter, and Maurice Tomlin, *The Furnishing and Decoration of Ham House* (London, 1980)

Thornton, Peter, *Authentic Décor, The Domestic Interior 1620–1920* (London, 1984)

Thornton, Peter, *Form & Decoration: Innovation in the Decorative Arts, 1470–1870* (London, 1998)

Thuillier, Jacques, and Jennifer Montagu, *Charles Le Brun 1619–1690: peintre et dessinateur* (Versailles, 1963)

Thurley, Simon, *Hampton Court: A Social and Architectural History* (New Haven, CT, 2003)

Tijou, Jean, *A New Booke of Drawings Invented*

& Desined by John Tijou ... (London, 1693)

Tipping, H. Avray, 'The English silver plate of the Duke of Cumberland' in *Country Life* vol.55, no.1413 (2 February 1924), pp.162–3

Tipton, Susan, 'Playing instruments from the past: Opernhäuser des Barock. Aus Anlass einer Bayreuther Ausstellung und Tagung', in *Kunstchronik* LIII (2000), pp.368–79

Tiricanti, Giulio, *Il Teatro Argentina* (Rome, 1971)

Toman, Rolf (ed.), *Baroque: Architecture, Sculpture, Painting* (Königswinter, 2004)

Torrione, Margarita, 'Decorados teatrales para el Coliseo del Buen Retiro en tiempos de Fernando VI: cuatro oleos de Francesco Battaglioli' in *Reales Sitios* vol.37, no.143 (2000), pp.40–51

Tozzi, Simonetta, *Incisioni barocche di feste e avvenimenti: giorni d'allegrezza* (Rome, 2002)

Treasures from Chatsworth: the Devonshire Inheritance (National Gallery of Art, Washington, exhib. cat., 1979)

Trusted, Marjorie, 'Moving Church Monuments: Processional Images in Spain in the Seventeenth Century', *Church Monuments X* (1995)

Trusted, Marjorie, *Spanish Sculpture: A Catalogue of the Post-medieval Spanish Sculpture in wood, terracotta, alabaster, marble, stone, lead and jet in the Victoria and Albert Museum* (London, 1996)

Trusted, Marjorie, *The Arts of Spain: Iberia and Latin America 1450–1700* (London, 2007)

Turner, Jane (ed.), *Grove Dictionary of Art*, 34 vols (London, 1996)

Tydén-Jordan, Astrid, *Kröningsvagnen: konstverk och riksklenod en studie i barockens karossbyggnadskonst* (Stockholm, 1985)

Ugolini, Cecilia (ed.), *Il Teatro per la Città: Teatro Comunale di Bologna* (Bologna, 1998)

Union latine: Petit Palais, Musée des beaux arts de la ville de Paris, *Brésil baroque: entre ciel et terre* (exhib. cat., 2000)

Urrea, Jesús, *Pintura italiana del siglo XVIII en España* (Valladolid, 1977)

Van Der Stock, J. (ed.), *Antwerp: Story of a Metropolis, 16th–17th Century* (Antwerp, 1993)

van der Wall, Fauke, *François Spierre. Ein lothringischer Maler und Stecher des 17. Jahrhunderts* (Würzburg, 1987)

Vasco Rocca, Sandra, et al., *Roma Lusitana – Lisbona Romana* (San Michele a Ripa, Rome, exhib. cat., 1990)

Vassallo e Silva, Nuno, 'Os relicários de S. Roque' in *Oceanos* no.12 (November 1992), p.117

Veenendaal, Jan, *Furniture from Indonesia, Sri Lanka and India during the Dutch Period* (Delft, 1985)

Verdi Webster, Susan, *Art and Ritual in Golden Age Spain* (Princeton, 1998)

Verdon, T., and J. Henderson (eds), *Christianity and the Renaissance. Image and Religious Imagination in the Quattrocento* (Syracuse, NY, 1990)

Verlet, Pierre, *French Royal Furniture: an historical survey followed by a study of forty pieces preserved in Great Britain and the United States* (London, 1963)

Verlet, Pierre, *Le mobilier royal français* (Paris, 1990–94)

Victoria and Albert Museum, London, *William & Mary and their Time* (exhib. cat., 1950)

Villa Hügel, Essen, *Barock in Dresden* (exhib. cat., 1986)

Viller, Marcel (ed.), *Dictionnaire de spiritualité ascétique et mystique: doctrine et histoire* (Paris, 1995)

Viterbo, Francisco Marques de Sousa, and R. Vicente d'Almeida, *A Capela de S. João Baptista Erecta na Egreja de S. Roque* (Lisbon,

1900; reprinted 1902, 1997)

Vlnas, Vit, *The Glory of the Baroque in Bohemia: Art, Culture and Society in the 17th and 18th Centuries* (National Gallery, Prague, exhib. cat., 2001)

Voltaire, *Dictionnaire philosophique* (1764)

von Corswant-Naumburg, Inga, *Huvudbaner och anvapen under stormaktstiden* (Uddevalla, 1999)

Von Kerssenbrock-Krosigk, Dedo, *Rubinglas des Ausgehenden 17. und des 18. Jahrhunderts* (Mainz, 2001)

Von Philippovich, E., *Elfenbein* (Munich, 2nd rev. edn 1982)

Von Saldern, Axel, 'Schlesische Hochschnittgläser aus der Werkstatt von Friedrich Winter' in Guntermann, Ingrid, and Brigitte Tietzel (eds), *Festschrift für Brigitte Klesse* (Berlin, 1994)

Von Watzdorf, Erna, *Johann Melchior Dinglinger. Der Goldschmied des deutschen Barock*, 2 vols (Berlin 1962)

Wackernagel, Rudolf H., *Der französische Krönungswagen von 1696–1825. Ein Beitrag zur Geschichte des repräsentativen Zeremonienwagens* (Berlin, 1966)

Wackernagel, Rudolf H., *Staats-und Galawagen der Wittelsbacher: Kutschen, Schlitten und Sänften aus dem Marstallmuseum Schloß Nymphenburg* (Stuttgart, 2002)

Waddy, Patricia, *Seventeenth-century Roman Palaces: Use and the Art of the Plan* (Cambridge, MA, and London, 1990)

Waddy, Patricia (ed.), *Nicodemus Tessin the Younger: Sources, Works, Collections; Traictè dela decoration interieure 1717* (Stockholm, 2002)

Walker, Stefanie, and Fredrick Hammond (eds), *Life and the Arts in the Baroque Palaces of Rome: Ambiente Barocco* (New York, 1999)

Walpole, Horace, *Anecdotes of Painting in England* (London, 1786)

Walton, Guy, *Louis XIV's Versailles* (Harmondsworth, 1986)

Watanabe-O'Kelly, Helen, *Triumphall Shews. Tournaments at German-speaking Courts in their European Context 1560–1730* (Berlin, 1992)

Watanabe-O'Kelly, Helen, and Pierre Béhar, *Spectaculum Europaeum: Theatre and Spectacle in Europe, 1580–1750* (Wiesbaden, 1999)

Watanabe-O'Kelly, Helen, and Anne Simon, *Festivals and Ceremonies: A Bibliography of Works Relating to Court, Civic and Religious Festivals in Europe, 1500–1800* (London and New York, 1999)

Watanabe-O'Kelly, Helen, 'Early Modern Festivals – Politics and Performance, Event and Record' in Mulryne and Goldring (2002)

Watanabe-O'Kelly, Helen, 'The Early Modern Festival Book: Function and Form' in Mulryne, Watanabe-O'Kelly and Shewring (2004), I, pp.1–17

Waterer, John W., *Spanish Leather, a History of its Use from 800 to 1800* (London, 1971)

Webb, G., 'Sculpture' in *Spanish Art* (London, 1927)

Webb, Michael, *The City Square* (London, 1990)

Weigert, Roger-Armand, 'Le meuble brodé de la salle du trône du Grand Roi à Versailles' in *Revue de l'art ancien et moderne* vol.62 (November 1932), pp.97–108

Weigert, Roger-Armand, 'Un meuble à retrouver: une pendule d'après Jean Berain' in *Revue de l'art ancien et moderne* vol.67 (1935), pp.43–8

Weigert, Roger-Armand, *Jean I Berain, dessinateur de la chambre et du cabinet du roi (1640–1711)* (Paris, 1937)

Weihrauch, Hans R., *Die Bildwerke in Bronze und in anderen Metallen: mit einem Anhang, Die Bronzebildwerke des Residenzmuseums* (Bayerisches Nationalmuseum, exhib. cat., 1956)

Weil, Mark S., 'The devotion of the forty hours and Roman baroque illusions', *Journal of the Warburg and Courtauld Institutes* 37 (1974)

Weiss, Allen S., *Mirrors of Infinity: The French Formal Garden and Seventeenth-Century Metaphysics* (New York, 1995)

West, S. (ed.), *Italian Culture and Northern Europe in the Eighteenth Century* (Cambridge, 1999)

Weston-Lewis, Aidan, *Effigies & Ecstasies: Roman Baroque Sculpture and Design in the Age of Bernini* (National Gallery of Scotland, Edinburgh, exhib. cat., 1998)

Wheeler, Daniel (ed.), *Princely Taste: Treasures from Great Private Collections* (Jerusalem, 1995)

Whinney, Margaret, *Grinling Gibbons in Cambridge* (Cambridge, 1948)

Whinney, Margaret (rev. Physick), *Sculpture in Britain 1530 to 1830* (London, 1988)

Whistler, Catherine, 'G.B. Tiepolo and Charles III: the Church of S. Pascual Baylon at Aranjuez' in *Apollo* vol.121, no.279 (May 1985), pp.321–7

Whistler, Catherine, 'Decoro e devozione nelle pale di Giambattista Tiepolo ad Aranjuez' in *Arte Veneta* vol.52 (1998), pp.70–85

Whistler, Catherine (ed.), *Opulence and Devotion: Brazilian Baroque Art* (Oxford, 2001)

Whitaker, Lucy, and Martin Clayton, *The Art of Italy in the Royal Collection: Renaissance & Baroque* (London, 2007)

Wilk, Christopher (ed.), *Western Furniture 1350 to the Present Day* (London, 1996)

Willes, Margaret, *And So to Bed* (London, 1998)

Williams, Sheila, 'The Pope-Burning Processions of 1679, 1680 and 1681' in *Journal of the Warburg and Courtauld Institutes* XXI, 1/2 (January–June 1958), pp.104–18

Williamson, Paul (ed.), *European Sculpture at the Victoria and Albert Museum* (London, 1996)

Wilson, Gillian, et al., *French Furniture and Gilt Bronzes. Baroque and Régence. Catalogue of the J. Paul Getty Museum Collection* (Los Angeles, 2008)

Wilson, Joan, 'A Phenomenon of Taste: The china ware of Queen Mary II' in *Apollo* vol.96, no.126 (August 1972), pp.116–23

Wind, E., 'The revolution in history painting', *Journal of the Warburg and Courtauld Institutes* II (1938–9)

Winterbottom, M., ' "Such massy pieces of plate": silver furnishings in the English royal palaces 1660–1702' in *Apollo* vol.156, no.486 (August 2002), pp.19–26

Wisch, Barbara, and Susan Scott Munshower (eds), *'All the world's a stage…': Art and Pageantry in the Renaissance and Baroque* (Pennsylvania, 1990)

Wittkower, Rudolf, *Bernini: The Sculptor of the Roman Baroque* (Milan, revised edn 1990)

Wittkower, Rudolf (rev. Connors, J., and J. Montagu), *Art and Architecture in Italy 1600–1750* (New Haven, CT, and London, 1999)

Wölfflin, Heinrich, *Renaissance und Barock* (Munich, 1888), trans. Murray, Peter (London, 1964)

Wood, Bruce, 'Purcell's Odes: a Reappraisal', in Burden (1995)

Woodbridge, Kenneth, *Princely Gardens: The Origins and Development of the French Formal Style* (New York, 1986)

Wren, Christopher (Jnr), *Parentalia* (London, 1750)

Wright, A.D., *The Counter-reformation. Catholic Europe and the Non-Christian World* (Aldershot, 2005)

Wynne, Michael, *Later Italian Paintings in the National Gallery of Ireland: the Seventeenth, Eighteenth, and Nineteenth Centuries* (Dublin, 1986)

Yans, Geneviève Barboni, 'Teatro a Mantova all'inizio del Seicento – le feste del 1608 descritte dal Follino – contributo alla ricostituzione pratica del teatro di corte', in Schnapper (1982)

Zandvliet, Kees (ed.), *The Dutch Encounter with Asia, 1600–1950* (Amsterdam, 2003)

Ziskin, Rochelle, 'The Places de Nos Conquêtes and the Unravelling of the Myth of Louis XIV', in *Art Bulletin* LXXVI, 1 (March 1994), pp.147–62

Zdenka, Flaskova, *The Castle Theatre at Český Krumlov* (Český Krumlov, 2001)

Zollikofer, Kaspar, *Berninis Grabmal fur Alexander VII: Fiktion und Repräsentation* (Worms, 1994)

Zucker, Paul, Space and Movement in High Baroque City Planning in *Journal of the Society of Architectural Historians* XIV, 1 (March 1995), pp.8–13

Manuscript Sources

'Manufacture des Gobelins: administration, états de fabrication, comptes, personnel, correspondance générale' (1659–1720), A.N. O1 2040 A–B

Spezifikation 1706

Specificatio derjenigen Praetiosen, Welche sieder im Monat Januar: 1706. in Hamburg gewesen, in Monath Octobt: 1714. aber wiederuhm in die Geh: Verwahrung, oder so genanntes Grüne Gewölbe geliefert worden (Dresden, SächsHStA, Loc. 896, fol. 37r–38v)

Pretioseninventar 1725–33 (Nachtrag)

Nachtrag zum Pretieussen Cabinet Stücken=Inventario

Pretioseninventar 1725

Inventarium derer Königl: Pretiosen welche sich in den Königl. Grünen Gewölbe befinden (besiegelt am 5. Januar 1725)

Inventar Pretiosenzimmer 1733

Inventarium über das Pretiosen-Zimmer in der geheimen Verwahrung des Grünen Gewölbes zu Dreßden. Anno 1733 (besiegelt am 31. Oktober 1733)

Inventar Kaminzimmer 1818

Inventarium über das Camin-Zimmer in der Geheimen Verwahrung des grünen Gewölbes zu Dresden 1818

Select Bibliography

The literature on the subjects covered in this book is enormous. This bibliography presents a selection of the more important and useful books, many of which contain further bibliographies. Its limited scope does not allow the coverage of individual artists, architects, designers and makers. For these a good general starting-point is Jane Turner (ed.), *The (Grove) Dictionary of Art* (published by Macmillan, London, in 1996) in 34 volumes, which is also available on-line (http://www.groveart.com).

1. Context and Background
Anderson (1998)
Blanning (2007)
Brown and Tackett (2006)
Hsia (2007)
Parry (1990)

2. General Works
Bazin (1968)
Careri and Ferranti (2002)
Harbison (2000)
Panofsky (1995)
Thornton (1998)
Toman (2004)

3. Places
Asia (and Asian styles in Europe)
Bailey (1999)
Berliner Festspiele (1985)
Cassidy-Geiger (2004)
Honour (1961)
Impey (1977)
Irwin and Brett (1970)
Jackson and Jaffer (2004)
Pereira (2000)
Veenendaal (1985)
Zandvliet (2003)

Central and Eastern Europe
Bourke (1963)
Brusatin and Pizzamiglio (1992)
Gaehtgens et al. (2006)
Gilberto (1992)
Grossmann (1998)
Hempel (1965)
Kaufmann (1995)
Mojser (1993)
Schmidt and Syndram (1997)
Von Watzdorf (1962)

France
Amarger, Arnaud et al. (2007)
Blunt (1973)
Burke (1992)
Centre Culturel Suédois (1985)
Constans and Salmon (1998)
Dee and Walton (1988)
Galéries nationales du Grand Palais (2002)
Hoog (1992)
Lablaude (1995)
Walton (1986)

The Netherlands
Baarsen et al. (1988)
Bowett (1999)
Rosenberg et al. (1991)
Slive (1995)

Italy
Bowron and Rishel (2000)
Detroit Institute of Arts (1974)
Fagiolo and Portoghesi (2006)
González-Palacios (1984)
González-Palacios (1986)
Walker and Hammond (1999)
Wittkower (1999)

Spain and Portugal
Delaforce (2002)
Levenson (1993)
Levenson (2007)
Trusted (2007)

South and Central America
Bailey (*Jesuit Missions*, 1999)
Bailey (2005)
Levenson (2007)
Rishel with Stratton-Pruitt (2006)
Union latine (1999)

Sweden
Alm et al. (1997)
Laine and Magnusson (2002)
Olín and Henriksson (2004)
Snickare (2002)
Waddy (2002)

4. Particular topics
Architecture
Blunt (1979)
Blunt (1982)
Millon (1999)
Norberg-Schulz (1986)

Carriages and sledges
Bessone (1993)
Kreisel (1927)
Tydén-Jordan (1985)
Wackernagel (1966)
Wackernagel (2002)

Ceramics and glass
Aken-Fehmers et al. (2001)
Aken-Fehmers (2007)
Archer (1997)
Cassidy-Geiger (2007)
Graves (2002)
Honey (1952)
Kräftner (2005)
Liefkes (1997)
Von Kerssenbrock-Krosigk 2001

Court culture
Adamson (1999)
Brocher (1934)
Elias (1983)
Girouard (2000)
Jarrard (2003)
Klingensmith (1993)
Walker and Hammond (1999)

Court workshops
Giusti (2006)
Keisch and Netzer (2001)
Lankheit (1962)

Eating
Brett (1968)
Brown (2001)
Bursche (1974)
Keisch (1997)
Musée national des châteaux de Versailles et de Trianon (1993)
Ottomeyer and Völkel (2002)
Strong (2002)

Festivals and performance
Mulryne, Watanabe-O'Kelly and Shewring (2004)
Mulryne and Goldring (2002)
Watanabe-O'Kelly and Béhar (1999)
Watanabe-O'Kelly and Simon (1999)
Wisch and Munshower (1990)

Furniture and woodwork
Baarsen (2000)
Bimbenet-Privat (2002)
Bowett (1999)
Bowett (2002)
Cirillo and Godi (1983)
Colle (2000)
Esterly (1998)
Kreisel (1968)
Kreisel (1970)
Lunsingh-Scheurleer (2005)
Pradère (1989)
Saule and Arminjon (2007)

Gardens
Conan (2005)
Hunt and Willis 1975
Hunt and de Jong (1988)
Hunt and Conan (2002)
Hyde (2005)
Mosser and Teyssot (1990)
Mukerji (1997)
Weiss (1995)
Woodbridge (1986)

Ornament
Clifford (1999)
Fuhring (1989)
Fuhring (1998)
Fuhring (2004)
Gruber (1996)
Hauglid (1950)
Kimball (1943)

Palace planning, interior decoration and furnishing
Baillie (1967)
Beard (1986)
Entwisle (1960)
Rutherford (1992)
Scholten (1989)
Thornton (1978)
Thornton (1984)
Waddy (1990)
Waddy (2002)
Waterer (1971)

Sculpture
Montagu (1996)
Physick (1969)
Souchal (1977–93)
Weston-Lewis (1998)
Whinney (1988)
Wittkower (1990)

Silver, jewellery and metalwork
Arnold (2001)
Baumstark, Seling and Seelig (1994)
Bimbenet-Privat (2002)
Bottineau and Lefuel (1965)
Diamantmuseum Antwerp (1993)
Frederiks (1952)
Fuhring (2001)
Hayward (1959)
Hernmarck (1977)
Oman (1970)
Ottomeyer and Pröschel (1986)
Scarisbrick (1994)
Seling (1980)
ter Molen (1984)

Textiles and Dress
Campbell, T. (2007)
Jenkins (2003)
Rangström (2002)
Ribeiro (1984)
Ribeiro (2003)

Theatre
Bjurström (1961)
De la Gorce (1986)
Küster (2003)
Lenzi and Bentini (2000)

Picture Credits

Images and copyright clearance have been kindly supplied as listed below (in alphabetical order by institution or surname). All other illustrations, unless otherwise stated, are © V&A Images

Archivio Fotografico della Soprintendenza Speciale per il Patrimonio Storico, Artistico ed Etnoantropologico e e per il Polo Museale della città di Roma: 1.38
Archivio Fotografico della Soprintendenza Speciale per il Patrimonio Artistico ed Etnoantropologico e per il Polo Museale della città di Roma / Galleria Nazionale d'Arte Antica di Roma, Palazzo Barberini: 5.21
© Archivio di Stato di Parma: 3.3
Courtesy of Banco de Crédito del Peru: 4.57
© Bayerisches Nationalmuseum, München: 3.28, 5.14
© Bayerische Verwaltung der staatlichen Schlösser, Gärten und Seen, München: 3.22, 5.18, 5.35
Courtesy of the Biblioteca Nacional de España: 1.13
© Bibliothèque Nationale de France: 2.5, 3.26, 5.46, 5.60, 5.67
© Bildarchiv Monheim GmbH / Alamy: 1.53, 4.17, 4.22
© Barnabas Bosshart / CORBIS: 1.33, 1.36
© bpk / Hamburger Kunsthalle / Elke Walford: 2.66
bpk / Kunstbibliothek, Staatliche Museen zu Berlin / Photo: Dietmar Katz: 5.29
© Bridgeman: 2.35
© The Trustees of the British Museum: 1.14, 1.15, 1.47, 1.49, 1.52, 3.33, 4.41, 5.30
Château du Grand Trianon, Versailles / Bridgeman: 5.10
Château de Versailles, France / Bridgeman: 1.24, 2.26, 2.64, 5.1, 5.13, 5.43, 5.50, 5.51, 5.65, 5.72, 5.79
Colección del Marqués de los Balbases: 4.59
Cooper-Hewitt, National Design Museum, Smithsonian Institution, Museum purchase from General Acquisitions Endowment Fund, 1988-4-48 / Photo: Matt Flynn: 2.83
© CuboImages srl / Alamy: 5.52
© Gianni Dagli Orti / CORBIS: 2.6
© Fridmar Damm / zefa / Corbis: 5.9
Das Neue Grüne Gewölbe, Staatliche Kunstsammlungen Dresden: 2.72
© DeAgostini Picture Library / Scala, Florence: 5.20
Courtesy of Deutsches Theatermuseum: 3.20
© The Devonshire Collection / Reproduced by permission of the Trustees of the Chatsworth Settlement: 5.77
Collection of The Trustees of the 9th Duke of Buccleuch's Chattels Fund: 5.81, 5.82
Reproduced by kind permission of His Grace the Duke of Marlborough, Blenheim Palace Image Library: 1.6
Reproduced by kind permission of His Grace the Duke of Marlborough, Blenheim Palace Image Library; Photography by Peter Smith: 1.9
© The Duke of Northumberland, Alnwick Castle: 2.63
© English Heritage Photo Library: 3.25
© ephotocorp / Alamy: 1.34
Founders Society Purchase, Ralph Harman Booth Bequest Fund Photograph © The Detroit Institute of Arts: 4.42
© The Francis Frith Collection / Scala, Florence: 2.16
© Fundación Televisa AC: 4.49
Galleria dell' Accademia, Venice, Italy /

Bridgeman: 1.56
Gemäldegalerie der Akademie der bildenden Künste Wien: 3.47
Getty Images: 1.7, 1.42, 2.18
Grünes Gewölbe, Staatliche Kunstsammlungen Dresden / Photo: Jürgen Karpinski: 2.1, 2.71, 2.73, 2.74, 4.12
© Guildhall Library, London: 3.32
© Helsinki City Museum; Photo: Mika Peltonen Valokuvaaja
© Historisches Museum Basel: 1.55
David Hoxley at Technical Art Services: pp.10-12, 2.12. 4.19, 5.22, 5.23
© Iconotec / Alamy: 4.26
Instituto dos Museus e da Conservação, I.P / Photo: Carlos Monteiro: 2.42
Instituto dos Museus e da Conservação, I.P. / Museu Nacional de Arte Antiga, Lisboa: 3.63, 4.4
isifa Image Service s.r.o. / Alamy: 4.11
Stephen Johnson / Getty Images: 4.10
© Wolfgang Kaehler / Alamy: 4.26
© Gisselfeld Kloster: 5.45
Courtesy of Koninklijk Museum voor Schone Kunsten, Antwerp: 3.40
© Kungl.biblioteket / The National Library of Sweden: 1.12
Kunstgewerbemuseum, Staatliche Kunstsammlungen Dresden / Photo: Hans-Peter Klut: 2.82
Kupferstich-Kabinett, Staatliche Kunstsammlungen Dresden, Photo: Herbert Boswank: 3.30, 3.36, 3.38, 3.39, 3.43
© Massimo Listri / CORBIS: 5.66
© Livrustkammaren / Photo: Göran Schmidt: 3.44, 5.63
© LSH / Skoklosters Slott, Stockholm / Photo: Jens Mohr: 1.4, 1.5, 2.30, 2.55, 2.68, 3.46, 5.60
© Louvre, Paris, France / Peter Willi / Bridgeman: 1.51, 3.27
© The Marquess of Salisbury, Hatfield House: 5.39
The Metropolitan Museum of Art, The Crosby Brown Collection of Musical Instruments, 1889. (89.4.2929) Image © The Metropolitan Museum of Art: 2.32, 3.11
The Metropolitan Museum of Art, Purchase, Rogers Fund, Isabel Shults Fund and Irene Lewisohn Bequest, 1991. (1991.6.1a-c) Image © The Metropolitan Museum of Art: 5.62
The Metropolitan Museum of Art, Victor Wilbour Memorial Fund, 1959. (59.32) Image © The Metropolitan Museum of Art: 4.3
Collection Musée de Cambrai / Photo: Hugo Maertens, Bruges: 1.8
Musée de la Ville de Paris, Musée Carnavalet, Paris, France / Bridgeman: 4.29, 5.2
Museo de América, Madrid: 1.17, 4.13
© Museo di Roma: 2.2, 3.31
© Museo Nacional Colegio de San Gregorio. Valladolid / Photo © Andrés de Solanes : 4.58
Courtesy of Museo Nazionale di Palazzo Venezia: 4.46
Museo Nacional del Prado, Madrid: 2.70, 4.6
Museu de Arte Sacra de São Paulo-Organização Social de Cultura/Secretaria de Estado da Cultura/Governo do Estado de São Paulo – SP – Brasil / Photo: Rômulo Fialdini: 4.48
Museu Nacional de Arte Antiga, Lisboa: 1.28, 4.5
Museum Sejarah Jakarta, Indonesia: 2.48
Národni památkový ústav, Castle of Český Krumlov / Photo: M. Halama: 3.8
© Národni památkový ústav, Castle of Český Krumlov; Photo Ladislav Pouzar: 3.9

© Národni památkový ústav, Castle of Český Krumlov, Photo: Veroslav Skrabanek: 3.6, 3.7
Courtesy of The National Gallery of Ireland / Photo © National Gallery of Ireland: Frontispiece; 3.29
© The National Gallery, London: 1.31, 1.43, 2.29
The National Gallery, London / Bridgeman: 1.62
Photo © National Gallery in Prague 2008: 4.52
Courtesy of the National Gallery of Scotland: 4.53
Courtesy of the Board of Trustees, National Gallery of Art, Washington: 2.19
© National Maritime Museum, Greenwich, London: 1.11
© Crown copyright. National Monuments Record: 1.64
Nationalmuseum, Stockholm: 2.59, 3.14, 5.4, 5.31, 5.32, 5.44, 5.47, 5.56, 5.61, 5.69, 5.71
© Norsk Folkemuseum: 4.43
Norsk Folkemuseum / Photo: Anne-Lise Reinsfelt: 4.24
North Carolina Museum of Art, Raleigh, Purchased with funds from the State of North Carolina: 1.32
© NTPL / John Hammond: 1.50, 5.24, 2.60, 5.58, 5.74, 5.76
© NTPL / Andreas von Einsiedel: 2.79, 5.57, 5.74
Courtesy of Palazzo del Municipio, Parma: 5.25
PCL / Alamy: 4.1
Nicholas Pitt / Alamy: 5.6
Private Collection / Courtesy of Sotheby's Picture Library: 1.10
Private Collection / The Stapleton Collection / Bridgeman: 5.5, 5.7
Provincia d'Italia della Compagnia di Gesù: 2.36
© RIBA Library Drawings Collection: 3.21
© RIBA Library Photographs Collection: 4.18
© Rijksmuseum, Amsterdam: 2.34, 2.53, 2.54
Ringsaker Church, Norway: 4.25
© RMN / Agence Bulloz: 5.64
© RMN / Michèle Bellot: 4.47
© RMN / Philippe Bernard: 5.11
© RMN / Gérard Blot: 1.21, 5.12, 5.40
© RMN / Les frères Chuzeville: 2.43
© RMN / Thierry Le Mage: 3.15
© RMN / Hervé Lewandowski: 3.45
© Royal Castle, Warsaw, Poland / Maciej Bronarski / Bridgeman: 4.54
The Royal Collection © Her Majesty Queen Elizabeth II: 1.45, 2.4, 2.11, 2.78, 3.13
The Royal Collection © Her Majesty Queen Elizabeth II / Photo: A.C. Cooper: 1.40
© The Royal Collections of Sweden / Photo: Alexis Daflos: 2.62, 4.27
© The Royal Collections of Sweden / Photo: Håkan Lind: 2.61
The Royal Danish Collections, Rosenborg Castle, Copenhagen: 1.46, 2.69, 2.77
David Russell / Alamy: 4.44
Rüstkammer, Staatliche Kunstsammlungen Dresden / Photo: Hans-Peter Klut: 3.37
Rüstkammer, Staatliche Kunstsammlungen Dresden / Photo: Elke Estel / Hans-Peter Klut: 3.42
© The Samuel Courtauld Trust, The Courtauld Gallery, London: 1.54, 2.15
© Samuel Courtauld Trust, The Courtauld Gallery / Bridgeman: 2.27
San Carlo alle Quattro Fontane, Rome, Italy / Alinari / Bridgeman: 2.10
Santa Casa da Misericórdia de Lisboa / Museu

de São Roque / Photo © Júlio Marques: 3.50, 3.51, 3.53, 3.54, 3.55, 3.57 – 3.62, 3.64, 3.65, 4.63
Santa Casa da Misericórdia de Lisboa / Museu de São Roque / Photo © Victor Silva: 3.56
Scala, Florence: 1.3, 1.30, 1.38, 1.48, 2.13, 2.14, 2.20, 3.1, 3.49, 4.9, 4.15, 4.23
Scala, Florence / BPK, Bildagentur für Kunst, Kultur und Geschichte, Berlin: 3.19, 5.70
Scala, Florence / Fondo Edifici di Culto-Ministero dell'Interno: 1.41, 2.9, 2.20, 2.23, 2.24, 4.32, 4.34
Scala, Florence / Courtesy of the Ministero Beni e Att. Culturali: 1.1, 1.22, 1.23, 1.29, 1.37
Scala, Florence / Luciano Romano: 1.2
Schloss Charlottenburg: 3.16, 5.84
Schloss Weissenstein, Pommersfelden: 5.53, 5.86
SCML / Núcleo de Audiovisuais e Multimédia / Photo: Santa Casa da Misericordia de Lisboa / Museu de São Roque / Photo © Carlos Sousa: 3.48
Scottish National Portrait Gallery, Edinburgh, Scotland / Bridgeman: 1.63
Leonid Serebrennikov / Alamy: 4.33
Soprintendenza Speciale per il Patrimonio Storico, Artistico ed Etnoantropologico e per il Polo Museale della città di Firenze Gabinetto Fotografico / Museo Degli Argenti, Palazzo Pitti, Firenze: 1.27, 4.37
Staatliche Kunstsammlungen Dresden: 3.34, 3.35
© Staatliches Museum Schwerin: 2.21
© Stiftsbibliothek, St. Gallen: 4.20
© Stiftung Preussische Schlösser und Gaärten Berlin-Brandenburg: 5.41
© Stift Melk / Photo: P. Jeremia: 4.21
Charles Stopford Sackville: 5.83
© Temple Newsam House, Leeds Museums and Galleries: 5.33
Courtesy of the Master and Fellows of Trinity College, Cambridge: 2.45
Uppsala University Library Collections: 1.25
© Västerås Cathedral, Church of Sweden / Photo: Magnus Aronson: 4.30
© Roger Viollet / Getty Images: 4.14
Viscount Coke and Trustees of Holkham Estate: 2.17
Viscount De L'Isle MBE DL: 5.78
Whitehall, London / Bridgeman: 1.20
Julie Woodhouse / Alamy: 4.8
Gari Wyn Williams / Alamy: 4.16

Index

The index does not include the Summary
Catalogue; figures in *italics* refer to illustrations.